Shakespeare Studies

Advisory Board

$\mathcal{S}$hakespeare $\mathcal{S}$tudies

AN ANNUAL GATHERING OF
RESEARCH, CRITICISM, AND REVIEWS

I

Edited by

J. LEEDS BARROLL

Inaugurated under the Sponsorship of
THE UNIVERSITY OF CINCINNATI
1965

*Contributions offered for publication
should be addressed to:
The Editor, Shakespeare Studies, The University of Cincinnati,
Cincinnati, Ohio and
should be accompanied by unaffixed return-postage.
Annual subscription is eight dollars*

Contents

Contributors

Don Cameron Allen.
　Sir William Osler Professor of English, The Johns Hopkins University.
Jonas A. Barish.
　Assistant Professor of English, the University of California, Berkeley.
Sylvan Barnet.
　Chairman of the Department of English, Tufts University.
Ronald Berman.
　Associate Professor of Literature, the University of California, San Diego.
Dennis Biggins.
　Senior Lecturer in English, the University of Newcastle, New South Wales.
Edward Clinkscale.
　Assistant Professor of Music, the University of California, Riverside.
Stanley Cooperman.
　Associate Professor of English, Simon Fraser University,
　Vancouver, British Columbia.
Giles E. Dawson.
　Curator of Books and Manuscripts, the Folger Shakespeare Library.
Franklin M. Dickey.
　Professor of English, the University of New Mexico.
John R. Elliott, Jr.
　Assistant Professor of English, the University of California, Santa Barbara.
Russell A. Fraser.
　Chairman of the Department of English, Vanderbilt University,
　Nashville, Tennessee.
R. A. Foakes.
　Professor of English, the University of Kent at Canterbury, England.
Charles R. Forker.
　Associate Professor of English, Indiana University, Bloomington.
Dean Frye.
　Assistant Professor of English, McGill University, Montreal, Canada.
Terence Hawkes.
　Lecturer in English, University College, Cardiff, Wales.
F. David Hoeniger.
　Associate Professor of English, the University of Toronto, Canada.
Charles K. Hofling.
　Department of Psychiatry, College of Medicine, The University of Cincinnati.
Dr. Leslie Hotson.
　Northford, Connecticut.
Cyrus Hoy.
　Professor of English, the University of Rochester, New York.

G. K. Hunter.

    Professor of English, the University of Warwick, Coventry, England.

Robert A. Kimbrough.

    Associate Professor of English, the University of Wisconsin.

Hilton J. Landry.

    Assistant Professor of English, the University of California, Davis.

Clifford Leech.

    Professor of English, the University of Toronto, Canada.

Ruth M. Levitsky.

    Assistant Professor of English, the University of Waterloo, Ontario, Canada.

Barbara Kiefer Lewalski.

    Associate Professor of English Literature, Brown University, Providence, Rhode Island.

Joseph Margolis.

    Chairman of the Department of Philosophy, the University of Western Ontario.

Derick R. C. Marsh.

    Senior Lecturer in English Literature, the University of Sydney, Australia.

Charles Mitchell.

    Assistant Professor of English, San Diego State College, California.

Kenneth Muir.

    King Alfred Professor of English Literature, the University of Liverpool.

Robert Ornstein.

    Professor of English, the University of Illinois, Urbana.

Burton R. Pollin.

    Associate Professor of English, the Bronx Community College, New York.

Eleanor Prosser.

    Professor of English, San Jose State College, Los Altos, California.

Charles T. Prouty.

    Professor of English, Yale University, New Haven, Connecticut.

Norman Rabkin.

    Assistant Professor of English, the University of California, Berkeley.

William O. Scott.

    Associate Professor of English, the University of Kansas, Lawrence.

Hallett D. Smith.

    Chairman of the Department of Humanities, the California Institute of Technology.

Rolf Soellner.

    Associate Professor of English, Kansas State University, Manhattan.

Robert K. Turner, Jr.

    Associate Professor of English, the University of Wisconsin, Milwaukee.

Helen C. White.

    Professor of English, the University of Wisconsin, Madison.

The Turning Away of Prince Hal

by Jonas A. Barish

The rejection of Falstaff,[1] like much else in Shakespeare, has tended to turn a searchlight on us, and make ourselves reveal ourselves either as moralists or as sentimentalists. Shakespeare preserves such a delicate balance, throughout the two parts of *Henry IV,* between authority and rebellion, business and pleasure, sobriety and negligence, that the final episode almost invites us to view them in the light of our own deep preferences. If we range ourselves naturally on the side of authority, with its promise of order and justice, we will tend to endorse the casting off of the embodiment of disorder, the enemy-in-chief of the Lord Chief Justice. We will be gratified by the reckoning with misrule that has been so long in coming. We will subscribe to the authorized versions of the incident—to Prince John of Lancaster's opinion, for example, that his brother, the new king, has behaved handsomely to his old associates. If, on the other hand, our instincts prompt us to range ourselves more strongly on the side of freedom and spontaneity, we may tend to remember the vitality in Falstaff more than his lawlessness; we may recall his panegyric to sack more vividly than his fleecing of Shallow, and we will doubtless compare it in its favor with the official treachery practised by Prince John in Gaultree Forest. We will then find the rejection scene an affront, Hal a preaching humbug, and the whole episode a distasteful illustration of the incompatibility of kingship with kindness.[2]

Either of these formulations certainly oversimplifies, but my own instincts lead me to suspect that the latter view is the truer one, and that Bradley's essay still remains the soundest statement of the case. Bradley, it will be recalled, felt that the planned deterioration of Falstaff in *2 Henry IV,* carried out by Shakespeare with remarkable thoroughness, still could not prevail over the vitality intrinsic to the character (who embodies "the bliss of freedom gained in humour"); and that, conversely, the fact that the rejection is indeed necessary to the welfare of the kingdom, and that the Prince has, in some sense, been rejecting Falstaff all along, could not dispel our feeling that the terms of the rejection are too peremptory and too scathing.[3]

I should like to ask whether we do not arrive at much the same view if we take a different route, and consider the incident not so much as a detail in a Bradleyan character analysis as in the light of Shakespearean dramaturgy in general, by measuring it against the pattern of other plays, especially the comedies. I think that when we do, we find Bradley's strictures confirmed. We find that the false notes struck by the new king in his speech to his old tavernmate—the sanctimoniousness, the dishonest retrospective revision of the relations between himself and

9

Falstaff, whereby the latter is turned into his "misleader," so that he can be more stingingly dismissed, and the king appear correspondingly more magnanimous — that these notes ring especially false because they impose a constricting rather than a liberating interpretation on all that we have witnessed up to this moment.

They also transfer us forcibly from the domain of comedy to the grimmer realm of history. In so doing, they help us to see what differentiates comic drama from history play. History, it would seem, lends itself better to the shape of tragedy than of comedy. In historical plays like *Richard III* and *Richard II,* tragic structure seems to arise naturally from chronicled event. As the erring kings reach the period of their acts or sufferings, they seem to crystallize almost without pressure into tragic protagonists; the playwright need only follow the grain of history. But as Falstaff, the greatest comic character in Shakespeare, nears the end of *his* reign, the comic mould must be broken by violence, and the comic resolution harshly suppressed. C. L. Barber has shown how Falstaff recreates the figure of the Lord of Misrule who must, for the health of the community, be cast out once his moment of triumph has passed.[4] It only remains to underline the fact that the realization of this pattern, in which the Lord of Misrule becomes a scapegoat, is not a comic but a tragic fulfillment.

In the comic world, it is those whom Barber designates as the kill-joys — the putters-down of mirth, the sour-faced guardians of authority or censorious moralism — who are chased from the stage so that joy may reign unconfined. Given the choice between a drunken sensualist like Sir Toby Belch and a prescriptive authoritarian like Malvolio, comedy opts for the former: the sensualist, however chastened and curbed of his disruptive tendencies, remains to participate in the communal festivities of the finale, while the foiled authoritarian stalks furiously from the scene. Similarly, at the end of *The Merchant of Venice, Much Ado about Nothing,* and *As You Like It,* it is the masquers and revellers who command the stage, while the enemies of pleasure — Shylock, Don John, the melancholy Jaques — hold themselves aloof, or take flight, or retreat into sterile solitude. The enemies of pleasure, we notice, are two of them villains: inability to enter into the festive mood is closely bound up with an inability to respond warmly to others, to form close attachments, to give freely and lovingly of oneself. But history imposes a bleaker design: at the end of *2 Henry IV* it is the kill-joys who win out, and the spirit of Carnival who is gorgonized by a stony British stare, and placed under lock and key in the Fleet.[5]

I have labelled these remarks "The Turning Away of Prince Hal" to underscore the element of *self*-rejection involved in the new king's action. The just-crowned Henry V declares with no slight emphasis that he is not the thing he was, that he has turned away his former self, and expects to do as much with those who kept him company. For a Shakespearean hero, this is an oddly self-mutilating declaration. Shakespearean drama normally works toward a synthesis, in which characters find themselves enhanced in their sympathies and more varied in their responses than before. The range of their appreciation has widened; they have learned to value things they once slighted; in tragedy this enlarged appreciativeness often constitutes a partial compensation for the protagonist's loss of worldly greatness.

Shakespearean comedy customarily finds its characters in a moment of idleness, in a recreative suspension of what has been or will be their "normal" life. After the games and improvisations of *Love's Labor's Lost,* the death of the Princess' father comes to recall us, along with the characters, to a sterner world of adversity and business. In *A Midsummer Night's Dream* the young lovers live through a spell of bewitchment, of abandonment to the irrational and quirky depths in themselves, before waking to daylight and normalcy. Waking, they recall in wonder the strange shapes traced on their memories by the events they have dreamed overnight.

In both these cases the interval of play or dream is conceived as a positive experience. The pleasant proclivities in themselves to which the young heroes and heroines of *Love's Labor's Lost* give rein—for wit and impromptu ceremony, for love and poetry and disguise, for feasts of language and masques of folly—are presented in the most attractive terms. These activities are conceived not only as suitable to the youth of the participants, but as enriching. The first sign of wisdom in the young men is not the little academe they aspire to found, but their renunciation of it, their surrender to the presence of the ladies and the delights of the season. If, in their wooing and revelling, they proceed a new way into folly, it is a folly that involves a happy attentiveness, however incomplete, to others beside themselves, a potential lessening, at least, of the egoistic self-absorption with which they took up their roles as philosophers in the academe. When at the height of the festivity, the shadow of death falls on the mirth, it does not repudiate the mirth, but places it within a larger perspective, renders it doubly precious by underscoring its fragility, even as it hints at its inadequacy. The twelve-month penance proposed by the Princess is not intended to wipe out the memory of the "courtship, pleasant jest, and courtesy" (V.ii.789)[6] offered to the ladies, but to chasten its extravagances, to put it to the test under severer conditions. There is no doubt that the young lords require a lesson in humanity—this much is proved by their callousness toward the rustics during the pageant of the Worthies, and reiterated by Rosaline's last words to Berowne—but no one suggests that the holiday interlude has in itself been reprehensible or immoral.

In *A Midsummer Night's Dream,* even more explicitly, the dream sequence proves potent enough to cast a prospective richness over the future lives of the lovers. Hermia will be the more loved by Lysander for his having momentarily strayed to Helena, and Helena will be the more cherished by Demetrius for his having yielded to a freak of folly, and courted Hermia. Demetrius' folly, we should notice, begins before the play does, and supplies the basis for its action. The enchantments of the night in the palace wood return him not to the condition he was in when he entered the wood, but to where he was before the play began, in love with his first love, his true love, Helena. The confusions provoked by the magic flower-juice have simply allowed the capricious and vagrant impulses in the lovers to play themselves out at farce tempo, as in a movie speed-up. At dawn the lovers do not merely come to their senses, or to themselves; they come to selves renewed and refreshed by the night's adventures. The sound of horns and hunting that fills the wood as Theseus takes to the chase conveys us into the bracing air of daytime reality, but the nocturnal spell proves able to sustain itself. When Oberon and his train return at nightfall to scatter blessings on the newly wedded couples, we see the witchery of the preceding night continuing, visibly, to shed its benefits on the spirits of the lovers.

Prince Hal, like the king and courtiers in *Love's Labor's Lost,* has been on holiday, as he told us in his first soliloquy. Like the young lovers of *A Midsummer Night's Dream* he has been dreaming: he has "long dreamt of such a kind of man" (V.v.53). And it has been a dream of love: if the prince has not loved Falstaff, Falstaff has certainly loved the prince. As a symbol of "the supremacy of the imagination over fact,"[7] Falstaff has glittered as enticingly as the moonlight in the Athens wood; as the incarnation of play, he has outstripped the young lords of Navarre even in their most inspired moments of sonneteering and masquerading. Following the lead of the comedies, then, we would expect the dream, the holiday, the moment of love, to have left some precious residue in the prince's spirit. We might suppose that certain human propensities were better cultivated at Eastcheap than at court: the free pleasuring of the senses, the capacity to live in the present, undistracted by vain regrets over the past or empty wishes about the future, the love of wit and mirth, the invigorating skepticism toward received opinion and official rhetoric.

But unlike the heroes of the comedies, Hal is ashamed of his holiday, and he despises his dream. He recoils from his former lover with more of a shudder than Titania from the memory of Bottom. Nowhere does his final speech allow for the possibility that the sportive interlude was valuable. Where his counterparts in the comedies incorporate the holiday or the dream into their fuller waking lives, the new king dismisses it as a spell of "riot," a moment of worthless disorder. Instead of a synthesis, in which an enlarged sense of human possibility emerges from the dialectic between duty and holiday, or dream and waking, we have a forcible sundering of the two kinds of experience, and a walling of them off into the noncommunicating realms of Good and Bad.

The sundering is accompanied, inevitably, by a shrinking. Prince Hal is rightly said by Tillyard to be, in his tavern days, of a "comprehensive nature,"[8] responsive to the whole range of human potentiality. When he sounds the base string of humility in the company of the drawers, Hal is putting himself in vital touch with the whole spectrum of English life. He claims such a microcosmic comprehensiveness for himself when he announces that he is "of all humours that have showed themselves humours since the old days of goodman Adam" (*1H4,* II.iv.104-6). In Tillyard's gloss, he is claiming to be "ruled simultaneously by every human motive that exists." Now, his coronation accomplished, we find that he has cultivated this wide responsiveness only to disavow it and deliver homilies on it, that he is bent on rooting out of himself the variousness of feeling he once prided himself on—that, in short, his comprehensive nature is comprehensive no more, but partial and exclusive.

He now takes the attitude toward his tavern truancy that has always been taken in court circles. The main extenuation of his scapegrace ways, by sympathetic counsellors, has been the hope that he would at length reject them. The Earl of Warwick, comforting the sick Henry IV, tries to reassure him concerning Hal's wildness:

> The Prince but studies his companions
> Like a strange tongue, wherein, to gain the language,
> 'Tis needful that the most immodest word
> Be look'd upon and learnt; which once attain'd,
> Your Highness knows, comes to no further use
> But to be known and hated. So, like gross terms,
> The Prince will, in the perfectness of time,
> Cast off his followers; and their memory
> Shall as a pattern or a measure live
> By which his Grace must mete the lives of others,
> Turning past evils to advantages.   *(2H4,IV.iv.68-78)*

The prince, thus, is defended on the ground that he is getting to know the seamy side of life, acquainting himself with vices so as to hate and shun them, as men learn foul words in foreign tongues in order to purify their vocabularies. The only available justification for Hal's misbehavior is one that frankly regards it as a deviation into *evils*, immersion in an alien element from which, it is piously hoped, *advantages* may one day ensue. Hal is not thought to have anything in common with his tavernmates, nor have they anything to teach him except the unattractiveness of vice.

This remains essentially the approved view after the accession. The Archbishop of Canterbury, at the beginning of *Henry V*, describes the young king's reformation as a descent of grace. In the Archbishop's eyes the king has been a prodigal, who on reaching the throne renounced the sins for which wise men censured him when he was prince: "his addiction was to courses vain, / His companies unletter'd, rude, and shallow, / His hours fill'd up with riots, banquets, sports" (I.i.54-6). Banquets and sports, we note, the pastimes of the holiday world, are here made nearly synonymous with "riots," the key term of disapproval, for which no favorable senses occur in Shakespeare. Henry IV, wistfully comparing his son to Harry Percy, saw "riot and dishonour" staining his son's brow. In the eyes of the guardians of order, Falstaff himself symbolizes Riot.[9] The prince's tavern life was "vain" — frivolous and empty. His companions were "rude" and "shallow," capable only of being a coarsening influence. When the new king, at his coronation, adopts the same vocabulary, when he bids the Lord Chief Justice "speak to that vain man," when he charges Falstaff with having been "the tutor and the feeder of [his] riots," he serves notice that he has absorbed the viewpoint of the establishment; he now sees his acquaintance with Falstaff as a wholly negative experience, an initiation into evil that has taught him what to shun.

13

"How ill white hairs become a fool and jester!" Folly, in Shakespeare, usually proves to be an inescapable condition of life, to which no one is immune, and jesters, to quote a perhaps not altogether trustworthy witness, "do oft prove prophets." Those who most fiercely claim exemption from folly are usually those suffering from hubris, for whom comic chastisement or tragic humbling is in store: the young men in *Love's Labor's Lost,* the fiery Lear. Acceptance of one's folly amounts to an acceptance of one's own earthy composition, and that of others: in both comic and tragic actions it forms an indispensable stage on the road to self-fulfillment. The newly crowned Henry V, by his categorical dismissal of folly, pursues the reverse course: he seeks to disclaim what he formerly acknowledged, his proneness to error, his membership in the race of goodman Adam. The rejection of Falstaff is part of a process in which, in the words of the Archbishop of Canterbury, "Consideration like an angel came / And whipp'd th'offending Adam out of him" (*H5,* I.i.28-9)—whereby the king disclaims the component of common clay in himself and sets himself apart from the stock of Adam. We are hardly surprised when later on, at the battlefield in France, he approves the execution of Bardolph without a flicker of recognition of the former association between them.

Now it is true that Hal is not the hero of a comedy, or of a tragedy, and that the experiences of romantic love, usually central to the comic formula, or of worldly ruin, central to tragedy, are here beside the point. It is true also that comic and tragic heroes ordinarily suffer from some defect of vision or error of feeling— Berowne's excessive penchant for mockery, Demetrius' whimsical fancy for Hermia—that must be corrected by whatever humbling experiences the plot affords. Hal, it may be argued, as the hero of a history play, suffers from no such defect. His task, according to the chief moralistic view, is not so much to understand himself, or to reform himself in any substantial way, as to fit himself to be the kind of king who will rule England wisely, and he is from the start in possession of his own best course. Eastcheap is not for him a regenerative wood, but a school of squalor where he learns plain truths about his future subjects and his realm. Even his most expansive moments, it may be urged, such as that with the drawers, are tinged with calculation; Hal is practising sounding the base string so as to be able later to play the whole gamut of the viol of state. But the more we insist on the element of planning in the Eastcheap truancy, the more we turn Hal into a cardboard prince, incapable from the outset of responding to the vitality of Falstaff. Under these conditions, the sojourn in the tavern becomes little better than an empty masquerade, and the gratuitous emphasis of the rejection speech seems more bizarre and inappropriate than ever. If, on the other hand, we grant the reality of the lure of Falstaff, as we surely experience it, and if we acknowledge what we plainly observe to be the case, that Falstaff delights the prince, then we find the exigencies of the history play leading to a "reformation" that we can only feel as a dehumanization.

Doubtless by progressively transforming revelry into misrule, during the latter scenes of *2 Henry IV,* Shakespeare has done what he could to justify dramatically the moralistic position. Having chosen to make Hal into the hero-king, a combination of both human and political virtues, he prepares the way for the crisis by making *us* reject Falstaff first. But those critics who have espoused the fierce tone as well as the dogma of the rejection scene have tended to give the episode a purely institutional reading. They have subscribed to the official doctrine according to which the prince makes himself the mirror of all Christian kings by disowning his past self. But Shakespearean characters do not achieve greatness by self-truncation, nor by adopting a priggish tone toward their own past misdeeds (if misdeeds they have committed). To banish plump Jack is to banish what is free and vital and pleasurable in life, as well as much that is selfish and unruly—not all the world perhaps, but more of it than either we or Hal can do without.

History thus defeats those who would defy it by trying to live in a changeless present or an undiminished youth, or in a realm of pure play. It awards its favors to those who can make themselves its servants by curbing their own human fullness. The history play as a genre—the Lancastrian tetralogy at least—takes an optimistic view of the process. It strives to present it as benign, so that the irresponsibles, who would flourish in comedy, are felt to deserve their defeat, while the exponents of order, however repressive, are felt to warrant our allegiance. In a later Shakespearean play a similar dilemma turns to tragedy. Antony and Cleopatra attempt to integrate into their public selves precisely the folly that Hal excludes from his: feasting, sensuality, music, sport and idleness. In their case the spirit of the tavern is installed at the heart of their beings as monarchs; instead of being curbed and disciplined, it expands till it disables them as rulers. Their progress reverses Hal's: they start with business, empire, authority, the tyranny of time and the consciousness of limits, and end with play, sensuality, time transposed into eternity, and all limits obliterated and transcended. In their case holiday gradually invades the conduct of imperial business till it engrosses them utterly; the life of kingship gradually becomes the dream, the life of pleasure the engulfing, transcending reality. Where Hal fits himself as a ruler by scrapping part of his humanity, Antony and Cleopatra unfit themselves by fostering the totality of theirs. Only the Egyptian transvaluation by which things melt into and become each other's opposites permits them to translate their political failure into a spiritual victory.

This play too has tended to expose its readers as moralists and sentimentalists. Those who see in Falstaff chiefly a portent of disorder, to be rightly spurned by a repentant Hal come to his senses after a prodigal sowing of wild oats, also tend to see a cautionary tale in the story of Antony and Cleopatra, a homily against adultery and a warning against the neglect of serious business. Those who see in the sacrifice of Falstaff a near-tragic reproof of life by the tyrannical demands of state tend also to see in the deaths of Antony and Cleopatra a triumphant escape from the clutches of the same tyranny. In neither case, one suspects, can the conflicting forces be made to merge lastingly, or reach a stable equilibrium. Too many contradictory conditions exist to be satisfied. Life contains more than any given configuration in it can ever adequately embody, especially if that configuration straddles the public and private worlds as hugely as do the destinies of the English

15

throne or the dynastic concerns of Egypt and ancient Rome. One must accept the fact that in one case political success is achieved at the cost of a constricted sensibility, in the other that a magnified sensibility is achieved at the price of imperial defeat.

Notes:

(1) The present essay, in slightly different form, was delivered as a paper before the Shakespeare section of the Modern Language Association, at its annual convention, in New York, December, 1964.

(2) The New Variorum Edition of the play, ed. Matthias Shaaber (Philadelphia, 1940), pp. 584-99, provides plentiful examples of both views, but particularly of the second, or sentimentalist view, the moralistic position, in its fullest development, being a more recent phenomenon. The Summer, 1956 (VII, #3) issue of *Shakespeare Quarterly*, a Supplement to the New Variorum Edition of *1 Henry IV*, ed. G. Blakemore Evans, contains a survey of later comment, in the Appendix, pp. 78-94. To the work of the two chief moralist critics, J. Dover Wilson and E. M. W. Tillyard, one may add such footnotes as Hugh Dickinson, "The Reformation of Prince Hal," *SQ*, XII (1951), 33-46, and Peter J. Seng, "Songs, Time, and the Rejection of Falstaff," *ShS*, XV (1962), 31-40.

(3) A. C. Bradley, "The Rejection of Falstaff," *Oxford Lectures on Poetry*, 2nd ed. (London, 1909), pp. 247-73. I should add that in addition to Bradley and Barber (cited below), the critics who seem to me to have written most illuminatingly on Prince Hal and Falstaff are Harold C. Goddard, *The Meaning of Shakespeare* (Chicago, 1951), I, 167-213; Derek Traversi, *Shakespeare from Richard II to Henry V* (Stanford, 1957), pp. 162-165; and J. A. Bryant, Jr., "Prince Hal and the Ephesians," *Sewanee Review*, LXVII (1959), 204-19. The last-named essay, though it does not engage in debate with the moralist critics, constitutes one of the best rejoinders to them from a point of view explcitly Christian and theological. Goddard, II, 184-209, and Traversi, *An Approach to Shakespeare*, 2nd ed. (New York, 1956), pp. 235 ff., have also written penetratingly on the relations between love and power in *Antony and Cleopatra*, proposing a thesis essentially the same as that adopted in the final two paragraphs of the present essay.

(4) *Shakespeare's Festive Comedy* (Princeton, 1959), pp. 192-221. Barber's comments on the rejection scene (pp. 218-20) tend to corroborate Bradley. Barber's anthropological Falstaff had of course been anticipated by J. Dover Wilson, *The Fortunes of Falstaff* (New York, 1943), pp. 25-31, and J. I. M. Stewart, *Character and Motive in Shakespeare* (New York, 1947), pp. 135-9; and was reinforced by Philip Williams, "The Birth and Death of Falstaff Reconsidered," *SQ*, VIII (1957), 356-65.

(5) Nothing said of Falstaff in the present essay need invalidate the propositions about him as a dramatic character made by such psychoanalytic critics as Franz Alexander and Ernst Kris, or such students of Elizabethan theatrical convention as E. E. Stoll and Bernard Spivack. Falstaff doubtless does represent, as Alexander suggests in "A Note on Falstaff," *Psychoanalytic Quarterly*, II (1933), 592-606, "the wholly self-centered pleasure-seeking principle," "the deep infantile layers of the personality," which the prince must master in himself before becoming a fully balanced adult. And he doubtless represents as well a "depreciated father-figure," the psychological need to repudiate whom explains (without necessarily dramatically justifying) the "pointed cruelty" of the rejection scene (Ernst Kris, "Prince Hal's Conflict," *Psychoanalytic Quarterly*, XVII [1948], 487-506). He is, further, the braggart soldier described by Stoll in *Shakespeare Studies* (New York, 1927), pp. 403-490, and the Vice of the sixteenth cen-

tury stage psychomachia described by Spivack in *Shakespeare and the Allegory of Evil* (New York, 1958), pp. 87-91. But in all these guises he continues to incarnate "freedom gained in humour," as Bradley phrases it (p. 262), to whom we respond even in his deterioration; in whom vitality persistently triumphs over old age, vice, and disease; and who "cannot be crushed with a plot," even if the plot is devised by Shakespeare. I would subscribe to William Empson's feeling, in "Falstaff and Mr. Dover Wilson," *Kenyon Review*, XV (1953), 221, 256, that "the main fact about Falstaff . . . is that it is hard to get one's mind all round him," and that "it is hard to defend this strange figure without doing it too much."

(6) Citations from Shakespeare are to the edition of George Lyman Kittredge (Boston, 1936).

(7) Goddard, I, 179, 183.

(8) *Shakespeare's History Plays* (London, 1944), p. 274.

(9) See *The Fortunes of Falstaff*, pp. 17-25.

The Nature of Guilt in the Henry IV Plays

by Ronald Berman

Much recent criticism of *Henry IV* has as its object the exposure of the relationship that appears to obtain between character and historical event in these plays. We have come to see that while the entire Lancastrian tetralogy is "about" politics it displays also motifs of disease, imposture and inhumanity. These motifs are superstructural, but they affect the political substratum profoundly. The motif of disease has been treated by D. A. Traversi, who explored the general "consciousness of disease" in *2 Henry IV*.[1] Imposture has been examined by L. Dean in his study of the "theater of the state" and the roles it demanded: both Richard II and his rival attempted to fulfill—and failed to fulfill—the role of an ideal Christian king.[2] I hope to relate the motifs of disease and imposture to guilt in the sphere of politics, and to add to the studies I have cited some idea of the language of inhumanity in these plays.

It should of course be noted that such a study has its limitations. I emphasize that this is not strictly a study of images but rather of dominant motifs. I am more than ready to agree that "poetic imagery should be considered together with other factors in the play which share its functions; and together these constitute dramatic imagery."[3] The point I hope to make is that the language of *2 Henry IV* in particular indicates not mutation but evolution: its elements develop from earlier rhetorical patterns in the two preceding plays. This gives the play particular and acute powers of statement, for the play is saturated with terms that refer us back to their earlier uses. These terms function like the forms of iteration described by Una Ellis-Fermor in *The Frontiers of Drama*.[4] I suggest that in this specific case we move from early and almost unnoticed mentions of disease to a sense of great and epidemic conditions. Lines like these—

> No more the thirsty entrance of this soil
> Shall daub her lips with her own children's blood—[5]   *(1H4,I.i.5-6)*

bring to their context a sense of moral distortion. The context is that of peace and religion, but the extraordinary, half-defined metaphor is that of a primitive and mythological act of cannibalism. It forces us to envision inhuman and inverted relationships.

In *Richard II* we first saw such intimations of distortion:

> That blood already, like the pelican,
> Hast thou tapp'd out and drunkenly carous'd.   *(R2,II.i.126-127)*

Thus Gaunt to his nephew, the presumed murderer of Gloucester. The pelican is the bird of Christ which, in the world of emblems at least, feeds its young on its own blood. The language does not require much explication: the emblem of love becomes in Gaunt's witty rhetoric that of hatred and murder. Spiritual exaltation becomes transposed into drunken exaltation, so that in one compressed metaphor there is a sense of the meaning of the crime, and especially of the psychological state which it reveals. I think the ugliness and disproportionate wit are intentional. A terrible imbalance in Richard is suggested. Drunken ecstasy signifies an isolation within one's own emotions and senses. Beneath the image of royalty there is another reality.[6]

I should like to note at greater length how certain rhetorical patterns establish relationships to each other and to a larger meaning, and to do so I begin now a reading of 2 Henry IV.

This play begins with the entrance of Rumour, a figure which suggests the moral uncertainties that envelop the action:

> I speak of peace, while covert enmity,
> Under the smile of safety, wounds the world.   (2H4,Induction,9-10)

Rumour reminds us of the fears and hatreds, ambitions and jealousies which permeate the drama. Specifically, Rumour describes Northumberland, who now lies "crafty-sick" in his "worm-eaten hold of ragged stone." The first of the terms I wish to trace is brought out by this figure.

Northumberland has undergone a great and symbolic change. In *Richard II* he was the minister of the king's deposition. The "most mighty prince" as Richard called him carried the business of rebellion to a successful conclusion. He in fact managed the abdication. In that play Northumberland had in full the pragmatism which Bolingbroke himself opposed to the hieratic ideals of monarchy. His speech after the deposition is an authentic statement of *hybris:* "my guilt be on my head, and there an end!" Like Bolingbroke, Northumberland once thought that history could be dominated by reasonable intentions. Given cause a king could be deposed. Yet he now finds himself the victim of guilt which emanates from the past to determine the future. He finds himself too the victim of what Morton calls "stormy passion." Between mourning for his son and rejoicing that "in poison there is physic" Northumberland states the extremes of this passion. He describes himself as "enrag'd with grief," and uses the simile of a fever-maddened man "impatient of his fit" breaking loose from the arms of his keeper. Northumberland now has discovered the nature of prophetic as opposed to rationalistic insight. Guilt does not end with the consummation of an event; it is cyclical. This Richard warned in the past—but in the history plays it is characteristic that the truth of prophecy be ignored:

> The love of wicked men converts to fear;
> That fear to hate, and hate turns one or both
> To worthy danger and deserved death.   (R2,V.i.66-68)

When, in 1 Henry IV, Hotspur receives news of his father's defection, he uses the word "sickness" with calculated ambiguity: "Sick now? droop now? This sickness doth infect / The very lifeblood of our enterprise." It is in the idiom of disease —to become a universal and dominant theme—that Northumberland is delineated in *2 Henry IV*. In that play he appears as it were in full allegorical panoply. The skeletal earl in the "worm-eaten hold of ragged stone" is an ideological death's head. The metaphor with which he describes himself is that of the man maddened by fever. His physical and psychological states are in fact paradigms of his moral state. There is revealed in his speech the same sense of blind destructiveness and animal passion that D. A. Traversi investigated.[7] The language of Northumberland is intended to cause certain reverberations. He invokes the chaos of which rebellion is only a reflection:

> . . . let one spirit of the first-born Cain
> Reign in all bosoms, that, each heart being set
> On bloody courses, the rude scene may end,
> And darkness be the burier of the dead! *(2H4,I.i.157-160)*

There is a specific reason for the metaphors involving primal guilt. More is involved than the contrast of the rebel's egomaniacal grief and the ruler's anguish for his country. In order to be used here the motif of Cain has come a long journey through the earlier plays. It comments implicitly on the problem so easily disposed of long ago by the rationalistic "my guilt be on my head, and there an end!" *Richard II* began in guilt with the crime of Cain. Gloucester's blood, according to Bolingbroke,

> like sacrificing Abel's, cries,
> Even from the tongueless caverns of the earth. *(R2,I.i.104-105)*

It was to redress this crime that Bolingbroke first challenged Mowbray. In *Richard II* the crime of Cain attached first to Richard, but it is important to note that by the end of the play it refers to Bolingbroke. At the end of the play it is clear that Bolingbroke's tone is already that of a man matured in pain. He speaks to the murderer of his cousin, and it is with what I think is conscious and self-directed irony that he ends the play, as he began it, with the mention of Cain:

> With Cain go wander thorough shades of night,
> And never show thy head by day nor light.
> Lords, I protest my soul is full of woe
> That blood should sprinkle me to make me grow.
> Come, mourn with me for what I do lament,
> And put on sullen black incontinent.
> I'll make a voyage to the Holy Land
> To wash this blood off from my guilty hand. *(R2,V.vi.43-50)*

The condition of things has after all not been changed; it is only that different protagonists assume the same role. In the first play of this cycle the Bishop of Carlisle predicted that the "Christian climate" would become involved in guilt;

20

the plays on Henry IV bear this out. Northumberland's invocation of Cain, the richest and darkest expression of guilt in these plays, is cumulative in its effectiveness. It suggests that guilt has become endemic; first used in describing individuals it now intimates something of the nature of political causes.

The invocation of Cain is not the only rhetorical element which serves to augment the sense of universal guilt. Richard's prophetic address to Northumberland furnishes the idea of disease to which the following plays will allude:

> The time shall not be many hours of age
> More than it is, ere foul sin gathering head
> Shall break into corruption. Thou shalt think,
> Though he divide the realm and give thee half,
> It is too little, helping him to all.   (R2,V.i.57-61)

The rhetoric embraces both the fact of rebellion and the greedy condition of the human will. We sense in its organic form a process which is inevitable and natural; it will break out literally in symbolic "corruption." When the vulpine Worcester alludes to "raising of a head" in *1 Henry IV* he permits himself a significant double meaning:

> And 'tis no little reason bids us speed,
> To save our heads by raising of a head;
> For, bear ourselves as even as we can,
> The king will always think him in our debt,
> And think we think ourselves unsatisfied,
> Till he hath found a time to pay us home.   (1H4,I.iii.283-288)

Self-preservation is for him the highest good. Hotspur too finds in "this head of safety" the answer to the supposed injustice of the king (1H4,IV.iii.103). When finally the imagery is used again by the king it brings to bear all the meanings its use has by now subsumed:

> . . . God knows, I had no such intent,
> But that necessity so bow'd the state
> That I and greatness were compell'd to kiss—
> 'The time shall come,' thus did he follow it,
> 'The time will come that foul sin, gathering head,
> Shall break into corruption': so went on,
> Foretelling this same time's condition.   (2H4,III.i.72-78)

The recapitulation of Richard's metaphor accomplishes several purposes. It indicates, for one thing, that Bolingbroke has come to understand and share the viewpoint of his dead enemy. The iterative use of the "head" image welds together some apparently disparate meanings. Some men raise a "head" of rebellion; others allege a "necessity" to assume greatness. All their intentions are subsumed by the expanded metaphorical meaning of a "head" of vile and corrupt matter, a sore which erupts on the body of the state.[8]

When Henry IV considers the state of the kingdom and says, "then you perceive the body of our kingdom, / How foul it is; what rank diseases grow," he gives emphasis to an idea of moral and physical disease linked by a single figure of speech. The theme of disease foliates in the speeches of other characters. In response to Northumberland his follower Morton has this to say:

> The lives of all your loving complices
> Lean on your health; the which, if you give o'er
> To stormy passion, must perforce decay.   (2H4,I.i.163-165)

He reminds the earl that he "cast th'event of war" when he said "Let us make head."

The dialogue which follows in the next scene takes up the same subject; the speakers there are Falstaff and the Lord Chief-Justice. Although in the language of comedy, this dialogue deals with issues of great seriousness, and is pitched upon the connotations of disease. The oppositions that are awakened in this interchange are those characteristic of the play as a whole. The "apoplexy" of the king is also that of Falstaff: it retains its fundamental meaning of paralysis. The paralysis from which Falstaff suffers is a moral one, the king's is both moral and physical. The Lord Chief-Justice is envisaged as the physician, imprisonment as the potion, and Falstaff as the patient. Falstaff rejects not only the prescription but the symptoms themselves. The moist eye, dry hand, yellow cheek and all other parts "blasted by antiquity" are disposed of by heroic sophistry. Yet the substance of the dialogue has been to introduce the theme of decay even where it seems least likely.[9]

After the words of the Lord Chief-Justice Falstaff thinks of the human condition itself as defined by characteristic diseases in time: "a man can no more separate age and covetousness than 'a can part young limbs and lechery; but the gout galls the one, and the pox pinches the other." He discourses now not of sack and food but of age, impotence, disease and death. He ends the scene with a speech of some importance, for it is thematic:

> A pox of this gout! or, a gout of this pox! for
> the one or the other plays the rogue with my great
> toe. 'Tis no matter if I do halt. I have the wars
> for my colour, and my pension shall seem the more
> reasonable. A good wit will make use of anything.
> I will turn diseases to commodity.   (2H4,I.ii.273-279)

The motif of disease includes the man who rebels from all ideological and moral claims, just as it includes all those who justify themselves by those claims. The last phrase of the speech indicates that, like certain other characters, Falstaff is ready to make his aberration the servant of his will. "Commodity" and "diseases" are concepts of some magnitude in this last play on Henry IV. The first (as in *King John*) crystallizes the intentions of all those concerned in profiting from the condition of the realm; the second suggests their values.

22

The Archbishop of York is the spokesman for the rebels in *2 Henry IV*, and his language accelerates the energy of the disease motif. "We are all diseas'd," he says,

> And with our surfeiting and wanton hours
> Have brought ourselves into a burning fever,
> And we must bleed for it; of which disease
> Our late King, Richard, being infected, died.　　*(2H4,IV.i.54-58)*

Like a "physician" he comes to "diet rank minds, sick of happiness" and "purge" the obstructions in the "very veins of life." The uses of the physician metaphor have been various: the Lord Chief-Justice applies it to himself when he rebukes Falstaff; Poins adds that "the immortal part" of Falstaff in fact needs a "physician," but "that moves not him." Warwick hopes that the kingdom, like a distempered body, "to his former strength may be restor'd / With good advice and little medicine." We ought perhaps to recall its first usage; as is the case with other figures of speech cited it derives from *Richard II*:

> Wrath-kindled gentlemen, be rul'd by me;
> Let's purge this choler without letting blood.
> This we prescribe, though no physician;
> Deep malice makes too deep incision.
> Forget, forgive; conclude and be agreed;
> Our doctors say this is no month to bleed.　　*(R2,I.i.152-157)*

When the metaphor is first used it is taken seriously by neither hearers nor speaker. It is taken with more and more seriousness in the succeeding plays, in which the vision of civil "madness cured" is so long unattainable.

When the Archbishop speaks of the causes of rebellion he combines the idea of sickness with images of distorted behavior. Like the imagery of the pelican in *Richard II* and the cannibalistic vision of blood on the lips of Earth in *1 Henry IV* his speech describing the "beastly feeder" (which is the "sick" commonwealth) intensifies the concept of the dehumanization of men. "Sickness" has become inseparable from bestiality. When the Archbishop speaks of the guilty commonwealth we may bring to mind the Bishop of Carlisle's speech in *Richard II*, in which the involvement of the "Christian climate" itself in the great crime is foreseen. From this "obscene" deed will come the "disorder" and "horror" which he predicts. "Disorder" is to be taken quite literally; it implies the deformation of the nature of life itself. Men are no longer images of God but of the beasts whose practices they imitate.

1 Henry IV opened on such a note. The king conceives of the civil war as a literal form of cannibalism. He makes a fervent and powerful contrast between the nature of war and the peace of Christ. Yet, when he invokes the "blessed cross" and the "holy fields" of Jerusalem it is only to have this vision invalidated by the reality of "civil butchery."[10] Westmoreland enters and describes the desecration which has occurred in Wales:

> A thousand of his people butchered;
> Upon whose dead corpse there was such misuse,
> Such beastly shameless transformation,
> By those Welshwomen done as may not be
> Without much shame retold or spoken of.   *(1H4,I.i.42-46)*

The prayer is the illusion, this is the reality. It gives dramatic power to the nightmare vision of Earth in one of the less pleasant versions of the Titan myth, her lips covered "with her own children's blood." There are, I think, two choices for the literal interpretation of Westmoreland's speech. One is that the bodies of the English have been dealt with as the body of Hotspur is later treated by Falstaff. The more likely alternative is that they have been sexually violated. The pattern of excess informs the event. Again the idea of "butchery" is involved—men are often dealt with in the world of this play like the animals they subsist on. They are the subjects of acts which are "beastly" and "shameless"—Carlisle had predicted that the new world would be "obscene." The sense of shame is insisted upon, and there is an equal emphasis on the "transformation" from men to corpses, from life and virility to symbolic devaluation.

The universality of guilt figured in excess may be noted in a variety of passages. Gadshill intimates that the *actions* of Falstaff are not wholly comic: "they pray continually to their saint, the commonwealth, or rather, not pray to her, but prey on her, for they ride up and down on her and make her their boots." The ribald sexual puns are easily noted; the equivocation between morality and rapacity may pass unobserved. But it is an equivocation representative of the activities of many other characters on this historical scene. It is one of the great themes of rebellion, political and otherwise. Even Hal and Hotspur are visualized, by the time of *2 Henry IV*, in the context of excess. Hotspur is now recalled by his ally, Lord Bardolph, as the man who

> with great imagination,
> Proper to madmen, led his powers to death
> And, winking, leapt into destruction.   *(2H4,I.iii.31-33)*

The prince, according to his father, is "humorous as winter." His passions are "like a whale on ground" and "rage and hot blood" are his counsellors. We are ultimately caught up in a universal view of the condition of nature. When Gloucester speaks of the natural world it is to reveal that, like the world of man, it has changed itself to a mysterious and loathly form:

> The people fear me, for they do observe
> Unfather'd heirs and loathly births of nature.
> The seasons change their manners, as the year
> Had found some months asleep, and leapt them over.   *(2H4,IV.iv.121-124)*

We are left with a sense of the universal transformation from order to chaos, from higher to lower forms of life, from the control of human nature to its unleashing.

24

This will be the world of "rotten times" until God puts "the world's whole strength / Into one giant arm."

The relationship between rhetoric and fact in the Henry IV plays is a problematic one. This we may see when Morton comments on the Archbishop of York:

> But now the Bishop
> Turns insurrection to religion.
> Supposed sincere, and holy in his thoughts.　　　*(2H4,I.i.200-202)*

The language, like the character of York, is quite ambiguous. "Supposed" holy (Morton is speaking of an ally), the bishop engages in what must be called a kind of ideological transubstantiation. In a sense what the bishop attacks, what is attacked with great frequency, is the idea of truth itself. The personification introducing the second play is, we remember, that of Rumour itself. "I have the wars for my colour" Falstaff said, and this kind of counterfeit intention permeates the plays. Indeed the word "counterfeit" will be used with iterative force. Revelations of counterfeit intentions come with great rapidity, causing us to revalue (and devalue) our opinion of agents and motivations. The description of Northumberland in *2 Henry IV* was adumbrated; we might note too the new information on Hotspur furnished by his widow and by Lord Bardolph's speech above. There is the well-known revelation of the rapacity of Falstaff to bear in mind. Something besides this may be noted: in Falstaff's reaction to Shallow we find an intense relationship between main and sub-plot. The past recaptured, we find, becomes the past stripped of illusion. When Falstaff says, "Lord, Lord, how subject we old men are to this vice of lying," we are, I think, intended to extrapolate. The speech refers not only to the other old men in these plays—Shallow, Falstaff himself, Northumberland, York, the king—but serves as a prelude to the scenes which follow. Falstaff's generalizations are always at least half-truths. Act IV, scene i, immediately following the declaration of Falstaff, tends to validate it. The Archbishop, "whose beard the silver hand of peace hath touch'd," is yet able to "dress" the "ugly form" of insurrection with the "true, native, and most proper shape" of truth. Lancaster later speaks of him as a counterfeiter "turning the word to sword, and life to death." He intimates the failure of belief itself:

> O, who shall believe
> But you misuse the reverence of your place,
> Employ the countenance and grace of heav'n,
> As a false favourite doth his prince's name,
> In deeds dishonourable? You have ta'en up,
> Under the counterfeited zeal of God.　　　*(2H4,IV.ii.22-27)*

Our sense, then, is of the oldest and presumably most moral agents in this world, the rulers spiritual and secular, as the direct causes of the subtle and corrupt changes in the total nature of *res publica*.

York has certainly not been alone in counterfeiting moral issues. Worcester in the first play and Lancaster in the second are also authors of deception. Perhaps Worcester needs no more to formulate him than the unconscious betrayal of his own rhetoric:

> Your son in Scotland being thus employ'd,
> Shall secretly into the bosom creep
> Of that same noble prelate.   *(1H4,I.iii.265-267)*

His sinuous personality is expressed in terms of a certain kind of realism. In response to the king's "liberal and kind offer" of pardon Worcester shows only suspicion and invective. His rhetoric (1H4,V.ii.8-21) reminds us of the strain of imagery which refers to men as if they were literally and figuratively beasts. In his essay on "Simulation and Dissimulation" Bacon praises the ability to keep secrecy, but "false profession" he calls "culpable," for it destroys "trust and belief." Worcester is guilty of this in many ways: as the man who deludes his king, his allies, and eventually his own nephew. Under the mask of the good counsellor is, to use his own term, the "fox" of treason. Lancaster, the brother of the prince, is concerned in a dialogue of "love and amity" near the end of the second play. The first thing Lancaster does after the truce of Gaultree Forest is to break the solemn pledge; the second is to order the rebel leaders executed; the last is to order the pursuit and butchery of the "scatt'red stray" of the opposing army, who have left the field "like youthful steers unyok'd," like a "school broke up." Like his father, Lancaster achieves political success and moral failure. His is the mask of friendship.

The theme of imposture is elaborated in comedy as well as in tragedy, so that we get a full conception of the possibilities of its meaning. The first scene of *1 Henry IV* raises quite seriously the issue of transformations of the soul and of the human image. It raises, in fact, the whole issue of the moral identity of the prince. The scene following reveals Hal's intention to transform himself. He does exorcize Hotspur, take on Hotspur's own quality of "honour," and progresses as far as from idler to military hero by the end of the first play. In the second play he moves from this to the more mature "royal image."[11] The career of Falstaff parodies this progression. It is a series of transformations of which he is quite conscious. He plays the role of hero on the highway, which is rapidly changed to coward. He is by turns sophist and actor, masquerading first as the king and then as the prince. He plays the role of corpse during the battle. He envisions himself as reforming, in a mockery of Hal's own intentions: "If I do grow great, I'll grow less; for I'll purge, and leave sack, and live cleanly, as a nobleman should do." In short, he vivifies the concept of imposture, for he undergoes every variety of transformation, from "Fortune's steward" to the last role, prisoner in the Fleet.

One of Falstaff's functions is to clarify the relationship of fact and ideal. He divests things of their ideological masks. When he questions ideals like those of honor they cannot survive the honesty of comic realism. He acts as a comic reagent on honor, truth and all the ideals of the world of order which, in these plays, often serve as the delusions covering criminal motives and acts. One of the things he demonstrates is that these ideals must be judged by their actual embodiment. He is as quick to penetrate their false appearance in politics as in the apparition of

Pistol at the Boar's-Head.

Our general impression is that of a world in which ideals fail men, and men fail ideals. Certainly the most important thing that substantiates this impression is the imposture of the king himself. The much-vaunted quality of honor as it relates to the king is seen precisely as Falstaff sees it when we learn of the counterfeits who are hunted down by Douglas. The king is in a sense the apotheosis of the idea of the counterfeit in these plays. On the field of battle he plays the role of leader, only to have Douglas comment with penetrating exactitude, "what art thou / That counterfeit'st the person of a king?" Douglas is, of course, for the first time that day of battle finally speaking to Henry IV. Is it mere accident that just after Douglas twice uses the word "counterfeit" in talking to and about Henry IV it should be the subject of a dissertation by Falstaff? The fat knight uses the word eight times in a short speech in which he accepts the idea of being a "counterfeit." We see here the relationship partially explained by Empson between the king and mock-king, except that *both* are mock kings.[12] The prince says to Falstaff, "thou art not what thou seem'st," and it is a statement the truth of which will be applied by the king to himself.

In seeking popular support the usurper offered the image of a humility not at all native to him. In 1 *Henry IV* he spoke with pride of having "dress'd" himself in humility. He "stole" courtesy from heaven and won through adroit use of promise and presence "allegiance from men's hearts." The man hid beneath the mask of state—he uses the term "a robe pontifical" to express the external quality of his conduct. He "show'd," he says, like a "feast." Later, in the second play, the usurper no longer feels pride but shame. He cannot, he says, "steep my senses in forgetfulness." Eventually it is with a tragic sense of self-knowledge that he comments on his actions to his son:

> God knows, my son,
> By what bypaths and indirect crook'd ways
> I met this crown. *(2H4,IV.v.184-186)*

His last speech reveals his sorrow for the honors he has "snatch'd with boist'rous hand." Perhaps the most explicit of his statements on the usurpation is that which reveals his sense of guilt: "How I came by the crown, O God forgive."

The "cold blood" which Falstaff saw operant in the sons of Bolingbroke effectively and I think ironically masters the passions of rebellion. The tense fifth act of 2 *Henry IV* is in its way a vindication of "cold and temperate blood." But if it is ideologically proper it has other aspects. The return to the world of order envisioned by the father is accomplished by the son. It is made, however, at the expense of something necessary but almost indefinable. Perhaps it may best be stated this way: Henry V begins as less than a man, and ends as more than one. He sees that the only way to escape the guilt which attaches to his inheritance is to abandon his personal being, to assume the role of father and brother to his countrymen. The last of the transformations in these plays is from man to "royal image."

Notes:

(1) D. A. Traversi, *Shakespeare From Richard II to Henry V* (Stanford, 1957), p. 116. Cf. R. J. Dorius, "Prudence and Excess in *Richard II* and the Histories," *Discussions of Shakespeare's Histories* (Boston, 1964), p. 25.

(2) L. F. Dean, *"Richard II:* The State and the Image of the Theater," *Shakespeare: Modern Essays in Criticism* (New York, 1961), pp. 159-168. Cf. G. Bonnard, "The Actor in Richard II," *SJ,* LXXXVII (1952), 87-101.

(3) R. A. Foakes, "Suggestions For a New Approach to Shakespeare's Imagery," *SS,* V (1952), 89.

(4) Una Ellis-Fermor, *The Frontiers of Drama* (London, 1945), pp. 77-95.

(5) This and succeeding quotations from the G. L. Kittredge edition (1936).

(6) *Vide* R. S. Berman, *"Richard II:* The Shapes of Love," *Moderna Språk,* LVIII (1954), 5.

(7) Traversi, p. 111.

(8) *Vide* F. Fergusson's study of "the hidden 'imposthume' which is poisoning the life of Claudius' Denmark" in *"Hamlet:* The Analogy of Action," *Hudson Review,* II (1949), 165-210; C. Spurgeon's study of "the distempered body of the kingdom" of *Henry IV* in *Shakespeare's Imagery* (Cambridge, 1935), p. 160; W. Clemen's study of "this canker of our nature" in *Hamlet* in *The Development of Shakespeare's Imagery* (Cambridge, Mass., 1951), p. 118.

(9) *Vide* Traversi, pp. 123-124 and J. Dover Wilson, *The Fortunes of Falstaff* (Cambridge, 1943), pp. 99-101.

(10) It is to be noted that some readers do not accept the sincerity of Henry's piety or his intention to go on a crusade.

(11) *Vide* R. S. Berman, "Shakespeare's Conscious Histories," *Dalhousie Review,* XLI (1961-62), 491-495.

(12) W. Empson, *Some Versions of Pastoral* (Norfolk, n.d.), p. 43. For additional references to the "counterfeit" king I am obliged to Professor Robert Daniel.

Scorpions, Serpents, and Treachery in Macbeth

by Dennis Biggins

Editors and commentators have, in general, passed over Macbeth's anguished but cryptic remark to Lady Macbeth: "O, full of scorpions is my mind, dear wife!" (III.ii.36).[1] Furness does not say anything about it in the New Variorum revised edition, nor does Dover Wilson in the New Cambridge. Kenneth Muir, in the revised Arden edition (London, 1959) merely notes a suggestion that there is a reference to the superstition that the plant basil propagated scorpions (p.86).

This suggestion was made by Roland M. Smith, who quotes or refers to various authorities for the belief that smelling basil breeds scorpions in the brain.[2] Mr. Smith's main concern is to show that the *Cyme* of V.iii.55 in the Folio text is *ocyme*, or Basil, which he thinks is also the "sweet oblivious antidote" (V.iii.43) that Macbeth seeks for his wife's sufferings; he suggests that Shakespeare was thinking of the notion that basil propagates scorpions in the brain when he gave Macbeth the exclamation "O, full of scorpions is my mind." It may be that there is a reference to this belief in Macbeth's utterance, but it is hardly relevant to the context. Macbeth's anguish is surely not to be referred, even marginally, to the effects of excessive basil-snuffing.

What does Macbeth mean when he says his mind is full of scorpions? Earlier in the scene Lady Macbeth reproachfully asks her husband why he keeps alone,

> Of sorriest fancies your companions making,
> Using those thoughts which should indeed have died
> With them they think on? Things without all remedy
> Should be without regard. What's done is done. *(V.iii.9-12)*

Perhaps Macbeth's metaphor is merely a powerful expression of his anguished brooding on Duncan's murder, which stings his mind like the tails of scorpions. Or there may be a suggestion of the Biblical "my father chastised you with whips, but I will chastise you with scorpions" (II *Chronicles*, x.11; cf. also I *Kings*, xii.11). In *A Worlde of Wordes, Or Most copious, and exact Dictionarie in Italian and Englishe* (London, 1598), John Florio defines one sense of *scorpion* as "a kinde of whip hauing plummets of leade at the ends of the cords to whip slaues and offendors with" (p.357). But although there are a number of Biblical echoes in the play,[3] I do not think that we simply have to do with one here. The scorpions in Macbeth's mind emblematize not remorse or the pangs of conscience, but rather fear. One does not have to accept Miss Lily B. Campbell's argument in *Shakespeare's Tragic Heroes: Slaves of Passion* (London, 1930), that the play is "a study in the complementary pair of passions of rash courage and fear" (p.238), to agree with her that from the murder of Duncan onward what motivates Macbeth's actions is fear.[4] In the immediate context of III.ii.36 the reference is to his fear of Banquo; Macbeth dreads that Banquo will in turn apply to him the example of treachery to one's sovereign that Macbeth has afforded in the murder of Duncan. The mention of scorpions occurs in a passage that links it with the treachery motif, which is expressed in the images of dissembling, false flattery and deceit that run through the play. When Lady Macbeth urges her husband to mask his brooding and to be "bright and jovial" at the banquet, he replies:

> So shall I, love; and so, I pray, be you.
> Let your remembrance apply to Banquo;
> Present him eminence both with eye and tongue—
> Unsafe the while, that we
> Must lave our honours in these flattering streams
> And make our faces vizards to our hearts,
> Disguising what they are.
> *Lady.*   You must leave this.
> *Macb.* O, full of scorpions is my mind, dear wife!
> Thou know'st that Banquo, and his Fleance, lives.   *(III.ii.29-37)*

The particularity of language with which Macbeth utters his thoughts is a notable feature of Shakespeare's presentation of him. Emotions and ideas are expressed in vivid visual metaphors. Through the striking image of the scorpions Macbeth makes concrete firstly, the notion of dissembling and flattery, of that hypocrisy which he and his wife have so well employed to snatch the crown, and secondly, the living menace embodied in Banquo and Fleance. It is symptomatic of the moral confusion that pursuing his ambition has wrought in Macbeth that, while admiring Banquo's "royalty of nature" (III.i.50), he simultaneously sees him in the same treacherous light as himself. Banquo may do to Macbeth what Macbeth has done to Duncan.

The connexion between scorpions and treacherous behaviour is not as tenuous as at first glance it may seem to be. Macbeth thinks of himself, and of Banquo and Fleance, as scorpions, I would suggest, because in medieval and Renaissance thought the scorpion is the emblem *par excellence* of flattering treachery. There is abundant literary documentation of the idea. The earliest example of it that I have found in English occurs in the *Ancrene Riwle* (c. 1200): "þe scorpiun is ones cunnes wurm þet haueð neb ase me seið sumdel iliche ase wummon. ᴣ is neddre bi-hinden. makeð feir semblaunt: ᴣ fikeð mid te heaued. ᴣ stingeð mid te teile."[5] Chaucer's contemporary, Dan Michel of Northgate, remarks that when a man praises and at the same time dispraises another, "þes is þe scorpioun þet makeþ uayr mid þe heauede.   and enueymeþ mid þe tayle."[6] Chaucer himself uses the image of the flattering but treacherous scorpion several times, most notably in *The Merchant's Tale*, where fickle Fortune is apostrophized as

Lyk to the scorpion so deceyvable,
That flaterest with thyn heed whan thou wolt stynge;
Thy tayl is deeth, thurgh thyn envenymynge.

. . . . . .

O monstre, that so subtilly kanst peynte
Thy yiftes under hewe of stidefastnesse,
That thou deceyvest bothe moore and lesse![7]

Caxton's version of Aesop's fable "of the wolfe the shepeherde and of the hunter" ends with the admonition that "men must nat trust in hym that hath two faces & two tunges for suche folke is like & semblable to [the] scorpion the whiche anoynteth with his tunge and pricketh sore with his tayle."[8]

Shakespeare could have got the notion of the treacherous scorpion from Chaucer,[9] or from Caxton, or simply from his own contemporaries. John Maplet says that the scorpion is "a Serpent of the earth, stinging deadly with his taile and of some is called flatering worme, for faire face shewed and friendly countenance. But if any man come neare hir behinde she payeth him home."[10] Edward Topsell echoes the anonymous author of the *Ancrene Riwle* in finding a resemblance to a woman's face in the scorpion's head, "the countenaunce whereof is fawning, and virgin-like. . . . Notwithstanding the fayre face, it beareth a sharpe sting in the tayle."[11] Topsell also remarks on "the crafty disposition of this Scorpion, and the great subtiltie and malice that it is indued withall in nature" (*ibid.*, p.226).

Possibly Shakespeare may have derived this conception of the falsely friendly scorpion from an Elizabethan revision of the English translation, by John of Trevisa, of the *De Proprietatibus Rerum* of Bartholomew Anglicus. This is Stephen Batman's *Batman vppon Bartholome*, which Shakespeare seems to have drawn upon occasionally. Trevisa-Batman explains that the scorpion is so called in Greek "for it stingeth with the tayle. . . . And this maner scorpion commeth of *Scorte* that is sweet, and of *Pogo*, . . . that is to seine, for before he feineth pleasance."[12]

The word "scorpion" appears in two other places in Shakespeare's writings: *2 Henry VI*, III.ii.85-87, and *Cymbeline*, V.v.43-45. In the former passage the context includes the idea of treachery; in the latter of hypocrisy. As used in *Macbeth*, in its apparent primary significance the word focuses the play's major theme of false appearances, while at the same time in its cryptic ambiguity it emblematizes the equivocation on which the action turns.

To the Middle Ages and to the Renaissance alike, scorpions belonged to the serpent family, and in the literary uses of "scorpion" and "serpent" there is frequent recourse not only to the common qualities of falsity and deceitfulness ascribed to these creatures, but also to their embodiment in the archetypal serpent-scorpion, the Devil. The Devil as serpent, of course, goes back to the earliest ideological traditions of Christianity. In Biblical exegesis scorpions also signify the Devil or his agents. In his *De universo Libri XXII*, Rabanus Maurus, for example, says that *coluber, cerasta, serpens, aspis, vipera, basiliscus* and *draco* all stand for the Devil or wicked men, and he also says: "Scorpio diabolum significat vel ministros," as in *Luke,* x, xi.[13] The association "scorpion-serpent-Devil" also appears elsewhere. In the fifteenth-century French *Mistére du Viel Testament,* Judith, after having slain Holofernes, is abused by his followers as

> Dyablesse pleine de diffame,
> Escorpion, oeil basilique,
> Chef cornu, gueulle draconique?
>
> . . . . .
>
> Monstre de beau semblant inique
> Fiction faulce et desloyalle, —
> D'avoir ung chef si manifique
> Occiz soubz equité loyalle![14]

Judith's behaviour is seen here as (a) diabolical; (b) scorpion-like; (c) serpent-like ("oeil basilique . . . gueulle draconique"—up to at least the seventeenth century basilisks and dragons were regarded as serpents); (d) masking treachery under an affectation of goodness and loyalty. The Tudor chronicler Edward Hall uses the scorpion and the serpent as emblems of treacherous and diabolical envy in this passage, recounting Henry the Fifth's address to the traitors Scrope, Gray and Richard Earl of Cambridge: "although some priuate Scorpion in your heartes, or some wild worme in your heades hath caused you to conspire my death and confusion, yet you shuld haue spared that deuelish enterprice as long as I was with mine army. . . ."[15] The Devil appears as deceitful scorpion in the sixteenth-century French poet du Bartas, as rendered by Joshua Sylvester:

> Thou play'st the Foxe when thou doost faine a-right
> The face and phrase of some deepe hypocrite,
> True painted toombe, dead-seeming coales, but quick;
> A Scorpion fell, whose hidden taile doth prick.[16]

The collocation of serpents and scorpions with false appearances or with the Devil, or both, is also found, to take some random examples, in Dunbar, Lyly, Chapman and Milton.[17] In the light of these associations, the scorpions in Macbeth's mind take on an added colouring highly appropriate to the play's undercurrent of diabolism.

To the Middle Ages and the Renaissance, then, scorpions and serpents were alike symbolical of deceit and malice, of the treacherous masquerading, after the Devil's way, as the well-intentioned. Both scorpions and serpents were used as images of mocking the time with fairest show, of the false face hiding what is known to the false heart. Serpents are frequently associated in Shakespeare, as in Elizabethan thought generally, with hypocrisy and treachery.[18] The references to serpents in *Macbeth* join with the scorpion image in III.ii.36 as metaphors of these evil qualities. The thematic importance of these images seems to have been overlooked hitherto, and their meaning has not always been properly understood. In the first of the serpent metaphors the central theme of the play is stated with epigrammatic vividness: Lady Macbeth adjures her husband to "look like the innocent flower, / But be the serpent under't" (I.v.66-67), to be, in fact, Chaucer's "scorpion so deceyvable," or Maplet's "flatering worme." It is to the strain of keeping up the role of scorpion, as well as to the fear and sense of insecurity that make it necessary, that Macbeth recurs in the speech I have already quoted (III.ii.29-37). Duncan is out of the way, but Malcolm, and more immediately Banquo, are living reminders of Macbeth's uneasy title to the throne, and an ever-present threat to his enjoyment of it.

It is this threat that Macbeth is obsessed with in his previous speech in III.ii, which incorporates the second serpent image found in the play:

> We have scotch'd the snake, not kill'd it.
> She'll close, and be herself, whilst our poor malice
> Remains in danger of her former tooth. *(III.ii.13-15)*

G. R. Elliott supposes that this passage shows Macbeth struggling with remorse. "The insidious insistence of conscience—the implicit subject of this present speech as a whole (13-26)—is a 'Snake' which his 'poore' strength has 'scorched' (slashed) in vain: he remains exposed to its poisonous 'Tooth' (13-15)."[19] The single word "malice," which Mr. Elliott glosses as "strength," surely forbids such an interpretation of the passage. It clearly refers to the act of regicide. Elliott later describes the "scorpions" filling Macbeth's mind as "offspring of the 'Snake' above (13)"; that is, they likewise represent, as Walter puts it, "pricking of conscience." But it is not *conscience* that prompts Macbeth's talk of snakes and scorpions; it is *fear*—fear that, in the upshot, the murder of Duncan was *not* "the be-all and the end-all here" (I.vii.5). The snake that has been merely "scotch'd" and not killed is precisely that rightful title to the throne, that true royalty, which must inevitably assert itself, and which, treacherously thrust aside in Duncan, confronts Macbeth in Malcolm, and in Banquo, the progenitor of future kings who kept his "allegiance clear" (II.i.28). It is characteristic of Macbeth's warped sense of values that he should envisage the true kingliness he has struck at as a snake—just as, a little later, he thinks of Banquo and Fleance as scorpions. Fair is indeed foul, as foul was fair. It was not conscience, but the foredoomed search for security, that led Macbeth, in the previous scene, to arrange the murder of Banquo and Fleance:

> To be thus is nothing,
> But to be safely thus. Our fears in Banquo
> Stick deep; and in his royalty of nature
> Reigns that which would be fear'd. *(III.i.48-51)*

Macbeth's preoccupation here is with a chimerical security—"to be safely thus"—and with the fear that Banquo may indeed plague him with those "Bloody instructions" (I.vii.9) he himself has taught. It is the same preoccupation that runs through his speeches in III.ii.; this it is that makes him envy the dead Duncan:

> After life's fitful fever he sleeps well.
> Treason has done his worst. Nor steel nor poison,

Malice domestic, foreign levy, nothing,
Can touch him further.   *(III.ii.23-26)*

In these lines Macbeth rehearses, not so much the perils Duncan is now free of, as the various forms of reprisal haunting the "terrible dreams / That shake us nightly" (III.ii.18-19). "Malice domestic" clearly harks back to "our poor malice," a few lines earlier. If Macbeth could play the scorpion, why not Banquo too? And, although more remote than the fear of "malice domestic," there is also the apprehension that Malcolm may yet return with "foreign levy."

Hence the third serpent image appears in Macbeth's reaction to the news of the partial success of his murderous plot against Banquo and Fleance:

There the grown serpent lies; the worm that's fled
Hath nature that in time will venom breed,
No teeth for th' present.   *(III.iv.29-31)*

Resuming his previous line of thought, Macbeth comforts himself with the reflection that one immediate source of danger—the potential traitor Banquo, like Macbeth himself, "the smylere with the knyf under the cloke," maybe—has been eliminated, although Fleance represents a future menace. Again we have the moral involution: the serpent-traitor Macbeth sees those who threaten his usurped crown as traitors, and so, as serpents. This corruption of the moral judgment is, of course, part of his punishment, of his damnation, as some critics will have it. As Macbeth pursues his desperate attempts to anchor himself on his stolen throne, his distorted moral vision sees treachery at every turn. Macduff flees, and his family, "and all unfortunate souls / That trace him in his line" (IV.i.152-153), are slaughtered as traitors by contamination. The difficulty of separating the traitor from the true subject is a dominant concern of Act IV, as indeed it is of the whole play. Under the tyrant, Scotland becomes a land where men grow bewildered in their fear, and cannot grasp the distinction between treachery and truth. Her husband's equivocal flight, Lady Macduff says, "was madness. When our actions do not, / Our fears do make us traitors" (IV.ii.3-4). Ross observes that "cruel are the times, when we are traitors / And do not know ourselves" (IV.ii.18-19). Malcolm's elaborate testing of Macduff in the next scene (IV.iii) acts out pragmatically Duncan's observation in I.iv: "There's no art / To find the mind's construction in the face" (IV.ii.11-12).

The play's final serpent images appear appropriately in the weird sisters' recital of ingredients for their cauldron; the charm that ushers in the last fatal "equivocation of the fiend, / That lies like truth" (V.v.43-44) includes "Fillet of a fenny snake," "Adder's fork, and blindworm's sting," and "Scale of dragon" (IV.i.12,16,22).

One of the play's great ironies is that once Macbeth has played the snake and acted the scorpion in the murder of Duncan, until his final hardening in spiritual death, when life itself is a tale told by an idiot, he sees a serpent under every innocent flower. Having once torn up the bond of social, political and individual human trust with bloody hand, Macbeth cannot piece it together again. The ancient

34

proverb, *sub omni lapide scorpius dormit,* was commonly misinterpreted in the Renaissance. It is correctly explained by Henricus Stephanus in his notes on the *Adagia* of Erasmus: "Omni in loco reperiuntur dolosi homines: nullum est hominum genus cui non admixti sint aliqui fraudulenti: inter omnes homines, cujuscunque conditionis sint, insidiosi & fallaces aliqui reperiuntur."[20] After enacting the role of the proverbial scorpion, Macbeth might well lament, "O, full of scorpions is my mind!" To him, in his lonely eminence, all who fail to bow the knee may be, like himself, "dolosi . . . fraudulenti . . . insidiosi & fallaces." The crime of treason, the sin of treachery bear their own punishment along with them: the isolation of the damned, or of the Devil himself.

Notes:

(1) Shakespeare citations and references are to the *Complete Works,* ed. G. L. Kittredge (Boston, 1936). In other quotations I have silently expanded contractions, where necessary.

(2) "Macbeth's *Cyme* Once More," *MLN,* LX (1945), 33-38.

(3) See Muir, Arden ed., pp. 51, 57, 80, 160, and *Shakespeare's Sources I: Comedies and Tragedies* (London, 1957), pp. 179-180. In his ed. of *Macbeth* (London, 1962), J. H. Walter glosses *full . . . mind* as "(a) pricking of conscience, (b) jealousy of Banquo, (c) tortures of fear," and suggests that there is an echo of *Revelation,* ix.3-5, which describes "locusts," to which "was given power, as the scorpions of the earth have power" to hurt "those men which have not the seal of God in their foreheads" (p. 116). There may well be such an echo present, but the line is more pregnant than this. See also below, n. 13.

(4) Cf. Ruth L. Anderson, "The Pattern of Behavior Culminating in *Macbeth,*" *Studies in English Literature 1500-1900,* III (1963), 172.

(5) *The English Text of the Ancrene Riwle, Edited from Cotton MS. Nero A.XIV,* ed. Mabel Day EETS, O.S. 225 (London, 1952), p. 92, ll. 5-8.

(6) *Dan Michel's Ayenbite of Inwyt, or, Remorse of Conscience,* ed. Richard Morris, EETS, O.S. 23 (London, 1866), p. 62.

(7) *CT* IV(E) 2058-64: *The Works of Geoffrey Chaucer,* ed. F. N. Robinson, 2nd ed. (Boston, 1957), p. 123. Cf. also *MLT,* II(B¹) 404-406; *MancT,* IX(H) 271; *BD* 636.

(8) *The Fables of Esop, in English* (London, 1500?), sig. I 2ᵛ.

(9) There are some (admittedly slight) parallels between *Macbeth* and *The Man of Law's Tale.* In both works treacherous murders are committed under cover of hospitality; in both, murderers try to implicate the sleeping innocent by leaving bloody knives near them. There are affinities between Chaucer's "Sowdanesse" and Lady Macbeth: both are dissemblers, ruthless in their purposes, who deny their femininity; both are likened to devils.

(10) *A greene Forest, or a naturall Historie* (London, 1567), fol. 101ᵛ.

(11) *The Historie of Serpents* (London, 1608), p. 224.

(12) *Batman vppon Bartholome, his Booke "De Proprietatibus Rerum,"* newly corrected, enlarged and amended (London, 1582), fol. 380ᵛ. The original Latin reads: "sic grece dictus eo quod cauda figat. . . . Et dicitur scorpio a scorte quod est dulce. et poio . . . id est fingere quia in anteriori parte blandicias fingit. in posteriori pungit." *De proprietatibus rerum*

(Cologne, 1481), fol. 407ʳ. For Shakespeare's possible indebtedness to *Batman vppon Bartholome*, see Francis Douce, *Illustrations of Shakspeare and of Ancient Manners*, 2 vols. (London, 1807).

(13) *PL*, CXI, col. 232 B-C. The Biblical term "scorpions" is often used figuratively to mean malicious, crafty and diabolical persons or forces, as in, e.g., *Deuteronomy*, viii.15, *Ezekiel*, ii.6, *Luke*, x.19, *Revelation*, ix.3,5,10.

(14) *Le Mistére du Viel Testament*, publié . . . par le Baron James de Rothschild, SATF (Paris, 1878-91), V, 349, ll. 44201-08.

(15) *Hall's Chronicle* (London, 1809), p. 61.

(16) *Bartas his Deuine Weekes and Workes* (London, 1605), pp. 309-310.

(17) See, e.g., *The Flytyng of Dunbar and Kennedie*, ll. 55-58, 249-252 in *The Poems of William Dunbar*, ed. John Small, STS (Edinburgh and London, 1893), I, 13, 19; *Euphues and The Triumphs of Trophes*, ll. 33-40 in *The Complete Works of John Lyly*, ed. R. Warwick Bond (Oxford, 1902), II, 146, ll. 18-23, III, 429; *Hero and Leander*, 4th Sestiad, l. 296 in *The Poems of George Chapman*, ed. Phyllis Brooks Bartlett (New York, 1962); *Samson Agonistes*, ll. 355-360, 997-998 and *The Doctrine and Discipline of Divorce*, Ch. 5 in *The Works of John Milton* (New York, 1931-38), I, part ii, III, part ii, 448, ll. 12-21.

(18) See, e.g., *2H6*, III.ii.264-269; *R2*, III.ii.129-132; *RJ*, III.ii.73-74; *Ham.*, I.v.39-40; *Oth.*, V.ii.285; *Lear*, V.iii.82-84; *Cor.*, III.i.287. Anthony G. Petti points out that in contemporary literature "Mary Queen of Scots, among many other things, was a venomous serpent." ("Beasts and Politics in Elizabethan Literature," *Essays and Studies by Members of the English Association*, 16 [1963], p. 75.)

(19) *Dramatic Providence in "Macbeth"* (Princeton, 1958), pp. 117-118.

(20) *Desiderii Erasmi Roterodami Opera Omnia* (Leiden, 1703-06), II, col. 164 D-E.

Shakespeare's Anti-Hero: Hamlet and the Underground Man

by Stanley Cooperman

I swear gentlemen, that to be too conscious is an illness—a real, thoroughgoing illness . . . an intelligent man cannot become anything seriously . . . Let us suppose, for example, that it feels insulted . . . To come at last to the deed itself, to the very act of revenge. Apart from the one fundamental nastiness the luckless mouse succeeds in creating about it so many other nastinesses in the form of doubts and questions, that there inevitably works up around it a sort of fatal brew, a stinking mess . . . maybe it will begin to avenge itself too, but as it were, piecemeal, in trivial ways, from behind the stove, incognito, without believing either in its own right to vengeance, or in the success of its revenge . . . Can a man of perception respect himself at all?   Dostoevsky, Notes from the Underground.

Knowledge, and the ability to act upon knowledge, are qualities essential for the Hero—the man who knows that life is real and earnest; who rescues the maiden, foils the villain, exposes wrongdoing. The tragic Hero, of course, is not quite so successful; yet he too is a man of action and knowledge—defeated by fate, perhaps, or treachery, a flaw in his own character or an emotional myopia which prevents him from focussing his attention on the real enemy. In any event, the Hero takes himself and his world quite seriously, and we rejoice at the nobility of his success or feel the tragic power of his defeat.

The man, however, who mocks himself no less than others; who burlesques his own postures; who sees all action as absurd and all inaction as sterile; who makes a fetish of his own inconsistency; who takes a perverse pride in his own suffering; who sees men (including himself) as puppets and the world as a bloated carcass; who makes plans while proclaiming the futility of any plan and achieves results which often negate the plans themselves; who wishes himself well out of the disease of human society but devotes himself, even at the risk of his life, to finding a cure for it; who desperately searches for goodness while convinced of the impossibility of goodness; who laughs, weeps, snarls, blesses and curses in all but the same breath—what can become of such a man? In the character of Hamlet, and in the literary existentialism of the nineteenth century, he becomes the Anti-Hero.

It is, of course, a long way from Jacobean England to nineteenth century Europe, and any attempt to set up exact parallels would be absurd. There are, however, points at which the two worlds intersect, and it is perhaps for this reason that *Hamlet* of all Shakespeare's works has so fully captured the imagination of readers and audiences during the past century. Times of metaphysical and moral crisis produce a literature of crisis, and the hero of action gives way to the hero of inaction; with the "revelation that all hope of atonement and salvation is illusionary,"[1] the human quest lies not so much in what to do as in what to be—the infinite and terrible examination of existence itself. Precisely because the examination is so painful, however, Anti-Heroes such as Hamlet or Dostoevsky's Underground Man[2] are accused of being anti-social, immoral and impious. Good people are likely to see them as either irrational or diseased, for orthodoxy presents comfort which they perversely refuse, and practical respectability suggests a status quo which they foolishly disturb.

The Renaissance came late to England, but when it did arrive the impact was enormous. Of course, one cannot define the syndrome rather loosely known as Jacobean pessimism in terms of any single factor; as Henri Fluchère suggests, however, the importance of Machiavelli must not be underestimated. "Never before had the human mind turned such a crude and destructive light upon the moral conscience"[3]—human motivations were exposed as corrupt appetites which often feed upon their own destruction; the simple dualism of good and evil itself became a paradox:

> If one considered everything carefully, one will find something which seems to be virtue, and to follow it would be ruin; and something else which seems to be vice, but ultimately security and prosperity come of it.
>
> If our religion never recommends force to us, it wants us to be readier to suffer than to do a great deed. This way of life, consequently, seems to have debilitated the world and to have delivered it up to wicked men. They are sure to have control of it, knowing that most men, to get to heaven, think more of submitting to blows than of avenging them.[4]

Like Machiavelli, both Hamlet and the Underground Man perceive the moral corruption of any submission which enables evil to flourish. (Unlike Machiavelli, however, they also perceive the absurdity of becoming evil in order to oppose it; this is, as I hope to demonstrate, the very basis of their existential dilemma.) Hamlet despises the practical and reasonable exhortation to accommodate himself; to "live and feed" upon the dunghill of a corrupt world. Dunghills may indeed be nourishing, but only if men first turn themselves into insects, and this is a metamorphosis which the Anti-Hero finds difficult—far more difficult than do the safely orthodox and stupidly (or shrewdly) philistine. The image of the insect is common to all existential literature, for the Anti-Hero sees only corruption where the reasonable gentlemen rejoice in a healthy status quo.[5] As a result, the Anti-Hero is nauseated to his very soul; there is the "sickness unto death" of Kierkegaard, a spiritual gagging on the excrement which sensible, ignorant or flesh-ridden persons find nourishing enough. The blessing of awareness brings the curse of existential disgust and despair; things "rank and gross in nature" live complacently in an "unweeded garden," the insects feed upon the tumor, the "imposthume," the rottenness and discharge from a cankered world.

38

The existential drama of the Anti-Hero does not, of course, refer merely to formal, philosophical Existentialism per se. My use of the term "existential" for Hamlet's suffering, nausea, and final affirmation, is rather a description of spiritual isolation in which affirmation itself is achieved not through simple action, ready-made orthodoxies, or socio-political calculations, but rather through perception into the total responsibility of the individual for action, together with the realization that—given such responsibility—action itself is both irreversible and absolute. The Anti-Hero, in short, is aware both of the absurd nature of action in a corrupt world, and the absurdity of inaction as well. The result is that heroic process is defined by *perception* rather than by action. Such a heroism—in worldly terms—must indeed seem inept, fumbling, or merely "negative," and for this reason the Anti-Hero (the hero of spiritual perception rather than action) tends to be mocked, or attacked, by those for whom accommodation is the supreme truth, and "efficiency" the supreme virtue.

Why not, as G. Wilson Knight suggests for Hamlet, pursue "forgetfulness" as the analgesic to obtain "peace of mind"?[6] Certainly both Hamlet and the Underground Man are suffering and would welcome an analgesic; but about them they see the philistine and hypocrite "forgetting" corruption, proceeding as though appearance were truth, and painting the truth for the sake of appearance. Peace of mind on a dunghill, after all, is itself disgusting:

> I will not take a hen-house for a mansion. The palace of crystal
> may be an idle dream, it may be that it is inconsistent with the
> laws of nature and that I have invented it through my own stu-
> pidity . . . But what does it matter that I am inconsistent? . . . I
> know, anyway, that I will not be put off with a compromise, with
> a recurring zero, simply because it is consistent with the laws of
> nature and actually exists.[7]

The result is "chemical disintegration," all meaning "flies off into the air," the only course is "to beat the wall as hard as you can"; given a choice between a nauseating inactivity or a frenzied activity which "repels consciousness at least for a time," one is left with the realization that "the sole vocation of any intelligent man is babble, that is, the intentional pouring of water through a sieve."[8] In a situation permitting no way out, faced with a corrupt world unaware of its own corruption, the Anti-Hero becomes an actor, a "disturbing influence," and ridicules himself for being both:

> And of course he knows himself that he is doing himself no sort
> of good with his groans; he knows better than anyone else that
> he is only harassing and lacerating himself for nothing; he knows
> that even the audience before whom he is making his efforts,
> and his whole family, listen to him with loathing, and do not put
> a ha'porth of faith in him, and inwardly understand that he might
> moan differently, more simply, without trills and flourishes.[9]

So the Underground Man describes his existential "toothache of the soul," and one is immediately reminded of Hamlet as we first meet him: disagreeable, lethargic, and misanthropic in the midst of what Mr. Knight sees as "the healthy bustle of the court,"[10] repulsing his family's overtures and resenting the implication that his "particular" grief borders on affectation. Hamlet, however, knows all too well that the bustle of the court is the stir of parasites feeding upon Claudius' corruption. It is the Anti-Hero, not the "positive man" who knows that the world is out of joint, and the result, as Mr. Fluchère remarks of *Hamlet*, is despair:

> Weariness creeps in, discouragement oppresses those who do not plunge heart and soul into matter, and who are beset by ingratitude, injustice, treachery, violence and cruelty. The best of characters are weighed down by the consciousness of imperfection . . . There are so many pitfalls, such a swarming of vice, a sabbath of witches riding men's foul egoisms, a mad rhythm of passions in pursuit of power and pleasure, ending dizzily with the hero crushed against the wall.[11]

When the play opens, Hamlet is already in the grip of existential nausea: "the disgust revealed in his first soliloquy . . . precedes rather than derives from his external situation."[12] As we shall see, this emotional torment cannot be explained simply by his mother's remarriage; the causes of despair are grounded in Hamlet's idealization and generalization, which in turn spring from the moral innocence which cannot accommodate to the painted dunghill of the court. And in this situation a clear-cut statement of fact provides no relief; indeed, while for some men the Ghost's call to action would have come as a resolution, for Hamlet it adds still another dimension of despair: "external diseases and inner disaffection, far from finding resolution in the prospect of action . . . exasperate each other in mutual aggravation."[13] The Anti-Hero finds it impossible to affirm life—while he knows it to be parasitic upon corruption; he cannot, as Harold Goddard so blandly advises Hamlet, either reconcile himself to it or set about "regenerating" it.[14]

There is no doubt, again, that the Anti-Hero is "negative"; he denies the world because he sees it as corruption, and for those who have a stake in the corruption, who feed upon it knowingly or unknowingly, this negativism is dangerous. Mr. Knight's judgment on Hamlet, for example, is precisely the judgment made against the Underground Man by clerical and secular philistines who are "human" enough to nourish themselves on a diseased status quo. Hamlet, says Mr. Knight, represents "inhuman cynicism," he is "deadly and venomous":

> Hamlet is not of flesh and blood, he is a spirit of penetrating intellect and cynicism and misery, without faith in himself or anyone else, murdering his love for Ophelia, on the brink of insanity, taking delight in cruelty, torturing Claudius, wringing his mother's heart, a poison in the midst of the healthy bustle of the court . . . he has walked and held converse with death,

and his consciousness works in terms of death and the negation
of cynicism. He has seen the truth not only of humanity, but of
the universe: and the truth is evil. Thus Hamlet is an element of
evil in the state of Denmark . . . It was the devil of the knowledge
of death which possesses Hamlet and drives him from misery
and pain to increasing bitterness, cynicism, murder and
madness.[15]

There is a remarkable syllogism here: Hamlet sees the truth, the truth is evil,
hence Hamlet's insistence upon truth is also evil; it would be far kinder and more
comfortable to avoid the truth altogether. This is, precisely, the solution of the
philistine, for whom life itself, at its most desirable level, is a form of analgesic.
The Anti-Hero, however, insists that evil lies not in perception of truth, but rather
in its avoidance; only when truth is faced can virtue exist. It is his insistence on
truth that calls down upon his head the indictment of the worldling; the Anti-
Hero is mad, cruel, inhuman—even unchristian. (One remembers the good clergy-
men denouncing Kierkegaard as a threat to respectable religion.) For the clerical
or secular philistine, all is easy and clear-cut, including the essential principle
that successful evil—by reason of its success—becomes virtue; hence Hamlet's
insistence upon truth is immoral. Such is the paradox implicit in Mr. Knight's
judgment, and one would almost imagine that Hamlet had it in mind when he
bitterly remarks:

> Forgive me this my virtue,
> For in the fatness of these pursy times
> Virtue itself of vice must pardon beg.   (III.iv.152-154)

Most certainly Hamlet *has* seen death; he has seen the death's head beneath the painted surface of Claudius' smile, he has seen the entire court—
including his friends, his mother, and the girl he wished to love—not as "eminently
likeable people" but rather as the tools and creatures of corruption. He has seen
death and so can define the life about him, while those who have failed to see
death—or even avoid it for "peace of mind"—become parasites upon evil. The
parasite, however, cannot recognize the disease upon which he feeds; this recognition is the tormented privilege of the Anti-Hero, who is attacked precisely
because of his awareness. Hence the terrible irony of Guildenstern's compliment to Claudius:

> Most holy and religious fear it is
> To keep those many many bodies safe
> That live and feed upon your Majesty.   (III.iii.7-10)

The "flights of angels" are ultimately invoked for Hamlet and Hamlet alone;
whether this is "ironic" as Roy Battenhouse maintains, or whether it is indeed
the final testimony to spiritual heroism and anguish, depends to a great extent
upon the nature of Claudius' court. If the court represents health, then the disease

most certainly is Hamlet's; if the world of appearance is a fine place after all, the Anti-Hero's emphasis upon corruption defines nothing more than his own neurosis, and the Underground Man is less a seer than a patient.

Mr. Battenhouse sees Claudius as a good and effective king; his crime is past, and given the proper cooperation Claudius may, in time, earnestly repent to the general welfare of Denmark and the satisfaction of all concerned. Mr. Goddard complains that Hamlet should have attempted to "regenerate" the king, who—like all sensitive men that poison their brothers—is commendably conscience-stricken; while Mr. Knight notes with approval that the king behaves as successful murderers ought to if they are decent fellows: he is kind and generous to the members of his court. Mr. Knight, indeed, insists that whatever treachery Claudius ultimately resorts to, the corrupting factor is Hamlet himself—the "inhuman" and misanthropic "death-force" compelling the king, despite the latter's basic benevolence and "life-force," into self-tormenting evil.

Certainly the nature of Claudius is the very crux of the play; if indeed the king is a representative of life-force, if indeed he poisons "with no offense i'the world," then Hamlet's Anti-Heroic role is destructive and nothing more. If, on the other hand, Claudius is the embodiment of murderous hypocrisy (the imagery of which is developed throughout the play), then his own amiability and the neatness of his court cover the deepest damnation; what Bishop Hall referred to as "noisesome carrion," a stench in the nostrils of God, perverting society for its own ends.[16]

Granted that Claudius is a diplomat, a man of smiles and "efficient action," it is hardly possible to deny that the horror of assassins and hypocrites is due precisely to their efficiency and fair appearance. Certainly Claudius can "dispose of business with no unnecessary circumstance, and so leave himself time for enjoying the good things in life"[17]—even his assassination of the elder Hamlet was a thing of admirable efficiency (no less admirable than his later corruption of Laertes, the competence of which Mr. Knight praises so highly). No waste motion in that earlier business: a smooth filip of a vial; a neat elimination of a brother. What sort of man, after all, chooses poison as his weapon? As Mr. Bradley points out, the poisoner is nothing if not subtle and diplomatic; indeed, he may dislike the very sight of blood or sound of violence.[18]

Throughout the first half of the play, from the very moment we hear Claudius in his ambiguous speech of "discrete sorrow," there is the slow building up of corruption's smooth, painted and plausible face. There is, as yet, no direct statement of Claudius' hypocrisy; the progression is gradual, and all subsequent action refers back to the smoothness and amiability in the first scenes. Claudius' pious offer to be a "father" to Hamlet creates only repugnance when we understand the delicate assassination which has made the offer possible. We see him use "common sense" to stop Hamlet's mourning; and no less plausibly, no less honestly, use common sense to enflame Laertes' passion. Indeed, when it suits him Claudius is the lawyer who can support any side of a question according to the demands of his purpose.

With Hamlet, Claudius plays the "kindly uncle," with Laertes, he plays Hamlet; it is unmanly to remember the common fate of fathers, it is unmanly to forget it.

Both arguments are plausible and easy—no less easy, indeed, than pouring a bit of liquid into a king's ear. Shakespeare, of course, often parallels physical poison with moral poison, both administered the same way: through the victim's ear. Lady Macbeth, for example, says: "Hie thee hither that I may pour my spirits in thine ear and chastise thee with the valour of my tongue"; Iago, planning the downfall of his master, will "pour this pestilence into his ear." So Claudius follows his physical poisoning of the elder Hamlet with the moral poisoning of Laertes; either verbal or liquid, the deadly agent produces the same result. At once the manipulator of and source for such "pestilence," Claudius has by the end of the play reduced an entire court to the status of panderers to his own appetite.[19]

As the surface of murderous hypocrisy, Claudius' fair behavior early in the play (which Knight, Battenhouse, Goddard et al. find so impressive) is only to be expected; hypocrisy with a foul surface would seem to be a contradiction in terms. The action of the play, however, bares the pollution of hypocrisy not merely within Claudius, but within the court which "feeds" upon him; there is the horror of a master of corruption who "by virtue of his position and his seeming splendour can pervert not merely his queen, but the entire land."[20] It is Hamlet alone who sees the filth beneath the gilt, the disease on which the world is feeding. For the parasites, this negation makes no sense; for Claudius it makes too much sense, and he "affectionately" wishes this despairing, bitter, and newly acquired son to remain within his sight—and if need be, within his reach.

In addition to, and running parallel with the imagery of disease and disgust which Caroline Spurgeon so accurately listed, there is throughout the play the imagery of hypocrisy—and this imagery is itself emphasized by action. The corruption of Claudius' first speech, for example, does not become evident until the king's true relation to Gertrude and Hamlet is revealed. Even before the revelation of the crime which is the foundation of Claudius' reign, however, the speech seems unsavoury; it is defensive and calculating; its devotion "doth protest too much"; and its ambiguous smoothness of language and reconciliation of paradox (after the ominous atmospheric effects, the "sickness" and "eruption" of the play's opening) is unmistakeable:

> Though yet of Hamlet our dear brother's death
> The memory be green, and that it us befitted
> To bear our hearts in grief and our whole kingdom
> To be contracted in one brow of woe,
> Yet so far hath discretion fought with nature
> That we with wisest sorrow think on him
> Together with remembrance of ourselves.
> Therefore our sometime sister, now our Queen,
> The imperial jointress to this warlike state,
> Have we, as 'twere with a defeated joy—
> With an auspicious and a dropping eye,
> With mirth in funeral and dirge in marriage,

> In equal scale weighing delight and dole—
> Taken to wife. Nor have we herein barred
> Your better wisdoms, which have freely gone
> With this affair along. For all, our thanks.   *(I.ii.1-16)*

This first impression of Claudius cannot be passed off as usual court formalism: Shakespeare calculated his effects very closely in first speeches, the introduction of a character serving as a guide for audience attitude. We see Hamlet, for example, alienated and in black, and his first words—a bitter pun—are totally characteristic of the man. The ambiguous introduction of Claudius is no less characteristic, and as a result we certainly feel—before any further data is offered— an element of counterfeit among the polished gold of the king's words.

The impression of ambiguity—of undefined hypocrisy—is immediately reinforced by Hamlet's pun ("A little more than kin and less than kind") and by his explicit reference to the "seems" of counterfeit emotion ("actions that a man might play"). The king responds with a "wooing" speech; he praises Hamlet's "sweet and commendable" grief, but calls upon Heaven, nature, and common sense to prove that it is "unmanly." (Later, of course, he is to take precisely the opposite position with Laertes.) Furthermore he begs Hamlet, in the name of "love," to "think of us as a father"—again pointing to the terrible revelation of Claudius' true relationship—and asks the prince to remain at court for "cheer and comfort." As the play progresses we remember this scene, and the reality behind the gentle appearance is repulsive: a successful assassin, enjoying the fruits of crime surrounded by an amiable and unsuspecting court, is faced with the as-yet-vague suspicions of the murdered man's son; certainly Claudius wishes Hamlet to remain at court—an efficient poisoner would be a fool to let a potential source of opposition out of his sight. Hamlet must be either won over or destroyed.

Finally, going to his carouse, the king speaks of the "jocund health that Denmark drinks today"—and the ambiguity and irony are complete: coming after the "sickness" which Shakespeare so carefully introduced, the king's good-fellowship, his hail-and-well-met posture itself creates foreboding, reinforced by Hamlet's soliloquy on rankness and grossness, the "unweeded garden" and existential disgust of the Anti-Hero. And at this point the audience must share rather than judge Hamlet's "suspicion"—his insistence upon some as-yet-undefined foulness.

The theme of hypocrisy is further developed by almost every speech in Scene Three. And just as the king had neatly woven his paradoxes and antitheses in his first address to the court, so Polonius, in advising Laertes, follows the same formalism—a balanced and artificial prose. Moreover, the basis of his advice is calculation for effect, for appearance; morality itself is reduced to a patterned and vacuous surface. After this advice, the very essence of which is calculated falsity, Polonius (with unconscious irony) adds:

> This above all: to thine own self be true,
> And it must follow, as the night the day,
> Thou canst not then be false to any man.   *(I.iii.78-80)*

Thus the speaker reveals his own hypocrisy, which he fails to recognize for what it is. A parasite upon authority based upon corruption, Polonius is at home in his environment—it is no wonder that he is the first to be convinced that Hamlet is mad (the parasite philistine must always see the Anti-Hero as "abnormal"); it is no wonder that Hamlet refers to the veteran worldling as a "chameleon," which in Elizabethan terms was the very symbol of hypocrisy.

It is in this scene too that falsity envelopes Ophelia. Both Laertes and Polonius warn the young girl that Hamlet is far above her; that it would be impossible for them to marry, and that the prince must be avoided. In Act Five, however, the Queen remarks over Ophelia's grave:

> I hoped thou shouldst have been my Hamlet's wife,
> I thought thy bride-bed to have decked, sweet maid,
> And not strewed thy grave. *(V.i.238-240)*

There was, in other words, clear expectation that Hamlet would marry Ophelia, and politics was obviously no barrier. In speaking to the Queen about Hamlet's "love-madness," however, Polonius acts as though the courting were both a well-kept secret, and politically impossible. He righteously—and hypocritically—proclaims that as a man of "faith" he had warned Ophelia that Hamlet was "out of thy star." Polonius' true concern, of course, is that Ophelia's innocence might spoil the negotiations for the very marriage which he swears, upon his faith and honor, is wrong. If Hamlet were to win Ophelia too quickly he might tire of her—a consummation devoutly to be avoided, for then Polonius would not be father to a queen. Hence the ironic relevance, and pathos, of Ophelia's mad song:

> By Gis and by Saint Charity,
>> Alack, and fie for shame!
> Young men will do't, if they come to't,
>> By cock, they are to blame.
> Quoth she, before you tumbled me,
>> You promised me to wed.

He answers:
> So would I ha' done, by yonder sun,
> An thou hadst not come into my bed.

Ophelia too has been used as a tool—and ultimately destroyed—by hypocrisy, the dunghill stench of which permeates the entire court of Denmark. On one level we have the basic corruption and painted face of the assassin; beneath him, and feeding upon him, is the corruption of the parasite. Something indeed is "rotten in the state of Denmark," and even by the time Marcellus speaks the lines the audience more than half suspects that the rottenness sits upon the throne or pledges allegiance to it.

The entire court, with the exception of Hamlet, becomes the tool of this corruption. Rosencrantz and Guildenstern—whom Hamlet welcomes as friends; Ophelia —whom he wishes to love; Polonius—who served his father; Gertrude—who gave

him life: all find their nourishment, and ultimate death, in corruption. And throughout the play Hamlet's bitter puns, asides, and ironies are not the discharge from a
sick mind, but rather the commentaries of a perceptive one. He tells Polonius that
"you yourself, Sir, should be as old as I am, if, like a crab, you could go backward."
(II.ii.205) And the crab-image for Polonius could hardly be more accurate. To
Rosencrantz and Guildenstern he says "there is nothing either good or bad, but
thinking makes it so" (II.ii.255-56), ironically recapitulating the moral standards
of the courtiers surrounding him, who insist that if only Hamlet would buck up
and join the jolly boys, all would be well. (This is, of course, very much the advice
of those critics who attack Hamlet's "negativism," who see no reason why corruption cannot be made comfortable, and find little wrong with the court except Hamlet's "disturbance" of it.)

It is Polonius, however, who speaks the most direct comment upon hypocrisy,
and does so to Claudius; there is obvious irony as he issues his little sermon on
the very vice which he, in a parasitic position, and his listener, in a primary position, represent at every move:

> We are oft to blame in this—
> 'Tis too much proved—that with devotion's visage
> And pious action we do sugar o'er
> The Devil himself. (III.i.46-49)

The passage has two functions: on one hand it serves as ironic emphasis of hypocrisy; on the other it points directly to the king's celebrated prayer-scene, which
Mr. Knight sees as "the fine flower of the human soul." Polonius, however, refers
to piety which "sugars o'er" the Devil; here again is the image of the false posture,
the painted face, which Claudius—in his aside—explicitly describes:

> How smart a lash that speech doth give my conscience!
> The harlot's cheek, beautied with the plastering art,
> Is not more ugly to the thing that helps it
> Than is my deed to my most painted word.
> Oh, heavy burden! (III.i.49-53)

To be sure, the king's conscience has been "lashed"; the assassin has been
forced to see—by the lurking danger of Hamlet—the rottenness of his own face.
While Polonius babbles Claudius suffers, but this very suffering, far from preventing further assassination, merely confirms its necessity; indeed, the ultimate
result of Claudius' prayer is a determination to eliminate the rod which has been
lashing his conscience all through the play—his "chiefest courtier, cousin, son."
In some ways like Macbeth, Claudius is capable of suffering, but attempts to
relieve this suffering by attacking the threat (therefore the insecurity) which
provokes it. Certainly the king's conscience is hurt, but this fails to make him
contrite; his concern is solely to provide an analgesic, and if further treachery
and murder are the only methods to achieve "peace of mind," why, they must be
employed, distasteful as they might be. Claudius, moreover, as efficient as ever,

46

wastes neither time nor effort reflecting upon the means he must adopt if he is to remain secure:

> That we would do
> We should do when we would, for this 'would' changes
> And hath abatements and delays as many
> As there are tongues, and hands, are accidents . . .
> But to the quick o' the ulcer. *(IV.vii.119-124)*

This is not to say that the king decides lightly upon another assassination; a sensitive man, quite happy to live and let live when policy permits, Claudius resorts to murder only when he feels it is quite necessary. "All may be well," he says at the end of his prayer. With the death of Polonius, however, it becomes obvious that Hamlet is a dangerous opponent, and there is no hesitation; Claudius typically battens upon Hamlet's friends to provide a plausible surface, and sends Hamlet away to "protect" the prince. And when this fails, Claudius uses Laertes. In both cases human relationships are perverted by Claudius in pursuit of his own ends: he plays upon the maternal affection of the Queen to secure her consent to Hamlet's exile, and uses Hamlet's old friendship for Rosencrantz and Guildenstern to allay suspicion; he later perverts Laertes' loyalty and grief into further tools of assassination, relying, furthermore, on Hamlet's own naïvete and honesty to make the final act of treachery possible.

During his prayer, the king equates himself with Cain; his crime "hath the primal eldest curse upon it." Cain, one remembers, despairs after his crime—but this despair is not contrition; indeed, Bishop Hall, in his commentary upon the Biblical murder, remarked: "Consciences that are without remorse are not without horror: wickedness makes men desperate."[21] Even on his knees Claudius is pathetic only to the modern audience; as Mr. Joseph suggests, the Elizabethan would have seen him as blasphemous, in terms of Bulwer's description of hypocrites at prayer— the men who lie "groveling on the earth, and by a contradiction of gesture, bear witness against themselves."[22]

It is during this prayer that Claudius himself describes the court of Denmark, wooed and won by corruption:

> In the corrupted currents of this world
> Offense's gilded hand may shove by justice,
> And oft 'tis seen the wicked prize itself
> Buys out the law. *(III.iii.57-60)*

He also tells the audience that "my offense is rank, it smells to heaven"—and one thinks immediately of the warning, early in the play, that "something is rotten in the state of Denmark." At this point we know indeed of what the rottenness consists, and the horror of an entire court that feeds upon it; we perceive the terrible meaning of Guildenstern's parasitic comment, replete with "piety":

> Most holy and religious fear it is
> To keep those many many bodies safe
> That live and feed upon your majesty. *(III.ii.8-10)*

47

When Hamlet describes Rosencrantz and Guildenstern as "adders fanged" he is not "dehumanizing" them, for they have already dehumanized themselves; they are indeed the fangs, the tools of the serpent infecting Denmark. And Claudius' attempt at self-justification itself becomes a terrible ambiguity:

> Diseases desperate grown
> By desperate appliance are relieved
> Or not at all. *(IV.iii.9-11)*

For Claudius, Mr. Knight's "kindly uncle," is himself the disease, a malignant organism grown "desperate" in all meanings of the word.

Assuming, then, that the court of Claudius is a stew of corruption, it is possible to see Hamlet's strange and "anti-social" behavior as something more than simple negativism. Surrounded by parasites who are unaware of the dunghill which their social order represents, Hamlet is in the classic position of the Anti-Hero: bitter, despairing, nauseous to the very depths of his soul, and confused. There is no way for him to communicate his awareness of disease; again, for the "agreeable," worldly, and spiritually infected philistines, the disease itself is health, while Hamlet's attack upon it becomes disease.

Moreover, there is no point upon which Hamlet can actually stand, nothing he can demonstrate to prove that the status quo, painted in the image of Claudius, is rotten. People are "getting along," and it is only common sense to accept both the world and his father's death. Hamlet has no clear reason for his nausea; it is quite true that mortality is the fate of all men, and also true that many women remarry. As for the matter of incest—that has all been settled legally and respectably; both the church and the court are satisfied, and the law has given its sanction to the marriage of his mother. Nothing is wrong . . . and everything is wrong: the crop-full flesh of the appetites surrounding him; the smooth courtier who has seduced his mother and the divine and human institutions smiling upon the seduction; the trumpets calling all men to drunkenness. Hamlet, in the grip of existential disgust which he cannot justify even to himself; revolted by the complacent lechery and feeding flesh; sensing unhealth he cannot name in the bustle of the court; is left, like the Underground Man, an eccentric figure in black, digesting and redigesting what Dostoevsky's protagonist calls "revolting conclusions on the everlasting theme":

> You are yourself to blame, though again it is as clear as day you
> are not to blame in the least, and therefore grinding your teeth
> in impotence, sink into luxurious inertia, brooding upon the fact
> that there is no one even for you to feel vindictive against, that
> you have not and perhaps never will have an object for your
> spite, that it is a sleight-of-hand, a bit of juggling, a card-
> sharper's trick, that it is simply a mess, no knowing what and no
> knowing who, but in spite of all these uncertainties and jug-
> glings, there is still an ache in you, and the more you do not
> know, the worse the ache.[23]

When we meet Hamlet he is already in the very depths of his own "sickness unto death": in his first soliloquy, when as yet there has been no call to irreconcilable action, even before any crisis of choice, he wishes an end to his "too too solid flesh"; the world is an unweeded garden arousing disgust so great it cannot be adequately described; his heart is "fretted in its very substance . . . neither faith nor reason can survive it."[24] And so, baffled in his despair, baffled by his despair, Hamlet makes an unpleasant spectacle of himself (one remembers Gertrude's almost impatient "why seems it so particular with you?") and like the Underground Man, suffers from a "toothache of the soul."

Hamlet's disgust at this point, one must remember, cannot be reduced to his external situation. It is not simply his mother's remarriage which he protests, but rather the bland and comfortable animality of the respectable which he cannot stomach. There is a revulsion against flesh itself; the natural law which has triumphed over his father and now mocks his memory with "incestuous sheets." Under the stress of this revulsion, this spiritual outrage, the material world itself is disgusting, and when Hamlet recalls Gertrude's relationship to her first (not her "incestuous") husband,

> The impression conveyed is not that of a particular, unlawful
> relationship, nor even in the several weaknesses which have
> born fruit in his mother's infatuation for Claudius, but of a
> corruption present in the heart of passion.[25]

Hamlet, in this first soliloquy, is not simply comparing a virtuous passion with an unvirtuous one; the image he uses is parasitic: "she would hang on him as if increase of appetite had grown by what it fed on." As the play progresses, this parasitic imagery is repeated and developed; but here, before specific knowledge of Claudius' crime, we are given Hamlet's revulsion against all parasitism. There is something in Gertrude, and so in all women, in all flesh, in the world itself, which reduces human ideals to the image of pneumatic feeding.

A. C. Bradley refers to this condition as "melancholy"—a word which no more describes the heartwrack of existential despair than "discomfort" describes the physical pain of a victim in an auto-da-fe. It is precisely through this despair, however, that Hamlet achieves the terrible clarity of the Anti-Hero. His perception into and ultimate triumph over corruption come not by means of reason, but rather by means of a disturbed and extremely sensitized spirit; both the disturbance and the sensitivity are beyond the reach of those "many many bodies" feeding upon the diseased majesty of Claudius. The king and his parasites—not Hamlet—are the reasonable men in the play; the prince, indeed, is guided by spiritual antennae, and so his behavior is incomprehensible to the courtiers.

Precisely because existential despair is a spiritual rather than an intellectual state, analyses based upon Hamlet as a "confused intellectual" produce an inadequate reading. The soliloquies, for example, are too often taken as though Hamlet were facing himself with all the deliberation and finesse of a scholastic debater; critics have then pointed to rational inconsistency, theological weakness or doc-

49

trinal error, and have proceeded to define the prince as a rationalist ruined by "passion,"[26] a theologian examining canon law,[27] or a "natural man" and "pagan" whose tragedy is that of the "Unbaptized Man."[28] The arguments, reasons, and comments, however, which Hamlet makes in his soliloquies (or in scenes such as Claudius' prayer or Polonius behind the arras), are superimposed upon the same spiritual awareness and feverish sensitivity which itself produced his "sickness unto death" early in the play; the soliloquies are "transient emanations of his subtle irritability rather than continuous revelations of his character,"[29] and the result is that "the conflicts in Hamlet's mind are no longer arguments but states of experience."[30] It is only when the essential positions are reversed, when the state of experience is made subordinate to logical or theological argument, that Hamlet—like the Underground Man—is reduced to rational and doctrinal incompetency.

Hamlet, then, from his first appearance on the stage, is suffering from spiritual nausea for which he cannot account clearly, and which by public reason and institutional law is unjustified. His colour is black, while the rest of the court— with the quick irridescence of insects upon corruption—is all brightness, and the brightness in turn deepens Hamlet's disgust. It is essential, however, to realize that this negativism, suspicion, and harshness toward those whom Mr. Battenhouse call his "neighbors," is not basic to Hamlet, but rather is the result of the existential shock produced by what he senses is the triumph of corruption. As a result of shock, Hamlet is in despair, but it was precisely his lack of suspicion, his innocence and abstracting idealism, which created the shock in the first place.

Innocence and idealism are the qualities essential to Hamlet, and account for both the bitterness of his alienation, and for his despair when after the Ghost's revelation, he realizes that he is to be the sole vehicle for the cauterization of the disease infecting Denmark. The shock of Gertrude's seduction, and the news of his father's murder, are among the factors plunging Hamlet into despair; a suspicious and naturally misanthropic individual, however, would have taken the first as proof of human depravity he had always suspected, and the second as a simple call to destructive action. Hamlet's innocence, furthermore, accounts directly for the violence against his mother, against Ophelia, against Rosencrantz and Guildenstern, against Polonius, and most certainly against Claudius. These reactions come not as a result of suspicion, but rather as a result of understanding; a series of painful perceptions which repeatedly torment a mind essentially without suspicion at all.

Hamlet's first greeting to Rosencrantz and Guildenstern, for example, is generous and unsuspecting; for him they are "excellent good friends," and "good lads." He asks, "in the beaten way of friendship," why they have come, and the simple question oddly disconcerts them. Hamlet notices their flustered appearance, and asks that "by the rights of our fellowship, by the obligation of our ever preserved love," they deal frankly with him. There is no bitterness or harshness here; these come only when Hamlet is all too aware that Rosencrantz and Guildenstern have renounced their fellowship and love, indeed their very humanity, for roles as "adders fanged"; by Act Four Hamlet knows that each of his "friends" is a sponge to the discharge of Claudius' corruption, a sponge which "soaks up the king's countenance, his rewards, his authorities":

> But such officers do the king's best service in the
> end. He keeps them, like an ape, in the corner of
> his jaw, first mouthed, to be at last swallowed.
> When he needs what you have gleaned, it is but
> squeezing you and, sponge, you shall be dry again.   *(IV.ii.16-23)*

So too Ophelia's role as pawn or "sponge" of corruption maddens him beyond endurance; so Claudius' crime—and even more than his crime, the whited sepulchre of his hypocrisy—shatter the basis of Hamlet's universe: he sees love either perverted, sold or denied wherever he turns. The result, certainly, is disease—but the disease is Denmark's; for Hamlet, placed in a situation where all alternatives involve contamination, motivated by idealism which abstracts evil just as it once abstracted good, there is nausea, paralysis, desperation, and ultimate resignation—resignation which, destroyed by Claudius' treachery, nevertheless provides the final affirmation of the play.

Within his situation of existential despair, compounded equally of moral innocence and moral perception (the oversensitized spirit which perceives corruption), and his idealizing mind which understands the inevitable proliferation of evil, Hamlet is ordered to act. The spirit of his father, who had been quietly and efficiently poisoned by Claudius, demands vengeance. Hamlet's first reaction is one of relief; his vague and formless nausea now has a focal point of infection; the canker in the state and the cause of his own revulsion have at last been diagnosed. "O, my prophetic soul!" he exclaims, certain now of the basis for his disgust, despite the complacency of the entire court, at Claudius' "good fellowship." Immediately after the impact of the revelation, however, Hamlet surrounds himself with ambiguities, with Prufrockian "visions and revisions," with the Anti-Hero's "stinking mess" serving not to relieve, but to deepen his despair.

Many critics have seen Hamlet's indecision at this point as the cause of his tragedy. Interestingly enough, however, while some readers proceed on the assumption that he clearly ought to have revenged his father (and so interpret the play, in the traditional 19th century view, as a tragedy of the over-intellectual man), others see the tragedy arising from Hamlet's failure to perceive the "immorality" of revenge, a totally destructive and negative act. Mr. Knight brands dedication to revenge as "death force" (compared to the "life force" of the court); Mr. Battenhouse is concerned with Hamlet's "sub-Christian" behavior and argues that the Ghost is a "pagan" apparition; Mr. Goddard piously recommends that the young prince, faced with the revelation that his new father is an assassin and a hypocrite, ought to have set about reforming him.

It seems to me, however, that the solemn debates on the act of revenge, and the extensive and learned theological arguments upon the nature of the Ghost, involve the wastage of much critical fire-power. The drama is not a sermon on "The

Christian Attitude to Revenge," nor is it a discussion of "The Dangers of Procrastination." The emphasis is rather upon Hamlet as a man involved in choosing action, with the action subordinated to his awareness of the realities within existential choice—that is, the choice of existence itself. *Hamlet* is no more a play about the "right" attitude toward revenge, than *Othello* is a case for reasonable caution before one strangles an unfaithful wife. The Ghost's command (and indeed, his very presence) is a mechanism which makes possible Shakespeare's examination into the ambiguities of choice which must be made without the support of either secular or clerical authority, since both the secular and clerical authorities have assented to the corruption of which the Anti-Hero alone is aware. As Mr. Traversi remarks:

> there is . . . no question of the rightness or wrongness of revenge. Hamlet's task interests Shakespeare as an act which requires unity of purpose and sentiment in a harmonious personality. But, as the entire action shows, it is precisely this lack of union which constitutes Hamlet's problem.[31]

One must quickly add, however, that it also constitutes his heroism and ultimate affirmation; the "harmonious" personalities, the individuals without a "problem," are precisely the ones who fit most comfortably into the role of parasites upon the corruption which Claudius represents.

As the unworldly man, as what David Daiches calls the Moral Innocent,[32] Hamlet has been unable to accept the surface reality of Claudius' court; he cannot "forgive and forget" the corruption of the world because both the forgiveness and forgetting involve assent to the corruption itself. His very awareness, however, prevents the reduction of his situation to any single, therefore inadequate pattern of action; he knows, even in the first flush of his father's revelation, that action must involve corruption—the renunciation of ideal values. So his reply to the Ghost is itself ambiguous:

> Haste me to know it, that I, with wings as swift
> As meditation or the thoughts of love,
> May sweep to my revenge.   (I.v.28-30)

At the very peak of his emotion, Hamlet is all too aware of the price of action—immersion into the world which he refuses to accept, together with renunciation of the very ideals which alone had prevented him from succumbing to the whited sepulchre of Claudius' hypocrisy. In contrast, how do the "men of action" (or for that matter, the Machiavellian moralists) respond? Dostoevsky's Underground Man, with his characteristic blend of envy and scorn, explains:

> Why, when they are possessed . . . with the feeling of revenge,
> then for the time being there is nothing else but that feeling left
> in their whole being. Such a gentleman simply dashes for his
> object like an infuriated bull with his horns down . . . through

his innate stupidity (he) looks upon revenge as justice pure
and simple.[33]

Not so with Hamlet; he knows too well that physical purgation of evil involves precisely the adoption of the evil itself. And so his initial reaction is an attempt to abstract the entire problem of Claudius and his punishment: first, in a characteristic gesture, he scribbles an aphorism in his notebook:

> My tables—meet it is I set it down
> That one may smile, and smile and be a villain.   *(I.v.107-108)*

Then in a gesture equally characteristic, but this time of his naïvete, he begins a public accusation: "There's ne'er a villain smiling in all Denmark . . ." The public announcement, of course, would produce public justice; an abstract justice in which Hamlet need not put on falsity of his own in order to purge the falsity of Claudius. Immediately, however, there comes the inescapable and pathetic realization that all action, as well as all responsibility, must be his and his alone, and so what began as an accusation ends as a cryptic and crippled sentence: ". . . but he's an arrant knave." A public accusation is impossible because the court, the law, and the church have all been infected by the king's corruption. They have accommodated themselves to Claudius, and before removing themselves from the comfort of this accommodation, would demand proof. What proof does Hamlet have? The testimony of a Ghost and his own spiritual awareness; they would call him mad. Furthermore, a public charge would be dangerous. Claudius is no villain to react with rage or anger: the result would be gentle sorrow, injured innocence, fatherly concern—and efficient death lurking in a glass of wine or placed quietly upon the dinner table.

There is no way out, no easy alternative. Hamlet must either commit himself to both violence and hypocrisy (for action against an opponent such as Claudius demands adoption of his methods if it is to be effective); or he must wash his hands of the problem itself, taking what satisfaction he can from his awareness but tormented by the realization that inaction is itself a sanction of evil. Here is the neither/nor of a situation in which all choices become degrading or absurd, and the result is the terrible mockery, the despair and desperation of the Anti-Hero, the "wild and whirling words" of which Horatio complains:

> Why you are i' the right,
> And so, without more circumstance at all,
> I hold it fit that we shake hands and part—
> You as your business and desire shall point you,
> For every man has business and desire,
> Such as it is. And for my own poor part,
> Look you, I'll go pray.   *(I.v.126-132)*

So great is Hamlet's despair at the conflict between his own "business" and "desire," so great is the conflagration of heartsick mockery, that Shakespeare actually breaks the dramatic illusion for his audience:

> Ah Ha Boy! Say'st thou so? Art thou there truepenny?
> Come on. You hear this fellow in the cellarage,
> Consent to swear.
>   *(I.v.150-152)*

It all becomes a shrug, a terrible jest; as in Dostoevsky's novel, the structure of the work itself is splintered, and the Anti-Hero and his problem reduced to absurdity: action and inaction alike are impossible to a spirit perceiving the consequences of both.

So Hamlet attempts to abstract himself out of the corrupt world, but is chained to it by relationships which alternately attract and disgust him (as he becomes aware of their roles as tools of corruption); by a duty which is at once explicit in the world and incompatible with his ideals. The ideals, however, are themselves impotent without the world—which plunges him into incompatible action if he deals with it on its own terms. Hence the ideal and the material are both rejected. But the rejection is sterile, and Hamlet is forced to make his commitment: "He has an acute understanding of evil and consequently a hatred of evil, borrowing from evil its own weapons to defeat it and having no other resource than to do evil."[34] This "borrowing of weapons," however, itself compounds his disgust, and the result is the wild, nihilistic posturing, the levity of a rictus, the "prodigious display of mental gymnastics born of despair":

> At great crises, confronted with the insoluble problem of his triumph or his fall, of his triumph *in* his fall, the Jacobean hero [or Anti-Hero!] mocks, curses, willfully mutilates himself. He resorts to inflamatory words, flashing images, a breathless sustained rhythm . . . the stars, the seasons, witchcraft, nature, disease provide him with the fullest understanding of his own malady.[35]

From the moment that Hamlet realizes that choice of action must be his own—that he himself must decide upon his existential commitment—his desperation grows until it reaches fever-pitch. All is confused and mixed: tenderness and cruelty (note, for example, the remarkable scenes with Ophelia and Gertrude); bombast and self-mockery (the inflated rhetoric of the "rogue and peasant-slave" soliloquy followed by merciless self-deflation and the fantastic scene with Laertes in Ophelia's grave); and callousness alternating with conscience.

Hamlet's remarks upon the body of Polonius, for example, are brutal; yet in the midst of his brutality he sees himself as "Heaven's scourge"—only to turn once again (when facing Claudius) to the nauseating bitterness so inappropriate, in terms of complacent sentimentality, to death. The major objection to Hamlet's language at this point is his refusal to employ euphemisms; the Anti-Hero, however, the Underground Man, always makes this refusal—a basic reason why respectable personages find his talk so disgusting. (Osric, and certainly Claudius, would have had another vocabulary for death—much prettier, much more pleasant, and infinitely more delicate.) Polonius' death, however, itself was the inevitable product of the corruption which the courtier had been serving. It was not Hamlet's sword but rather Claudius' poison which had killed Polonius—just as surely as the king's poison on the tip of Hamlet's rapier, and not the rapier itself, later kills Laertes. The parallel is unmistakeable: both men are destroyed not by Hamlet, but by their own succumbing to corruption; each falls after agreeing to serve as a tool for Claudius, and each loses his life as a result of the agreement. For this reason Laertes forgives Hamlet for his own death and that of his father; he realizes—too late—that he has been serving his own mortal enemy no less than Hamlet's. So too Hamlet says that he will "answer well" for the death of Polonius; so he remarks, upon the deaths of Rosencrantz and Guildenstern, that:

> they did make love to this employment.
> They are not near my conscience, their defeat
> Does by their own insinuation grow.   *(V.ii.57-59)*

Polonius, Rosencrantz and Guildenstern, Laertes, Gertrude, Ophelia—all are victims of the adder on the throne of Denmark, the serpent whose "venom" contaminates innocent and guilty alike.

Because Hamlet, like the Underground Man, is consistent only in his inconsistencies, the irrelevant speculations which delight him (most notably the long passage on the state of the contemporary drama), his free-wheeling juggling of paradox, even his ironies appear incomprehensible to those who approach his pyrotechnic brilliance, born of mockery and despair, with the solemnity of social or theological scientists. Mr. Battenhouse, for example, sees the apostrophe on man as a serious Platonic inquiry, as a sort of philosophic speculation providing a major clue to the tragedy of Hamlet's "sub-Christian" framework of values. The apostrophe itself, however, is ironic; from the beginning of the play Hamlet has been convinced that the world is an "unweeded garden." He has long seen it as anything but a "goodly frame"—it is an excrescence; indeed, a moment before the apostrophe he punctures Rosencrantz' hypocritical depreciation of ambition by observing: "then are our beggars bodies, and our monarchs and outstretched heroes the beggars' shadows." All is absurd, and in the apostrophe Hamlet is not "inquiring," but rather ironically deflating the facile assumption of a pretty universe and human nobility; he knows too well that one is a "foul and pestilent congregation of vapours" and the other a painted surface for calculated or uncalculated feeding on the pestilence itself. The tone of the apostrophe is sarcastic rather than speculative; he is burlesquing optimistic humanism, not attempting to affirm it. It is, basically, the same irony with which the Underground Man misleads, confuses and irritates the good citizens who solemnly try to deal reasonably with his contradictions:

> A direct person I regard as the real normal man, as his mother
> nature wished him to be when she graciously brought him into
> being on the earth. I envy such a man until I am green in the face.

This is, certainly, a judgment, an expression of yearning for effective and direct action, a confession of inadequacy. In his next breath, however, the Underground Man demolishes all that went before:

> He is stupid. I am not denying that, but perhaps the normal man
> should be stupid, how do you know? Perhaps it is very beautiful,
> in fact.[36]

As the continuous statement and counterstatement weaves along, there is ironic, and — to sensible individuals convinced of their own importance — thoroughly exasperating refusal to *stand still.* So Hamlet solemnly discusses Thespian propriety as a matter of considerable importance, and at the same time ridicules Polonius' sage judgments, noting that it is all a conceit, a dream, an imitation which is itself nothing. So he "unpacks his heart" with rhetoric, ridicules himself for doing so, demands that the actor who is to speak his "mousetrap" avoid making a spectacle of himself with melodramatic posturing, and later leaps into Ophelia's grave with Laertes, mouthing extravagant similes and fashionable (classical) allusions, burlesquing his own bombast. So he seriously instructs the actor to speak his lines as though they were great art: yet refers to his "creation" as a mousetrap, and punctuates his comments on the play with ironies, with bitter jests, with irreverent puns, and generally behaves so unlike an author, that he creates an inexplicable disturbance. After the mousetrap has served its purpose, there is the wordplay with Horatio — itself a burlesque on the pompous advice he had given the unwilling player:

> Would not this, sir, and a forest of feathers, if
> the rest of my fortunes turn Turk with me, with
> two Provincial roses on my razed shoes, get me a
> fellowship in a cry of players, sir?
> *Horatio:* Half a share.
> *Hamlet:* A whole one, I.

(III.ii.285-290)

The ambiguities of the player scene proliferate in several directions, all of which relate in turn to the ambiguities within Hamlet himself. Aeneas' tale to Dido, for example, can in one sense be taken as a model for revenge; certainly Hamlet remembers it, and uses it to spur his flagging purpose. Far too much is made of this, however: the lines themselves contain value judgments on the very action for which the prince remembers them. Pyrrhus, certainly, as a model of a "man of action" is a repulsive figure, bloody and hellish:

> The rugged Pyrrhus, he whose sable arms,
> Black as his purpose, did the night resemble
> When he lay couched in the ominous horse,
> Hath now this dread and black complexion smeared
> With heraldry more dismal. Head to foot
> Now he total gules, horridly tricked
> With blood of fathers, mothers, daughters, sons,

> Baked and impasted with the parching streets
> That lend a tyrannous and damned light
> To their lord's murder. Roasted in wrath and fire,
> And thus o'ersized with coagulate gore,
> With eyes like carbuncles, the hellish Pyrrhus
> Old grandsire Priam seeks.   *(II.ii.474-486)*

Pyrrhus himself is a "painted tyrant" (whose "eyes like carbuncles" are half ludicrous, half horrible); he disregards the "milky head" of "reverend Priam," slaughtering the "old grandsire" and making "malicious sport" with the limbs of aged royalty. His "aroused vengeance," indeed, is compared to a monstrous Cyclops; and the result "would have made milch the burning eyes of heaven." The vengeance, in short, is a bloody and revolting deed, with overtones of savage absurdity, while the revenger himself is surrounded with the fumes of hell. If Aeneas' tale is indeed a "model," it is a singularly repulsive one, and would hardly have been chosen by a man convinced that the justice of his personal revenge were an established fact. That it is not an established fact, for Hamlet, is precisely why the lines move him so deeply; they speak not to his simple desire for revenge, but rather to his anguish and insoluble dilemma which, as I have indicated, is itself the product of his revulsion against personal revenge, and of his knowledge that if he is to purge Denmark of Claudius, he must make room in his conscience for the diseased "efficiency" of the king.

The actual "mousetrap" is no less difficult to place within a single framework of explication. On the one hand the test is a delay—a further reliance, despite Hamlet's denial, upon words rather than action. On the other hand, it is quite literally an attempt to prove the guilt of Claudius not to the court, but to Hamlet himself. The prince's first impulse, remember, upon hearing the Ghost's indictment, was to reveal all and so secure public or abstract punishment of the serpentine Claudius. This was manifestly impossible. Hamlet immediately perceived that the burden must be placed entirely upon his own back, that he himself must serve as both judge and executioner, and must accept—with complete existential commitment—the consequences of this burden. Nevertheless, he is tormented by the lack of abstract and impersonal justice which a direct accusation and trial would have provided. By means of the "mousetrap" he places Claudius in a position where the king, in effect, may convict—or acquit—himself. In short, he provides a trial in which Claudius is his own judge, and so removes part of the intolerable burden of both judgment and action which the Ghost's revelation had pressed upon him. Hence the frenzied lightness with Horatio after the king has shown his hand; Hamlet is indeed doing a spiritual jig; his heart for the moment is lighter by half than it was before.

The jubilation, however, is short-lived. Precisely because Claudius has convicted himself, action—if Hamlet is to commit himself to action at all—can no longer be delayed. But this action is no less revolting than it appeared before the test; still before Hamlet is the revolting, the ambiguous figure of Pyrrhus. Judg-

ment has been abstracted by means of the mousetrap, but execution of this judgment must plunge Hamlet back into the concrete world, must corrupt him because
execution can in no way be abstracted without becoming futile. Once again, his
situation—after a brief interlude of relief—is the neither/nor of existential despair,
in which both action and inaction are alike absurd: the one repugnant and the
other futile.

Almost immediately after the play-within-a-play comes the celebrated scene
with Claudius at prayer. I have earlier discussed this scene as a demonstration
not of Claudius' piety, but of his blasphemous hypocrisy; it now remains to clarify
Hamlet's position. Critical opinion on this point, of course, has varied enormously.
Many readers—like Dr. Johnson—feel that the episode is too terrible to dwell
upon; others have taken it as proof of Hamlet's religious orthodoxy; still others
maintain that Hamlet's inadequate (or "sub") Christianity is here established.

I would suggest, however, that the scene—like Aeneas' tale—contains ambiguities which are intrinsic to Hamlet's existential dilemma, and which therefore
cannot be reduced to any simple analogy. The very fact that Hamlet cannot perform an execution before an altar, for example, contrasts directly with the dialogue
between Laertes and the king, neither of whom has any such compunction:

> *King.*   What would you undertake
> To show yourself your father's son in deed
> More than words?
> *Laer.*   To cut his throat i'the church.
> *King.* No place indeed should murder sanctuarize.
> Revenge should have no bounds.   *(IV.vii.125-129)*

A sacred place—or for that matter, a sacred posture—would be no more an inhibi-
tion to Laertes and Claudius than would the necessity for revenge plunge them
into despair, as it does Hamlet. So great, however, is Hamlet's revulsion against
the role of Pyrrhus, that even the image of Claudius in the role of Priam destroys
his resolve, itself made only after long torment and in the white-heat of desperation. Hamlet's commitment to action, remember, came in the midst of, and indeed
was only made possible by the spiritual disgust aroused by the corruption of Denmark. Unlike Claudius, Hamlet cannot cooly involve himself in such corruption;
he can proceed only in terms of reaction, when the choice is solely between corrupt
but purgative action and absolute sterility. His responsibility is spiritually shattering; he can act upon it only when the criminal is manifestly condemning himself:

> When he is drunk asleep, or in his rage,
> Or in the incestuous pleasure of his bed—
> At gaming, swearing, or about some act
> That has no relish of salvation in't—
> Then trip him, that his heels may kick at Heaven
> And that his soul may be as damned and black
> As Hell, whereto it goes.   *(III.iii.89-95)*

This condemnation, however, is couched in spiritual terms; it must be without the "relish of salvation." And precisely in spiritual terms Hamlet, with the terrible clarity of the Anti-Hero, perceives that Claudius is, at the moment of his prayer, beyond the reach of punishment; in the act of contrition, Claudius would achieve Heaven—"hire and salary" would be provided by the very hand striking at the evil which he represents. This truly would reduce the action to an absurdity.

Claudius, of course, is not in the act of contrition at all; as I have already suggested, his position is clearly like that of Cain, whom Bishop Hall described as being desperate rather than contrite. Claudius, like Cain, most certainly is sorry—for himself; he admits that in the "wicked currents of this world" he has triumphed, but knows too well that he cannot "buy out the law" of Divine Justice. The total effect is not one of repentance for what has been done, but rather of a desperate awareness that there are limits to the buying power of his success; one feels that if there were a way to "buy out" Heaven, Claudius would not hesitate a moment in putting out the cash.

Hamlet, then, is mistaken; he is fooled by a pious surface, just as he is—in the duel of Act Five—taken in by a sociable one. The error, however, is characteristic of the basic innocence and naïvete of Hamlet, who is repeatedly plunged deeper into despair because of disillusion which would be impossible to a more suspicious or a more callous individual. The shock of his mother's seduction, his despair at Ophelia's desertion, the disgust at Rosencrantz and Guildenstern's subordination of friendship to political ambition; each opens a fresh wound in his spirit. And upon his return from England, after experiences and insights enough to make a saint suspicious, Hamlet—despite the pleading of Horatio and the warning of his own heart—plays directly, and openly, into the trap laid for him by Claudius.

Hamlet, in short, never learns to be suspicious; he persists in believing the best until shown the worst, and for him a man at prayer is necessarily, if only for the moment, in communion with holiness. He has seen too well that love, friendship, and loyalty can be corrupted, but that prayer—the deepest reaches of a man's spirit—can also be corrupted, he has not been shown, and cannot even imagine. To a less innocent man, certainly, or to a less religious one, a villain at prayer would be simply a villain.

It is Hamlet alone, then, among all the major figures of the play, who is aware of spiritual values beyond ambition, lust, and self-protection: Claudius' prayer is hypocritical; Rosencrantz and Guildenstern's piety is parasitic; Laertes has nothing to do with religion at all except to hurl insults at the hapless priest officiating at Ophelia's burial; Gertrude speaks of repentance only after being awakened by Hamlet's mixture of tenderness and reproach ("my heart and tongue be hypocrites in this," he says of his chastising speech); Polonius remarks only that a sanctimonious surface can cover the Devil.

From his first appearance on the stage Hamlet is deeply concerned with religion: even in the depths of existential despair and nausea, for example, he refuses to take Ophelia's way out because the "Everlasting" had "fixed his canon 'gainst self-slaughter." Throughout the play it is Hamlet who refers to God: "Angels and ministers of Grace defend us" he prays when the Ghost appears (I.iv.39); "so grace and mercy at your most need help you," he tells Horatio and Marcellus (I.v.180); "in thy orisons be all my sins remembered" he whispers while coming to Ophelia (III.i.89); "Save me and hover over me with your wings, you heavenly guards!" he cries when he sees the Ghost in his mother's chamber (III.iv.103). It is in this moving scene with Gertrude that Hamlet calls for repentance and confession, promises to ask Heaven's blessing for her, and points out that his harshness has been only for the good of her soul. Throughout the play Hamlet, from his first appearance to Horatio's final choral comment, is surrounded by the aura of Christian spirituality, deepened and made heroic precisely because of his suffering.

One may well ask why Hamlet, as a religiously aware individual, did not turn to the Church for advice. As I have already observed, there could be no ready-made solutions to his problem of total commitment; the Church as well as secular institutions had succumbed to Claudius' corruption; indeed, had given it sanction. Certainly nothing could have been easier and more comfortable than to accept their judgment; it is both the blessing and the curse of the existential man, how-ever, that the comfort of "peace of mind" is inadequate motivation. For this reason — for his insistence that one must face truth, death and the chaos of being itself before affirmation is possible — the existential man is incomprehensible to the worldling; again, his spiritual heroism becomes worldly anti-heroism. Hamlet, long on the rack of his own conscience and spiritual awareness, faced with the necessity of a total choice in which all alternatives are repugnant, arrives, finally, at the peace which is the result of not avoiding truth, but of accepting it. When we see him in Act Five, Scene Two he has come to understand both that "there is a divinity which shapes our ends" and that human action is meaningful only as an integral part of some vaster purpose. One cannot foresee consequences because they are shaped and hewn by divinity; nevertheless one acts, and on this basis action demands the exercise of profound faith and ultimate affirmation.

As Hamlet shows Horatio the king's letter calling for his murder, there is none of the frenzy met with earlier in the play; there is no longer the anguish of immedi-ate commitment. Hamlet now has the means for public accusation, and — as he tells Horatio — "the interim is mine." The period of dissembling and corruption is past and Hamlet can now act as a public accuser rather than as a private avenger; even Horatio, the choral and objective figure in the play, for the first time is fully aware of the king's villainy. ("What a king is this!" he exclaims.) The seduction of Denmark has all but run its course, and it is in this spirit of resigna-tion and inner peace that Hamlet, despite his own anxiety and Horatio's warning, enters the duel with Laertes.

In the first court scene, to which the final episode is a parallel, we met Hamlet as a dark, alienated figure, nauseated with a sense of corruption he could not clearly identify; here, however, the basic corruption has been made clear not only to the audience, but to Hamlet himself. As the two young men prepare for their sport, there is none of the bitterness, the terrible irony which set Hamlet's charac-ter from the beginning. He is sociable and even humble, and his wit is charming rather than deadly; even his behavior toward the king is dutiful. The evil days of Claudius are numbered; the burden of private revenge has been lifted from Hamlet's soul; another social order will come when Divinity determines it should come, and "the readiness is all."

The crisis, however, arrives sooner than Hamlet expects: in rapid succession follow the Queen's death, his own and Laertes' wounds, and the king's sordid end. Not with desperation, but with a certainty and the knowledge of his own justice, Hamlet turns Claudius' venom upon himself; and Laertes, recognizing at last the "foul practice," sees the "poison tempered by himself" destroy the serpentine king whose corruption still—even in its death-struggle—surrounds itself with murder. It is in these final lines that Shakespeare presents the ultimate judgment upon his characters: the Queen dies after one last expression of maternal concern:

> Here, Hamlet, take my napkin, rub thy brows,
> The Queen carouses to thy fortune, Hamlet.

Claudius meets his death weeping for his own flesh: "Oh yet defend me, friends, I am but hurt"; and Laertes forgives Hamlet as a "gentleman" and basically honest man: "Mine and my father's death come not on thee, nor thine on me!"

It is Hamlet alone, however, who ends his life with spiritual affirmation. He invokes Heaven to bless Laertes' plea for forgiveness; with his last strength he saves the life of Horatio (in direct contrast to Claudius, whose concern and "love" for Gertrude quickly leave his mind when he himself is injured); and with his dying breath he gives his vote to Fortinbras, thus securing Denmark from further conflict, and ensuring honorable order for his nation—an order which, although indeed based upon material ambition, is nevertheless without the spiritual corruption which made of Claudius' "efficiency" a reign of damnation.

"Suffering is the sole origin of consciousness," the Underground Man says, and this is perhaps the most fitting epitaph for Hamlet. It is only through consciousness that choice can be made, and without total choice religion is an empty gesture, a pursuit of respectability, a request for analgesic. Faith itself, then, finds its sole origin in suffering, and for this reason the tortured Anti-Heroes of Dostoevsky, like Hamlet himself—Shakespeare's Anti-Hero—are alternately despised or explained away as psychological or spiritual monsters. And if *Notes from the Underground* is usually read as a case history of neurosis, Hamlet has been played too often as a bloody revenger, a pale, romantic, and womanish figure, complete with "poet's collar" and much sighing, or a violent madman. The spiritualism and existential symbolism of Shakespeare's drama, however, like that of *Notes from the Underground*, can be reduced to no comforting formula. Its truth is the realization that affirmation—that faith itself—is based upon consciousness and suffering. It is this truth which Samuel Johnson, sensing its presence, nevertheless found too terrible to face; it is this truth which critics, moralists, and theologians too often attempt to deny.

Notes:

(1) Henri Fluchère, *Shakespeare and the Elizabethans* (New York, 1953), p. 53.

(2) In *Notes from the Underground*. All references to text are from the Dial Press edition, *The Short Novels of Dostoevsky*, (1953).

(3) Fluchère, p. 46.

(4) *The Prince*, quoted by Fluchère, pp. 45, 47.

(5) Kafka's hero turns into a cockroach; in *The Brothers Karamazov* eternity is conceived as one corner of a bathhouse with spiders running about. Even Vachel Lindsay, despite his bombast, conceived of the world as "the soul of a spider."

(6) *Wheel of Fire* (New York, 1956), p. 19.

(7) *Notes from the Underground*, p. 153.

(8) *Ibid.*, p. 140.

(9) *Ibid.*, p. 138.

(10) *Wheel of Fire*, p. 38.

(11) Fluchère, p. 54.

(12) D. A. Traversi, *An Approach to Shakespeare* (New York, 1956), p. 87.

(13) *Ibid.*, p. 89.

(14) *The Meaning of Shakespeare* (Chicago, 1951), p. 382.

(15) *Wheel of Fire*, p. 38.

(16) Quoted by Bertram Joseph, *Conscience and the King* (London, 1953), p. 68

(17) See *Wheel of Fire*, pp. 33-39.

(18) In *Shakesperean Tragedy* (New York, 1955).

(19) See Frances Fergusson, *The Idea of a Theater* (Princeton, 1949), p. 138.

(20) Joseph, p. 64.

(21) *Ibid.*, pp. 64-65.

(22) *Ibid.*, p. 66.

(23) *Notes from the Underground*, p. 137.

(24) Fluchère, p. 61.

(25) Traversi, p. 87.

(26) See Lily B. Campbell's discussion of Hamlet in her *Shakespeare's Tragic Heroes* (Cambridge, 1930).

(27) Notably Fredson Bowers, "Hamlet as Minister and Scourge," *PMLA*, LXX (1955), 740-49.

(28) Roy Battenhouse, "Hamlet's Apostrophe on Man," *PMLA*, LXVI (1951), 1073-1113.

(29) J. O. Halliwell-Phillips, *Memoranda on the Tragedy of Hamlet* (London, 1879).

(30) Traversi, p. 83.

(31) *An Approach to Shakespeare*, p. 100.

(32) See "Guilt and Justice in Shakespeare," *Literary Essays* (New York, 1957).

(33) *Notes from the Underground*, pp. 134-35.

(34) Fluchère, p. 59.

(35) *Ibid.*, p. 59.

(36) *Notes from the Underground*, p. 135.

Shakespeare and the Double Image
of King John

by John R. Elliott, Jr.

I

The study of the sources of literary works is usually, and with good reason, confined to books which the author in question can be demonstrated to have known.[1] Unless we are fortunate enough to have a record of his library, the only direct knowledge we can have of an author's sources is through the palpable impression that they make upon his works: books that he ought to have known, ideas and opinions that he might have known, analogues that we wish he had known may furnish comparisons that help us to evaluate his work but cannot contribute to our understanding of either his intentions or his creative processes. There is one circumstance, however, in which the term "source" may usefully be applied to material not specifically to be found in the work itself, and this is when a work depends on the special knowledge of its readers or audience for its effect. If, for instance, a Fourth of July orator were to mount a platform in Philadelphia and proceed to deliver a eulogy on King George III, the effect of his speech upon his audience would not have been produced solely by the actual words that he had spoken. Here, as often, the irony depends on a discrepancy between what the audience expects and what it receives, and thus the audience's knowledge that George III was not an American patriot must certainly be considered an essential "source" of the speech's meaning, even in the unlikely case that the speaker himself was unaware of the fact. Furthermore, an historian of the year 2364 who was to read the speech without that knowledge would certainly be guilty of misreading the historical significance of what the speaker had said, if not the speaker's conscious intentions. When, however, the historian had ascertained not only the difference between George III and George Washington but the fact that the orator himself must have known this difference, he would be entirely justified in concluding that the conscious intent behind the speech was ironic, if not subversive.

Such an exemplum helps to clarify the problem faced by the modern literary historian in interpreting the significance and intent of Shakespeare's English history plays. Shakespeare wrote for an audience at least as knowledgeable about the chief figures of English history as American audiences today are about George Washington. Consequently the knowledge which the audience brought with it to the theater must be considered as much a "source" of the plays' original significance—as large a factor in Shakespeare's calculations—as the material which he confronted in his specific historical and literary sources. In addition to asking how Shakespeare adapted this material, what he selected, what he omitted, and

64

what he added, students of Shakespeare's "sources" ought also to ask to what extent the finished product corresponded or failed to correspond to the expectations of Shakespeare's audience. Indeed, the audience's prior familiarity with their subjects makes the English history plays a unique opportunity for modern scholars to reconstruct with some degree of accuracy what may have been Shakespeare's intentions and what his audience may have perceived these intentions to be.

In the Arden edition of *King John,* E. A. J. Honigmann remarks that "the reign of John was an open book to Shakespeare's first audience."[2] The contents of this book, however, have been only partially indexed by cultural historians and Shakespearean scholars.[3] In actuality there were two, quite distinct "books" of the reign of King John, existing side by side in Shakespeare's century, in one of which John was portrayed as a villainous failure, in the other as a national hero. The history of the contents of these two books and of Shakespeare's selection of material from them in *King John* helps to explain the significance of this much neglected play in the development of Shakespeare's political attitudes and provides some surprising new insights into Shakespeare's relationship to orthodox Tudor opinion.

II

In historical actuality, King John's career on the throne was a series of anticlimaxes, of partial victories and partial defeats.[4] In character John seems to have been irascible enough to be impressive, clever enough to be admirable, and indecisive enough to be despicable. The chief issue of his reign as seen by historians prior to the seventeenth century was, of course, not Magna Carta but John's defiance of the Pope, the Interdict laid upon England, and the eventual surrender of the crown to the Papal legate, Pandulph. In the hands of the medieval chroniclers, many of whom, like Roger of Wendover, felt it their purpose to be the recording of anecdotes "for the imitation of succeeding times and admonition to the faithful,"[5] John's reputation sank lower and lower in the three centuries following his death. The results of his defiance of the church were held up as a warning to future rulers of the fruits of impiety. Furthermore, he was accused of having usurped the throne from his nephew and chief rival, Arthur, and later of having murdered him, though the evidence is obscure on both points. Nevertheless, anecdote after anecdote piled up in the chronicles to illustrate John's personal and political vices. He is said to have reveled in cruel and unusual punishments such as slitting noses, plucking out eyes and teeth, and crushing bodies under lead weights. He extorted money, seized property, and raped the wives and daughters of his barons. He despised Christianity and even, according to Matthew Paris, concocted a scheme to make England subservient to the Moslem ruler of North Africa in return for the latter's protection against the Pope.

Given the didactic purposes of both medieval and Renaissance historians, however, it is hardly surprising that the sixteenth century, with its far-reaching political and religious changes, soon contrived for itself a very different interpretation of this monarch, and that it was this new and favorable image of John which came to dominate the mind of the average Englishman of Shakespeare's time.

The earliest attack on the Catholic chroniclers with specific regard to King John seems to have been made by William Tyndale in *The Obedience of a Christian Man* in 1528. "Consider the story of King John," wrote Tyndale, "where I doubt not but they have put the best and fairest for themselves, and the worst of King John: for I suppose they make the chronicles themselves."[6] On at least one occasion (in 1533) Henry VIII compared his task to that of John,[7] and his enemies did likewise: in 1535 a priest named John Hale was tried for treason for, among other things, praying that Henry's "death I beseech God may be like to the death of the most wicked John, sometime King of this realm, or rather to be called a great tyrant than a King"[8]—an obvious allusion to the legend that John was poisoned to death by a monk.

It is highly significant that these early favorable references should come from sources—Tyndale and Henry VIII—which inevitably gave to this new image of John an aura of official orthodoxy, both political and religious, for it was with this aura that the new image passed into popular and polemical Protestant literature. As early as 1529, for instance, a pamphlet by Simon Fish entitled *A Sypplicacyon for the Beggars,* addressed to the King, attacked the clergy on the grounds that they were about to do to Henry VIII as they had done "unto your nobill predecessour king John . . . suche a rightuous [sic] kinge."[9] This work was part of a politically-inspired pseudo-historical literature whose purpose was to show that the clergy, in violation of Christ's commandment, have "translated all rule, power, lordishippe, auctorite, obedience and dignite from your grace [i.e. Henry VIII] unto theim."[10] Other similar works, such as the anonymous *Treatise proving by the King's Laws* published in 1538, sought the legal roots of Henry's supremacy in the precedents set by his "most noble progenitors," including King John.[11]

Accordingly, chronicle accounts of John's conflict with the Pope were quickly revised in order to make them conform to the new official version. For example, Pynson's edition of Fabyan in 1516 had described John's "cruelnesse agayne holy churche," and had lamented that even the Pope's interdict "myght not move the kyng frome his erroure."[12] The 1533 edition, however, deleted the phrase "frome his erroure," as did all subsequent editions. Another passage stating that John was "accursyd" for his "dysobedience to the churche," together with some verses celebrating God's punishment of him, were unaccountably overlooked and left standing in 1533, but deleted in the edition of 1542.[13]

The new image of John as an heroic king and Protestant martyr soon made him one of the most popular of English historical figures. One testimony to this popularity is the fact that he became the hero of the first English history play, John Bale's *King Johan,* around 1536. Strictly speaking, of course, *King Johan* is not so much a history play as a political morality play, Bale having chosen a patriotic historical subject rather than a Biblical or homiletic one only because he did not want his work identified with "popetly playes,"[14] i.e., religious moralities enforcing Romish doctrines. Indeed, to deviate from the new interpretation of John after Bale's work would have been tantamount to heresy, for Bale's tone suggests that his interpretation has become a part of Protestant dogma.

Bale attributes all the troubles of John's reign to foreign intervention—particularly by the Pope—in English affairs, comparing John to Moses withstanding the "Egyptyanes," and Henry VIII to "Josue," who "clerely brought us in to the lande of mylke and honye" (1100-1103). John had only righteous intentions, but they were undermined by the "usurped power" of the Pope and by the sedition of the Nobles:

> Upon a good zele he attempted very farre
> For welthe of thys realme to provyde reformacyon
> In the churche therof, but they ded hym debarre
> Of that good purpose . . . by excommunycacyon.   *(1083-1089)*

Of special interest to us is the fact that Bale repeats Tyndale's charge against the chroniclers. Nobility says to Clergy:

> Yt is yowr fassyon soche kyngs to dyscommend
> As yowr abuses reforme or reprehend.
> You pristes are the cawse that chronycles doth defame
> So many princes, and men of notable name,
> For yow take upon yow to wryght them evermore;
> And therfore Kyng Johan ys lyke to rewe yt sore,
> Whan ye wryte his tyme, for vexyng of the Clargy.   *(575-581)*

In particular, Bale attacked Polydore Vergil, who, as we shall see, was primarily responsible for continuing the adverse medieval view of John into the sixteenth century. Polydore had already been attacked by the patriotic antiquary John Leland for his debunking of the Brut and Arthur legends,[15] and now Bale took Polydore severely to task for his treatment of King John:

> I assure ye, fryndes, lete men wryte what they wyll,
> Kynge Johan was a man both valiaunt and godlye.
> What though Polydorus reporteth hym very yll
> At the suggestyons of the malicyouse clergye,
> Thynke yow a Romane with the Romanes can not lye?
> Yes; therefore, Leylande, out of thy slumbre awake,
> And wytnesse a trewthe for thyne owne contrayes sake.[16]   *(2145-2151)*

Here we see clearly the religious and patriotic associations with which the image of King John was imbued in the sixteenth century. Bale's close friend, John Foxe, incorporated Bale's views of John's reign in his enormously popular *Book of Martyrs* (1563), and explained that John "was far from deserving that, for the which he hath been so ill reported of divers writers, who, being led more with affection to popery, than with true judgment and due consideration, depraved his doings more than the sincere truth of the history will bear."[17] Similarly, Richard Grafton, who copied many passages *verbatim* from Foxe, sought in his *Chronicle at Large* (1569) to rehabilitate John's reputation by simply omitting, as Bale had done, any references to John's usurpation of the throne or to his murder of Arthur. Like Foxe, Grafton justified this rewriting of history with the claim that he was only delivering "our Countrie men and the subjects, but specially the princes therof, . . . from slaunderous reportes of foreyne writers."[18]

Bale and his followers, then, "corrected" history by bringing the light of the Reformation to illuminate what they considered to be the real issue of John's reign, and their influence helped to set the pattern for the popular conception of John throughout the century. As a result of Bale's work, and of that of Grafton and Foxe, John became firmly identified with a set of religious-political doctrines that were at the heart of official Tudor policy: hatred of the Pope, obedience to the King, resistance to foreign intervention, and intolerance of all forms of civil dissension. Indeed, John became the standard symbol for English Protestant writers of the patriot-martyr.

For example, the reign of King John was one of the principal exempla employed by the "Homily against disobedience and wylfull rebellion," which was assigned to be read in all English churches after the northern rebellion of 1569, and which, as Alfred Hart has shown, was almost certainly known to Shakespeare.[19] In order to prove his lesson that "rebellion is both the first and greatest, and the very roote of all other sinnes,"[20] the homilist cites the example of the revolt of the barons against King John. The barons were duped by the Pope because of their ignorance of "their dutie to their prince, the Byshop of Rome having no right." In consequence, they alone were responsible for the lamentable events that followed: the expulsion of the king "out of the greatest part of Englande," the surrender of the crown to a "false forraigne usurper," the invasion of the Dauphin, who "kept the possessioun a great whyle," and the ensuing "tyrannie, raveny, and spoyle of the most greedie Romish wolves," together with the worship of "the babylonicall beast of Rome."[21] In all this, John is the innocent and heroic victim: there is no mention of his usurpation and murder of Arthur, of his oppression of his subjects, or of his later abject alliance with Rome against his own nobles.

One further example will serve to indicate how ingrained the image of John as a national hero had become in the Elizabethan historical consciousness. In 1599 the legal historian Richard Crompton published a treatise entitled *The Mansion of Magnanimitie, wherein is shewed the most high and honorable acts of sundrie English Kings.* The subject of the work was the praise of soldiers who had protected their country against foreign enemies, and it was dedicated to the Earl of Essex so that he might "thereby be encouraged to followe their steppes."[22] Crompton devotes parts of two chapters to King John, one on the evils of rebellion, the other on the treachery of nobles, and for his details closely follows the "Homily against disobedience," even occasionally copying the phrasing of the latter work, though omitting its anti-Catholic bias. As we might expect, Crompton ignores John's political weaknesses and the barons' grievances, and finds in their revolt against their king only the familiar Tudor moral that civil war opens the gates of the country to foreign invaders, in this case the French, who "greatly indomaged the said king, and got the possession of diverse castels, townes, and other places, and so became strong within this realme" (sig.F$_4$^{v}). When the Dauphin in turn plots to betray the barons after they have helped him to invade England, Crompton comments that this is a fitting reward for those who would rebel against their "high and honorable" sovereign.

Although Geoffrey Bullough has noted that "the reputation of King John had undergone some changes before the fifteen-nineties,"[23] the full extent to which John had become associated in the popular mind with orthodox Tudor political doctrines has not generally been recognized. *The Mansion of Magnanimitie* is only one of at least a score of didactic patriotic works of the 1580's and 1590's which display the heroic Tudor image of King John.[24] Nor is it true, as M. M. Reese has claimed, that "in official circles the beatification of John proceeded no farther than the express condemnation in the Homilies of the subjects who had revolted from him."[25] As we have seen, the reinterpretation of John's reign had begun with Henry VIII himself and his earliest supporters, and in Shakespeare's time the rehabilitation of John's image was still being continued by such representatives of the Tudor establishment as Crompton.[26]

III

In spite of the rehabilitating efforts of the Tudors, however, the image of King John that we find in Shakespeare's play is much closer to the older, medieval interpretation of that monarch, a tradition kept alive in Shakespeare's age by a small number of professional chroniclers who were less skeptical of the veracity of the medieval chroniclers than Bale and Tyndale had been. Ironically enough, the chief responsibility for perpetuating the medieval view of John into the sixteenth century belongs to the very man to whom Henry VIII had entrusted the historical justification of the Tudor accession—Polydore Vergil.

Polydore Vergil's *Anglica Historia* was written before the break with Rome, though it was published in the same year as the Acts of Succession and Supremacy, 1534. Polydore was well aware of the controversial nature of much of his material for the *Historia,* and he made several changes in his manuscript for political and religious reasons between the completion of a first draft around 1515 and the first printed edition.[27] Nevertheless, the hostile view which he had gathered from the monastic chroniclers of the reign of King John not only passed intact into his work but was even intensified there.[28] John's right to the throne, for instance, had seldom been seriously questioned, even by his enemies. Tradition held that Richard on his death-bed had declared John his heir, forgiving him for his past disloyalty and rescinding an earlier bequest of the throne to Arthur. Polydore, however, makes it clear from the start that he regards John as an unqualified usurper. John "snatched" the throne and barred the rightful owner, Arthur, from it ("Ioannes Ricardi frater ... regnum arripit: excluso Arthuro cui regnum debebatur").[29] According to Polydore, Arthur possessed the throne not only by lineal descent but by virtue of Richard's will ("Ricardi nepotem quem ille testamento haeredem fecerat").[30] Though recounting all the other details of the second will made by Richard on his death-bed, Polydore omits entirely the bequest of the throne to John.

Consequently, at John's coronation, Polydore writes, quite unhistorically, that many of the "right-minded" English nobles ("qui recte sapiebant") were amazed that John should defraud Arthur, whom they considered an excellent young man ("optimum adolescentem"), of his grandfather's kingdom against the law of men and nature ("contra jus fasque" [p. 343]).

The rest of Polydore's account follows the familiar medieval pattern. John is indolent, cowardly, avaricious, and cruel, and he oppressed his people mercilessly. Concerning the means of Arthur's death, Polydore admits that his "sources differ," but feels that the most reliable rumor is that he was put to death by John ("magis constans fama est, a Ioanne morte affectum" [p. 347]). Concerning the religious conflict, Polydore, an Italian Catholic, sides unequivocally with the Pope. He even introduces some new anecdotes to illustrate the "vices and tyranny of the man" ("hominis vitia ac tyrannidem" [p. 355]), as a result of which the Pope's council voted unanimously to deprive John of his kingdom as a man "who held religion in contempt, who scorned the papal warnings, nay even those of Christ, which were conducive to his safety and that of his people" ("qui ita religionem contemptui haberet, qui monita pontificia, imo Christi, quae ipsius populique conducerent saluti" [p. 355]).

Polydore was not writing religious propaganda, however, and John's submission to the Pope does not, as one might have expected, change Polydore's attitude towards him. John takes advantage of the Pope's support to exploit his subjects at home, and Polydore writes sympathetically of the barons' grievances, attributing to them the most patriotic of sentiments. It is only after John has granted their demands and again fails to keep his promises that the barons appeal to France for help "against an unjust tyrant who made a mockery of his princes and of his citizens" ("adversus iniquum tyrannum, qui ita suos principes, suos cives ludificatus esset" [p. 366]).

In short, Polydore Vergil treats John from the point of view of a continental Catholic who frequently shows traces of his affection for his adopted land. He sympathizes with Arthur's claim to the throne supported by France and the Pope, but he can also understand the English barons' exasperation at learning that John's tyranny over them is supported by Rome. In politics, Polydore displays a traditional view of the reciprocal duties and rights of the feudal system, including the right of the nobility or magistrates to curb abuses of power by the king—this in spite of the fact that his work is dedicated to Henry VIII, *Potentissime Rex* (p.[6]).

The fact that Polydore based his criticism of King John not totally, or even mainly, on sectarian religious grounds made it possible for his characterization of this monarch to interest Protestant writers like Stowe and Holinshed (though we should perhaps note that Stowe was occasionally suspected of being "insufficiently Protestant"[31]). In Stowe's *Annals* (1582), for instance, we again find the charge, invented by Polydore, that John usurped the throne. Stowe makes it clear that in his opinion "the succession of inheritance belonged not to John," but that "John . . . after the death of his brother Richard, took on him the kingdom disin-

70

heriting his nephews Arthur and Elianor the true heirs."[32] This is of some importance, since the issue of John's usurpation is a major one in Shakespeare, though
it does not appear in any other Elizabethan treatment of King John.[33]

The most important stage in the transmission of the adverse medieval view of
John from Polydore Vergil to the later Elizabethans, however, was Holinshed's
Chronicle, where the older estimate is to be found strangely mixed together with
the more popular image. M. M. Reese has recently asserted that "Holinshed, who
was usually content to accept whatever he read in the medieval chronicles, rejected their version of a king who, in his view, 'had a princely heart in him and
wanted but faithful subjects.'"[34] Holinshed does indeed show numerous traces
of the nationalistic and Protestant fervor which shaped the popular interpretation
of John's reign, but he also tempers his account and the morals to be drawn from
it with a full knowledge of the older chroniclers, especially Polydore Vergil (there
are more marginal citations of Polydore in Holinshed's account than to any other
historian, with the exception of Matthew Paris). Although Holinshed occasionally
suspects that much of his information about John consists of the "Coniectures of
such writers as were evill affected towards the kings cause,"[35] he decides not to
make over the reign of King John in the Tudor image but to "content our selves
with this unfreendlie description of his time" (339).

The result is a more carefully qualified statement of familiar Tudor political
lessons than is to be found in popular and homiletic literature. Like Bale and his
followers, Holinshed points out the dangers of foreign, especially Papal, intervention into England's affairs. Philip is an ambitious "fraudulent league-breaker"
and Arthur is "wilfull" and "presumptuous" in demanding John's kingdom (284).
Holinshed even shares Foxe's delight in punning on the Pope's name, calling him
"Nocent" instead of "Innocent" (316).[36] Unlike Polydore, Holinshed does not suppress Roger of Hovenden's account of Richard's death-bed will making John his
heir. Thus for Holinshed John is a lawful king, and so he paints the familiar picture
of the evils of "domesticall or homebred broils, the fruits of variance," and laments
John's lack of "faithfull subiects" (337-339). Holinshed shows the barons as being
"negligent and slothfull in aiding him," and he reports approvingly the sermon
of a divine who preached "a doctrine most necessarie in that dangerous time [that]
the people were by Godes lawes bound in dutie to obeie their lawfull prince, and
not through any wicked persuasion of busie heads and lewd discoursers, to be
carried away to forget their loiall allegiance, and so to fall into the damnable sinke
of rebellion" (300).

Nevertheless, Holinshed does not hesitate to follow Polydore in placing much
of the blame for John's catastrophes on the character and conduct of the King himself. John's treatment of Arthur was a deed of "heat and furie . . . reprochful to a
prince" (286). John made "warre with his subjects pursses at home, emptieng them
by taxes and tallages, to fill his coffers, which alienated the minds of a great number of them from his love and obedience" (279-280). Though Holinshed gives a tinge
of heroism to John's defiance of the Pope, he feels that John's initial oppression
of the clergy was a rash and unnecessary act "which he might have prevented

and withstood, if he had beene so qualified with discretion as to have seene what was convenient and what inconvenient for his roiall estate" (289). Similarly, despite the fact that he has entitled one section of his work "The sawcie speech of proud Pandulph the popes lewd legat" (306), Holinshed also repeats Matthew Paris's judgment that John's loss of his baggage train in the Wash was a "punishment appointed by God, that the spoile which had beene gotten and taken out of churches, abbeies, and other religious houses, should perish, and be lost" (335).

According to Holinshed, then, the story of John's reign is the story of the wrong man at the wrong time. John would not have made a good king under the best of circumstances: he was a man who "wanted discretion . . . , as one not able to bridle his affections . . . and thereby missed now and then to compasse that which otherwise he might verie well have brought to passe" (339). But his natural shortcomings were also aggravated by circumstances beyond his control: the "manie molestations, anguishes & vexations [which he] procured against himselfe" might have been "withstood if fortune had beene favourable" (337). Holinshed's summary statement takes both of these factors into account:

> All which presupposed plagues concurring, what happinesse
> could the king arrogate to himselfe by his imperiall title, which
> was through his owne default so imbezelled, that a small rema-
> nent became his in right, when by open hostilitie and accursed
> papasie the greater portion was pluckt out of his hands.   *(337)*

Thus in Holinshed material was found from both the old and new interpretations of King John by the two playwrights who were to dramatize his reign—Shakespeare and the anonymous author of *The Troublesome Reign of King John*. In all likelihood Shakespeare based his play on the dramatic model provided by *The Troublesome Reign*. The order of incidents in the two plays is strikingly similar, though verbal correspondences are few. E. A. J. Honigmann has argued, I think unconvincingly, that an early version of King John preceded *The Troublesome Reign*, and that the latter is a corrupt, probably pirated version of Shakespeare's work. It is not necessary, however, to posit the chronological priority of *King John* in order to argue the artistic independence of Shakespeare's work: in following the older play as a dramatic model, Shakespeare thoroughly changed its emphases in a way that reveals a sensitivity to and knowledge of the ambiguities and complexities of sixteenth-century interpretations of King John. The significance of Shakespeare's selection from this material can best be seen through a fresh comparison of these two plays.

IV

Shakespeare wastes no time in informing his audience that the play before them will not dramatize the familiar image of King John that they have learned from the "Homily against disobedience" and its polemical progeny. His John is first presented to us as a usurper who has schemed to supplant the legitimate owner of the throne and must now maintain his position against King Philip of France, who has championed Arthur's cause. In charging John with usurpation and in considering John's claim to the throne as the first of the "issues" of his reign, Shakespeare is deliberately following the older, less popular tradition of Polydore Vergil and Stowe, as we have seen. Furthermore, Shakespeare's interest in John's usurpation goes considerably beyond even that of his predecessors. In Polydore the subject had merited only a couple of pages, in Stowe a mere two or three sentences. In *King John*, however, John's illegality is the central dramatic problem of the first act and of much of the second, and is kept before the audience throughout the play.

King John opens with a challenge to John's legitimacy and authority. Chatillon, the French ambassador, brings an insulting greeting to "the majesty, the borrow'd majesty, of England" (I.i.4).[37] Such a slur is, of course, to be expected from John's foreign rival, but John tacitly admits the truth of the charge by refusing to defend himself. When Eleanor retorts to Chatillon that it is "a strange beginning: 'borrow'd majesty!'," John cuts her off with the words, "Silence, good mother, hear the embassy" (I.i.5-6). Similarly, when Chatillon proceeds to claim all of John's lands for Arthur, John advances no counter-claim whatever, but merely inquires "what follows if we disallow of this?" (I.i.16). Finally, when in private conversation John attempts to encourage his mother by citing his "strong possession and our right," Eleanor reminds him to trust "your strong possession much more than your right, / Or else it must go wrong with you and me" (I.i.39-41).

In stressing John's illegitimacy in this opening scene, Shakespeare diverges widely from *The Troublesome Reign*. That play opens not with Chatillon's challenge but with a speech by Eleanor conferring the crown upon John in rightful succession to his brother, Richard, followed by a noble speech of acceptance by John—"a warlike Christian and your Countryman,"[38] as the Prologue had called him. When Chatillon does present his demands, instead of remaining cynically silent, John is incredulous that a King should be requested to give up his rightful possessions. In *TR*, even the French refrain from accusing John of usurpation and they implausibly pay him the tribute that "sooner would he scorne Europaes power, / Than loose the smallest title he enjoyes, / For questionless he is an Englishman" (I.ii.449-451). Correspondingly, Philip offers no justification of Arthur's "right," and his tone implies pure opportunism: "Now gin we broach the title of thy claime Yong Arthur in the Albion Territories" (I.ii.422-423).

Shakespeare, however, never lets the fact that John is an Englishman obscure his illegality. In his first speech to Arthur, Philip refers bluntly to "the usurpation of thy unnatural uncle, English John" (II.i.9-10), and later in the same scene he eloquently defends Arthur's right to the throne according to both natural and divine law:

> That Geoffrey was thy elder brother born,
> And this his son; England was Geoffrey's right,
> And this is Geoffrey's; in the name of God

How comes it then that thou art call'd a king,
When living blood doth in these temples beat,
Which owe the crown that thou o'ermasterest?   *(II.i.104-109)*

Similarly, Shakespeare dramatizes a dispute over King Richard's will, which according to Holinshed disinherited Arthur and named John as heir. In *TR*, which also includes such a dispute, Queen Eleanor has the last word in the debate, claiming "justice" on her side, but in Shakespeare it is Constance, Arthur's mother, who ends the argument by belittling the document, calling it a "wicked will . . . a canker'd grandam's will!" (*TR*,I.ii.545;*John* II.i.193-194).

Thus Act I and the first half of Act II in Shakespeare's play have as their main subject the illegality of John's rule. The rest of this portion of the play is taken up by the "subplot" involving the Bastard, Faulconbridge, and this subplot, as is usual in Shakespeare's plays, reinforces the theme of the main plot.

Like King John, the Bastard has no legal status. The physical fact of his parentage, all too apparent in his face, and the will of Lord Faulconbridge assigning his lands to his younger son, Robert, both prove Philip's illegitimacy. (There is no mention of this will in *TR*.) Questions of legality are, however, of no more interest to the Bastard than they are to King John. In *TR* the Bastard is quick to oppose his brother's challenge to his legitimacy because he considers it a "shamefull slaunder of my parents" and a "dishonor of myself" (I.i.89-90), but Shakespeare's Bastard is almost indifferent to the matter. Whether he is "as *true* begot" as his brother he does not care, but "that I am as *well* begot, my liege . . . compare our faces and judge yourself" (I.i.75-79). He is, then, interested only in his natural endowments, not in social distinctions, and even after he has shown himself to be pleased at discovering his royal blood he repeats the sentiment that "I am I, howe'er I was begot" (I.i.175). Thus, whereas the *TR* Bastard stays behind at the end of the scene to force his mother to "resolve me of my sire" and to cure his "grose attaint" (I.i.334,329), Shakespeare's Bastard remains to assure his mother that, whoever he may have been, "with all my heart I thank thee for my father!" (I.i.270).

Furthermore, just as King John had relied on his "strong possession much more than [his] right," so the Bastard finds himself unhindered by his lack of legal status. Applying the same standard that he had applied to himself, John decides (I.i.120-129) that the Bastard has a de facto claim upon the Faulconbridge lands, regardless of his origins (Tillyard unaccountably calls this the administration of "excellent justice to the brothers Faulconbridge"[39]). Even so, the Bastard prefers to rely on his own innate merits and accepts Eleanor's offer to be the "reputed" son of Richard, "Lord of thy presence and no land beside" (I.i.137)—a phrase repeated by John when he demands that the citizens of Angiers recognize the true King of England

In us, that are our own great deputy,
And bear possession of our person here,
Lord of our presence, Angiers, and of you.   *(II.i.365-367)*

King John then, fairly revels in the illegitimate and the unconventional, and most of what Shakespeare has invented in the first two Acts serves to reinforce this theme. The Bastard satirizes "worshipful society," of which he is now a member, for being "too respective and too sociable" (I.i.184-216), too irrationally hierarchical and obsequious, and he vows to practice its pretensions only to "strew the footsteps of my rising." In parallel fashion, John too is aloof to traditional, proper society, a fact which Shakespeare emphasizes through the imagery describing the lawlessness and impetuosity of his followers to France:

> With them a bastard of the king's deceas'd,
> And all th'unsettled humours of the land;
> Rash, inconsiderate, fiery voluntaries,
> With ladies' faces and fierce dragons' spleens,
> Have sold their fortunes at their native homes,
> Bearing their birthrights proudly on their backs,
> To make a hazard of new fortunes here.   *(II.i.65-71)*

(Here Shakespeare is expanding on a single phrase in *TR*, describing the Bastard as being "a hardy wilde head, tough and venturous;" the rest of John's followers are called by *TR* simply "many other men of high resolve" [I.ii.491-492].)

We can, therefore, hardly agree with Tillyard that in *King John* Shakespeare became "weary of the theme of the succession of the crown."[40] One suspects that Tillyard's interpretation is based on the fact that John is not made to pay the consequences for his "rape upon the maiden virtue of the crown" (II.i.97-98)—in other words, that Shakespeare does not seem to be repeating the lesson of the *Henry VI* plays and *Richard III*. Instead, he seems now to be dramatizing the fact that, as the Bastard jocularly comments to his mother, "some sins do bear their privilege on earth" (I.i.261)—a remark which, recognizing the elaborate parallel drawn between the two characters, the audience could not help but apply to John's sins as well.

Indeed, the emphasis on John's illegality is not for the purpose of condemning him as king, any more than the parallel plot concerning the Bastard is intended to condemn illegitimacy. In Polydore Vergil and Stowe, of course, this had been true. Shakespeare, however, though refusing to mitigate the shadiness of John's behavior, capitalizes as well on the patriotic image of John created by the Tudors in order to encourage the audience to sympathize with his hero. One consequence of this peculiar blending of the two traditions is the fact that none of John's political difficulties results from his usurpation of the throne. Rather, it is the selfish designs of those who claim legitimate ends that threaten John's success. Furthermore, we may note that the Bastard's sarcastic remarks on the "mad world" and its "mad kings" (II.i.561)—which are often taken as criticisms of political immorality —are never directed against John's usurpation. Rather, they begin only after Hubert has suggested the politic marriage between Blanche and Lewis. J. Dover Wilson has found the Bastard's resentment at Lewis's wooing of Blanche unintelligible without reference to *TR*, where it is explained by the fact that the Bastard has been wooing Blanche for himself.[41] Wilson, however, fails to consider the

Bastard's role in Shakespeare's scene, which is that of a detached observer of political "commodity." A personal interest in one of the issues would obscure this function, and this is the reason why Shakespeare omits jealousy as a motive. In *TR* the Bastard had indeed objected to the truce only because it took Blanche away from him, and his tone was angry:

> If Lewes get her, well, I say no more:
> But let the frolicke Frenchman take no scorne,
> If Philip front him with an English horne.   *(I.v.797-799)*

Shakespeare's Bastard, however, is a realistically-minded satirist impatient with pretension, and it is altogether in character for him to criticize Hubert's speech not simply for suggesting Blanche's betrothal but for its obvious insincerity and pretentiousness:

> Zounds! I was never so bethump'd with words
> Since I first call'd my brother's father dad.   *(II.i.466-467)*

It is precisely this hypocrisy that both John and the Bastard are refreshingly free of, but which consistently characterizes those who base their claims not on ability but on legality.

Thus in *King John* the theme of usurpation leads Shakespeare not into the type of political morality play that he had created in *Richard III* but into an analytical study of political pragmatism and of the realities of the political world. The speeches of John and Philip before Angiers (II.i.206-266), for example, present a contrast between practical expediency and hypocritical righteousness. John offers the citizens protection against the "iron indignation" and "merciless proceeding" of invasion, and cites the accomplishment of his "painfull" and "expedient march" in saving the city from the French. That is, he concentrates on the here and now, on the inevitable and necessary facts of the present situation. Philip, on the other hand, offers an unctuous, inflated plea for the "downtrodden equity" of Arthur, whose protection he has "most divinely vow'd"—a vow, however, that he is soon to break for his own personal advantage. Philip's speech reveals him to be a man much like Machiavelli's description of Alexander VI, as it was translated by an anonymous Elizabethan:

> There was never anie man woulde affirme a thinge with more
> substantiall reasons, or sweare it with more solempne religion,
> or perfoorme it with soe sleight regarde, yet did he reape *com-
> moditie* with his crafte.[42]

It is even possible that the Bastard's later humorous diatribe against "Commodity" echoes this passage, though the echo is probably coincidental.[43] What is clear, however, is that Shakespeare is developing an interest in the same political phenomena that the *real* Machiavelli treated, as opposed to the Elizabethan stage-Machiavellism that had infused *Richard III*. Philip is not a malignant spirit masquerading as beneficent and delighting in the destruction of others, he is merely shrewd, self-seeking, and unprincipled. Thus, just as Machiavelli goes on in the same passage to note that a Prince "should seeme with greate reverence to extoll and imbrase Pittie, Fayth Honestie Courtesie & Religion, and speciallie the laste," so Shakespeare's Philip is careful to interlace his address with pious words and phrases—"divinely," "religiously," "zeal," "clouds of heaven"—and to deal liberally in "Amens."

In fact, piety in *King John* is almost always tainted by hypocrisy. Honigmann has noted the frequent use of the word "zeal" in the play, which connoted to Elizabethans the hypocritical religious fervor of the Puritans, and he points out "the hypocrisy of France, beneath whose hot zeal cold calculation presides."[44] Furthermore, in *King John* it is always the enemy who resort to the pious clichés which in *Richard III* had been the sole property of the saint-like Richmond. Austria, that contemptible coward who is insulted off the stage by the Bastard, almost paraphrases Richmond's battle oration when he announces before Angiers that

> The peace of heaven is theirs that lift their swords
> In such a just and charitable war. *(II.i.35-36)*

The very vagueness of the sentiment is proof of its inapplicability to the present situation. John has already pointed out that it is Austria and France who have "beat His peace to heaven" (II.i.88) and that their "charity," as King Philip later admits, is undertaken only for their "own vantage" (II.i.550).

It is not surprising, then, that the exhortations of Philip and Austria, eloquent as they are, have little effect on the pragmatic Hubert, representing the citizens of Angiers, who decides that "he that proves the king, / To him will we prove loyal" (II.i.270-271). By "prove" Hubert means a physical, not a legal, test, as is shown by his subsequent comment on the strength of the armies:

> Both are alike, and both alike we like.
> One must prove greatest: while they weigh so even,
> We hold our town for neither, yet for both. *(II.i.331-333)*

As the scene continues, Shakespeare makes even more explicit the conflict between abstract legal fictions and pragmatic political reality. The two kings again present their claims: Philip that he represents the true king, Arthur, who has the "right;" John that he needs no "deputy" since he stands in physical possession of the crown and bears "possession of our person here." To this Hubert replies:

> A greater power than we denies all this;
> And till it be undoubted, we do lock
> Our former scruple in our strong-barr'd gates:
> Kings of our fear, until our fears, resolv'd
> Be by some certain king purg'd and depos'd. *(II.i.368-372)*

The Folio assigns this entire speech to Philip, and though modern editors are undoubtedly correct in giving the last four lines to Hubert, the Folio is possibly correct in giving the first line to Philip.[45] The word "we" is capitalized in the Folio,

77

possibly indicating the "royal 'we'," just as the word "us" had been capitalized in John's preceding speech. With this emendation, Hubert's reply is a characteristically prudent, and humorous, one to Philip's typically pompous boast of divine protection. If, on the other hand, we follow the usual modern reading, we have Hubert himself piously referring the quarrel to God and then ironically awaiting concrete proof of superior power.

The world of *King John,* then, is not the black and white one of *Richard III.* The difference in the relationship between abstract right and actual merit in the two plays is further illustrated by a device carried over from *Richard III* but used for different effect in *King John*—the female lamentation. Constance, like Queen Elizabeth in the earlier play, pitifully bewails the fate of her innocent son, identifies him with divine favor, and calls for revenge on his enemies:

> His grandam's wrongs, and not his mother's shames,
> Draws those heaven-moving pearls from his poor eyes,
> Which heaven shall take in nature of a fee;
> Ay, with these crystal beads heaven shall be brib'd
> To do him justice and revenge on you.   *(II.i.168-172)*

The unctuous banality of these and other lines by Constance, however, is totally unlike the grim, ritualistic curses of *Richard III,* nor is it to be found in *TR.* Though perhaps wishing to remind us of the similarity between Arthur and the murdered princes, Shakespeare makes Constance a self-pitying, possessive, hysterical "bedlam" (II.i.183), who takes a masochistic pride in the magnitude of her grief, thus betraying her selfish motive in championing the claim of her son:

> I will instruct my sorrows to be proud,
> For grief is proud an't makes his owner stoop.
> To me and to the state of my great grief
> Let kings assemble; for my grief's so great
> That no supporter but the huge firm earth
> Can hold it up: here I and sorrows sit;
> Here is my throne, bid kings come bow to it.

Irving Ribner has written that "the lamentations of Constance . . . are Shakespeare's dramatic means of swaying the sympathies of his audience away from King John in the third act, and when this has been accomplished Constance drops out of the play."[46] This, however, is the act in which John reaches his greatest heights—his defiance of Pandulph and his scattering of "a whole armado of convicted sail" (III.iv.2)—and so Constance's laments can hardly be expected to have the effect of smearing John's character in the opinion of the audience. Furthermore, her last series of lamentations, in III.iv, are directed not against John but against Philip's "shame" ("Lo, now! Now see the issue of your peace!" [III.iv.21]) and against Pandulph's hypocritical reassurances ("Thou art not holy to belie me so" [III.iv.44]). In this way Shakespeare shifts any scorn felt by the audience from John to Philip and Pandulph.

78

Constance's proud lamentations, then, hardly have the same effect of raising political issues to moral ones that Queen Elizabeth's did in *Richard III*. Rather, they look forward to Richard II's melodramatic self-pity ("You may my glories and my state depose, / But not my griefs; still am I king of those" [IV.i.192-193]), both being equally excessive and ineffectual in a world dominated by political realism. As Philip exasperately comments, "You are as fond of grief as of your child" (III. iii.92). We may note, furthermore, that although in public Constance calls to heaven for aid, in private she acknowledges that Arthur is the victim not of evil but merely of fortune.

> Nature and Fortune join'd to make thee great:
> Of Nature's gifts thou mayst with lilies boast
> And with the half-blown rose. But Fortune, O,
> She is corrupted, chang'd and won from thee;
> Sh' adulterates hourly with thine uncle John.   *(II.ii.52-56)*

Indeed, Constance has betrayed a mistrust of heavenly justice all along, as when she declared that "with these crystal beads heaven shall be *bribed* / To do him justice and revenge." She realizes that although evil is subject to punishment by the hand of God, fortune is unpredictable, amoral, and "treads down fair respect of sovereignty" (II.ii.58) as often as it holds it up.

Thus when we come soon afterwards to the scene in which John reluctantly requests Hubert to remove Arthur—that "very serpent in my way" (III.ii.71)— we are prepared to sympathize with John's own struggle with misfortune, however reprehensible the act is by moral standards. Having regarded John throughout the play as acting in the best interests of England, and by the only standards possible in a world so beset with "thorns and dangers" (the phrase is the Bastard's), we are virtually forced by Shakespeare to recognize the political necessity of the act:

> John hath seiz'd Arthur; and it cannot be
> That, whiles warm life plays in that infant's veins,
> The misplac'd John should entertain an hour,
> One minute, nay, one quiet breath of rest.
> A sceptre snatch'd with an unruly hand
> Must be as boisterously maintain'd as gain'd
> And he that stands upon a slipp'ry place
> Makes nice of no vild hold to stay him up:
> That John may stand, then Arthur needs must fall;
> So be it, for it cannot be but so.   *(III.iii.131-140)*

This accurate, though characteristically cynical, analysis of the situation is by Pandulph; it is entirely lacking in *TR* and is a measure of the political complexity which Shakespeare has added to the story by his manipulation of the rival traditions. Thus, while the "murder" of Arthur—had it occurred—would have been a private sin upon John's head, which "must be answer'd, either here or hence" (IV.ii.89), it is only the adverse political effect of Arthur's death which leads to the revolt of the barons. Pembroke had asked for Arthur's freedom, not out of mercy but out of policy:

> That the time's enemies may not have this
> To grace occasions, let it be our suit
> That you have bid us ask his liberty;
> Which for our goods we do no further ask
> Than whereupon our weal, on you depending,
> Counts it your weal he have his liberty. *(IV.ii.61-66)*

Likewise, the decision of the nobles to desert John after they are informed of Arthur's death is based on their realization that "This will break out / To all our sorrows, and ere long, I doubt" (IV.ii.101-102).

Shakespeare, then, has taken advantage of the Tudor image of King John to influence his audience to sympathize with a hero who is both a usurper and a potential murderer—both of which are aspects of John's character that Shakespeare has retained from the medieval tradition. His purpose in so doing seems to be to emphasize the tragic ambiguity of John's situation. Either alternative spells doom for John. As long as Arthur lives, John cannot enjoy "one quiet breath of rest," and so "Arthur needs must fall" (III.iii.134,139). At the same time, Arthur's death can provide only "Bloody safety and untrue" (III.iii.148). The inevitable fatality of this impasse is only emphasized the more by the cruel irony that John is in fact not responsible for Arthur's death. In fact, John's personal responsibility is of only minimal importance in influencing either Arthur's death or the reactions to it. The Bastard decides to return to John before he can be certain that John was innocent of the deed (indeed, he never finds out for sure) and despite the fact that he realizes that in Arthur "the life, the right and truth of all this realm / Is fled to heaven" (IV.iii.144-145). Likewise, the barons continue their flight to the Dauphin even though they have been assured by Hubert that "'Tis not an hour since I left him [Arthur] well" (IV.iii.104). In jumping to the conclusion that John must have murdered Arthur, the barons are vainly attempting to place a simple moral interpretation on a complicated political conflict.

Having made sure that his audience will neither praise nor blame John for superficial reasons, however, Shakespeare can now continue to use the hostile medieval tradition to show John's faults as a king, basing his criticism on the same pragmatic standards by which he has established John's worthiness. For instance, John lacks the essential accomplishment of a king, the subordination of his passions to calm, deliberative reason. He is consistently characterized, even in his triumphs, as being motivated by fiery, rash emotions:

> France, I am burn'd up with inflaming wrath;
> A rage whose heat hath this condition,
> That nothing can allay, nothing but blood,
> The blood, and dearest-valued blood, of France. *(III.i.266-269)*

80

Shakespeare thus follows Holinshed in criticizing John's "want of discretion," as when Eleanor tells John that Constance's opposition "might have been prevented and made whole, / With very easy arguments of love" (I.i.35-36). It will be noted that Eleanor's emphasis is not on the Christian doctrine of charity *per se*, but on its practical results, though fortunately the two coincide in this case, as indeed Shakespeare is to discover that they frequently do. Henry V is a wiser king than John because he knows that "when lenity and cruelty play for a kingdom, the gentler gamester is the soonest winner" (*H5*,III.vi.118-120).

In *King John*, then, Shakespeare has drawn material from the two conflicting Elizabethan images of his subject in such a way as to produce a fresh and thought-provoking treatment of a familiar subject. To an audience prepared to sympathize with John as an early nationalistic patriot-martyr Shakespeare presents a John who is also a usurper and a potential murderer. The unconventionality of such a juxtaposition of details may easily be seen by comparing it to Shakespeare's treatment of similar political situations in the earlier play *Richard III*. Like Richard, John is an evident usurper, and though not so hypocritical as Richard, is not above maintaining his position by fraud and deceit. Unlike Richard, however, in *King John* the acknowledged usurper ironically stands for the best interests of England, and the barons who revolt from him are traitors to their country, not redeemers of it. Ironically too, John's rival for the throne, though identified like Richmond with both legal right and divine favor, is in reality merely a tool in the hands of foreign powers whose pious arguments conceal their selfish ambitions. Finally, like Richard, John even goes so far as to hire a murderer to assassinate his nephew, but instead of losing his kingdom because of the heinousness of the deed, John retains the loyalty of his chief supporter and dies a martyr's death in attempting to expel the Pope and the French from his land.

It is perhaps time, then, to revise the usual estimate of Shakespeare as a writer who used the form of the history play principally to glorify his nation's past and to preach from the stage the clichés of orthodox Tudor political doctrine. In *King John*, at least, Shakespeare chose deliberately to dramatize the most controversial material to be found in his sources, and revealed to his audience a mind sensitive to the complexities of politics, the ironies of history, and the ambiguities of human nature.

Notes:

(1) A much abridged version of this article was read before the Renaissance Comparative Literature Group of the Modern Language Asociation in Chicago, Dec. 28, 1963.

(2) *King John*, The Arden Shakespeare (London, 1954), p. xxv.

(3) For accounts of King John's reputation in the sixteenth century see Ruth Wallerstein, *King John in Fact and Fiction* (Philadelphia, 1917); Geoffrey Bullough, *Narrative and Dramatic Sources of Shakespeare* (New York, 1962) IV, 3-6; and Honigmann, Arden *John*, pp. xxvi-xxvii.

(4) The most recent account of the historical King John is W. L. Warren, *King John* (New

York, 1961); see also Wallerstein, *op. cit.,* and Charles Petit-Dutaillis, *Le Roi Jean et Shakespeare* (Paris, 1944).

(5) Roger of Wendover, *Chronica sive Flores Historiarum,* ed. H. O. Coxe (London, 1841-4), I, 1-2 (my translation).

(6) William Tyndale, *Doctrinal Treatises,* ed. Henry Walter (London, 1858), p. 338; quoted in Irving Ribner, *The English History Play in the Age of Shakespeare* (Princeton, 1957), p. 39.

(7) *Letters and Papers Foreign and Domestic of the Reign of Henry VIII,* ed. James Gairdner (London, 1882), VI, 109. I am indebted to Dr. Barry Adams for calling my attention to this reference.

(8) *Ibid.,* VIII, 230.

(9) Simon Fish, *A Supplicacyon for the Beggars,* ed. Edward Arber (London, 1880), p. 6.

(10) *Ibid.,* p. 6.

(11) *A Treatise proving by the King's Laws* . . . (London, 1538), sig. A₃.

(12) Robert Fabyan, *Concordance of Histories,* ed. Henry Ellis (London, 1811), p. 317.

(13) Fabyan, pp. 322-3.

(14) John Bale, *King Johan,* ed. J. H. P. Pafford, Malone Society Reprints (London, 1931), p. 417. All quotations are from this edition. I have regularized spelling and punctuation.

(15) John Leland, *Assertio Inclytissimi Arthurii* (London, 1544); for an account of the dispute over the Arthur legend see Edwin Greenlaw, *Studies in Spenser's Historical Allegory* (Baltimore, 1932).

(16) Pafford (pp. xv-xvi) finds evidence that these lines were written between 1546 and 1552, i.e., during a revision of the play and after Leland's attack on Polydore. Thus they probably constitute a request for him to take up the gauntlet again, this time specifically on behalf of King John. The "slumbre" probably refers to the insanity with which Leland was afflicted in his later years.

(17) John Foxe, *Acts and Monuments* (London, 1563), p. 71.

(18) Richard Grafton, *A Chronicle at Large, and Meere History of the Affayres of Englande* (1569), ed. H. Ellis (London, 1809), I,xv.

(19) Alfred Hart, *Shakespeare and the Homilies* (Melbourne, 1934), p. 122.

(20) "An homilie against disobedience and wylfull rebellion" (London, 1571), sig. A₂.

(21) "Homilie against disobedience," sigs. J₂ᵛ-J₃.

(22) R. Crompton, *The Mansion of Magnanimitie* (London, 1599), sig. A₃ᵛ.

(23) Geoffrey Bullough, *Narrative and Dramatic Sources of Shakespeare* (New York, 1962), IV, 3.

(24) A partial list of these works may be found in Honigmann, Arden *John,* pp. xxvi-xxvii.

(25) M. M. Reese, *The Cease of Majesty* (London, 1961), p. 265.

(26) Crompton was a lawyer, a member of Gray's Inn, and a judge, who early retired to private life in order to compose treatises on Elizabethan jurisprudence. His most notable work was "L' Authoritie et Jurisdiction des Courts de la Maiestie de la Roygne" (1594), which upheld the authority of the Star Chamber.

(27) F. A. Gasquet, "Some Materials For A New Edition of Polydore Vergil's 'History'," *Trans. Roy. Hist. Soc.*, New Series, XVI (1902), 1-17; Denys Hay, "The Manuscript of Polydore Vergil's *Anglica Historia,*" *Eng. Hist. Rev.*, LIV (1939), 240-251.

(28) A few, but only a very few, of the details concerning John's excesses were omitted from the second and third editions of the *Historia* in 1546 and 1555, presumably out of deference to the new Tudor opinion of King John; see Denys Hay, *Polydore Vergil, Renaissance Historian and Man of Letters* (Oxford, 1952), pp. 123, 190.

(29) Polydorus Vergilius, *Anglica Historia,* ed. J. Thysius (Leyden, 1651), p. 341. This edition is based on the second, revised edition (Basle, 1546), and is the most recent and access-ible complete edition of the *Anglica Historia*. All quotations are from this edition, but have been checked against the Folger Library copy of the 1534 edition.

(30) *Anglica Historia,* p. 341. The actual designation of Arthur as heir is described in the account of Richard's reign, p. 319, without mention of John's possible claim to the throne.

(31) C. S. Lewis, *English Literature in the Sixteenth Century* (Oxford, 1954), p. 298.

(32) John Stowe, *Annales, or, A Generall Chronicle of England* (1580), ed. and continued by Edmund Howes (London, 1631), pp. 150, 160. The reference to "Elianor" is puzzling. Arthur's sister is said by Grafton to have been named "Brecca." Stowe's mistake may have come from a misreading of the passage in Grafton, which also relates that John had a daughter named "Elianor" (Grafton, *op. cit.*, I, 232).

(33) Honigmann, therefore, appears to be wrong in his assertion that "John's 'usurpation' is Shakespeare's fiction, for his 'right' is not seriously questioned in the chronicles" (Arden *John,* p. xxvii). On Shakespeare's sources for the issue of John's usurpation, see John R. Elliott, Jr., "Polydore Vergil and the Reputation of King John in the Sixteenth Century," *ELN,* II (1964), 90-92.

(34) Reese, *Cease of Majesty,* pp. 264-265.

(35) Raphael Holinshed, *Chronicles* (London, 1807), II, 319. Further references indicated in the text are to this edition and volume.

(36) Foxe had printed some Latin verses, said to be contemporary, along with an English translation, beginning: "Non est Innocentius, imo nocens vere,..." ("Nocent, not inno-cent, he is ..."). *Acts and Monuments* (1576), pp. 257-258.

(37) All references to Shakespeare's *King John* are to the revised Arden edition, ed. E. A. J. Honigmann (London, 1954).

(38) All references to *The Troublesome Reign of King John* are to the text printed by Bul-lough, *Narrative and Dramatic Sources of Shakespeare,* IV, 72-151. I shall follow the customary practice of abbreviating the title of *The Troublesome Reign* to "TR."

(39) E. M. W. Tillyard, *Shakespeare's History Plays* (London, 1956), p. 223.

(40) Tillyard, p. 221.

(41) *King John,* ed. J. Dover Wilson (Cambridge, 1936), p. xxi.

(42) *Machiavelli's "The Prince": An Elizabethan Translation,* ed. Hardin Craig (Chapel Hill, 1944), pp. 76-7 (my italics). The translation probably dates from c. 1584.

(43) The similarity of Shakespeare's later history plays to Machiavelli's *Prince,* or at least to the kind of secular, analytic approach to politics which that work represents, has been suggested by Irving Ribner, "Bolingbroke, A True Machiavellian," *MLQ,* IX (1948),

177-183; and J. F. Danby, *Shakespeare's Doctrine of Nature* (London, 1949), ch. 3. Ribner compares in detail Bolingbroke's rise to the throne in *Richard II* with Machiavelli's analysis of the rise to power of a new prince. Danby finds some general qualities of Machiavelli's Prince in the Bastard, Bolingbroke, and Prince Hal.

There is no concrete evidence that Shakespeare read Machiavelli's works, but that he was familiar in some form with Machiavelli's actual ideas (as opposed to the distortions attributed to him by Gentillet) is quite possible. For the genuine interest in and knowledge of Machiavelli's works in Elizabethan England see Napoleone Orsini, "Le traduzioni elisabettiane inedite di Machiavelli," in *Studii Sul Rinascimento Italiano in Inghilterra* (Florence, 1937).

(44) Arden *John,* II.i.19n.; II.i.53n.; II.i.477-9n.

(45) See J. Dover Wilson, New Cambridge *King John,* p. 122, n. 368.

(46) *King John,* ed. Irving Ribner, The Pelican Shakespeare (Baltimore, 1962), p. 20. Ribner follows most modern editors in putting the Folio "Actus Secundus" (Honigmann's II.ii) at the beginning of Act III.

Shakespeare's Chronicle Plays as Historical-Pastoral

by Charles R. Forker

The best actors in the world, either for tragedy, comedy, history, pastoral, pastoral-comical, historical-pastoral, tragical-historical, tragical-comical-historical-pastoral.

Hamlet, II.ii.415-418

I

The critic who invokes the failing mental powers of Polonius in matters of literary terminology no doubt risks impaling himself upon the point of his own irony. Nevertheless, the risk is worth taking, for there is a sense in which the old counselor's words go beyond their immediate context to describe the modes of Shakespeare's own artistic practice. Elizabethan drama is nearly always "impure art," and Polonius's final category is more applicable than has generally been recognized to Shakespeare's ten plays on English kings from *1 Henry VI* to *Henry VIII*. It is the "pastoral" element in these histories that I want specifically to discuss in this essay, but perhaps, by way of laying the necessary foundation, I may be permitted a few general comments on the unity of the history plays as a group and the generic principles that appear to inform that unity.[1]

Although the individual plays have their own dramatic unity and have been acted independently ever since they were first presented at the Globe,[2] it is obvious from the arrangement of the Folio, where they are grouped according to the chronology of reigns, that their plots and characters are related and that they share common thematic and political interests. All the plays are crowded with action, comprise a more or less continuous drama covering roughly a century and a half of political and military history, and therefore project an image of great temporal and spatial extent. Because the emphasis is political, they usually present ambiguous conflicts between characters or groups of characters who represent opposed systems of value, partial or complementary mixtures of good and evil, so that our moral sympathies necessarily hover between the different sides of an issue. And in all the plays, too, Shakespeare raises the complex question of order in both its political and metaphysical aspects.

The so-called Tudor myth with its orthodox teleological and providential assumptions about the movement of history might support the idealistic position that political order was ultimately an aspect of divine order. Tillyard has shown how importantly that essentially medieval tradition influenced Shakespeare. Yet the equally forceful and more modern notion that man might, in some sense, be a shaper of his own destiny, that political goods and evils could and *did* result directly from the strength or weakness of individual leaders, cut precisely the other way; it seemed to suggest, with disturbing Machiavellian import, that the two orders had little practical connection and might in fact conflict. The struggle between Richard and Bolingbroke in *Richard II* obviously owes something to both attitudes.

It has been usual ever since A. W. Schlegel's *Lectures on Dramatic Art and Literature* (delivered in 1808) to take the plays together as comprising a national epic in dramatic form, a great panorama involving some two hundred different characters from both high and low life, a great patriotic celebration of "This happy breed of men . . . This blessed plot, this earth, this realm, this England" (*R2*, II.i. 45-50).[3] Although the epic qualities of the series have been generally granted, critics on the whole have been somewhat vague in their use of the term. One might begin the search for a clearer definition by noting that Tasso's summary of epic requirements (though of course the Italian poet was thinking not of drama but of the romantic-heroic poem in the tradition of Ariosto) fits Shakespeare's histories surprisingly well in a general way. The essentials for Tasso, apart from the orthodox classic purpose of inspiring admiration in the audience and delighting it through instruction, were: "The authority of history, truth of religion [i.e., specifically Christian values], the license of fiction, suitability of period [i.e., a period neither so remote as to appear uncivilized by contemporary standards nor so close to the present as to hamper unduly the poet's freedom of invention], and grandeur and mobility in the incidents."[4]

The plays include, of course, elements of both comedy and tragedy, but, taken as a cycle,[5] they define the ideal leader, the public man, the English hero in peace as well as war. There could not be, of course, as in classical epic, one central hero, and Tillyard, in fact, has tellingly restated the old notion that Shakespeare's real hero was the nation itself. In a general sense this is undeniable, but it is surely possible, without contradicting him, to say that Shakespeare builds up through the ten plays, as Spenser does in *The Faerie Queene*, a kind of composite hero through examples both negative and positive. Richard III and Henry V may represent the most obvious extremes, but the plays present us with a succession of heroic types, some of them very limited and hardly any unflawed, who nevertheless embody some of the qualities desirable in a public man—physical valor, patriotism, honesty, wisdom, generosity, loyalty, responsibility, justice, humility, as well as other qualities that Shakespeare numbered among the king-becoming graces.[6] The constant allusion to the heroes of classical epic as well as to such illustrious native figures as Richard the Lion-hearted, Edward III, and the Black Prince has the effect of heightening the heroic tone. The great profusion of stirring exhortations of troops, formal challenges flung back and forth, and speeches of diplomatic exchange have a similar effect. With the succession of heroic types goes a whole chain of anti-heroes, many of whom are very moving or humorous in their weaknesses. Shakespeare's interest in the histories, then, is not limited to the figure of the ideal king, but includes the loyal public servant, the wise counselor, the brave soldier, and the righteous churchman as well. It might be added that the medium of blank verse was ideally suited to such epic celebration, for it had after all been used first in English by the Earl of Surrey, himself a courtier and man of action, for his famous translation of Virgil's *Aeneid*.

But Shakespeare found it necessary to show the personal and private side of his public men, not only for the sense of depth and wholeness that would be missing without it, but in order to capitalize upon the tension between epic generality and detachment on the one hand, and comic or tragic involvement on the other—in other words to reconcile epic with dramatic requirements. Shakespeare's two most tragic kings in the cycle, Henry VI and Richard II, are tragic because they are temperamentally unsuited to bear public responsibility, and his most comic king, Richard III, is even more unsuited to bear it because he turns the acquisition of power into a monstrous private joke.

The tension between public and private worlds in the histories relates to another contrast fundamental to the series—that between order and chaos; for this conflict too may be seen in terms of epic or ideal order violated by comic or tragic disruptions. Almost all the important thematic contrasts of the history cycle—Peace against War, Love against Hate, Rise against Fall, Divine against Human power, Legitimacy against Illegitimacy, Strength against Weakness, Pleasure against Duty, Ceremony against Informality, Innocence against Guilt—can be subsumed under the two principal contrasts already mentioned: Order vs. Chaos and Public vs. Private Life.

The subtle and complex dramatic form which the greatest Elizabethan plays exemplify is based not on unity of action (in the Aristotelian sense) but on multiple actions related to each other, as musical themes are related, by repetition and variation—by a system of ironic contrasts and parallels. This principle of organization, though of course Shakespeare uses it elsewhere, was perhaps especially significant to him in the history plays because of the special problems of ordering in dramatic compass the epic sweep and multitudinousness of the chronicle source material.

What I propose to argue in this essay is that Shakespeare often found it convenient to organize his system of contrasts and parallels in the histories with reference to another traditional literary dichotomy—one exploited almost contemporaneously by Tasso in *Jerusalem Delivered*, Spenser in *The Faerie Queene*, and Sidney in *The Arcadia*—that between epic and pastoral. I must warn readers at the outset that I am using the term "pastoral" very elastically, for to the formal pastoral drama of Tasso and Guarini, the drama that Jonson and Fletcher were later to imitate in England, Shakespeare owed comparatively little. His tradition was rather the rustic, spontaneous, and popular pastoralism of his native country—the tradition to which the medieval nativity plays, the popular romances, the Robin Hood ballads, and other folklore contributed much, and in which the word "shepherd" could suggest a various world of lovers, poets, holiday humor, nobles disguised as peasants, and Christian simplicity.[7] The familiar Renaissance contrasts of court vs. country and art vs. nature, for instance, lie very close to its heart. My central point is that by drawing upon this pastoral tradition directly and also indirectly by making the audience aware of nature and the natural world through language, character, action, and setting, Shakespeare was able to dramatize more effectively some of the ironic contrasts between public and private life and between order and chaos that give the history plays their special richness.

II

Shakespeare introduces the pastoral tradition most schematically in the earliest plays—those that make up the *Henry VI* trilogy. Probably the most obvious and familiar example occurs in the third part where "Holy Harry of Lancaster" (as he was sometimes called in the sixteenth century) contemplates the advantages of the shepherd's life as the battle of Towton rages around him. He sits upon a molehill which reminds us ironically of another molehill earlier in the play upon which the ambitious York aspirant to the crown, Richard Plantagenet, has been ritually mocked, crowned with paper, and murdered. As the king sits, meditative and withdrawn, wishing he had only sheep to tend instead of warring subjects, he watches an emblematic little morality play on the unnaturalness of civil war in which a son kills his father unwittingly and a father kills his son:

> This battle fares like to the morning's war,
> When dying clouds contend with growing light,
> What time the shepherd, blowing of his nails,
> Can neither call it perfect day nor night.
>
> . . . . .
>
> Here on this molehill will I sit me down.
> To whom God will, there be the victory!
>
> . . . . .
>
> Would I were dead, if God's good will were so!
> For what is in this world but grief and woe?
> O God! methinks it were a happy life
> To be no better than a homely swain;
> To sit upon a hill, as I do now,
> To carve out dials quaintly, point by point,
> Thereby to see the minutes how they run—
> How many makes the hour full complete,
> How many hours brings about the day,
> How many years a mortal man may live;
>
> . . . . .
>
> So minutes, hours, days, weeks, months, and years,
> Pass'd over to the end they were created,
> Would bring white hairs unto a quiet grave.
> Ah, what a life were this! how sweet! how lovely!
> Gives not the hawthorn bush a sweeter shade
> To shepherds looking on their silly sheep
> Than doth a rich embroider'd canopy
> To kings that fear their subjects' treachery?
> O yes, it doth! a thousandfold it doth!

88

> And to conclude, the shepherd's homely curds,
> His cold thin drink out of his leather bottle,
> His wonted sleep under a fresh tree's shade,
> All which secure and sweetly he enjoys,
> Is far beyond a prince's delicates,
> His viands sparkling in a golden cup,
> His body couched in a curious bed,
> When care, mistrust, and treason waits on him.   *(3H6,II.v.1-54)*

Shakespeare is dramatizing several ideas in this scene. Henry represents the timorous warrior and incompetent king who retreats from the harsh realities of his reign into an imaginary, golden world where "the lion fawns upon the lamb" (*3H6*, IV.viii.49). But the king's pastoral daydream characterizes him also as a kind of Holy Idiot (like Dostoevsky's Prince Myshkin). The molehill is an emblem of his humility (just as the contrasting molehill was a bitter mock of his Yorkist rival's reaching at mountains). His meditation throws the unnatural savagery of the civil war into vivid relief, and Shakespeare forges a symbolic link between the golden world of pastoral and the eternal world of Henry's religious commitment. A few scenes later, King Henry, now unsuccessfully disguised, becomes a deer in his own deer-park and is taken prisoner by two of his own gamekeepers to be delivered over to the new York claimant, Edward IV. He is only too willing to make a spiritual kingdom of his cell, where he may be a king, as he says, "in mind":

> My crown is in my heart, not on my head;
> Not deck'd with diamonds and Indian stones,
> Nor to be seen. My crown is call'd content;
> A crown it is that seldom kings enjoy.   *(3H6,III.i.62-65)*

The pastoral motif here betokens Shakespeare's concern with the conflict between private and public values and their relation to order in the universe, the state, and the individual soul. Henry's golden world, his "crown of content," contrasts finely with Richard of Gloucester's idea of a golden world. For him, as for Tamburlaine, the perfect bliss and sole felicity is the sweet fruition of an *earthly* crown ("the golden time I look for") and, like one "lost in a thorny wood," he will hew his way to it "with a bloody axe" (*3H6*, III.ii.127-181). In the penultimate scene of *3 Henry VI* the worlds of force and spirit are effectively juxtaposed through metaphor: Richard murders Henry in the Tower of London, and Shakespeare transforms the pastoral associations used earlier into ritual sacrifice. The protective jailer, suddenly dismissed from the room, becomes the timorous shepherd driven from his charge, and Henry, "the harmless sheep," "yield[s] his fleece" (V.vi.8) and "make[s] a bloody supper" (V.v.85) for the ravenous wolf. Such imagery becomes nearly automatic throughout the early tetralogy. Peace, order, and innocence are repeatedly thought of in terms of the shepherd with his sheep; and the ruthless forces of power that turn the pastoral landscape into a scene of slaughter are imaged in terms of preying wolves and foxes.

The idea of the king as shepherd is very old. Northrop Frye[8] tells us it can be traced to ancient Egypt; but for European writers it derives mainly, of course, from Biblical tradition, for Christ was the prototype of the good shepherd (the *bonus pastor*) who was also king of the universe. To Elizabethan audiences who were used to being told that kings were a sort of gods on earth, deputies elected by the Lord, anointed, crowned, planted many years, the analogy would not have seemed in the least strange. Furthermore, it was useful to poets and dramatists because, by enshrining a paradox, it focussed upon a fundamental conflict in the nature of kingship—the conflict between power and humility. Hall's *Chronicle* (1548) calls so warlike a king as Henry V "a shepherde whom his flocke loued and louyngly obeyed";[9] nor is it surprising to find the figure employed in history plays by Shakespeare's contemporaries. In Greene's *James IV* (1589-92) Douglas laments the king's defection from responsibility ("Oh haplesse flocke whereas the guide is blinde" [II.ii.2][10]), and Robert of Artois in *Edward III* (1592-95) refers to his sovereign as "the true shepeard of our commonwealth" (I.i.41).[11] James Shirley elaborates the idea in one of his early plays, *The School of Compliment* (1624):

> A shepherd is a king, whose throne
> Is a mossy mountain, on
> Whose top we sit, our crook in hand,
> Like a sceptre of command.
> Our subjects, sheep grazing below,
> Wanton, frisking to and fro.[12]　　　　　　　　　*(IV.ii)*

Shakespeare gradually modifies this idea in the later history plays until the rather artificial and conventional image of the shepherd disappears, but the pastoral longing for escape from public duty to a quieter, simpler, more anonymous and contemplative world, continues throughout the histories until it merges with the potentially tragic concept of kingly isolation.

Prince Arthur, the rightful heir to England's crown but a helpless pawn in the game of international power-politics, dreams of the pastoral life in *King John*:

> By my christendom
> So I were out of prison and kept sheep,
> I should be as merry as the day is long!　　　　*(IV.i.16-18)*

The Lady Constance bemoans her lost hopes for him, sitting like the shepherds of pastoral elegy, upon a grassy knoll:

> my grief's so great
> That no supporter but the huge firm earth
> Can hold it up. Here I and sorrows sit;
> Here is my throne, bid kings come bow to it.　　*(III.i.71-74)*

Even when Shakespeare drops the pastoral imagery and puts the longing for humble anonymity in more realistic and varied terms, he seems repeatedly to have his royal characters express attitudes which may be called "pastoral" in the sense of anti-heroic — when they imagine themselves as monks, beggars, and commoners or indulge themselves in escapist roles such as that of poet or tavern roisterer. Crookback Richard, who describes himself as "a plain man" of "simple truth" (*R3*, I.iii.51-52), and who is forever glancing heavenward with such utterances as "I thank my God for my humility" (II.i.72), parodies Henry VI's desire for the contemplative life with mordant irony as he woos the London citizens:

> Alas, why would you heap this care on me?
> I am unfit for state and majesty.   *(III.vii.204-205)*

This is the man of whom Buckingham has just said with such comic unction:

> When holy and devout religious men
> Are at their beads, 'tis much to draw them thence,
> So sweet is zealous contemplation.   *(III.vii.92-94)*

Richard II, Shakespeare's first study in depth of a man caught tragically between his ceremonial image of himself and his own private emotions, lapses periodically into a kind of sentimental pastoral role. Returning from Ireland, he stoops to pat the gentle earth of his kingdom in affectionate greeting while his active fantasy conjures up a poetic landscape in which nettles, adders, and toads annoy the feet of Bolingbroke's invading army; he threatens to exchange his sceptre for a palmer's walking staff and his gorgeous palace for a hermitage. Or, again, he half welcomes "worldly loss":

> Say, is my kingdom lost? Why, 'twas my care;
> And what loss is it to be rid of care?   *(III.ii.94-95)*

For a moment, he recognizes, like Wolsey, "the blessedness of being little" (*H8*, IV.ii.66). Becoming a spectator at his own tragedy, he sits upon the ground (like a shepherd) to tell sad stories of the death of kings, he muses on the theme of time (as Henry VI does on his molehill), and comes at last, unlike Henry, to the perception that he has played "in one person many people, / And none contented."

> Sometimes am I king:
> Then treasons make me wish myself a beggar,
> And so I am. Then crushing penury
> Persuades me I was better when a king;
> Then am I king'd again; and by-and-by
> Think that I am unking'd.   *(V.v.31-37)*

In *Richard II,* the pastoral idea of escape from responsibility is connected with Richard's feeling for the beauty of his emerald isle and his love of words and artificial postures. For Richard, as for Duke Senior in *As You Like It,* "sweet are the uses of adversity."

The insomniac Henry IV expresses a familiar pastoral attitude when, weighed down under a crown that has become a "polish'd perturbation," a "golden care" (*2H4*, IV.v.23), he wishes for the uncomplicated condition of an ordinary subject

(III.i.4-31). And his son takes up the same theme when, wandering incognito among his soldiers in the dark hours before Agincourt, he ruminates half-enviously upon the lackey who "all night / Sleeps in Elysium" (*H5*, IV.i.290-291). "Uneasy lies the head that wears a crown" (*2H4*, III.i.31) captures a sentiment that Shakespeare's own sovereign probably appreciated, for Walton in his idyllic treatise on fishing records the story "that our good Queen *Elizabeth* did . . . often wish her self a Milkmaid all the moneth of *May,* because they are not troubled with cares, but sing sweetly all the day, and sleep securely all the night."[13]

In the last play of the ten, Shakespeare returns to the more conventional symbolism of pastoral. There we see Henry VIII, not as a second Bluebeard or the heavy, brooding figure of Holbein's familiar portrait, but as a monarch young and buoyantly romantic. He interrupts Wolsey's gay banquet in the masquing costume of a French shepherd and, temporarily forgetting matters of state, loses his heart to pretty Anne Bullen. For Shakespeare, then, in the history plays, the worlds of pleasure, naturalness, contemplation, carelessness (in the root sense), art, and romance may all be seen as versions of pastoral. They remind us of that "infinite heart's-ease" (*H5*, IV.i.253) which, all too often, kings must neglect and private men may enjoy.

But pastoral symbolism may also serve ironically to emphasize disorder and unnaturalness. Since pastoral values typically suggest some sort of peaceful, civilized social norm, the abandonment or perversion of these values usually signifies anarchy. It is as if Shakespeare were reminding us that particular historical disorders may be rooted in some fundamental crime against Nature herself, in a violation of natural law. Some such purpose seems to lie behind Shakespeare's portrayal of Joan of Arc, whose dark character in Holinshed he manages to blacken further. Although she is "by birth a shepherd's daughter" who "waited on . . . tender lambs" (*1H6*, I.ii.72-76), she repudiates the pastoral world that is her lot, and, assisted by hellish powers, helps to turn a peaceful land into a battlefield. Shakespeare makes her into a sort of female Tamburlaine (who was also a shepherd to begin with)—a conqueror, not only of the English, but of her own sovereign. The Dauphin inverts traditional order in one scene by acknowledging her his vanquisher:

> Thou art an Amazon
> And fightest with the sword of Deborah.
>
> . . . . .
>
> Let me thy servant and not sovereign be.   *(1H6,I.ii.104-111)*

At the end of the play she is revealed to be not only a witch but a lascivious hypocrite arrogant enough to claim that royal blood runs in her veins. Shakespeare makes the moral contrast between order and disorder unmistakable when her own father, a humble shepherd content with his lot, curses Joan as unnatural, and reflects that it would have been better if "some ravenous wolf had eaten thee" "when thou didst keep my lambs afield" (V.iv.30-31).

Jack Cade, "born under a hedge" (*2H6,* IV.ii.55), is another of Shakespeare's falsely aspiring and misplaced rustics. His rebellious energies create the very chaos that Henry VI's inept rule has courted and portend the even greater chaos that the rising house of York already threatens. Cade, like Joan, claims royal descent with a bogus tale of mixed-up twins that might come straight out of some pastoral romance. His watchwords are ignorance and brute force, and he sits on London Stone, a kind of surrogate king, and imagines a silly communist utopia where the exercise of reason in any form is a hanging offense and where "the pissing conduit" shall "run nothing but claret wine this first year of our reign" (IV.vi.3-5). The frightening commonwealth that Cade dreams of is a sort of peasant's brave new world, a parody version of the legendary golden world that Gonzalo later imagines in *The Tempest* (II.i.147-156) and that Shakespeare partly derived from the fifteenth book of Ovid's *Metamorphoses* and Montaigne's delightful essay on cannibals. But Cade's imaginary order is really the very opposite of Gonzalo's idyllic primitivism. Cade's idea of the state of nature, because it is uncultivated by art or learning, is savage and unnatural. Dick Butcher cries out in his enthusiasm for reform, "let's kill all the lawyers" (*2H6*, IV.ii.83); and Cade says to his rabble army, "then are we in order when we are most out of order" (IV.ii.199-200).

The priestly function in medieval and Renaissance life was traditionally idealized, of course, as the Christian pastor's cure of souls, his selfless responsibility for the spiritual health of his flock. If this standard could be met by such lowly men as Chaucer's country parson ("He was a shepherde" able to "drawen folk to hevene by fairnesse" and "good ensample" who "waited after no pompe and reverence"), how much more was it to be enjoined upon the great prelates of the church whose very symbol of episcopal authority was the crozier or shepherd's crook. The mere presence of the lords spiritual in the histories reminds us of the historic pastoral commitment to be *in* the world without quite being *of* it, but of course many of Shakespeare's ambitious clerics fall very short of this ideal and behave in fact like lords temporal. Malicious or worldly churchmen like Cardinal Beaufort in *Henry VI*, Cardinal Pandulph in *King John*, the Archbishop of York in *Henry IV*, or Wolsey in *Henry VIII* dramatize the great gulf between an order based upon Christian grace and charity (the order of the Good Shepherd) and the perverted greed for riches, power, and privilege that makes a mockery of their pastoral calling. Such are the corrupt clergy that Milton was later to attack through St. Peter's words in *Lycidas*—those who "for their bellies' sake, / Creep and intrude, and climb into the fold," or "scramble at the shearers' feast / And shove away the worthy bidden guest." Prince John of Lancaster strongly, if a little smugly, rebukes Archbishop Scroop's perversion of his pastoral function:

> My Lord of York, it better show'd with you
> When that your flock, assembled by the bell,
> Encircled you to hear with reverence
> Your exposition on the holy text
> Than now to see you here an iron man,

Cheering a rout of rebels with your drum,
Turning the word to sword, and life to death.   *(2H4,IV.ii.4-10)*

We see the true standard of Christian behavior when Henry VI, more a priest
than a king, prays for the soul of Cardinal Beaufort, who has served him so treacherously, or when Wolsey moralizes on his own fate:

O Cromwell, Cromwell!
Had I but serv'd my God with half the zeal
I serv'd my king, he would not in mine age
Have left me naked to mine enemies.
. . . . .   Farewell
The hopes of court! My hopes in heaven do dwell.   *(H8,III.ii.454-459)*

When Shakespeare is not reinforcing the various aspects of the pastoral theme
by contrasts in action and characterization, he often seems to do so obliquely by
evoking a sense of ideal landscape through imagery and setting. One cannot read
the histories consecutively without being struck by the constant prevalence of
natural imagery. As early as *Titus Andronicus* Shakespeare had begun "to warble
his native woodnotes wild," and, indeed, we are never very far from the out-of-
doors throughout Shakespeare's poetry. But in the history plays especially, landscape is often symbolic of moral attitude rather than merely decorative or
atmospheric. Shakespeare shares with Wordsworth that pastoral impulse that
makes poets turn to the countryside for reflections on man's experience in the
bustling world, that looks to Nature as a teacher. Certain stock metaphors constantly recur. Health and unhealth in the body politic are regularly imaged by
figures drawn from husbandry. Commonwealths as well as individual fortunes
bud, ripen, and wither.[14] Another of Wolsey's speeches illustrates Shakespeare's
typical practice:

Farewell, a long farewell, to all my greatness!
This is the state of man: to-day he puts forth
The tender leaves of hopes; to-morrow blossoms
And bears his blushing honours thick upon him;
The third day comes a frost, a killing frost,
And when he thinks, good easy man, full surely
His greatness is a-ripening, nips his root,
And then he falls, as I do.   *(III.ii.351-358)*

Weeds in gardens, caterpillars eating leaves, and cankers in roses stand, of
course, for various evils. Genealogical relationships are traditionally associated
with trees or vines, and one gets in the histories the constant linking of blood
with growth and vegetation. Bolingbroke, at the end of *Richard II*, sees himself
as a plant watered by the scarlet rain of his rival's murder:

Lords, I protest my soul is full of woe
That blood should sprinkle me to make me grow.   *(V.vi.45-46)*

94

The landscape mirrors the values of peace and war, so that, typically, cedars (like Warwick) yield "to the axe's edge" (3H6, V.ii.11), branches (like Rutland) are "lopp'd" when their "leaves put forth" (3H6, II.vi.47-48), and "sweet" plants (like Prince Edward) are "untimely cropp'd" (3H6, V.v.62). The soil of England "daub[s] her lips with her own children's blood," "trenching war channel[s] her fields" and "bruise[s] her flow'rets with . . . armed hoofs" (1H4, I.i.5-8), soldiers "Make boot upon the summer's velvet buds" (H5, I.ii.194), a "crimson tempest . . . bedrench[es] / The fresh green lap of fair King Richard's land" (R2, III.iii.46-47), or a dynastic crisis changes the complexion of England's face to "scarlet indignation" and "bedew[s] / Her pastures' grass" with blood (R2, III.iii.98-100). If Shakespeare had liked Stendhalian titles, he might have called the entire cycle "The Red and the Green."

Seasonal imagery is of course vital to the pastoral tradition (The Shepheards Calendar springs instantly to mind), and accordingly in the history plays glorious summers succeed winters of discontent. But sometimes, as in Richard III, what ought to be a rebirth turns out to be a hideous storm of terror. In Richard II, the Duchess of York, referring to the new king's favorites, asks her son: "Who are the violets now / That strew the green lap of the new-come spring?" York warns him:

> Well, bear you well in this new spring of time,
> Lest you be cropp'd before you come to prime.   (V.ii.46-51)

Political mutability has its familiar analogue in the cycles of nature, and Shakespeare puts it to eloquent use.

Security, coolness, ease, natural order are traditionally associated with the countryside, but for Shakespeare ideal landscapes are populated, controlled by human beings, methodized (as Pope might say) so as to analogize natural law. Behind this symbolism, of course, lies the Christian Neo-Platonic habit of regarding nature as a second book of revelation. Shakespeare's attitude often seems akin to that of Duke Senior in As You Like It who,

> exempt from public haunt,
> Finds tongues in trees, books in the running brooks,
> Sermons in stones, and good in everything.   (II.i.15-17)

There was also the possibility of analogy, often ironically employed, between the green landscape of England and the Biblical garden of Paradise. Shakespeare exploits this parallel in the famous allegorical garden scene of Richard II where a pair of gardeners, following the pastoral tradition that goes back to Virgil, discuss their betters and moralize at length upon the misgovernment of England in the language of pruning, weeding, and the propping up of limbs. The land which Gaunt earlier describes as "This other Eden, demi-paradise" has fallen from its prelapsarian state to the condition of a mere "pelting farm" (II.i.42-60). Under Richard's slovenly care, as the names of his sycophants, Bushy and Green, may help to symbolize, it has become an unweeded garden. Things rank and gross in nature possess it merely.

The Duke of Burgundy in a lovely speech from *Henry V* sees the disordered countryside of France, that "best garden of the world," in the same terms:

> all her husbandry doth lie on heaps,
> Corrupting in it own fertility.
> Her vine, the merry cheerer of the heart,
> Unpruned dies; her hedges even-pleach'd,
> Like prisoners wildly overgrown with hair,
> Put forth disorder'd twigs; her fallow leas
> The darnel, hemlock, and rank fumitory
> Doth root upon, while that the coulter rusts
> That should deracinate such savagery.
> The even mead, that erst brought sweetly forth
> The freckled cowslip, burnet, and green clover,
> Wanting the scythe, all uncorrected, rank,
> Conceives by idleness and nothing teems
> But hateful docks, rough thistles, kecksies, burrs.   (*V.ii.36-52*)

War has its heroic side in *Henry V*, but here it is seen as a violation of natural law revealed in a landscape that forfeits "both beauty and utility."

So often in Shakespeare a scene is placed in a garden or forest,[15] not for the sake of realistic background or local color but for ethical or thematic suggestiveness.[16] This partly explains why ordinarily we get no complete and sometimes no clear impression of place in the verse.

One of the most illuminating examples of Shakespeare's use of emblematic setting occurs in the famous Temple Garden scene of *1 Henry VI*, where with ingenious wit and ceremonial rhetoric he dramatizes the growing faction between the red rose of Lancaster and the white rose of York. The whole episode is an extended metaphysical conceit in dramatic form. The plucking of the red and white roses with its accompanying verbal quarrel constitutes both a prophecy and a pastoral reduction of the fratricidal war to follow. In this sense it serves as an analogue to the Fall. The garden setting establishes, in fact, a whole complex of interrelated ironies. As in *Richard II*, it is a foil to set off the sickness and chaos in the state against the health and order in nature. Indeed, this contrast becomes the more emphatic because the garden adjoins an ancient school of law. Moreover, the garden is rich in connotations that go back to medieval literary tradition. We recall the gardens of Chaucer's *Troilus* and *Canterbury Tales* that often mingle the erotic associations of *The Romance of the Rose* with the idea of gardens as types of Eden and therefore allegories of sacred order, divine love, and human charity.[17] The birth of a national blood feud therefore takes place in a setting that normally connotes love, whether secular or religious. In the great chain of being, the rose was traditionally at the top of the floral hierarchy and hence analogous to royalty. This idea became associated in medieval religious tradition with the symbolism of martyrology,[18] and Shakespeare seems to draw upon this association again in later plays when he describes the kissing lips of the little princes in the

Tower as "four red roses on a stalk" (*R3*, IV.iii.12) and calls Richard II "My fair rose" (*R2*, V.i.8) or again, "that sweet lovely rose" (*1H4*, I.iii.175). The color contrast is symbolic too: Shakespeare exploits its ironic possibilities when he makes the traditional symbolism of white for innocence and red for love prefigure pale fear and gory death:

> Rich. Now, Somerset, where is your argument?
> Som. Here in my scabbard, meditating that
> Shall dye your white rose in a bloody red.
> Rich. Meantime your cheeks do counterfeit our roses;
> For pale they look with fear, as witnessing
> The truth on our side.
> Som. No Plantagenet!
> 'Tis not for fear, but anger, that thy cheeks
> Blush for pure shame to counterfeit our rose.   *(1H6,II.iv.59-66)*

The plucking of the roses, then, becomes the emblem of natural law violated. It expresses in iconographic form the same sentiment that one of the remorseful murderers in *Richard III* utters:

> We smothered
> The most replenished sweet work of nature
> That from the prime creation e'er she fram'd.   *(IV.iii.17-19)*

King Henry, sitting on his molehill, later notices "The red rose and the white . . . The fatal colours of our striving houses" (*3H6*, II.v.97-98) on the mangled face of the boy slain by his father.

Gardens, orchards, parks, and forests keep reappearing in the history plays. In her husband's garden the Duchess of Gloucester (*2H6*, I.iv) dabbles with black magic by involving herself with the notorious witch Margery Jourdain and two sinister priests.[19] There by blasphemous invocations and other occult ceremonies —to the accompaniment of thunder and lightning—they raise "a spirit" who, in riddling fashion, foretells the deposition of the king and the deaths of York, Somerset, and Suffolk. Richard Plantagenet allies himself with Warwick the kingmaker in another garden scene (*2H6*, II.ii). Strolling together in a "close walk" (II.ii.3), later described as "this private plot" (II.ii.60), they plan to root up the red rose and plant the white, biding their time until their enemies "have snar'd the shepherd of the flock / That virtuous prince, the good Duke Humphrey" and the hour be ripe to stain their swords "With heart-blood of the house of Lancaster" (II.ii. 66-74). The walled garden or *hortus conclusus* (as it was called in the Middle Ages) is traditionally the place for quiet contemplation and retirement. Yet here the contemplation runs on political murder—as it does later for Brutus in still another garden. The ordered gardens become ironic settings in which to mirror impending chaos, to commune with evil forces, to sow seeds of destruction, to contemplate the annihilation of all that's made with green thoughts in a green shade. Shakespeare gives us a comic scene of ambitious contemplation later on when Falstaff tells Shallow in the latter's "arbour" (*2H4*, V.iii.2) that "the laws of England are at my commandment" (V.iii.142).

In Shakespeare, as in Spenser (cf. the episodes in Book VI of *The Faerie Queene* where Serena is nearly devoured by cannibals or in which Pastorella is kidnapped by brigands and her father murdered), violence and savagery seem constantly to menace the idyllic aspects of the green world. In *2 Henry VI*, Alexander Iden (one can scarcely overlook the symbolic overtones of a name spelled "Eden" in the 1587 edition of Holinshed) contemplates his own garden in a typically pastoral vein:

> Lord, who would live turmoiled in the court
> And may enjoy such quiet walks as these?
> This small inheritance my father left me
> Contenteth me, and worthy a monarchy.
> I seek not to wax great by others' waning,
> Or gather wealth, I care not with what envy.
> Sufficeth that I have maintains my state
> And sends the poor well pleased from my gate.   *(IV.x.18-25)*

When Jack Cade leaps the garden wall in order to steal food (see IV.x.8-9), we have chaos breaking in upon order, and Iden has to kill him in order to re-establish the natural equilibrium. Perhaps Shakespeare suggests in this scene as he does later in *As You Like It* that the separation between the world of affairs and the pastoral world can never be complete.

Of course, all the Shallow scenes in *2 Henry IV* with their delightful local color serve to underscore the traditional pastoral contrast of court with country. The rambling chatter about grafting pippins, sowing the headland with red wheat, settling debts with "a couple of short-legg'd hens" (V.i.28), and selling "a score of ewes" (III.ii.55) or "a good yoke of bullocks at Stamford fair" (III.ii.42) dramatizes a world removed from civil war and indicates that the distance between Gloucestershire and Westminster Palace, where the king lies stricken, is more than a matter of miles. The point, incidentally, has not been lost on producers of the play. Sir Frank Benson in 1864 brought out the country quality of the scenes at Shallow's "through the visible and vocal presence of sheep, pigeons, and fowls," and subtler modifications of his idea have marked more recent productions.[20]

Richard of Gloucester sends the Bishop of Ely to order strawberries from a garden in order to break up a council meeting and suddenly change the atmosphere from one of natural amity and established law into a little reign of terror. The contrast between the strawberry garden outside and Richard's shrunken arm inside, "like a blasted sapling, wither'd up" (*R3*, III.iv.68), points one of the morals Shakespeare desires us to draw from the scene. Indeed, the strawberry itself, as Lawrence J. Ross has recently shown in a significant article, was emblematic of both "the good or uncorrupted man" and "the seemingly good man, the hypocrite."[21] He traces the symbolism of the strawberry as an apparent good which conceals evil to a passage in Virgil's *Eclogues* (III, 92-93), and also points out the idyllic connotations of the fruit in classical and Christian literature and art. For instance, in Ovid's *Metamorphoses* (I, 104) the strawberry typifies the food of the pastoral Golden Age; and, as signifying the fruit of the spirit, it traditionally "appears near the blessed or in the Eden of unfallen Adam and Eve in representations of the celestial or earthly paradise."[22] King John dies in an "orchard" whither he has been brought in the hope that "the open air . . . would allay the burning quality / Of that fell poison which assaileth him" (V.vii.7-10). The fresh air of the orchard cannot restore his health, but the shift of the final action to a natural setting does foreshadow the cure of England's ills and the restoration of natural order to the state. In both plays, details of setting with "pastoral" overtones help to define moral contrasts that are significant in the total structure.

Natural settings sometimes seem to agree with actions in the later plays too. The rebels of *2 Henry IV* are betrayed into dispersing their forces at a place in Yorkshire called Gaultree Forest. Holinshed's spelling ("Galtree") again brings out more clearly the ironic connotations of the name. Queen Katherine's lady-in-waiting in *Henry VIII* tries to cheer her mistress's heavy heart by singing a pastoral lyric in which Orpheus creates a poetic landscape as different as might be from the dolor of her palace apartment:

> Orpheus with his lute made trees
> And the mountain tops that freeze
>   Bow themselves when he did sing.
> To his music plants and flowers
> Ever sprung, as sun and showers
>   There had made a lasting spring.   *(III.i.3-8)*

But a little later in the scene the queen seems to identify herself with the flower of a poetic landscape, herself indulging in the pathetic fallacy that is so marked a feature of the song:

> Like the lily
> That once was mistress of the field and flourish'd,
> I'll hang my head and perish.

The reverse symbolism appears in Cranmer's great prophecy where Shakespeare compliments James I by identifying him with a cedar of Lebanon with its obvious biblical overtones:

> He shall flourish
> And like a mountain cedar reach his branches
> To all the plains about him. Our children's children
> Shall see this and bless heaven.[23]   *(V.V.53-56)*

Symbolic weather is an adjunct of natural setting, and Shakespeare frequently employs it in the same way—that is, to point up how the actions of men are reflected or prophesied in physical nature. Richard III notices that the sun "disdains to shine" on Bosworth field and draws the ironic inference: "A black day will it be to somebody" (V.iii.279-281). The bloody sun appearing "Above yon busky hill" (V.i.2) at Shrewsbury foretells the "dread correction" (V.i.111) that waits upon the rebel forces in 1 Henry IV: "The southern wind / Doth play the trumpet . . . And by his hollow whistling in the leaves / Foretells a tempest and a blust'ring day" (V.i.3-6). The blasted bay trees in Richard II are obviously related to the same literary technique, for Shakespeare includes them among the portentous and unnatural "signs" that "forerun the death or fall of kings" (II.iv.15).

To summarize then, Shakespeare uses the pastoral motif and its extension in details of landscape, imagery, and setting both to mirror and to challenge ideas of order and disorder in the great world of affairs. The green world becomes for Shakespeare what Northrop Frye has called a "complex variable," a kind of archetypal symbol which functions in such a way as to express a continuing tension between the ideal and the actual as it affects both the individual and the state. The "pastoral" emphasis shows us, as it were, the underside of epic. It permits points of rest between the excursions and alarums. By allowing for reflection, sometimes choric reflection, upon the action, it helps to evoke what is timeless in the context of speeding time. The contrast partly enables Shakespeare to dramatize history in both long and short perspective at once—and in a way that ultimately humanizes the grand as well as the trivial in the lives of men and nations. To put it another way, the complementary relationship of epic and pastoral in the history plays illustrates afresh the truth of Dryden's wise and splendid words about Shakespeare:

> He was the man who of all modern, and perhaps
> ancient poets, had the largest and most compre-
> hensive soul. All [my italics] the images of Nature
> were still [i.e., ever] present to him. . . .[24]

As Shakespeare's dramatic powers matured, he relied less and less exclusively on traditional and iconographic devices, and was able more and more to realize contrasts between the private and the public, between order and chaos with greater psychological subtlety—that is to say, through the creation of richly contrasting and complementary characters. Time and again throughout the history plays, comic or semi-comic actions and characters are used to parody the heroic and tragic aspects of the story and thereby to qualify simplistic attitudes. By this means orthodox political and moral notions that a less humane poet might accept uncritically are constantly re-examined and submitted to new tests of validity. Pistol's nearly meaningless bombast, a tissue of shreds and patches from theatrical rant, does not cancel the stirring effect of Henry V's great martial speeches, but it does force us to reconsider them in a new light. Faulconbridge's wiseacre remarks, interjected while international diplomacy is being conducted, make us aware of the pretension and hypocrisy that public utterances so often cloak. The two Henry IV plays, as C. L. Barber has shown persuasively in a recent book,[25] are Shakespeare's greatest achievement in this way. There we watch Prince Hal grow up by experiencing what is best and worst in the divided but linked worlds of tavern and court, the two kingdoms of Falstaff and Bolingbroke. The point, of course, is that each of the two kingdoms deepens and qualifies our understanding of the other by virtue of the dramatic interaction between them. William Empson, in fact, has suggested that structures of this kind are built upon a version of pastoral;[26] but the element of parody in the histories is a subject in itself and deserves full discussion in a separate essay.

The reflection of order and disorder through pastoral and through the evocation of physical nature in the history plays raises but does not answer some of the great metaphysical questions of the Renaissance. Nature in one of its aspects suggests the possibility of an ordered and harmonious cosmos in Hooker's terms— a great universal garden created, tended, and brought to ultimate fruition by a supreme and loving Gardener. This is the kind of order that critics have usually seen as lying behind Shakespeare's histories. But the plays, though they have their moments of peace, are never very far removed from war, which, if it involves heroism, also involves butchery of the innocent. The savage realities of dynastic struggle, of power, of the human ego asserting itself politically, do not permit us to forget that, in its other aspect, nature is Hobbesian—red in tooth and claw.

Many of the characters in the histories, from Henry VI to Katherine of Aragon, die patiently confident of a Christian heaven; yet the total dramatic action of the plays in which these characters appear, as well as of the other histories written in between, puts more emphasis upon the vanity of human wishes than upon man's eternal hopes. In *Henry VIII*, to be sure, Queen Katherine is vouchsafed a supernal vision. Figures in a sort of pastoral ballet hold a garland of bays above her head in an action clearly meant to symbolize spiritual victory. But Shakespeare wrote that play only three years before his death, and, in any case, many scholars still think Fletcher's hand was stronger in it than his own. The earlier plays are concerned more with Nature and less with Grace, and they are not so affirmative in tone. They contain that which points forward to the half-sunny world of Arden Forest and beyond it to the pastoral sweetness of *Cymbeline* and the "great creating nature" of Perdita's flower garden. But the histories also anticipate a view of nature in which Ophelia, driven mad by disorders she cannot comprehend, can drown beneath a willow in a weeping brook—in which Lear can stagger about a heath, "Crown'd with rank fumiter," with "hardocks, hemlock, nettles, cuckoo flow'rs, / Darnel, and . . . all the idle weeds that grow / In our sustaining corn" (IV.iv.3-6).

When we learn from Hostess Quickly that Falstaff died babbling "of green fields" (*H5*, II.iii.17),[27] it is moving to think of that loveable reprobate departing this world with that most pastoral of psalms, the twenty-third, on his lips. We should like to think that the Lord is his shepherd and that he comes at last to lie down in green pastures. But Nell Quickly, who is outrageously sentimental and no theologian, may very well miss the point. Surely it is not without significance that she mistakes Abraham's bosom for Arthur's. There is much in the history plays that looks forward to the great tragedies—those profound dramas in which man's hopes about universal order are so terribly shaken. Shakespeare does not let us forget that in *this* world—the world of history—we fear evil even as we create it, and that we walk through the valley of the shadow of death.

Notes:

(1) Readers familiar with the voluminous scholarship on Shakespeare's histories will recognize my considerable indebtedness to such important standard works as J. D. Wilson's introductions to his New Cambridge editions of the individual plays, E. M. W. Tillyard's *Shakespeare's History Plays* (London, 1951), Irving Ribner's *The English History Play in the Age of Shakespeare* (Princeton, 1957), Alfred Harbage's *As They Liked It* (New York, 1947), M. M. Reese's *The Cease of Majesty* (London, 1961), and L. B. Campbell's *Shakespeare's "Histories": Mirrors of Elizabethan Policy* (San Marino, 1947). I have also found useful W. W. Greg's *Pastoral Poetry and Pastoral Drama* (New York, 1959), Edwin Greenlaw's "Shakespeare's Pastorals," *SP*, XIII (1916), 122-154, and Madeleine Doran's *Endeavors of Art* (Madison, 1954). The text of Shakespeare cited throughout is *The Complete Works*, ed. G. L. Kittredge (Boston, 1936).

(2) Only once, I believe, in the English speaking theatre have all ten plays been consecutively performed when the Pasadena Playhouse of California acted them in 1935. Stage and television performances of parts of the cycle have become much more common recently, both in England and America. The Royal Shakespeare Theatre at Stratford-upon-Avon devoted its four hundredth anniversary season (1964) to a series of seven plays which embraced both tetralogies; the three parts of *Henry VI* were abridged into two plays, the second being renamed *Edward IV*.

(3) One of the best modern discussions of this aspect of the histories, to which I am indebted in what folows, is Una Ellis-Fermor's "Shakespeare's Political Plays" in *The Frontiers of Drama* (London, 1948), pp. 34-55.

(4) I quote Graham Hough's translation of Tasso's words from his illuminating analysis of the Italian poet's *Discorsi dell' Arte Poetica e in particolare sopra il poema eroico;* see *A Preface to "The Faerie Queene"* (New York, 1963), p. 55. Tasso's remarks appear to have served him as a prolegomenon to *Jerusalem Delivered*.

(5) Some critics of course have tended to ignore *Henry VIII* as a history play, influenced in most cases by the much disputed claim for Fletcher's partial authorship and by the play's remove in time and style from the earlier histories. An influential exception is G. Wilson Knight's important essay in *The Crown of Life* (London, 1948), pp. 256-336, which argues with force, incidentally, that the play is Shakespeare's unaided work. But Tillyard omits it from consideration in *Shakespeare's History Plays*, as does Lily B. Campbell in *Shakespeare's "Histories*," while R. A. Foakes in his New Arden edition asserts "that it cannot be fitted into the scheme of the earlier histories" (p. xlii). Reese in *The Cease of Majesty* says that "In the main" it "is conceived in the spirit of the later romances, with a good deal of pageantry and spectacle" and that here Shakespeare "does not trouble to revive the political themes" of the earlier plays (p. 333). No one, I think, would now deny the important thematic and stylistic relationship to Shakespeare's other "last plays," but from the standpoint of genre in the Renaissance sense, such considerations are secondary. Heminge and Condell classed *Henry VIII* with the other English histories because obviously it contained historical characters, dealt with historical events, and in the birth of Elizabeth and Cranmer's prophecy dramatized the fulfillment of those national hopes for "smiling plenty, and fair prosperous days" (*R3*, V.v.34) that had concluded the preceding play in the Folio collection. And if this were not sufficient reason to group *Henry VIII* with the other histories, there were additional grounds, for the most prominent theme of the drama, the rise and fall of persons of state, was one that had preoccupied Shakespeare continuously throughout all nine of the earlier dramas.

(6) In *Macbeth* Malcolm speaks of these,

> As justice, verity, temp'rance, stableness,
> Bounty, perseverance, mercy, lowliness,
> Devotion, patience, courage, fortitude.

(IV.iii.92-94)

(7) It is often forgotten that even within the somewhat frigid conventions of the formal pastoral, touches of realism and humor have a way of creeping in. Jerry H. Bryant in *"The Winter's Tale* and the Pastoral Tradition," *SQ*, XIV (1963), 387-398, helps correct the usual oversimplification.

(8) *Anatomy of Criticism* (Princeton, 1957), p. 143.

(9) (London, 1809), p. 112.

(10) *Specimens of Pre-Shakespearean Drama*, ed. J. M. Manly (Boston, 1897).

(11) *The Shakespeare Apocrypha*, ed. C. F. T. Brooke (Oxford, 1918).

(12) *The Dramatic Works and Poems of James Shirley*, ed. W. Gifford and A. Dyce (London, 1833), I, 65.

(13) *The Compleat Angler, or, The Contemplative Man's Recreation*, ed. John Thompson (New York, 1962), p. 72. It is interesting that Venator's reminiscence is provoked by a singing of Raleigh's popular pastoral lyric, "Come live with me, and be my Love."

(14) Caroline Spurgeon in *Shakespeare's Imagery* (New York, 1936), pp. 216-224, calls attention to the vegetative imagery that pervades the histories. She fails, however, to explore its significance very deeply. Richard D. Altick's "Symphonic Imagery in *Richard II*," *PMLA*, LXII (1947), 339-365, contains a splendid treatment of the earth-husbandry imagery and its relation to other themes in the single play he discusses.

(15) The quartos and Folio, of course, rarely specify locations of scene in the form of stage directions; garden settings, like most other settings in Shakespeare, are more reliably and more effectively established by references to place in the dialogue itself. In the following analysis I have tried to provide the necessary evidence of setting in each case by means of appropriate quotation or, at least, specific reference to Shakespeare's own words.

(16) Though I would argue that this technique has a special appropriateness to the history plays, where the theme of social and political order is so heavily stressed, it is by no means unique there, for Shakespeare also uses natural settings symbolically in both the comedies and tragedies. In *The Merchant of Venice* (V.i), for instance, a landscape near Portia's house stirs the romantic Lorenzo to lyrical reflections on the relationship of love, music, and cosmic harmony. Clearly the idyllic atmosphere in which the wind "gently kiss[es] the trees" (V.i.3) and "the moonlight sleeps upon this bank" (V.i.54) reinforces an ideal of natural moral order against which the unnatural values of Shylock are ultimately measured. And it is not difficult to find similar examples in the tragedies. The romantic orchard in *Romeo and Juliet* where the moon "tips with silver all these fruit-tree tops" (II.ii.108) serves to emphasize the central contrast between young love and old hatred; and Shakespeare heightens the unnaturalness of King Hamlet's murder by having the crime committed with symbolic irony in an orchard. Kyd in *The Spanish Tragedy* had already used the latter device: Horatio is suddenly hanged in the leafy arbor where he has been making love to Belimperia, and his grief-crazed mother later chops it down and curses the entire garden in an act of symbolic retribution.

(17) See E. R. Curtius, *European Literature and the Latin Middle Ages*, trans. W. R. Trask (New York, 1953), pp. 183-202; also D. W. Robertson, Jr., "The Doctrine of Charity in

Mediaeval Literary Gardens: a Topical Approach through Symbolism and Allegory," *Speculum,* XXVI (1951), 24-49.

(18) Frye goes so far as to recognize "a secular Eucharist symbol in the red and white rose" *(Anatomy of Criticism,* p. 284); he points to their historical union in "the reigning head of the church" (p. 195) and quotes *Richard III* (p. 363): "And then, as we have ta'en the sacrament,/ We will unite the White Rose and the Red" (V.v.18-19).

(19) The quarto specifies that the conjurors are brought "to the backside of [Eleanor's] Orchard" (I.ii) and mentions a tower to which she ascends. The Folio omits this detail, but it is clear from the action that the same setting applies. In the sixteenth century "garden" and "orchard" were often interchangeable terms (see *OED*).

(20) See A. C. Sprague, *Shakespeare's Histories* (London, 1964), pp. 88-89.

(21) "The Meaning of Strawberries in Shakespeare," *Studies in the Renaissance,* VII (1960), 229.

(22) *Ibid.,* p. 233.

(23) See R. A. Foakes's New Arden edition of *Henry VIII* (London, 1957), pp. xxxi and 176.

(24) "An Essay of Dramatic Poesy" in *Essays of John Dryden,* ed. W. P. Ker (Oxford, 1961), I, 79.

(25) *Shakespeare's Festive Comedy* (Princeton, 1959), pp. 192-221.

(26) *Some Versions of Pastoral* (London, 1950), pp. 27-86. I am heavily indebted to the chapter entitled, "Double Plots: Heroic and Pastoral in the Main Plot and Sub-Plot."

(27) Theobald's famous emendation has of course been challenged, but no one has yet suggested words so appropriately in character. Falstaff knew his Bible, as he reveals when he refers to "Pharoah's lean kine" (*1 H4,* II.iv.520) and to "Dives that lived in purple" (III.iii.36), and he could imagine himself as a weaver singing psalms (cf. II.iv.146). Sir Walter Greg has defended the reading persuasively on paleographical grounds in "Principles of Emendation in Shakespeare," *Aspects of Shakespeare* (British Academy, 1933), pp. 129, 155, 172.

Commentary in Shakespeare: the Case of Coriolanus

by Dean Frye

The critic of Shakespeare can avoid weighing the commentary within a play only if he takes a radically ironic view of that play, which usually means that he holds such a view of drama as a whole. Unless, that is, he considers that an audience is *never* properly led to accept the judgments of *any* character as valid, he must decide when it is that such acceptance is likely. Sometimes this audience must be thought of as characteristically Elizabethan, but more often the critical question is dramatic, not historical. The Elizabethan audience that would have responded to all dramatic actions according to a limited, rigorous and ungenerous set of gnomic catchphrases is too handy to be believable and often is apparently the product of nostalgia for an imaginary time of correct—or anyway settled—belief. Elizabethan literature hardly supports the idea that its readers were much less ready than we are to respond to the same general situation—the rejection of parent by child, say—in widely different ways. They were influenced, like us, not only by extenuating circumstances, but also by the characters involved, by the kind of story in which they appeared, and by the attitudes of others in that story. There are limits to the range of judgments which a work admits as relevant. We should not find Celia culpable for causing her father possible anxiety by going with Rosalind to Arden. We might conceivably do so if anyone in the play expressed such a notion, but then that would be a different sort of play.

An emphasis on testimony, on judgments by one person in a play of the actions or character of another, has been a basic element of one strain of twentieth-century Shakespeare criticism. Those writers who have stressed the conventional nature of Elizabethan dramaturgy, and have deplored the naturalistic expectations of earlier critics, have naturally made much of "choral" commentary. Such critics have taught us not to think of the Shakespearean character as one thinks of real people. This means, in the first place, that speeches need not always be seen as expressive of personality; First and Second Gentlemen may be given a few roughly indicated traits, but we should never feel that two other gentlemen might have said something very different. Also, the "character" of a protagonist may necessarily be created in part by the comments of others upon him; he cannot be isolated from this context. Such principles, combined with a general expectation that Shakespeare will be working through convention, have increased our readiness to take testimony seriously as orientation for the audience, and therefore as guidance for the critic.

"The comment of others," says Stoll, "is one of Shakespeare's chief means of characterization."[1] S. L. Bethell writes later in the same tradition: "Shakespeare and other dramatists in the popular tradition solve the problem [of characterization in poetic drama]... by presenting us with an authentic outline of each important character, clearly stated either by himself or by another."[2] A change within this line of criticism, indeed a reversal, can be seen in the difference between Schücking and Bethell. The latter sees great dramatic advantages in the conventions he is describing, while the former generally considered them unfortunate primitive vestiges. Still, Schücking's description of the dramatic facts is similar to Bethell's: "the poet is very careful... not to mislead us about the behaviour and the character of the hero by remarks of persons who have a wrong or biased conception of him."[3] Again, Arthur Colby Sprague is a more cautious generalizer, but his emphasis is the same: "so remarkable is the credibility of the witnesses in Elizabethan drama that unless they are contradicted, or are known to have a reason for departing from the truth, we are usually justified in believing whatever they say." He is referring here not only to testimony as to facts, but also to "explanations of motives and events."[4] All these critics have called attention to undeniable facts about Shakespeare's plays, and in fact seem at times too cautious in limiting the application of their principles to plays of only certain times or types. Even quite naturalistic drama uses such techniques as commentary to establish audience response. Yet a danger in all these observations is that they may encourage an oversimplified approach to situations in which one character comments on another, especially when what he says squares with what a critic believes anyway.

For this problem of testimony is a tricky one. The rules of evidence here are not at all those that apply in courts of law, or even in everyday life, at least when we are at our most objective. The primary problem for the critic is not the ethical validity of testimony, perhaps not even its factual truth, but the effect it will have on an audience. We do not believe everything that anybody says, even in highly conventional drama. We do usually believe, or accept as a postulate, something that *everybody* says or assumes, and this is a most important, if scarcely noticeable, effect of commentary. But often there is discrepancy in the testimony. Like any dramatist, Shakespeare must provide a set of assumptions, ethical as well as factual, in order to make his play work, and the most important means of doing so are to see that no one questions these assumptions and, perhaps, that someone states them. But part of the interest of his better plays comes from the clash of attitudes, the conflict among ways of looking at things, which deepens the particular antagonisms of the plots. A preference for Shakespeare over Shaw should not obscure what they both share with so much great drama, this wider conflict which provides much of what goes by the name of "universality."

Two simple ways out of the problems raised by such conflicts are not promising: the ironic approach ("Shakespeare looks with the great artist's philosophical amusement or pity upon the comedy of life with its irreconcilable standards and desires"), and the approach through Elizabethan orthodoxy ("however at sea our morally confused age may be, Shakespeare is explicable according to the following commonplaces from Elyot and Hooker"). Most of the plays should engage the sympathies of the audience, so that Olympian detachment is either the result of a bad performance or evidence of self-conscious resistance to the experience they are designed to produce. Through such involvement, a play creates its own morality, or pseudo-morality, which may coincide with the most influential ethical writings of its time, or may be subtler and more humane than anything which can be communicated abstractly, or may—we must realize—be unacceptable as real, working ethics because the play isolates and simplifies a situation so as to give the audience an opportunity to respond according to idealistic and absolute standards which put aside the probabilities of real life in a fallen world. The critic, then, must ask how and where the sympathies of the audience are allotted, and part of the answer lies in comments within the play on its situations and characters. At the same time, he must recognize the complexity of the problem, even if he is not willing to go as far as Alfred Harbage: "Whenever in a play by Shakespeare there is a commentator on the worth of the other characters or the significance of the action, there is always something about him to prevent our relying too implicitly upon his words."[5]

Coriolanus is a particularly interesting case in point for several reasons. Today, at least, its hero has little immediate appeal, so that uncomplimentary commentary about him is not apt to conflict, as with some of the other heroes, with a modern audience's own predispositions. He is seen, moreover, almost entirely in his social role[6]—this is, in fact, part of the reason that the audience fails to take him to its heart. As Arthur Sewell has argued so persuasively, the great tragic heroes can transform the vision of an audience so that "social and political judgements (though never wholly abrogated) tend to break down."[7] Such an effect partly depends upon our involvement in their internal lives. Even Brutus in *Julius Caesar* occasionally puts on his gown and shifts our attention from his public responsibilities to his private uncertainties. But we see little of Coriolanus's purely personal life, which is to say that he has little. When he is with his wife and mother it is always in public, and what is said is rarely intimate. He seems most at home in battle, and since his fame comes from fighting, battles are part of his public life. On the other hand, he is constantly in conflict with one part of his society or another. Its members are not merely observers whose interests have an important claim; they are active antagonists in the conflicts of the plot. As such, they may be seen as speaking from their own motives and limited viewpoints. Their testimony does not have the immediate weight of, for instance, the defenses of the public interest by the Lord Chief Justice in *2 Henry IV*.

"The tragic flaw of Coriolanus," says Willard Farnham, "is pride, as we are told by other characters in the play again and again."[8] Certainly we are told so often enough, as we are told so many things about Coriolanus; the play is full of commentary. And certainly he is proud. It does not follow, however, that he is either detestable or comic. What matters is the attitude that the play induces towards this pride, for it is surely wrong to say that all plays, or even all plays by Christians, work on the settled assumption that pride is bad and humility good. "Ever since the critics discovered the sin of pride," Edward Hubler reminds us, "the concept of honor has been getting very short shrift, although Shakespeare's high regard for honor is demonstrated on almost every page he wrote."[9] If all the commentators in the play agree that Coriolanus is proud, moreover, they express varying attitudes towards his pride, so that the unanimity of the testimony is partly illusory. Much depends upon how the audience will react to the comments of each of the main groups in the play.

It can hardly be denied that we see little of the action from the point of view of the citizens. As usual in Shakespeare, the populace is too giddy to provide weighty testimony. As they change their minds about Coriolanus under instructions from the tribunes, and then again when danger threatens, they are presented sardonically: "though we willingly consented to his banishment, yet it was against our will" (IV.vi.144-145).[10] As soldiers, they act pretty much as Coriolanus says they do. Their belligerence in the first scene fades quickly when the news arrives that the Volsces are in arms, and, according to the stage direction at least, they "steal away" when Marcius invites them to follow him (I.i.255). They later refuse to follow him within the gates of Corioli (I.iv.46-47)—though they are roused to a kind of valor when he has been successful (I.vi.76-80)—but are quick to seize a chance to loot the city (I.v.1-3). The tribunes know that, disliking Coriolanus, "they / Upon their ancient malice will forget / With the least cause these his new honours" (II.i.243-245). Such forgetfulness is foolish, for even if the play recognizes the necessity of both military and civic virtues, Coriolanus's soldiership is indispensable to Rome. And too, as one of the citizens says at a time when they are least the pawns of the tribunes, "for the multitude to be ingrateful were to make a monster of the multitude" (II.iii.10-12).

The people are not, it is true, presented as are Cade's followers in 2 Henry VI. They are more unwise than vicious and are the victims of their tribunes. When we first see them, in fact, in the first scene of the play, we are prepared to believe that they have some justice on their side, though Menenius's fable seems designed to put them in the wrong. Their hunger demands charity from the patricians if indeed there is corn available, a question which the play never clearly answers. In a play about Rome, rebellion may not have evoked automatic censure even from an Elizabethan audience, and Menenius's placatory tone, at least, probably seems the correct one. We are, in these circumstances, given the first comments on the hero, and on the whole they are derogatory. It is true, and worth noting, that the Second Citizen reminds the others of "what services he has done for his country" (I.i.30-31), and suggests that they speak "maliciously" (I.i.35), but there is general agreement that Caius Marcius is "a very dog to the commonalty" (I.i.28-29) who "pays himself with being proud" (I.i.33-34), and we know nothing to offset the effect of such a description.

This raises an important question, the force of such early commentary. There is no doubt that it has considerable weight at the time when it is delivered. The audience is trying to get its bearings, to learn the facts that it will need and, unconsciously perhaps, to absorb the ethical climate of the play. The early scenes potentially offer exposition, not only for understanding the plot, but also for making judgments and allotting sympathies. And an Elizabethan audience was closer than we are to a drama in which characters were regularly "placed" early in a play by their names, by their own extra-dramatic self-identifications, or by definitive statements by others. Much has often been made of the fact that Shakespeare's characteristic method is one of irony, which demands an audience which has been oriented early, rather than one of suspense and surprise, which keep the audience expectant rather than knowing. So, for example, we find as one of Schücking's italicized first principles that *"the first mention in the drama of things which are important for the action or the characterization of the central figure must never be allowed in the interest of the characterization of secondary figures to distort the representation of the facts."*[11] In the case of *Coriolanus,* as in others, the hero's first entrance is in a manner to confirm the picture of him which the early commentary has provided,[12] or rather, since he does nothing that clearly conflicts with that picture, and since we can understand and judge what he does do according to it, we tend to do so. At this point, the play may turn out to be about the unfeeling warrior and the suffering plebians.

The "primitive" element in Shakespeare's drama can, however, be seriously overestimated. An audience may be trying to find its footing at the beginning, but it is also aware that it has much to learn. It is prepared, at the time of these early scenes, to discover more than it yet knows. Most drama could hardly operate if this were not so, and Shakespeare's audience does not seem to have been unique in this respect. Surprise and suspense are more frequent in Shakespeare than critics who are already familiar with the plays sometimes remember. That Othello will murder Desdemona is inevitable only in a specialized sense. To respond properly to *Hamlet,* an audience must reverse the impression left by Claudius's very plausible first speech. In *Julius Caesar,* there is a strong element of debate, and the audience probably changes its mind about the conspiracy often enough to make it wary. Early impressions are far from everything. We must change our first conception of Angelo in *Measure for Measure,* and Orsino's opening speech in *Twelfth Night* by no means defines the values or the emotional tone of that play. One cannot assume, then, that the first scene of *Coriolanus,* or of *Antony and Cleopatra* or of any other play, produces an attitude towards the hero which is by the rules of Shakespeare's dramaturgy unalterable, or even of special authority.

Not that anyone would deny that Coriolanus is proud or that he is contemptuous of the people. But the battle scenes that rapidly follow this first scene provide considerable justification for both these aspects of his character, and the praise he receives in the Capitol balances the earlier adverse commentary (II.ii). As for the citizens, they are seldom seen again when they are not totally swayed by the tribunes. The main exception is the first part of Act II, scene iii, where Coriolanus appears in the gown of humility, and the effect of this scene will depend considerably upon how the audience receives the custom which the hero must follow. Democratic presuppositions may be particularly dangerous here. On the other hand, Coriolanus is certainly churlish, and the citizens gain a certain simple dignity by the contrast. This effect, however, depends upon their granting of their voices; otherwise they would be ungrateful and unmindful of genuine worth. The power to deny him their voices, the Third Citizen says, "is a power that we have no power to do" (II.iii.5). Once they succumb to the tribunes' handling of them, they lose all standing as commentators and largely justify the judgments that all the patricians constantly make upon them.

Sicinius and Brutus raise the special problem of testimony from villains. It is true that they are not Iagos or Edmunds, but they are self-serving Machiavellians who use their power as tribunes for their own ends and who purposely bring about the occasion, at least, for the hero's fall. Despite Kenneth Muir's defense of them, where he oddly identifies their interests with "the cause of the people,"[13] there is really no reason to withhold the term "villain" from either of them. They are particularly distasteful as they change the minds of the citizens about Coriolanus's consulship — the people have been "lesson'd" (II.iii.185), but have forgotten their lesson — while arranging that the patricians shall think that they have been on his side: "Say you ne'er had done't / (Harp on that still) but by our putting on" (II.iii. 259-260). Such practices may be sound politically, but it is always difficult to make an audience favor such misrepresentation in the theatre, and special pains, which Shakespeare certainly does not take here, are necessary to turn the trick. By the end of Act IV, scene vi, the tribunes are discredited as politicians as well. After some self-congratulation about "a happier and more comely time" (IV.vi.27) since Coriolanus's banishment, which is heavily ironic for an audience that knows what the hero is doing off stage, and an airy summary of his faults (IV.vi.29-33), they hear news of the Volscian campaign, refuse to believe it (IV.vi.47-56), concoct fatuous explanations of the report (IV.vi.69-70), and are next seen pleading with Menenius, whom they have been close to patronizing, to save the situation (V.i.33-60). H. J. Oliver suggests that a comparison of the play with Plutarch shows "that the blame for the banishment of Coriolanus is clearly taken by Shakespeare from the shoulders of the hero and put on those of the tribunes."[14] Certainly the patricians come to allot the blame in this way, and they do so in a reiterated chorus unusual in Shakespeare: "You have done a brave deed" (IV.ii.38); "You have made fair work!" (IV.vi.88,100); "You have made good work!" (IV.vi.79,95,146-147; V.i.15). Shortly afterward, the citizens turn against the tribunes and threaten them (V.iv.38-42).

Now, realistically speaking, there is no reason why such men as the tribunes may not speak the truth when they tell Menenius that Coriolanus is "insolent, / O'ercome with pride, ambitious past all thinking, / Self-loving" (IV.vi.30-32). Why should we reject their testimony that he is "poor in no one fault, but stor'd with all. Especially in Pride. And topping all others in boasting" (II.i.20-23), though he almost painfully avoids the last charge? Life can easily arrange itself so that the most accurate view of a situation is expressed by someone whose motives are suspect and whose way of looking at things in general is detestable. Here is a delectable irony which the Olympian philosopher-artist may well savor. But reflection, I think, convinces one that this is a rare situation in drama, and that

Shakespeare is not so very different from other playwrights, only better. The mere fact that a judgment comes from a character whose approach to life the audience dislikes tends to discredit it, unless the character is being consciously plausible. If prudence, in a play, is regularly counselled by the mean-spirited, or if conventional moral judgments always come from the sanctimonious, or if democratic sentiments are primarily the tools of demagogues, the effect is to infect the sentiments with the unpleasantness of the speakers. The Devil can quote Scripture, but his application is by definition faulty. An advantage of plays as propaganda is that even a spectator who would ordinarily agree with some assertion may hiss it when it comes from a villain; the problem for the propagandist is that in plays the response to opinions is so colored by action and character that the spectator may not recognize his own thought and so may escape conversion.

The normal effect of testimony from villains can be counteracted, but this generally requires a comment from some reasonably certified character that contrary to expectations they speak wisely in a certain instance. Usually, the critic should beware of views of the play that coincide with sincere remarks by such characters as the tribunes, or Goneril and Regan, because the expression of a judgment by such people places it among the attitudes which the action defines as, for this play, valueless. It is generally agreed, for instance, that Brutus's opinion that Coriolanus is willing to serve under Cominius only in order that any failures will be blamed on the general (I.i.267-274) is later shown to be unjustified and finally tells us more about the tribune than about the hero. Many villainous characters in Shakespeare can assume a self-satisfied, righteous air which is a travesty of moral feeling and a parody of sanctimonious public hand-washing. To turn them into authoritative commentators is to resist the play.

In fact, of course, it is usually felt that neither the attacks of the citizens nor those of the tribunes would have much weight by themselves, and that Menenius, especially, performs such a choric function that his judgments on both groups work effectively to discredit them. When he wishes that the tribunes—"Because you talk of pride now" (II.i.28)—could see themselves as others see them, he seems to express the view of the audience: "a brace of unmeriting, proud, violent, testy magistrates (alias fools)" (II.i.46-48). Then the news of Coriolanus's triumph arrives and Menenius taunts the two: "Marcius is coming home. He has more cause to be proud" (II.i.160-161). It is they who are proud in the derogatory sense; what they attack in Coriolanus is knowledge of proven worth. Throughout, the patricians are contemptuous of citizens and tribunes. But later they have their own adverse comments to make on Coriolanus, and these, coming from friends, have particular force as testimony. They relate to the hero's inability or refusal to placate the citizens; "What the vengeance," says Menenius, "Could he not speak 'em fair?" (III.i.262-263). All the main patricians counsel prudence, and all are persuasive. As a general, Cominius demonstrates that the advice is not inconsistent with valor; Volumnia's opinion requires the suppression of all her prejudices and instincts. This last is an important point. Comments are often understood to be the expression of personality and are judged accordingly; when a character

111

speaks uncharacteristically, what he says seems to have the force of the incontestable. If, in the face of all this counsel, Coriolanus remains unalterable, he may well appear inflexible and self-absorbed, so set in a self-conscious posture as to be almost a comic figure.[15] Throughout Acts II and III the patricians provide a running commentary to this effect, and this is potentially the most damaging testimony against the hero.

It is well to remember what the patricians *don't* say. There is no defense from them of the rights of the people to a voice in government, or even to courtesy. That is why Gordon Ross Smith can call them all "sado-masochistic authoritarians."[16] The champions of popular rights are the tribunes, who preach them for their own ends. Unless one assumes that democratic ideals formed a basic standard for Shakespeare or his audience, they are largely irrelevant to the play. The patricians speak for civil peace, not egalitarianism, and for the policies which they think will insure it. They want Coriolanus to be consul although they are fully aware of his views and although he does not wish it for himself (II.i.218-220). They only want him to go prudently about getting elected. Volumnia, at least, seems to think of soft-spokenness as only temporarily necessary, wishing "You had not show'd them how ye were dispos'd / Ere they lack'd power to cross you" (III.ii.22-23). "Before he should thus stoop to th'herd," says Menenius, "but that / The violent fit o' th'time craves it as physic / For the whole state, I would put mine armour on" (III.ii.32-34).

The patricians express no adverse judgments on Coriolanus except that he is imprudent. There may be a note of exasperated sarcasm in Menenius's "His nature is too noble for the world" (III.i.255), though it is not demonstrable, but Volumnia makes a similar point seriously: "You are too absolute: / Though therein you can never be too noble, / But when extremities speak" (III.ii.39-41). The play is full, indeed, of commendatory speeches on the hero; few characters in Shakespeare receive more straightforward praise on stage. It comes especially from Cominius, a character whose lack of any ax to grind and of any striking personality to express makes him appear an objective, if militarily minded, observer. His address to the Senate (II.ii.86-126) seems by its very length to insist upon the nobility of this hero. An audience which resisted it while believing Sicinius and Brutus would be incredibly perverse. When Coriolanus is banished (IV.i), there is no reproach from any of the patricians, only regret and expressions of esteem. Cominius and Menenius wish they could accompany him (IV.i.38-44,55-57); Volumnia curses Rome (IV.i.13-14).

The patricians' idea of him is of a noble character who, beset by enemies in a troubled time, has been too absolute to let "Honour and policy . . . grow together" (III.ii.42-43). Their impatience with him is largely well-meant impatience with one who stubbornly works against his own best interests, although they also have their own reasons for wanting him to be consul and need him as a warrior. Menenius's description of him as "a limb that has . . . a disease" (III.i.296) is part of an appeal to the tribunes and agrees with little else that he says. The patricians consider the hero's pride not so much inordinate as something to be concealed at a certain

112

moment. They may be wrong, of course, and Coriolanus may be more guilty than they can realize, but in that case who is right? Really only Shakespeare and the spectator, sharing a perception that is granted to no sympathetic character in the play.

As for the patricians' practical cautions, they may seem sound at the time, but the matter is complicated. There is surely a tendency in an audience to respect a hero who works his own undoing though a concern for his integrity or for some principle. The impulse to think that every man has a duty to himself, to his family, or to the nature of things, to be a practical success if he can, is not strong in the theater. His friends may wish him to compromise just this once, but the audience can approach the fiction of the play more idealistically. Drama is generally "escapist" at least to that extent. When it isn't, and the personal and social dangers that attend idealism are what is stressed, the playwright must present the alternative, ironic attitude sympathetically, acted out, or at least expressed, by characters who can draw the audience after them into a new way of looking at things. If Major Barbara is not to be Saint Joan, there must be Undershaft. Otherwise, the hero's world may come to be judged by his standards, or at least by its failure to make room for such a man.

Coriolanus does not argue with his friends solely on the basis of his honor or of his hatred of the citizens. It is too often forgotten that he makes a political point, and makes it at length. He alone clearly grasps that the tribunes have been plotting against him (III.i.38-41), and he sees his own situation as a danger to the patricians. The granting of tribunes to the people under duress was, he says, a mistake, since it suggested weakness (III.i.119-139). Under any circumstances it would have been unwise, because it made orderly government impossible:

> where gentry, title, wisdom
> Cannot conclude but by the yea and no
> Of general ignorance — it must omit
> Real necessities, and give way the while
> To unstable slightness. *(III.i.144-148)*

Confusion must follow "when two authorities are up, / Neither supreme" (III.i. 109-110). The people are led astray by their tribunes, "On whom depending, their obedience fails / To th'greater bench" (III.i.166-167).

Whatever these speeches may be, they are not merely prideful railing. Granting the assumptions which he shares with the patricians, in fact, Coriolanus is justified by events, though he himself comes to represent the chief danger that the patricians' policy creates. The only public act which we see the tribunes perform is the banishment of Coriolanus, which causes a weakness in the state which the Volscians hope to capitalize on before there is any thought of Coriolanus's joining them (IV.iii.16-19). Of course, the danger might not have developed if he had followed the patricians' prudent advice, though the tribunes were determined to be rid of him. But what is important here is that when the peril appears the patricians blame, besides the tribunes, not him but themselves. "We lov'd him," says

113

Menenius, "but, like beasts / And cowardly nobles, gave way unto your clusters" (IV.vi.121-122). By choosing caution they have lost both honor and safety, or so they seem to think. "Who is't can blame him?" asks Cominius (IV.vi.105). "'Tis true," says Menenius,

> If he were putting to my house the brand
> That should consume it, I have not the face
> To say 'Beseech you, cease.' You have made fair hands,
> You and your crafts! You have crafted fair! (IV.vi.114-118)

In banishing Coriolanus, he believes, they failed to respect the gods (V.iv.34-37). "If he could burn us all into one coal, / We have deserv'd it" (IV.vi.137-138).

There is, again, a realistic way of looking at all this. In such circumstances, people may foolishly blame themselves and regret an action which was in fact proper. But for an audience there can scarcely be weightier testimony than that of a character who announces that he now realizes he was in the wrong. Such an admission is frequently part of the conclusion of comedy, when truth is recognized and common sense is restored. Even Shakespeare would be hard put to it to make an audience feel at this point that it is the admission that is misguided while the earlier criticism of Coriolanus was correct. Even while agreeing with Sewell that we do not "see the universe through" Coriolanus's eyes,[17] and that he thus has no power to wrench our vision from its normal focus on society in time, we can still feel that the question of what society does to the hero may be as important as the question of what the hero does to society. Here, the most sympathetic segment of his society comes to feel that it has done badly by the hero and that, even in this political world, honor had its claims, and might, ironically, have pointed the most practical course. Their acceptance of their own culpability will make the audience accept it as well and would be senseless were not the audience already prepared to accept it.

This is not to say that Coriolanus's threat to Rome is approved of by the audience. We "can't blame him" in the sense that his reaction to his banishment and to the failure of his friends to stand by their principles and by him is understandable to us. We do blame him in another sense, and Volumnia's speeches to him in the Volscian camp partly express our feelings. Coriolanus, like some other tragic heroes in Shakespeare, lacks the worldliness to understand at first what has happened to him. Political realities and human ingratitude so shock him that he becomes unable to see virtue anywhere, and like Lear and Timon he embraces the moral chaos that seems to confront him with an anguished, perverse nihilism:

> But out, affection!
> All bond and privilege of nature, break!
> . . . . . I'll never
> Be such a gosling to obey instinct, but stand
> As if a man were author of himself
> And knew no other kin. (V.iii.24-25;34-37)

Such a reaction is not morally repulsive. The moment when reality breaks in on innocence is this terrible only for someone who is serious about moral distinctions. If innocence is a dangerous or almost sinful quality, there is still more to distrust in the man who is always perfectly at home in the world. Nevertheless, we recognize the need for balance; Coriolanus must not stay as he is. To that extent the judgment on him is socially based. Volumnia's appeal is in part personal, asserting claims which we accept, and in part a statement of our own attitude at this point:

> Think'st thou it honourable for a noble man
> Still to remember wrongs?
> . . . . .   Say my request's unjust,
> And spurn me back. But if it be not so,
> Thou art not honest,   (V.iii.154-155;164-166)

These speeches have their effect, and Coriolanus yields although he recognizes the danger.

Two more sources of testimony may be mentioned. One is Aufidius, but it is hard to decide how to take much of what he says. He is an unusually inconsistent character and everything depends upon how he is played. In Act IV, scene vii, however, having hinted at some plan against Coriolanus, who is standing in his light (IV.vii.19-26), he goes on to discuss the banishment, and what he says that is favorable to the hero will have the force of unwilling praise. Sprague, at least, considers him a "chorus character" at this point.[18] Aufidius mentions "pride" (IV.vii.37), "defect of judgment" (IV.vii.39), and lack of flexibility (IV.vii.41-45) as faults of which Coriolanus has "spices . . . not all" (IV.vii.46), but he still considers the banishment unjustified: "he has a merit, / To choke it in the utt'rance" (IV.vii.48-49). "So our virtues / Lie," he concludes, "in th'interpretation of the time" (IV.vii.49-50). Aufidius also ends the play with a final bit of praise of Coriolanus: "he shall have a noble memory" (V.vi.154). Since he has just conspired at his death, this might be seen as unexampled hypocrisy or miraculous repentance, but the tragedies generally end with such a speech about the hero.

More important is the testimony of two characters who discuss the hero at the beginning of Act II, scene ii. The main plot of the play is about to be set going, the stage having been set and the situation established, but first there is this brief moment of rest and recapitulation. Here, for once, Coriolanus is talked about by characters who are neither friends nor enemies, and the talk is dispassionate and judicial. Like the three gentlemen of *The Winter's Tale*, or the two gardeners of *Richard II*, or the three "strangers" of *Timon of Athens*, these two officers are anonymous commentators whose testimony is colored neither by an individual point of view nor by involvement in the antagonisms of the plot. It might be objected that they too are citizens and so have a stake in the questions they discuss, but they are capable of a special detachment, and provide a clear contrast to "the people," who, as the Second Officer says, "love they know not why, [and] hate upon no better a ground" (II.ii.11-12). And although it is sometimes assumed that they are military men, and thus have a specialized outlook, it is doubtful that any-one would think of them as soldiers on the basis of what they say, and "officers" is at least ambiguous. Essentially, they are spokesmen for what Harbage calls the "safe majority" of Shakespearean characters,[19] the well-meaning, fair-minded community of the normal. Watching a play with as public a hero as Coriolanus, the spectators respond largely within the area of social judgment, as Sewell says, but it is this community, not necessarily the specific society of the hero's time and place, which defines such a social view.

The overall tendency of the testimony of these two commentators is to remove blame from the hero. It is true that the First Officer speaks of his pride and his hatred of the people, but the effect is not really even that of a balanced appraisal of defects and virtues. He is after all the *first* officer, and the second has answers to his charges. As there is an advantage to being the replier in a debate, so the Second Officer, who also speaks more lines, has the greater influence as he shifts attention to questions of society's treatment of the hero. For Coriolanus, he says, "neither to care whether [the people] love or hate him manifests the true knowl-edge he has in their disposition" (II.ii.13-15). He also offers an implied criticism of the tribunes and of the later acquiescence of the patricians in the banishment:

> He hath deserved worthily of his country; and his ascent is not by
> such easy degrees as those who, having been supple and courteous
> to the people, bonneted, without any further deed to have them at
> all into their estimation and report; but he hath so planted his
> honours in their eyes and his actions in their hearts that for their
> tongues to be silent and not confess so much were a kind of ingrate-
> ful injury; to report otherwise were a malice that, giving itself the
> lie, would pluck reproof and rebuke from every ear that heard it.   *(II.ii.27-38)*

The ingrateful injury of the people, the malice of the tribunes, and the failure of the patricians to make reproof and rebuke effective: all are judged in this bit of extremely weighty testimony with which such characters as Menenius and Cominius sooner or later agree entirely. The First Officer replies only: "No more of him, he's a worthy man" (II.ii.39).

Among the comments on Coriolanus' pride, his authoritarian principles, and his inability or refusal to placate the people, then, those which can be expected to have the greatest weight with an audience are also those which, while admitting faults in the hero, see more to praise than to blame. The idea that his fall is im-posed for his crimes by a just universe is, of course, specifically a villainous idea. The idea that the laws of social dynamics which lead to that fall are somehow right because inevitable is not one that is admitted as relevant. The claims of peace and order are regarded as primary by the most weighty testimony, but the appli-cation of this principle is ultimately in the hero's favor. Coriolanus brings about his own destruction in the sense that a different man would not have suffered his fate, but the most persuasive commentary finally presents this uncomfortable hero as most importantly a test which his society has failed, and it provides no

116

support for the comfortable attitude that he deserves what he gets. This commentary is not, of course, authoritative by itself. Testimony provides only one source of dramatic meaning and to consider nothing else in a play is not remotely adequate criticism. But if we are to consider it at all, and to quote bits of it in support of our interpretations, we must determine how the testimony actually functions within its dramatic context.

Notes:

(1) Elmer Edgar Stoll, *Shakespeare Studies* (New York, 1927), p. 140.

(2) *Shakespeare and the Popular Dramatic Tradition* (London, 1944), p. 73.

(3) Levin L. Schücking, *Character Problems in Shakespeare's Plays* (London, 1922), p. 66.

(4) *Shakespeare and the Audience* (Cambridge, Mass., 1935), p. 164.

(5) *As They Liked It* (New York, 1947), p. 110.

(6) This has frequently been noted. See, for instance, Mark Van Doren, *Shakespeare* (New York, 1939), p. 282; Arthur Sewell, *Character and Society in Shakespeare* (Oxford, 1951), p. 122.

(7) *Character and Society*, p. 76.

(8) *Shakespeare's Tragic Frontier* (Berkeley and Los Angeles, 1950), p. 207.

(9) "The Damnation of Othello: Some Limitations on the Christian View of the Play," *SQ*, IX (1958), 298.

(10) References are to the *Complete Works*, ed. George Lyman Kittredge (New York, 1936).

(11) *Character Problems*, p. 71.

(12) William Rosen notes this and stresses the effects of such early scenes in *Shakespeare and the Craft of Tragedy* (Cambridge, Mass., 1960), pp. 174-185. He emphasizes the importance of commentary throughout this book, though with different results from mine in the case of *Coriolanus*.

(13) "In Defence of the Tribunes," *EIC*, IV (1954), 332.

(14) "Coriolanus as Tragic Hero," *SQ*, X (1959), 57. Professor Oliver suggests several of the points I make here.

(15) Oscar James Campbell, as is well known, considers the play a satire, "full of the spirit of derision." *Shakespeare's Satire* (New York, 1943), p. 199.

(16) "Authoritarian Patterns in Shakespeare's *Coriolanus*," *Literature and Psychology*, IX (1959), 45-51.

(17) *Character and Society*, p. 124.

(18) *Shakespeare and the Audience*, pp. 228-229.

(19) *As They Liked It*, pp. 163-173.

Notes on Shakespeare's Cymbeline

by Charles K. Hofling

The line of thought which I shall develop here is speculative and hence, no doubt, of limited appeal, but the matter does have a certain relevance if one continues to assume that the study of Shakespeare may be influenced by a familiarity with matters not precisely literary.[1]

When one considers the possible utility of knowledge in the field of modern depth psychology to the study of Shakespeare, one does not think primarily of applicability to the critical interpretation of his writings. I am persuaded that such an applicability exists, as, for example, in a discussion of the plausibility of a given piece of characterization. It is, however, when one arrives at the realm of biography that psychoanalytic considerations are most clearly appropriate.

Biography is, of course, seldom a sharply defined form. Too often it seeks for the facts as recorded in the documents of the time and then speculates, by recourse to certain elementary and naive inferences, as to what it was "probable" or "natural" that Shakespeare wanted to be doing at this or that time. Now insofar as biography occupies a respectable place in Shakespearean scholarship, what it is my aim to suggest here is how the attempt to account for the life of a human being may be brought up-to-date with the newer knowledge of human psychology and, in particular, the psychology of unconscious motivational forces. Otherwise, Shakespearean biography is likely to remain at a state resembling that which textual scholarship occupied in the days of Rowe.

In point of fact, there has been, in recent years, an increasing amount of what might be called psychoanalytic literary criticism. Nearly all of it—including several pieces of my own—has been confined to psychoanalytic journals. While it is just possible that this circumstance primarily results from the preference of the various authors, it is a likelier inference that the material is where it is because it is objectionable to most professional literary scholars.

There is, for example, the frequently valid objection that the psychoanalytic critic, in his reliance on "universals," gives insufficient weight to significant particulars, e.g., time-bound cultural factors. This does not mean solely that he may read too much into this material, as is often charged, but that he may read too little into it. (As a specific instance, he may miss the implication of effeminacy in Aufidius's taunt of Coriolanus, "Name not the god, thou boy of tears," not realizing that the Jacobeans divided the members of society into two categories, men, and women-and-boys.) More importantly, there is the charge that the psychoanalytic critic may, in his comments, blur the dividing lines between three psychologies: that of the protagonist of a literary work taken as an actual person, that of the author of the work, and that of the audience. To observe the distinctions would be, for example, to say that, whereas *Oedipus Rex* is, among other things, evidence that Sophocles underwent an exceptionally poignant oedipal experience, it does not contain much evidence that the same can be said of Oedipus considered as a person. As for the members of an audience of this play, all one can say in this connection is that, for any individual member, the intensity of his emotional reaction to the play is likely to correlate with the intensity of his own oedipal experience to a degree beyond that of mere chance.

In addition to these and several other legitimate criticisms, however, there are criticisms which seem primarily to indicate a misunderstanding, born of anxiety. These criticisms vary widely in content, but the misunderstanding is unvarying, namely, that the psychoanalytic criticism represents an attack upon some person, some function, or some value with which the professional critic is identified. The anxiety is that which human beings invariably experience when first confronted with interpretations based upon awareness of unconscious mental processes. It is quite impossible to deal with this anxiety by means of logic or persuasion, as every psychiatrist can aver from his own experience. Hence there is an irreducible minimum of resistance to psychoanalytic interpretations, which should be accepted in advance and uncomplainingly by every author attempting to offer such interpretations in print. Fortunately for the author of this essay, who is not especially fond of controversy, the material to be presented is almost entirely of a benign— although, it is hoped, not of a banal—nature.

The psychological truisms upon which the present essay rests are basically few in number and anything but startling in nature, namely, that unconscious forces may be of great significance in human life, that any extended effort a person makes is in some measure characteristic of him, and that human nature has not changed in any fundamental way in three hundred and fifty years. The second of these points may warrant a bit of discussion here in connection with the application of it made in this essay, the reading of biography from art.

In actuality, nearly all critics—and most other folk as well—do draw biographical inferences from creative works; the questions are, by what processes of thought, with what degree of specificity, and with what amount of speculation? Thus, long before the present author studied psychiatry, he was cured of a tendency toward adherence to the Baconian theory of the authorship of Shakespeare's plays by a careful reading of Bacon's essays. The thought, "This is not the kind of mind that could have produced *Romeo and Juliet* or *Hamlet*," is, in fact, a biographical inference from works of art. It has, I daresay, been shared by most of my readers. Here the process is intuitive. The biographical statement, that Bacon did not write Shakespeare's plays, is a general one. There is certainly an element of speculation.

The thought, "The mind which created *Coriolanus* had achieved a greater degree of *conscious* insight into certain aspects of the mother-son relationship than it possessed when it created *Hamlet*," is again a biographical inference drawn from creative works. Here the process of making the inference is less intuitive, the inference itself somewhat more specific, and the speculation a bit greater than in the previous example. The basis for this inference is that in *Coriolanus* Shakespeare offers his audience a *kind* of information not offered in *Hamlet*. In *Hamlet* there is considerable information as to the major current conflicts in the mind of the protagonist (what a psychiatrist would call "Hamlet's psychodynamics") but relatively little information as to the influences which one is to think of as having shaped his character (Hamlet's "psychogenetics"). In *Coriolanus* Shakespeare gives the audience vivid and revealing glimpses of certain influences which were of critical significance in making the hero what he is as the play opens. These influences are shown to have emanated from the hero's mother, Volumnia. A review of the pertinent material will serve both to illustrate the basis for the inference of which we are speaking and to furnish background for the present essay.

It is of interest to note that Volumnia has been mentioned in Shakespearean criticism in terms of considerable admiration. She has been considered to typify the noble Roman matron of the early days of the Republic. A careful reading of the play, however, reveals that Shakespeare visualized Volumnia as having exerted an influence upon Coriolanus which was what we might today call "traumatic." Volumnia is first introduced in Act I, Scene iii. Her long initial speech affords a basis for extensive insight into her personality.

> *Vol.* I pray you, daughter, sing; or express yourself in a more comfortable sort. If my son were my husband, I should freelier rejoice in that absence wherein he won honor than in the embracements of his bed where he would show most love. When yet he was but tenderbodied and the only son of my womb, when youth with comeliness plucked all gaze his way, when for a day of kings' entreaties a mother should not sell him an hour from her beholding, I, considering how honor would become such a person, that it was no better than picture-like to hang by th' wall, if renown made it not stir, was pleased to let him seek danger where he was like to find fame. To a cruel war I sent him; from whence he returned, his brows bound with oak. I tell thee, daughter, I sprang not more in joy at first hearing he was a man-child than now in first seeing he had proved himself a man.

Volumnia thus is presented as an unfeminine, non-maternal person, one who sought to mold her son to fit a preconceived image gratifying her own masculine strivings. Her method, the audience learns from the above speech and others, was to withhold praise and the scant affection she had to give from any achievements except aggressive and exhibitionistic ones. She also gives lip-service to "honor," but her attitude proves to be hypocritical. During the political crisis of Acts II and III, she urges her son to adopt craft and pretense until he has won power.

Volumnia's influence upon her son's developing personality is shown to have

120

been the more intense by reason of the facts that Coriolanus lost his father in infancy and, so far as we are told in the play, had no brothers or sisters. There are two points here: the boy's emotional needs had no source of satisfaction except his Amazonian mother, and there was no guiding influence to counterbalance hers.

The same scene as that from which Volumnia's long speech has been quoted contains an episode of crucial importance in estimating the effects of the mother-son relationship. Valeria inquires about Coriolanus's son and thus, indirectly, gives the audience a glimpse into the hero's own childhood.

> *Val.* How does your little son?
> *Vir.* I thank your ladyship; well, good madam.
> *Vol.* He had rather see the swords and hear a drum than look upon his schoolmaster.
> *Val.* O' my word, the father's son: I'll swear, 'tis a very pretty boy. O' my troth, I looked upon him o' Wednesday half an hour together; has such a confirmed countenence. I saw him run after a gilded butterfly; and when he caught it, he let it go again; and after it again; and over and over he comes, and up again; catched it again; or whether his fall enraged him or how 't was, he did so set his teeth and tear it. O, I warrant how he mammocked it!
> *Vol.* One on's father's moods.
> *Vir.* A crack, madam.

Following immediately the lines in which Volumnia has spoken of Coriolanus as a child and of the standards she imposed upon him, this vignette can only mean that Volumnia is trying to repeat the process with her grandson with some success, and that, in effect, little Marius can be taken to represent Coriolanus, himself, at a similar age. The incident of the butterfly shows childish curiosity and desire for mastery turning into sadism.

Shakespeare reintroduces the butterfly theme, with extrordinary effectiveness, in Act IV, Scene vi, in the description to the tribunes of the advance on Rome of Coriolanus and the Volscian Army.

> *Com.* He is their god. He leads them like a thing
> Made by some other deity than nature,
> That shapes men better; and they follow him
> Against us brats, with no less confidence
> Than boys pursuing summer butterflies,
> Or butchers killing flies.

Thus it would seem evident that the boyhood frustrations of Coriolanus, considered as a person, stand—and are seen by Shakespeare to stand—in a cause-effect relationship to what is, in effect the unleashing of furious aggression in adult life. Furthermore, it would seem evident that Shakespeare wished to share this insight with his audience and took pains to do so.

Although *Hamlet* is, of course, by far the greater play, it does not contain any comparable glimpse of the forces at work upon the hero's character in its formative years. Thus the statement that a greater degree of conscious insight into certain aspects of the mother-child relationship is displayed in *Coriolanus* than in *Hamlet* is purely factual. The biographical inference, that Shakespeare acquired this insight during the time between the writing of the two plays, is speculative. The speculation is, however, a fruitful one since it invites one to look at the available biographical data from a new perspective.

To take an analogy from mathematics, the situation is somewhat like that in which one is looking at a sheet of paper on which the location of quite a few points has been determined, but on which relatively little has emerged in the way of a pattern. A biographical inference, such as the one which has been under discussion, may be compared to a line, at first imaginary, which is traced upon the paper on the basis, let us say, of experience in some comparable situation. If one then finds that a significant number of known points fall upon the line, one may be justified in using the line to help determine the probable location of new, and hitherto unsuspected points.

To come closer to the theme of the present essay, one may note that, in addition to its intrinsic interest as a tragedy of character and to the particular psychological dimension just considered, *Coriolanus* merits attention because of its pivotal position in Shakespeare's life and works. The best evidence indicates that the play was written at a time close to the death of the poet's mother and just before his retirement from London to Stratford. It is the last of the tragedies and is followed by several plays of a different *genre*, the final comedies.

At almost the same point of time, then, that Shakespeare's relationship to his mother is altered (by her death or impending death) and that his relationship to his wife is altered (by the return to Stratford), the poet writes a play in which emphasis is placed upon the mother-son relationship and, as Goddard has ably pointed out, upon the husband-wife relationship. One must either accept all this as an extraordinary set of coincidences or seek the most plausible interpretation of the interconnection between the facts. In the latter attempt, it is natural to think of looking just beyond the pivotal point and considering the first play written after it, to see whether or not some of the ideas suggested in *Coriolanus* undergo further development, to see if additional correlations between the poet's life, experiences, and writings are feasible, and, if they are, to determine if they support and clarify the correlations already made.

The plays which probably followed *Coriolanus* are *Pericles* (1608), *Cymbeline* (1609 or 1610), *The Winter's Tale* (1611), *The Tempest* (1611), *Henry VIII* (1613), and *The Two Noble Kinsmen* (1613).[2] Of these dramas, the first four are, of course, conventionally grouped as the final comedies. It is unfortunately the case that *Pericles*, which according to these dating assumptions was very likely written next after *Coriolanus*, is not really suitable for the purposes of the present study, inasmuch as, like *Henry VIII* and *The Two Noble Kinsmen*, it may have been in considerable part the work of a collaborator. Moreover, critics are not in agreement as to where Shakespeare's work ends and the collaborator's begins. Accordingly let us select *Cymbeline* as the play upon which to base the present inquiry. (Here, too, it is sometimes suggested that Shakespeare did not write the entire play; however, the extent of his authorship appears to be reasonably well established and it includes the decisive features of plot and characterization.)

Cymbeline has been called "Shakespeare's most recapitulatory play." It is of interest to note certain of the echoes of the great tragedies in *Cymbeline*. This interest is heightened by the recognition that at least one such echo is obviously conscious and deliberate, a circumstance which raises the likelihood that a number of others were introduced in the same manner. *King Lear* and, to a slightly lesser extent, *Othello* are the plays of which the echoes appear to be the clearest and most significant. Not only is a father-daughter relationship of great importance in *Cymbeline*, as in *Lear*, but there is considerable correspondence in details of the situation. Cymbeline, like Lear, is an early British king; like Lear he is quick-tempered; like Lear, he trusts the wicked and rejects the loyal. Imogen, like Cordelia, is the third child of her father; like Cordelia, she is warm-hearted and sincere; she loves her father, but will not permit him to dominate her to the loss of her own self-respect. Like Lear, Cymbeline is influenced by an immoral woman, an influence which is to the detriment of himself and the heroine. Like Lear, Cymbeline becomes separated from all three of his children. As in *Lear*, there is in *Cymbeline* a reconciliation between father and virtuous daughter.

Echoes of *Othello* are scarcely less striking. The one which is unmistakably deliberate is the name of the principal villain. Iachimo is literally "little Iago." Although the personality of Iachimo is not merely an echo or repetition of that of Iago, there are manifest similarities, such as the misogyny, the shrewdness, and the dishonesty. The entire "wager-plot" in *Cymbeline* is closely analogous to the main plot of *Othello*. In both instances, the villain manages so effectively to misrepresent a faithful wife as to rouse murderous rage in a previously loving husband. There is even a correspondence in certain smaller details of the situation. For example, in both *Othello* and *Cymbeline* the heroine has married against her father's wishes a man whom the father considers socially inferior. In both plays the villain uses a piece of the heroine's personal property to clinch his argument. In both plays the article was originally given the wife by her husband and then stolen from her by the villain or his agent.

This brief review does not begin to exhaust the list of echoes of previous writings to be found in *Cymbeline*, a list which includes material from *Romeo and Juliet*, *Hamlet*, *Macbeth*, and *Coriolanus*, as well as some of Shakespeare's non-dramatic poetry, but it is of almost equal interest to realize the close relationship of *Cymbeline* to the other romances: *Pericles*, *The Winter's Tale*, and *The Tempest*. In the first part of each play a father loses a daughter through his own poor judgment and instinct-ridden behavior. A considerable portion of the action in each play is devoted to the suffering and/or remorse following from this estrangement. In the end, the child is reconciled with the father and becomes an instrument of a more general reconciliation. Since *Cymbeline* is the first of these plays (apart from *Pericles*), one might reasonably expect to be able to make out certain psychological implications regarding the author with particular clarity. In a general way, these links with other plays before and after it attest to the psychological significance of *Cymbeline*. More specifically, some of the links enable one to postulate certain psychological developments in the author, a matter which can only be discussed, however, after a glance at the characterization of Imogen.

One of the several telling arguments which have been advanced against the old idea that the romances gave evidence of Shakespeare's failing powers is that the dramatist never showed a firmer grip on characterization than is revealed at times in these last plays. *Cymbeline* furnishes a number of examples of this strength in characterization, of which the most outstanding is Imogen. In the opinion of a number of critics, Imogen has but one rival among Shakespeare's women—Cleopatra—in the richness of her portrayal. Other critics feel that she has no rival.

In expressing a woman's point of view, Margaret Webster[3] writes: "Imogen is she whom every woman in love would wish to be—free, generous, sane, miraculously happy in the expression of her love. Over and over again she puts feeling into words so just that she seems to express the emotion for all time." Goddard has pointed out that Imogen, "like Hamlet, is an epitome, uniting in herself the virtues of at least three of Shakespeare's types: the naive girl (in boy's costume part of the time), the queenly woman, and the tragic victim. It is as if the poet had consciously set out to endow his heroine with the finest traits of a dozen of her predecessors: 'from every one The best she hath, and she, of all compounded, Outsells them all.'"[4]

Examples of the intensity and beauty of Imogen's love are frequent in her speeches. Her first words to Pisanio after the banishment of Posthumus (Act I, Scene iii) are typical.

> I would thou grew'st unto the shores o' th' haven,
> And question'dst every sail: if he should write
> And I not have it, 't were a paper lost
> As offer'd mercy is.

At times, when speaking of Posthumus, as a little further on in this same scene, Imogen shows a fresh and youthful quality reminiscent of Juliet.

> I did not take my leave of him, but had
> Most pretty things to say. Ere I could tell him
> How I would think on him at certain hours
> Such thoughts and such, or I could make him swear
> The shes of Italy should not betray
> Mine interest and his honor, or have charg'd him
> At the sixth hour of morn, at noon, at midnight,
> To encounter me with orisons, for then

I am in heaven with him; or ere I could
Give him that parting kiss which I had set
Betwixt two charming words, comes in my father
And like the tyrannous breathing of the north
Shakes all our buds from growing.

It is of importance to realize that Imogen is not a paragon—certainly not just a paragon—but a young woman of very human qualities. She has married without her father's consent, a rather serious offense in Elizabethan days, and as Granville-Barker says, "has been a clandestine wife for some while . . . under Cymbeline's very nose, which shows . . . some ability in deception." Moreover she speaks out to her father at times with a forthrightness verging on disrespect.

I beseech you, Sir,
Harm not yourself with your vexation:
I am senseless of your wrath.

Imogen is capable of humor, as in the "shes of Italy" line in the long speech quoted above; of gracious courtesy, as in her reception of Iachimo, thinking him her husband's friend, and of flashing anger, as in response to Iachimo's attempt at seduction. She can be free with contempt, as in speaking to the foppish and and cowardly Cloten. She is no unreal, superhuman tower of strength: given the cruel shock of finding, as she supposes, Posthumus beheaded, she sinks, after her initial, near-hysterical outburst, into a dazed state. To the Roman's question, "What art thou?" she can answer only, "I am nothing: or if not, Nothing to be were better."

Perhaps most significantly of all, Imogen is *capable of hope*. To a certain extent one may ascribe Imogen's belief that matters will eventually work out well for herself and for Posthumus to a realistic appraisal of certain strengths in his character and in her father's, but one is still left with the question of what enables her to maintain this appraisal in the face of very adverse circumstances. To perceive the crucial significance of this quality of hope, one must consider what is technically the central scene of the play, Act III, Scene iv, toward the end of which Imogen rallies from near-despair and achieves an attitude of hope which sustains her throughout the rest of the play. It is the outcome of this scene which determines that the play is to be a tragi-comedy and not a tragedy. Imogen and Pisanio are on the road to Milford Haven, when Pisanio breaks down and shows the princess the letter he has received from his master, Posthumus.

Imo. (Reads.) "Thy mistress, Pisanio, hath played the strumpet
in my bed. . . . I speak not out of weak surmises, but from
proof as strong as my grief and as certain as I expect
my revenge. . . . Let thine own hands take away her
life. . . ."

Pis. What shall I need to draw my sword? The paper
hath cut her throat already.

Imogen's first reaction is pure anguish. This is quickly succeeded by honest anger.

> *Imo.* False to his bed! What! is it to be false
> To lie in watch there and to think on him;
> To weep 'twixt clock and clock; if sleep
>   charge nature,
> To break it with a fearful dream of him,
> And cry myself awake? That's false to's
>   bed, is it?

This hostility is temporarily "directed inward," as Imogen expresses the wish for Pisanio to carry out his order; but not entirely so, even in this moment of great stress; a certain amount of honest self-respect remains (as well it may in view of the largely unambivalent character of her love for Posthumus).

> *Imo.*   Do his bidding; strike.
> Thou mayst be valiant in a better cause,
> But now thou seem'st a coward.
> *Pis.*   Hence, vile instrument!
> Thou shalt not damn my hand.
> *Imo.*   Why, I must die;
> And if I do not by thy hand, thou art
> No servant of thy master's. Against self-
>   slaughter
> There is a prohibition so divine
> That cravens my weak hand. Come, here's
>   my heart,
> (Something's afore't,—soft, soft! we'll
>   no defense)
> Obedient as the scabbard. What is here?
>   [Draws the letters from her bosom.]
> The scriptures of the loyal Leonatus,
> All turned to heresy? Away, away,
> Corruptors of my faith! you shall no more
> Be stomachers to my heart.

Pisanio is unwilling to carry out his commission, but suggests that Imogen play for time, and the heroine quickly picks up the suggestion. When Pisanio advises her to return to her father, Imogen is too proud to accede, but she continues actively thinking of possible plans.

> *Pis.*   If you'll back to th' court—
> *Imo.* No court, no father; nor no more ado
> With that harsh, noble, simple nothing,
> That Cloten, whose love-suit hath been to me

                    As fearful as a siege.
Pis.   If not at court,
          Then not in Britain must you bide
Imo.   Where then?
          Hath Britain all the sun that shines?
            Day, night.
          Are they not but in Britain? I' th' world's
            volume
          Our Britain seems as of it, but not in't
          There's livers out of Britain.

Pisanio then hits on the plan of Imogen's dressing like a boy and joining
the expedition of Caius Lucius, a move which is likely to bring her eventually
to Rome and the vicinity of Posthumus. Imogen accepts this idea with fortitude
and hope.

      Imo. There's more to be consider'd; but we'll even
            All that good time will give us. This attempt
            I am soldier to, and will abide it with
            A prince's courage.

So it is the emotional health, and particularly the capacity for hope, in Imogen
which, at this decisive point, makes the difference between tragedy and comedy.
Imogen adopts none of the courses which would lead to a morbid outcome: submission to her father and step-mother, marriage to Cloten, suicide, revenge on
Posthumus. Instead she is amenable to the one course which gives eventual promise of a healthier outcome.

This matter of hope warrants further consideration, but to round out this sketch
of Imogen's personality, two other incidents should be noted. The diffuse material of Act IV, involving events at the mountain retreat of Belarius and the young
princes, does not contribute appreciably to the portrayal of Imogen's personality. It is almost solely concerned with the romantic-narrative aspects of the
play. The last scene of Act V, however, yields significant glimpses of Imogen. The
first of these occurs when Imogen notices the ring she had given Posthumus on the
finger of Iachimo. She asks a boon of the king that Iachimo be required to give an
explanation of the circumstance. Dazed, shaken and heartbroken as she has been
rendered by the horrendous events in Act IV, Imogen retains the strength to
resume her goal-directed behaviour as soon as she realizes that somehow Posthumus is still alive. Then, in the final surge of relief after Iachimo has confessed
and Posthumus has recognized her, Imogen speaks three charming lines, playful,
affectionate, and sensual all at once, which complete the portrayal of her
personality.

      Imo. Why did you throw your wedded lady from you?
            Think that you are upon a lock, and now
            Throw me again.

Having reviewed briefly the position of the play among Shakespeare's works, its connections with some of the other plays, its complicated plot, and the personality of its leading character, we may now consider the difficult task of exploring the psychological relationship of *Cymbeline* to its author and, in particular, the continuity of development between the psychological status of the author of *Coriolanus* and that of the author of *Cymbeline*. To this effect, it may be well to note at the outset Shakespeare's biographical data at the period of his life just before and during the presumed time of writing of *Cymbeline*.

1. On June 5, 1607, Shakespeare's older daughter, Susanna, married John Hall, a Puritan physician of Stratford, eight years older than she.

2. February, 1608. A daughter was born to this union.

3. September, 1608. Shakespeare's mother died.

4. Late in 1608 or early in 1609 *Coriolanus* was written.

5. During 1609 the *Sonnets* were published.

6. Late in 1609 or in 1610, *Cymbeline* was written.

7. In September, 1610, Shakespeare retired to Stratford, occupying the house he had previously purchased, New Place, which had once been the home of Sir Hugh Clopten, one of the town's most distinguished former citizens.[5]

To this list should be added several other items of a biographical nature having a possible bearing on the significance of *Cymbeline*. For example, it is clear that the period of twenty years was of particular significance in the life of Shakespeare being (approximately) the length of time that he lived in London as an actor and playwright. Twenty years was also the approximate length of time between the postulated critical period in Shakespeare's early childhood (see Ella Sharpe's work, discussed in the following section) and the known critical period in his young adult life, at which he left home and went to London.

Another biographical feature of possible relevance is the likelihood that Shakespeare and Anne Hathaway lived as man and wife for some little time before their wedding (possibly having a "pre-contract").

It may also prove of interest that there were important similarities—or identification points—between Shakespeare and his daughter Susanna. Susanna was, in fact, spoken of as being very like her father, "witty above her sex."[6] Like his daughter, Shakespeare had married a person eight years older than himself and with Puritan leanings. (The latter circumstance is a possible reason for Anne not accompanying her husband to London and becoming a part of his life in the theater.)

Finally, while Shakespeare was not literally one of three children—his mother having borne eight—yet there were situations within the family in which a *sense* of being one of three children must have assumed significance. Shakespeare was the third child of the family, yet, for awhile, the only child, since the two elder had died in infancy. Then, during a highly significant developmental period—age five to age seven and one-half—Shakespeare was one of three living children in the family. It is also true that he, himself, had three children, the boy Hamnet, and two daughters.

If we return to *Cymbeline*, certain correlations between the foregoing biographical material and events depicted in that play become interesting to the student of psychology. The theme of reunion and reconciliation so prominent in the final comedies and especially striking in *Cymbeline* does tend to reflect events in the poet's own life. In the play, no fewer than five characters—Imogen, Posthumus, the two princes, and Cymbeline—in effect "share" certain experiences with Shakespeare. Like the princes, Shakespeare returns home after twenty years: indeed, he comes home to what amounted to a palace, one of the finest houses in town. But more importantly, we may observe the shape of family-relationships. Shakespeare's own childhood situation offers certain similarities to the composition of Imogen's family, and, as far as the poet's later life is concerned, his romance with Anne is reminiscent of the relationship between Imogen and Posthumus. The drama is marked, too, by the absence, through death, of one mother and the current death of another, and we are perhaps reminded that Shakespeare's career, being obviously marked by an absence from his own mother, is to a certain extent affected by her death in that this is followed by a decision to return to Stratford. Finally, we have suggested Imogen as somewhat atypical (p.124) in that her existence as a composite of womanly types is not characteristic of Shakespeare's other figures.

Other parallels can be found, but these are perhaps sufficient to show that *Cymbeline*, unlike many of the other plays, presents matters of some basic concern to Shakespeare's own emotional life, no matter how removed from his work we may assume an artist to be. For the events of this period of the dramatist's life are such as to emphasize his relationships with significant women. There are the death of his mother, the marriage of his daughter, the return to his wife, and even —through the publication of the Sonnets—some reminiscence of his relationship (whether real or only in fantasy) with the "dark lady."

Before going further with the attempt to discern what Shakespeare may have been revealing about himself in the play *Cymbeline*, it may be well to return for a moment to a consideration of the psychological truism presented on p.119, namely, that any extended effort a person makes is in some measure characteristic of him. Modern depth psychology teaches that all creative writing is in some measure a projection of certain facets of the author's personality. The view is that one cannot create realistically except out of one's self, that one cannot, to be more specific, create a fictional character of vitality and significance except insofar as something within one's own personality is in resonance with the strivings and the defenses of the character. On this view, one might say of Shakespeare (or any other great writer) that any given work—let us say, to take an extreme case, *Love's Labor's Lost*—expresses the emotional conflicts of its author. There is, I should think, truth in such a statement, but it involves an over-simplification so great that the attendant error exceeds the truth. In the productions of a great master, such as Shakespeare, one can find expression of essentially all of the fundamental conflicts of which human beings are capable. If all of these conflicts had been of personal importance to Shakespeare, his mind would have been not one of the most highly organized the world has ever seen, but quite disorganized. Thus, one is led to the conclusion that it is possible for a very great artist to create entertainingly, beautifully, realistically, without being *deeply* involved in a personal way. On the other hand, when it is a matter of his greatest masterpieces, the case appears to be different quantitatively. Without knowing anything of Shakespeare's personal life, most persons would surmise that the creation of *Hamlet* arose out of more moving personal experiences of the author than did *Love's Labor's Lost*. And indeed, a study of Shakespeare's life gives some evidence to support such a contention.

Three plays which seem particularly to belong together psychologically and to reflect a developmental sequence in the author are *King Lear, Coriolanus,* and *Cymbeline*. Some of the evidence for postulating a significant relationship between *King Lear* and *Cymbeline* has been given on p.123. Initially the reasons for suspecting a significant psychological relationship between *Coriolanus* and *Cymbeline* were that the two plays were (barring *Pericles*) written in quick succession within a short time of the death of Shakespeare's mother and that they lie, so to speak, on either side of a point which marks striking changes in Shakespeare's *genre* of expression and in his personal life.

I do not propose to offer here a psychoanalytical investigation of *Lear*. This has been done, however, with great technical competence by Ella Freeman Sharpe.[7] Taking Miss Sharpe's essay at face value—which is surely the wisest course, in view of her undoubted integrity—one finds that the validity of its speculations is attested by its author's being able to deduce, solely from a careful reading of *Lear*, that Shakespeare had been, for a while, an only child, that one of his siblings had been born when he was about two years of age, and that another sibling had been born at a time when he was able to walk about the neighborhood independently. In *King Lear*, Miss Sharpe finds evidence of reactivation in Shakespeare, at the time of writing the tragedy, of intense conflicts from his early childhood, conflicts which involved what a psychoanalyst would call "pre-oedipal strivings," i.e., strivings for gratifications of the sort of paramount importance to a child below the age of three years. In the reactivation, these conflicts are, of course, considered to have been completely unconscious.

In *Coriolanus*, as I have pointed out in an earlier essay,[8] the principal conflicts of the protagonist are at an early oedipal level. Insofar as this circumstance may be taken to indicate a similar shift in the author's principal conflicts at the time, one may say that, if there has been an emotional retreat of the sort suggested by Miss Sharpe, it has begun to be reversed. If the ideas offered previously are accepted, then one may add that the psychological healing was accompanied by a certain amount of personal insight. What is relatively certain is that the writing of *Coriolanus* was shortly followed by a definitive change in the author's literary productions and style of personal living. While the destructive mother figure occupies the center of the stage for a large portion of the time in *Coriolanus*, there are clear glimpses of a wholesome woman figure in the person of Virgilia. Although in the play Virgilia is the wife of Coriolanus, nevertheless her significance as a mother figure is unmistakable (through interaction with her son as well as in her having partially reversed the effects of Volumnia's personality on Coriolanus).

Cymbeline may be considered the third term in a series of which *Lear* and *Coriolanus* are the first and second terms, with the series being thought of as reflecting changes in the psychological position of the author.

In examining *Cymbeline* from this point of view, the most conspicuous factor is surely the characterization of Imogen. This portrayal is not only rich but almost completely unambivalent. Moreover it is not appreciably touched by the effects of psychological defenses in the author; that is to say, it is not sentimental, not rigid, not idolatrous. It might be called an oedipal or post-oedipal portrait, in the sense that such an image of a woman is characteristically held only by a man of considerable personal maturity. Its richness appears to indicate that the portrait was drawn from marked breadth and depth of experience, probably involving the four women figures in Shakespeare's life mentioned on p.128.

At first consideration, one might think that, although rich and genuine, the characterization of Imogen as an ideal woman is incomplete since specifically maternal features are not included. This is, however, only partially true. It is a well-known fact of human psychology that emotions and attitudes—particularly if they are to some extent repressed—of a woman toward her father or of a man toward his mother are frequently revealed in emotions and attitudes experienced toward a child of the same sex as the parent in question.

> *Lear.* When were you wont to be so full of songs, sirrah?
> *Fool.* I have used it, nuncle, ever since thou mad'st thy daugh-
> ters thy mother, for when thou gav'st them the rod, and
> puttest down thine own breeches . . .

Miss Sharpe is of the opinion that Shakespeare expressed deep-seated, largely unconscious feelings about his mother through the characterization of Lear's three daughters. The close parallels between *Cymbeline* and *Lear,* and the fact that *Cymbeline* was written rather soon after Shakespeare's mother's death, suggest to me that the same process of substitution is in operation in this play. On this view, the reconciliation of Cymbeline and Imogen is not only one of father and daughter but also of son and mother. The son, as it were, forgives the mother, and the mother reaffirms her loyalty to the son.

This line of thought suggests a closer look at the relationship between Shakespeare and his daughter, Susanna, and invites speculation upon it. In view of the documented resemblance between them, it is a reasonable inference that the bonds were strong despite the infrequency of contacts during Susanna's later childhood and adolescence. On the other hand, it seems likely that there was some basis for negative feelings in Shakespeare toward his daughter, partly conscious and partly unconscious. Clearly the playwright had some reason for irritation toward Susanna for her marrying Doctor Hall, inasmuch as he was a Puritan and therefore strongly opposed to the theater. To speak of unconscious factors, it is a permissible inference that there was some old resentment toward Susanna for having been born at all, thus terminating the idyllic phase of Shakespeare's relationship with Anne, for having begun to reconstitute the situation which Shakespeare, according to Miss Sharpe's analysis, found so difficult in his own early childhood, namely the advent of rivals for the affection of the woman figure in his life. At least one knows that Shakespeare left his home for London shortly after the birth of his second and third children. (The conscious rationale for a young man's going to London to seek his fortune is, of course, in no sense contradictory to the idea that Shakespeare's leaving Stratford was also running away, since it is quite possible to run to something and away from something else at the same time.)

Yet these negative feelings must clearly have been counterbalanced by some other force or forces during the period in which the ideas for *Cymbeline* were germinating. Again it is possible to speak of conscious and unconscious factors. It seems reasonable to surmise that Shakespeare was thinking in terms of a male heir at this time. Indeed, all of the elaborate provisions of his will seem to have been designed with the purpose of seeing that his wealth would be concentrated in the hands of such an heir. With Anne well past the age of childbearing, it was to Susanna or Judith that he must look for such an heir, and Susanna was the elder and his favorite. (The will makes it quite clear that if Susanna has a son, he will become Shakespeare's heir.) Further, it seems reasonable to assume that this child-to-be was thought of by Shakespeare as his own (consciously, in a figurative sense; unconsciously, in a literal sense), and that the wish for a child by daughter had become fused unconsciously with the common oedipal wish for a child by mother.

Susanna had shown herself to be fertile and doubtless was delighted with her father's intentions with respect to her son-to-be. Thus there was every reason for the relationship between father and daughter to become increasingly cordial and mutually pleasant.

There seems little reason to doubt that, in addition to the psychological forces just mentioned, Shakespeare's mastery over the feelings of bitterness and near-despair which were given expression in *Lear* was fostered by, as well as expressed in, a favorable trend in his relationship with Anne, his wife. (Anne may well have been one of the sources of the "queenly" characteristics of Imogen.)

Here again one should consider both conscious and unconscious factors in the situation. To think first of conscious factors, one must recall something of Anne's position. Like Shakespeare's mother, Anne was of a highly respectable background, having come from a family of landowners. There seems to have been something dignified about Anne which made her quite suitable as a wife to one who aspired to become and did become a member of the gentry. While her leanings toward the Puritan faith produced a definite incompatibility with her husband during the years when he was an actor in London, this factor must have faded markedly in significance with Shakespeare's acquisition of property and status in Stratford, and may well have become inconsequential by the time now in question, when he had become established as a gentleman resident of Stratford.

132

It would have been only natural for Anne to have been appreciative of the mounting evidence of Shakespeare's intention to reestablish himself in Stratford and to give up the stage. Her positive feelings may well have been gratifying to Shakespeare and so, no doubt, was her continuing loyalty, a virtue highly prized by the author of the *Sonnets*.

On an unconscious level, the mother-transference which seems to have caused difficulty to Shakespeare in the early years of the marriage may now have become a source of gratification. The conflicts mobilized by the advent of the children would have quieted since they were no longer in childhood or adolescence. Shakespeare may well have come to feel reinstated as Anne's first concern. Then, too, the transference would have been somewhat diluted at this point, with Susanna being its partial recipient.

III

Up to this point, in the consideration of certain psychological sequences in Shakespeare, the person, only material deriving from a study of the characterization of Imogen (in relation to biographical data) has been utilized. To supplement the line of thought which has been developed, one may now turn to a consideration of certain aspects of the plot of *Cymbeline* together with a look at certain of the other figures in the story.

First, the plot of the wager and the slandered lady. The action of this portion of the play primarily involves Imogen, Posthumus, and Iachimo. The names of the two male characters are surely significant. The name, "Iachimo," clearly represents a conscious and deliberate attempt to call to mind the villain, Iago from the tragedy, *Othello*. The name, "Posthumus," clearly represents a conscious and deliberate effort to call to mind the parentless state of this protagonist.[9] The latter circumstance is completely irrelevant to the action of the play,—but *Shakespeare* became parentless with the death of his mother at the beginning of the pivotal period which saw the writing of *Coriolanus* and *Cymbeline*. (Mary Shakespeare died in September, 1608. The plays were written in the period of late 1608 to early 1610.)

The choice of the name, "Iachimo," has a superficial explanation, no doubt valid so far as it goes: the wish to remind the audience of the highly successful villain in the highly successful play, *Othello*, and thereby to increase the interest in the action to follow. On the other hand, the question of the similarity in names merges with the question as to the similarity in plot between this portion of *Cymbeline* and the Othello-Iago-Desdemona action in Othello, and this leads into deeper waters.

It has been postulated that if one wishes to study *Othello* from the point of view of a series of projections of its author's conflicts, it is appropriate to consider Othello and Iago as two aspects of a single personality, with Iago representing certain unquenchable hostile and homoerotic id forces and Othello the struggling ego. It is not possible to draw a tight analogy between the Othello-Iago-Desdemona plot and the Posthumus-Iachimo-Imogen plot because of the enormous shift in importance in the heroine of the latter plot. On the other hand, one can go so far as to say that this portion of Shakespeare's message in *Cymbeline* is that, given time and hope, the disruptive id forces (which destroyed Othello) can be brought under control.

The significance of the time element is shown in one of Shakespeare's modifications of the plot as found in his source. Unlike the situation in Boccaccio— and unlike that in *Othello*—Posthumus has time for his ego to assert itself before tragedy has occurred. On returning to England, Posthumus repents of his instructions to Pisanio *while still under the impression of Imogen's guilt*. The message further implies that hostility need not be quenched in revenge, not even in being shown to be groundless, but by the ability to love.

The significant element of hope (together with a healthy aggressivity) is, of course, principally manifested not in Posthumus but in Imogen (p.127). Put Imogen in Desdemona's place and the tragedy of *Othello* would not have occurred. Put her in Cordelia's place and the tragedy of *Lear* would not have occurred. If one considers the characters of *Cymbeline*, like those of *Othello* and *Lear*, from the standpoint of their being projections of strivings and attitudes of their creator, one may say—on the basis of the portrayal of Imogen alone—that Shakespeare's bitterness and near-despair have been vanquished by hope.

To summarize and rephrase what has been said of the implications to be found in the character of Imogen and the action in which she is involved, one may begin by saying that she is consciously represented as both a wife and a daughter. Both husband-wife and father-daughter reconciliations are thus represented in the last scene. These correspond to Shakespeare's renewed gratifying relationships with wife and daughter. Unconsciously (for the dramatist), Imogen, like Cordelia, represents a mother. This facet of the situation corresponds to Shakespeare's being able (unconsciously) to forgive and be reconciled with his memory representations of his mother.

Imogen is taken back to the palace; Shakespeare installs Anne in New Place and deeds it to Susanna. Reduction in a sense of guilt, reconciliation, and hope for the future are all linked.

What has thus far been worked out appears internally consistent and consistent with the facts that are known. It is possible, however, to view the central portion of the play in a more speculative way, one which touches deeper layers of the poet's unconscious. In this view, the figure of Imogen is, perhaps, best considered as one with whom Shakespeare is identified. We have noted (p.125) that the pivotal point of the play is Act III, Scene iv. Actually, it would be more nearly correct to speak of a pivotal area, since the fourth scene is surrounded by two others, the third and sixth, which supplement it and, taken in sequence with it, furnish the basis for the reconciliations in the final scene of the play. These three scenes take place in the Welsh hills in and around the secret cave. It is necessary to view these scenes in a more symbolic fashion that much of the rest of the play to appreciate fully their significance. When, however, one takes such a view, the material is seen to be fully consonant with the interpretations previously derived from the play.

In effect, one may say that the descending or tragic component of the action is arrested during this sequence of scenes and the successful (in this sense, comic) resolution of the difficulties begins or is prepared for. The setting of the cave strongly suggests that an unconscious reference is being made to the mother's womb. From the cave issue the two young princes—sibling figures. It seems a reasonable inference that Shakespeare was here unconsciously symbolizing the critical periods in his life when he was in danger of experiencing a pathogenic regression.

There seem to have been three such periods. The most recent was the potential regression discussed by Miss Sharpe (and others) as being in relation to the writing of the great tragedies. The intermediate one was the occasion of Shakespeare's going from Stratford to London following the birth of his second and third children. The original occasion may well have followed the birth of Shakespeare's sister, Joan (the second sibling to succeed him). The idea of these scenes' representing a regression is reinforced by the circumstance that, in a sense, they involve a turning back of the clock by twenty years. Belarius and the princes are, so to speak, figures of the past.

The important new element represented in these scenes—as contrasted, say, with the message of Lear—is that love appears at the critical moment for Imogen (and, by inference, in Shakespeare's view of life at this time). Love reigns in the primitive surroundings of the cave. It affects Imogen, the princes, and Belarius. In other words, Shakespeare seems now to have succeeded in getting through the (psychic residuals of the) stressful periods of his early childhood, detected by Miss Sharpe in Lear, back to (the psychic residuals of) a still earlier period, rock bottom, at which there were love and reason for hope, and to have succeeded in reversing the regression through this knowledge. With the reversal, the love and hope begin to infiltrate later periods, bringing with them the possibility of a reconciliation between Shakespeare and sibling figures and between Shakespeare and his offspring.

One thus returns to the key element of hope. Indeed, if one were to epitomize the significance of the play, Cymbeline, insofar as it is a representation of its author's psychological position, one could scarcely do better than to say that it is his fullest expression of an unambivalent picture of woman and of the power of hope. Furthermore, one is led strongly to suspect that the two expressions are here (as usually) dynamically connected. St. Paul says, "Faith is the substance of things hoped for, the evidence of things not seen," and where—if he is fortunate —does everyone first find this faith but in the ministrations of a woman, a mother, whose availability to her small child does not cease when she leaves the room?

Thus the meaningful sequence, Lear, Coriolanus, Cymbeline, is completed. In Lear the good woman (mother figure) is visualized but is ineffectual (Cordelia); in Coriolanus, she is partially effective (Virgilia); in Cymbeline, she is fully effective (Imogen). One is led to postulate that there were two sets of factors which contributed to Shakespeare's achievement of this final position. The first is surely the self-induced catharsis of the writing of the tragedies, beginning with Julius

135

Caesar and ending with *Coriolanus*. In Miss Sharpe's words, "The poet is not Hamlet. Hamlet is what he might have been if he had not written the play of *Hamlet*." One is inclined to agree that "The massive cycle of the tragic plays gives the impression of a renewed attempt to master every phase of development."[10] In the writing of the great plays there was an element of regression, but it was truly what psychoanalysts call a "regression in the service of the ego," that is to say, a controlled regression which is ultimately of value to the whole personality. The regression achieved its purpose by reason both of the poet's marvelous endowment and of the fact that the first years of his childhood were, by and large, happy and successful ones.

Hand in hand with the reassertion of ego control—favored by it and fostering it—went the second set of factors, the real-life developments referred to previously in this paper. As Dover Wilson put it, "Wordsworth recovered by falling in love a second time with the Lake Country; Shakespeare by falling in love a second time with Stratford." To this should be added that it was not merely Stratford that was effective, but circumstances involving the women figures in Shakespeare's life: the death of his mother, the loyalty of Anne, and the coming of age and marriage of Susanna.

The immediate (psychological) effect of the death of Shakespeare's mother is, perhaps, not known, but a proximal effect was exemplified in the writing of *Coriolanus* and a later effect in the writing of *Cymbeline*. An effective mourning must have contributed toward halting the poet's regression and fostering—in combination with other events—a return to a more mature orientation. Shakespeare's early childhood strivings were not fully abandoned but were attenuated and merged into strivings more nearly capable of fulfillment in the real world. At the same time, circumstances in that world were developing to bring some fulfillment and the promise of additional fulfillment.

Notes:

(1) The above article is the first of a series to be offered in *Shakespeare Studies* by authors whose fields of professional competence may have relevance to the disciplined study of Shakespeare.—The Editor.

(2) I use here the dating of E. K. Chambers, *William Shakespeare* (Oxford, 1923), I, 484 ff.

(3) Margaret Webster, *Shakespeare without Tears* (Cleveland, 1955), p. 271.

(4) H. C. Goddard, *The Meaning of Shakespeare* (Chicago, 1951), pp. 635-636.

(5) For these well-known facts, see Chambers, I, 86 f.; 555 ff.; II, 4 ff.

(6) Chambers, II, 12.

(7) E. F. Sharpe, "From *King Lear* to the *Tempest*," *Collected Papers on Phychoanalysis* (London, 1950).

(8) "An Interpretation of Shakespeare's *Coriolanus*," *American Imago*, XIV (1957), pp. 407-435.

(9) See *NED*, "posthumous," meanings *a-c*.

(10) Sharpe, "The Impatience of *Hamlet*," in *Papers*.

Taking Shakespeare at His Word

by Leslie Hotson

Convinced that such a course will greatly profit us, I am here going to argue for taking Shakespeare at his word. For experience has shown me that our failure or refusal to follow that course in centrally important matters has kept us groping in the dark, or (what is worse) adopting mare's-nests as acceptable living quarters.

But before we can take him at his word on any given point, we must first be sure that we know approximately what he is saying. And this demands unremitting study of Elizabethan idiom and Elizabethan life: something we are evidently not going to get from the advancing academic multitude. To quote *The Times Literary Supplement*, "The emphasis is being taken off the study of language and our early traditions, and is being subtly transferred . . . to the here-and-now. The effects of this change to the modern are bad." No one will deny that our modern criticism, when it first took hold, gave us a stimulating shake, needed and welcome. But both the direction it has come to take and the results it has produced are open to question.

If "trained by modern poetry and modern criticism" we perceive in Shakespeare a novel aspect which our up-to-date mind values and thinks valid, we call this an "insight", and congratulate ourselves on having got "closer to the truth". For if a modern-trained eye can see it, we assume that Shakespeare must have put it there, consciously or otherwise.

But *truth is what man troweth*: truth is what we think or believe. Whether what we believe coincides with something which once existed in our author is a point much easier to assume (or to ignore) than to examine. Can we be large enough to remember that every age was once modern? that the modern minds of the twelfth and thirteenth centuries had their insights too? In Virgil they detected exciting necromantic powers. And their great Dante, even more penetrating, perceived that Virgil's work was divinely inspired. Here indeed was a notable break-through of criticism—to a truth, a new dimension never suspected either by the Augustans or by Virgil himself.

To prove to the shade of Dante that this "divine inspiration" (which he found valid) was a notion of his own, and not an authentic Virgilian phenomenon, might be no easy task. And he might counter, with the brilliant obliqueness of a Lascelles Abercrombie, Why not let Virgil mean all he *can* mean? To me, Dante, his meaning holds divine inspiration.

Without a doubt Dante got more spiritual stimulus and suggestion out of the text than any one of Virgil's Augustan readers did. On the other hand, clearly those contemporaries *understood* the *Aeneid* more fully and accurately than any thirteenth-century mind could ever do. Necessarily so, since its assumptions were their assumptions, its words their words, its connotations their connotations.

So also with Shakespeare, the Elizabethans, and ourselves. However much we learn, we shall never understand Shakespeare as only they could understand him. As for the subtlest and most imaginative approach from our latter-day complex of beliefs—what will it give us? The product may well be very significant illumination of the modern mind; but will it be more light on Shakespeare? More than a generation ago our wisest Dante scholar, Charles Grandgent, outlined our human limits: *Wherever we go, whatever we look at, we see what is in our own minds, or what our mind is capable of assimilating. . . . the critic exhibits himself more than he strips his victim.*

Naturally we cannot, even remotely, become Elizabethans. Nevertheless we can still cast more light on Shakespeare. It will be done not by applying novel critical formulas, but by assimilating more of the Elizabethans' thought, by learning more of what they took for granted, by recovering more of the connotations of their words. An endless process; and slow, for want of trained scouts able and willing to explore. This is why the poetic country of the original Shakespeare is still a land of opportunity.

To give one small example: critics from the eighteenth century onward have learnedly discussed the rapt rhetoric of Hotspur's famous speech

> By heaven, methinks it were an easy leap
> To pluck bright honour from the pale-fac'd moon

without ever thinking to ask why—unless he is lunatic—it is especially in *the moon* that Harry Percy sees bright honour, for him to pluck and "wear without corrival". But Shakespeare's audience—who in "this most bloody *boar*" at once recognized Richard Crookback—knew why.

For the identifying badge which every Percy wears is his family's *silver crescent moon*: displayed both in *The Battle of Otterburn* and in Drayton's

> The noble Percy in that dreadful day
> With a bright Crescent in his guidehome [guidon] came.

Before Shrewsbury fight the poet again presents the renowned Percy Moon— similarly unseen by the modern eye—in the King's stern demand of Thomas Percy Lord Worcester,

> Will you
> . . . . .
> . . . move in that obedient orb again
> Where you did give a fair and natural light?

And third and last, at the climax when armed Rebellion confronts Rule—Harry Percy meets Harry Monmouth:

> I am the Prince of Wales; and think not, Percy,

138

To share with me in glory any more.
Two stars keep not their motion in one sphere,
Nor can one England brook a double reign
Of Harry Percy and the Prince of Wales.

The two great stars which cannot move in one sphere are Shakespeare's *moist star* or *wat'ry star*—the Moon of Harry Percy, and the majestic rising *day-star*—the coming Sun or King, Henry, "this Star of England".

In sum, moon, planet, and star—which we took to be three bodies far away in space—in fact all present one familiar English symbol, the Percy Moon. Recovery of this unified concept—what does it show us? That Hotspur's honour-seeking leap spells rebellion, not a mere flight of moon-struck fancy; and that the inescapable Ptolemaic astronomy of the two other passages is likewise focussed by King and Prince upon that mutinous Moon whose exorbitant pull makes the tension of this political drama. Once more we are shown that Shakespeare chooses his images with precision to enhance the play in hand; once more that much other lost significance in Shakespeare must still be waiting to be seen. And this brings us to our major matter.

For if we ask the primary question, *When were the Sonnets written?* we still find the replies of the Shakespeare handbooks agreeing only in uncertainty. Yet for the future of our knowledge it would be hard to name a guidepost which—once located—would point the way to more advantage and profit than the correct answer.

I believe that my years of active thought and search devoted to this question have led me to the answer. And I am further persuaded that this long labor would not have been needed, had my predecessors in the enquiry taken Shakespeare at his word.

But of course when I began I didn't take him at his word either. How could I, brought up in ancestral assumptions—assumptions which by endless repetition had come to be received articles of faith? To begin with, in the face of all the testimony of his own time to Shakespeare's astonishing quickness, we modern students were instructed to see him as a slow developer, a lagging follower of the fashion, an imitator of his contemporaries. Why was this? Solely because his early plays were assumed—on no firm evidence—to be late; and the Sonnets, being obviously maturer work, in consequence later still: that is, curiously stale productions of the middle or late nineties, when, as C. S. Lewis remarks, the sonnet was in its senility.

Unobtrusively turning the Mercury-quick Shakespeare of history into a case of arrested development, this question-begging logic accordingly gave us the egregiously backward Shakespeare of the lecture-room, our old familiar Mumpsimus Shakespeare, handed on by rote.

Now when a conjectural hypothesis logically followed lands us in the absurd, it is time to look for a substitute which will not end in an insult to intelligence. And the authoritative source in which to seek it is Shakespeare himself.

If we pause to think of it, we know that the typical Elizabethan sonneteer was under twenty-five years of age. And we also know that these youths in their sonnets adopted the young Petrarch's paradoxical senility—representing themselves with old age's wrinkles and white hairs. Shakespeare, in doing the same (Sonnets 22, 62, 63, 73), similarly witnesses to his own youth. And in Sonnet 138, while fashionably insisting on this preposterous old age, he lets the truth slip out—namely, that (if he acts gullible) he might be taken for a *simple* young man, *some untutor'd youth:* merely reiterating his statement in *my pupil pen* that he is young, as Samuel Daniel so often does in his *Delia.*

In short, whatever else the Sonnets may be, we have it on their author's testimony that they are—like those of his fellows—the work of a youth, a young man under twenty-five, the Mercury-quick poet his contemporaries knew. This means that they were completed about 1589. It is to this cardinal fact that the dating of his other early works must sooner or later be accommodated.

Similar disregard of Shakespeare's words in the chief "dating sonnet"—107—has in the past been responsible for failure to recognize the tremendous occasion which called it forth. Critics have disregarded his opening picture of the instant mental scene. He begins by recalling both his own recent fears and the world-wide apprehension of a doom foretold which would sweep away both his Friend and himself in the universal death.

No such appalling world-prophecy overhung either 1596 or 1603. The *only* year of the Shakespearean age to which these words can apply is the long-foretold and

> *fatal year of fearful Eighty Eight,*
> *Forethreat'ning falls of empires, realms, and kings,*
> *Out-breathing bale to every earthly wight* (Kyffin, 1588).

And the *mortal* or deadly *Moon* whose suffered eclipse has now instead ushered in joyful Peace for England is naturally not the royal *Sunne of the world . . . Great Gloriana* (Spenser), not the majestic *Sun, Elizabeth our Queen* (Aske, 1588), but the deadly Crescent, the Moon-shaped Armada of 1588, defeated by Queen Elizabeth, the Woman *clothed with the Sunne . . . and having the Moone . . . placed under her feete* (Hellwis, 1589).

The offered objection that "the crescent moon cannot be eclipsed" is as unfortunate as it is thoughtless. For notoriously the moon in any phase can be eclipsed—"cloudes Gan to eclips Lucinas siluer face" (Greene and Lodge)—just as the sun can: "Although the Sunne be oft Eclipst in cloudes" (Chr. Middleton). Also, as for enemy crescents enduring eclipses by shattering defeats at sea,

> The silver crescents in the tops they [the Turks] carried
> . . . from his fury suffer'd sad eclipses. (Fletcher, *A Wife for a Month*)

And again, at Lepanto,

> when the Turks *Moon* light
> Was so eclips't that the proud *Ottoman*
> Resign'd his title to the Ocean. (Gayton, *Pleasant Notes . . .*)

140

Sir Walter Raleigh rightly said "we can never find Shakespeare talking in vague and general terms of that which lay beyond his ken. He testifies of what he knows." And I should add, since he means to be understood, he writes what his readers can recognize. Thus when he calls his Friend of the Sonnets a King, and speaks of his royal canopy, he is not rhapsodizing, but reporting.

His friend Will *was* a King, a sovereign well known to Elizabethan London. And Shakespeareans would have recognized him long ago, had they taken the poet at his word. I can recommend this novel approach. It will be found rewarding.

Rightly to be Great

by Ruth M. Levitsky

I

What is honorable behavior for a man who finds himself in an intolerable situation? Shall he submit to the forces which have placed him in this situation—and, if so, how can he submit with dignity? Or shall he resist—and, if so, how can he resist honorably? Here are the components of Hamlet's fundamental question—how rightly to be great—a question increasingly vexed during the period when Shakespeare was at the height of his career as a dramatist.[1] To bear the unbearable is doubtless the burden of any tragic hero, but Hamlet's problem is peculiar precisely because in Shakespeare's day the question of what constitutes true nobility had come to the fore as it could not have done in a less-unsettled age.

This is not to say that complete unanimity of opinion as to the nature of noble action existed during the Middle Ages; but a peace of sorts had been made with Aristotle, and the influence of Stoicism had not yet been felt in any significant way. Toward the end of the sixteenth century, however, the changing picture of the world brought with it speculation on moral, ethical, and religious questions not heretofore considered respectable. The rising interest in Stoicism[2] invited the thinking man to examine its tenets in the light of the accepted religious teaching as well as of the received tradition of Aristotelian ethics.

The thesis advanced in the present study is that Hamlet's dilemma is occasioned by the fact that each of these sometimes-contradictory philosophies is partially "honorable" and partially "dishonorable" in the eyes of the Renaissance gentleman.[3] Inasmuch as the distinctions between these three schools of thought have (through more than three centuries of further eclecticism) become more and more obscured, it is perhaps advisable to present at this point a somewhat detailed analysis of what the Aristotelian, the Stoic, and the Christian ethic demanded of a great man.

The leading features of Stoicism with which we are here concerned are 1) the belief that the emotions can and should be completely controlled by the Reason and the Will, 2) the conviction that such control will lead to a sublime state of indifference to the evils of this life, 3) contempt for all life's "goods" except virtue, and 4) scorn of (and ultimate defiance of) the deity who controlled these other "goods." As Zeller points out, the demands of the Stoic system "developed to their legitimate consequences, require the complete extirpation of the whole sensuous nature."[4]

Theoretically a Renaissance man might very well agree with Seneca that "there is nothing so difficult and dangerous, which a man's mind cannot overcome, and that continuall meditation bringeth not in use, and no affections are so fierce and obstinate which are not tamed by discipline."[5] Put in less abstract terms, however, the doctrine might be difficult for a gentleman of honor to embrace.

> shall not a good man be angrie, if hee see his Father stroken, his Mother ravished? He shall not bee angrie, but revenge and defend them.[6]

Here, Seneca has intended to suggest the greatest possible motive for man's anger and yet to deny him the right to that emotion.

The Stoics did, however, recognize the right—or more accurately—the *duty* of revenge, the avenger being required to approach his task deliberately and unemotionally.

> A good man executeth his offices without confusion or feare, and in such sort will perform those thinges that are worthie a good man, that he will do nothing unworthie a man. Shall my Father be murthered? I will defend him. Is he slaine? I will burie him, not because I am sorrie therefore, but for that I am bound thereunto. . . . But this is a worthie matter, and well beseeming a man to shew himselfe a protector of his parents, his children, his friends, and his Countrie: not by violence, or passion, but voluntarily with judgement, and discretion, with prouidence [sic] and moderation.[7]

Plutarch wholeheartedly agrees with Seneca concerning the frame of mind proper to the executioner:

> neither hath he need to use choler as a sauce or deintie dish for to get him a stomacke and appetite to correct: but even when he is farthest off from desire of revenge, then of necessitie he is to make use of reason and wisdome to direct him.[8]

To neglect the duty of punishment entirely is to Plutarch an even graver error than to punish in anger:

> For certeinly it is not a thing so much to be blamed, for to punish one in anger, as not to punish when anger is past and alaied, and so to be retchlesse and desolute.[9]

The common people, Plutarch observes, mistake "peevish and froward unrulinesse to be fortitude and strength," whereas a true "act of rare valour" would be to extinguish ire completely.[10]

What, then, of courage? A courageous man, says Cicero, is marked by a characteristic attitude and characteristic action. The proper attitude is one of indifference to outward circumstances—this indifference resulting from the convictions that 1) nothing but moral virtue is worth striving for, and 2) one ought not to be

143

subject to the passions or to the accidents of fortune. A proper action is one which, arduous and fraught with danger, has as its end "great entreprises, and those same right profitable." Cicero admits that all the glory, honor, and profit are in the action: "but the cause, and meane that makes manlie men, is in the former [i.e., the attitude]. For in it is that, which maketh excellent corages, and such as despise the world's vanities."[11]

Though the ideal to which the Stoics aspired was a state of perpetual calm, their sanction of suicide was virtually an admission that this felicitous state is seldom if ever achieved:

> Shall we take pleasure to remain in so loathsome a prison? Shall we counsaille our selves to continue under the yoake of murtherers? Contrariwise, we will make it knowne, that in all oppressions the way of libertie is laid open to us . . . on what side soever thou turnest thy selfe, there is an end of these miseries. Seest thou yonder steepie place? from thence mayest thou descend to thy libertie. Seest thou that sea? Seest thou that River or that Pit? Libertie sitteth in the bottom thereof. Seest thou thy throat, thy wesand-pipe, thy heart? These are the meanes to escape servitude. . . . Enquirest thou which is the way to libertie? Every veine in thy bodie.[12]

In spite of their vaunted indifference, the fact of the matter is that the Stoics did recognize one enemy whom they found it possible to endure only by asserting their freedom to escape through suicide. This was the goddess Fortuna.[13] Although she had no power to pervert a man's will or corrupt his virtue, this goddess governed (and dispersed capriciously) all worldly goods—including wealth, health, life, death, and fame. Seneca is consistently bitter in his references to Fortuna. She will maltreat man's body with violence and insult; things deserved and undeserved he must suffer just as she wills for she is capricious both in rewards and in punishments.[14] The safest course with such a deity, Seneca finds, is to reduce the number of one's treasures so as to be less exposed to her injuries.[15]

Here is an attitude not properly labeled indifference; it is rather indicative of a desire to outwit the goddess. The only sure way of outwitting Fortuna, however, is to take one's own life, thus depriving her of the pleasure of her sport. Suicide is for Seneca more than an escape, more than martyrdom: it is a glorious act of defiance. It is, as Zeller puts it, "the crowning point over destiny, the highest triumph of the human will."[16]

The Roman Stoic whom Shakespeare knew[17] could hardly have failed to hold some fascination for the dramatist of the late Renaissance. Serious-minded, virtuous, proud, courageous, beset by inescapable ills—the Stoic hero must eventually face the fateful question: whether it is more noble to maintain an attitude of indifference toward outrageous Fortune or to oppose her in the only way possible —by taking arms against oneself. He might cast aspersions upon such a deity, or he might console himself that all men were in like situation. But he would not rage, he would not weep, he would not forfeit his dignity: relying upon his own Reason and his own Will, he would control the only fate that mattered—his virtue. He would administer punishment or submit to punishment alike without emotion. But there existed a point beyond which it was neither brave nor wise to remain indifferent to Fortune's blows. At this point he would substitute defiance for indifference and go to his death proud in the knowledge that he had overcome his lifelong enemy.

A basic distinction between the fortitude of the Stoic and the patience of the Christian is seen in the latter's capacity for suffering. The gospels teach that Christ himself felt pain in a very human fashion, and the Christian is generally convinced with Thomas à Kempis that, if there had been a better way to salvation than through suffering, Christ would have shown it.[18] Far from insensitive, the follower of Christ endures "in spight [sic] of the reluctance of sense."[19] Indeed, the magnanimity of Christian forgiveness lies largely in the fact that the injured party does truly suffer. "I will not," says Bishop Hall, "be a Stoic, to have no passions; for that were to overthrow this inward government which God hath erected in me; but a Christian, to order those I have."[20]

The passion of anger has its sanction for the Christian, Hall finds, in St. Paul's injunction, "Be angry and sin not" (Eph. iv.6), and in Christ's whipping the money-changers out of the temple.

> Sure [concludes Hall] if we be not thus angry we shall sin. If
> a man be so cool, as without any inward commotion, to suffer
> God's Honor to be trod in the dust, he shall find God justly angry
> with him for want of anger.[21]

Though the Christian admits anger, he (along with the Stoic) disparages honor. The "ethnicks," says John Woolton,

> avoided vice, and followed virtue through desire for praise,
> honor, and glory or through desire of dignity and authority,
> or for common concord and quietness; or else through rever-
> ence of men and fear of laws, or some such like matter: whereas
> the Christians direct all their doing to the glory of God and the
> profit of their neighbor.[22]

Bishop Hall finds that many men who recognize the worthlessness of riches nevertheless set much store by "honor." That honor is any worthier goal than riches, however, he considers the "confused opinion of those that know little," for ... "a distinct and curious head shall find an hard taske to define what point the good-nesse thereof consisteth."[23]

It is not difficult to see why honor, either as a goal or as an inner sense, might be discouraged in a doctrine that preached humility, a virtue unacceptable to both Stoic and Aristotelian. The pagan, whether he sought retribution or disdained to do so, was motivated by pride and governed by his own Reason.[24] The Christian, on the other hand, humbly relied upon the grace of God to furnish him with both strength to endure and wisdom to act. The Elizabethan schoolboy would have been told:

> My sonne, knowe this, that thou arte not hable to do these thinges of thy self, nor to walke in the commaundements of God and to serve him, without his speciall grace, which thou must learne at all times to cal for by diligent prayer.[25]

Sixteenth-century sermons and tracts abound with epithets to remind man of his lowly estate.[26] For the man who accepted his lot as a mere clod or worm, life could be a matter of sheer perseverance. As a Christian, however, he must persevere; he had no choice but to "go on in [his] course of life, here on earth in holy prayers."[27] He must never have any greater desire to die than had St. Paul when he prayed "to be loosed and to be with Christ."[28]

Personal affliction, insult, and injury must then simply be endured, neither escape through suicide nor solace through retribution being permitted. By means of the homilies the Elizabethan church-goer was repeatedly reminded of the fact that he must not only endure injury but must love the evil-doer.

> Christian charity is to love every man, good and evil, friend and foe and whatsoever cause be given to the contrary, yet never the less to bear good will . . . to every man.[29]

Shall evil then go unpunished? The homilist anticipates this question and is ready with his answer: "to an evil man they [plagues and punishments] be both good and necessary, and may be executed with charity."[30] Though vengeance must be left to God, steps must be taken by God's ministers to deter evil or correct the evil-doer. That the Prince was God's foremost minister of justice was generally accepted: he had not only the right but the duty to punish evil. The homily, "On Charity," teaches that the rebuking of vice is to be executed diligently—"the Preacher with the word, and the Governor with the sword."[31]

Certain tenets regarding Christian behavior emerge clearly from this examination of Renaissance commentary on the subject. First, the Christian does not attempt to extirpate the passions: he is grieved and angered because of the evil in the world. Secondly, evil must be punished by the proper authorities, but not in the spirit of revenge or with a concern for honor. Thirdly, the Christian does not rely primarily on his own Reason as a guide: humility teaches him to put his trust in a wisdom and goodness beyond that of which mere man is capable. Fourthly, he does not endeavor to escape his earthly trials; he must fulfill his mission on earth and await his release from suffering in God's own time.

With respect to the question of patience, both Stoic and Christian find themselves at odds with Aristotle. For Aristotle is the advocate of the mean, and it must be admitted that both the Stoic's indifference to pain and injury and the Christian's bearing of good will to every man "whatsoever cause be given to the contrary" represent extremes. According to Aristotle's definition of virtue, patience would be at its highest or best when it was at the mean:

146

> Virtue ... is a state of character concerned with choice, and
> lying in a mean, i.e. the mean relative to us, this being deter-
> mined by a rational principle by which the man of practical
> wisdom would determine it. Now it is a mean between two
> vices, that which depends on an excess and that which depends
> on defect; and again it is a mean because the vices respectively
> fall short of or exceed what is right in both passions and actions,
> while virtue both finds and chooses that which is intermediate.[32]

The passion with which we are most concerned here is anger; fortunately Aristotle chooses the use of this passion to exemplify his doctrine of the mean. A man
is not blamed, says Aristotle, because he feels anger, but because he feels it in
a certain way, for a certain reason, etc.:

> For those who are not angry at the things they should be angry
> at are thought to be fools, and so are those who are not angry
> in the right way, at the right time, or with the right persons;
> for such a man is thought not to be pained by them and since
> he does not get angry, he is thought unlikely to defend himself;
> and to endure being insulted and put up with insult to one's
> friends is slavish.[33]

This passage clearly reveals the distinction between Aristotelian and Christian
"uses" of anger: to be thought a fool or to have one's forbearance designated
"slavishness" does not distrub the Christian. It will be seen, then, that the Christian, sanctioning anger, and the Stoic, denying anger, are nevertheless allied
against Aristotle with regard to the question of Honor.

Whether it be a sense of honor or the Italianate exaggerated code of honor, its
ultimate sanction as a "good" can be traced to Aristotle's *Nicomachean Ethics,*
where honor is discussed together with its (for Aristotle) necessary concomitant,
anger. A brave man does not act merely from anger, but this passion "is often
called to the assistance of man." Citing some lines from Homer, Aristotle observes:

> these passages imply that the excitement of anger is auxiliary
> to courage, which, however, in man ought to originate in a sense
> of honor ... of all passions anger is the most nearly allied to
> this virtue [of manly courage] and would entirely accord with
> it if directed by maxims of honor.[34]

The greatest possible courage is that shown "in encountering death in battle,
and setting warlike dangers at defiance"; the brave man meets and defies death
and wounds "because it is honorable to do so." Thus it will be seen that courage,
honor, and anger were for Aristotle inextricably intertwined and that all were
essential to the highest kind of action.

Elizabethan scholars, divines, and courtiers were much exercised about the
question of the relative merits of Christian, Stoic, and Aristotelian concepts of

honor and the use of the passions. The homily, "On Contention," reveals the threat to Christian patience seen in Stoic fortitude:

> Histories be full of Heathen Men that took very meekly both opprobrious and reproachful words and injurious and wrongful deeds. And shall those heathen excel in patience us that possess Christ, the teacher and example of all patience.... Is it not a shame for us that possess Christ, to be worse than a heathen people, in a thing chiefly pertaining to Christ's religion? Shall philosophy persuade them more than Christ's word shall persuade us? Shall natural reason prevail more with them than Religion shall with us?[35]

That Sir Thomas More should have felt the need to write a treatise explaining why "the comfort devised by the old paynem philosophers was unsufficient"[36] may be counted a sign of the times. It is significant, too, that Erasmus declares a philosopher and a Christian to be synonymous[37] and that Elyot's ideal Governour and his Wise Man are both essentially Stoic.[38]

Toward the end of the century appeared the works of Guillaume Du Vair and Justus Lipsius, both presumably earnest Christians, who were nevertheless impressed with the discovery that the heathen had coped so well with a problem which the sixteenth-century Christian was finding all too difficult. Du Vair wholeheartedly endorses the doctrine of indifference, professes infinite faith in man's ability to rule his own Will through his own Reason, and asserts the necessity of studying philosophy as an aid to "ordering the affections."[39] Lipsius' definition of "constancie," if not wholly Stoic, is nevertheless not quite Christian:

> Constancie is a right and immoveable strength of minde, neither lifted up nor pressed downe with external or casuall accidents ... the true mother of Constancie is Patience and lowliness of mind, which is a voluntary sufferance without grudging of all things whatsoever that can happen to or in a man. This being regulated by the Rule of Right Reason, is the very roote whereupon is settled the high and mightie bodie of that fair oake Constancie.[40]

Lipsius speaks as confidently as does Du Vair of the state of felicity to be attained through indifference; and he sees that this indifference precludes all emotions, including hope and love.[41]

Joseph Hall, some few years later, manifests a similar admiration for the Stoics in his *Heaven upon Earth* (1606) and *Characters of Vertues and Vices* (1608). His Valiant Man "undertakes without rashnesse and performes without feare";[42] as for his Patient Man, "all things befall him alike; and he goes with the same mind to the shambles, and to the fold."[43] Christianity is, of course, superior to Stoicism, and the good Bishop mingles pity with envy as he reads over "the morall writings of some wise heathen, especially those of the Stoicall profession."[44]

148

If the Stoic morality enjoyed a revival of interest around the turn of the century, it must be remembered that it had a formidable enemy in the Aristotelian concept of the Golden Mean. Lipsius complains that Aristotle is accepted everywhere and the Stoics neglected.[45] Sir Thomas Elyot, whom we have observed praising the Stoics, had nevertheless defined fortitude as a "mediocrity between two extremes, the one in surplusage, the other in lack."[46] Magnifycence, the chief character in an early sixteenth-century play dramatizing Aristotle's philosophy of the virtues, had declared: "Measure shall never depart from my sight."[47] Even Latimer, perhaps best remembered for his extremes of Christian patience, had paid lip service to this ideal of the mean.[48] That Hall, at the beginning of the new century, has not abandoned Aristotle is evident from his description of the Wise Man: ". . . his passions are so many good servants . . . ready to be commanded by reason, by Religion."[49]

The doctrine of the mean was liable to criticism, however, with respect to the passion of anger. In *The Anatomy of the Mind*, Thomas Rogers, having already condemned the Stoics for "taking out also vertue" in the process of eliminating vice, turns upon the Peripatetics, who "also fall into error by allowing sin in some degree."[50] To buttress his charges against Aristotle, Rogers could have found support in both Cicero and Seneca. Cicero, though in general he approves of the doctrine of the mean, wishes that the Peripatetics did not "comende angrinesse and say that it is profitablie given of nature."[51] Seneca, in his essay "On Anger," refers at least three times to the harm Aristotle has done by encouraging this passion.

> Anger, saeth Aristotle, is necessarie, neither can any thing
> be atchieved without her, except she encourage the minde,
> and enkindle the spirit. But we are to use her not as a Captaine
> but as a Souldier: which is false.   *(Lib.3,ch.III.)*

> Thinke not . . . I employ my selfe unprofitably in defaming
> Anger. . . . I doe it because there are some found amongst Phi-
> losophers of the greatest note and reputation, who hath pleaded
> for her and said that she is profitable, and animateth the mind
> unto battel.   *(Lib.1,ch.IX.)*

> Aristotle stands forth, and pleads for Anger, and willes us not
> to extinguish it wholly in us. He alleadgeth that it is the spurre
> of vertue, and that if man be deprived thereof, his heart is dis-
> armed, and he becommeth recreant, idle, and unable to execute
> any great attempts.   *(Lib.2,ch.XII.)*

With the Renaissance authors of courtesy books and manuals for the education of gentlemen, however, Aristotle found much favor. These manuals, though intended to educate the complete gentleman, emphasize deeds of valor; and the honor which they declare to be the greatest of all external goods is the honor attained by feats of arms. The "principal and true profession" of Castiglione's courtier is that of arms,[52] and the author finds it impossible to pursue honorable actions without the aid of anger. When Lord Ottavanio advises a "temperance unperturbed — which renders the mind calm and full of rest, adorns it with tranquility so serene that it is never ruffled and becomes in all things obedient to reason,"[53] he sounds so much like a Stoic that Gonzago promptly challenges him:

> I do not know what virtues befitting a lord can spring from this temperance, if it is the one which removes the passions from the mind as you say. Perhaps this would be fitting in a monk or a hermit: but I am by no means sure whether it would befit a prince (who was magnanimous, liberal, and valiant in arms) never to feel whatever might be done to him, either wrath or hate or goodwill or scorn or lust or passion of any kind, or whether he could without this wield authority over citizens or soldiers.[54]

Whereupon Lord Ottaviano assures his hearers that he did not mean to suggest the complete eradication of the passions, for "even the passions contain some element of good." It is concluded, then, by these gentlemen that the passions can be helpful—wrath to aid strength, hatred of evil to aid justice—and that if these passions were wholly removed, they would leave the Reason weak, "so that it could effect little, like the master of a vessel, abandoned in great calm."

Torquato Tasso, in his explanation of the allegory of *Jerusalem Delivered*, manifests this same desire to refute the deprecators of the "ireful virtue." His Rinaldo, lover of honor, has his place in the scheme of things as well as his Godfrey, lover of wisdom. And it is clear that Rinaldo is aided in his duties by the passion of anger rather than by Reason:

> the reasonable part [argues Tasso] ought not,—for herein the Stoics were much deceived—to exclude the ireful from actions, nor usurp the offices thereof, for this usurpation would be against nature and justice.[55]

It is true that anger ought to be subjugated to Reason, but for Godfrey to attempt daring and dangerous deeds without the help of Rinaldo would be arrogant.

In England, the sanction of honor as a possession to be defended or a goal to be sought is readily seen in such manuals and tracts as Sir William Segar's *Book of Honor and Arms* and Robert Ashley's *Of Honor*. Segar, while admitting that Christian law requires men to be "of so perfect patience" as to endure quietly the most violent actions and injurious words, nevertheless recognizes the necessity of setting aside this law because none "or verie few" have attained this perfect patience.[56] Ashley's book takes issue not so much with the patient Christian as with the indifferent Stoic. His aim is

> to prove against the dul and heavye spirited, and against the abject and baseminded, that a modest desire for honor is not

150

only convenient, but above all things (virtue only excepted whych yt usually accompanieth) to be preferred.[57]

Ashley is alarmed that in his own day men are denying the claims of honor: he has even heard some say that they do not know what honor means—"that it is only a word." Such talk sounds to him more like "the voyce of a beast or of some heavy brutish and insensible creature than that of a man." That his quarrel is with the Stoics he does not leave us long in doubt: neither the Cynic, Diogenes, "nor any other Stoyck" is to be commended who teaches that honor is to be despised. If we take away honor, then magnanimity, fortitude, moderation, and decency will perish. Nobody would embrace virtue "with so great labor and paynes as yt bringeth with yt yf there were no pricks of honor to awake and stir up our minds to the study thereof."[58]

An acquaintance with the neo-chivalric code of Ashley's day, however, may help to explain why many young men were tempted to embrace this despicable doctrine of the "Stoycks." Honor had in some circles been elevated above either Reason or Christian sufferance: the code demanded the duel upon the slightest provocation and frequently called for revenge-murder of the cruelest kind.[59] These attitudes and actions depart so radically from the prescribed "mean" that it would be misleading to call them Aristotelian without some qualification. Since, however, the code depended upon the sanctions of honor and anger and upon a set of rules as to when, how long, with whom, and to what degree to exercise that anger, they may at least be designated as pseudo-Aristotelian.

The dilemma in which a Renaissance gentleman might find himself as a result of the various opinions propounded by scholars, courtiers, and divines is well summed up by one of Shakespeare's contemporaries, Sir William Cornwallis:

> About nothing do I suffer greater conflicts in my selfe then about induring wrongs; for other duties—though perhaps I seldome performe them, yet I am resolved they be done; and it is not the fault of my meditation but of my negligent flesh. But heere is set up Reputation as the Garland appointed, and he that revengeth not is not capable of this glorie ... I know what Divinitie, what Philosophie perswades; I know these wrong-doers to be wretched creatures, rather in truth to be pittied than maliced; and yet for all this I dare not yield. . . . I have not yet any outward witnesse of my valour. . . . Upon receipt of a wrong and an honest determination to forgive, I am whispered in the eare that this lenitie is injustice, that I nourish sinne with not cutting it up when I see it grow, that though I effet revenge, and revenge could do no more, yet it is not revenge—it is justice. Pitifull abuse. Anger is the mother of injustice and yet justice must lackey her Errands, fight battailes, and give her the victorie. I cannot reconcile these

together, but even in the behalfe of Truth and mercy, I will combat a received tradition.[60]

We have seen that Philosophy and Divinity are sometimes difficult to reconcile, that Philosophy itself is divided, and that Divinity prescribes different actions under differing circumstances. If Elyot and More, Lipsius and Du Vair, Hooker and Hall, Ashley and Cornwallis were aware of these discrepancies in the various respectable codes of the day, it is not surprising that Shakespeare should have allowed Hamlet a measure of confusion as to the precise nature of a "great" action.

II

How does Shakespeare dramatize this dilemma and make it basic to the tragedy of Hamlet?[61] In the background always (and sometimes in the foreground) is a distinct awareness of the Christian ethic, and Hamlet is never allowed to forget its precepts.[62] But those characters whose presence inclines him now toward honor and passionate action, now toward suicide, *apatheia*, or the cool execution of duty—these characters find their sanctions not in Christianity but in the pagan philosophies of Greece and Rome. Whether Stoic or Aristotelian, the laws by which they are guided are clear, definite, well-formulated. Hamlet, on the other hand, sees his mission as unique, his duty as peculiarly his own; and he must discover for himself how rightly to be great.

Although the debate over the relative merits of the Stoic, Christian, and Aristotelian attitudes occurs within the hero's own mind and is often revealed through his soliloquies, the issues are made clearer both for him and for us by the presence in the play of representatives of these various attitudes. Claudius and Polonius spout Aristotelian platitudes concerning the via media; the ghost, though serving as a grim reminder of the Christian after-life, bases his appeal primarily upon the argument from "nature"; the First Player shames Hamlet out of his aspirations toward a Stoic insensitivity, while the presence of Horatio inspires in him an envy of that blissful state; Fortinbras' reckless pursuit of fame underscores honor as possibly a worthy spur to action, while Laertes' behavior furnishes a perfect example of the slavery to which this honor-seeking can lead. In addition, there are recurring reminders that Hamlet has been brought up in (and indeed still lives in) at least a nominal Christian society; and finally, there is the experience of the sea voyage, as a result of which Hamlet abandons that firm reliance upon Reason taught by both Stoic and Aristotelian. The "action" of the play consists almost entirely in Hamlet's working his way through these conflicting impressions toward an understanding of what constitutes noble action.[63]

Hamlet's very worth as a human being depends upon his making the correct decision in this matter. For here is no mere academic exercise: he has come face to face with the reality of evil and the problem of how to cope with it. Very early in the play we learn (and perhaps Hamlet is only just then learning it) that the textbook prescriptions for behavior which are adequate for practically everyone

152

else in the play are inadequate for a man of his temperament in his situation.[64] Both Gertrude and Claudius reprimand him for his failure to accept what is "common" and to behave in the commonly-accepted manner. With the whole stock of Claudius' proverbial wisdom, Hamlet would have been familiar since childhood:

> you must know, your father lost a father;
> That father lost, lost his, and the survivor bound
> In filial obligation for some term
> To do obsequious sorrow: but to persever
> In obstinate condolement is a course
> Of impious stubbornness; 'tis unmanly grief;
> It shows a will most incorrect to heaven,
> A heart unfortified, a mind impatient,
> And understanding simple and unschool'd:
> For what we know must be and is as common
> As any the most vulgar thing to sense,
> Why should we in our peevish opposition
> Take it to heart? Fie! 'tis a fault to heaven,
> A fault against the dead, a fault to nature,
> To reason most absurd;   *(I.ii.87ff.)*

In effect, Hamlet is charged with not grieving by the book—not indeed by *any* of the books: he does not accept the will of God, he lacks Stoic fortitude, and he breaks the rules dictated by Reason through his failure to grieve in the right degree, at the right time, and for the right reason.

We are shortly to hear Polonius deliver himself of some "few precepts" gleaned from the measure-in-all-things school. Though Hamlet does not hear this harangue, he is well acquainted with Polonius and the Polonius ethic. After Shakespeare has presented these characters with their hypocritical mouthings and shallow discernments, he promptly takes us into another world where Hamlet calls Horatio's attention to the fact that philosophy does not have all the answers. The lines given to Hamlet in response to the ghost's demand for revenge express a disillusionment with all copy-book maxims: he will wipe from his memory

> all trivial fond records,
> All saws of books, all forms, all pressures past,
> That youth and observation copied there;   *(I.v.99ff.)*

Whatever these "saws of books" are, they are now seen by Hamlet as trivial, foolish, indeed *base* (l.105). They do not, in other words, suffice for a man charged with the duty of avenging a father killed and a mother "stained." How much less adequate must they appear to a man who sees his mission—as Hamlet shortly will—as extending beyond mere personal revenge.

Initially, however, Hamlet responds to the ghost's demand in the same spirit in which it was delivered—i.e., in a spirit of revenge:[65]

> If thou didst ever they dear father love —
>
> . . . . .
>
> Revenge his foul and most unnatural murder.
>
> . . . . .
>
> If thou has nature in thee, bear it not.   *(I.v.23,25,81)*

Hamlet will "sweep to [his] revenge," a revenge which means the destruction of the "damned, smiling villain" against whom he has a personal grievance (I.v.31, 109).

Yet, before the end of the scene we are aware that here is no ordinary revenge tragedy. Hamlet, in addition to the duty to avenge his father's death, recognizes a duty to set right the state of affairs in Denmark (I.v.189-190). The assumption of this added duty is to be made clearer later in the play, immediately after Hamlet has inadvertently killed Polonius; there he will call himself God's "Scourge and Minister,"[66] albeit in the same scene recognizing once more his duty to avenge his father (III.iv.107ff;175).

To this double motivation for the hero's action, Shakespeare has added the conflict in the mind of Hamlet concerning *how* this action may properly be pursued, a conflict pointed up for the audience by the ghost's injunction:

> howsoever thou pursuest this act,
> Taint not thy mind,   *(I.v.84-85)*

There is in the play no question, it seems to me, of whether Hamlet should act — only a question of *how* he should act.[67] What bothers Hamlet, trained in many theories and little practice, is how to perform this deed and taint not his mind.[68]

Hamlet has at some time in the recent past been a student at the University in Wittenberg, where he doubtless learned a good many "saws of books" which he might have expected to use as a guide to action in later life. Among other things, he undoubtedly learned something of the Stoic philosophy. The first conversation between Hamlet and his old school-fellows, Rosencrantz and Guildenstern, is essentially a battle of wits in which the weapons are philosophical jargon. It is a conversation which would be meaningful only among those who understood the Stoic counsel to remain indifferent to the gifts of Fortuna:

> *Ham.*   Good lads, how do ye both?
> *Ros.*   As the *indifferent* children of the earth.
> *Guil.*   Happy, in that we are not over-happy;
>   On fortune's cap we are not the very button.
> *Ham.*   Nor the soles of her shoe?
> *Ros.*   Neither, my lord.
> *Ham.*   Then you live about her waist or in the
>   middle of her favours?
> *Guil.*   'Faith, her privates we.
> *Ham.*   In the secret parts of fortune? O, most
>   true; she is a strumpet.   *(II.ii.231ff.)*

This is Seneca's capricious goddess whose blows can be averted only by reducing one's possessions and desires. The tone of levity here forbids our taking seriously any of this banter, including Hamlet's famous speech a few lines later: "There is nothing either good or bad, but thinking makes it so" (II.ii.255). The scene serves a dramatic purpose, however, in providing a signal for the audience that Hamlet and his schoolfellows are all "learned" in the Stoic philosophy.

That Hamlet has seriously been striving for just such an attitude as that expressed in his "Nothing either good or bad" speech nevertheless seems likely in view of his reaction to the First Player's portrayal of the passion of Hecuba. "The instant burst of clamour that she made," the Player recites,

> Unless things mortal move them not at all,
> Would have made milch the burning eyes of heaven,
> And passion in the gods. *(II.ii.538ff.)*

The description of old Priam's cruel slaughter and his wife's impassioned grief thereat is a speech Hamlet has for some time "chiefly loved" (II.ii.468). Recited now by this player, who "lives the part," it has the effect of making Hamlet thoroughly ashamed of his own apparent dispassionateness. How much more noble does Hecuba's grief—or even that of the Player—seem to Hamlet than the indifference of a "dull and muddy-mettled rascal" like himself. Hamlet does not merely berate himself, however; he makes plans for action, action which will presumably not be carried out with cool prudence, now that he has been given "the cue for passion" (II.ii.587).

The next time we see Hamlet—and that is very soon indeed (II.i.56ff.)—there can be no doubt about the seriousness with which he is examining the validity of the Stoic morality. His soliloquy opens with the question which every Stoic in adversity must answer for himself: is it nobler to suffer the outrages of a capricious and cruel Fortune than to escape in the only way possible—i.e., through suicide?[69] Hamlet puts the question as if he were a full-fledged Stoic, but his answer turns out to be Christian. In the midst of his musings on the nothingness of death, he catches himself up with the query: what if death be something more? He never answers his original question at all: which is nobler—to suffer or to escape? There is no escape for Hamlet; the Everlasting has fixed his canon against it.

Having just witnessed Hamlet's renunciation of dispassionateness and suicide—both of which are basic to the Stoic philosophy—how are we to account for his panegyric on Horatio's Stoicism in the very next scene? In effect, Hamlet pays tribute here to a kind of fortitude which it is not in his own nature to achieve. But is it a more noble attitude than his own? Does Hamlet find it so? Does he find in it the answer to his question—how rightly to be great? Let us examine this tribute:

> Since my dear soul was mistress of her choice
> And could of men distinguish her election,

> S'hath seal'd thee for herself; for thou hast been
> As one, in suffering all, that suffers nothing,
> A man that fortune's buffets and rewards
> Hast ta'en with equal thanks: and blest are those
> Whose blood and judgement are so well commeddled,
> That they are not a pipe for fortune's finger
> To sound what stop she please. Give me that man
> That is not passion's slave, and I will wear him
> In my heart's core, ay, in my heart of heart,
> As I do thee.   *(III.ii.68ff.)*

Hamlet has apparently known Horatio for some time; for he has admired him ever since he has been sufficiently mature to distinguish between the admirable and the contemptible. Why? Because by remaining at all times in complete control of his emotions and by accepting with indifference whatever came—good or evil—Horatio has managed to avoid suffering. A man who can do this, says Hamlet, is indeed happy, and "I will wear him in my heart's core." But how does such a man measure up to the demands made upon the hero? What is his dramatic use in the play?

That Hamlet feels a certain envy for the Stoic Horatio seems obvious; that he is not himself ever to be such a Stoic seems equally obvious. At this point it must also have been apparent to Hamlet. In his youth (at Wittenberg, perhaps?)[70]—i.e., before life forced him to face reality with more than saws of books, he had doubtless imagined himself capable of acting quite dispassionately, with the cool prudence of a Horatio. But, put to the test, he finds not only that he is constitutionally unable to dispense with the emotions, but that he is no longer sure indifference, *apatheia,* is noble. Though he may envy the Stoic (wear him in the very core of his heart), we have seen him renounce both suicide and dispassionateness as incompatible with his own nature and his own view of life. We are later to see him renounce the third basic tenet of Stoic morality—the reliance upon human Reason.

Horatio's cool, rational outlook makes him a valuable accomplice for Hamlet in his effort to "catch the conscience of the King" by means of the mousetrap play. In this play occur two lines of extraordinary significance,[71] because they sum up Hamlet's discovery about his own nature:

> What to ourselves in passion we propose,
> The passion ending, doth the purpose lose.   *(III.ii.204-205)*

Hamlet is undeniably a passionate individual: he grieves deeply, he loves ardently, he hates intensely; he cares about his friends, his parents, his country, his reputation. And he can act only when stirred by passion. He cannot bring himself to act purely according to rules or precepts, as presumably Horatio or Laertes can.

Yet he is still attempting to act from such rules when he passes up his opportunity to kill Claudius at prayer. Both a modern and an Elizabethan audience would surely agree that these are not very noble rules.[72] But the attitude expressed here was one familiar to Elizabethans: it sums up the morality of the Italian *bella vendetta*[73]—a practice which depends for its success upon the coldness of the Stoic.[74] Hamlet's analysis of the situation in these cold-blooded terms serves an important purpose: it shows up in all its horror what the eradication of the emotions can lead to. The Elizabethan audience must have reacted to this calculated cruelty in very much the same manner as a modern audience; and this must have been exactly what Shakespeare intended. Little by little the dramatist is piling up evidence to indicate that a truly great action is not performed in the Stoic manner. If he does not "preach" about it, this simply means that he is writing drama and not a treatise. He is portraying a heroic character *in action*—in the process of discovering for himself how to act. If Hamlet still thinks he can pursue revenge in this Italianate manner, this merely indicates that he does not yet know himself.

Hamlet was angry when the mousetrap play was over—so angry that he had to calm himself down before he went to his mother. Once there, however, he becomes so incensed by what appears to be one more evidence of Claudius' craftiness (as well perhaps as his mother's perversity) that he strikes with no thought of the *ultimate* in revenge. The Claudius he thinks he is killing is not "drunk asleep," "in his rage," or in "the incestuous pleasures of his bed." He is, however, where a man who means Hamlet well ought not to be, and Hamlet can kill him in the heat of passion or in self-defense.

Hamlet's castigation of his mother is surely a part of his duty as Heaven's scourge and minister.[75] Here, if ever, he makes both an earnest and an effective effort to set right the rotten state of affairs in Denmark. He is indignant, he is angry, he is harsh; but he is—so far as we can see—successful in his efforts to save his mother. He can now "leave her to heaven"[76]—as he departs for England.

Before Shakespeare allows Claudius to send Hamlet off to England, however, he causes Fortinbras—on his way to seek glory in battle—to cross the hero's path. If Horatio served to remind Hamlet of the Stoic way rightly to be great, Fortinbras exemplifies the Aristotelian way. But note that Hamlet is not shown as condoning Fortinbras' action: it is quarreling over a straw or an eggshell; it will mean the unnecessary death of thousands of men; it is action pursued for the sake of a "fantasy or trick of fame" (IV.iv.32). It is, in short, entirely irrational and not entirely ethical. The sequence of Hamlet's thoughts is difficult to follow. But the gist of the soliloquy is discernible: the two faculties which set man apart from the beasts—namely, Reason and a sense of honor—operate in opposition to each other, the former causing man to think too precisely on the event and let action go, the latter causing man to think too little and act rashly. Hamlet concludes that, in spite of its irrationality, action motivated by a true sense of honor *is* great action provided the argument is great; and conversely, the argument *is* great if honor is truly at the stake. Though at the end of the scene, we may agree with Hamlet that there is something to be said for honor, surely we also agree with him that Fortinbras' argument is not great. Again Shakespeare has drawn a contrast between the action called for by his hero and that of another character in the play.[77] And in so doing he has brought Hamlet one step further on his way to understanding what is required of him.

In Laertes we have a character motivated by still another kind of "honor," a character whose situation invites comparison with that of Hamlet. Surely *his* argument is great—it is much the same as Hamlet's—and yet his action is manifestly unheroic. Laertes exhibits both of the seemingly-contradictory extremes of behavior fostered by the neo-chivalric code of honor: the rash, headlong action prompted by desire for revenge at any cost and the controlled action prompted by a set of rules. As was pointed out above, this code derives ultimately from—though it greatly distorts—Aristotle's emphasis upon honor together with his recommendations for exercising anger at the right time, with the right person, in the right degree, etc.

By contrast with Hamlet's efforts to approach his problem calmly, we have Laertes' "That drop of blood that's calm proclaims me bastard." By contrast with Hamlet's anxiety lest he proceed unjustly against one in the seat of authority, we have Laertes' "To hell, allegiance!" And by contrast with Hamlet's respect for the Christian canon, we have Laertes'

> Conscience and grace, to the profoundest pit!
> I dare damnation. To this point I stand,
> That both the worlds I give to negligence,
> Let come what comes; only I'll be revenged
> Most thoroughly for my father.   *(IV.v.132ff.)*

In declaring what he *will* do, Laertes virtually sums up what Hamlet is at great pains *not* to do. To Hamlet, conscience, grace, and calm Reason are forces which help determine what constitutes noble action: he cannot therefore brush them lightly aside and rush blindly forth to be revenged "most thoroughly for [his] father." Such action is as impossible for him as is the cold-blooded approach of the Stoic.

Laertes' deliberation over the acceptance of Hamlet's apology appears at first glance quite inconsistent with his former rash behavior. Actually, he is in both instances concerned with acting according to the rules: he already *knew* what the code demanded of a son whose father had been murdered; but he was uncertain of the rules concerning the acceptance of apologies. "I am," he declares, "satisfied in nature,

> but in my terms of honour
> I stand aloof; and will no reconcilement,
> Till by some elder masters, of known honour,
> I have a voice and precedent of peace,
> To keep my name ungored.   *(V.ii.255ff.)*

Once more, the dramatist has provided us with a scene which underscores the very standards of conduct which Hamlet finds inadequate. "Saws of books" are again tried and found wanting. Hamlet's problem is an individual one which must be solved according to his own best insights.

158

But are these insights to be derived from Reason alone? At the time of this scene
with Laertes, Hamlet has at last discovered a more reliable guide to action than
mere passion, the sense of honor, the code of honor, dispassionate Reason, or any
combination of these. The formula for great action which he had adopted in the
course of his reflections upon Fortinbras' attitude has been superseded by one
which finds a place for faith in a Divine Providence. For Hamlet has had a remarkable experience during his enforced sea-voyage—an experience further proving
what he has sometimes appeared to have forgotten: that there are more things in
heaven and earth than are dreamed of in philosophy. Upon his return to Denmark
he attempts to describe this experience to Horatio. He was, he says, trying to
sleep when something prompted him to get up and take measures to save his life.
That this "something" was not Reason he makes perfectly clear:

> Rashly,
> And praised be rashness for it, let us know,
> Our indiscretion sometimes serves us well,
> When our deep plots do pall.   *(V.ii.6ff.)*

Hamlet sees in this incident proof that "there's a divinity that shapes our ends,
Rough-hew them how we will."[78] And the consequence of his wonderful experience is a calm acceptance of whatever is in store for him. This acceptance is stated
in terms which, though sometimes reminiscent of Stoic resignation, nevertheless
indicate a reliance upon a wise and benevolent God[79] rather than a submission
to the unjust and capricious ways of Fortuna:

> there's a special providence in
> the fall of a sparrow. If it be now, 'tis
> not to come; if it be not to come, it will
> be now; if it be not now, yet it will come:
> the readiness is all: *(V.ii.230ff.)*

Here is a readiness not felt by the Hamlet of the "too, too solid flesh" or the "to
be or not to be" soliloquies. Hamlet's calm acceptance of his destiny is not a mere
readiness to die, but a readiness to act in the knowledge that that action is the
highest and best of which he is capable and that the consequences can safely be
left to a Providence that has a care for the fall of a sparrow. The Divine Will is still
carried out by human agents, however, and Hamlet's readiness in no way relieves
him of his responsibility. Does not the responsibility of destroying this evil man
fall upon me? he has asked Horatio. And will I not be damned if I allow "this canker
of our nature [to] come / In further evil?" (V.ii.69-70). The Elizabethan homilist
could have answered Hamlet: the rebuking of vice is to be executed diligently—
"the Preacher with the word, and the Governor with the sword."

But Horatio could *not* answer this question—or at least he *did* not. This Stoic,
whose philosophy should have supplied him with all the answers, apparently has
none for his friend's dilemma. It is important to examine closely what Shakespeare
does with Horatio, because he has for so long and by so many scholars been con-

sidered the model hero whom Hamlet should have emulated.[80] Here, as elsewhere, we see Horatio unburdened by the dilemmas of real-life situations. His Stoic creed can remain intact precisely because he is not, like Hamlet, forced to put it to the test. We cannot know what he would have done had he had a father killed, a mother whored, and a kingdom taken from him. Within the context of the play he is called upon neither to suffer nor to act until the very end. And what is the role given him there? He would prove his Stoic fortitude by committing suicide. This in spite of the fact that he has already been requested to vindicate the honor of Hamlet by revealing the truth to the people of Denmark.

If you are a man, says Hamlet, do not seek to escape from this harsh world; but live and "report my cause aright" (V.ii.350). This request, coming from Hamlet as death approaches, reveals a concern which ought not to bother either a Stoic or a Christian, but which the Aristotelian has freely admitted—i.e., the concern for reputation, for "good fame," for honor.

As Hamlet's commission had included both personal revenge and purgation of the State, at death he is anxious both about his good name and the future of Denmark. And he provides for both. Life must begin anew, and who is to assume the burden of kingship? Why does Fortinbras have Hamlet's "dying voice"? There may well be some significance in the fact that Fortinbras, motivated as he was by an irrational sense of honor, seems to Hamlet most nearly fit to govern his country. Whatever significance there may be must be sought in Hamlet's experience earlier in the play; for after he casts his vote, "the rest is silence."

Let us, then, briefly review that experience as the playwright has presented it. Hamlet, seeing himself both as Heaven's scourge and minister and as the avenger of his father's murder, ruminates on the question of how to execute his commission without tainting his mind. In spite of an admiration for and an envy of a character within the play who appears able to handle problems of life and death alike with cool prudence, Hamlet is made to discover that neither in suicide nor in dispassionateness lies the true nobility: Heaven has ordained that he live and act; and though his passions may render him less than a god, they raise him above the level of a beast. Placed also in juxtaposition with characters who on the one hand act rashly and on the other, according to set rules, Hamlet reacts in such a way as to cast doubts upon their greatness. If Reason alone is not the answer, neither is passion-plus-honor. Nor is it a simple combination of these elements. Hamlet's sea-adventure as he relates it reveals the source of his final readiness: it is a reliance upon something quite irrational and quite unakin to a sense of honor. This readiness is a state not properly labeled either Stoic *apatheia* or Aristotelian measured control.

Is Hamlet at the end, then, merely the Christian magistrate performing his duty to the State? One has only to observe the manner in which he addresses the dying King to answer this question:

> Here, thou incestuous, murderous, damned Dane,
> Drink off this potion! Is thy union there?
> Follow my mother. *(V.ii.336ff.)*

This is not the voice of Christian charity. There is here an unequivocal expression of satisfaction in having avenged the wrongs perpetrated against a father and a mother. When Hamlet pours the poison down the throat of Claudius, he is not following a code of honor nor is he exercising cool prudence. His killing of Claudius is neither merely an act of duty nor merely an act of vengeance: it is both and it is something more. Having suffered with Hamlet in his long struggle to act without tainting his mind, we understand why at the end, "the soldier's music and the rites of war / Speak loudly for him" (V.ii.410-411).[81]

Hamlet has discovered how rightly to be great. As Cicero has said, it is the attitude and not the action "that makes souls preëminent." But that this attitude can be entirely devoid of human passion or entirely governed by human Reason, *Hamlet* denies. Passion combined with Reason, sensitivity combined with circumspection, faith in Divine Providence combined with faith in oneself—all these go into the final attitude and the final action, which transcend the received traditions as represented by Claudius, Laertes, the elder Hamlet, Horatio, and Fortinbras.

Notes:

(1) This article is a part of a larger project which is intended to deal with Shakespeare's changing concept of heroic behavior.

(2) The importance of the Stoic morality to the Elizabethan-Jacobean playwright was first called to my attention by certain works of Hardin Craig. See, for example, his *An Interpretation of Shakespeare* (New York, 1948), esp. pp. 179-181. See also Henry Osborn Taylor, *Thought and Expression in the Sixteenth Century* (New York, 1920), pp. 274-362.

(3) With all due respect for the valuable research done on the Elizabethan humor-psychology in interpreting Shakespeare's drama, I am more in sympathy with the sentiments expressed in an article by Louise C. Turner Forest to the effect that by relying too heavily upon Elizabethan psychology, we have "shrouded in a mist of humors the firm clear ethics on which its tragedy depends." "A Caveat for Critics," *PMLA*, LXI (1946), 651-672.

(4) E. Zeller, *The Stoics, Epicureans, and Sceptics* (London, 1870), p. 273.

(5) "Of Anger," Lib. 3, ch. XII, *The Workes both Morall and Natural of Lucius Annaeus Seneca*, trans. T. Lodge (London, 1614).

(6) *Ibid.*, Lib. 1, ch. XII.

(7) *Ibid.*

(8) The *Philosophie Commonlie Called the Morals*, trans. Philemon Holland (London, 1602), p. 127.

(9) *Ibid.*

(10) *Ibid.*, p. 124.

(11) *Thre Bokes of Duties*, (London, 1556), fol. 27. Cicero's philosophy is, of course, quite eclectic. His definition of courage seems to me to warrant putting him in the Stoic camp with referance to the question of honor as well as to the passions. C. B. Watson, however, claims that "his attitude toward honor, reputation and glory is, in all essentials, similar to that of Aristotle." *Shakespeare and the Renaissance Concept of Honor*, (Princeton, 1960), p. 25. R. M. Wenley, on the other hand, says: "We know that Cicero, ... went over to Stoicism at last." *Stoicism & Its Influence*, (New York), p. 141.

(12) Seneca, *"Of Anger,"* Lib. 3, ch. XV.

(13) See Howard Patch, "The Tradition of the Goddess Fortuna in Roman Literature," *Smith College Bulletin,* III (1922), 133.

(14) "To Marcia," 10.VI.

(15) "On Tranquility," 16.IV.

(16) Zeller, p. 317.

(17) It is not necessarily suggested that Shakespeare knew all of these sources at first hand. If he knew Montaigne, he had a fairly accurate transcription of sections of Plutarch and Seneca. See, for example, *The Essays of Montaigne done into English by John Florio* (London, 1603), III.x.263 and 276. Other possible sources available to Shakespeare will be referred to from time to time within the text of this article. As for Shakespeare's access to Cicero, see Watson, *op. cit.,* especially p. 301.

(18) *The Following of Christ,* trans. Whitford, (London, 1545?), Bk. II. ch. III, fol. ix.

(19) Richard Allstree, *The Works of the Author of the Whole Duty of Man* (London, 1682), p. 2. By contrast, Seneca describes the truly great mind as one which is not even aware of the injury ("Of Anger," 3.V). For a further comparison of these two attitudes see J. B. Lightfoot, *St. Paul and Seneca,* bound with *Epistle to the Philippians* (London, 1913), pp. 200 ff.

(20) Joseph Hall, "Meditation VII," 457, quoted by Audrey Chew in "Joseph Hall and Neo-Stoicism," *PMLA,* LXV (1950), 1137.

(21) "Medit. VI," 437-438, quoted by Chew, p. 1137.

(22) *A Christian Manual* (Cambridge, 1931), p. 200.

(23) *Heaven upon Earth and Characters of Vertues and Vices,* ed. Rudolf Kirk (New Brunswick, 1948), p. 119. No less a person than Richard Hooker in *Works* (London, 1821), II, 324, however, expressed this "confused opinion." Whether Hooker is more or less representative of Elizabethan Christianity than is Hall is not basic to my argument in this essay. The point is that the conflict which Hall saw between Christian and Aristotelian values would have been felt by many Elizabethans who did not possess Hooker's synthesizing ability.

(24) The effort to maintain an even balance between Christian humility and pagan pride was closely allied to the attempt to reconcile Reason and religion. For a discussion of this problem, see Hiram Haydn, *The Counter-Renaisance* (New York, 1950), chs.I and II.

(25) *The Booke of Common Prayer* (1549), quoted in T. W. Baldwin, *Shakespeare's Petty School* (Urbana, 1943), p. 50.

(26) Helen C. White, *English Devotional Literature* (Madison, 1931), p. 200

(27) Peter de la Primaudaye, *The French Academie* (London, 1618), p. 698.

(28) J. Norden, *A Pensive Man's Practice* (London, 1610), p. 190.

(29) *Certain Sermons or Homilies Appointed to be Read in the Time of Queen Elizabeth* (Dublin, 1767), p. 64. Both Alfred Hart, in *Shakespeare and the Homilies* (Melbourne 1934), and Alfred Harbage, in *Shakespeare and the Rival Traditions* (New York, 1952), p. 139, have called attention to the importance of the homilies in the early training of any person growing up in the Age of Elizabeth.

(30) *Certain Sermons,* p. 51.

162

(31) *Certain Sermons*, p. 52.

(32) *Nicomachean Ethics*, II.6.1107a.

(33) *Ibid.*, IV.5.1125b.

(34) *Ibid.*, III. 7-8.

(35) *Certain Sermons*, p. 113.

(36) *The Dialog of Comfort Against Tribulation* (New York, 1910), p. 310, first printed in 1533. The "times" referred to here are obviously earlier than the period when Shakespeare was dealing with the problem.

(37) However, Erasmus satirizes the Stoics in his *In Praise Of Folly* (Oxford, 1913), pp. 56-58; and his first requirement of his Prince, in *The Education of A Christian Prince* (New York, 1936), p. 150, is that he be a Christian.

(38) Elyot asserts that, nevertheless, "for this form of patience we need not go to the Greeks, for there were frequent examples of martyrs who for true religion sustained torments exceeding those of Zeno." *The Knowledge that Maketh a Wise Man* (Oxford, Ohio, 1946), p. 178; *The Book Named the Governor* (London, 1834), p. 211.

(39) *The Moral Philosophy of the Stoicks*, ed. Rudolf Kirk (New Brunswick, 1951), p. 150.

(40) *Two Books of Constancie* (New Brunswick, 1939), p. 11. Duvair and Lipsius, like More and Elyot, hoped to achieve a synthesis of Christian and Stoic morality.

(41) He commends as "lofty poesie" the phrase "neither with hope nor with fear" as a maxim to aid one in passing through the world without being infected with its sorrows (p. 84).

(42) *Heaven Upon Earth*, p. 153.

(43) *Ibid.*, p. 156.

(44) *Ibid.*, p. 86.

(45) See J. L. Saunders, *Justus Lipsius: The Philosophy of Renaissance Stoicism* (New York, 1955), pp. 73-75.

(46) *The Governour*, p. 200.

(47) *The Poetical Works of Skelton and Donne*, ed. Alexander Dyce (Boston, 1881), I. 190.

(48) *Sermons* (New York, 1906), II. 18.

(49) *Heaven Upon Earth*, p. 148.

(50) Quoted by Willard Farnham, *Shakespeare's Tragic Frontier* (Berkeley, 1950), p. 350.

(51) *Thre Bokes of Duties*, fol. 35.

(52) *The Book of the Courtier* (New York, 1929), p. 25.

(53) *Ibid.*, p. 254.

(54) *Ibid.*, p. 255.

(55) Quoted in Hiram Haydn, *op. cit.*, p. 584. I have been unable to locate an edition of *Jerusalem Delivered* which contains Tasso's explanation of his allegory.

(56) Quoted by Sr. Mary Bonaventura Mroz, *Divine Vengeance* (Washington, 1941), p. 43.

(57) (San Marino, 1947), p. 43.

(58) *Ibid.*, pp. 31-46.

(59) Paul N. Siegel, in "Shakespeare and the Neo-Chivalric Cult of Honor," *The Centennial Review*, VIII (1964), 39-70, makes clear the important distinction between the neo-chivalric cult of honor and the Christian Humanist ideal of honor. See also M. C. Bradbrook, "Virtue is the True Nobility," *RES*, I (Oct. 1957), 289-301.

(60) "Of Patience," *Essays*, ed. Don Cameron Allen (Baltimore, 1946), pp. 14-15.

(61) I am aware of the many facets of the controversy concerning the nature of Hamlet's tragedy and, indeed, of tragedy in general. Although it would be impossible to give an adequate definition of tragedy here, some notion of the view of tragedy upon which this study is based is perhaps essential to an appreciation of my analysis of the play. The following quotation from R. B. Sewall's *The Vision of Tragedy*, (New Haven, 1959), pp. 47-48, will suffice as a reasonably accurate expression of that view:
"Only man in action, 'man on the way,' begins to reveal the possibilities of his nature for good and bad and for both at once. And only in the most pressing kinds of action, action that involves the ultimate risk and pushes him to the very limits, are the fullest possibilities revealed. It is action entered into by choice.... And it leads to suffering— but choice of a certain kind and suffering of a certain kind. The choice is not that of a clear good or clear evil; it involves both, in unclear mixture, and presents a dilemma. The suffering is not so much that of physical ordeal ... but of mental and spiritual anguish as the protagonist acts in the knowledge that what he feels he must do is in some sense wrong . . . This kind of suffering presupposes man's ability to understand the full context and implications of his action, and thus it is suffering beyond the reach of the immature or brutish, the confirmed optimist or the confirmed pessimist, or the merely indifferent.... Only the hero suffers in this peculiar, ultimate way. The others remain passive, make their escape, or belatedly rally to the hero's side.... Suffering of this kind does more than prove man's capacity to endure and to perceive the ambiguity in his own nature and in the world about him. The Greeks and the poet of Job saw the suffering endured by these men of heroic mold to be positive and creative and to lead to a reordering of old values and the establishing of new."

(62) Although I see the Christian elements in the play as highly significant, it will be apparent from n. 61 that I do not look upon *Hamlet* as a "Christian tragedy"; (indeed, I question whether there is such a thing as "Christian tragedy"). I see this play as closely akin to Greek tragedy, but by Greek tragedy I do not mean one which follows Aristotle's "rules." See F. L. Lucas, *Tragedy, Serious Drama in Relation to Aristotle's Poetics* (New York, 1958) and H. D. F. Kitto, *Greek Tragedy, A Literary Study* (London, 1961).

(63) The thesis of G. K. Hunter's "The Heroism of Hamlet," *Hamlet* (London, 1963), p. 94, is remarkably similar to mine: " . . . in *Hamlet* all the possibilities reflect back to the hero; we are asked to note not only the variety of potentially heroic attitudes, but also to consider their relationship within one mind, and the possibility of choice between them. . . . his self-consciousness (especially seen in the soliloquies) is the means by which Shakespeare is enabled to collate and compare modes of heroism which (objectively considered) are essentially disparate...." I was well into my final draft of this paper before I discovered Mr. Hunter's article, but I wish to acknowledge a debt to him for having helped to clarify certain points concerning Shakespeare's dramatic devices and for affording moral support. No less a scholar than E. E. Stoll, however, in *Shakespeare Studies, Historical and Comparative in Method* (New York, 1942), pp. 136-139, denies that the "conflict in the mind" of Hamlet is the basis of the tragedy.

(64) In this respect Hamlet fits H. D. F. Kitto's description of the hero of antiquity: "He is bound to stand out above the crowd; his must be the choice at the crisis; he, the individual, must be seen at grips with his destiny." *Greek Tragedy*, (London, 1961), 3rd ed., p. 29.

(65) My view of the nature of the ghost will become clearer in the ensuing analysis of the play. Suffice it to say here that that view is for all practical purposes consonant with the opinion expressed by Robert West in "King Hamlet's Ghost," *PMLA*, LXX (1955), 1107-17. Readers interested in other views are referred to Sr. Miriam Joseph's "Discerning the Ghost in *Hamlet*," SQ, XIV (1961), 493-502; J. A. Bryant's *Hippolyta's View* (Lexington, 1961), p. 127; Sidney Warhaft's "The Mystery of Hamlet," *ELH*, XXX, (1963), 193-208.

(66) The lines read as follows: "heaven hath pleased it so,/ To punish me with this and this with me,/ That I must be their scourge and minister" (III.iv.175-177). F. T. Bowers, in "Hamlet as Minister and Scourge," *PMLA*, L (1955), 740-749, considers the conventional interpretation of these lines as offering only a "meaningless redundancy." Although he admits that some Elizabethan writers used the terms interchangeably, there was, according to him, "a general tendency to distinguish them": the *scourge* was an instrument of punishment necessarily evil and necessarily damned, whereas the *minister* was an instrument of divine retribution. Bowers' argument, if I understand it correctly, is that Heaven originally appointed Hamlet minister, albeit with the foreknowledge that he would not properly carry out the duty of a Heavenly minister (n., p. 746). Heaven, therefore, so ordered events that Polonius should be behind the arras at such a time as to receive his death blow from Hamlet—this act of murder being Hamlet's punishment for failure to delay action until Heaven was ready for him to strike. "The 'this,' " says Bowers, "with which he is punished is certainly the body of Polonius...." Hamlet, then, is punished *for his impatience* by being allowed to commit murder; he is subsequently punished *for the murder* by having his appointment as Minister converted to that of Scourge. In this manner, Professor Bowers explains the "syntactical relationship between the first statement about the double punishment, and the second, 'That I must be their scourge and minister.' "

My own explanation of these lines is much simpler: I accept the terms "scourge and minister" here as constituting a redundancy. The first "this" in question I take to refer to the noun clause, "That I must be their scourge and minister." (The second "this" refers to Polonius—"this wretched, rash, intruding fool"). Hamlet designates his appointment as scourge and minister a punishment for the same reason that he has earlier (I.v. 189-190) termed it a "cursed spite" that ever he should have been the one born to set right what was "out of joint" in Denmark.

(67) I am indebted to Hardin Craig for the germ of my thesis. A sentence in his *An Interpretation of Shakespeare* (New York, 1948), p. 188, was the starting point of my investigation: "It must be remembered that action alone will not satisfy the demand; it must be wise and fitting action."

(68) The complete sentence reads as follows: "But, howsoever thou pursuest this act,/ Taint not thy mind, nor let thy soul contrive/ Against thy mother aught; leave her to heaven,/ And to those thorns that in her bosom lodge, "To prick and sting her." Paul Siegel, in "Discerning the Ghost in Hamlet, *PMLA*, LXXVIII (1963), 148, suggests that "taint not thy mind" points *not* back to "howsoever thou pursuest this act" but forward to "against thy mother aught." The expression, however, becomes strangely awkward in this case: "Taint not thy mind ... against thy mother aught." Siegel may have in mind some relationship between the folio version and that of the 1603 Quarto: "If thou hast nature in thee, beare it not,/ But howsoever, let not thy heart/ Conspire against thy mother aught," (ll. 527-9).

(69) I am aware that the currently popular interpretation of "to be or not to be" is "to act or not to act" rather than "to exist or not to exist." This I take to be a reflection of the contemporary interest in existentialism, a philosophy which makes "being" synony-

mous with acting—with being engagé. The obvious link with Stoicism, however, seems to me a sound argument for the traditional reading.

(70) A. C. Bradley has an interesting note on the question of how long Hamlet has been away from Wittenberg. See his *Shakespearean Tragedy* (New York, 1904), p. 323.

(71) On the whole, I am in sympathy with Morris Weitz's objection to the practice of making one passage from the play a statement of its "philosophy." Weitz, in *Philosophy in Literature* (Detroit, 1963), pp. 46-49, cites Lily B. Campbell's *Shakespeare's Tragic Heroes* (New York, 1960), p. 136. Miss Campbell sees in the passage containing these lines the dominant idea of the play. Her interpretation differs considerably from mine, however.

(72) Bowers, in his *Elizabethan Revenge Tragedy* (Gloucester, Mass., 1959), pp. 90 ff., makes the point that a hero who used the Italianate revenge devices would not elicit a favorable reaction from the audience. Stoll seems to agree with this view. (See his *Shakespeare*, p. 71).

(73) Jacob Burckhardt describes the vendetta in part as follows: "Cool-headed people declared it [the act of vengeance] was most worthy of praise when it was disengaged from passion and worked simply from motives of expedience.... [It demanded] a combination of circumstances for which it was necessary to wait patiently." *The Civilization of the Renaissance in Italy* (New York, n.d.), pp. 267-268.

(74) Plutarch had advised "when the storme is overblowne,... then if upon mature deliberation, when our mind is staied and our senses settled, the thing appears to be naught [i.e. evil], we are to hate and abhor it; and in no wise either to for let or put of [sic] or altogether omit or forbeare correction." *The Morals*, pp. 125 and 127. It is by no means suggested that Plutarch or any other Stoic had in mind any such cruelty as Hamlet's plan reveals. But the calculating manner required for the successful execution of this type of revenge surely has its source in just such dispassionateness as the Stoics recommend. The relationship of the vendetta to Stoicism is perhaps roughly that of the neo-chivalric code to the true Aristotelian concept of honor.

(75) It is difficult to understand why Sr. Miriam Joseph, in *SP*, LIX (1962), 129, considers Hamlet's behavior to his mother both an act which "brings upon him ... an avalanche of sorrows" and a violation of the ghost's command. The ghost's injunction is "nor let thy soul contrive/ Against thy mother aught." Surely Hamlet is not here contriving against his mother: he is doing his best to save her. The ghost goes on to say, "leave her to heaven" and her conscience, but it seems pretty obvious that Gertrude's conscience needed stirring up. Hamlet is cruel only to be kind.

(76) It is important to note the Christian advice Hamlet gives his mother: repent, confess, in the future abstain from lust. Here and in many other places (e.g. Hamlet's and Laertes' mutual forgiveness in V.ii. 340 ff.) we are made aware of the all-pervading Christian influence in Hamlet's upbringing. Nevertheless, I do not think Shakespeare had in mind any Christian "message" in this play. Roland M. Frye has recently published a valuable book on the subject of Shakespeare's use of Christian doctrine, *Shakespeare and Christian Doctrine* (Princeton, 1963). It is to be regretted, however, that he selected almost exclusively Protestant sources to buttress his argument.

(77) G. K. Hunter (*op. cit.,* pp. 94-96) puts very aptly Shakespeare's achievement here: "The admirable qualities of Fortinbras are focused in the ... soliloquy, 'How all occasions ...,' and it is clear enough from this why Hamlet admires Fortinbras ...; but one can see from it why Fortinbras cannot be the hero of the play ... In the life of the play Fortinbras' efficient kind of heroism is fairly insignificant.... We can hardly regret that Hamlet has failed to be like him."

166

(78) Harold C. Goddard in *The Meaning of Shakespeare* (Chicago, 1951), p. 376, undertakes to show that in this passage "divinity" is merely made a justification for Hamlet's callous action in sending Guildenstern and Rosencrantz to their deaths. He misses the point, it seems to me, concerning the parenthetical clause with its apostrophe to rashness.

(79) The Stoic did not believe that Divine Providence was concerned about the individual. (See Zeller, *op. cit.*, p. 167). For a large body of comment on this question, see S. F. Johnson, "The Regeneration of Hamlet," *SQ*, III (1952), 187-207.

(80) D. G. James' assertion may be taken as an example of the many expressions of admiration for Horatio: "the moral and intellectual confusion of Hamlet, and then the calm and impregnable bearing of Horatio, are driven hard home as the inner spiritual setting of the ensuing climax of the play." *A Dream of Learning* (Oxford, 1951), p. 52.

(81) Patrick Cruttwell, in "The Morality of Hamlet," *Hamlet* (London, 1963), pp. 119, 128, rightly points out that "[The critics] have forgotten that Hamlet is at war" and that "war and murder are not synonymous for Shakespeare." Hamlet, says Cruttwell, "has done things, as we all do in wars, he would rather not have done; but he believes it to be a just war, and all in all, he has borne himself well. That this is how Shakespeare saw it,. the ending of the play convinces me; for why else should

> The soldier's music and the rite of war
> Speak loudly for him?"

Thematic Patterns in Twelfth Night

by Barbara K. Lewalski

Twelfth Night achieves astonishing success in fusing a great multiplicity of elements into an organic whole, a poetry-filled, song-drenched world that stubbornly resists analysis. To isolate one or more thematic or dramatic strands for commentary in any Shakespearean play is inevitably to simplify, but this must seem especially true in regard to that intricate and perfectly wrought artistic universe that is Illyria. Yet precisely because the play dazzles by its shimmering surface, its richly variegated texture, and its subtlety of nuance and meaning, its fundamental thematic patterns have proved elusive. Without intending to restrict the meanings of the play to the themes derived herein by analysis of action and language, I would argue that these thematic patterns display a dimension not usually recognized in criticism of the work —a core of unified, cohesive meaning and a carefully articulated dramatic and poetic structure through which that meaning is adumbrated.

Recent studies linking the play with traditional holiday celebrations have greatly illuminated its mood and theme. Leslie Hotson has advanced the plausible theory that the play may have been written for and first performed at a Twelfth Night celebration before the Queen at Whitehall on January 6, 1601, at which a visiting Italian nobleman, Don Virginio Orsino, was a guest. Hotson points out that the play is generally understood to have been written either shortly before or shortly after 1600, that the character Orsino may have been intended as a compliment to the visitor, and that one of Don Orsino's letters mentions that he saw on the Twelfth Night occasion a "mingled comedy, with pieces of music and dances."[1] The evidence is suggestive but not conclusive. At any rate, though, we know from the diary of John Manningham that the play was performed at the Middle Temple on another Christmastide festival occasion, the feast of Candlemas, February 2, 1602.[2]

Whether the play was specifically written for the 1601 Twelfth Night celebration at Whitehall or not, it reflects, as C. L. Barber has pointed out,[3] the spirit and form of traditional Christmastide festivities at court and in the great houses of England, festivities which derive ultimately from the pagan Saturnalia held at approximately the same period. The primary feature of the celebrations for the twelve days of Christmas and especially those for Twelfth Night or Epiphany involved the creation of a *Festus*, or "Lord of Misrule" to preside over the maskings, interludes, music, song, and other merrymaking; he embodied the release provided by the holiday occasion from the social and psychological restraints of everyday, a deliberate fooling and disruption of decorum which seems to be a kind of madness but which may lead to a reintegration of self and society on a more perfect level. In the play Sir Toby Belch assumes the role of a Lord of Misrule (Malvolio declares that he keeps "uncivil rule" in the night hours) and the Clown Feste is by his very name identified as the embodiment of the festival spirit.

Moreover, though the point has received little attention, I believe it can be shown that the central themes and motifs of this play contain something of the religious significance associated with Epiphany and with the spirit of Christmastide. By this statement I do not imply that the play is an allegory in which characters and incidents are designed to stand for or mean abstract qualities or religious personages. Nor is Shakespeare's method here much like Plato's mode of allegory, in which a particular sensible object (here the dramatic fiction) has its own kind of reality but yet reflects or images forth something in the realm of Forms or Archetypes which is more real. Rather, Shakespeare's method resembles, and was probably formed by, that other tradition of allegorical interpretation which was still influential in the Renaissance, namely the tradition of Christian typology, whereby certain real historical events and personages from the Old Testament and (more significantly for the present purposes) from certain classical fictions such as the *Metamorphoses* or the *Aeneid* were seen to point to aspects of Christ and of the Gospel story without losing their own historical or fictional reality.[4] This mode of reading could and sometimes did lead to a swallowing up of the type, the particular historical event or classical fiction, in the antitype, but such emphasis was not inevitable: one might also focus primarily upon the typical event or story, deepening its meaning and significance by allusion to the antitype which restates, fulfills, and perfects all its themes. In *Twelfth Night* Shakespeare's incorporation of certain religious significances into his dramatic fiction rather resembles the typological treatment of some classical stories and completely reverses the Platonic emphasis, being incarnational rather than transcendent in focus. In Shakespeare's play the particular story, the created fiction, draws into itself and embodies larger meanings and significances but the focus remains always on the dramatic microcosm: the word is made flesh and continues to dwell among us. However limited or widespread such a mode of vision may be in Shakespeare's total work,[5] it is obviously wholly appropriate in a play celebrating the Christmas festival.

Illyria is one of several idealized locales in Shakespeare's romantic comedies and romances, a "second world" markedly different from and in most respects better than the real world by reason of its pervasive atmosphere of song and poetry, its dominant concern with love and the "good life" (that is, the life of revelry), and its freedom from any malicious villany. Other idealized locales such as the Forest of Arden, the forest of *A Midsummer Night's Dream*, Prospero's island, and Perdita's pastoral refuge, present what Northrop Frye terms "green worlds" or John Vyvyan labels "retreats in the wilderness"[6] into which characters move from the world outside, within which they establish new comic relationships and clarifications, and from which they then return to the real world. But the case with Illyria is different: the characters who enter it from outside, Viola and

Sebastian, do not leave it again; moreover they are not formed or altered by it, or in it, or under its influence, but they are themselves the chief agents in reordering and perfecting Illyrian life.

Something of the special quality of Illyria is indicated by the first use of the name in the dialogue, as Viola specifically contrasts Illyria with Elysium:

> *Viola:* What country, friends, is this?
> *Captain:* This is Illyria, lady.
> *Viola:* And what should I do in Illyria?
> My brother he is in Elysium. (I.ii.1-4)

At the same time, however, Illyria is related to Elysium through the melodic, romantic sound of the two words and their identical syntactical positions. Indeed the dominant Illyrian concern with song, music, poetry, good cheer, and love gives the place an idyllic, Elysium-like atmosphere. This idyllic aspect may be more precisely defined when one considers that the avowed antagonist of Illyria's accustomed life and activities is Malvolio—Bad Will—whose name is justified and interpreted by Olivia's comment, "O, you are sick of self-love, Malvolio, and taste with a distempered appetite. To be generous, guiltless, and of free disposition, is to take those things for birdbolts that you deem cannon bullets" (I.v.85-88). If Malvolio's "Bad Will" (self-love) constitutes the antagonistic force to the life of Illyria we may be directed by this fact to the recognition that the Elysium-like quality of this place emanates from a festival atmosphere of *Good Will* which has banished active malice and radical selfishness and has created a genuine community. These terms invite recall of the Christmas message proclaimed by the angels, rendered in the Geneva bible as "peace on earth, and towards men good will," and in the Rheims New Testament as "on earth peace to men of good will."[7] Illyria would seem to be a realm ready for, open to, and perhaps already experiencing in some measure the restoration and "peace" promised in the angelic message: the charity of the play's spirit is such that Malvolio himself is invited at the conclusion to share in this special condition. This context gives significance to the full title of the play, "Twelfth Night: Or, What you Will." Instead of being merely an invitation to whimsical response and interpretation the subtitle would seem to point to the thematic opposition of Good and Bad Will in the play, and to the fact that the promises of the Christmas season attend upon or include the spirit of Good Will.

But if Illyria is in some respects related to Elysium as a place of Good Will exhibiting the spirit of the season, it is also a place much in need of the restoration and peace of the Christmastide promises. The name Illyria may be intended to suggest *illusion* in the sense of distortion, disorder, and faulty perception of self and others; at any rate, as J. R. Brown has pointed out, these are all dominant features of Illyrian life.[8] Barber notes that "madness" is a key word in this play:[9] almost every character exclaims about the madness and disorder afflicting other people and sometimes himself as well. Malvolio coming to stop the midnight revels of Sir Toby and Sir Andrew asks, "My masters, are you mad?" (II.iii.80). Sir Toby in his cups is said by Olivia to speak "nothing but madman" (I.v.101-102). Malvolio's ridiculous behavior after he is gulled by Maria's letter is termed a "very midsummer madness" (III.iv.51). Olivia identifies her love-madness with what she thinks to be Malvolio's real lunacy, "I am as mad as he, / If sad and merry madness equal be" (III.iv.13-14). Orsino describes his fancy as "high fantastical" (I.i.15). Sebastian subjected to the apparently gratuitous attack of Andrew Aguecheek asks, "Are all the people mad?" (IV.i.25). Feste asks the supposed lunatic Malvolio, "tell me true, are you not mad indeed? or do you but counterfeit?" (IV.ii. 110-111). This pervasive "madness," while it is not malicious or vicious and may even be in some respects restorative, nevertheless leads each person whom it afflicts towards a culpable self-centeredness and a potentially dangerous indulgence of emotional excess. Illyria is badly in need of restoration to order and peace, but such a restoration as will also preserve the merriment, sponteneity, and sense of human community displayed in the "mad" state.

Malvolio, by repudiating any share in the Illyrian "madness" shows himself more lunatic than any, for he repudiates thereby the greatest goods of human life and the common bonds of human kind, love and merrymaking. His fundamental "bad will" is shown both in his attempted repression of merrymaking which calls forth Sir Toby's immortal comment, "Dost thou think, because thou art virtuous, there shall be no more cakes and ale?" (II.iii.105-106), and in his loveless, wholly ambition-motivated aspiration to wed his mistress Olivia. His dislike of revelry, his sober garb and deportment, his trick of ascribing his apparent success in social climbing to the direct intervention of God—"It is Jove's doing, and Jove make me thankful" (III.iv.69)—substantiate Maria's tentative identification of him as "sometimes . . . a kind of Puritan" (II.iii.128). But she further observes that he is not a Puritan as a matter of principle, but is rather a "time-pleaser," and "an affectioned ass" who spends his time "practicing behavior to his own shadow" (II.iii.135, II.v.14-15). He is victim not so much of Maria's trick as of his own self-delusion and hypocrisy, for he speculates about advancing himself by marrying Olivia well before he discovers the faked letter, and he quickly discards his solemn dress and sober deportment when he thinks Olivia has urged this course as a means to his advancement. One whose self-regard, self-delusion, and absurd ambition cause him to exclude himself deliberately from human merriment and human love is obviously a greater madman than the most abandoned reveller or the most fantastic lover in Illyria, and Maria's trick, which causes Malvolio to be taken for a lunatic, points symbolically to the real lunacy of his values. Since he so richly deserves his exposure, and so actively cooperates in bringing it upon himself, there seems little warrant for the critical tears sometimes shed over his harsh treatment and none at all for a semi-tragic dramatic rendering of his plight in the "dark house."

Sir Toby Belch, Sir Andrew Aguecheek, and Fabian represent the life dedicated to good cheer and merriment, song and revelry, which is constantly escaping from "the modest limits of order" (I.iii.7-8). But though usually engaging and harmless this love of disorder and revelry also shows a less attractive side: Toby reveals his capacity for selfish manipulation in defrauding his boon companion Andrew

Aguecheek out of his fortune on the pretext that Andrew has a chance for Olivia's hand, and Andrew demonstrates the same trait by aspiring to Olivia chiefly as a means to recoup the fortunes wasted on revelry. Also, Toby's jests sometimes have a potential for unconscious cruelty: witness the pain caused to Viola disguised as Cesario when Toby engineers a duel between Cesario and Andrew.

Olivia displays two varieties of disordered passion. Her melancholy takes the form of excessive grief and ostentatious mourning rituals for her dead brother, appropriately described in Valentine's exaggerated language: "The element itself, till seven years' heat, / Shall not behold her face at ample view; / But like a cloistress she will veilèd walk, / And water once a day her chamber round / With eye-offending brine" (I.i.27-31). This melancholic grief gives her some common bond with that scorner of pleasure and love, Malvolio: she herself declares that his "sad and civil" demeanor is appropriate to her state (III.iv.4-5), and he suggests the same point when he denies her any community of feeling with Sir Toby, "she's nothing allied to your disorders" (II.iii.89). But Toby knows well that he is "consanguineous," that he is "of her blood" (II.iii.71). That Toby has the right of it is clear when Olivia falls madly in love with Viola-Cesario, developing hereby a new madness which acts in some ways as a restorative in that it draws her away from the bad will, the self-love that Malvolio represents and fixes her devotion upon a worthy object. But this new "most extracting frenzy" of love which afflicts her is attended by delusions regarding the object (her Cesario is the disguised Viola), and a self-regarding determination to have Cesario whether he will or no, using any means, even bribery, to win him: "How shall I feast him? What bestow of him? / For youth is bought more oft than begged or borrowed" (III.iv.2-3).

The Duke Orsino, indulging his unrequited passion for Olivia, is in the throes of another kind of madness—love-melancholy—characterized by giddy appetite, unregulated fancy, self-indulgence. His graceful opening speech reveals his self-indulgent posturing in the role of love-sick swain: he desires "excess" of music to feed the appetite of love even to surfeiting, he fancies himself an Acteon turned to a hart and pursued by his desires, he seeks out "sweet beds of flow'rs" as the appropriate setting to promote his "love-thoughts." He gives way to, and indeed takes pride in the "unstaid and skittish" behavior which he thinks proclaims him a lover, and seems oblivious to the self-contradiction in his logic when he first proclaims to Cesario that men's fancies in love are "more giddy and unfirm, / More longing, wavering, sooner lost and worn, / Than women's are," and a few moments later observes that women's love lacks "retention. / Alas, their love may be called appetite, / No motion of the liver but the palate, / That suffers surfeit, cloyment, and revolt" (II.iv.17, 32-34, 95-98). Orsino's disorder also has its darker side: it is based upon self-delusion, for the viewer sees that Orsino is in love with *love* rather than with Olivia; it leads to disregard of the lady's feelings in being unable to love him, manifested especially when he urges Cesario to "leap all civil bounds" in pressing his suit; and it leads finally to a frenzy of jealousy and hurt pride wherein he offers violence to his beloved page Cesario: "I'll sacrifice the lamb that I do love / To spite a raven's heart within a dove" (V.i.124-125).

Opposition to the forces of self-love and disorder in Illyria is offered by certain characters who embrace wholeheartedly the human activities of love and merry-making but who are preserved from "madness" by positive ordering principles within themselves and who project these principles as forces to restore and re-order the community.

Maria embodies one such restorative force within Illyria: sheer wit. Early in the play Feste points to her special quality, terming her "as witty a piece of Eve's flesh as any in Illyria" (I.v.25-26). Maria employs her wit as contriver and executor of the masterful plot against Malvolio: her faked letter is cleverly framed so as to confirm Malvolio's self-delusions about Olivia's regard for him, and the letter's recommendations that Malvolio affect yellow stockings, cross-garters, constant smiles, and surly behavior are brilliantly calculated to insure his self-exposure. The power of Maria's wit is thus addressed to the revelation and punishment of the "madness" involved in self-delusion, self-love, and hypocritic affectation of virtue. Maria's wit becomes an instrument for further reformation when Sir Toby Belch out of sheer delight in her witty plot offers to marry her: there can be little doubt from her success in managing Sir Toby and his associates throughout the play that she will succeed henceforward through wit in controlling Toby's ex-cesses without in the least repressing his gaiety.

The clown Feste is the second force working from within to reorder and perfect Illyria. In many respects he is Malvolio's opposite, incarnating the spirit of festival Good Will. He frequents Orsino's court as well as Olivia's house, takes part in the midnight revels of Sir Toby, and masquerades as Sir Topas the clergyman coming to exorcise "Malvolio the lunatic," explaining this ubiquity in the following terms, "Foolery, sir, does walk about the orb like the sun; it shines everywhere" (III.i.37-38). His foolery is a consciously adopted and controlled foolery which is a far cry from the madness and disorder rampant in Illyria; it is compacted of wit and song and is firmly aligned with the forces of love and merrymaking, but is conscious also of other perspectives and harsh realities.

One aspect of Feste's restorative role is his function as "licensed Fool" exer-cising his wit to stalk wise men's folly: as Viola declares, "This fellow is wise enough to play the fool, / And to do that well craves a kind of wit. / . . . For folly that he wisely shows, is fit; / But wise men, folly-fall'n, quite taint their wit" (III. i.58-66). Feste's jest displaying Olivia as a fool in mourning for a brother whom she believes to be in heaven, achieves considerable success: its curative effect upon Olivia is immediately evident in her compliment to his wit, her defense of the fool's role against Malvolio's diatribe, and her keen insight into Malvolio's "self-love." But Orsino is less responsive to the fool's jest upon his giddy love melancholy—"Now the melancholy god protect thee, and the tailor make thy doublet of changeable taffeta, for thy mind is a very opal" (II.iv.72-74)—although his discordant passions are often soothed by that other important aspect of the fool's role, his song. Feste also undertakes the care of the reeling Sir Toby when his drunkenness has progressed to the stage of "madness," declaring, "the fool shall look to the madman" (I.v.131-132).

Finally, Feste in the guise of Sir Topas the curate (the topaz stone was traditionally thought to cure madness)[10] endeavors to cure Malvolio's "lunacy" by witty mockery designed to point out the true madness of his attitudes. Responding to Malvolio's constant protestations of his sanity, Feste replies, "Madman, thou errest. I say there is no darkness but ignorance, in which thou are more puzzled than the Egyptians in their fog" (IV.ii.42-44). The exchange about Pythagoras' opinion concerning the transmigration of souls is not merely comic dialogue since it deals with the sources of Malvolio's lunacy: lack of sensitivity to others, lack of concern for any life beyond his own. Feste accordingly declares that Malvolio should be left alone in darkness until he embraces Pythagoras' opinion, "and fear to kill a woodcock, lest thou dispossess the soul of thy grandam" (IV.ii.57-59). Sir Topas also mocks Malvolio as one possessed of the devil or as himself a kind of comic Satan cast into a dungeon dark "as hell" (IV.ii.34-35). Assuming the tones of an exorcist he calls, "Out, hyperbolical fiend!" (IV.ii.25), and again, "Fie, thou dishonest Satan. . . . I am one of those gentle ones that will use the devil himself with courtesy" (IV.ii.31-33). These exchanges are brilliant comedy, but they also point to the fact that Malvolio's ill will derives ultimately from the Satanic principle: self-love directed toward self-advancement. Finally, resuming his own form, Feste achieves Malvolio's release by carrying a letter from him to Olivia—identifying himself in this action as the "old Vice" of the morality-play tradition serving the "goodman devil" (IV.ii.121, 128).[11]

The forces of wit and festival—of Good Will—can do much to reorder and restore Illyria but they cannot do everything. They can in large part reclaim Olivia from melancholic surrender to excessive grief, they can control and care for Sir Toby, they can expose the real "lunacy" of Malvolio and cast him forth as comic Satan into the bondage and darkness which was supposedly the fate of Satan himself at the nativity of Christ.[12] But they cannot reform Malvolio, they cannot deal effectively with the love disorders of Orsino and Olivia, and they cannot restore the community as a whole to the "peace" that is the special promise of the season. For this a force must come from outside, presenting a pattern of perfect love and perfect order, and having power to produce these qualities in the community. Such a force enters the Illyrian world in the persons of the twins, Viola and Sebastian.

Though the two are dramatically separate, Viola and Sebastian represent thematically two aspects of the same restorative process. This fact is suggested partly by an identity in their physical appearances so absolute that they themselves recognize no differences: Viola declares, "I my brother know / Yet living in my glass. Even such and so / In favor was my brother, and he went / Still in this fashion, color, ornament" (III.iv.359-362), and Sebastian seeing Viola in her disguise as Cesario asks, "Do I stand there" (V.i.218). More important, there is a remarkable identity in the events of their lives: both endure a sea tempest, both are saved and aided by good sea captains, both are wooed by and in a manner of speaking woo Olivia, both are forced to a duel with Andrew Aguecheek, both give money to Feste, both are in the end betrothed to their proper lovers. By these parallels the twin motif is made to do much more than to provide occasion for comic misapprehension and misunderstanding, though it does that also in good measure.

Viola, disguised throughout the play as the page Cesario, is the embodiment of selfless love (as Maria is the embodiment of wit and Feste of festival foolery); as such she provides a direct contrast to the self-centered passions of Orsino and Olivia and at length inspires both to a purified love. Herself desperately in love with Orsino from her earliest encounters with him, Viola-Cesario acts with perfect selflessness in her difficult position as his emissary in wooing Olivia. Though she endeavors to talk both Olivia and Orsino out of their hopeless passions, she is above any duplicity to serve her own interest: rather she presses hard her master's case with Olivia, she can pay just tribute to the beauty of her rival, she is moved to pity rather than mockery when she discovers Olivia's unlucky attraction to her disguised self, she never betrays or scorns Olivia's foolish manifestations of affection, and she is even willing to be sacrificed by Orsino in his fit of jealous rage. This pattern of selfless love acts finally to inspire right love in Olivia and Orsino: Olivia's attraction to the 'outside' but also to the inner worth of Viola-Cesario brings her to discard completely her self-indulgent grief and readies her for the final transfer of her affection to Sebastian, Viola's alter ego and the right recipient of her love. Orsino is inspired almost at once to love of his "boy" Cesario (Valentine comments on the suddenness and depth of the affection in I.iv.1-3) and is so moved by the story of Viola's constant love and hard service undertaken for him that he loves her at last in her own person.

Because her love is selfless, Viola is able to embrace love fully, freely, and at once, to share in the common human turbulence of feeling attending upon love without ever giving way to the madness and disorder that accompany the selfish passions of Orsino and Olivia; she is thus a pattern of the ordered self as well as of selfless love. In this respect Viola is specifically contrasted with Olivia: both have lost (as they suppose) dearly beloved brothers, but Olivia has disordered herself and disrupted her household by giving way to excessive grief whereas Viola steels herself to act in accordance with the needs and necessities of her situation. Viola is also directly contrasted with Orsino: both are victims of unrequited love, but whereas Orsino gives way to love-sick posturing and giddy behavior, Viola can endure with patience. Viola-Cesario's playful description to Orsino of 'his' sister's pining away from unrequited love suggests the strength of her own affection for Orsino but also offers a significant contrast to her own behavior:

> She never told her love,
> But let concealment, like a worm i'th'bud,
> Feed on her damask cheek. She pined in thought;
> And, with a green and yellow melancholy,
> She sat like Patience on a monument,
> Smiling at grief. *(II.iv.109-114)*

Viola is patient and smiles at grief, but she poses on no monuments: she does not pine, she does not give way to melancholy of any color, and her damask cheeks apparently retain their bloom.

175

Also, because she is ruled by selfless love Viola can wait patiently upon time for the manifestation, the epiphany which must resolve the difficulties. This waiting observes the finest balance between inaction and precipitancy. Viola never retreats to inaction despite the difficulties of her situation: immediately after the shipwreck she laments, "O that I . . . might not be delivered to the world, / Till I had made mine own occasion mellow, / What my estate is" (I.ii.42-45), but she nevertheless determines upon a course of action. Having determined, she never supposes that her own action will in itself resolve all difficulties but commits the event to "time": "What else may hap, to time I will commit" (I.ii.60). Or again, "O Time, thou must untangle this, not I; / It is too hard a knot for me t'untie" (II.ii.39-40). But in thus waiting upon time she never forces any issue: after her encounter with Antonio who mistakes her for Sebastian (III.iv) she is reasonably sure that her brother is alive—"O, if it prove, / Tempests are kind, and salt waves fresh in love" (III.iv.363-364). But despite the steadily mounting pressure upon her resulting from the mistaken identities—Antonio's rage, Olivia's chiding, Orsino's offer to kill her—she gives no hint that she has a twin brother who may hold the key to the confusions. The epiphany must be allowed to come when it will, and she endures in patience until the revelation is given.

Sebastian's role is to bring to determination the issues which Viola begins, and to resolve the difficult situations which she must endure until his manifestation. Whereas Viola must constantly give selfless love and service to others. Sebastian is able at once to inspire selfless, devoted love for himself: his friend Antonio risks danger and imprisonment to minister to Sebastian's needs in the strange town, and later risks life itself for him in undertaking a duel in his supposed defence. The pattern is repeated when Olivia (thinking him Cesario) proclaims her love for him at first sight and proposes a betrothal. His immediate decision to accept that betrothal despite his perception that it is grounded in some error, and his forthright response to the attack of Andrew and Toby in which he gives each a "bloody coxcomb" show a power of firm determination which make possible the restoration of order to the land.

The complementary roles of Viola and Sebastian in Illyria may on the basis of what has been said be seen to reflect the dual nature and role of the incarnate Divine Love, Christ, in accordance with the Christmastide theme implied in the play's title. Recognition of such a dimension does not, it should be reëmphasized, make the Viola-Sebastian story an allegory of Christ's action in the world, but rather presents this dramatic fiction as a type of that ultimate manifestation of Divine Love—a reflection, an analogue, another incarnation of it.

The dual nature of Christ as human and divine, and the two modes in which his role was executed—his humiliation as suffering servant and his exaltation as divine king—were constantly emphasized in Epiphany sermons and commentaries on the gospel appointed for the Feast of the Epiphany, Matt., ii. 1-12. Almost all commentators dwelt upon the paradox of the lowly, helpless child receiving testimony to his Kingship and Divinity by the tribute of the Magi and the miracle of the star. A note to Matt.,ii.1-12 in the Geneva Bible states that "Christ a poore child, layd down in a crib, and nothing set by of his owne people, receiveth not-withstanding a noble witnesse of his divinity from heaven [the star], and of his kingly estate of strangers."[13] Calvin, commenting on the same passage, observes,

> Here is to be noted a notable harmonie of thinges seeming to be
> repugnant. The starre from heaven declareth him to be a king,
> whose throane is the beastes stall . . . His maiestie shineth in
> the East, which not onely appeareth not in Iudea, but is also
> defiled with many reproches. . . . Because they [the wisemen]
> certeinly appoint that he shal prove otherwise then he yet ap-
> peared, they are no whit ashamed to give him kingly honour.[14]

An Elizabethan "Postill" or exposition of the Gospel for Epiphany also points to the paradoxical duality of Christ's manifestation to the Magi: "For as the Maunger in which he lay, argueth that his kingdome is not of this world: so the starre ap-pearing from Heaven declareth him to bee a heavenly king. And like as the Maun-ger sheweth him to be base in the sight of the worlde: even so the starre setteth out the maiestie of his kingdome for us to behold."[15] Indeed the three gifts pre-sented by the Magi were often taken as symbolizing the multiple aspects of Christ's role. The annotations to the Rheims New Testament state that the Magi gave "the Gold, to signifie that he was a King. the frankincense, that he was God: the myrrhe, that he was to be buried as man," and Luther in an Epiphany sermon translated into English in 1578 also interprets the gifts as testifying that "this child is a king, and not a king onely, but also God, and . . . mortall man."[16] Accordingly, an audi-ence would be prepared through the significances commonly associated with the Epiphany message to find in a play entitled *Twelfth Night* and presenting twins who embody complementary aspects of the role and power of love, a reflection of the dual manifestation of Christ's action in the world as Divine Love incarnate.

In *Twelfth Night* Viola's role alludes to the human dimension, Christ's role as patient servant, willing sufferer, model of selfless love. Her offer to Orsino, "And I, most jocund, apt, and willingly, / To do you rest a thousand deaths would die" (V.i.126-127) is perhaps the most direct verbal reference to this role. Sebastian reflects the divine dimension, pointed up especially in Antonio's language to and about Sebastian: "I do *adore* thee so / That danger shall seem sport" (II.i.42-43) and again, "to his image, which methought did promise / Most venerable worth, did I *devotion*" (III.iv.342-343), and then in disillusionment, "But, O, how vile an *idol* proves this *god*"[17](III.iv.345). The bloody pates dealt out to Toby and Andrew present Sebastian in the role of judge and punisher, and the final betrothal to Olivia suggests Christ's role as destined "husband" of the perfected soul and of the reordered society, the Church.

In the "epiphany" in the final scene when Sebastian is at length manifested and the double identity is revealed, some of the language points directly to the theo-logical dimension here noted, but at the same time resists simplistic allegorical equations. When the twins are first seen together by the company the Duke's comment suggests and reverses the usual formula for defining Christ as incorporating two natures in one person, observing that here is "One face, one voice, one habit, and two persons" (V.i.208). Antonio makes a similar observation, "How have you made division of yourself? / An apple cleft in two is not more twin / Than these two creatures" (V.i.214-216). But the other formulation, a mysterious duality in unity, is suggested throughout the play in Viola's dual masculine-feminine nature, and is restated in the last scene in Sebastian's words to Olivia, "You are betrothed both to a maid and man" (V.i.255). Elsewhere in the final scene Sebastian denies any claim to "divinity" in terms that at the same time relate him to such a role: "I never had a brother; / Nor can there be that deity in my nature / Of here and everywhere" (V.i.218-220). And again, "A spirit I am indeed, / But am in that dimension grossly clad / Which from the womb I did participate" (V.i.228-230).

Sebastian and Viola do indeed bring the "peace" of the season to Illyria through a reordering of its life and its loves. The seven years' peace throughout the Roman world before the traditional date of Christ's birth was commonly seen as a sign of that peace: as Lyly declared, "Christ would not be borne, untill there were peace through-out the whole worlde."[18] But the peace pronounced in the Angelic message, "Glory be to God in the high heavens, and peace in earth, and towards men good will" had much more profound and ideal dimensions. Commenting upon that message Luther declared in a nativity sermon, "[The] maner of peace of Christians Esay declareth, and sayth; *No man shall doe evill unto an other, no man shall destroy an other in my holy hill* . . . They shall breake their swordes into mattocks, & their speares to make sythes . . . Christ is called the king of peace."[19] In the conclusion of the play Fabian virtually echoes the Isaiah prophecy in pointing to the wondrous peace established in Illyria: "let no quarrel, nor no brawl to come, / Taint the condition of this present hour, / Which I have wond'red at" (V.i.346-348). The right betrothals are made though Viola may not yet put off her disguise: that must wait upon finding the sea-captain who has her "maids garments" and who "upon some action / Is now in durance, at Malvolio's suit" (V.i.267-268). When we remember that Malvolio has been identified as comic devil the line seems to point to the condition of mankind held in durance by the devil's "suit" as a result of the Fall, and reminds us that only after the atonement for that Fall has been made may Christ's passive, suffering servant's role be put aside. Sir Toby and Sir Andrew have endured the token punishment for their disorders meted out by Sebastian, Toby will wed Maria and reform, and even Malvolio is freed and invited to participate in the general "peace" if he will, "Pursue him and entreat him to a peace" (V.i.369). The Duke's concluding statement shows him taking firm hold of affairs in his kingdom for the first time since the play began, auguring well for the preservation of the land in order and peace. And the Duke's declaration that the weddings will take place when "golden time convents" suggests that the reordering made possible by this fictional embodiment of the significance and themes of Christmastide looks forward to the reëstablishment of the golden age, or in Christian terms, to the millennium.

Feste's final song, contrary to much critical opinion, is integrally related to the themes of the play, as developed above. Its opening lines,

When that I was and a little tiny boy,
With hey, ho, the wind and the rain,
A foolish thing was but a toy,
For the rain it raineth every day.
But when I came to man's estate,
With hey, ho, the wind and the rain,
'Gainst knaves and thieves men shut their gate,
For the rain it raineth every day   (V.i.378-85)

seem to allude to I Cor.,xiii.11, "When I was a childe, I spake as a childe: I under-stoode as a childe, I thought as a childe: but when I became a man, I put away childish things."[20] This echo also recalls Paul's classic definition of Christian love which immediately precedes the verse cited and which needs only to be quoted in part for its relevance to the play to be apparent:

Love suffereth long: it is bountifull: love envieth not: Love
doth not boast it selfe: it is not puffed up:
It doth no uncomely thing: it seeketh not her owne things: it is
not provoked to anger: it thinketh no evill:
It suffereth all things: it beleeveth all things: it hopeth all
things: it endureth all things. (I Cor.xiii.4-7)

And the verse just following the echo mentioned, "For nowe we see thorow a glasse darkely: but then shall wee see face to face. Nowe I know in part: but then shall I knowe even as I am knowen" (I Cor.xiii.12), with its graphic symbol for the imperfections of the present life in relation to the ideal fulfillment of love in the future state relates to the tone and burden of Feste's song. His sad and haunting references to the wind and the rain, the thieves and the tosspots, the swaggering and the drunken heads which have been part of life from birth to death since the world began set the play suddenly in a new perspective, that of the real world. Bringing the Twelfth Night celebration to a close, Feste reminds us that the world we live in is a very great distance from the land of good will that is Illyria, that the restorative forces which had a comparatively easy time there have much more resistant materials to work upon in the real world, and that the golden age fore-seen as imminent at the end of the play is in the real world only a far-off apoca-lyptic vision.

Notes:

(1) Leslie Hotson, *The First Night of "Twelfth Night"* (New York, 1954). I do not regard the follies of the character Orsino as a serious drawback to the play's possible perform-ance before the real Orsino. After all, everyone in the play is afflicted by love follies of one sort or another; Orsino actually fares very well in the end, being matched with one of the most delightful of Shakespeare's heroines; and in any event the spirit of the Twelfth Night festivals called for a challenge to the usual decorums.

(2) See Charles T. Prouty, ed., *Twelfth Night* (Baltimore, 1958), "Introduction." All quota-tions from the play are taken from this edition.

(3) C. L. Barber, *Shakespeare's Festive Comedy* (Princeton, 1959), pp. 3-35.

(4) Erich Auerbach, *Mimesis,* trans. Willard Trask (New York, 1957), p. 171, makes this point most emphatically: "A figural schema permits both its poles—the figure and the fulfillment—to retain the characteristics of concrete historical reality, in contradistinction to what obtains with symbolic or allegorical personification, so that figure and fulfillment—although the one 'signifies' the other—have a significance which is not incompatible with their being real. An event taken as a figure preserves its literal and historical meaning. It remains an event, does not become a mere sign." Roland M. Frye, *Shakespeare and Christian Doctrine* (Princeton, 1963), pp. 63-69, denies that Renaissance writers found religious meanings in classical and secular literature, citing Golding's commentary on Ovid's *Metamorphoses* as an example of the avoidance of such meanings. But in fact there is a widespread Renaissance tradition (carried over from the Middle Ages) of reading classical myths as imperfect types of biblical events, and of taking such analogous episodes as Noah's Flood and Deucalion's Flood, Samson's exploits and Hercules' labors, Orpheus' descent to Avernus to rescue his bride Eurydice and Christ's descent to Hell to rescue his bride the Church, as proof that the classical myths in fact derived ultimately from the Bible. This approach to classical myth is to be found in Boccaccio's *Genealogia Deorum Gentilium* (Venice, 1547), XIV.8, XIV.13, XV. 7-8, foll. 252, 257^v-259^v, 275, 276^v; Pierre de Ronsard, "L'Hymne de L'Hercule Chrestien." *Oeuvre,* V (Paris, 1584); Giles Fletcher, *Christs Victorie, and Triumph* (Cambridge, 1610), III, st. 6-7, and in very many other Renaissance works. Indeed, despite Frye's claim, Golding's verse epistle to his edition of the *Metamorphoses* in *The XV Bookes of P. Ovidius Naso* (London, 1587) itself states the rationale for typological reading, and invites to it:

> I trust there is alreadie shewd sufficient to detect
> That Poets tooke the ground of all their chiefest fables out
> Of Scripture:
>
> . . . . .
>
> If Poets then with leasings and with fables shadowed so
> The certaine truth, what letteth us to plucke those visers fro
> Their doings, and to bring againe the darkened truth to light
> That all men may behold thereof the cleerenes shining bright?
> The readers therefore earnestly admonisht are to bee
> To seeke a further meaning than the letter gives to see.

Obviously, the tendency to read classical literature typologically had not died away in Shakespeare's time, and there was no such sharp distinction between secular literature and religious truth as Frye suggests. This does not prove Shakespeare's concern for such meanings, but does indicate that such concern is by no means impossible.

(5) I have elsewhere traced a somewhat similar mode of vision in Shakespeare's MV, "Biblical Allusion and Allegory in *The Merchant of Venice*," *SQ,* XIII (Summer 1962), 327-43.

(6) Northrop Frye, "The Argument of Comedy," *English Institute Essays* (New York, 1949), pp. 58-73; John Vyvyan, *Shakespeare and Platonic Beauty* (London, 1961), pp. 105-106.

(7) All biblical quotations not otherwise specified are from the Geneva-Tomson version, *The Bible, That is, The Holy Scripture conteined in the Old and New Testament* (London, 1599). The Rheims New Testament used is *The New Testament of Jesus Christ* (Antwerp, 1600). Richmond Noble, *Shakespeare's Biblical Knowledge* (London, 1935) notes that Shakespeare's biblical allusions are usually drawn from one of the following versions—Geneva, first ed. (1560), Geneva-Tomson, first ed. (1576) and the Bishops Bible, first ed. (1568). Lawrence J. Ross, "Two Supposed Defects in Shakespeare's Biblical Knowledge," *N&Q,* CCIII (Nov. 1958), 462-463, calls attention to the fact that not

only the biblical text but also traditions of biblical interpretation and notably the still viable medieval allegorical tradition are important for understanding Shakespeare's allusions.

(8) John Russell Brown, *Shakespeare and His Comedies* (London, 1957), pp. 160-182. Brown's perceptive essay calls attention to the complex moral dimensions of Shakespeare's conception of love in the play—its generosity of spirit, its ordering power, its capacity for perception of truth.

(9) Barber, pp. 242-244.

(10) See Reginald Scot, *The Discoverie of Witchcraft* (1584), XIII.vi, p. 294: "A Topase healeth the lunatike person of his passion of lunacie."

(11) Bernard Spivack points out in *Shakespeare and the Allegory of Evil* (New York, 1958), pp. 202-203 that Feste's song taunting Malvolio "recaptures the typical features of the comic passages between the Vice and the Devil, whenever in the moralities the former comes to the aid of the frustrated demon . . . and badgers him unmercifully."

(12) Cf. Milton, "On the Morning of Christ's Nativity," ll. 167-72:

> from this happy day
> Th'old Dragon under ground,
> In straiter limits bound,
> Not half so far casts his usurped sway,
> And wroth to see his Kingdom fail,
> Swinges the scaly Horror of his folded tail.

(13) Geneva Bible, note to Matt., i.1.

(14) John Calvin, *A Harmonie upon Matthew, Mark, and Luke*, trans. E. P. (London, 1584), p. 84.

(15) Nicholas Heminge, *A Postill, or Exposition of the Gospels that are usually red in the Churches of God, upon the Sundaies and Feast dayes of Saincts*, trans. Arthur Golding (London, [1569]), fol. 36 v.

(16) Rheims New Testament, note to Matt., ii; Luther, "A Sermon . . . of the Epiphanie, or Appearing of Christ, Matth. 2.1-12," in *Special and Chosen Sermons of D. Martin Luther*, trans. W. G. (London, 1578), pp. 24-26. See also Immanuel Tremellius' edition with annotations by Theodore Beza, *Jesu Christi Domini Nostri Novum Testamentum* (London, 1585), notes to Matt., ii.

(17) Italics mine.

(18) John Lyly, *Euphues and His England*, ed. Edward Arber (London, 1868), p. 456.

(19) Luther, "A Sermon . . . of the Nativitie of Christ," *Special and Chosen Sermons*, pp. 15-16.

(20) Noble, pp. 212-213, also notes this echo.

Interpretation and Misinterpretation: the Problem of Troilus and Cressida

by Derick R. C. Marsh

The only point on which there seems to have been anything even approaching general agreement on that contentious play, *Troilus and Cressida,* has been its inclusion in a group with *Measure for Measure* and *All's Well That Ends Well,* the group of the Dark or Problem Comedies. Even this has recently been questioned,[1] but despite arguments for the dissolution of the grouping, there does still seem to be something to be said for considering these plays together and as comedies, provided that one recognises the difficulty of applying any simple notion of comedy to any of them, and particularly to *Troilus and Cressida.*[2] The fact that it has not been easy to find an exact descriptive label for this play, that more words than one would care to reckon have been devoted to showing that it is a comedy, or a tragedy, or a defective tragedy, or a morality, or a problem play, or a satire, or any combination of any of these, points to the root of the trouble: a general uncertainty in interpretation. Interpretation is, after all, a major part of the critic's business, classification largely a convenience of terminology. Where there has been general agreement on the sort of play being written about, as there has been with, say, *King Lear* or *Twelfth Night,* critics have been able to devote their energies to the elucidation of the plays themselves; their interpretations, though naturally different, have been useful in each contributing to a fuller understanding of the plays' total meanings. With *Troilus and Cressida,* where there has been no such agreement, interpretation has often been directed by the need to argue a case, and the play has sometimes been distorted to make it fit the desired classification. What this essay will suggest is that the main problem of *Troilus and Cressida* is in fact one of interpretation rather than of classification, and that misinterpretations have frequently arisen from attempts either to make the play accord with some preconceived theory of *genre,* or from the operation of an over-nice sensibility, resulting in a reluctance to allow the play to read as disturbingly as it actually does. It will be argued that if the play is accepted for what it is, and not racked on some Procrustean bed, many of the problems disappear, for the control of one's responses, though subtle, is as firm as that exerted by any play in the Shakespearean canon.

It is probable that Shakespeare's use of so well-known a story has occasioned some further confusion. Many critics appear to believe that Troilus must be the model of the perfect lover, Hector a hero noble beyond reproach, Cressida the pattern of infidelity, because tradition has it so. Some even argue that since the Elizabethans, and therefore Shakespeare, had inherited mediaeval attitudes to the Trojan war, it is necessary in this play to see the Trojans as the heroes and the Greeks as the villains. Hardin Craig may serve as a spokesman for those who share this view, when he claims, in his introduction to the play in his 1961 edition of the *Complete Works*, that the Romances, through which the stories would be familiar to the Elizabethans, all share an obvious feeling of affection for Troy. He goes on: "*Hence, it is easy to see* that Shakespeare and his audience sided with the Trojans"[3] (my italics). Such sympathy for the legendary founders of Rome and Britain, either presumed in the author, or felt by the reader, seems to have directed many responses to the play, but it is surely safer to be guided by the attitudes the play itself expresses, even if they are at variance with the conventional beliefs of the time, no matter how clearly established. Whatever the views and beliefs of that sometimes convenient fiction, the average Elizabethan, may have been, they were no more binding on Shakespeare than the necessity to portray Creseyde as the most perfidious of all women was on Chaucer. Certain proprieties are observed, as they must be whenever so familiar a story is used, for what may not be altered is the general sequence of events. The author must abide by the accepted outcome, but the emphasis and interpretation given to that chain of events is his own, and is what distinguishes one work of literature from all others based on the same story. With *Troilus and Cressida,* this principle has apparently been difficult to accept. Even Coleridge, (who clearly felt that he had a smack of the Trojan in him as well) is surprisingly ready, in a play so patently concerned with the difference between appearance and reality, to accept the Trojans at their face value. He supposes Shakespeare's purpose to have been to oppose "the inferior civilization but purer morals of the Trojans to the refinements, deep policy, but duplicity and sensual corruption of the Greeks."[4] Clearly, if one approaches the play having already made up one's mind, for whatever reason, on what one is going to find there, the results are likely to be surprising. Wilson Knight, for instance, is so charmed by the notion of the gallant, sensitive, intuitive Trojans that he can see the conception of Pandarus (leering, syphilitic, and taking a vicarious pleasure in the sexual encounters of his niece and Troilus) as "one of the most exquisite things in this play" and his humour as "health-bringing sunshine."[5] For him, the play is the tragic destruction of Trojan values by the policy, materialism and brute force of the Greeks. It is true that one of the points made by the play is how much of value is lost in the destruction of Troy and in the war in general, but to see it as principally the tragedy of Troy's fall is to give it a wholly false emphasis.

Other critics[6] have suggested a central concern with Time as the great destroyer, and contended that the play is tragic because nothing human can withstand this process of decay. This, too, is a valid comment, but one that is only partially useful in a reading of the play, for while the story of love and war is seen against the background of Time's destruction, an awareness of the transience of all things, and particularly an awareness of man's vulnerability, is characteristic of all of Shakespeare's plays, and of many other plays of the period. G. S. Knowland, in a penetrating article in *Shakespeare Quarterly,*[7] has questioned the real importance for this play of the notion of Time the Destroyer, pointing out that it is the lovers themselves who betray and destroy their love, and that if one needs to seek for some external force directing the action, it is to the intervention of Fate and Chance that one must look, rather than to the simple severing and decaying force of Time. Knowland points out, too, that there are at least as many similarities between Greeks and Trojans as there are differences, and is generally convincing in his demolition of many of the misconceptions that seem to have accumulated around the play. To his assessment of the play as a whole, and of Troilus in particular, I shall return later.

To arrive at an interpretation of *Troilus and Cressida* that is not governed by preconceptions of one kind or another is admittedly not easy, but one profitable approach may be by considering the relation of the play's structure to the twin concerns of love and war. It is, I believe, demonstrable that the play has a structure rather like that of *Measure For Measure* or, to a lesser extent, *All's Well That Ends Well.* That is to say, the principle of construction is one of anti-climax, of deflation, through the technique of ironic juxtaposition. Character, incident and motive are explored in depth in the usual way, but in addition, they are frequently used to provide ironic comment on other characters, incidents and motives. Pretention, illusion and deceit are gradually stripped away, and the ugly self-interest of human motives exposed. What is revealed may not be reassuring or pleasant to contemplate, but that is no excuse for refusing to recognise what is being done. If this *is* recognised, and if the principle of ironic juxtaposition is accepted, another major cause for misinterpretation is removed, for there is then no need to feel that the play must endorse the characteristics and attitudes of Greek or Trojan, or for that matter, of any individual, for such a construction does not require an embodied centre, or even a point of view that can be loosely identified with any group of characters in the play. The total awareness which the play creates for the audience or reader may contain, by implication and contrast, a positive set of values, but it does not need to do so. What is vital for the understanding of *Troilus and Cressida* is that one should recognise and accept that the awareness created by the whole play transcends the awareness of any of its characters.

Until quite recently, the customary approach to the play has been to enlarge on the differences between the two warring camps, and this in spite of the fact that the sequence of events effectively shows up their similarities. In the usual classification of the Trojans as the upholders of honour, imagination, idealism and intuition, and the Greeks as the possessors of practicality, policy and power, Troilus the lover and Ulysses the schemer are taken as the representative and opposing figures, even though they are actually neither wholly typical nor wholly opposed. Certainly the Trojans talk a great deal about Honour, Value, Beauty, Courage, Love and similar great abstractions, but then the Greeks talk too, of Honour and of Order, and Courage and Duty. On both sides, almost invariably, these admirable abstractions are presented in a context which reveals the contamination of the ideals by the self-interest of the speakers who profess them. Consider, for instance, the presentation of the opening scene, in which Troilus appears in the character of the typical courtly lover, proclaiming that he cannot bring himself to fight outside the walls of Troy, when he finds

> such cruel battle here within. *(I.i.3)*

The conventional expression of the pangs of disprized love is not the chief point to be noticed here, although it does strengthen the hint of artificiality that the scene conveys. More importantly, one is made disturbingly aware of the gap between what Troilus thinks is his situation, and what it actually seems to be. Both he and his emotions are being offered for criticism, for there is a level of meaning in his speeches of which he is not conscious. After Pandarus' bawdy jokes, one cannot take very seriously Troilus' complaint that his friend is reluctant to help in the wooing of Cressida, or indeed that she

> is stubborn-chaste against all suit. *(I.i.100)*

Whatever explanation it may be possible to accept later for Cressida's betrayal of Troilus, any audience must know that Cressida cannot be "stubborn chaste." Nor, indeed, does Troilus' later behaviour give any indication that he really believes her to be so, but in this opening scene, the view of himself as the disappointed but persevering lover suits the part he sees himself as playing. His speech, like Orsino's opening speech in *Twelfth Night,* without being insincere, expresses an appropriate emotion, not unmixed with self-satisfaction, rather than a deeply-felt one. For Troilus, though, it is a dangerous satisfaction, for it is purchased at the expense of a refusal to see Cressida as she is. The audience's awareness of the extent of his delusion must cast doubts on the force of the already somewhat fanciful image of himself as the merchant and Pandarus as the ship, sent to purchase Cressida, the pearl beyond price. (It is worth noticing that Troilus is later to apply this pearl image to Helen, whom he here dismisses as a blood-rouged doll.) What, too, is one to make of the alacrity with which he abandons the role of lover for that of warrior, in spite of his emphatic avowal that he is so much love's servant that he cannot bring himself to fight? He has castigated the savagery and senseless waste of war in the shocking image of Helen, splattered with the blood of the slain;

> Helen must needs be fair
> When with your blood you daily paint her thus. *(I.i.93)*

but now this attitude is abandoned, the battle is "sport" and he will join it, for lack of better sport at home, since "would I might" with Cressida is not yet "may." In an astonishingly rapid transition, his own account of his love has moved from the meticulously-phrased high courtly mode, in which the lover serves without hope of reward, to a "sport" based on physical appetite. The value of all his earlier protestations of love must be set against his apparent unawareness that what he feels is determined by what he thinks he ought to feel and by what he wants to feel. Troilus is not consciously hypocritical, but the audience is already being given a greater understanding of him than he has of himself, and being accustomed to viewing him in this critical way.

185

One can see this process of ironic reversal, of deflation and anti-climax at work in the play as early as the Prologue. After the high-dramatic and grandiloquent opening, the "princes orgulous", "their high blood chaf'd", with "their crownets regal", who have come to rescue the "ravish'd Helen, Menelaus' queen", the whole romantic pretence collapses. Helen does not want to be rescued; she sleeps contentedly with "wanton Paris"—"And that's the quarrel". This abrupt summary, with the pause the sense and rhythm demand, gives sharp emphasis to the full ironic effect. All the parade of pomp, all the cruelty and loss, are expended in a quarrel over the possession of a strumpet, and the crowning irony is that not even the realization that this is so can halt the destruction. As Diomedes later says of Helen, when taunted by Paris,

> She's bitter to her country: hear me Paris:
> For every false drop in her bawdy veins
> A Grecian's life hath sunk; for every scruple
> Of her contaminated carrion weight,
> A Trojan hath been slain: since she could speak
> She hath not given so many good words breath
> As for her Greeks and Trojans suffer'd death.   *(IV.i.67)*

Such a judgement of Helen must reflect back on the value claimed for her by Troilus in the Trojan council, and, because of the sustained parallel between her situation and that of Cressida, must reflect too on the value which Troilus places on his own love. (It is, by the way, quite typical of the play that Diomedes, clear-sighted enough about Helen, should later believe that Cressida is worth having.)

This ironic structure persists throughout the play. Ulysses' famous speech on order, with its plea for the observance of degree, for the recognition that Agammemnon the king is like

> the glorious planet Sol
> In noble eminence enthron'd and sphered   *(I.iii.89)*

is followed immediately by the entrance of Aeneas, bearing a challenge from Hector, and looking for Agammemnon;

> How may
> A stranger to those most imperial looks
> Know them from eyes of other mortals?   *(I.iii.223)*

he asks. As his insulting question implies, the ideal is not easily recognisable in the actual human situation. He does not enjoy his superiority for long though, for as a spokesman for the chivalric ideal, his pretensions are punctured by the Greek response to the challenge. This play never minimizes the cruelty of the war, and Cassandra's predictions should be a constant reminder to the Trojans that this is a war of survival. Nevertheless they, and Hector particularly, persist in regarding it as some sort of sport. When Hector's challenge offers to break a lance for the beauty of his lady, Agammemnon's reply exposes the unreality

186

that lies behind its romantic phraseology,

> This shall be told our lovers, Lord Aeneas;
> If none of them have soul in such a kind,
> We left them all at home.   *(I.iii.284)*

The Greeks are hardly likely to be upset by the charge that their "dames are sunburnt". War is not a tournament, as the absurdity of the aged Nestor's offer to prove that his lady is fairer than Hector's grandmother, and (with the caution of his greater experience) "as chaste / As may be in the world" serves to emphasise. Hector is Troy's strongest defence, but his insistence on trying to fight the war as if it were a knightly tournament, (the play's anachronism does not seem out of place, because it so clearly characterises Hector's attitude) succeeds only in getting him butchered by Achilles' henchmen.

Perhaps the clearest illustration of the way in which one attitude is used to criticise another, without either attitude necessarily being endorsed, is to be found in the exchange between Troilus and Hector, shortly before the latter's death.

> *Troil.* When many times the captive Grecian falls
> Even in the fan and wind of your fair sword
> You bid them rise, and live.
> *Hect.* O, 'tis fair play.
> *Troil.*   Fool's play, by heaven, Hector.
> *Hect.* How now! how now!
> *Troil.*   For the love of all the gods
> Let's leave the hermit pity with our mothers
> And when we have our armours buckl'd on,
> The venom'd vengeance ride upon our swords
> Spur them to ruthful work, rein them from ruth.
> *Hect.* Fie, savage, fie!
> *Troil.*   Hector, then 'tis wars.   *(V.iii.40-49)*

Here there is obviously something to be said for and against both attitudes. The view of Troilus is the more realistic, (more Grecian than Trojan, perhaps, in the usual classification,) for war is shown to be an essentially savage business, as Hector's death will soon re-emphasise, yet one can hardly argue that this acceptance of the savagery by Troilus, his determination to go on killing until he is himself killed, because this fits his present mood of disillusionment, is in any way more admirable than Hector's standards of honourable conduct and civilized behaviour, even though these standards can only be held to by ignoring the cruel realities of war. This sort of juxtaposition of attitudes, with their comments on each other, seems to me to make it quite unnecessary to look for some individual worthy of sustained admiration, whose conduct can provide a consistent standard by which to judge the shortcomings of others.

This notwithstanding, there have been persistent attempts to lighten what some critics feel to be the pessimistic tone of the play by finding a hero, the most popular candidates being Troilus, Hector and Ulysses. Of these, Troilus is clearly the most formidable contender. He is the most important person in the play, and more than anyone else, unites in his actions and feelings the play's dual concern with love and war. When forced to acknowledge Cressida's infidelity, he is put in a situation in which he might achieve that painful progression to greater self-knowledge that seems to distinguish the tragic hero, yet even at this point, one's sympathy for his suffering is not allowed to outweigh one's critical awareness of his determined clinging to his illusions. One remembers that from the first, the suggestion has been that his valuation of Cressida has been a hopelessly false one, a suggestion that has been ironically emphasised by Troilus' own comments on intrinsic and extrinsic value in the Trojan council. Yet the fact that he is wrong in what he thinks of Cressida is clearly less important than the way in which he is shown to be wrong about himself. In the first scene, he has enjoyed his role as courtly lover. Later, when he waits for Pandarus to conduct him to Cressida's bed ("Expectation whirls me round") he appears to relish something too much his coming role as voluptuary. It seems unnecessary to go as far as those readers who see him as a practised sensualist; nevertheless, it is pertinent to ask how aware Troilus is himself of the element of lust in his love. The importance of the bawdy offices of Pandarus, with his persistently lascivious comments, the equally persistent parallels drawn between the characters and behaviour of Cressida and Helen, which Troilus himself insists on, combine to make the audience aware of how large a part physical appetite plays in the action, despite the claims the lovers make for the ideal and transcendental quality of their emotions.

All this serves to demonstrate that the central critical question about Troilus is not really whether one agrees with the view of Knowland that

> It is pointless to say that Troilus' love is flawed by his inability to see the real worth of Cressida, that his passion lacks the reason to guide and control it. Love is like that, sometimes.[8]

or feels with Traversi that Troilus' passion "for all its surface intensity, has no adequate foundation",[9] for both propositions are demonstrably true. What the play insists on is that Troilus is so unaware of the real nature of his feelings, that when the test comes, what he has thought of as his controlling passion is proved inadequate, either as a value to live by or as something worth dying for, as is the love of Romeo and Juliet or Antony and Cleopatra. Troilus feels strongly, it is true, but he appears to feel at least as strongly for himself, as the betrayed lover, as he does about the loss of Cressida's love. The self-regarding quality, which has been apparent in him from the beginning, and which has made his love less idealistic than he himself believes it to be, becomes hysterically insistent when he is confronted with proof of Cressida's infidelity.

That the play demands this sort of judgement of Troilus is nowhere more apparent than in the scene in which he observes Cressida and Diomedes together. Here he is given the opportunity, as it were, to attain to the stature of a tragic hero, but fails to do so. When he is confronted with Cressida, who has apparently already forgotten him, and is embarking with no great reluctance on a new sexual liaison with Diomedes, he is also confronted with a radical choice, which, in dramatic terms, constitutes the crucial test of his integrity. He can either accept that he has been wrong about Cressida, which will involve the admission that he has been wrong in his opinion of himself and of the world around him, or he can retain these illusions about himself and invent some other reason for his betrayal. He chooses the latter course, for only so can he escape the humiliating realization that he has, to put it bluntly, made a fool of himself. The nature of his confusion is made clear in the unconscious echoing of his words to the Trojan council. There he made an impassioned appeal ("What's aught but as it is valu'd?") for the primacy of the will. "I take today a wife" went his example, where the image of the senses as the "traded pilots 'twixt will and judgement" carries the suggestion that it is the function of the senses to mediate between the opposed will and judgement. Reason·is explicitly rejected. Helen appears to be worth keeping, even if judgement advocates her surrender. The will to keep her, then, must prevail over the reason that advises letting her go. Thus the normal order, the weighing of information received from the senses by the judgement, and the translation of this into the will, is inverted; once the order is upset, the will may impose its desires on the senses, and see only what it wants to see. His advice, and the equally interested advice of Paris and Hector to retain Helen, is as disastrous for Troy as his insistence that Cressida is what he wants her to be is for himself. His will, no matter how powerful, cannot refashion the world to his desires[10] and, as is the case with all those Shakespearean characters who see only what they want to see, he must suffer a cruel confrontation with reality. When this happens, as it does in this scene, he cannot admit that his will has misled him, for to do so would be to question the basis of all his values, his belief in himself. His pain and bewilderment are intense, but this intensity of suffering should not be allowed to obscure the principal dramatic effect of the scene. His utterances sound theatrical, which with Shakespeare is usually a clear indication that the poetry does not seek to carry any great depth of emotion. He feels acutely, but it is his image of himself that has received the blow, rather than his heart.

At first Troilus affects not to believe the evidence of his senses, trying still to make his will their master:

> yet there is a credence in my heart
> An esperance so obstinately strong,
> That doth invert the attest of eyes and ears,
> As if those organs had deceptious functions
> Created only to calumniate.
> Was Cressid here? (V.ii.120)

The language throughout the scene has a clotted quality which reflects the turnings and twistings of Troilus' mind as he tries to escape from the inescapable. He denies that this is the Cressid *he* loves, a denial that is comforting only to his

189

wounded vanity, as is the hysterical charge that if she is false, so then too are all her sex. (Cressida too has tried to evade responsibility for her action by blaming her sex, but has done so in a much more perfunctory manner, as if she hardly felt the need to excuse her behaviour.) The way that one is intended to view Troilus' suffering ought to be impossible to miss, for Shakespeare has provided two commentators, not only the scurrilous Thersites, but Ulysses as well, who has by this stage of the play established himself as an acute observer of the follies of others. Here, his cool, matter-of-fact replies, his "I cannot conjure, Trojan", with its double implication that he, unlike Troilus, lacks both the ability to call up phantoms to deceive, and the inclination to evade the realities of the situation by juggling with words, and his sardonic question, "What hath she done, prince, that can soil our mothers?" provide the reasonable standard by which to measure Troilus' rantings and ramblings. Thersites, as one would expect, is even more brutally direct in his comments:

> Will he swagger himself out on 's own eyes? (V.ii.136)

He rightly sees the vanity ("swagger") that lies behind Troilus' passionate self-deception. If Troilus can convince himself that fidelity does not exist, anywhere, that all men are deceived in love, then his own deception is less culpable. The distortion of a vision that would rather see the whole world as corrupt than admit its own error is typical of many other characters in the plays, for instance Leontes, and Posthumus,[11] but while these suffer for their mistakes, as Troilus does, they go on through suffering to realize the nature of those mistakes, which Troilus never does. He finds it easier to seek solace in the belief that all others are deceived as well, that it is the nature of love to be deceptive, and to let the matter rest there rather than risk any further self-examination.

The exact sense of the long speech in which Troilus declares that all order, all integrity have been negated by Cressida's defection is not easy to follow, for he is anything but clear in his own mind, (he cannot afford to be) about what he thinks and feels, but it is possible to recognise as the obvious and major flaw in his reasoning the same flaw that his thinking has so consistently shown. His argument is that if one as beautiful as Cressida has been proved false, then all beauty is deceptive, all truth falsehood, all integrity, all value in love destroyed. In essence, what he is saying is that things should be what they appear to be. There is, of course, no reason, except that in his love for her he desires it to be so, that Cressid should be sexually honest simply because she is beautiful, and in fact the Greeks seem to recognise her for what she is without any difficulty, but in Troilus' disappointment it is love itself, and not his own failure to see the truth, that he condemns. Immediately after this, he does make the gesture of declaring that he still loves Cressida; the views he holds of the function of his will and of his honour—

> how may I avoid,
> Although my will distaste what it elected

> The wife I chose? there can be no evasion
> To blench from this and to stand firm by honour. *(II.ii.65)*

—compel him to do so. But this "love" is only used as a measure of his hatred for his supplanter, and he never really speaks of love again. Now all seems chaos around him, for he cannot or will not admit that he has been mistaken in his point of reference, and all remains chaos and violence around him to the end of the play. His speeches with their verbal contortions, incoherent rhythms and confusion of sense mirror the chaos he feels about him, but one must not forget that this assumption of chaos is itself an escape from a realization that he seems to find even more painful than confused despair. His love for Cressida and her fidelity had seemed inseparable, but now they divide "more wider than the sky and earth." In an image that compounds and confuses the entangling web of the spider and Ariadne's clue of thread, the point is made that he is incapable of taking the only way out of the maze of his thoughts and vanities. Self-knowledge is the only way out of his dilemma, but self-knowledge is what his pride makes him shun, and so, like the spider's victim, he is ensnared, and the only life that remains for him is a struggle and a waiting for death. All the sexual bitterness that he feels at his betrayal must be directed against externals, and comes out in the ironic echo of his earlier, confident

> the remainder viands
> We do not throw in unrespective sieve, *(II.ii.70)*

Now the bonds of heaven have been replaced by the knot of Cressid's hand, "five-finger-tied" to that of her new lover, and she herself is rejected with revulsion, because

> The fragments, scraps, the bits and greasy relics
> Of her o'er-eaten faith, are bound to Diomed. *(V.ii.169)*

Some critics[12] feel that Troilus' love is strong enough to survive the shock of disillusion, but this vital scene suggests just the opposite. Henceforth Troilus will think only of revenge, on Diomed, on the Greeks, on the world, and the vigour with which he hurls himself into the battle is not that of a man fighting for an ideal, or even for self-preservation, but rather the fury of a mad dog, doing as much destruction as it can before it too is destroyed. These are not the actions of a hero, nor can I see any evidence of his love having survived the shock. Even when the opportunity for revenge offers itself, in the chance meeting with Diomedes on the battlefield, Troilus cannot put into execution his horrendous threats, and is denied any kind of satisfaction or resolution. They fight inconclusively, with Thersites at hand to comment

> Hold thy whore Grecian!—now for thy whore, Trojan! *(V.iv.24)*

and when they meet again, Diomedes has stolen Troilus' horse as well, and it is this theft, and not the loss of Cressida, over which Troilus waxes passionate.

> O traitor Diomed! turn thy false face, thou traitor,
> And pay the life thou owest me for my horse! (V.vi.5)

Troilus' love could hardly be exposed to a grosser deflation than to have to yield place to this quarrel, with its obscenely ironic suggestions, over a horse.

As a lover then, Troilus does not seem to be able to command the unqualified admiration or even the sympathy of the audience. As a warrior, he is not much more impressive. He is reputed to be an excellent fighter—so is Ajax—but the encounters he is shown to have end inconclusively. He is not even allowed to make a good end, dying heroically in battle, but is last seen mouthing threats at the Greek camp. Fighting and killing, which he has himself criticised early in the play, or, at another stage, defended as a means to honour and glory, become finally a futile end in themselves. It is an end that the play as a whole thoroughly discredits, for not only is the overall destruction and loss caused by the war repeatedly stressed, but the other legendary heroes, who might dignify this theme of war, are unsympathetically presented. Ajax is a dolt, and vain as well, Paris conceited, and little interested in the war he has caused, and the great Achilles proud, indolent, and guilty moreover of the cowardly murder of Hector. Hector himself, the warrior who comes closest to filling the role of hero, or at least to providing a centre of sympathy in the play, is equally carefully placed, and one's sympathy for him is carefully controlled and modified. He is undoubtedly presented as being brave, noble, gentle, intelligent, the main shield of Troy, loved by his countrymen and respected by the Greeks, but he too, is shown to be the victim of his own pride, and of his inability to see beyond what he wants to see. His blindness costs him his life.

These shortcomings notwithstanding, it is true to say that of all the Trojans, Hector is the most clear-sighted. Soberly, with sound judgement and clear reasoning, he discusses in the Trojan council the rights and wrongs of the war, pointing out that moral law, reason, common humanity, all demand that the Trojans should accede to the latest Greek demand for the return of Helen, and thus end the frightful ravening destruction of what Priam calls the "hot digestion of this cormorant war." So far so good, but even as he speaks, and demolishes the interested arguments of Paris and Troilus, he knows, and the audience knows, that he has already decided to act the other way.

> Hector's opinion
> Is this in way of truth; yet ne'ertheless
> My spritely bretheren, I propend to you
> In resolution to keep Helen still,
> For 'tis a cause that hath no mean dependence
> Upon our joint and several dignities. (II.ii.189)

This remarkable reversal can only be explained by an examination of Hector's concept of honour, for it is by this that he lives, and, in the end, dies. The complexity of the Renaissance concept of Honour has been demonstrated at length by

192

Curtis Brown Watson.[13] Simple reputation formed an important part of it, and from contemporary records it is clear that this was a matter of great concern to Elizabethan noblemen. On the other hand, humility was one of the traditional values of chivalry,[14] since chivalry was itself based largely on the Christian ethic. The conflict between these apparently opposed values was a subject for much Elizabethan debate, and it is not therefore surprising to find, in this and other plays[15] that the simple equation of honour with fame is not uncritically accepted. It is in this simple and limited sense, however, that the Trojans, including Hector, and many of the Greeks too, think of honour. It explains the motivation of Hector's challenge to the Greeks, and is, together with his natural magnanimity, the reason for his chivalric conduct on the field of battle, when he refuses to take what he considers to be an unfair advantage over his enemies. But in the light of his death, the inadequacy of these values in the situation of the battle is one of the things that the play forces on one's attention. That this is so may be regrettable, and an indictment of the cruelty of war, but it must surely be an indictment of Hector as well, who has advised the continuance of the war simply in order to have more opportunity for the demonstration of his chivalric behaviour. It is his thirst for this sort of "honour" that has prevented him, in the Council scene, from acting in the way that his intelligence and his moral sense tell him is right. As is the case with Troilus, will, led by pride, has directed the action despite the opposition of the judgement. It is pride that makes even Hector think that honour and renown are synonymous, and it is pride, symbolised most clearly perhaps, in his desire for the rich armour of the Greek he meets in the field, that takes him out to meet his death, despite the pleas of Priam, Andromache and Cassandra. Hector's war is not the war that is so clearly revealed by the play, the cruel and bloody struggle for survival, but a sort of game, an opportunity to win fame by his courage and his chivalry. When he is confronted with the brutal facts of war, it is quite futile to say "fie, savage, fie", just as, at the moment of his ignominious death, unarmed, at the hands of the Myrmidons, it is futile to expect from the enraged Achilles the sort of courtesy and fairness he would himself have shown. Pride clouds his perceptions, obscuring what he most needs to know, just as it does with Troilus, with Ajax and with Achilles, and each suffers for it.

The attitude to Hector that is required from the reader by the play is a complex and subtle one, for the absolute values of humanity, of fairness, mercy and courage are not discredited. One is meant to admire these qualities in Hector, and also to feel disgust for the action of Achilles, but one is not meant, surely, to admire Hector himself without reservation. When these admirable qualities are made to serve his desire for glory, they are shown to be tainted with the same self-interest that contaminates the ideals of Troilus or the reasoning of Ulysses. Ideal values are used as means to other, less idealistic, ends, and, whether consciously or not, as justification for the selfish desires of the characters who profess them. Hector's self-deception is not as gross as that of Paris, arguing that the retention of Helen is an excellent thing for Troy, but the element of self-interest cannot be ignored, and must largely destroy Hector's claim to the role of even a minor tragic hero.

The Greeks have not in general been popular with critics who look for a centre of approval in the play, but Ulysses has had some support. He demonstrates a clearer insight into human behaviour than anyone else in the play; he is shrewd, discreet, an accomplished orator, and in his speech to the Greek council, the enunciator of the need for order, one of the great recognised Shakespearean positives. He has been called wise and statesmanlike, but with little better claim to the titles than, one suspects, most of the people to whom such a combination of epithets is applied, for his wisdom and statescraft do not seem to be directed to any purpose other than the winning of a war. To the Greek leaders he offers an opinion on why Troy has resisted successfully for so long: he ascribes it to Achilles' refusal to join the battle, and prescribes a return to order and discipline in the Greek camp, not necessarily for their own sakes, but so that Achilles may be forced back into the fight. Even then, he has so little confidence in the efficacy of his own remedy, that he immediately afterwards suggests a plan to Nestor that will bring Achilles back, not by persuading him to accept his responsibilities, but by playing on his vanity. Had this plan been successful, its end would have been more bloodshed, more disorder, with only lip-service paid to the ideal on which Ulysses' eloquent discourse to the Greek generals is based. His purpose is to win the war, and he does not much care how this is done. This may show a sound practical sense, but it is hardly the sort of attitude that can be elevated to stand as a high moral positive. Thus his aims and his proposals for action form an ironic comment on the wisdom he is reputed to show, as do the circumstances of Achilles' eventual return to the battle, for when this does occur, it is not because he accepts the need for some ideal order, nor even directly because of Ulysses' attempt to work on his vanity, but because of his passionate grief and rage over the death of Patroclus.

It is undeniably true, nevertheless, that in his address to the Greek generals, and in his attempt to persuade Achilles of the need to keep his honour brightly furbished, Ulysses is given some of the most powerful poetry in the play. In the particular structure of this play, this need not be a source of confusion; no matter what ulterior motives Ulysses may have, what he says remains a valid and trenchant comment on the whole world of the play:

> Take but degree away, untune that string,
> And hark, what discord follows! (I.iii.109)

His speech describes what the play shows, a world where everything is seen in terms of power and appetite, will uncontrolled by any operation of reason or judgement.

> Power into will, will into appetite;
> And appetite, an universal wolf
> So doubly seconded with will and power,
> Must make perforce an universal prey
> And last eat up himself. (I.iii.120)

This is what happens to Troilus, to Achilles, to Ajax, even to Hector and to Troy itself, but in spite of this there does not seem to be any indication that Ulysses himself is conscious of the wider implications of what he says. He is diagnosing a particular malady in the Greek camp; if he believes in order for its own sake, or allows its dictates to shape his thoughts and actions, he gives little indication of this in the course of the play. Like Isabella's "Man, proud man / Drest in a little brief authority" in *Measure for Measure*, what he says is more in the nature of a choric comment on the whole play, than a revelation of his own feelings.

His discussion of honour with Achilles,

> Time hath, my lord, a wallet at his back
> Wherein he puts alms for oblivion.   (III.iii.145)

despite its urging of the exercise of virtue, of the need to keep "honour bright" as the only possible defence against the jealousy of others and the erosion of time, with its destruction of reputation, works in the same way. One's reaction to it must be considerably modified by one's awareness that this is a calculated argument, and very definitely not the expression of any equivalent sentiment to Milton's "I cannot praise a fugitive and cloistered virtue, unexercised and unbreathed." Ulysses is working on Achilles' vanity, making him fear for the preeminence of his reputation. He is stating no absolute value, but offering a piece of carefully planned rhetoric, designed to anger Achilles, whom incidentally he despises as a mere engine of war, and to goad him back into battle. In order to do this, he makes use of the typically Trojan notion of honour, arguing for it, not as a code of behaviour, but as something to be jealously guarded and only to be retained by outdoing one's would-be emulators. The use of this argument by Ulysses, and its acceptance by both Achilles and Ajax cannot but help to reveal the deficiencies of this view of honour in Hector, who shares it with them. Thus, in the end, the role of Ulysses in the play, like that of Thersites, is one of chorus or commentator. His craft in politics is directed to the winning of the war, but the war itself is so degraded by the sordidness of the quarrel, and by the savagery and futility of its course, that it is impossible to see Ulysses' skill and acumen as directed to any worthy cause. One is tempted to construct a neat antithesis by setting Hector, principle without practicality, against Ulysses, practicality without principle, but to do so is to oversimplify their roles, and is in any case misleading, for Ulysses' practicality is shown to be as unsuccessful in execution as Hector's principle is contaminated in the holding.

It has already been remarked that the themes of love and war are used to cast an ironical and critical light upon each other. The war is fought over the possession of a whore, for Helen is presented as little better than that. The behaviour of Cressida, the comments of Pandarus, and his part in the love story, make this too, concerned with the possession of a whore. After Cressida's departure for the Greek camp, Troilus and Diomedes, with Greek and Trojan roles reversed, re-enact the quarrel of the war. Thersites points up the obvious parallel, commenting in his ribald fashion now on the combat between Troilus and Diomed, now on that between Paris and Menelaus. The balance is exact: for a faithless Greek, Helen, a faithless Trojan, Cressida, and so on. Both love and war, suitable themes for romance and renown, are revealed as riddled with deceits, vanities, lusts and greeds. Blind to the truths they most need to know, the truths about themselves, most of the characters seem to rush headlong to their disastrous but futile ends. Not even friendship escapes the imputation of ulterior motive. Pandarus obviously derives a vicarious sexual pleasure from helping his friend into his niece's bed, and is bitterly repudiated for his pains when Cressida proves faithless. The friendship of Achilles and Patroclus, too, is criticised, defiled in the "mastic jaws" of Thersites.

The question that poses itself then, is that if the world of the play is shown to be devoid of genuine honour, love and integrity of any kind, is one to take the raillery of Thersites as providing a point of view from which everything must be judged? The answer, as it so often is with Shakespeare's plays, when one asks this sort of direct question, must be both yes and no. Thersites' cynical view of the action, and of the posturings of the other characters is justifiable. His summary of "Lechery, lechery; still, wars and lechery; nothing else holds fashion" (V.ii.190) undoubtedly provides a more accurate picture of what happens than anything that emerges from the romantic self-deceit of Troilus or the chivalric delusions of Hector, but on the other hand, Thersites is himself to some extent discredited. He is a coward of a particularly unattractive kind. He is foul-mouthed by habit, by profession and by inclination, and so his blanket condemnation of mankind loses force. The very violence of his abuse, and the depraved pleasure he seems to take in corruption of all kinds, generates an opposite sort of reaction, strengthening in the reader the feeling that despite all that the play shows, all love need not be lechery, all honour vanity, nor all action stupid, brutal and futile.

It is of course true that an implied positive can be claimed for any work of a satirical nature, though this claim cannot always be successfully sustained by reference to the work itself. For *Troilus and Cressida,* though, such a claim is securely based. Hector may not fully understand his own motives, but his gentleness, his courage, his moral sense, even if he does not obey its dictates, do point to the existence of values other than those that rule the world of the play. Ulysses, too, may not reflect in his own actions those standards of honour and order that he speaks of, but his references to such things do suggest some existence better than that represented in this squalid and drearily permanent war. This remains true, even if, as we have seen, he means something different, something less admirable, by the words which convey this suggestion to the reader, for the different levels of awareness in the poetry allow the reader to catch a meaning not operative in the context of Ulysses' scheming. Even the speech on Honour is so constructed that it provides its own comment on the notion that it advances. Heroes can still be imagined to exist, although nobody in this play lives a hero's life or dies a hero's death.

It is something of a platitude in Shakespearean criticism to point out that in comedies and tragedies alike, there seems to be an advance, in those characters capable of it, to a better understanding of themselves and of their position in the world around them. Thus one accepts that Beatrice and Benedict seem likely to achieve happiness because they are aware both of themselves and of each other. Lear, and the other great tragic figures, too, learn through suffering and disaster, though perhaps they learn too late; they learn what they are, what they believe in and care about. No such learning process seems to distinguish any character in *Troilus and Cressida*. In those spheres of the deepest personal involvement, love and war, no human quality is discovered that is pure enough to withstand the corrosion of self-interest, or the corruption of time. Human behaviour is shown as self-delusive, vain, shallow, contemptible and futile, so that it seems only fitting that the action of the play should tail off into a slack and meaningless disorder, with the last, inconclusive word given to the syphilitic Pandarus. Nevertheless, those critics who find the play distasteful, or those who feel compelled to read it in such a way as to mitigate its indictment of human folly, which is really the same thing, miss the point. The play does not claim an exclusive truth, or profess an universal cynicism and despair. The consequences of a corrupt notion of honour, of the failure to recognise the true nature of love, and therefore the failure to love truly, of the lack of order, are horrifyingly shown, but to gather from this that the play declares that honour, love, and order cannot exist, is to react in the same way as Troilus when confronted with an unpalatable truth. It is, in a way, a tribute to the play's savage power that so many critics should react as if all human integrity were being denied. It is not, but these are the sorts of challenges that all human integrity must meet.

Notes:

(1) E. Schanzer; *The Problem Plays of Shakespeare,* (New York, 1963) has recently pleaded for a regrouping, wishing to reserve the term Problem Play for *Measure for Measure, Julius Caesar* and *Anthony and Cleopatra.* He uses the term in a different sense from that usually found in Shakespeare criticism.

(2) Oscar J. Campbell's well-known work *Comicall Satyre and Shakespeare's Troilus and Cressida* (San Marino, 1938) makes out a strong case for the play's having been recognised in its own time as a "Comicall Satyre", and offers an analysis of the play for which all subsequent readers have cause to be grateful.

(3) *Op. cit.,* p. 863.

(4) From some manuscript notes and marginalia on *Troilus and Cressida.*

(5) G. Wilson Knight, "The Philosophy of *Troilus and Cressida*" in *The Wheel of Fire* (New York, 1960), p. 61.

(6) Notably L. C. Knights and G. Wilson Knight.

(7) Vol. X (1959).

(8) Knowland, *op. cit.* p. 364.

(9) D. Traversi, *An Approach to Shakespeare* (New York, 1956) p. 67.

(10) Note the difference here from Antony's situation. He can recognise what Cleopatra is,

but loves her for it, and even the cynical Enobarbus acknowledges her fascination. In *Troilus and Cressida* all the "objective" judgement is against Cressida.

(11) The situations are reversed, in that in these plays Hermione and Imogen are actually innocent, but the attitudes the characters reveal are strikingly similar.

(12) See Knowland, *op. cit.* p. 365. "There is disillusion, but disillusion has led to truth, and Troilus is strong enough to survive the shock."

(13) *Shakespeare and the Renaissance Concept of Honour* (Princton, 1960).

(14) See, for instance, Chaucer's Knight.

(15) For example, in the treatment of Hotspur in *I Henry IV*.

Coriolanus: Power as Honor

by Charles Mitchell

Although there seems to be little internal drama in *Coriolanus* and much conflict in events, these events unravel within the hero a drama of honor.[1] The absence of a verbally articulated inner drama results from the character of the protagonist, who is a man not of mind or sensitive feeling, but of action. Nearly all of his feeling is reserved for himself, and selfish feeling divorced from selfless feeling becomes, as Shakespeare shows, a kind of un-feeling. Coriolanus' lack of feeling transforms him into a destructive lifeless object: when his soldiers take him up in their arms Coriolanus crows, "O, me alone, make you a sword of me?" But the moral and theatrical dramas benefit from the fact that in Coriolanus' recognition of the concept of selfless honor, there remains enough of the feeling of conscience to generate an internal conflict.

Coriolanus' lack of feeling is an essential element of the general ethical problem of valorous action: "physical prowess is not only admirable in itself, but symbolical of spiritual strength. Since bravery in battle is often closely allied to the most unfeeling cruelty, however, the soldier is often a confusing symbol."[2] Coriolanus has lacked feeling from his youth; never a boy, but a man almost from birth, he was sent to manly battle ere feeling could be nurtured. Coriolanus has equated feeling with femininity and youthfulness, and so rejected it:

> My throat of war be turn'd,
> Which choir'd with my drum, into a pipe
> Small as an eunuch's, or the virgin voice
> That babies lull asleep! The smiles of knaves
> Tent in my cheeks, and schoolboys' tears take up
> The glasses of my sight![3]   *(III.ii.112-117)*

By serving as objective embodiment of his condition Coriolanus' mother indicates the absence of feeling in her son; she represents the feminine (feeling) become masculine (unfeeling). She is much like Lady Macbeth, who exhorts the supernatural spirits to "unsex me here." Not only is Volumnia the cause and symbol of Coriolanus' own femininity transformed into masculinity and so lost—buried in a childhood never lived—but also he serves her as her own masculinity vicariously fulfilled.

The supplanting of human feeling with war's unfeeling is described by Volumnia when she says that a man should make war instead of love:

> I should freelier rejoice in that absence wherein
> he won honour than in the embracements of
> his bed where he would show most love.   *(I.iii.3-5)*

199

It is an oversimplification, the play indicates, to devaluate love in this way and to exclude it from the realm of what is nobly human; on the other hand, the espousal only of war hardens the heart, which is the seat of love and conscience:

> Now put your shields before your hearts, and fight
> With hearts more proof than shields.   *(I.iv.24-25)*

Nevertheless, Coriolanus is alleged, surprisingly, to be guided by feeling for others; many times it is said about and by him that he fights for the love of country:

> I have done
> As you have done, that's what I can; induc'd
> As you have been, that's for my country.   *(I.ix.16-17)*

The purpose of the play's introductory scene seems to be to make the audience wonder whether such a motive is possible in such a man:

> I say unto you, what he hath done famously, he did it to that
> end. Though soft-conscienc'd men can be content to say it
> was for his country, he did it to please his mother, and to be
> partly proud; which he is, even to the altitude of his virtue.[4]

That honor is the reward of selfless action poses no problem for the selfless man. Upon quoting Erasmus' opinion that no one is "fit to rule who has not assumed the role unwillingly and only after persuasion," Arnold Stein comments that "To desire power is to disqualify oneself as foolish, ignorant, or wicked."[5] Cominius seems to describe a virtuous Coriolanus who spurns the proffered rewards of action:

> Our spoils he kick'd at,
> And look'd upon things precious as they were
> The common muck of the world. He covets less
> Than misery itself would give, rewards
> His deeds with doing them.   *(II.ii.128-32)*

Such a reaction would seem to mirror the fundamental moral truth that virtue is its own reward; but in Coriolanus' case, the fact that action is its own reward is not true in an ethical way, since he acts valiantly primarily to exhibit his power and since his action contains a built-in self-praise. Coriolanus' acceptance of the rewards normally bestowed not only might question his motive for action, but would also belittle the action by implying that the reward were commensurate with the action (see II.ii.51-52). John Palmer seems to imply such an analysis when he asks, "And does not the admiration of these little men diminish rather than increase his stature: Are they really big enough to praise him?"[6] Coriolanus' rejection of reward simultaneously protects his motive and increases the sought reward by preserving the action at a height above reward. For Coriolanus *vertu* is virtue: power contains its own honor.[7] He has no difficulty in disguising even from himself his motive—the desire for the reward of honor—so long as he rejects reward and does not openly become his country's enemy.[8] But the disguise fails when, having earnestly sought reward at Corioli but been deprived of it at Rome, Coriolanus attacks his country. That is, Coriolanus finally and unmistakably succumbs to temptation when the consulship is offered, because it, if no other reward, seems capable of measuring and reflecting his action. The consulship would confer recognition of his superiority to all other men. When during the electioneering scene Coriolanus conceals his self-centered motive from himself, a dramatic inner conflict develops—between concealed private interest and publicly avowed purpose.

Menenius' fable of the belly, which establishes the framework for the action of the play, has far-reaching implications, both in what Menenius says and leaves unsaid. Although Menenius uses the belly as a trope of order and although the belly had an old history as fable for the harmonious working of the body politic, it had an older and wider history as symbol of selfish appetite, and it is to this older interpretation that the citizens give preference when they speak of the "cormorant belly." The immediate political facts do not concur with Menenius' generalistic interpretation,[9] for while he has the belly tell the citizens that they

> From me do back receive the flour of all,
> And leave me but the bran,

the belly-like nobility have, in fact, refused the plebeians grain, "suffer[ing them] to famish, and their storehouses crammed with grain." Thus the citizens' interpretation of the image applies in general to the nobility; as the play shows, it applies in particular to Coriolanus, who enters now to deny the people grain even as the nobility are prepared to grant it to them.[10]

A master symbol in the play, the belly poses the problem of honor: whereas Menenius' interpretation concentrates on the benefits of the belly's action, the pleb's interpretation focuses on its motive. Although Menenius argues rightly that the belly nourishes the body, he does not affirm that the belly is motivated by concern for the whole body. Similarly, Coriolanus benefits his country while feeding his own appetite for military glory. Associated with Coriolanus throughout the play, the belly symbol characterizes and evaluates his actions, defining martial action as the good with which he satisfies his great appetitive love of self.

That he is not genuinely a lover of country but is potentially its enemy,[11] Coriolanus himself brusquely reveals in his first scene:

> They say there's grain enough!
> Would the nobility lay aside their ruth
> And let me use my sword, I'd make a quarry
> With thousands of these quarter'd slaves as high
> As I could pick my lance.   (I.i.200-04)

Shortly thereafter Coriolanus betrays a selfish motive in what is thinly disguised as courteous sentiment: upon learning that the Volsces are marching against Rome, he announces,

Were half to half the world by th'ears and he
Upon my party, I'd revolt, to make
Only my wars with him. He is a lion
That I am proud to hunt.   *(I.i.232-40)*

This witty remark about his revolt against his country confirms the introductory statement that "Caius Marcius is chief enemy to the people" (I.i.6), for it places personal motive before, even against, public interest.

The progress of his relation to his opponent Aufidius externalizes a major pattern of Coriolanus' dramatic development. Whereas in the beginning Coriolanus seems to be enemy to Aufidius and friend of Rome, these relationships are reversed in Act IV as Coriolanus becomes friend of Aufidius and enemy to Rome. The change is only external, since Coriolanus changes outwardly from Rome's friend to its enemy, while inwardly he remains its enemy; similarly, he remains inwardly the friend of Aufidius while outwardly he changes from his enemy to his friend. To Menenius, Coriolanus and Aufidius appear diametrically unlike, enemies to the core:

He and Aufidius can no more atone
Than violent'st contrariety.   *(IV.vi.72-73)*

Yet as the action manifests, and as Aufidius remarks to Coriolanus, there exists between them a close interior friendship:

A thousand welcomes!
And more a friend than e'er an enemy.   *(IV.v.151-52)*

Coriolanus loves Aufidius because to some extent his imagination has fashioned Aufidius into an image of his own ideal self,[12] so that his love for Aufidius mirrors his love of himself. That Coriolanus has transmuted Aufidius into his outer image is indicated by the discrepancy between the real Aufidius and Coriolanus' conception of him. Coriolanus' description of Aufidius' nobility and bravery is too elevated for the real man, who is shown to be neither brave nor noble; for example, during their first encounter, Aufidius flies away the moment his fellows give him the opportunity. Furthermore, Coriolanus may elevate Aufidius also in order to have a worthy opponent, since without a worthy one, Coriolanus' martial achievement is not praiseworthy. Because there is no opponent worthy of Coriolanus except Coriolanus himself, he must forge Aufidius into the image of himself. More than he loves his country, Coriolanus loves his enemy, because it is the enemy who gives him the opportunity to display himself through martial achievement. War is Coriolanus' peace, just as peace, it turns out, is his real war; because it is the personal achievement, less than the public service, which interests Coriolanus, he who is enemy to Rome is friend to Coriolanus. So Coriolanus condenses the enemy into one man, contracts the public to the private significance by transforming the military battle into a duel, and elevates to the image of his own self the man who, by serving as formidable opponent, serves best as a means of

202

fulfilling self through action. Coriolanus' recreation of Aufidius seems like a symbolic manifestation of his wish to be "author of himself" (V.iii.36).

Because he has a personal rather than a public interest in war, Coriolanus regards war as a kind of love:

> O, let me clip ye
> In arms as sound as when I woo'd, in heart
> As merry as when our nuptial day was done
> And tapers burn'd to bedward! *(I.vi.29-32)*

Since Rome is being attacked, the present war is technically a defensive action, but Volumnia views it as an offensive and thus an occasion for merriment because it will lead to the celebration of one man's achievements:

> Methinks I hear hither your husband's drum;
> See him pluck Aufidius down by the hair;
> As children from a bear, the Volsces shunning him.
> Methinks I see him stamp thus, and call thus:
> "Come on, you cowards! you were got in fear,
> Though you were born in Rome." *(I.iii.32-37)*

Volumnia's stress is not on Rome, the public, but on Aufidius, the personal.

The personal nature of Coriolanus' interest in the war is shown by his eager searching for an encounter with Aufidius before he has yet struck a blow in defense of country and also by his reacting in wounded personal pride to the public attack:

> They fear *us* not, but issue forth their city.
> . . . . .
> They do disdain us much beyond our thoughts,
> Which makes *me* sweat with wrath. *(I.iv.23-27)*

We should not be so stunned by the quantity of Coriolanus' courage that we neglect to question its quality. One soldier describes Coriolanus' action as "fool-hardiness" (I.iv.46), a term echoed by Cominius when he describes their retreat in a manner which contrasts coolly with Coriolanus':

> Breathe you, my friends; well fought. We are come off
> Like Romans, neither foolish in our stands
> Nor cowardly in retire. Believe me, sirs,
> We shall be charg'd again.[13] *(I.iv.1-4)*

Coriolanus' great single-handed action contrasts sharply with Cominius' behavior. For similar actions, Cominius commends, whereas Coriolanus condemns, his men:

> You souls of geese,
> That bear the shapes of men, how have you run
> From slaves that apes would beat! Pluto and hell!

> All hurt behind! Backs red and faces pale
> With flight and agued fear.[14]   *(I.iv.34-38)*

Since Coriolanus expects others to act as valiantly as he, he considers all retreat to be cowardice, even hinting cowardice to Cominius, his military superior: "Are you lords of the field? If not, why cease you till you are so?" Not led but leading, Coriolanus, before whom "the nobles bended, / As to Jove's statue," has taken the place of the gods, whereas Cominius, who fights truly for country (the higher purpose) is humbly guided by the gods (the higher power); hence Cominius modestly solicits,

> Whiles we have struck,
> By interims and conveying gusts we have heard
> The charges of our friends. Ye Roman gods!
> Lead their successes as we wish our own,
> That both our powers, with smiling fronts encount'ring,
> May give you thankful sacrifice.   *(I.vi.4-9)*

Some fear may be allowed such a man ("Believe me, sirs, / We shall be charg'd again," he says), for it expresses properly an awareness of both his mortal limitations and his self-sacrifice for country. Fear should be present but should be mastered—through trust in the gods and for the love of country. But that during this great action, which outwardly benefits his country, Coriolanus is inwardly its enemy, is suggested when at the height of battle the defeated Cominius calls his men "friends" and the victorious Coriolanus addresses his men as enemies:

> He that retires, I'll take him for a Volsce,
> And he shall feel mine edge.

The problem of self-love grows during the battle when Coriolanus begins to manifest his desire for leadership. Coriolanus joins the second defensive flank in a great rush to gain further glory, twice asking "Come I too late?" and then requesting permission from Cominius to assume Cominius' command:

> I do beseech you,
> By all the battles wherein we have fought,
> By th'blood we have shed together, by the vows
> We have made to endure friends, that you directly
> Set me against Aufidius and his Antiates;
> And that you not delay the present.   *(I.vi.55-60)*

That is, while his men stop to gather the trivial rewards of action—the booty which he spurns (I.v.1-15)—Coriolanus will pursue the higher honor contained in still greater action.

Like his relation to Aufidius, Coriolanus' relation to Cominius provides a significant measure of the progress of Coriolanus' self-love.[15] Not only is Cominius' military behavior in sharp contrast to Coriolanus', but so also is his motive, his ideal selflessness:

I have been consul, and can show for Rome
Her enemies' marks upon me. I do love
My country's good with respect more tender,
More holy and profound, than mine own life,
My dear wife's estimate, her womb's increase
And treasure of my loins.

Ironically, it is Cominius' place to which Coriolanus aspires. In the beginning Cominius is first, and Coriolanus second, in command:

Lart.   [To Com.] Lead you on.
[To Mar.] Follow Cominius; we must follow you;
            Right worthy you priority.

The prejudiced tribunes offer a biased forecast of the shift in the relationship:

Half all Cominius' honours are to Marcius,
Though Marcius earn'd them not, and all his faults
To Marcius shall be honours, though indeed
In aught he merit not.   *(I.i.277-80)*

Though the tribunes speak here out of hate and fear, they forecast events with a grim irony.[16] Though second in command before the battle, already Coriolanus has "Half all Cominius' honours." And after the battle, Coriolanus accepts Cominius' horse:

Therefore be it known,
As to us, to all the world, that Caius Marcius
Wears this war's garland; in token of the which
My noble steed, known to the camp, I give him.

While rejecting the other rewards grandly, Coriolanus accepts Cominius' horse, "known to the camp," although Coriolanus as we know (see I.iv.1-7), already has an especially fine horse. The final stage in Coriolanus' aspiration is marked by his acceptance of the consulship, held at the time by Cominius (see II.ii.47). After Coriolanus is voted in, Cominiuᵔ, the mirror image of what Coriolanus sought to be, addresses him as "Lord Consul" (III.i.6).[17]

As he gradually ascends toward Cominius' place, Coriolanus tries to conceal from himself his interest in self. Although earlier Coriolanus had admitted that in his youth praise motivated his action (III.ii.107-10), now, in maturity, he denies that motive:

Pray now, no more. My mother,
Who has a charter to extol her blood,
When she does praise me grieves me.   *(I.ix.13-15)*

For now Coriolanus realizes that overeagerness for the reward invalidates the ethical value of both the action and the reward; hence he thinks to conceal his private motive by publicly disclaiming it:

> You shout me forth
> In acclamations hyperbolical,
> As if I lov'd my little should be dieted
> In praises sauc'd with lies.
> (I.ix.50-53)

By means of the *As if,* Coriolanus attempts to turn fact into fiction; moreover, he knows that these acclamations are not lies, because the hyperbolical praises measure his hyperbolical actions. Although Cominius tells him, "Too modest are you," Coriolanus' modesty is too violent—or hyperbolical—for that false modesty which seeks to kindle praise by disclaiming it. The violence of the response (see I.ix.41-47) seems symptomatic of Coriolanus' effort to control his desire by defaming the thing desired—the praise.

Yet at the same time that he seeks praise, Coriolanus sincerely shuns it. He hates praise because it is often merely verbal, the word divorced from the thing (see I.ix.43-44). He distrusts words because they are the mere shadows of actions, sometimes given liberally to undeserving, inferior men. So Coriolanus spurns the reward of words just as he does those of horses and treasure:

> Our spoils he kick'd at,
> And look'd upon things precious as they were
> The common muck of the world.
> (II.ii.128-30)

These offers he spurns because they, too, are not equivalent to the action they are meant to reward.[18] Coriolanus understands that reward measures the value of action:

> See here these movers that do prize their hours
> At a crack'd drachma!

But though praise is cheap and many may receive it, Coriolanus would still fain have it, not only in order to prove and prolong his achievement, but also to immortalize it. Since he does not want to be "the grave of [his] deserving," when a very special kind of verbal praise—the appellation "Coriolanus"—is now awarded him, he gladly accepts it. Likewise he will later accept Cominius' horse and political position, since these, too, are rewards which seem equivalent to his merit. Thus Coriolanus reluctantly discloses his interest in reward by accepting reward when it is made so attractive—equal to self—that to deny it would almost be to deny self.

The ethical difficulty of Coriolanus' character is brought out by the political entanglement in which he finds himself, for he now discovers that his action, independently performed, depends for its reward on the despised commonalty. At this time the images of wound and tongue pair into a symbol which defines the moral problem of the political issue. Wound is naturally and easily identified with action; and tongue with praise or reward, that is, the consulship for which Coriolanus requires the votes, or voices, of the plebeians. They state, "if he show us his wounds and tell us his deeds, we are to put tongues into his wounds and speak for them." Coriolanus, to the contrary, claims that his wounds need no tongue because they speak for themselves. Inasmuch as the wound-tongue symbol correlates with the virtue-honor relationship, he contends that his action does not depend on others for its honor but speaks for itself.

"Action is eloquence," says Volumnia, who first introduces the wound (blood) as its own reward (the gilt on the trophy):

> Vir. His bloody brow! O Jupiter, no blood!
> Vol. Away, you fool! it more becomes a man
>   Than gilt his trophy.   *(I.iii.41-43)*

During the battle Coriolanus associates the bloody wound with praise:

> Lart.   Worthy sir, thou bleed'st
>   Thy exercise hath been too violent for
>   A second course of fight.
> Cor. Sir, praise me not.   *(I.v.15-17)*

Because they manifest the measure of his achievement, Coriolanus goes on to describe his wounds not as pains, but as pleasures:

> My work hath yet not warm'd me; fare you well.
> The blood I drop is rather physical
> Than dangerous to me.

During the battle, attention is several times called to Coriolanus' wounds:

> Cor.   Come I too late?
> Com. Ay, if you come not in the blood of others,
>   But mantled in your own.   *(I.vi.27-29)*

> Though I could wish
> You were conducted to a gentle bath
> And balms applied to you. . . .   *(I.vi.62-64)*

> 'Tis not my blood
> Wherein thou seest me mask'd.   *(I.viii.9-10)*

After the battle, Coriolanus refers to his wounds three times, on each occasion preventing others from speaking for his wounds in order that they may speak for themselves. The first time, Coriolanus offers his wounds as an excuse for rejecting the praises which Cominius offers him:

> I have some wounds upon me, and they smart
> To hear themselves rememb'red.   *(I.ix.28-29)*

When Cominius offers material reward, Coriolanus rejects that, too, again adducing his wounds:

> For that I have not wash'd
> My nose that bled, or foil'd some debile wretch.

Even when Coriolanus finally does accept the more attractive rewards — Cominius' horse and the name "Coriolanus" — he first adduces his wounds:

> I will go wash;
> And when my face is fair, you shall perceive
> Whether I blush or no.

Indeed, even while it professes modesty, this remark calls attention to the blood in such a way as to suggest some open self-praising of the wounds. Each time he refers to his wounds, Coriolanus sets the self-reward contained in them against the reward offered by others: each time, he refuses to let Cominius put tongue into wound, preferring to let his wound speak with its own tongue. But finally, to a rather special temptation, Coriolanus succumbs, letting the others put tongues into his wounds:

> For what he did before Corioli, call him,
> With all th'applause and clamour of the host,
> CAIUS MARCIUS CORIOLANUS!

To sum up, let us recall that when he wishes to deny that his motive for action is the common one of interest in reward, Coriolanus exclaims, "I . . . cannot make my heart consent to take / A bribe to pay my sword." Yet though he cannot be bribed with the common rewards, he can be swayed with uncommon reward. For example, although he rejected the common horses, he accepts Cominius' horse, and similarly though he rejected the yelling of "Marcius," he accepts the shouting of "Coriolanus." It is evident that though Coriolanus' wounds are wounded by common praise, they are healed by uncommon praise.

By surrendering to the temptation of praise, Coriolanus has placed himself in a position of dependence. From this situation arises the dramatic tension wherein his ingrained independence conflicts with his newly imposed outward dependence. When his reward is enlarged to include the consulship, his problem displays itself with powerful urgency, for now though the people have become the tongues politically, Coriolanus tries to deny that they now have the power to elect him: literally, by denying that their political power has validity; ethically, by arguing that he should not have to beg for the reward since he deserves it; and symbolically, by concealing his wounds so that they may not put their tongues into them: "No, no; no man saw 'em." The plebs' refusal to grant him his reward unsolicited forces him to confess openly his desire for it. No longer able to conceal the knowledge from himself, Coriolanus revolts against those who made him aware of it. Moreover, since he cannot accept the consulship without admitting that he is limited by dependence upon their voices, he can preserve his seeming divinity only by rejecting their dependent reward for his independent action. When his refusal results in his banishment, Coriolanus seems bent on revolting against Rome in order to satisfy the outrage to his unlimited superiority by destroying those who have imposed limits on him.[19]

Although a political leader should be both master and servant, Coriolanus can endure only to be master. Even when fighting for that part of country (the nobility) which is primarily an externalized image of self,[20] he uses country as an excuse. During his moments of greatest service, he is best described as master:

> as weeds before
> A vessel under sail, so men *obey'd*
> And fell below his stem.[21]   (II.ii.109-11)

The great service to country is described as a master's personal acquisition: "brings 'a victory in his pockets?"

Coriolanus' return from the war is heralded by Menenius' and Volumnia's grotesque anticipation of new wounds and recounting of old ones. In effect, they are adding up the total to determine whether Coriolanus has enough to *pay for* the consulship:

> *Men.* Is he not wounded? He was wont to come home wounded.
> *Vir.* O, no, no, no.
> *Vol.* O, he is wounded; I thank the gods for't.
> *Men.* So do I too, if it be not too much. Brings 'a victory in his
>   pocket? The wounds become him.   (II.i.131-36)
> *Men.* Where is he wounded? God save your good worships!
>   Marcius is coming home; he has more cause to be proud.
>   —Where is he wounded?
> *Vol.* I'th'shoulder and i'th'left arm. There will be large cica-
>   trices *to show the people, when he shall stand for his*
>   *place.* He received in the repulse of Tarquin seven hurts
>   i'th'body.
> *Men.* One i'th'neck, and two i'th'thigh,—there's nine that I
>   know.
> *Vol.* He had, before this last expedition, twenty-five wounds
>   upon him.
> *Men.* Now it's twenty-seven; every gash was an enemy's
>   grave.   (II.i.157-72)

As symbol of the moral fact that he must serve, the consular candidate is required to don the robe of humility; further, he must ask the people for the power to rule them. Ruler and ruled—each is both master and servant: the material of the "[wooluish] toge" identifies it, and thus the consul, with the people, described by Coriolanus as "woollen vassals."[22] Although Coriolanus does not realize it, the consulship is both the reward for the act of service and the continuation of service. Just as his service in the past was not essentially selfless, so neither is it in the present. Coriolanus looks on the consulship in terms of the "sway" and the "high office and the honour," that is, as reward for personal achievement, not as the opportunity for further service given for past service.

Whereas the mode of war permits Coriolanus to command, the mode of peace requires him to become obedient. The robe of humility denotes an inferiority of rank diametrically opposite to his conscious superiority. Hence Coriolanus cannot accommodate his warlike character to the mode of peace by transforming his mastery into self-mastery. Aufidius remarks that Coriolanus lost the consulship because Coriolanus' nature would

> Not . . . be other than one thing, not moving
> From th'casque to th'cushion, but commanding peace
> Even with the same austerity and garb
> As he controll'd the war.
>
> *(IV.vii.42-45)*

For some time, as we have seen, martial success has hardened Coriolanus' heart. His resulting adamant hate for his plebeian inferiors makes him emotionally incapable of perceiving the moral truth of his changed political position. Since, as the play informs us, the heart is needed to advise the head, Coriolanus is without a necessary source of knowledge. Even though they disagree about the aims of the belly in the body-politic metaphor, the plebs and Menenius agree about the function of the heart; the plebs refer to the "kingly-crowned head" and "counsellor heart," and Menenius describes the course of the blood as flowing "even to the court, the heart, to th'seat of the brain." Menenius and the plebs concur because both parties seem to feel strongly for the whole commonwealth. Though the plebs lack judgment, they have sufficient *feeling*, even for the man who hates them, to perceive the deep paradoxical truth about virtue and honor, master and servant:[23]

> 1. *Cit.* Once if he do require our voices, we ought not to deny
>   him.
> 2. *Cit.* We may, sir, if we will.
> 3. *Cit.* We have the power in ourselves to do it, but it is a power
>   that we have no power to do; for if he show us his
>   wounds and tell us his deeds, we are to put our tongues
>   into those wounds and speak for them; so if he tell us
>   his noble deeds, we must also tell him our noble ac-
>   ceptance of them. Ingratitude is monstrous, and for the
>   multitude to be ingrateful were to make a monster of
>   the multitude; of the which we being members, should
>   bring ourselves to be monstrous members.
>
> *(II.iii.1-14)*

In "childish friendliness" they give Coriolanus their loves, but lacking feeling, he cannot perceive their truth and so he asks,

> Why in this [wooluish] toge should I stand here
> To beg of Hob and Dick, that do appear,
> Their needless vouches?
>
> *(II.iii.122-124)*

His martial mind, alienated from his heart, gropes for an answer:

> Custom calls me to't.
> What custom wills, in all things should we do't,

> The dust on antique time would lie unswept,
> And mountainous error be too highly heapt
> For truth to o'erpeer.[24]   *(II.iii.124-28)*

It is really no answer at all, and Coriolanus does not understand its meaning, but merely recites it as an excuse for going on.

The plebs give Coriolanus their feeling, and in return expect his. In fact, they ask for what they ought to have been able to assume was already there. But Coriolanus leaped over his childhood, when the tenderer feelings are nurtured, and so the plebs, who know that the motive has never been strongly present in him, can only hope that it may appear after the reward is given, even if not before. At best they can only hope for that inverted version of the ethic of honor:

> so his gracious nature
> Would think upon you for your voices and
> Translate his malice towards you into love,
> Standing your friendly lord.   *(II.iii.195-98)*

Until the public election, Coriolanus manifests what appear to be the conventional forms of humility, rejecting the proffered "things precious" and leaving the senate while his praises are being read. Even on being told that the senate have made him consul, Coriolanus can react with apparent modesty ("I do owe them still / My life and services") because their offer comes unrequested. But when he is forced to ask the plebs for the consulship, he drops his assured mask of selflessness, and the angry selfishness bursts terribly into view. The breakthrough occurs when to the plebs' question, "tell us what hath brought you to't" (II.iii.70), Coriolanus replies, "Mine own desert." If the deserver claims desert, he thereby overeagerly becomes his own judge in order to possess a positive judgment for its own, rather than for virtue's, sake. The plebs indicate as much when they inform Coriolanus, "You have deserved nobly of your country, and you have not deserved nobly."[25]

Honor rewards virtue, and also tests it. Because the nobility view honor primarily as the recognition of *achievement*, they praise rather than test, Coriolanus' action. But the plebs offer honor as recognition of *service* and thus unwittingly test Coriolanus' virtue by requiring that he profess the proper motive for action. Coriolanus wants the consulship when it is offered by the nobility, for then he may graciously ascend toward it; but should he accept the consulship when it is offered by the plebs, he would have to descend to it, suffering a severe loss of dignity. A citizen reveals the terrible truth that "The price is to ask it kindly." The pun on "kindly," that is, naturally, suggests the complexity of the moral truth Coriolanus would have to recognize in submitting politically to the *common* people of the *common*wealth.

Coriolanus does know that it is the "popular man" who craves consulship whereas the noble man is above the craving, and so he recognizes that his interest in reward is an expression of weakness. Yet Coriolanus' understanding of even this belief is limited to a literal explanation that to beg for a thing is degrading primarily because one thereby resembles petty men. He does not understand the more serious paradox that to lower oneself in service is to ascend in virtue but that to elevate oneself in power is to lower oneself into evil.

Coriolanus avoids cognizance of his own pettiness, and evil, by a subtle imaginative effort of evasion. He argues that he does not *desire* the consulship, but *deserves* it (II.iii.70-71) and that he only pretends to desire it (II.iii.108) in order to get what he deserves. He refuses to be like popular men, who desire but pretend to deserve; Coriolanus argues that he deserves, but pretends to desire. Thus in pretending to pretend, he intends to avoid the common pretense: "I will practise the insinuating nod and be off to them most counterfeitly; that is, sir, I will counterfeit the bewitchment of some popular man."[26] Unable to admit to himself that he is like other men, Coriolanus tells himself that he only pretends to be like them, only pretends, that is, to be the very thing he is.[27] He is still pretending and yet straining against pretense when more citizens appear:

> Here come moe voices.—
> Your voices! For your voices I have fought;
> Watch'd for your voices; for your voices bear
> Of wounds two dozen odd; battles thrice six
> I have seen and heard of; for your voices have
> Done many things, some less, some more. Your voices.
> Indeed, I would be consul.

The reality of intense desire rends the guise of pretense, and the unbidden truth darts out in the ironic last line.[28]

In Act I Coriolanus acts and in Act II receives the reward for his action. In the first half of Act II, because the nobility confer on him the consulship, he may show a proper reluctance to accepting it; but when in the second half of Act II he must ask the plebs for that reward, his reluctance disappears. Deprived of the consulship in the first half of Act III, Coriolanus tries to deny the plebs their power; but in the second half, on learning that he cannot, Coriolanus once more submits to the people to gain the consulship. In Act II, he merely wore the robe of humility; but in Act III, he must become in fact "humble as the ripest mulberry." The first occasion makes Coriolanus confess his desire for the reward; but on the second occasion he will not submit further to the consequent knowledge that his reward is dependent on his inferiors. The first occasion reveals his interest in reward, and the second tests the strength of that interest. Coriolanus passes the test not because he is less a self-lover than others, but more. Our response to his decision is ambivalent: we admire the quality in Coriolanus which allows him to spurn a consulship, but condemn it since it is not his virtue which remains superior to reward, but his will which remains superior to limitation (see II.iii.53-54). Self-sacrifice, which is involved in the former, is more difficult and hence more admirable, than self-assertion. Moreover, as Seneca shrewdly remarks in *Of Benefits,* "To refuse a good office, not so much because we do not need it, as because we would not be indebted for it, is a kind of fantastical ingratitude, and somewhat akin to that nicety of humour, on the other side, of being over-grateful"(Ch.XVIII).

In the first half of Act III, the dominant concern is power: Coriolanus contends that rebellion has been prepared

> By mingling them with us, the honour'd number
> Who lack not virtue, no, nor power, but that
> Which they have giv'n to beggars.[29]   *(III.i.72-74)*

He believes that power should reside not in the ruled, but the ruling, arguing his own case (his desire for power) under the guise of the public—that is, aristocratic—interest. In effect, for Coriolanus public power signifies personal honor, and since he is protecting his own power, Coriolanus cannot concede the possibility of power's being divided between master (the aristocrat) and servant (the plebeian).

Since Coriolanus is obsessed with power, his mind is preoccupied with corn because it becomes for him the symbol of power. When the plebs hunger for corn in Act I, the Senate granted them tribunes to argue their case, for the first time conceding power to the plebs. Related to the corn image are those of belly and feeding, and of sowing and reaping, which together form a complex symbol preeminently applicable to Coriolanus. He is described as a powerful mower by Volumnia:

> His bloody brow
> With his mail'd hand then wiping, forth he goes,
> Like to a harvest-man that's task'd to mow
> Or all or lose his hire.   *(I.iii.37-40)*

The presentation of war as the grain which feeds the belly of self-love is stronger in Cominius' description of Coriolanus' desire to fight Aufidius:

> Yet cam'st thou to a morsel of this feast,
> Having din'd before.   *(I.ix.10-11)*

In his study of the food imagery in the play, Maurice Charney does not indicate that the image of selfish feeding applies to Coriolanus as well as to the plebs. He argues that "The imagery of food and eating . . . . calls attention to the appetitive nature of the plebeians, while the negative images of temperance and austerity represent an heroic aristocratic ideal" and that "the people are not concerned with honor in battle but only with 'provand,' a base image of the animal appetite. The contrast is clearly drawn in II, III."[30] Charney errs by reading the symbol literally, since appetite applies literally to the plebs and figuratively to Coriolanus.

Coriolanus associates himself negatively with the belly hungry for praise of power (see I.ix.50-53, quoted earlier). Aufidius associates feeding with his and Coriolanus' military encounters, which satisfy their hunger for glory:

> Five times, Marcius,
> I have fought with thee; so often hast thou beat me,

213

And wouldst do so, I think, should we encounter
As often as we eat. *(I.x.7-10)*

When Coriolanus attacks Rome, the evil inherent in the feeding image becomes explicit; here again he is described as mower: "He will mow all down before him, and leave his passage poll'd" (IV.vi.215). And here his encounter with Aufidius is recalled in terms which make the symbolic almost literal:

> 1. *Serv.* He was too hard for him directly, to say the truth on't.
> Before Corioli he scotch'd him and notch'd him like a
> carbonado.
> 2. *Serv.* An he had been cannibally given, he might have
> boil'd and eaten him too.[31]   *(IV.v.197-201)*

The destruction of Rome is to be as a great feast cooked to satisfy the enemy's hungry belly: " 'Tis as it were a parcel of their feast, and to be executed ere they wipe their lips" (IV.vi.232). The Volsce soldiers associate Coriolanus' military prowess with the belly:

> Your soldiers use him as the grace 'fore meat,
> Their talk at table, and their thanks at end.[32]   *(V.vii.2-3)*

Just as Coriolanus approaches Aufidius' camp so that he may feast on Rome, Aufidius is feasting.[33] In fact, Coriolanus' attack on Rome is described as his own dish: "I think he'll be to Rome as the osprey to the fish." Finally as Coriolanus awaits the attack which will give him a bellyful of power, Menenius says of him, "He was not taken well; he hath not din'd" (V.i.50). Menenius, who speaks the first and last lines on the belly, makes more explicit in this last remark the association only implicit in this fable.

Coriolanus argues against delivering power to the plebs by presuming that they do not deserve corn gratis:

> They know the corn
> Was not our recompense, resting well assur'd
> That ne'er did service for't; being press'd to th'war,
> Even when the navel of the state was touch'd,
> They would not thread the gates. This kind of service
> Did not deserve corn gratis.   *(III.i.120-25)*

Even from an Elizabethan standpoint, it might appear inhuman to assume that a man must first *deserve* before he be fed, that he prove his right to live before he be allowed to live. Coriolanus holds the people

> In human action and capacity,
> Of no more soul nor fitness for the world
> Than camels in the war.   *(II.ii.265-67)*

Coriolanus would forbid them not only power, but also the power of life, symbolized by the corn which feeds it.

214

For some reason, Coriolanus bears the plebs a hate that seems inexplicable: "he seeks their hate with greater devotion than they can render it [love] him, and leaves nothing undone that may fully discover him their opposite. Now, to seem to affect the malice and displeasure of the people is as bad as that which he dislikes, to flatter them for their love" (II.ii.20-25). As the preceding quotation indicates, Coriolanus seems to hate the plebs because they represent for him the image of man become animalistic through loss of spirit. In his mind they correlate with the finite, physical part of dualistic human nature, that part which he has eliminated from his composite self in order to free his infinite spirit of limitation:

> You speak o'th'people
> As if you were a god to punish, not
> A man of their infirmity. *(III.i.80-82)*

Menenius refers to the plebs as the "common body" (II.ii.51), and indeed, they are related to their aristocratic rulers, and especially to Coriolanus, as body to spirit. To begin with, Coriolanus' own will completely masters his body:

> When, by and by, the din of war 'gan pierce
> His ready sense, then straight his doubled spirit
> Re-quick'ned what in flesh was fatigate. *(II.ii.119-21)*

Furthermore, Coriolanus thinks to manifest his spirit's mastery by refusing to wear the woollen robe—the emblem of the plebs and of his finiteness:

> I will not do't
> Lest I surcease to honour mine own truth
> And by my body's action teach my mind
> A most inherent baseness.

Sicinius remarks of Coriolanus that he "disdains the shadow / Which he treads on at noon," thereby identifying earth with the body which Coriolanus disdains. When he fights, Coriolanus disregards his body even though it is wounded repeatedly. Moreover, it seems possible that war is for Coriolanus the major gesture whereby he eliminates his own body symbolically by destroying others. Only while it is in motion does the will seem infinite, and Coriolanus' will is in perpetual motion when he is fighting, when he is destroying the mass symbol of human limitation—human bodies:

> from face to foot
> He was a thing of blood, whose every motion
> Was tim'd with dying cries.
> . . . . .
> And to the battle came he, where he did
> Run reeking o'er the lives of men, as if
> 'Twere a perpetual spoil. *(II.ii.112-24)*

Nevertheless, while it is meant to elevate Coriolanus, his excessive valor, as we have seen, has lowered him. According to Renaissance ethics, "the soldier may avoid the danger of effeminacy only to incur the still greater danger of brutishness. . . . True manhood is a comprehensive ideal, growing out of the familiar Christian concept that man is between the beasts and the angels in the hierarchy of creation. To be worthy of this station a man must show more than the physical valor which characterizes the soldier and traditionally distinguishes the male of the species."[34]

For as long as Coriolanus feels the need to conceal personal motive behind service to country, that is, for as long as he seems to remain loyal to Rome, his arrogant will is checked by the humanizing emotion of conscience. Even in his soliloquy following his banishment the feeling which Coriolanus expresses would seem to be a manifestation of his conscience. The structure of his argument is lucidly simple: 1) friends become enemies for no reason at all, 2) likewise, enemies become friends for no reason at all, and 3) so with Coriolanus, he does become both enemy to his friends and friend to his enemies;

> So with me;
> My birthplace hate I, and my love's upon
> This enemy town.

But although the progression of the argument is clear, its terms are not. Because his hate for his birthplace cannot exclude the plebs, we can be sure that those whom Coriolanus now hates are "The beast with many heads [which] butts me away," but according to his present argument, those he hates are those whom he has loved. Since his hate is for those he has loved, he seems to be including the plebs amongst those whom he has loved. Although consciously he rejects unity between himself and the plebs, his moral feeling may include his acceptance of that unity:

> Friends now fast sworn,
> Whose double bosoms seem to wear one heart,
> Are still together, who twin, as 'twere, in love
> Unseparable, shall within this hour,
> On dissension of a doit, break out
> To bitterest enmity.   *(IV.v.12-17)*

The referent of "friends" who love him is unclear, but Coriolanus had already said that "I shall be lov'd when I am lack'd." Perhaps we might say of Coriolanus at this stage what Eugene Waith observes of Macbeth: "His mental torment grows out of a conflict between the narrow concept of man as the courageous male and the more inclusive concept of man as a being whose moral nature distinguishes him from the beasts."[35] In the soliloquy, Coriolanus' conscience can express itself only indirectly by determining the way his imagination figures the rightness of union with country ("twin . . . in love / Unseparable") and describes the awfulness of union with the enemy ("fellest foes").

One reason for Coriolanus' plan to destroy Rome may be a wish to recover his honor by destroying those who have ruined it. But a second or underlying reason may be that for so proud a man, the prick of conscience can best be relieved by destroying those who invoke it in him. Coriolanus' need to affirm his identity by destroying his accusers is perhaps explained by some related remarks by Erich Fromm: "The deepest need of man, then, is the need to overcome his separateness, to leave the prison of his aloneness. The absolute failure to achieve this aim means insanity, because the panic of complete isolation can be overcome only by such radical withdrawal from the world outside that the feeling of separation disappears—because the world outside, from which one is separated, has disappeared."[36] Similarly Coriolanus would "depopulate the city and / Be every man himself."

Act IV, scene v, where Coriolanus appears in the Volscian camp, has a certain likeness to the electioneering scene. In effect, Coriolanus is again garbed in a robe of humility ("in mean apparel," according to stage directions), but whereas before, Coriolanus involuntarily wore the robe of humility and would not admit that his acts were intended as services to his countrymen, he now wears it voluntarily and offers service to their enemy. However, in a practical sense, Aufidius will be serving him, since Coriolanus will use Aufidius' forces to satisfy his own purpose, which is to destroy Rome. In fact, Coriolanus assumes leadership from Aufidius when attacking Rome, just as earlier he had assumed leadership from Cominius in attacking Corioli:

> Tullus Aufidius,
> The second name of men, obeys his points
> As if he were his officer.

Paradoxically, Coriolanus' stature seems to have grown by his banishment from Rome. There is now an increased emphasis on his divinity. Aufidius addresses him as "thou Mars" and calls him "most absolute sir" (IV.v); a servant describes Coriolanus as son and heir to Mars, and Cominius describes him as become the "god" of the Volsces (IV.vi). Coriolanus has steadily progressed through the play toward an increased greatness of self; as Menenius puts it, "This Marcius has grown from man to dragon; he has wings" (V.iv.12-13). Coriolanus has gradually freed himself from mortal limitations, ascending from officer to consul to god. Indeed, the consulship was rather an impediment in this progression, because it entailed humility and loss of freedom. Since his unchanging warlike nature cannot accommodate itself to peace, Coriolanus ascends higher by reverting to what he was before becoming consul—a martial leader. He becomes a general again, but now he is a godlike general—or Mars—who would destroy now not merely his enemies, but even his country, and all the forms of dependence that inhere in true patriotism. By destroying Rome, Coriolanus would achieve complete freedom. In a single stroke he intends to destroy all the forms of limitation embodied in symbolic Rome: conscience (the motive of country), and consulship (as service and as reward), and peace itself, the state of harmony which, established during his absence, is inimical to his freedom.[37]

Like Milton's Satan, Coriolanus inverts the ethical relationship between good and evil, as the evil man must do in order to deceive his conscience. Just as Satan says to himself, "Evil be thou my good," Coriolanus says, "Let it be virtuous to be obstinate" (V.iii.26). Having reversed his human values by viewing war as good, and love as bad, Coriolanus must also reverse his moral values, namely, justice and injustice. Coriolanus now sits in judgment upon his countrymen: for their justice in banishing him he will punish them with his unjust justice. Act V—in which Coriolanus is visited by Cominius, Menenius, and the three women—is a kind of trial scene in which Coriolanus sits as judge, rejecting the pleas of those who beg him to suspend sentence. In a kind of terrible heroic reversal, individual conscience has supplanted collective conscience. Coriolanus acts as jury, judge, and executioner. He judges Rome guilty of an offense against himself, sentences it to the supreme penalty, and prepares to execute that penalty himself. To cook this feast, he intends to use fire—an ancient symbol of destructive will.

Although Coriolanus changes from friend to enemy when he leaves Rome, he remains steadfast to himself by again becoming a soldier. His relation to Rome undergoes yet another conversion when he relents and spares it. This reversal is, of course, in the opposite direction to the earlier one, yet Coriolanus changes not only from enemy to friend, but at the same time from god to child. The first reversal had taken him to the enemy, and thus, in letting him be true to himself, it was less a reversal than a step forward in his growth of power. But the second reversal points him backward, all the way back to that stillborn time of his childhood.

The second reversal begins slowly, with the approaches of Cominius and then Menenius, which gradually soften Coriolanus. At the approach of the three women and the child, Coriolanus' hard will must confront for the first time his own tender feelings. The significance of Coriolanus' past and present actions, indeed, the essence of his character, he spells out in the great speech he delivers as the women approach. First of all, the speech is electrical in its tension between will and feeling, expressed by the sudden vacillations from one to the other. The speech defines clearly what Coriolanus' will would make of him and what it has cost in feeling to make himself godlike. Even Coriolanus now identifies himself as a god:

> What is that curtsy worth? or those doves' eyes,
> Which can make gods forsworn.

Amphibian man is both divine and bestial, but to purify his divinity, Coriolanus tries to sunder from it the last particle of his natural self: "But out affection! All bond and privilege of nature, break!" The act of breaking the bond of nature—which ties together the body and the soul—expresses the essence of his character. Since according to Plato's myth, man was originally male and female, maleness became associated with spirit, and femaleness with the body; hence the inward bond between man's divine and natural aspects could be expressed outwardly by the union between man and woman. When she now approaches, Coriolanus addresses his wife as "best of my flesh." Furthermore, the inner bond between man's male and female natures is mirrored also in the relation of individual to

218

country—to Rome, which includes the base plebeians. Thus it is appropriate that Rome be described as Coriolanus' wife (IV.iii.33) and as "our country . . . / Whereto we are bound." Now in surrendering momentarily to feeling, Coriolanus identifies the forces which oppose his concept of the unlimited self: feeling, nature, earth, family, and country. He identifies his inner earth with the outer earth of Rome: "I melt, and am not / Of stronger earth than others"; but then he reverts to his former concept of self: "Let the Volsces / Plough Rome and harrow Italy." In effect, he would destroy his natural self by destroying Rome. The act of destruction is for the demented will an act of creation, even self-creation:

> I'll never
> Be such a gosling to *obey* instinct, but stand
> As if a man were author of himself
> And knew no other kin.

Near the close, however, Coriolanus is made to realize that no man can be "author of himself"; he interprets his whole life as a kind of sham or play-acting, remarking, "like a dull actor now I have forgot my part." He now considers that the concept of his divine self has been but a stage role and that his compassionate nature, which earlier he had considered his stage role, is his true self. Dressed earlier in the costume of humility, Coriolanus believed that he was play-acting. When at that time he was told to become milder for the plebs, he asked,

> Why did you wish me *milder*? Would you have me
> False to my nature? Rather say I play
> The man I am. *(III.ii.14-16)*

The rhetoric of this past answer becomes truth in Act V when he becomes truly mild: "These eyes are not the same I wore in Rome." Appearance and reality of self become inverted when by expressing tenderness, Coriolanus becomes the child he never was in his youth. In his childhood, what he was in reality could only appear as a stage role: "When he might act the woman in the scene. He prov'd best man i'th'field," but in yielding now before his own son, he becomes temporarily the child, filling the omission in his nature.

There are three distinct, but related and cumulative arguments which must be advanced before Coriolanus can arrive at the limited understanding which makes him yield at last to compassion. The appeals which Volumnia makes in V.iii, are to personal feeling (V.iii.22-86), to protection of country (V.iii.87-131), and to regard for personal honor (V.iii.131-182). The appeal to feeling is inadequate, for at its end Coriolanus turns the pleaders away. To this first appeal is added that of patriotism, the old public excuse for action: "the father tearing the country's bowels out," "we for our country pray," "Alack, or we must lose / The country . . . or else thy person / Our comfort in the country," "tread on thy country's ruin," and "March to assault thy country" (V.iii.102-123). But the combined appeals of feeling and country prove inadequate also:

> Not of a woman's tenderness to be,
> Requires nor child nor woman's face to see.
> I have sat too long.

Only when the first two appeals are combined with the third—to honor as reward—do they become effective.[38]

There is an evident similarity between this scene (V.iii) and the earlier one (III.ii) where Coriolanus responded to his mother's rhetoric by humbling himself.[39] Not only does he relent each time, but the cause for relenting is the same: the main issue of both her arguments is the loss of Coriolanus' honor (as in the earlier scene, she reiterates the word *honor* four times: V.iii.135, 149, 154, 164). In some other ways, however, the occasions are directly opposite: earlier, he had to remind *her* that he was about to lose his honor, but now she must remind *him*. Thus she makes him suddenly aware that by destroying Rome he would lose rather than preserve his honor. Although on both occasions Volumnia shows Coriolanus how to retain his honor, her two arguments are different in that the earlier one is specious and the latter one true. It is a misreading of the latter scene to say that Coriolanus, "unconvinced by her arguments, yield[s] at once to her displeasure," that he "does not succumb to his mother's arguments but . . . to the rough edge of her tongue."[40] It is essentially the content of Volumnia's speech, not the familial authority of the speaker to which Coriolanus responds.

Having saved her strongest argument until last, Volumnia now probes Coriolanus' weakness by forcing him to realize that he will lose what he prizes best, his honorable name, if he destroys Rome in order to preserve it:

> if thou conquer Rome, the benefit
> Which thou shalt thereby reap is such a *name*
> Whose repetition will be dogg'd with curses,
> Whose chronicle thus writ: "The man was noble,
> But with his last attempt he wip'd it out,
> Destroy'd his country, and his *name* remains
> To th'ensuing age abhorr'd."

Coriolanus' honor has become identified with his name: initially he was given his name as honorable reward, and he now cherishes it as symbol of his honor:

> My name is Caius Marcius, who hath done
> To thee particularly and to all the Volsces
> Great hurt and mischief; thereto witness may
> My *surname*, Coriolanus. The painful service,
> The extreme dangers, and the drops of blood
> Shed for my thankless country are requited
> But with that *surname*; a good memory
> And witness of the malice and displeasure
> Which thou shouldst bear me. Only that *name* remains.   *(IV.v.71-79)*

But in burning down Rome, he would sear from the self that name which makes him dependent for his honor. That process is part of making him the "author of himself":

> Coriolanus
> He would not answer to; forbade all *names*;
> He was a kind of nothing, *titleless*,
> Till he had forg'd himself a *name* of'th'fire
> Of burning Rome. *(V.i.11-14)*

Coriolanus thinks that the object can be its own subject and that power contains honor. To put it another way, he thinks his will places him beyond morality, as their divinity does remove the gods. But his mother drives home the fact that human greatness (fixed in an honorable reputation) is dependent upon other men. Coriolanus cannot forge his own name; he can forge only the action, but the name is branded on the action for him. Menenius, who has said that a man's honor resides in the grateful beneficiaries of his action, has made it clear that there is even a kind of divine immortality in honor:

> Now the good gods forbid
> That our renowned Rome, whose gratitude
> Towards her deserved *children* is enroll'd
> In Jove's own book, like an unnatural dam
> Should now eat up her own! *(III.i.290-94)*

Volumnia stresses this truth when she tells Coriolanus now of his awful "chronicle thus writ." Coriolanus is made to realize that to retain his honor, he must rely upon others for it; upon submitting to that cornerstone of ethics, he receives back his former name, and the people put their tongues again into his old wounds: "Unshout the noise that banish'd Marcius! / Repeal him with the welcome of his mother."[41]

Coriolanus responds to his mother as symbol of the masculine precepts of honor and to her final argument as the expression of her symbolism, though he responds to her also as dear person:

> O, my mother, mother! O!
> You have won a happy victory to Rome.

But in placing on Volumnia all the responsibility for his decision, Coriolanus is simplifying his motives. In overemphasizing his filial motive, he may be concealing another, namely that in large part he relents because he must do so in order to regain his past honor. He cannot openly admit that fact because he would be further dishonored for betraying the honor of his new state, Volscia, to preserve his personal honor. Thus Coriolanus is willing to admit, even stress, the weakness of filial love in order to conceal the more dishonorable weakness of committing treason to preserve the self's honor.

Though Coriolanus understands and submits to the galling fact that honor is dependent, to further limitation than that he will not surrender. He will not return to Rome and thereby become one with the symbol of his lower self. The rejection of the opportunity to return to Rome corresponds with his rejection of those elements within his nature which Aufidius implies in his charge that Coriolanus is a boy. But perhaps part of Coriolanus' reason for returning to the Volsces is his sense of guilt—for both his treason against Rome and his treason against Volscia. He foresees that death awaits him at the hands of the Volsces, for he tells his mother:

> Most dangerously you have with him prevailed,
> If not most mortal to him.

As John Palmer notes, Coriolanus dies a little too easily.[42] But in satisfying his conscience by paying his debt to both Romans and Volsces, he cleans the guilt from his honor. Just as after his banishment he had presented his throat to Aufidius, he now presents it to all the Volsces:

> Cut me to pieces, Volsces; men and lads
> Stain all your edges on me.

When he attempts to deny Coriolanus the honored name which Coriolanus has just secured, Aufidius introduces the issue of honor which Coriolanus has tactfully left submerged:

> Dost thou think
> I'll grace thee with that robbery, thy stol'n name,
> Coriolanus, in Corioli? (V.vi.88-90)

Coriolanus dies defending his right to the name he had regained by recognizing dependence; yet at the same time, his evident assertion seems a defiance of that dependence. Two acts, of rejecting the title "Boy" and retaining the title "Coriolanus," occur simultaneously:

> "Boy!" False hound!
> If you have writ your annals true, 'tis there
> That, like an eagle in a dove-cote, I
> Fluttered your Volscians in Corioli;
> Alone I did it. "Boy!"

In Cominius' remarks about young boys' playing the female roles on stage, the child was associated with the female and with feeling (Coriolanus' own boy is present with the three women when he relents), and so Coriolanus has, in effect, denied once more the bond of nature. Yet in this very act of defending his right to the name "Coriolanus," he admits dependence, for he has renewed the name which before he had renounced: Coriolanus' reference to the Volsces' having "writ your annals true" reverses Volumnia's previous forecast about Coriolanus' infamous "chronicle thus writ." The terse laudation on which Aufidius concludes the play awards the dead Coriolanus the undying honor which he hoped to salvage by salvaging Rome: "Yet he shall have a noble memory."

Notes:

(1) E. E. Stoll says, "The inner struggle, however, is not clearly presented, and appears mainly in deeds." *Art and Artifice in Shakespeare* (New York, 1962), p. 148.

(2) Eugene M. Waith, "Manhood and Valor in Two Shakespearean Tragedies," *ELH,* XVII (1950), 262.

(3) The text I am using is in *The Complete Plays and Poems of William Shakespeare,* ed. W. A. Neilson and C. J. Hill (Boston, 1942). Italics are mine.

(4) Critics generally conclude that Coriolanus acts either for self or for country. The following citations illustrate the common contention that Coriolanus is prompted by egotism: Derek Traversi, *An Approach to Shakespeare* (Garden City, 1956), p. 234; D. J. Enright, *"Coriolanus: Tragedy or Debate?" EIC,* IV (1954), 13; and John Palmer, *Political Characters in Shakespeare* (London, 1952), pp. 258 and 283. On the other hand, William Bowden and Maurice Charney contend that Coriolanus' valor is moved by virtue: see William Bowden, "The 'Unco Guid' and Shakespeare's Coriolanus," *SQ,* XIII (1962), 41-48; and Maurice Charney, *Shakespeare's Roman Plays* (Harvard University Press, 1961), Ch.V. Such exclusiveness eliminates much of the complexity to be found in Coriolanus.

(5) Arnold Stein, *Heroic Knowledge* (Minneapolis, 1959), p. 32. Milton's understanding of ethical problems is not irrelevant to Shakespeare's.

(6) Palmer, p. 265.

(7) Eugene Waith quotes a relevant passage from Plutarch's life of Coriolanus: "Now in thos dayes, valliantnes was honoured in ROME above all other vertues: which they called *Virtus,* by the name of vertue selfe, as including in that generall name, all other speciall vertues besides. So that *Virtus* in the Latin, was as muche as valliantnes." Waith goes on to say that "Machiavelli's praise of *virtu,* that uncompromising strength of mind and will essential to the successful prince, is a Renaissance reflection of the Roman attitude noted by Plutarch. To the more conservative contemporaries of Machiavelli such an identification of force and virtue was repugnant, if not actually (along with the rest of his ideas) Satanic." (*Op. cit.,* 262-63).

(8) Not only does Coriolanus fool himself and others within the play, but he also has deceived a number of critics. William Bowden asserts that Coriolanus is "painfully honest" (*op. cit.,* 46), and Charney feels that he is "deeply honest" (*op. cit.,* p. 161). Charney argues that Coriolanus "cannot betray the truth of his own nature," which Charney classifies as "a narrowly aristocratic ideal." Yet steadfast fidelity to one's self-love is not the property of a social aristocracy, and such honesty to one's self-love admits of, and even necessitates, a wide range of deception. Contrary to other critics, John Palmer says that Coriolanus "does not . . . know himself as we have learned to know him" (*op. cit.,* p. 283). The points of view of Coriolanus and of the audience should not be confused.

(9) Thus Traversi notes that "Menenius criticizes justly the failure of the populace to play a proper part in the social organism; but the figure he chooses to elaborate his point turns the argument equally against his own position" (*op. cit.,* p. 221). Although Traversi notes the pejorative application of the belly image to the aristocrats, he leaves unnoticed the specific application to Coriolanus. J. C. Maxwell has wrongly declared its irrelevance to him: the belly image's "prominence makes us notice its irrelevance to the concerns and outlook of the central character." "Animal Imagery in 'Coriolanus,'" *MLR,* XLII (1947), 418.

(10) Many critics have been unable to explain why *Coriolanus* is a tragedy; unable to establish that Coriolanus is a tragic hero, they argue that he is a representative of his trag-

ically flawed society. See especially Enright, 19, who follows Traversi (see p. 233). See also Brents Stirling, *Unity in Shakespearean Tragedy* (New York, 1957), pp. 190-91. Such a view, which posits that Coriolanus' tragic flaw is his unbending sense of aristocracy, neglects to observe how unlike Menenius, Cominius, and even Volumnia, Coriolanus is in his violation of the code of his own aristocratic class.

(11) G. W. Knight says that "Coriolanus had ever the seed of treachery in his pride, unsubdued as it was to love of country or kin." *The Imperial Theme* (London, 1961), p. 134.

(12) Eugene Waith feels that Coriolanus "considers [Aufidius] almost an alter ego." *The Herculean Hero* (Columbia University Press, 1962), p. 131. For his useful discussion of Coriolanus as Herculean hero, see pp. 121-43.

(13) During the electioneering scene, Cominius applies the judgment directly to Coriolanus: "manhood is called foolery when it stands / Against a falling fabric" (III. i. 246-47). See also IV. vi. 104-05, where Cominius refers to the concept again.

(14) Charney distorts Shakespeare's balance when he remarks that Coriolanus' independence in battle "emphasizes Marcius' valor as contrasted with the cowardly soldiers who remain behind" (*op. cit.*, p. 178).

(15) The observations in this paragraph prevent us from reaching James Phillips, Jr.'s misguided conclusion that Coriolanus "never ... expresses any desire for political power." *The State in Shakespeare's Greek and Roman Plays* (New York, 1940), p. 163.

(16) John Palmer stresses the validity of the tribunes' observations here (*op. cit.*, pp. 259-260); in fact, Palmer attempts a wholesale justification of all they do.

(17) Historically, two consuls governed jointly (see Coriolanus' reference to plural "consuls" at III. i. 108), although some historians agree that there may have been only one at the time (at III. i. 108, Coriolanus may be speaking generically). For dramatic purposes and to ensure the relevance of past history to contemporary society, Shakespeare seems to create the illusion that Coriolanus will become sole consul: "affecting one sole throne" (IV. vi. 32).

(18) G. W. Knight says perceptively, "He instinctively rejects thanks. Partly, perhaps, because he knows his deeds are not done for Rome, or, if he does not yet know it, fears he may be forced to know it and would rather turn his mind from the matter; and, partly, because the giving and receiving of praises is a kind of payment, a levelling of differences, a mingling with inferior beings who cannot have anything to give him worth his attention. ... He is embarrassed, ungenerous, in receipt of tangible honours. And this ungenerosity, at root, springs from one fact: his pursuit of honour as an end in itself. He would not have it desecrated idolatrously by fits and praises: it is to him the divine reality. Superficially a fine attitude, it yet secretes its own insidious poison" (*op. cit.* p. 169).

(19) Charney points to the important issue of limitation when he says that Coriolanus' "pride in deifying itself rejects the ordinary limits of man" (*op. cit.*, p. 187).

(20) Thus Phillips says that "It can be charged, moreover, that he acts not for the welfare of the whole state, but for that of his own class alone. Much has been written of Coriolanus' patriotism. ... But loyalty to one class must be distinguished from that concern for all degrees which should characterize a governor. Little is said specifically of Coriolanus' selfish class interest, but it is the logical implication of his notorious contempt for the common people. And in an aristocratic form of government, political action for the benefit of the privileged few is tantamount to political action for the selfish interests of the ruler" (*op. cit.*, p. 160).

224

(21) As Palmer succinctly puts it: "Marcius served Rome, as long as he could count himself one of her masters" (*op. cit.*, p. 286).

(22) See III, ii. 9 and II. iii. 122. The exact spelling of the adjective modifying *toge* is uncertain. Neilson accepts Collins' amendation to *woolless*, but, as Charney notes, "the Folio spelling 'Wooluish,' would suggest to a reader the base woolen material of the gown" (*op. cit.*, p. 182). Charney accepts the Folio spellings to read as modern *wolvish*, and goes on to argue strangely that wolvish toga "suggests that the people are trying to make Coriolanus seem to be a wolf by clothing him in a sheep's wool." *Wolvish toga* would have to suggest that its wearer resembles a wolf, not, as Charney contends, a wolf in lamb's wool. The context seems to suggest that the robe is made of wool. Hence he who serves country serves it as a lamb, perhaps even as a sacrificial lamb: see II. i. 1-16, where Menenius argues with the people that Coriolanus is a lamb to the state. In short, Coriolanus has to demonstrate that he is a lamb to the state by wearing its wool.

(23) Erasmus identifies the king with the mind: "the rule of a prince over his people is no different from that of the mind over the body," while at the same time he identifies him with the heart: "What the heart is in the body of a living creature, that the prince is to the state." As embodiment of mind, the king is raised above his subjects, but as embodiment of heart, he is lowered to their level: "The heart is situated in the very middle of the body. Just so should a prince always be found among his own people." Desiderius Erasmus, *The Education of a Christian Prince*, trans. Lester Born (New York, 1936), pp. 175-76 and 208.

(24) See Phillips' comments on the importance of custom as a principle of ethics (*op. cit.*, p. 43). In discussing Coriolanus' speech Palmer observes that it "is a strange observation to fall from the lips of a conservative nobleman, but it is entirely in character. The contempt of Marcius for the people is rooted neither in concern for his country, which he betrays, nor in allegiance to an ordered system of government, which he is prepared to reject in any particular if it does not happen to please him" (*op. cit.*, pp. 269-70).

(25) The subtle ethic of desert has been overlooked by critics who are misled by Coriolanus' argument about desert. For example, Charney says that "Coriolanus should not have to beg for a reward that is rightly his. Either he deserves to be consul or he does not, but this is not a question to be decided by the base plebeians" (*op. cit.*, p. 181). Charney compares Coriolanus favorably with the Prince of Arragon in *The Merchant of Venice*, in that "neither has any doubts about his own intrinsic worth." Charney neglects to add, however, that as a result of his choice based on desert Arragon loses Portia and gains a fool's head.

(26) Charney interprets the scene favorably to Coriolanus, arguing that Coriolanus nobly refuses to become the popular man like Bolingbroke in *Richard II*, who gained his position through "dishonest flattery" (*op. cit.*, p. 183). The inverted analogy does not apply, however, for Bolingbroke has to flatter the common people in order to become ruler, whereas Coriolanus does not. The dishonor which attends flattery's deception is not an issue in *Coriolanus* since the protagonist deserves and has already received his position. Rather than demean him morally, Coriolanus' "flattery" of the people would debase him socially, he feels, and elevate the plebs. It is the debasement, the equalizing of himself with the plebs, which enrages him. Charney had earlier introduced the better answer when he said that Coriolanus' "costume is a violation of social decorum" (p. 180).

(27) Charney notes that "The ability to act or to dissemble is one of the chief resources of the Machiavel," but that "For Coriolanus images of acting and the theater are used

negatively to stress his honesty" (*op. cit.*, p. 170). Charney does not consider that the very act of only pretending to pretend may itself be a kind of pretense.

(28) Eugene Waith's contention that Coriolanus "has political convictions rather than ambitions" damages the drama by erasing one of the terms of Coriolanus' conflict *(The Herculean Hero,* p. 129).

(29) See also the references to power at III. i. 97, 116, and 172.

(30) Charney, pp. 143 and 151.

(31) Charney manages to escape the implications of the servants' exchange by generalizing the referent of "he": "both images develop the violence of the war-as-devourer theme" (*op. cit.*, p. 154).

(32) Of this appearance of the image, Charney remarks, "The association of Coriolanus with eating is curiously positive here" (*op. cit.*, p. 155). Only from a narrow perspective is the association positive: what is positive from the point of view of soldiers about to destroy Rome, is negative from the audience's point of view.

(33) Charney says of the stage details only that "It is undoubtedly good dramatic economy to keep this feast off-stage, since it only serves as background for the appearance of Coriolanus" (*op. cit.*, p. 186). In fact, Charney would have the audience view this background feast, not as a thematic correlative but as a contrast to Coriolanus' condition: "At the very beginning of this scene a strong contrast is made between Coriolanus 'in mean apparel, disguis'd and muffled' and the sound and bustle of the feast going on offstage" (p. 154).

(34) Eugene Waith, "Manhood and Valor," pp. 62-63.

(35) *Ibid.*, p. 266.

(36) Erich Fromm, *The Art of Loving* (London, 1962), p. 14.

(37) As Palmer notes, Shakespeare has altered his source at an important place in the drama: "The shock, when it comes, is the more tremendous in that Shakespeare's Marcius entertains a design which goes far beyond anything in Plutarch. The historical Marcius had no inteniton of burning Rome. His quarrel was with the popular party and his plan was to ally himself with the nobility of Antium in order to recover for himself and his friends their old ascendency in the Roman republic" (*op. cit.*, p. 284).

(38) The timing of Coriolanus' reactions to the triple appeal will not allow us to conclude that he capitulates merely because of love for his mother, as Coriolanus, and many critics, would have us believe.

(39) Palmer notes the similarity of the two scenes when he says that "in this scene, where she lashes him into submission, there is a fore-shadowing of the greater scene when, at the climax of the play, she will use her terrible authority over her son to save Rome and drive him to his death" (*op. cit.*, p. 280).

(40) Palmer, p. 297. All other critics concur.

(41) A question which George Eliot asks in *Middlemarch* neatly frames Coriolanus' present situation: "Who can know how much of his most inward life is made up of the thoughts he believes other men to have about him until the fabric of opinion is threatened with ruin?"

(42) Palmer observes that "He died calling for six Aufidiuses on which to use his lawful sword. But one Aufidius was enough to compass his death" (*op. cit.*, p. 307).

226

The Text of Othello

by Kenneth Muir

The relationship between the 1622 quarto of *Othello* and the text printed in the First Folio is now well established.[1] F is based on a copy of Q imperfectly collated with "an authoritative manuscript."[2] This is proved not so much by the odd spellings—which might have survived the processes of transmission—as by the frequent agreement of the two texts in ending preterites and past participles with t or d.[3] Miss Alice Walker, on the assumption that "one quarto error out of every ten escaped notice," believes that there may be "fifty or sixty errors common to the two texts."[4] This is, of course, a mere guess. The accuracy with which the collation was carried out, even if we could be certain that only one person was responsible, depends on the legibility of the manuscript, the care of the collator, the time allowed for the task, and whether he was fresh or tired, completely sober or slightly fuddled. There may be hundreds of common errors—or hardly any.

Miss Walker believes that the relative badness of the Q text "was due not to scribal errors but to memorial contamination," the copyist (who was possibly the book-keeper) relying too much on his memory.[5] But Sir Walter Greg, E. Honigmann, F. R. Ridley and Nevill Coghill all believe that Miss Walker exaggerates the unreliability of Q[6] and that it preserves some genuine first thoughts of the poet.

Honigmann has shown good reason to believe that the copy for Q was provided by two copyists rather than one; and since the supposed memorial contamination is not confined to the pages copied by one of the copyists, it is unlikely that either was the book-keeper.[7] Honigmann has also shown that Q was set by two or three compositors.[8]

Coghill has recently argued that the Folio text represents Shakespeare's revision of the play, after it had been performed and that the passages which used to be regarded as cuts in Q were in fact deliberate additions by Shakespeare.[9] It would certainly seem to be true that the passages concerned—with one exception, as we shall see—could not have been deliberate cuts by the actors; the time saved is negligible—ten minutes at most, and probably a good deal less; some of the cuts (e. g. the Pontic Sea simile) would have been absurdly inept; and there are other passages which might have been spared.

The exception referred to above is the willow song. Referring to the echo by Emilia in the last scene of the play, which was also cut, Coghill comments:[10]

> Those who think these lines were cut regard it as evidence of
> the cutter's intelligence that, when he cut the Willow Song, he

remembered to cut its echo in Emilia's mouth; but once again this intelligent cutter dissolves on closer scrutiny into the clever-moron, for in this passage too we find care and carelessness, knowledge and ignorance, in an impossible mixture. We have only to turn to the Willow Song and its context to see at a glance that if this supposed cutter had cut from the beginning of Desdemona's speech . . . he would successfully have ousted *all* reference to the Willow Song whatever, without losing anything necessary to the flow of the dialogue.

The objection to this argument is that Coghill has to suppose that Shakespeare wrote the lines in which Desdemona refers to the song, without allowing her to sing it:

> My mother had a maid cald *Barbary*,
> She was in loue, and he she lou'd, prou'd mad,
> And did forsake her, she [had] a song of willow,
> An old thing 'twas, but it exprest her fortune,
> And she died singing it, that Song tonight,
> Will not goe from my mind—

It is surely difficult to believe that Shakespeare wrote these lines and only after the play's first performance added the song here, and Emilia's echo of it in the last scene, Coghill dismisses the usual theory that the song was cut later because the actor could not, or could no longer, sing, on the grounds that "it is not intended to be sung as a formal solo, but as a sort of *fredonnement* or singing-to-oneself." But if it was a cut, it would have been necessary to cut Emilia's echo (without anything more than average intelligence on the part of the cutter) and not absolutely necessary to cut the introductory lines. Indeed, if the speech had been cut, Emilia would have had little time to assist Desdemona to undress.

One omission from Q—not discussed by Coghill—was clearly unintentional. The speech in IV.ii. reads in F:

> Was this faire Paper? This most goodly Booke
> Made to write Whore vpon? What committed,
> Committed? Oh, thou publicke Commoner,
> I should make very Forges of my cheekes,
> That would to Cynders burne vp Modestie.
> Did I but speake thy deedes. What Committed?
> Heauen stoppes the Nose at it, and the Moone winks:

Q jumps from the second of these lines to the last, presumably because the compositor's eye jumped from the last word of the second line to the same word at the end of the sixth.

Another explanation of the cuts in Q has been put forward by Charlton Hinman. [11] He suggests that the copy was cast-off for the different compositors and that one or other of them omitted lines of the text when he found it impossible to fit them into the pages at his disposal. There are certainly signs of cast-off copy: unnecessary spacing and splitting of lines (e.g. D3^a) and the employment of various devices to save space (e.g. B4^a D1^b E4^a G2^b). But if we accepted Honigmann's division of the text between three compositors, we would expect compositor X to begin to get worried only when he reached Sig. F; and that compositor Y would have similar anxiety when he was nearing the end of his stint in Sig. M. In fact none of the larger cuts was made in these crucial pages. It is difficult to find an explanation of this conflict of evidence; but it would appear that the cuts in Q were not due to the attempt of compositors to fit the lines into insufficient space. Nor, as we have seen, does it seem plausible that most of the cuts were made by actors; nor that the passages concerned were added by Shakespeare after the first performance of the play. One is driven to suggest that most of the cuts were due either to sheer carelessness on the part of copyist or compositor or to the difficulty of deciphering Shakespeare's foul papers or the hurried copy made by the two scribes posited by Honigmann.

The editor of *Othello* is therefore faced with a complex problem. Although F must be his copy-text, there are many occasions when he must accept Q readings, and some occasions when he will reject both, either when both fail to make sense or when F has failed to correct a Q error.

Quarto readings are of the following kinds:

1. Shakespeare's first thoughts, on which he afterwards improved.
2. Shakespeare's first thoughts which are superior to his second thoughts.
3. The genuine text which was afterwards altered by someone other than the author.
4. Misreadings of Shakespeare's foul papers by the two copyists—some of which may be due to memorial contamination.
5. Errors of compositors.
6. Errors which were overlooked by F.

Folio readings are of the following kinds:

1. What Shakespeare wrote.
2. Shakespeare's second thoughts.
3. Errors carried over from Q.
4. Misreadings of Shakespeare's foul papers.
5. Sophistications.
6. Errors of compositors.

The editor's main difficulty, of course, is to decide in which category to place any particular reading; and, in the remainder of this article, an attempt will be made to consider some representative divergencies between Q and F. Variants which are unanimously preferred will be ignored.

(1) I.i.25

    Wherein the toged consuls can propose
    As masterly as he: (Q)
    Wherein the Tongued consuls can propose
    As Masterly as he.   (F)

Although F has its defenders, on the grounds that Iago is contrasting men of action with talkers ("mere prattle" is his complaint about Cassio), it is probable that the F compositor misread "toged" as "tōged", partly because the Q word was unfamiliar and partly under the influence of the context.

(2) I.i.29

    At *Rhodes*, at *Cipres*, and on other grounds   (Q)
    Christian and Heathen
    At Rhodes, at Ciprus, and on others grounds
    Christen'd and Heathen   (F)

Presumably F introduced two misreadings, "Christen'd" relating to "others".

(3) I.i.30

    must be led, and calm'd   (Q)
    must be be-leed, and calm'd (F)

Q is obviously wrong, and nearly all editors follow F. Heath and Staunton suggested "lee'd" for "be-leed" and this may well be the correct reading; but F makes good sense and the metrical irregularity of the line is not such as to require emendation.

(4) I.i.147

    To be produc'd, as if I stay I shall   (Q)
    To be producted, (as if I stay, I shall,) (F)

Presumably a misprint in F.

(5) I.ii.21

    provulgate   (Q)
    promulgate   (F)

Ridley is the only editor to follow Q here; but, as he rightly points out "On the *difficilior lectio* principle Q1 carries it away, since *O.E.D.* does not even recognize the word. . . . Further, *promulgate* has a certain connotation of publication by official authority which is not particularly appropriate to Othello's hypothetical action as a private individual in presenting the common people (*vulgus*) with the facts." As Greg says, the rarer word is "most unlikely to have been introduced by the transcriber." It is just possible that Shakespeare himself substituted later the commoner word, but it is more likely to be a misreading of *u* as *m*.

(6) I.iii.35

    inioynted with   (Q)
    inioynted them with (F)

It looks as though the F transcriber imagined erroneously that "inioynted" required an object.

(7) *I.iii.139*
> And with it all my trauells Historie;   (Q)
> And portance in my Trauellours historie.   (F)

Neither version is satisfactory. Q's "with it all" reads like a feeble substitution; but, although "Trauellours" has had its defenders, it would carry the implication of "tall stories" which Othello can hardly have intended.

(8) *I.iii.144*
> > men whose heads
> Doe grow beneath their shoulders: this to heare   (Q)
> > men whose heads
> Grew beneath their shoulders. These things to heare   (F)

It looks as though F, having correctly substituted "These things", realised that the line was irregular and tried altering the beginning.

(9) *I.iii.159*
> She gaue me for my paines a world of sighes;   (Q)
> She gaue me for my paines a world of kisses: (F)

The preposterous F reading was presumably a compositorial blunder.

(10) *I.iii.240*
> > As leuels with her breeding.
> *Du.*   If you please, bee't at her fathers.
> *Bra.*   Ile not haue it so
> *Oth.*   Nor I.
> *Desd.*   Nor I, I would not there reside.   (Q)
> > As leuels with her breeding.
> *Duke.*   Why at her Fathers?
> *Bra.*   I will not haue it so.
> *Oth.*   Nor I.
> *Des.*   Nor would I there recide.   (F)

Q makes three scanable lines, divided at "please", "so" and "reside", and both the Duke's and Desdemona's speeches as given by Q are better than those in F. Presumably F intended "Why! at her father's." It is possible, as Alice Walker implies, that in inserting the "Why", the compositor inadvertently omitted "If you please". In the last line of the passage the compositor telescoped "Nor I, I would not" into "Nor would I".

(11) *I.iii.250*
> My downe right violence, and scorne of Fortunes   (Q)
> My downe-right violence, and storme of Fortunes   (F)

Both "scorne" and "storme" make good sense, and since c/t and n/m are common misreadings either word could have been mistaken for the other. (Cf. *Lear,* III.i.10. where "out-scorne" may be a misreading of "out-storme".). I have shown in *Shakespeare's Sources I,* p.129, that Shakespeare may be echoing Lewkenor's Epistle Dedicatory to *The Commonwealth and Government of Venice*—a book he is known to have read—in which Lewkenor speaks of "the violence of my own fortune". This seems to tip the balance in favour of the F reading.

> (12) *I.iii.269*
>
> > when light-wingd toyes,
> > And feather'd Cupid foyles with wanton dulnesse,
> > My speculatiue and actiue instruments,　　　　　(Q)
> > > when light wing'd Toyes
> > > Of feather'd *Cupid,* seele with wanton dulnesse
> > > My speculatiue, and offic'd Instrument:　　　　(F)

Both versions make sense, as Knight pointed out. The speculative and active instruments are the eyes, the senses and, possibly, the limbs. The speculative and officed instruments—the plural is to be preferred—are the eyes. Shakespeare probably substituted "offic'd" for "actiue". He may originally have written "foyles", but this could be a misreading of "seeles".

> (13) *I.iii.278*
>
> > And speede must answer, you must hence tonight,
> > *Desd.* To night my Lord?
> > *Du.*　　This night.　　　　(Q)
> > And speed must answer it.
> > *Sen.*　You must away to night.　　(F)

Alice Walker comments on the Q version: "It does not seem to me in character that Desdemona should exclaim 'To night my Lord?', forestalling Othello's reply ['With all my heart'], which strikes quite a different note; and although editors have generally followed the quarto dialogue the Folio's omission of the interchange between Desdemona and the Duke strikes the right warrior note and was, I think, deliberate." Certainly the sense requires "it" in the first of these lines; but Desdemona's words can be a question rather than an exclamation and do not seem necessarily out of character. The three speeches of Desdemona, the duke and Othello make a single line. The F version has an alexandrine followed by a short line, or a short line followed by a pentameter. It is possible that the words "You must hence tonight" should be given to the Senator, and that the omission of Desdemona's speech by F was caused by a misunderstanding of this correction.

> (14) *I.iii.330*
>
> > ballance of our liues　(Q)
> > braine of our liues　　(F)

Q gives the correct meaning; F is nonsense as it stands but may, as Theobald suggested, be a misreading of "beame" (r/e, n/m).

(15) *I.iii.355*
> as acerbe as the Colloquintida   (Q)
> as bitter as Coloquintida   (F)

On the principle of *difficilior lectio* there is no doubt that Q gives the correct reading, especially as the word from which it is derived is used by Cinthio to describe [Iago's] hatred of Desdemona. Alice Walker argued that the commoner word was appropriate to Iago, but Harold Brooks showed that Iago uses uncommon words "in soliloquy or in talk with Roderigo—does not this help to mark that his bluff plainness is assumed, not native to him?" It is barely possible that Shakespeare himself substituted "bitter" because the other word caused difficulty; but it is more likely that the substitution was made by someone else.

(16) *II.i.11*
> For doe but stand vpon the banning shore,
> The chiding billow seemes to pelt the cloudes,   (Q)
> For do but stand vpon the Foaming Shore,
> The chidden Billow seems to pelt the Clowds,   (F)

Steevens urged that Q offers the bolder image: "the shore that execrates the ravage of the waves". But, as Delius pointed out, "chidden" is more logical than "chiding". Alice Walker argues that "banning" was suggested by the chidden billow. But I agree with Dover Wilson and Ridley that no scribe or actor would have introduced this word. It is probable, therefore, that "Foaming" was a F sophistication, but that "chidden" was an authentic correction derived from Shakespeare's foul papers (or, less probably, from his own second thoughts).

(17) *II.i.70*
> Traitors enscerped; to clog the guiltlesse Keele,   (Q)
> Traitors ensteep'd, to enclogge the guiltlesse Keele,   (F)

All editors assume that "enclogge" is wrong, but nearly all editors accept "ensteep'd" (i.e. submerged). Grant White, however, printed "enscarp'd" and afterwards changed his mind; and Steevens suggested "enscerped" was derived from "escarpe", "which Shakespeare, not finding congruous to the image of clogging the keel, afterwards changed". But it may be retorted that rocks, mentioned in the previous line, could not clog a keel, and that "ensteep'd" could be a misreading of "enscarp'd". As the passage was originally written, "escarp'd" referred to the gutter'd rocks and "clog" to the congregated sands. On the whole it seems likely that the change was made by Shakespeare for the reason given by Steevens.

(18) *II.i.96*
> So speakes this voyce: (Q)
> See for the Newes: (F)

The Q reading is an assent by Cassio to the Second Gentleman's words "This likewise is a friend". Later in the scene (l.122) Desdemona is told that one has gone to the harbour: Shakespeare (or someone else) may have noticed that no one had been sent and altered Cassio's words to remedy this omission.

(19) *II.iii.251*

What is the matter?   (Q)

What is the matter (Deere?)   (F)

Alice Walker believes that the F addition breaks decorum and that the term of endearment is more suitable for Othello to use. She therefore reads "All's well, dear sweeting" in the next line in place of Q "All's well now sweeting". I cannot see that there is anything indecorous in Desdemona's words; and the "Deere" was probably added by Shakespeare to show that Desdemona was still perfectly in harmony with her husband.

(20) *III.iii.39*

sneake   (Q)

steale   (F)

Nearly all editors follow F, which however appears to have substituted a more genteel word for the one Shakespeare wrote.

(21) *III.iii.123*

denotements   (Q)

dilations   (F)

Iago uses "denotement" earlier in the play (II.iii.310) where it means "indication". Shakespeare may have used it again here and afterwards altered it. Some editors read "delations" (meaning "accusations"). This emendation misses the point: "dilations" comes from the Latin "dilationes" or the French "dilations" and it means "pauses" or "delayings". It refers back to l.120:

Therefore these stops of thine, fright me the more.

Iago has broken off several times, as though he were unwilling to utter his thoughts.

(22) *III.iii.146*

As I confesse it is my natures plague,

To spy into abuses, and oft my iealousie

Shapes faults that are not, I intreate you then,

From one that so imperfectly coniects,

You'd take no notice,   (Q)

(As I confesse it is my Natures plague

To spy into Abuses, and of my iealousie

Shapes faults that are not) that your wisedome

From one, that so imperfectly conceits,

Would take no notice,   (F)

The syntax of the Q version is rather loose, but it is not un-Shakespearian. It seems probable that Shakespeare was also responsible for the tidying-up process, but that either his handwriting was difficult to decipher or the F compositor was careless. It is possible that it was Shakespeare who altered "oft" to "of" (which improves the speech) but unlikely that he would alter "coniects", which goes better with "imperfectly" than with "conceits". The F version of the third of these lines is metrically weak and Alice Walker is doubtless right in thinking that a word has dropped out—probably "then" as in the Q version.

(23) *III.iii.395*
  superuisor (Q)
  super-vision (F)
This is presumably a compositor's blunder.

(24) *III.iv.138*
  And it endues our other healthful members,
  Euen to that sence of paine; nay, we must thinke
  Men are not gods,   (Q)
     and it endues
  Our other healthfull members, euen to a sense
  Of paine. Nay, we must thinke men are not Gods (F)
Neither version is satisfactory. Although the Q lines are good in themselves they involve mislineation before and a short line. The F enjambement is ugly and it is not improved by Miss Walker's omission of "euen" which she thinks was caught from l.149. Shakespeare may have left the speech imperfect or his foul papers may have had corrections which were difficult to decipher. It is impossible to restore what he wrote from the rival texts, but one suspects one line should end with *paine* and that a word is missing from the next, e.g.
  Our healthfull members to a sense of paine.
  Nay, we must thinke [besides] men are not Gods.

(25) *III.iv.141*
  obseruances (Q)
  obseruancie (F)
Although the F word is not used elsewhere by Shakespeare, it is certainly authentic; and the Q misreading is doubtless due to the unfamiliarity of the original word.

(26) *IV.i.78*
  vnfitting (Q. uncorrected)
  vnsuting (Q. corrected)
  resulting (F)
This is apparently a blunder by the F. compositor.

(27) *IV.i.108*
  in *Bianca's* power, (Q)
  in *Bianca's* dowre, (F)

The F compositor blundered, possibly printing a p upside down, as Ridley suggests.

(28) *IV.i.213-4*

  Something from Venice sure, tis *Lodouico*,
  Come from the Duke, and see your wife is with him. (Q)
  I warrant something from Venice,
  'Tis *Lodouico*, this, comes from the Duke.
  See, your wife's with him.   (F)

Q makes better sense; but presumably the corrections in F, though they are bungled, should point to the correct reading. Alice Walker reads:

    I warrant, something from Venice.
            'Tis Lodovico!
  This comes from the Duke; and see your wife is
          with him.

She assumes that the first of these lines in Q was contaminated with Iago's words at V.i.90 "yes sure: O heauen *Roderigo"* and Gratiano's question "What of *Venice?"* But "this", which Miss Walker thinks was inserted in the wrong place, may have been added merely to fill out the line, the corrector or the compositor having mis-divided the lines. For the second of these lines it is therefore safer to follow Q.

(29) *IV.ii.53*

    but alas, to make me
  A fixed figure, for the time of scorne,
  To point his slow vnmouing fingers at—oh, oh, (Q)
    But alas, to make me
  The fixed Figure for the time of Scorne
  To point his slow, and mouing finger at.   (F)

Nearly all editors prefer the indefinite article at the beginning of the second of these lines and nearly all prefer "slow vnmouing" to "slow, and mouing" (a sophistication to remedy the apparent illogicality of the Q reading). Nearly all editors reject "oh, oh", which presumably represent Richard Burbadge's groans, and prefer "finger." But critics seem fairly evenly divided on the exact meaning of the lines. Some assume that "the time of scorn" means "the scornful world" (e.g. Kittredge); others think it is used in a temporal sense as in "time of tribulation" (e.g. Alice Walker). Some think the finger is the hand of a clock, and that "a fixed figure" is a number on the dial; others that it refers to the finger of Time or of the scornful world.

(30) *IV.ii.185*

  for your words,
  And performance are no kin together (Q)
  and your words and Performances are
  no kin together   (F)

(An uncorrected forme of F reads: "And hell gnaw his bones Performances." The first four words belong to Emilia's speech on the previous page.) Q "for" is clearly the correct reading and we should probably read "performance;" but the compositor mistakenly prints the speech as verse.

(31) *V.i.114*
      Hee's almost slaine, and *Roderigo* dead.   (Q)
      He's almost slaine, and *Rodorigo* quite dead (F)

Both texts are probably wrong. Most editors follow Q. Perhaps, as Ridley suggests, the corrector intended to substitute "quite" for "dead," but the compositor misunderstood. Even this would be a feeble line, whether Shakespeare was responsible for it or not.

(32) *V.ii.55*
         the strong conceit.
    That I doe groane withall: (Q)
         the strong conception
    That I do grone withall.   (F)

The F reading is superior as it links better with "groane," with its imagery of childbirth.

(33) *V.ii.209*
    reprobation. (Q)
    Reprobance. (F)

F gives the more unusual reading and probably the correct one, especially as it is better to end the speech on an accented syllable.

(34) *V.ii.317*
    nicke   (Q)
    interim (F)

This is doubtless a F sophistication.

(35) *V.ii.347*
    Indian (Q)
    Iudean (F)

Both readings have been warmly defended. The F reading would be a reference to Judas and it would link up with "I kiss'd thee ere I kill'd thee" in Othello's next speech. The more straightforward Q reading refers to the numerous accounts by travellers of the ignorance of natives of the value of gems, and it links up with Othello's earlier reference to the perfect chrysolite. Either word could be a misreading of the other; but perhaps "Indian" is more likely to be misread as "Iudian" than "Iudean" as "Indian."

It will be apparent from the above examples that it is not always possible to decide in which category the variants fall—whether they are errors of copyists or of compositors, Shakespeare's second thoughts or Folio sophistications. Sometimes both variants are wrong and sometimes F will have failed to correct a Q error. Although the Folio is generally more accurate than the Quarto, it is unsafe to adopt all the apparently "indifferent" F variants since a close analysis will often show that one is slightly better than the other. A list of all the variants in the first scene of the play will illustrate necessity of judging each variant on its own merits rather than on the assumption that because F is generally more accurate we should wherever possible adopt its readings.[12]

Line	Q reading	F reading	Text to follow
1	Tush	om.	Q
2	you . . . has	thou . . . hast	F
4	S'blood	om.	Q
10	Oft capt	Off-capt	F
15	In conclusion	om.	Q
25	toged	Tongued	Q
29	other	others	Q
30	Christian	Christen'd	Q
33	God	om.	Q
33	worships	Mooreships	F
39	assign'd	Affin'd	F
48	noughe	naught	F
65	Doues	Dawes	F
66	full	fall	Q
66	thicklips	Thicks-lips	Q
67	carry'et	carry't	F
69	streete	Streets	Q
72	out	on't	F
79	Seignior	Siginor	Q
84	all doore lockts?	your Doores lock'd?	F
86	Zounds	om.	Q
88	Euen now	Euen now, now	F
95	worse	worsser	F
100	brauery	knauerie	Q
102	in them	in their	Q
107	Zouns	om.	Q
108	you thinke	and you thinke	F
115	come	comes	F
115	now	om.	Q
122-38	om.	If't . . . yourself	F
140	this delusion	thus deluding you	F
146	pate	place	F
147	produc'd	producted	Q
150	cast him	cast-him	Q
153	not	none	F

238

Line	Q reading	F reading	Text to follow
154	hells	hell	F
154	paines	apines	Q
158	Sagittar	Sagitary	F
166	thou deceiuest	she deceaues	F
173	manhood	Maidhood	F
175	I haue sir	Yes Sir: I haue indeed	F
176	o that you	oh would you	Q
177	yon	you	F
181	leade me on	you lead on	F
183	night	might	Q

It would seem to follow that, despite the fact that F was based on a corrected copy of Q, a reasoned and controlled eclecticism should be the basis of a modern text. Even with *King Lear*, of which the quarto is manifestly corrupt, there has been a proper reaction in recent years against the view that the Folio readings should be accepted wherever possible; and the quarto of *Othello*, in spite of Miss Walker's strictures, is certainly more respectable than that of *King Lear*.

Notes:

(1) Cf. W. W. Greg, *The Shakespeare First Folio* (Oxford, 1955), p. 363; *Othello*, ed. Walker and Wilson (Cambridge, 1957), p. 128.

(2) A. Walker, *Textual Problems of the First Folio* (Cambridge, 1953), p. 156.

(3) *Ibid.*, pp. 153-6.

(4) *Ibid.*, p. 158.

(5) *Shakespeare Survey* 5 (1952), p. 24.

(6) W. W. Greg, *op cit.*, p. 368; N. Coghill, *Shakespeare's Professional Skills* (Cambridge, 1964), pp. 164 ff.; E. Honigmann, *The Stability of Shakespeare's Text* (London, 1965). pp. 107-9.

(7) *Op. cit.*, pp. 112 ff.

(8) *Op. cit.*, pp. 113 ff.

(9) Coghill, *op. cit.*, pp. 177 ff.

(10) *Ibid.*, p. 192.

(11) In a paper read at Stratford-upon-Avon, 1964.

(12) One is discussed above; and two indifferent variants have been omitted.

Hamlet, A Successful Suicide

by Burton R. Pollin

Hamlet's leap into the grave after Laertes and his subsequent words, "Be buried quick with her, and so will I," may be taken as symbolic of the hero's tendency throughout the play.[1] He speaks about suicide early in the first act and later presents it as an available alternative to the outwardly-directed action that the Elizabethan audience might expect. His efforts to end his own life will here be viewed as the integrative and dominant theme in the play. I intend to examine the causes for his ready acceptance of the fatal challenge in the light of contemporary writings which evaluated and linked suicide and melancholy, of the audience's general orientation to plays with avenging and melancholic characters, and of the direction of the successive episodes. I believe Hamlet's suicidal impulses to be fully adequate to explain his puzzling behavior and inconsistent speeches.[2] His intellect, sensitivity, and moral and religious scruples caused him to seek the least reproachable means of terminating an intolerable burden of existence. His death would ultimately have the virtue of exposing the real source of public corruption in Denmark.

It may be asserted that many tragic dramas are based on an action of self-sacrifice in which death is the hazard.[3] If the chances for survival are foreseen as negative, devotion to the highest principles may then be deemed an indirect, yet justified self-destruction. We may thus consider martyrdom, in which only the miraculous intervention of the Deity may preserve life. As we shall see, John Donne, following early Christian doctrine, expressed an evolving Elizabethan heterodoxy about suicide when he viewed martyrdom in exactly this light. As for the representation of opinion on the Elizabethan stage—whatever the nature of the fatal crisis, there is a great difference between a mere risk deliberately taken by the hero in overcoming obstacles and a plunge into certain death, after frequently entertaining the idea of self-destruction. Hamlet's allusions to suicide, his deteriorating state during the play, and his failure to achieve any of his purposes to the end— all stamp this drama as different from any conventional tragedy of noble self-sacrifice.

To gauge the real significance of suicide in this part of the Shakespearean canon, it is instructive to glance briefly at other plays of his into which it enters. Before *Hamlet* both *Romeo and Juliet* and *Julius Caesar* use the theme prominently; in the first, a play of Christian background, the theological and moral stigma is alleviated somewhat by the lovers' desperate or "mad" state as viewed by Friar Lawrence, who says of Juliet, "And she, too desperate, would not go with me, / But, as it seems, did violence on herself" (V.iii.263-264), and earlier of Romeo, "Hold thy desperate hand; / Thy wilde acts denote / The unreasonable fury of a beast" (III.iii.109-111). Romeo, at the moment of death, calls himself "desperate pilot" (V.iii.117). As is obviously true of Ophelia, madness, even temporary, might be used to exonerate the "self-murderer" as a Christian.

The pagan atmosphere of *Julius Caesar*, closest in style to *Hamlet*,[4] suggests another factor in the question of suicide. We remember Horatio's remark to the dying Hamlet, that he is more an "antique Roman than a Dane" (V.ii.328) and his comparison at the beginning between the "disjoint" state of Denmark and "the most high and palmy state of Rome" (I.i.113). To Shakespeare the Roman spirit was best exemplified in the refusal of a noble character to yield to ignomiy. "Elevation . . . invests the suicide of Brutus and Cassius" as it does that of Antony, Cleopatra, Charmian, and Iras in *Antony and Cleopatra*, dating probably from 1606-1607.[5] An effort to escape from disgrace as well as to inflict justice on himself prompts the suicide of the "pagan" Moor, Othello, but there is not a shred of Christian condemnation of the act in Cassio's "This did I fear, but thought he had no weapon, / For he was great of heart" (V.ii.361-362). Earlier Iago had cynically dissuaded the love-maddened Roderigo from suicide, chiefly through promising him the joy of eventually deceiving Othello. *Macbeth*, close to *Hamlet* in date of composition, is equivocal on the subject, since Macbeth, relying on the supernatural, disdains such a death: "Why should I play the Roman fool, / And die on mine own sword?" (V.viii.1-2). In *Lear* the attempted suicide of the blinded Gloster (IV.vi) appears as an act of resignation, more in the spirit of *Antony and Cleopatra* since the entire atmosphere is pagan, with the characters regularly invoking the "great" or "gentle" gods (I.i.117; IV.vii.17; V.iii.23). Moreover Gloster is specifically "in despair" according to Edgar, and despair is held a state of melancholy in Shakespeare's plays. The scene of ancient Britain in *Cymbeline* yields a last reference to suicide in Imogen's request to Pisanio, who has been sent by the deluded husband to slay her, for "gainst self-slaughter / There is a prohibition so divine / That cravens my weak hand" (III.iv.79-81); this is an anachronistic echo of the Christian prohibition mentioned in Hamlet's first soliloquy. Clearly in Shakespeare's plays a suicide may occur only when a noble pagan faces defeat and shame or when a Christian is driven into a state of dementia by accumulated woes, as in *Romeo and Juliet*. The latter has particular significance for *Hamlet*.

The mounting disasters which afflict Shakespeare's tragic protagonists might be termed forces of fate; in *Hamlet*, as has been said of *Julius Caesar*, there is a "climate of apprehension, of impending fatality . . . of man foredoomed from the outset."[6] The acceptance of a predetermined death as a kind of unavoidable justice, self-inflicted in suicide, accords with the spirit of Roman stoicism and of Greek ritualistic drama. Francis Fergusson, in comparing the Greek and Elizabethan theatres, maintains that Hamlet is equivalent to Oedipus in that "his death was the only adequate expiation for the evil of Denmark. Hamlet, however darkly and uncertainly he worked, had discerned the way to be obedient to his deepest values and accomplished some sort of purgatorial progress for himself and Denmark."[7] Those who stress the motif of the inherited tragic-flaw, following the lead of

241

Hamlet's "the stamp of one defect" (I.iv.31), can easily subscribe to this view. The hero's fatalistic acceptance of doom, however, from the beginning would subordinate the dramatic element of will unreasonably for an Elizabethan audience which demanded firm action from a strong although humanly fallible protagonist. The final action which deliberately invites the doom, as I view *Hamlet,* fulfills the demands for developing and solving the complex dramatic and philosophic tensions of this ambitious play.

There is, of course, a question of the extent to which the theme of suicide occupied the minds of the audience and authors of the age. Elements that need to be discriminated are the dramatic and psychological patterns that pointed to such an act, a general view of the ethical stand on the subject, and the consonance of such a theme with the spirit of the age. Undoubtedly, much caution is needed in making any claim about the degree of pessimism or disillusionment of any one period. While the reign of Elizabeth as a whole has seemed to past historians to be fraught with high hopes and the spirit of expansionism, there is an increasing shift toward the view maintained by G. B. Harrison and others, that the turn of the century was marked by gloom and discouragement among thoughtful Elizabethans. As causes he itemizes the wars with France and Spain or the constant state of wariness like that described at the beginning of *Hamlet;* the nationwide fear of internecine conflict over the undecided successor to the moribund queen; the death of great statesmen such as Walsingham, Hatton, and William Cecil; the revolt and execution of the popular Essex; and virulent plagues in the city of London.[8]

These and other events contributed to the development of that general feeling which George Williamson has aptly called "the metaphysical shudder . . . which 'brought death into the world' of early seventeenth century thought" and which Lawrence Babb calls "the despondency of the late English Renaissance." Following Professor Williamson's lead, Victor Harris has adduced many instances of the growing belief in the corruption and mortality of the universe, from the stars to man.[9] So widespread were these advocates of doom that George Hakewell was moved to publish in 1627 his "long-preparing" work, *An Apologie of the Power and Providence of God in the Government of the World.* Many were the sermons of despair, reflecting a fairly popular attitude; similarly, a large number of works intermingling ethics and psychology considered the causes and symptoms of melancholy, an evidence of increasing general interest. It may be granted at once that the Elizabethans held inconsistent and confused views in this area, as many commentators have cautioned.[10] Reference will be limited to a few of those works which, according to internal evidence in *Hamlet,* may well have engaged Shakespeare's interest. Even more pointedly, it must be limited to those writers who express opinions about the suicidal drives of melancholics: Montaigne, Cardanus, and Bright.

Only a few words need be said about Montaigne, long held a source for ideas in Shakespeare.[11] The popular essays were translated by Sir William Cornwallis and by John Florio for two separate editions in 1600. Classical stoicism is the keynote of this work, written during the extraordinary political and religious strife of

242

France under Catherine de Medici. Relevant to my theme is the third chapter of Book II, "A Custome of the Ile of Cea," which surveys individuals and groups who have preferred suicide to a life in pain or shame. A citation notes that "Agis being demanded how a man might do to live free, answered: 'Despising and contemning to die'" (p.307). Christian prohibition is ignored in the stipulation, "So am I nothing tied unto lawes made against murtherers, if I deprive my selfe of mine owne life" (p.309). The theme recurs in "Of Judging of Others Death" (II.xiii.), which concludes with an extensive citation of the death of Socrates, the slow self-destruction of Marcellinus as recorded by Seneca, and the death of Cato (pp.551-553).

The *Comforte* (of death) by Girolamo Cardanus, translated from the Italian by Thomas Bedingfeld (published 1573 and again 1576) was a probable source of specific passages in *Hamlet*. Hardin Craig and Lily Campbell fancifully propose it as the very book from which Hamlet was reading when accosted by Polonius (II.ii.).[12] Several of the pertinent sentences will give the flavor of this once popular work and show its relevance to the death-theme in *Hamlet*. Cardanus comments on man's resemblance to a shadow (sig.A4) and remarks, "In this lyfe there is nothing found that may justly be called good or evyll ... all things consysted in opynion. ... We are causes of oure own evill (sig.B). On death he notes, "As in sleeping and waking, we feel it not when it comes" (sig.D). He elaborates, "from Socrates," the comparison of death with "a sound sleape, a long journey, or destruction" (sig.D2) and speaks of the soul as "beinge let lose from prison of the bodye" so that we should not "eschew death" for "desyre of such heavenlye hapynesse." Very close is the resemblance in "fore there is nothing that doth better or more truly prophecy the ende of lyfe than when a man dreameth that he doth travayle and wander into farre countries and ... in countries unknown without hope of retourne" (sig.D3); also close is "Death dooth take away more evylles then it bringeth and those more certayne" (sig.D3). He speaks of life as compact of "toyle ... labour, suspicions and peril (sig.D4) and lists several of those who "have disdayned death and for lighte causes killed themselves," including Portia, Cleopatra, Lucretia, and Leonidas (sig.D10). Finally he observes that by death we shall "not be subject to injuries, and calamity" (sig.F). Fifty years after the first printing Cardanus, himself a suicide, was still being read as an authority, if we may judge from over one hundred references to his works in Burton's *Anatomy of Melancholy*.

Both Montaigne and Cardanus demonstrate the marked shift in the late sixteenth century from the medieval revulsion at the idea of self-murder to Donne's enlightened tolerance in his *Biathanatos*, written in 1608 and circulated in manuscript before Donne's accepting Holy Orders in 1614, although published by his son only in 1646. I shall cite it as a concrete embodiment of opinions current among the intellectuals of the age when *Hamlet* was being produced.[13] The *Biathanatos* is well summarized in its subtitle: "A declaration / of that / Paradox / or / Thesis, that / Selfehomicide is not so Naturally / Sinne, that it may never be otherwise / Wherein / the nature and the extent of all those Lawes / Which seem to be violated by this Act, / are diligently surveyed." Initially he explains that it is no "sinfull concurrence" or "brave scorn" or "faint cowardliness" that makes him undertake the subject, but merely the reflection that "whensoever any affliction assails me, me thinks I have the keyes of my prison in mine own hand ..." (p.19). First, he observes that it is condemned as (1) springing from "desperation," (2) as making a return to God "in this life" impossible, and (3) as precluding repentance for its implicit sin. Donne has no wish to attack the traditional Catholic and Anglican view that "desperation" or madness exonerates the suicide by depriving him of freedom of will. He wishes to refute only the last two articles. For example, he asserts that sacrifice through martyrdom is equivalent to suicide (pp.56-58) so that in the time of St. Cyprian it was deemed a deprivation of glory to die a natural death.[14] He returns again to the theme in citing Christ as giving "his life for his sheepe" (p.187), and he finds numerous "suicides" in the Old Testament, such as "Samson, Ionas, and Eleazar" (pp.196-205). He cites the negative evidence that only two church councils spoke against self-slaughter (pp.86-87) and attaches importance to the idea of man's preferring "a publique good ... before his private life" (p.141). The right to a sacrificial suicide is clear since "though we have not "dominum," we have "usum" of our own existence, which we may "lose ... when we will" (p.112). In short, Donne earnestly endeavors to find a justification for those instances which correspond to the goal of tragedy, i.e., self-abnegation for the service of mankind or of God to the point of annihilation.

Donne was primarily concerned with the ethics of suicide because of a keener current interest in the causes. The instances of suicide may not have been notably increasing until well into the Jacobean period, although statistics for the period are markedly unreliable,[15] but there is no question of an increase in one of the major acknowledged causes, namely various types of depression or melancholy. If the larger number of cases did not proportionately swell the suicide list, there must have been at least a greater popular concern with what Babb aptly terms "the Elizabethan malady." Many factors could have contributed to this in addition to the general despondency of mood mentioned above, one of the chief being the Italianate deportment of the young bloods, returning from the Continent and often finding their sources of advancement unresponsive despite their travel and education. Thus the "malcontent" type became a characteristic personality in the court and intellectual centers of London, as well as in the theatre.[16] As Professor Stoll and others have shown, Marston's The Malcontent reflected a major concern of the period and also antedated Hamlet in theme.[17]

The cynicism and generalized depression of the malcontent enlisted him in the large company of sufferers from the melancholy humors which afflicted the protagonists of the revenge tragedies in general. Critics have drawn a parallel between Hamlet and several of these, especially Kyd's The Spanish Tragedy.[18] I should like to point out unnoted similarities: Hieronimo commits suicide at the end, indeed with a "bare bodkin," after slaying the Duke, and Bel-Imperia takes her own life in a more definitive action than that of Ophelia. The prevalence of suicidal speeches and actions in the whole school of revenge tragedy clearly suggests Shakespeare's awareness of the popular acceptance of the connection between madness and suicide, as well as of its dramatic usefulness. The inclusion of three types of aberration in so popular a play as *Hamlet* indicates how readily the audiences accepted it as a substantive force in their drama. Melancholia was a useful temperament to give to a hero since, on the dubious authority of Aristotle, it was widely held that "melancholics were likely to be brave, witty, and thoughtful."[19]

I should like to examine briefly a few treatises on melancholy for the light shed either directly on suicidal concepts in *Hamlet* or indirectly on the opinions of the theatre-goers of the age. Timothy Bright's *Of Melancholie* (with two editions in 1586 and a third in 1613) has been suggested as a source of Shakespeare's lore on madness.[20] "Melancholy" was used by Bright and his coevals to indicate the disease itself and its symptoms, including depression, sadness, misery, hysteria, sullenness, hypochondria, morbidity, and frenzy (p. vi). We find a distinction between melancholy as despondency and madness as frenzy sometimes made in *Hamlet*: e.g., "make mad the guilty" (II.ii.537), "out of my weakness and my melancholy" (II.ii.577), and especially (from the king) "[His speech] was not like madness. There is something in his soul / O'er which his melancholy sits on brood" (III.ii.164-165), and "This something-settled matter in his heart, / Whereon his brains still beating puts him thus / From fashion of himself" (III.ii.178-180). However, this distinction is not consistently preserved in Shakespeare, nor made in Bright, as his title indicates. There was often little distinction made between a melancholic temperament and action.

A few references to Bright's treatise—several not previously noted—will show interesting parallels between the melancholy man in Bright and in *Hamlet* and underscore his suicidal tendencies. He asserts that "the causes of all diseases are either breaches of dutie ... or such accidentes as befall us in this life against our will, and unlooked for. From the same also do arise the works of melancholie" (p.242). Perhaps persons most conscious of their duty and sensitive in general are most liable, such as scholars, for "of the labours of the mind, studies have good force to procure melancholie" (pp.242-243). Hence it is not surprising that such persons sometimes "are found verie wittie, and quick [to] discern." They seem to have "that of a natural readiness which custom of exercise, and use hath found in them" (p.130). We remember that Hamlet tells Rosencrantz and Guildenstern that he has lost all his "mirth, foregone all custom of exercises" and lost delight in "this goodly frame, the earth" (II.ii.289-290). May not Hamlet's "custom of exercises" refer merely to the sallies of wit and the logic-chopping that keep the mind limber, as he had demonstrated earlier in the same scene, especially since the entire passage concerns his change of attitude, not of physical habits? The symptoms of Bright's melancholic and of Hamlet have much in common: e.g., "Their dreames are fearfull" (p.131) as Hamlet peripherally notes about the would-be suicide; they are "more exact and curious in pondering the very moments of things" and also "diligent and painefull, warie, and circumspect. ... Their resolution riseth of long deliberation because of doubt and distrust" (pp.130-131). He later elaborates on the theme which has become standard in *Hamlet* criticism, i.e., dilatoriness: "Thowe contemplations are more familiar with melancholic persons then with others, by reason they are not so apt for action ..." (p.200). We are reminded of Hamlet's witticisms and hysterical outbursts, anent Ophelia and spies set upon him when we read about "the sudden and capricious mirth" of the melancholic (pp.163-164) as well as his "sighing, sobbing, lamentation, countenance, demisse, and lowring" (p.135). Compare Hamlet's list of the qualities of the grief-stricken melancholic (I.ii.76-81).[21] The "flat despaire" into which the melancholic falls makes him especially aware of "the calamities of this life, not inferior to the pain of transgression of civill lawes" (p.185). He "distasteth much wholesome meate of consolation, and loatheth many plesaunt and fragraunt cuppes of comfort and counsell" (p.223), says the clergyman-writer. It is no wonder that in this condition, as Hamlet notes upon seeing the ghost, the melancholic is subject to "certaine blasphemies suggested of the Devill and laying of violent hands of themselves, or upon other neither moved therto by hate or malice or any occasion of revenge" (p.228). Much of Hamlet's cautiousness in action and suicidal impulse match this "textbook" of Elizabethan psychology.

It would be tedious and unnecessary to show in how many respects Robert Burton followed the lead of Timothy Bright in his great work, definitive for the period, *The Anatomy of Melancholy*, of 1621.[22] A few items will substantiate the view that Hamlet could have been readily accepted by Shakespeare's audience as a suicidal melancholic. May not this statement of Burton's stand as a motto for the entire play: "If they hear, or read, or see, any tragical object, it sticks by them; they are afraid of death, and yet weary of their lives; in their discontented humours they quarrel with all the world, bitterly inveigh, tax satirically, and because they cannot otherwise vent their passions, or redress what is amiss, as they mean, they will by violent death at last be revenged on themselves" (p.353)? Burton learnedly presents the many authorities who hold that "spirits, bad Angels, or Devils" can "cause Melancholy" (pp.157-176). He gives the many physical causes of the disease, including even bad air (pp.206-210), a factor which reminds one of Hamlet's "I am but mad north-north-west. When the wind is southerly, I know a hawk from a handsaw" (II.ii.360-361). This hearkens back also to Bright's "The ayre meet for melancholie folke, ought to be thinne, pure and subtile, open and patent to all winds; in respect of their temper, especially to the South and Southeast" (p.257). The subsections of Burton, dealing with the "Passions and Perturbations of the mind" (pp.217-282), include "Sorrow," "Shame and Disgrace," "Envy, Malice, Hatred," "Desire of Revenge," "Anger," "Discontents," "Concupiscible Appetite, as Desires, Ambition," and "Love of Learning, or overmuch Study." There is material of relevance also in his "Prognosticks of Melancholy" (pp.366-374), which section indicates the high incidence of melancholic suicide: "Seldom this malady procures death, except (which is the greatest, most grievous calamity, and the misery of all miseries) they make away themselves, which is a frequent thing, and familiar amongst them" (p.367). After citing most of the familiar instances from Biblical and classical literature, including examples of martyrdom, he adds a plea that suicides who, "deprived of reason, judgement, all, as a ship that is void of a pilot must needs impinge upon the next rock or sands and suffer

246

shipwrack," should not be censured (p.373). Many are the suicides of those suffering from Love Melancholy, a section which comprises almost the entire "Third Partition" of Burton's work (pp.611-866). Finally he discusses types of "Religious Melancholy," as does Bright in his last section, and pleads that "we must make the best construction" of the act of a man who puts "desperate hands upon himself, by occasion of madness or melancholy, if he have given testimony before of his Regeneration, in regard he doth this not so much out of his will, as from the violence of his malady" (p.949). We are thereby reminded of Horatio's statement —be it pious hope or assertion of belief: "Good night, sweet prince, / And flights of angels sing thee to thy rest" (V.ii.346-347).[23]

Keeping in mind a few of the factors which the "psychopathologists" of Shakespeare's day thought sufficient causes of melancholia, let us briefly examine in *Hamlet* seriatim the indications that Shakespeare intended him indeed to appear to the audience from the outset as a bona fide, grief-stricken melancholic. It should first be noted that although the malady may strengthen the tendency toward suicide, such an action by no means derives solely from it. There are several types of evidence: Hamlet's self-conviction in soliloquies and asides or in speeches to Horatio and others in those rare moments when he is not on guard; his words to others at times when they are subject to several interpretations, as to Polonius; statements made about him by other characters; actions which appear to spring solely from a state of desperation or hysteria and those which appear to be so contrary to discretion and caution as to imply irrationality. First, I shall consider the instances of the first and second types which seem least equivocal as indications of his rooted melancholy.

Our first view is of a man "of nighted colour" with "vailed lids," (in the words of Gertrude) who implies for himself an even greater extremity of grief: "Dejected haviour of the visage, fruitful river in the eye" etc. (I.ii.81-83). This "haviour" plus his dress led Anthony Scoloker, in his *Daiphantus* of 1604, to say: "Puts off his clothes / His shirt he only wears, / Much like mad Hamlet."[24] The speech leads directly into Hamlet's first soliloquy, opening on the theme of a frustrated tendency toward suicide and closing with the overwrought sentence, "But break my heart, for I must hold my tongue!" (I.ii.159). Later, upon his confronting the ghost, Horatio suggests that it might deprive his perhaps over-sensitive friend of reason and "draw [him] into madness" (I.iv.74-75), a suggestion which Hamlet adopts later. Somewhat ambiguously the ghost itself suggests it: "But, howsoever thou pursuest this act, / Taint not thy mind, nor let thy soul contrive / Against thy mother aught" (I.v.85-86). A "taint" of the mind need have no reference at all to matricide, but specifically to a type of deterioration into frenzy that the ghost witnessed on his second appearance to Hamlet.[25] Surely the spirit who was enjoining upon his son the soul-damning action of murder could not here be concerned with the infection of mere sin.[26] Next, in Hamlet's wild, soliloquizing response, with its almost hysterical jottings on the tablet concerning his uncle, he designates his head as "this distracted globe," the adjective being reserved throughout the play for "mad," as in "She is importunate, indeed distract" (IV.v.2). Horatio finds his words to be "wild and whirling" even before his declared intention to assume "an antic disposition" (I.v). In Act II Ophelia describes a man in "the very ecstasy of love," as Polonius reports him (II.i.102), whose antic disposition would have to encompass more skill than that of any of the players to be falsely so convincing: "Pale as his shirt, his knees knocking each other, / And with a look so piteous in purport" (II.i.81-84).[27]

Claudius, Polonius, and Gertrude give abundant evidence that Hamlet is "changed"; a mother's concern and scrutiny might well penetrate a mere deception carried on for weeks. Hamlet's letter, sent to Ophelia and read by Polonius (II.ii.115-119), while perhaps demonstrating as he says a sincere passion awkwardly expressed by one "ill at these numbers," might also be an instance of "wild words," especially if one believes that he had previously been taking leave of the girl and was heart-brokenly determined to turn her love aside for the sake of her safety.[28] Ambiguous are his statements to Rosencrantz and Guildenstern about "inability to reason" (II.ii.259) and being "mad-north-northwest" (II.ii.360), but in the soliloquy concluding the scene both the language and the intemperate passion charge him with madness; e.g., "I . . . peak / Like John-a-dreams" and "out of my weakness and my melancholy, as he is very potent with such spirits, / Abuses me to damn me" (II.ii.541-542 and 577-578).

At the beginning of Act III the "good friends" speak of his admitting to being "distracted" and recognize his "crafty madness" (III.i.5-8), a condition which, to the audience, might appear the feints of real madness as well as a deliberate deception. In "To be or not to be" the language itself might reveal one type of melancholy, according to Bright; thus: "the native hue of resolution / Is *sicklied* o'er with the *pale cast* of thought" (III.i.84-85), thought being Hamlet's self-confessed flaw. There is every reason to assume this to be a piece of self-analysis, as I shall show. We have already noted the king's reference to his "melancholy" as distinct from his dubious "madness." Later I shall consider the implications of such actions as his wild response to Horatio concerning the "Murder of Gonzago" (III.ii) and to the over-solicitous spying pair, as well as the implications of his self-inflammatory speech about speaking "daggers" to Gertrude. In his abusive speech then, he makes the interesting observation that "madness could not err, / Nor sense to ecstasy was ne'er so thrall'd / But it reserv'd some quantity of choice / To serve in such a difference" (III.iv.73-76). Is this perhaps a hint that even a melancholy hero can exercise judgment, show discretion at times, and execute a plan only as a victim?[29] Later, after the queen has been perplexed and alarmed by his dialogue with the ghost, he bids her conceal "That I essentially am not in madness, / But mad in craft" (III.iv.187-188). This does not disprove his melancholy, simply his present condition of frenzy, especially because of the possible qualification in the word "essentially." Gertrude certainly is not convinced that he is sane, to judge from her statements to Claudius (IV.i), nor does she show any signs of distrust of the king and compliance with Hamlet's plan until the moment of drinking the poisoned cup. The single, trifling exception is "He weeps for what is done" (IV.i.27), which might easily be spoken out of a motherly protection of a beloved madman who will need this extenuating circumstance.

In the final act, in addition to actions which spring from a disordered intelligence or frenzy, such as his outshouting Laertes at the grave, we note his long apology to Ophelia's brother, disavowing any culpability because of his madness (V.ii.216-231), a passage which obviously represents "the gentle entertainment to Laertes" previously requested by the queen (V.ii.194-195). There is a kind of sincerity in its self-abasement—"His madness is poor Hamlet's enemy"—which convinces the reader and auditor rather than the implacably vengeful Laertes.[30] Hamlet's last utterance, indeed, continues his own feeling of abuse, so to speak, in his reference to "this harsh world," which has thrust him, helpless although forewarned, into a fatal "springe" baited by the brother of that other innocent victim. (Two scenes—V.ii.293 and I.iii.115—show father and son using the same image.)

Hamlet's melancholy or strong discontent with the private and public aspects of the world is a "cantus firmus" which determines the direction of his thoughts and actions, even toward suicide as one of his options. Robert Burton reviewed the several causes of melancholy in the belief that each of them can turn the wits awry (pp.113-366); in Hamlet we find an imposing array of sources of keen distress, all of which enmesh his life and reason. Consider briefly his total condition. Recalled by the sudden death of his father from the quiet, academic atmosphere of Wittenberg, he is shocked by his mother's incestuous marriage[31] to his uncle, "the bloat king" (III.iv.182 and III.ii.89),[32] who soon proves to be his father's murderer. The morally corrupt court[33] has connived in the usurpation of the Prince's throne[34] and his two school friends, Rosencrantz and Guildenstern, lend themselves, like Polonius, to insidious probing and "knavery" (III.iv.205); the beloved Ophelia becomes an obedient lure at the disposal of his enemy,[35] even as does his mother in her chamber.[36] Is there any wonder that he feels corrupted in his own inner being, especially when torn between the obligations to his Christian ideals and to his father's spirit?[37]

To requite the murder of his father he is commanded or encouraged to slay his uncle according to the lex talionis which is so repugnant to his humanity and religion that he is still, in Act V, after proof of the king's deadly intentions toward himself, questioning Horatio about the justice of killing Claudius (V.ii.67-68). Surely it is proper to surmise that blood revenge was a cause in which he could not believe, despite his assurance to the ghost and occasionally to himself and Horatio.[38] Significantly, Horatio's "entreatment" to the ghost asks him to speak "if there be any good thing to be done, / That may to thee do ease, and grace to me" (I.iv.39-42). Obviously the ease of mind that the revenge will accomplish for the ghost will also destroy the hope of salvation for Hamlet's soul; we know how much his father's lack of absolution weighed upon Hamlet's mind. I conclude that Shakespeare intended his deep sense of religion to prevent him from deliberately ending either the life of his uncle or of himself.[39] Even his casual phrases are saturated with a religious stream of references. Since it is basic to major passages and to the entire question of suicide, the religious element in the play needs to be further explored.

Bradley moderately declares that while the play cannot be termed a religious drama, it makes a freer use of "popular religious ideas" than any other Shakespearian tragedy; Goddard insists that Hamlet was "made for" religion. Father Blackmore asserts that the delay in revenge stems from "a failure to transgress Christian principles of justice" and that the religious tone of resignation deepens with the progress of the action, a resignation which Bradley is more inclined to call fatalism. In Schücking's opinion Hamlet justifiably dwells upon his father's lack of time for repentance and Hankins sees most of Hamlet's endeavor as concerned with drawing his mother into a readiness for sincere contrition.[40] Hamlet sounds the religious note when first he speaks of the "canon" against self-slaughter, which is eventually underscored in the "maimed rites" tendered Ophelia and in the antecedent debate of the gravediggers on the degree of will involved in the suicide.[41] From the language of Hamlet it is possible to cull an impressive number of religious allusions, some of course directly suggested by the ghost but many uttered as gratuitous expressions of emotion or belief; even the interjections based on holy names have a special relevance at times. They are much more frequent proportionately in Hamlet's utterance than in Horatio's, for example. An almost random survey yields the following: in Act I, nine; in Act II, five; in Act III, thirteen; in Act IV, three; in Act V, seven.[42]

It may be argued that the third soliloquy, "To be or not to be," in its final form eliminates the religious element. In the 1603 Quarto, it continues the argument of the first soliloquy in "For in that dreame of death, when wee awake, / And borne before an everlasting Judge . . . ." The broad theme here of Hamlet's preoccupation is clear, but more questionable is the specific emphasis, that is, whether upon his own self-destruction or the elimination of Claudius.[43] Despite the mixed metaphors of the soliloquy it is easy to follow the argument and apply it to Hamlet himself. Continued existence entails enduring "outrageous fortune" whereas opposition to the "slings and arrows" can only mean invoking forces that will lead to the extirpation of one's troubles, probably together with life. "To take arms" might also mean, in a sense, taking up "a bare bodkin" for one's own death; the end is the same, whatever the meaning of the metaphor. As for the puzzling "conscience," it should be noted that in its common Elizabethan meaning of "clear knowledge" or "inward apprehension," devoid of any moral tone, it validates the non-action of staying alive, here regarded as cowardly by comparison with self-destruction. We must remember the purely neutral attitudes toward suicide seen in Montaigne, Donne, and Cardanus, in accepting this definition. It is rendered more likely by the referent of the preceding line: "than fly to others that we *know not of*" (III.i.82).[44] In short, our knowledge of present evils is more valid than our incomplete knowledge or mere suspicion of future evils, and therefore we resolve but fail to act. Significantly, the action may be that of suicide as is remotely intimated by his next remark—a request to Ophelia to pray for his sins. The manner of a suicide's advent to that "undiscovered country" might intensify the evils, as Ophelia's burial will indicate. Note also that the burdens of life enumerated by Hamlet may all be considered as relating directly to himself: the "dispriz'd (or "despis'd" of Quarto Two) love—of Ophelia; the law's delay in placing him on the throne; the "wrong," "contumely," "insolence", and "spurns," that he must "take" from the "unworthy" king. It is significant, surely, to find Hamlet on the day of the "mousetrap" presentation, reviewing the advantages of annihilation.[45]

The theme is always attractive to him, in his rational moods and in his deepest melancholy. Having secured the pledge from the two witnesses of the ghost, he regrets his very existence that requires him to set right the disjointed limb of the times. In his letter to Ophelia, shown to Claudius, he closes with "Thine evermore, most dear lady, whilst this machine is to him" a suggestion that his bodily being was unlikely to survive long. Polonius is struck by the trenchant reply, "Into my grave?" but fails to observe how much more apt is his thrice repeated "except my life." After slaying the garrulous old lord, he voices a series of macabral jests on the dissolution of corpses, and pursues the topic further upon his return from England when he takes up the skull of Yorick. Finally, there is the insistence of Hamlet, while his "prophetic soul" bodes ill, that "the readiness is all" (V.ii.210). Even this prophetic mood might appear melancholic to the Elizabethans.[46] Of this portion of the play I must say more in discussing the many risks taken by Hamlet in his course.

From my point of view, Hamlet is as much devoted to endangering his own position and courting an honorable death as he is to promoting that of Claudius. From his first entrance he directs inappropriate insult and mockery at his unscrupulous, hypocritical adversary. Ernest Jones is one of the few who mention that this course "can lead to no other end than to his own ruin," but he fails to follow up this aperçu.[47] From the rejection of consolatory "son," with its punning reference to his disinherited state (I.ii.67), to his last contemptuous pun on his uncle's "union," Hamlet scarcely ever speaks a wholly civil word to the king. But what is merely a sense of outrage and animosity before the appearance of the ghost becomes foolhardiness and self-defeat afterwards. He spares no opportunity to inform the king directly or through his agents of his antipathy, his ambitions for the throne, and his distress over the marriage. Many scenes of the play show this. Surmising almost at once that his two school-fellows have been suborned, he baits them with "Denmark's a prison" and "our monarchs [are]... the beggars' shadows," returning to the theme in "Beggar that I am ..." (II.ii.205). When the players enter, he initially and probably scornfully declares that the player king "shall have tribute of me" (II.ii.310); next he tells the pair about Claudius's former detractors who now pay dearly for his miniature. In the prearranged encounter with Ophelia, almost certainly recognized as such by Hamlet, he abuses her father for intruding into other people's affairs and pledges his opposition to the life of one married person.[48] After the play-scene he puns abusively on the "fare" given by the king in the promise of succession (III.ii.98-100). His references to "poison in jest" (III.ii.224), "the galled jade" (III.ii.232-233), and the "croaking raven" which "doth bellow for revenge" (III.ii.241-242) are broad hints. Afterwards, he tells the two probers about the violence of the purgation he would offer the king, mentions his lack of "advancement," and flings them off with the business of the recorders.

After the death of Polonius, he plainly shows his disdain for them as "sponges" of the king, whom he then calumniates as "a thing—of nothing" (IV.ii.). Directly he invites "your fat king" (cf. "the bloat king") as well as "your lean beggar" to feed maggots which will feed fish for the table. (Cf. his being a "poor beggar" in II.ii.266. Is this a covert death wish?). Finally he consigns the king to the lower regions and leaves him with a broad, insulting allusion to his marriage (IV.iii.).

In major episodes of the plot this inclination to alarm, warn, and menace the king is made clear. In the first, Hamlet presents "The Murder of Gonzago" after he has accepted the authenticity of the ghost for about two months. There was no need to insist upon so exact a dramatic parallel in murder in order to "tent him to the quick." A guilty conscience could be expected to show a response to a much less faithful representation.[49] Recognizing this, J. Dover Wilson has made an asset out of the enigma by insisting upon the primarily menacing nature of the whole sequence with the scornful interpolation by Hamlet. Yet, after a long exegesis, devoted to proving that Hamlet wishes to convince Claudius and the court of his homicidal mania, an aim counter to self-preservation, Wilson shuffles off the problem by submitting that "the mystery itself is an illusion" and the character of Hamlet "is a matter of 'make-up.'"[50] This is a tribute to Shakespeare's legerdemain, but not to his dramaturgy.

The next major episode, Claudius's prayer, demonstrates Hamlet's inability deliberately to kill the man who will attempt to murder him, as he has every reason to believe. Shortly before, Hamlet had announced that his "purgation would plunge him into far more choler" (III.ii.292-293), a pun also on the issue of blood. In typical fashion, Shakespeare is here spinning the thread that will more naturally serve to introduce the king at his own purgation. Whatever the reasons that prevent Hamlet from taking revenge at this convenient moment, he expresses no belief in the sincerity or effectuation of the king's repentance (III.ii.89-95). In the next scene Hamlet indicates his distrust of the commission that takes him to England, thus exposing the purely dilatory purpose of his previously expressed scruples. When Claudius rises to confirm Hamlet's belief, having failed to pray wholeheartedly, our fears for the Prince's safety increase abruptly. In Gertrude's chamber we observe that he places himself in further jeopardy by thrice insisting upon the horror of marrying a murderer (III.iv.28-30, 64-65, 97-101). To be sure, by the end of the scene Hamlet seems convinced of his mother's change of heart and intention to be secretive; yet, noting no estrangement between the king and queen in the last act, in the graveyard or at court, and with no interview held before the first meeting (as his ignorance of Ophelia's death proves), he has no assurance that his warning too has not been conveyed to Claudius. Thus his real danger from the king's fear-maddened thrust at his life is increased. It is reasonable to assume that basically this is a chance that he is more inclined to invite than to avoid.

One of the chief problems for criticism is the next episode, which carries a not unwilling Hamlet off to England in the company, or custody, of his "two schoolfellows, / Whom I will trust as I will adders fang'd" (III.iv.202-203; cf. their master as "the serpent that did sting thy father's life," etc., I.v.39). He obviously expects the worst "knavery" from their "mandate," and yet he makes no plan or opposition against his danger as a friendless victim on the sea or in England. One of the putative sources of *Hamlet* finds this circumstance, derived from Saxo, too incredible and shows the Prince as refusing to embark upon the high seas.[51] Nor does Hamlet later tell Horatio that he made a determined, purposeful investigation of that "mandate."[52] It was a whim, "rashness," that led him to the fearful truth, while only the fortuitous arrival of the pirate ship enabled him to return.[53] It may be claimed that assurance of execution would have been gratifying to his impulses toward self-extinction, but a craven's or felon's death could not fail to outrage his sense of pride and honor. The discrepancy between Hamlet's gnawing sense of duty toward his father and his compliance with Claudius's plans for a "sea-change" is intensified by the soliloquy on the passage of the troops of Fortinbras, with its amazing conclusion, as Hamlet proceeds to the port: "Oh, from this time forth, / My thoughts be bloody, or be nothing worth!" (IV.iv.65-66). These inappropriate sentiments may well have caused the dropping of the whole speech from the First Folio.

The next major event that illustrates the thesis that Hamlet continually courts death at the hands of Claudius has received much less critical examination than one would expect. Having been deposited on Danish soil by the pirates, perhaps a token of "the great love the general gender bear him" (IV.vii.18), Hamlet dispatches a curt letter to Claudius, to announce that he will on the morrow see those "kingly eyes" which were always offering a strange brand of "cheer and comfort" even in Act I. His first sentence offers the useful information that he is "set naked" on the shore and in a postscript he emphasizes "alone," "naked" being a word which the *Concordance* shows to mean "weaponless, especially when menaced."[54] The use to be made of this information might very well be a further threat against his life, a possibility that seems all the more likely with Laertes thirsting for vengeance at the side of Claudius. Hamlet might have inferred that the son would return with a desire for just such a revenge as he himself had verbally undertaken. However, the indirections and furtive practices of a poisoner appeal to Claudius more than the acceptance of the invitation or the challenge of the letter (if we interpret Hamlet's "alone" to mean, in Claudius's mind, the Prince's circumvention of the "mandate" plot), and so the end comes in the great hall where first we met the assembled family and court.

The final and most cogent example is Hamlet's accepting the challenge while fully aware of the implicit plot against his life. The attempt of Laertes to choke him at the grave fully revealed the brother's ill-will, and the enduring malevolence of Claudius is the subject of his discussion with Horatio just before the entrance of Osric. Consulting his friend about the justice of requiting his would-be murderer, he immediately shifts to the need for speed since a message from England will soon arrive. (In fact, this was chronologically possible only if we postulate an exceptionally slow return by the pirates.) Then, with complete disregard for this urgency of attack, he engages in scornful banter with Osric and accepts the challenge, which will delay further or else, and most significantly, play into the hands of his two opponents. Twice he refuses to postpone the match (V.ii.187-188 and 205-206) and yet confesses to Horatio, "Thou wouldst not think how ill all's here about my heart; / But it is no matter" (V.ii.200-201).

If it be argued that he sees in the match an opportunity to turn the treachery upon the king, there is no sign of his plan. It is always overlooked that Hamlet exhibits great prescience even about the form of the final contest when he mitigates this treachery against Guildenstern and Rosencrantz by explaining to Horatio: "'Tis dangerous when the baser nature comes / Between the pass and fell incensed points / Of mighty opposites" (V.ii.60-62). He envisions a last duel, surely the most honorable and frank way to meet an adversary; yet he carelessly takes the first rapier (and dagger too—V.ii.152) from Osric, the untrustworthy creature of the king, with a light query about the uniformity of blade lengths but without examining the tips. In a sense Hamlet chooses the instrument and Claudius through his henchman effects the release which Hamlet's moral and religious scruples prevent him from grasping himself; the bare bodkin is Laertes'.

The leitmotive of the "king's purpose" which has become Hamlet's purpose is strong evidence which has not received critical attention. After the death of Polonius, Claudius has told Hamlet that he is bound for England. "Good," says the Prince. "So is it, if thou knew'st our purposes," says Claudius. Hamlet's reply, "I see a cherub that sees them," expresses merely his sensible inference as to the uncle's animosity (IV.ii.47-49). On the same theme, after Hamlet's unexpected return, is Claudius's planning in concert with Laertes to poison him via the foil and the "chalice . . . whereon but sipping, / If he by chance escape your venom'd stuck, / Our purpose may hold there" (IV.vii.161-163). Now, in discussing with Osric the forthcoming fencing match, Hamlet takes up the theme: "Let the foils be brought, the gentleman willing, and the king hold his purpose, I will win for him if I can" (V.ii.169-171). A few lines later Hamlet tells the second emissary sent to him: "I am constant to my purposes; they follow the king's pleasure. If his fitness speaks, mine is ready; now or whensoever, / Provided I be so able as now" (V.ii.189-191). Indeed, it appears that in *Hamlet* "the readiness is all," and it is a readiness to fulfill the unmistakably deadly purpose of the king. A last chiming of the note is provided by Shakespeare in Horatio's penultimate statement about "purposes mistook / Fall'n on th' inventors' heads" (V.ii.372-373).

The "casual slaughters" to which Horatio refers are clearly linked to Hamlet's final performance. The critical view that adverse circumstances overwhelmed the Prince fails to account for the self-destructive intent of his antic disposition, his play-scene, his slaying of Polonius, his gibes, his self-defeating judgments, and his acquiescence. It seems to me that from the beginning to the end, his desperate desire to escape from an intolerable burden of life has motivated Hamlet. While his nobility of mind and spirit maintains him as the hero, the depth of his tortured feelings and the scope of his frustrated longings mark him as the epitome of mankind—too often a willing victim for its own, self-inflicted destruction.

254

Notes:

(1) *Hamlet,* ed. Horace Howard Furness, *New Variorum,* 2 vols. (Philadelphia, 1877), reprint (New York, 1963), V. i. 267. All references in the text are to this edition of *Hamlet* (Vol. I; commentaries in Vol. II), with spelling modernized. Only the First Quarto contains the stage direction for the leap into the grave.

(2) Hamlet's death-wish has long figured in criticism; e.g., see Caldecott, cited in *Variorum,* II, 205; Hartley Coleridge and Ludwig Tieck, cited in Augustus Ralli, *A History of Shakespearian Criticism* (London, 1932), I, 24 and 176; John Middleton Murry, *Shakespeare* (London, 1936), p. 247; and Ernest Jones, *Hamlet and Oedipus* (New York, 1949), p. 70. The motivating force of the suicidal impulse was suggested by Karl Polanyi in *The Yale Review,* XLIII (1954), 347, and Robert Speaight, *Nature in Shakespearian Tragedy* (London, 1955), p. 26. My brief preliminary study of the topic was published in *The English Quarterly* (Spring 1952), 20-28.

(3) This is the opinion of Richard Simpson, as represented by H. S. Bowden, *The Religion of Shakespeare* (London, 1899), pp. 310-311. See also G. Wilson Knight, *Principles of Shakespearian Production* (London, 1936), p. 222: "Each of Shakespeare's heroes is a miniature Christ," and J. A. Bryant, Jr., *Hippolyta's View* (Lexington, 1961), p. 120: "Shakespeare in reworking the story of Hamlet imitated an action which in the life of Christ found perfect realization in history." In his whole treatment of *Hamlet,* Bryant approaches my interpretation but avoids the idea that Hamlet willingly effects his own death (pp. 120-127).

(4) M. W. MacCallum, *Shakespeare's Roman Plays and Their Background* (London, 1910), p. 75; see also James Alexander Kerr Thomson, *Shakespeare and the Classics* (London, 1952), p. 116.

(5) James Holly Hanford, "Suicide in the Plays of Shakespeare," *PMLA,* XXVII (1912), 390. He considers that suicide is held sinful only in *Hamlet,* a point made by John Hankins in *The Character of Hamlet and Other Essays* (Chapel Hill, 1941), p. 222.

(6) J. Thomson, *op. cit.,* pp. 246 and 248. See Francisco's "I am sick at heart" (I.i.9) and Hunter's comment thereon *(Variorum,* I,4).

(7) F. Fergusson, *The Idea of a Theatre* (Princeton, 1949), (reprint New York, 1953), pp. 144-145; see the whole of Chapter IV, pp. 109-154. No one has noted that Hamlet's ranting challenge of Laertes at Ophelia's grave, introduced by the interjection " 'Swounds" for "God's wounds," equates him with Christ: "Woo't drink up esill" (V.ii.262 and 264). See *Variorum,* II, 408 for two allusions to Christ in citations; note also Florio's use of *wormwood* for *esill* and Hamlet's use of *wormwood* during the play scene (III.ii.171).

(8) G. B. Harrison, essay prefacing his edition of Nicholas Breton's *Melancholie Humours* (London, 1929), pp. 49-89, esp. pp. 49-58. Similar is the view of Henri Fluchère, *Shakespeare,* trans. Guy Hamilton (London, 1953). He maintains that British drama was then "death-ridden" (p. 31) and that "the time is out of joint" is symbolic of the whole age (p. 198).

(9) George Williamson, "Mutability, Decay and Seventeenth Century Melancholy," *ELH,* II (Sept. 1935), 121-150; Victor Harris, *All Coherence Gone* (Chicago, 1949), pp. 93-120; and Lawrence Babb, *The Elizabethan Malady* (East Lansing, 1951), p. 110.

(10) For the note of caution see Louise Forest, "A Caveat for Critics against invoking Elizabethan Psychology," *PMLA,* LXI (1946), 651-672. For their inconsistent views see Hardin Craig, *The Enchanted Glass* (New York, 1936), p. 233, and Lawrence Babb, "On

the Nature of Elizabethan Psychological Literature" in *Joseph Quincy Adams* (Washington, 1946), pp. 509-522.

(11) For Shakespeare's probable acquaintance with Florio's translation, see a passage from "An Apologie of Raymond Sebond," II,xi, in *The Essays* (New York, 1933), p. 396, and Hamlet's praise of nature and man (II.ii.290-300). Further references are to this edition of Montaigne. Alice Harmon, "How Great Was Shakespeare's Debt to Montaigne?" *PMLA*, LVII (1942), 988-1008, surveys studies which make the attribution and deprecates it herself, but she is cogently answered by George C. Taylor in *PQ* XXII (1943), 330-337.

(12) Girolamo Cardano, *Comforte/ Translated into English and published by Commaundement of the right hon. the Earle of Oxenford* (London, 1573), photofacsimile ed. (New York, n.d.). All references are to this edition. Francis Douce was apparently the first to note verbal parallels, in *Illustrations of Shakespeare* (London, 1839), II, 238. For more recent notice see Hardin Craig, "Hamlet's Book," *Huntington Library Bulletin,* VI (1934), 17-37, and Lily B. Campbell, *Shakespeare's Tragic Heroes* (New York, 1952), p. 133.

(13) John Donne, *Biathanatos* (London, 1700), Facsimile Text Society, fac. of 2nd ed. (New York, 1930). All references are to this edition. For an extensive discussion of this work see S. E. Sprott, *The English Debate on Suicide* (La Salle, Illinois, 1961), pp. 22-26; he fully presents views on suicide later than 1600.

(14) Gaston Garrison in *Le Suicide dans l'antiquité et dans les temps modernes* (Paris, 1885), p. 5, gives the standard view—that of St. Thomas Aquinas, that only the insane may be forgiven. The clowns in *Hamlet* (V. i. 1-27) discuss the Anglican view, for which see Sir Dunbar Plunket Barton, *Links Between Shakespeare and the Law* (London, 1929), pp. 51-54. See Louis I. Dublin, "The Christian Church and Suicide," *Suicide* (New York, 1963), pp. 118-119, for additions to St. Cyprian.

(15) Sprott, *op. cit.,* pp. 32-33 and 159-160, adduces statistics for his claim that 1640-1660 produced more suicides in England than earlier or later periods. Richard W. B. Lewis, *The Picaresque Saint* (New York, 1959), p. 24, claims that only Reformation Germany and Elizabethan England could provide a parallel with today's "wave of real and fictional suicides."

(16) E. E. Stoll, "Shakespeare, Marston and the Malcontent Type," *MP*, III (1906), 281-303. See also Paul N. Siegel, "Studies in Elizabethan Melancholy," *Harvard University Summaries of Theses for 1941* (Cambridge, 1945), pp. 341-344; and Babb, *op. cit.,* pp. 66-75.

(17) For the wide range of melancholic "types" see Babb, *op. cit.,* pp. 76-90 and the five categories given by Theodore Spencer in *Joseph Quincy Adams*, pp. 523-535.

(18) See Ashley H. Thorndike, "The Relations of *Hamlet* to Contemporary Revenge Plays, *PMLA,* XVII (1902), 125-220, esp. 143-151; Fredson T. Bowers, *Elizabethan Revenge Tragedy* (Princeton, 1940), pp. 90-100; and Percy Simpson, *Studies in Elizabethan Drama* (Oxford, 1955), pp. 138-178. In "Hamlet's Mad Soliloquy," *South Atlantic Quarterly,* LXIV (1965), 60-71, Linwood E. Orange holds that the genre established the link between suicidal tendencies and madness for the audience.

(19) For the association of melancholia with genius, wit, and scholarliness through Aristotle and Marsilio Ficino, see Babb, *op. cit.,* pp. 59-60, and 74, and Erwin Panofsky, *The Life and Art of Albrecht Dürer* (1943) reprint (Princeton, 1955), pp. 165-171; the far-flung influence of Dürer's "Melancholia I" throughout the century is worthy of note. Concerning the three types of aberration, one might tentatively label Hamlet's "manic-depressiveness," as does Dr. H. Sommerville, *Madness in Shakespearian Tragedy* (London,

256

1929), p. 39, that of Ophelia "schizophrenia," and that of Polonius "senile dementia." For the last, note Robert Burton's subsection on "Old Age a Cause" in *The Anatomy of Melancholy* (New York, 1945), pp. 183-184.

(20) Hardin Craig, in his preface to Timothy Bright's *Of Melancholie* (1586) Facsimile Text Society, fac. ed. (New York, 1940), p. vii. All references will be to this edition. For verbal echoes of the work in *Hamlet*, see also Mary O'Sullivan, *"Hamlet* and Dr. Timothy Bright," *PMLA,* XLI (1926), 667-679.

(21) For an ingenious explanation of the "sighs" of melancholics see the widely circulated *Discourse of . . . Melancholick Diseases* (1599), by André Du Laurens, trans. Richard Surphlet, Shakespeare Association Facsimiles, No. 15 (London, 1938), p. 94. See the entire discourse for many characacteristics of *Hamlet;* note especially, p. 89: abhorrence of the sun (cf. I. ii. 67); and pp. 72-73: man is "the modell of the whole world" and has "the sence or policy as the beasts; and understanding, as have the Angels; the chief and principall of Gods worke, and the most noble of all other creatures" (cf. II. ii. 295-299).

(22) Floyd Dell and Paul Jordan-Smith, eds., *An Anatomy of Melancholy* (New York, 1940), p. 121, point out the indebtedness of Burton to Bright. All references hereafter are to this edition.

(23) Christopher Devlin, *Hamlet's Divinity* (London, 1963), p. 26, derives this statement from the Catholic burial service, "In Paradisum deducant te Angeli"; see also pp. 30-32 for other parallels with the Latin liturgy. See also Bryant, *op. cit.,* p. 133.

(24) Given by J. D. Wilson in *Hamlet* (Cambridge, 1934), p. 170, and *Variorum,* II, 11.

(25) The *OED* gives two corroborative meanings, with examples: a) to injure or cause detriment to, as "Sure the man is tainted in's wits" *(T.N.* III. iv. 13) and b) diseased (for tainted) as "I am a tainted wether of the flock. Meetest for death" *(M.V.* IV. i. 114-115).

(26) Robert H. West, "King Hamlet's Ambiguous Ghost," *PMLA,* LXX (1955), 1107-17, states that no other ghost in drama comes from purgatory to make such a demand, and argues that the ghost can be declared "accursed." For this very "vexed" question see Roy Battenhouse, *SP,* XLVIII (1951), 161-192, who favors his being a pagan; as does Lily Campbell, *MP,* XXVIII (1931), 281-296; by contrast see I. J. Semper, *The Month,* N.S. IX (1953), 222-231, who argues that the ghost is merely carrying out divine judgment, as does Bowers in *PMLA,* LXX (1955), 740-749. Bowers chooses to ignore the ghost's statement in Gertrude's bedchamber about "This visitation" as intended "to whet thy almost blunted purpose," since he is arguing that Hamlet is too precipitate rather than dilatory in his action.

(27) See Burton, *op. cit.,* p. 726, for the long "gazes" common to those mad for love. Dr. Sommerville, *op. cit.,* pp. 24-25, n. 25, finds this episode to be Hamlet's "worst attack of mental confusion." For typical nineteenth century German criticism see L. Boerme, *Gesämmelte Schriften, Dram. Blätter* (Hamburg, 1829), II, 172, in *Variorum,* II, 291: "Does Hamlet *feign* himself mad? He *is* so. He thinks he is playing with his madness, and it is his madness that plays with him." Bernard Grebanier, in *The Heart of Hamlet* (New York, 1960), pp. 65-72, offers a survey of critiques on his madness, while he denies their validity.

(28) Patrick Cruttwell, in *The Shakespearean Moment* (London, 1954), p. 37, aptly calls the letter a "savage parody (sane or insane, it does not matter) of that early uncritical adoration."

(29) Hudson, *Variorum,* II, 226, aptly comments: "His sanity and madness shade off imperceptibly into each other, so as to admit of no clear dividing line between them."

(30) To my knowledge only G. W. Knight, *The Wheel of Fire* (London, 1949), p. 321, has commented on this passage as indicating Hamlet's abnormality. Gilbert Highet, *The Powers of Poetry* (New York, 1960), pp. 286-290, regards the graveyard ranting as one of many signs of Hamlet's "intermittent madness."

(31) See J. D. Wilson, *What Happens in Hamlet?* (New York, 1935), pp. 39-44. Rev. Gerard Bridge, *Shakespeare's Catholicity* (Beatty, Penn., 1926), p. 26, cites the two medieval church councils which expressly forbade such marriages, as does the *Biathanatos,* pp. 86-87.

(32) One wonders, so prominent is Hamlet's antipathy to drink, at the protest of Brander Matthews, in *Shakespeare as a Playwright* (New York, 1913), p. 212, that Hamlet's first objection (I. iv. 8-20) does not elucidate the atmosphere or the characters.

(33) Augustus Ralli summarizes many treatments of this theme in *A History of Shakespearian Criticism;* among the German critics alone, for provocative ideas we might single out Gustave Rümelin (I, 546), H. A. Werner (I, 523), Th. Gessner (II, 45), and Hermann Turck (II, 163). George Brandes, *William Shakespeare* (New York, 1898), p. xi, asserts: "[Hamlet] feels as if he must die because he cannot set [the disjoint state] right." See also Caroline Spurgeon, *Shakespeare's Imagery* (Cambridge, 1952), pp. 79 ff.

(34) Despite Blackstone's research, "The elective throne is a mirage," says J. D. Wilson, *op. cit.,* p. 30. May we not also surmise that just as Claudius nominates Hamlet for the kingship (I. ii. 108-112) and Hamlet, Fortinbras (V. ii. 342-343), so the "son of a dear father" (II. ii. 559) would have been nominated before the play began?

(35) J. D. Wilson, *op. cit.,* p. 128, reminds us that it is Ophelia who is "jilting" Hamlet, not he the girl.

(36) To my knowledge, no one has noted that Hamlet accuses Claudius to his mother only after stabbing through the arras. If he is unsure of her loyalty, as he seems to be, why does he reveal this information, thereby chancing even greater enmity from the king? As yet, he has only surmised the evil intentions in the mission to England. Should not his disgust with Gertrude grow greater at the thought of her tolerating a spy in her chamber? Perhaps as a result, save for one reported letter to her, Hamlet ceases to attempt to communicate with his mother until the end of the fencing match.

(37) J. D. Wilson, *op. cit.,* pp. 40-42, strongly urges "sullied" for the customary "solid" of the first soliloquy. Kittredge, *Five Plays of Shakespeare* (Boston, 1939), p. 246, cites a verbal parallel for "weary," "solid," and "melt" in *2 Henry IV,* III. i. 47-49 to support "solid" as the reading. Perhaps the First Folio's "foule" for the adjective of "his sole son" (III. iii. 77) is more consistent with Hamlet's self-disdain. Note the extreme position of Hankins, *op. cit.,* p. 34. Allardyce Nicoll, *Studies in Shakespeare* (New York, 1927), p. 73, postulates a sense of distress even over his own ambition to rule, although for a prince this seems no unreasonable claim. For Hamlet's uncalled-for confession of sinfulness see III. i. 88-90 and III. i. 124.

(38) G. B. Shaw asserts in *A New Postscript (1944) to Back to Methusaleh,* quoted in Roy Walker, *The Time Is Out of Joint* (London, 1948), p. 154, n. 13; "Born into the vindictive morality of Moses he has evolved into the Christian perception of the futility and wickedness of revenge and punishment." Harold C. Goddard, *The Meaning of Shakespeare* (Chicago, 1950), p. 370, also speaks of his antipathy to blood-revenge. Goddard (p. 349) and Hartley Coleridge, in Ralli, *op. cit.,* I, 176, point out the oddity of the ghost's urging murder after calling it "most foul, as in the best it is." Sister Miriam Joseph, in *"Hamlet, A Christian Tragedy,"* SP, LIX (1962), 119-140, stresses the religious nature of Hamlet's

dilemma, but tries to validate his revenge as just according to St. Thomas—a questionable attempt.

(39) The apparently cold-blooded sending to death of Rosencrantz and Guildenstern needs justification in this regard. Hamlet has told his mother his suspicions of their intentions (with confirmation told later to Horatio); his substitution of the mandate—now for their death—seems warranted, especially since their being allowed "shriving time" in England would have granted the pair an opportunity to tell the king of England about Claudius's plan, as sealed in the commission. The affair took place *before* the rescue by the pirates; therefore *immediacy* of their execution might have been Hamlet's only manner of escape in England. The subsequent discussion of their fate (V. ii. 56-72) is, possibly, a salve for his conscience. Dramatically, of course, their death was intended to heighten the audience's sense of the need for quick action against Claudius.

(40) A. C. Bradley, *Shakespearean Tragedy* (London, 1911), p. 174; H. C. Goddard, *op. cit.*, p. 333, n. 41; Father Blackmore, quoted in Williamson, *op. cit.*, pp. 372-374; Levin Schücking, *The Meaning of Hamlet* (London, 1937), p. 215. (This might also be said of Polonius and it was positively so ordered for Rosenkrantz and Guildenstern.); J. E. Hankins, *op. cit.*, pp. 207-213, n. 39. Hankins also makes much of Claudius's achievement of the first two stages of repentance, forgetting that it leaves no lasting effect on his conduct.

(41) For the suggestion that the Sixth Commandment must be the "canon" see Hankins, *op. cit.*, pp. 223-224, and *Variorum*, I, 131-132. The sexton echoes the counsel's argument in the famous case of Sir James Hales of 1554, which adumbrates Hamlet's statements on action throughout the play in maintaining that suicide consists of three parts: "Imagination, which is Reflection or Meditation of the Mind . . . the resolution or determination of the mind, and third, the perfection or execution of the resolution" (given in Kittredge, *op. cit.*, pp. 274-275, n. for V. i. 11ff, and in Barton, n. 14, *supra*).

(42) I. ii. 182; I. ii. 195; I. iv. 39; I. iv. 67; I. v. 132; I. v. 136; I. v. 147; I. v. 166; I. v. 180; II. ii. 172; II. ii. 298; II. ii. 505; II. ii. 551; II. ii. 574-576; III. ii. 29-30; III. ii. 122-125; III. ii. 353; III ii. 371-373; III. iii. 73-96; III. iv. 14; III. iv. 47-48; III. iv. 126; III. iv. 144-155; III. iv. 161-162; III. iv. 169; III. iv. 173-175; IV. iii. 34; IV. iii. 47; IV. iv. 36-39; V. i. 74-76; V. i. 247; V. ii. 10; V. ii. 48-49; V. ii. 67-70; V. ii. 312; V. ii. 330. For the explication of a few of these references in terms of Holy Writ, see R. Noble, *Shakespeare's Biblical Knowledge* (London, 1935), pp. 200-209. See also H. Mutschmann and K. Wentersdorf, *Shakespeare and Catholicism* (New York, 1952), pp. 363-365 for "proofs" of the Catholic ambience; also Bowden, *op. cit.*, p. 313.

(43) M. B. Allen, in "Hamlet's 'To Be or Not to Be' Soliloquy," *Shakespeare Association Bulletin*, XIII (1938), 195-207, examines a large sampling of Shakespeare criticism and concludes that the majority support the suicide theme as predominant. Cf. Adolphus A. Jack, *Young Hamlet* (Aberdeen, 1950), pp. 117-118.

(44) Both Bradley, *op. cit.*, p. 98, and G. W. Knight, *op. cit.*, p. 306, are inclined to rely on the last soliloquy (IV. iv. 40-41) for the interpretation of conscience, i.e., "reflection on the consequences of actions" as in "the craven scruple of thinking too precisely on the event." Therefore it seems inconceivable for Hamlet to imply by "enterprise" that of suicide, with so different a type of enterprise as that of Fortinbras brought into the reckoning. The *OED* also lists "reasonableness, understanding, sense" as possibilities, though rare.

(45) Johnson, on the contrary, remarks that he "mentions many evils to which inferior stations only are exposed"— cited in *Shakespeare Criticism*, ed. D. Nicol Smith (London,

1936), p. 196. See also *Variorum*, I, 212, and 206, and W. J. Lawrence, *Speeding up Shakespeare* (London, 1937), pp. 57-60.

(46) The "genius" view of melancholics in the period is confirmed by Du Laurens, *op. cit.,* p. 98, who declares that their writings "have oftentimes foretolde what afterward hath come to passe." Their being prone to "dreadfull dreames" (p. 82) is sometimes part of their prescience.

(47) Ernest Jones, *The Problem of Hamlet* (London, 1947), pp. 28-29, and *Hamlet and Oedipus,* p. 91. Robert Speaight *op. cit.,* pp. 29-30, comments on his recklessness in shouting about the marriage to the hidden king, but despite his asserting that he is "mad at moments" (p. 22), he holds that Hamlet represents "a norm of sanity" (p. 31).

(48) J. D. Wilson, *op. cit.,* pp. 129-134, offers the best support for this widely accepted view, using many points such as the oddity of Ophelia's chancing to have his gifts, the nature of her replies, and Hamlet's words themselves as well as his exits and entrances from the lobby in the hope of surprising the emerging king. See also Coleridge's agreement with the general view in *Variorum*, I, 216.

(49) See Carl Rohrbach, *Shakespeare's Hamlet Explained* (1859), cited in Ralli, *op. cit.,* I, 411-412: "He lets the king know too much through the mouse-trap and his mother."

(50) J. D. Wilson, *op. cit.,* pp. 137-197 and 229.

(51) In *Fratricide Punished* in which Hamlet also manages to eliminate his "conductors" through the unlikely expedient of dodging their shots so that they kill each other and then journeys by land back to court *(Variorum*, II, 137). H. Granville-Barker, *Prefaces to Shakespeare* (Princeton, 1952), I, 112, finds the announcement of the departure for England to be "a complete and ironic triumph for Claudius" with Hamlet brought in "as a prisoner" by the pair and with other attendants, like a jury about to sentence a dangerous, homicidal maniac. Now Hamlet is on the "defensive," he asserts (p. 114).

(52) G. F. Bradby, *Short Studies in Shakespeare* (New York, 1929), pp. 188-189.

(53) D. S. Savage, *Hamlet and the Pirates* (London, 1950), pp. 21-25, argues inconclusively that Hamlet had arranged the interception before he left Denmark—no mean feat before the use of radio and radar! He seems unaware that others have proposed this ingenious theory: S. A. Blackmore, *The Riddles of Hamlet and the Newest Answers* (Boston, 1917), pp. 391-393, D. J. Snider in *The Journal of Speculative Philosophy*, January, 1873, as cited in C. Williamson, *op. cit.,* pp. 125-126, and Miles, cited in *Variorum*, I, 353.

(54) See this use of the term in *3H6*, V.iv.42; *H8*, III.ii.457; *Caesar*, IV.iii.101; *Oth.*, V.ii.258; *Cym.*, V.v.4. The simultaneous arrival of Horatio alone at the shore, summoned also by a letter, need not have precluded a murderous attack by the king's henchmen, but would merely provide a witness for Hamlet. Concerning the larger frame of reference—his return from the toils of Claudius's original plot—Walker in *The Time Is Out of Joint*, p. 145, aptly comments that Hamlet comes back "to the death he has chosen through the graveyard." See Roland M. Frye, *Shakespeare and Christian Doctrine* (Princeton, 1963), p. 138, for Hamlet's readiness for death at the end.

Shakespeare, Montaigne, and *the Rarer Action*

by Eleanor Prosser

An interesting paradox has developed in recent Shakespearean scholarship. Almost all critics accept Montaigne's influence on Shakespeare as established, yet very few regard the supporting evidence as conclusive. Hundreds of parallels have been offered in proof, but only one has withstood the attack of sceptics. When Edward Capell in 1781 pointed to the essay "Of the Caniballes" as the source for Gonzalo's speech on the ideal commonwealth, he offered the only parallel to remain uncontested.[1]

Sceptics have had good reason for their doubts. Despite the imposing lists of parallels published by over a dozen scholars throughout the past century, not one has demonstrated the striking similarity in thought and diction that established Capell's citation as indisputable. In the wake of a mounting tide of Montaigne studies, as early as 1917 Pierre Villay warned that one hundred zeroes added together still make only zero.[2] Nonetheless, enthusiasm continued to swell in G. C. Taylor's *Shakespeare's Debt to Montaigne* (1925), a detailed study arguing the profound influence of Florio's translation on Shakespeare's diction and phrasing. The significance of Taylor and his predecessors—including G. F. Stedfield, Karl Elze, W. C. Hazlitt, J. M. Robertson, and Edward Dowden—can be seen in the ease with which Dover Wilson cited Montaigne, without question, as the source for many passages in his 1934 Cambridge edition of *Hamlet*.[3]

In Alice Harmon's carefully documented argument of 1942, the conservative position received new impetus.[4] Noting that the most frequent citations are of aphoristic material found in the works of classical authors, and thus available to both Montaigne and Shakespeare in *loci communes,* she cautioned against the danger of "influence-grafting." Despite Taylor's able defense,[5] Miss Harmon's warning has increasingly been heeded. Scholars have become wary of positing direct influence on the basis of parallels unless coincidences in diction as well as in idea are unmistakable, and unless such agreements cannot be found in other sources. To date, the only passage surviving this test remains that from *The Tempest.*

A recent chance discovery would seem to add one more parallel that passes Miss Harmon's test. While investigating Renaissance attitudes toward revenge, I was reading Montaigne's essay "Of Crueltie" in the Florio translation and was struck by an unmistakable echo of Prospero's speech of reconciliation:

> Though with their high wrongs I am struck to th' quick,
> Yet with my nobler reason 'gainst my fury

> Do I take part; the rarer action is
> In virtue than in vengeance.[6]

The relevant passage from the essay is quoted in full to give the necessary context.

> Methinks Virtue is another manner of thing, and *much more noble* than the inclinations unto Goodnesse, which in us are engendered. Mindes well borne, and directed by themselves, follow one same path, and in their actions represent the same visage that the vertuous doe. But Vertue importeth and soundeth somewhat I wot not what greater and more active than by an happy complexion, gently and peaceably, to suffer itself to be led or drawne to follow reason. He that through a naturall facilitie and genuine mildnesse should neglect or contemne injuries received, should no doubt performe *a rare action,* and worthy commendation: but he who being *toucht and stung to the quicke* with any *wrong* or offence received, should arme himself with *reason against* this *furiously* blind desire of *revenge,* and in the end after a great conflict yeeld himselfe master over it, should doubtlesse *doe much more.* The first should doe well, the other *vertuously:* the one action might be termed Goodnesse, the other Vertue. For it seemeth that the very name of Vertue presupposeth difficultie, and inferreth resistance, and cannot well exercise itself without an enemie.[7]

Even the most conservative, among whom I count myself, will agree that the parallel is incontestable. Moreover, diction and phrasing are so similar as to suggest that Shakespeare actually had Florio open before him as he wrote.[8]

Discovery of the passage enables us to do more than merely identify a probable source. It also helps to solve a minor problem of interpretation. Prospero's speech is somewhat cryptic, and editors often feel it necessary to gloss *rarer* as "nobler," and *virtue* as "forgiveness." On the whole, of course, they are right. The point is that they feel the passage to be slightly illogical as it stands. In the original Arden edition, Morton Luce comments, "antithesis and alliteration (in 'virtue' and 'vengeance') convey an impression that is almost superior to any articulate meaning";[9] and in the new Arden, Frank Kermode suggests that although the word "pardon" would, indeed, "suit" better, "*virtue* has a curiously positive and inclusive quality."[10]

When we compare Shakespeare's words with Montaigne's, we find nothing inarticulate, nothing curious. Montaigne is considering the motives that lead man to accept injury with patience, defining such motives according to the degree of virtue from which they spring. At the lowest level he places the man who does not retaliate because he has no desire to do so; he is simply good-natured. His choice of patience Montaigne classes as "goodness" (*bonte*), but not true "virtue." His choice leads him to do a "rare action" (*chose tresbelle*), but it arises basically from what Milton was to term "a blank virtue."[11] Above him, Montaigne places the man who feels an injury and furiously desires revenge, but does not retaliate because he puts passion under the control of reason. His choice leads him to "doe much more" (*beaucoup plus*); that is, to do a "rarer action." His choice, based as it is on mastery of temptation, is truly denoted as "virtuous."

Shakespeare's point is slightly different from Montaigne's. Prospero does not choose patience arising from rational control rather than passivity arising from an amiable nature. His "rarer action" is his choice of patience rather than vengeance. In so doing, he nonetheless exemplifies Montaigne's point: that "the very name of Vertue presupposeth difficultie, and inferreth resistance." Prospero is no Stoic. He still feels the injury. Shakespeare's meaning is not merely that Prospero "forgives," and such a gloss is slightly misleading. He means that Prospero's specific type of forgiveness is a "rarer action" than that of a patient Griselda, who forgives easily because she feels no anger. Prospero's choice is difficult, but in electing to take the part of his "nobler reason" despite the claims of his fury, to both Shakespeare and Montaigne he acts with true "virtue."

Apart from the light thrown on the meaning of Prospero's speech, discovery of this particular parallel would seem to be significant for two reasons. First, it suggests that Shakespeare did read Florio's translation and read it closely. If the entire case rested on the Gonzalo parallel alone, we would have to allow the possibility that Montaigne's vivid description of a primitive culture might have been widely copied and thus have been available to Shakespeare without direct reference to the essays.[12] The philosophical discussion in "Of Crueltie" was not the type to have been excerpted, and Shakespeare's use of its suggests that he was reading at least this one essay with close attention. Second, discovery of the parallel suggests that renewed investigation of Montaigne might prove profitable. To my knowledge, neither the given passage nor, indeed, any part of this essay has ever been noted in discussions of Montaigne's influence on Shakespeare. Recognizing the diligence of the many gleaners in the field, we may have assumed that all possible parallels have been unearthed and have limited our attention to those essays most frequently cited. Chance discovery of this one passage suggests that fresh attention to lesser known essays might turn up new finds. Undue weight should not, of course, be placed on one discovery. However, Pierre Villay would surely agree that one times one adds up to a definite one.

Notes:

(1) *The Tempest*, II. i. 147-156. Margaret T. Hodgen, in "Montaigne and Shakespeare Again," *HLQ*, XVI (Nov. 1952), 23-42, cast doubt on the inference that Shakespeare derived his ideas solely from Montaigne's description of barbaric cultures. Nonetheless, her evidence reinforced the probability that he used "Of the Caniballes" as his major source. In her study of the traditional formula by which the nonexistence of civilized features was conventionally described, she found no other example to correspond so closely with Shakespeare's diction. She thus agreed that Shakespeare probably used the Florio

translation. Her contribution was to establish that the ideas were common stock and that several details found in Gonzalo's speech, but not in Montaigne's essay, were available in many sources.

(2) "Montaigne et les poètes dramaticques anglais du temps de Shakespeare," *Revue d'histoire littéraire de la France,* XXIV (1917), 390.

(3) Wilson's assumption of direct influence is all the more remarkable when we realize that no one has yet grappled firmly with the problem of dates. Since Florio's translation was not published until 1603, its direct influence on *Hamlet* must be predicated on Shakespeare's having access to the manuscript. Such a possibility is conceivable, but are we prepared to assume that Florio would loan his personal manuscript for several months and perhaps even years? The type of argument offered by Taylor would require that Shakespeare had the essays at hand throughout the composition of *Hamlet* and, probably, its revision. Moreover, the same claims are made for *Troilus and Cressida.* Taylor's argument could be valid only if Shakespeare was able to refer closely to the manuscript for a considerable period of time—unless, of course, he had a photographic memory that retained total recall for a period of at least a year.

(4) "How Great Was Shakespeare's Debt to Montaigne?" *PMLA,* LVII (1942), 988-1008. In the following year, Frederick Page cast further doubt on Taylor's analysis. Studying the 750 words which Shakespeare first used after 1603 and which thus, according to Taylor, prove direct influence of the Florio translation, Page noted that over 620 were already in use in England before 1603. For this and further evidence see "Shakespeare and Florio," *N&Q,* CLXXXIV (1943), 283-285; CLXXXV (1943), 42-44, 107-108.

(5) "Montaigne—Shakespeare and the Deadly Parallel," *PQ,* XXII (1943), 330-337.

(6) *The Tempest,* V. i. 25-28.

(7) *World's Classics* (Oxford, 1904-1906), II, 119.

(8) Characteristically, J. M. Robertson, in *Montaigne and Shakespeare* (London, 1897), p. 168, attributed Prospero's speech to a passage from the essay "On Diversion" that is wholly unrelated in language and only loosely related in idea.

(9) (London, 1901), p. 125.

(10) (Cambridge, Mass., 1948), p. 114.

(11) Although some parallels in early plays may suggest that Shakespeare consulted the original French version of the essays, there can be no doubt that he was here using Florio. Note Florio's odd rendition of *chose tresbelle* as "rare action."

(12) Considering such a possibility might appear to be pushing scepticism beyond reason, but on the basis of just such an argument Frederick Page concludes that even the Gonzalo parallel offers no sure proof that Shakespeare actually read the essays.

Troilus and Cressida: the Uses of the Double Plot

by Norman Rabkin

To many in each generation *Troilus and Cressida* must seem, as it did once to Tennyson, "perhaps Shakespeare's finest play."[1] On the stage it has had memorable if all too infrequent successes; in the study its muscular and irridescent intellectuality, its language and characterization have earned it the constant attention of Shakespeare's critics. Yet critics repeatedly imply their sense that *Troilus and Cressida* is a failure, and find themselves obliged either to denounce it for its apparent idiosyncrasies or to explain them by seeing the play as a special phenomenon — an exercise for law students, a comical satire — not to be judged by the canons which we normally apply to Shakespeare. The range of statements that have been made about the play is as broad as can be imagined. Thus, for example, S. L. Bethell locates the problems of the piece in its "consciously philosophical" nature and Shakespeare's failure to merge the "story" and the "philosophy," so that "the story is an excuse for thought rather than the embodiment of thought"[2]; while on the other hand Robert Kimbrough explains what he finds anomalous in the play by arguing that "the plot has no central drive, no consistent argument": Shakespeare has been too little willing to sacrifice the conventions which he has inherited from several traditions to achieve an intellectually coherent whole. "War and lechery generally confound all, but this overall theme has no general reverberation or universal ring as developed in this play. It opens in confusion and merely moves through more confusion to less confusion."[3] The play is damned on the one hand for the primacy of its theme, on the other for its themelessness.

For both of these critics the heart of the problem is the relation of "theme" or animating idea to action; and it should be noted that such critics as have achieved a measure of success with the play — Una Ellis-Fermor and L. C. Knights, for example — have done so precisely by confronting the question of the involvement of the theme in the play.[4] Not to recognize the extent to which an underlying idea relates the discrete elements of *Troilus and Cressida* to one another and explains Shakespeare's disposition of events is dangerously to misunderstand both the play's technique and its meaning. Ideas have a life in this play that they rarely have on the stage. What gives them that life is the way in which, built into a double-plot structure, they are made dramatic. *Troilus and Cressida* is perhaps the most brilliant of all instances of the double plot, that convention which gives a play the power to convey a complex theme implicitly through action and ironic language.[5] Through the use of the double plot, as in other ways through other conventions, Shakespeare and his contemporaries turned ideas into theater so that the two could

265

scarcely be separated. Our understanding of the significance of the double plot has long since enriched our understanding of a number of Shakespeare's plays.[6] I should like to argue, by an analysis of the structure of *Troilus and Cressida*, that "the primary reason for [the play's] baffling, ambivalent final effect lies" not, as Professor Kimbrough claims, "with Shakespeare,"[7] but with our failure to recognize in Shakespeare's use of a dominant convention of his theater the key to the meaning of one of his greatest plays.

Despite the smoothness of the bond between them, *Troilus and Cressida* presents two distinct plots, as independent of one another as any in Shakespeare: the affair between Troilus and Cressida on the one hand, and the Greek ruse to bring Achilles back into the war and thus end it on the other. Each plot, or action, has its own beginning, middle, and end, and would in itself constitute a strong enough line for a play of its own; neither plot depends for its outcome on the course of the other. Even in such scenes as the Trojan council meeting, where Troilus irrelevantly speaks of the taking of a wife, or the exchange of the prisoners, which deeply concerns the progress of each action, the two plot lines remain separate. With its discrete plots which paradoxically seem to comprise a unified action, *Troilus and Cressida* resembles other plays in which Shakespeare modifies the convention of the double plot—*A Midsummer Night's Dream* and *King Lear*, for example, where we begin with a strong sense of separate plot lines only to learn that they are inextricably intertwined. Whether the illusion Shakespeare creates in a given play is that the actions are independent of one another or that they are, as in *Troilus and Cressida*, part of a complex and integrated whole, the result is always a structural sophistication so purely Shakespearean that perhaps we should not be surprised at the reluctance of centuries to recognize a shared convention in the double plots of Shakespeare and his contemporaries.

In *Troilus and Cressida* the double plot structure makes possible a thematic exposition, aesthetic rather than conceptual despite the philosophizing for which the play is so remarkable, that makes one realize most poignantly the inadequacy of rational analysis. Only by observing particulars in the order in which they appear, by considering each moment of the play in the contexts of both the whole play and the point at which it occurs, and by recognizing the effects achieved by the parallels between the autonomous plots can we stay clear of the traps into which the critic tempted to make *a priori* statements may fall. My concern is thematic, to be sure. I am not, however, interested in formulating a "one- or two-word subject about which the [play] makes an ineffable statement," but rather with determining by an inductive reading of the whole play the principle which unifies and gives meaning to its discrete elements.[8] The analysis of a work whose genius is primarily structural must itself be structural.

Like a glittering and intricate spiderweb, the totality of the play seems implicated in its every node. Almost any point will do for a start. Let us take the end of the second scene, for example. Watching the heroes return from battle, Cressida and Pandarus have been fencing with each other, Pandarus maladroitly attempting to arouse his niece's interest in a young man toward whom she shows every evidence of indifference. As her uncle leaves, however, Cressida tells us that she actually prizes Troilus more than Pandarus can praise him:

> Yet hold I off. Women are angels, wooing:
> Things won are done; joy's soul lies in the doing.
> That she belov'd knows naught that knows not this:
> Men prize the thing ungain'd more than it is.[9]   *(I.ii.312-315)*

Conveyed in the first sententious speech of the play, Cressida's pessimism comes as a greater shock than the more conventional cynicism she has been demonstrating to her uncle, and is an important touch in a character study which will attempt to explain a notoriously inexplicable infidelity. But, like many such speeches in Shakespeare, Cressida's scene-ending soliloquy does not merely characterize: it raises a question. Is she right? Has a moment no value beyond its duration? Is expectation more satisfying than fulfillment? Is there no survival value in achievement?

As might be expected, Shakespeare is not overtly setting out the thematic conclusion of the play, but he is preparing us for the exposition, sounding his theme in the minor so that we will think back, often and crucially, to Cressida's statement as new facets of the theme are revealed. Already we may be called back by the odd similarity of Cressida's self-justification to a remark that Troilus has just made, with savage irony, in the only other soliloquy so far in the play:

> Peace, you ungracious clamours! peace, rude sounds!
> Fools on both sides, Helen must needs be fair
> When with your blood you daily paint her thus!   *(I.i.91-93)*

Helen's value, that is, lies in the doing: if so many men fight for her, she must be worth fighting for. Like Cressida's soliloquy, Troilus' sardonic jibe merely foreshadows the arguments to come as to the subjectivity of value;[10] but like hers it has a dramatic significance that no one can miss who knows the old story, for, finding the fickle Helen "too starved a subject" for his sword, Troilus immediately and ironically turns to the praise of Cressida.

His theme adumbrated in the love plot, Shakespeare now begins to develop it in the war plot. Listening to the elaborate argumentation of the first Greek council scene (I.iii), the audience may be rather surprised to recognize in a discussion of matters that seem far removed from the love life of the Trojans a concern with the same questions that have already been raised within the walls of Ilium. Why have the gods prolonged the war for seven years? asks Agamemnon. The answer: because Jove wants to make trial of men. When fortune smiles all men seem alike in quality,

> But in the wind and tempest of her frown
> Distinction, with a broad and pow'rful fan,
> Puffing at all, winnows the light away,
> And what hath mass or matter, by itself
> Lies rich in virtue and unmingled.   *(I.iii.26-30)*

With comic alacrity the aged Nestor catches his commander's drift. Whatever it tells us about his intellectual independence, Nestor's repetition of the idea clarifies and reinforces it. He is neither the first nor the last Shakespearean character to make a statement which we must take more seriously than we do its speaker, and his performance here exemplifies Shakespeare's capacity simultaneously to strengthen dramatic illusion and to advance the theme. When the sea is smooth all boats seem equally competent, Nestor observes, but when it storms only the stoutest survive: "Even so / Doth valour's show and valour's worth divide / In storms of fortune" (I.iii.45-47).

Again a metaphysical question underlies the speeches: what is the value of a man? When can one be sure of that value? The answer suggested by Agamemnon and Nestor is that, as the medium in which fortune distributes adversity, time will ultimately distinguish true value. As the play develops, the idea of time as a process which defines and identifies value will grow increasingly complex and important as its role in both actions becomes clear; here it is being suggested for the first time, and as yet it may not seem particularly relevant.[11]

What follows immediately has all too often been taken as a formulation of the play's theme. Ulysses' great sermon on "the specialty of rule" delights the ear and lingers in the memory; it is a gorgeously imagined setting of an Elizabethan commonplace. Moreover, it is crucial in the play. Seldom if ever, however, does such a set piece explicitly enunciate the theme of a play by Shakespeare, and we should not simply assume that it does here. Brief reflection, in fact, should be sufficient for the realization that Ulysses' remarks do not hit dead center. What he does is to make us aware of the urgency of the Greeks' situation, of the dire condition of a society which has lost its old order, and of the dangers of surrendering reason to will, passion, and power. These concerns are indeed highly relevant to what goes wrong in both plots, and parallel in philosophical assumption to the debate about reason and passion; but they do not comprise the ultimate statement to be made about the universe of the play. When Ulysses so persuasively pictures the shaking of degree he is merely describing, not explaining; one might similarly account for juvenile delinquency by pointing out that many young people have lost their respect for established values. Ulysses' speech carries our attention from seven years of stalemate and the concern of the great generals to the delinquency of Achilles without allowing us to think of the latter as less important than the former, and this is a significant function: if the crucial understanding of Achilles' own attitude, at the center of the subplot, is reserved for a later point, its significance has at least been clearly signalled. But the comfortable ideas about order and disorder so often cited—most notably by Tillyard—as the chief importance of the speech do not really begin to answer the questions the play has been asking.

The idea which most looks forward to vigorous development in the play is that of time, whose winnowing function has been described by Agamemnon and Nestor. Already in this scene Ulysses, who is to make the play's most famous speech about time, speaks of it in an odd fashion as he proposes his trick to Nestor:

> I have a young conception in my brain;
> Be you my time to bring it to some shape. *(I.iii.312-313)*

Time is thus a midwife, attendant at an organic process. As he unfolds his plan, Ulysses continues to talk in the language of birth and growth:

> Blunt wedges rive hard knots. The seeded pride,
> That hath to this maturity blown up
> In rank Achilles must or now be cropp'd,
> Or, shedding, breed a nursery of like evil
> To overbulk us all. *(I.iii.316-320)*

The imagery of the nursery takes us back to Agamemnon's account of the seven years' failure:

> Checks and disasters
> Grow in the veins of actions highest rear'd,
> As knots, by the conflux of meeting sap,
> Infects the sound pine, and diverts his grain,
> Tortive and errant from his course of growth. *(I.iii.5-9)*

Ulysses' organic description of time finds its echo almost immediately in Nestor's response. Proposing an encounter between Hector and Achilles, the old man suggests that the success of the event

> Shall give a scantling
> Of good or bad unto the general;
> And in such indexes (although small pricks
> To their subsequent volumes) there is seen
> The baby figure of the giant mass
> Of things to come at large. *(I.iii.341-346)*

Thus, by the end of the first council scene our attention has been drawn to a question of value and to a notion of time. How these matters are to be related to the play's theme is a larger question that in characteristically Shakespearean fashion withholds its question until later. But after the scurrilous interlude in which we first see Achilles, Ajax, and Thersites, the play takes up these matters again. Once again the scene is a council meeting, this time within Troy. And once again, as if to underline the symmetry between I.iii and II.ii, rational men make a mockery of reason: as Ulysses in the Greek camp both praised and exemplified the reason that stands in opposition to the universal wolf of appetite, yet found no better use for his reason than to trick Achilles, so Hector in Troy sees and rationally understands what action is necessary, yet impulsively acts against his own decision. Like the scene before Agamemnon's tent, the scene in Priam's palace concerns the war plot, but at a crucial moment in the argument Troilus reveals that his own attitude toward the return of Helen is based on his attitude toward Cressida; and at this moment the developing theme of the play begins to coalesce.

269

Like the Greeks, the Trojans are reassessing their situation; and like them they discover almost immediately that the attempt to justify what is happening to them leads to a discussion of value.

> *Hect.* Brother, she is not worth what she doth cost
> The holding.
> *Tro.*   What's aught but as 'tis valu'd?

During the course of the argument, Troilus lets us understand what he meant, in the play's first soliloquy, by his jibe at Helen. To Hector, Helen's value is an objective quantity which, measured against the manhood lost in her defense, makes her surrender a moral necessity: "What merit's in that reason which denies / The yielding of her up?" Reason is the key word here, for objective evaluation is a rational process. And Troilus recognizes that reason is precisely the challenge he must answer:

> Nay, if we talk of reason,
> Let's shut our gates and sleep. Manhood and honour
> Should have hare hearts, would they but fat their thoughts
> With this cramm'd reason. Reason and respect
> Make livers pale and lustihood deject.

Distrustful of reason's ability to find excuses for selfish behavior—as indeed it does later when Hector backs out of his fight with Ajax on rational grounds—, Troilus self-consciously espouses an irrational position:

> I take to-day a wife, and my election
> Is led on in the conduct of my will,
> My will enkindled by mine eyes and ears,
> Two traded pilots 'twixt the dangerous shores
> Of will and judgment. How may I avoid,
> Although my will distaste what it elected,
> The wife I chose? There can be no evasion
> To blench from this and to stand firm by honour.

Judgment may err in choice; will is changeable. All that is left is commitment, fidelity to the choices one has made regardless of the consequences; and committed behavior actually creates the worth of the object to which it is committed. From the sarcastic "O theft most base, / That we have stol'n what we do fear to keep" (II.ii.93-94) it is a short distance to "But I would have the soil of her fair rape / Wip'd off in honourable keeping her" (II.ii.149-150). Helen has only such value as her defenders create—but that value is absolute.

Heroic, faithful, selfless, touching as Troilus' asseveration is, our accord with it is shortly to be subjected to considerable strain when we first meet Helen. From Euripides—perhaps even from Homer—to Giradoux the story of Helen's rape has captivated the literary imagination because it so neatly puts the question: should

270

the Trojan war, or any war, have been fought? This is the question that Shakespeare too is asking. Having set up Troilus' justification for the keeping of Helen, Shakespeare dramatically demolishes it within the same debate, even before Helen is introduced. "No marvel," Helenus remarks acidly to Troilus, "though you bite so sharp at reasons, / You are so empty of them" (II.ii.34-35); and Hector makes a similar charge:

> Or is your blood
> So madly hot that no discourse of reason,
> Nor fear of bad success in a bad cause,
> Can qualify the same? (II.ii.115-118)

Opposed to reason, after all, is will, almost synonymous in Shakespeare's English with blood. "The reasons you allege," Hector points out, "do more conduce / To the hot passion of distemp'red blood, / Than to make up a free determination / 'Twixt right and wrong" (II.ii.168-171). Hector objects that in rejecting reason in evaluation Troilus is committing himself to the dangers of subjectivity. "But value dwells not in particular *will*," he argues, because the value of an object resides within the object:

> 'Tis mad idolatry
> To make the service greater than the god;
> And the will dotes that is attributive
> To what infectiously itself affects,
> Without some image of th' affected merit.

Will is the issue, then. Is Hector right in arguing that reason perceives value, or is Troilus in proposing that will projects value upon the object? Shakespeare insists that we be at least aware of the consequences of Troilus' belief, for the hero's most persuasive argument (II.ii.61-96) is ended by the unanswerable screams of Cassandra:

> Our firebrand brother Paris burns us all.
> Cry Trojans, cry! a Helen and a woe!
> Cry, cry! Troy burns, or else let Helen go.

The compressed argumentation of II.ii., then, has spelled out a dialectic that we have already seen developed in the first council scene; even more interestingly, it has translated that dialectic from its first adumbration in the initial soliloquies of the hero and heroine of the love plot to parallel arguments about will by Ulysses and Hector in the political world of the war plot. Most interestingly of all, through a bold device Shakespeare calls attention to the symmetrically matched investigations of a single metaphysical question in the two plots. At the climax of Troilus' argument, the moment at which he must most convincingly advocate his proto-existentialist ethic, the willful hero makes an analogy between the two actions in which he is concerned:

271

> I take to-day a wife, and my election
> Is led on in the conduct of my will,
> My will enkindled by mine eyes and ears. . . .

As a recent editor shrewdly notices, "the analogy between Troilus' choosing a wife and the rape of Helen as an act of revenge is, of course, a very false one."[12] But—as it will take the rest of the play to show—the analogy has a point. Immediately one sees the similarity between Helen and Cressida as foci of action who by one standard are worthless, and by another infinitely valuable.

In the main plot Cressida is going to remain the focus of the question of value. In the subplot, however, the same question is going to be asked most insistently not about Helen but about Achilles. Thus, avoiding the symmetry another dramatist might have attempted, Shakespeare creates the illusion of a universe that is not only coherent but also multitudinously rich. The kaleidoscopic fashion in which the dramatist begins to formulate the theme in his subplot in terms of one character only to complete it in terms of another is one of the marks of his genius in the play.

The next scene begins as another depressing interlude in which Achilles, Ajax, Thersites, and company revile each other—note how little of the Troilus and Cressida plot has been generated so far—but the scene grows more significant as Troilus' question, "What's aught but as 'tis valu'd?" becomes Achilles' question. The warrior has "much attribute," Agamemnon concedes to Patroclus; yet, because Achilles does not regard his own virtues virtuously, because he is "in self-assumption greater / Than in the note of judgment," because he overvalues himself, Achilles is losing the respect of his colleagues. There is a fatal disparity between the actual, inherent value of the hero, and the opinion of that value which Achilles holds. "Imagin'd worth," in Ulysses' words,

> Holds in his blood such swol'n and hot discourse
> That 'twixt his mental and his active parts
> Kingdom'd Achilles in commotion rages
> And batters down himself.

Like Hector talking of Troilus, Ulysses identifies overvaluation with blood, and the notion of will runs through his entire criticism of Achilles; even Hector's charge of idolatry ("'Tis mad idolatry / To make the service greater than the god") finds an echo in Ulysses' "Shall he be worshipp'd / Of that we hold an idol more than he?" The question, what is Achilles? has not yet been formulated as it will be in coming scenes; but in the elaborately planned manner of *Troilus and Cressida* the materials have been gathered to make it possible.

In terms of both plot and theme, the exposition of the play is now over in both actions and the development section about to begin. Each plot has presented a woman who, because of the attitudes of those about her, raises the metaphysical question of value; and each has introduced as central male character a man whose patently exaggerated evaluation—of Cressida in Troilus' case, of himself in

Achilles'—has been attacked as willful, a matter of blood by a character notably concerned with reason and its relation to social order. As the third act opens, Shakespeare leads us back to the love plot. He does so, however, in such a way as to keep alive in his audience's mind its similarity to the war plot, for the scurrilous episode between Helen and Pandarus plainly parallels the similar episode with which the preceding scene opened. Two passages (others might be cited) exemplify Shakespeare's technique:

II.iii.

Ther. Agamemnon is a fool; Achilles is a fool; Thersites is a fool; and, as aforesaid, Patroclus is a fool.

Achil. Derive this, come.

Ther. Agamemnon is a fool to offer to command Achilles; Achilles is a fool to be commanded of Agamemnon; Thersites is a fool to serve such a fool; and Patroclus is a fool positive.

Patr. Why am I a fool?

Ther. Make that demand to the Creator. It suffices me thou art.

III.i.

Helen. In love, i' faith, to the very tip of the nose!

Par. He eats nothing but doves, love, and that breeds hot blood, and hot blood begets hot thoughts, and hot thoughts beget hot deeds, and hot deeds is love.

Pan. Is this the generation of love— hot blood, hot thoughts, and hot deeds? Why they are vipers! Is love a generation of vipers?

The alacrity of such critics as Professor O. J. Campbell to agree with Thersites that in *Troilus and Cressida* "all the argument is a whore, and a cuckold" is easy enough to understand when in contiguous scenes, set in the play's two worlds, reason is so symmetrically travestied.[13] But it is important to observe that the milieux of Achilles and Ajax and of Pandarus and Helen are, though strikingly similar, only one level of a play in which moral seriousness is almost ubiquitous: even Cressida's betrayal, it is clear, has its philosophical basis.[14]

As the scene in which Troilus and Cressida finally get together, III.ii stands at the center of the play. Not surprisingly, it picks up and develops the still emerging theme of the piece, once again simultaneously exposing a number of that theme's facets, but this time fully revealing it. In the first place, as everyone has noticed, the sensuality of Troilus' language gives away the quality of his love; more interestingly, it affirms the accuracy of Hector's unanswered charge that Troilus is moved by will, or blood, rather than by reason:

> I am giddy; expectation whirls me round.
> Th' imaginary relish is so sweet
> That it enchants my sense. What will it be
> When that the wat'ry palates taste indeed
> Love's thrice-repured nectar?

But this is not all. In his fear that expectation must exceed fulfillment—"This is the monstruosity in love, lady, that the will is infinite and the execution confin'd, that the desire is boundless and the act a slave to limit"—the lover shows himself in precise agreement with Cressida's initial reason for withholding herself from love: "Men prize the thing ungain'd more than it is."

Again: what is the relation between the thing and the value men place on it? Such repeated asking of the question—in relation to Achilles, his reputation, and his opinion of himself; to Helen, her intrinsic worthlessness, and the value that has already produced seven years of war; and now to the love of Troilus and Cressida—makes us recognize the justice of the epithet "problem play." As Troilus suggests a position new for him, the crucial scene hints at the play's answer to its basic question:

> Praise us as we are tasted; allow us as we prove. Our head shall
> go bare till merit crown it. No perfection in reversion shall have
> a praise in present. We will not name desert before his birth,
> and, being born, his addition shall be humble. *(III.ii.97-101)*

With its suggestion that time will tell, Troilus' speech recalls the words of Agamemnon and Nestor at the Greek council meeting; moreover, it picks up the organic metaphors in which first Agamemnon, then Ulysses, and finally Nestor couched their discussion of time. In a climactic scene of the love plot Shakespeare is beginning to draw such images together in a significant pattern. Though its meaning does not yet become clear, the pattern emerges dramatically in the words of Troilus. We have heard once before, in Agamemnon's opening speech, of the winnowing function of time. Now, hopefully, Troilus inquires as to the probability of a fidelity in Cressida that might withstand the decay of the blood: he wishes that his

> integrity and truth to you
> Might be affronted with the match and weight
> Of such a *winnowed* purity in love!
> How were I then uplifted! But, alas,
> I am as true as truth's simplicity
> And simpler than *the infancy of truth.*

The connection between Troilus and "unpractis'd infancy" (I.i.12), the establishment of Troilus as one who "with great truth catch[es] mere simplicity" (IV.iv.106), the notion of Troilus as innocent and faithful remain constants throughout the play. But of far greater significance is the picture of truth, like time, as an organic entity, something that has an infancy and a maturity. We shall hear more of it.

Immediately, however, follows one of the most striking dramatic moments in the play, and here it is that the argumentation of the play moves from dialogue into staged action as, through the use of a dramatic irony powerfully grounded in his audience's familiarity with the old story and the terms it has lent their language, Shakespeare allows a ritualistic tableau to act out for us what will happen when time, now in its infancy, shall grow old:

> *Tro.* True swains in love shall in the world to come
> Approve their truths by Troilus. When their rhymes,

274

Full of protest, of oath, and big compare,
Want similes, truth tir'd with iteration—
'As true as steel, as plantage to the moon,
As sun to day, as turtle to her mate,
As iron to adamant, as earth to th' centre'—
Yet, after all comparisons of truth,
As truth's authentic author to be cited,
'As true as Troilus' shall crown up the verse
And sanctify the numbers.

Cres.   Prophet may you be!
If I be false, or swerve a hair from truth,
When time is old and hath forgot itself,
When water drops have worn the stones of Troy,
And blind oblivion swallow'd cities up,
And mighty states characterless are grated
To dusty nothing—yet let memory,
From false to false, among false maids in love,
Upbraid my falsehood! When th' have said, 'as false
As air, as water, wind, or sandy earth,
As fox to lamb, or wolf to heifer's calf,
Pard to the hind, or stepdame to her son'—
'Yea,' let them say, to stick the heart of falsehood,
'As false as Cressid.'

Pan.   Go to, a bargain made! Seal it, seal it; I'll be the
witness. Here I hold your hand; here my cousin's. If
ever you prove false one to another, since I have taken
such pain to bring you together, let all pitiful goers-
between be called to the world's end after my name;
call them all Pandars. Let all constant men be Troiluses,
all false women Cressids, and all brokers-between
Pandars! Say 'Amen.'

The debates in *Troilus and Cressida* may well be the most magnificent staged
argumentation since Aeschylus. But the real measure of the play's greatness is
to be taken at such moments as this, where an argument which originates as an
abstraction from human experience is reëmbodied in such experience to give the
illusion of life. Shakespeare is not telling us about time's function in determining
value: he is showing us, and what he shows us is the theme of the play. The Troilus
who has seen "the infancy of truth" will live to see his Cressida betray him before
his eyes, and to exclaim "O withered truth" (V.ii.46). And what will have happened
in the time in which truth passes through its life-cycle will be the ironic fulfillment of each of the prophecies at the ritualistic ending of III.ii.

To suggest the nature and role of time in *Troilus and Cressida*, let me, recalling
the notion of the spiderweb-like structure of the play, move forward for a moment

to the beginning of IV.iii when Paris announces that the day of Cressida's removal to the Greek camp has arrived.

> It is great morning, and the hour prefix'd
> For her delivery to this valiant Greek
> Comes fast upon.

Steevens glossed "great morning" as "*Grand jour,* a Gallicism," and Delius noted in 1856 that the same phrase occurs in *Cymbeline,* IV.ii.62.[15] No other explanation of the lines has ever been offered. Editors might well have referred us to another sense of "great" in *Pericles,* V.i.107: "I am great with woe, and shall deliver weeping." In the passage in *Troilus and Cressida* as in the one in *Pericles,* "great" means "pregnant," indicating a condition that culminates in "delivery." The incessant personification of time in *Troilus and Cressida* is astonishing. Time is a monster, a witch, an arbitrator, a robber, a fashionable host; it is envious and calumniating, grows old and forgets itself, and walks hand in hand with Nestor. To recognize such a treatment of time, one need not agree with Professor G. Wilson Knight that time is the "arch-enemy," the issue on which the "love-interest turns";[16] but one must note the play's peculiar emphasis on the organic, almost personal nature of metaphysical process. The answer to Troilus' optimistic faith in the world's ability to meet his expectations of it is roundly answered by what the end of III.ii tells us: Cressida, like Troilus and Pandarus, is defined not by wishful thinking but by what each will become in time, and action which is not guided by that realization is going to come a cropper.[17]

At the center of the play, then, the theme which has been taking shape from the beginning has become full and clear. As if by design, Shakespeare chooses this moment to stage the turning point in the action of the main plot, the making of the bargain which will send Cressida to the Greeks. The trade of prisoners naturally involves the war as well as the private affairs of Troilus and so we are back in the war subplot almost immediately. Again, if the play's structure is not a matter of conscious design, one must marvel at the intuitive genius which arranges that, immediately after the climactic exposition of the theme of the relation of time to value in the main plot, that theme should be dramatized with equal emphasis and clarity in the subplot. Thematically, III.ii and III.iii, one in the main, the other in the subplot, are the crucial scenes of the entire play.

Ulysses' trick has worked, and the neglected Achilles is driven to investigate the cause of the derision he sees aimed at him. Merit, he sees, has little to do with reputation:

> And not a man for being simply man
> Hath any honour, but honour for those honours
> That are without him, as place, riches, and favour,
> Prizes of accident as oft as merit.
> . . . . .   I do enjoy
> At ample point all that I did possess

276

Save these men's looks, who do methinks find out
Something not worth in me such rich beholding,
As they have often given.

Claiming like Hamlet to paraphrase the book he is reading, Ulysses offers Achilles
an explanation of his predicament that Cassius had once given to Brutus (in *Julius
Caesar*, I.ii.52ff.): man "Cannot make boast to have that which he hath, / Nor feels
not what he owes, but by reflection." One perceives one's own value, that is,
by seeing it reflected in the opinions of others. Pretending to find the position
difficult to accept, Ulysses continues its exposition: if value is subject to the judgment of others, then "no man is the lord of any thing . . . Till he communicate his
parts to others." Therefore, Achilles' qualities are forgotten while those of Ajax,
"a very horse," receive universal admiration. "What things again most dear in the
esteem, / And poor in worth!" Ulysses exclaims. Having noticed that his deeds
do seem to have been forgotten, Achilles cannot deny what Ulysses has been saying, and he is ready to hear his shrewd opponent's explanation of the shortness
of reputation:

Time hath, my lord, a wallet at his back,
Wherein he puts alms for oblivion,
A great-siz'd monster of ingratitudes.
Those scraps are good deeds past, which are devour'd
As fast as they are made, forgot as soon
As done. Perseverance, dear my lord,
Keeps honour bright. To have done is to hang
Quite out of fashion, like a rusty mail
In monumental mock'ry.

How many moments of the play crystallize here: not only what Agamemnon and
Nestor have already told us about time's determination of value, but also all that
we have learned in the last scene; not only Achilles' discovery that what he has
done will not retain its lustre but must be constantly renewed, but also Cressida's
intuition of the ultimate reality of process ("Things won are done"):

Let not virtue seek
Remuneration for the thing it was! for beauty, wit,
High birth, vigour of bone, desert in service,
Love, friendship, charity, are subjects all
To envious and calumniating Time.

Ulysses' speech is profoundly pessimistic. For if the love plot has been telling
us that value resides not in the valuer (Troilus, Achilles), but in the true nature
of the object (Cressida, Achilles), the war plot makes explicit what the ritual at
the end of III.ii dramatized: even the value in the object itself will be defined —
and generally that definition is by a process of erosion — by time. By the kind of
irony that the double plot in the hands of a master makes possible, the point is
dramatically reinforced. As Achilles laments the course his career has taken in

time, arrangements are in the making to take Cressida away from Troilus while simultaneously the lovers are enjoying what they take to be the sealing of their love's compact. When we next see Troilus he will be innocent of his impending loss, and the irony will recur. And when Troilus discovers the grim irony of his happiness, he will respond to it in a terse remark that Achilles might as well have made to Ulysses: "How my achievements mock me" (IV.ii.71).[18]

His theme established, Shakespeare will vary it for the rest of the play in ways that it is not necessary, after so much analysis, to describe. A few points, however, in which the double-plot structure continues to make itself felt deserve brief notice. One is a new version of the question of merit, noteworthy because it applies—and is applied by the audience—even more vividly to a character in the main plot than to the subplot character it ostensibly describes. Paris asks Diomedes whether Menelaus or Paris himself "deserves fair Helen best." Diomedes, who as everyone in the audience knows is going to be Cressida's next lover—her Paris, as it were—answers as follows:

> Both alike.
> He merits well to have her that doth seek her,
> Not making any scruple of her soilure,
> With such a hell of pain and world of charge;
> And you as well to keep her, that defend her,
> Not palating the taste of her dishonour,
> With such a costly loss of wealth and friends.
> He like a puling cuckold would drink up
> The lees and dregs of a flat tamed piece;
> You, like a lecher, out of whorish loins
> Are pleas'd to breed out your inheritors.
> Both merits pois'd, each weighs nor less nor more;
> But he as he, the heavier for a whore. *(IV.i.54-64)*

The words precisely describe Cressida as the play's Thersites-voice might describe her in transit between Troilus and Diomedes. The predominant and unpleasant imagery of eating and drinking is only a version of Troilus' characteristic language in love.[19] The dregs to which Helen is reduced in masculine opinion hark back too neatly to be overlooked to an earlier prophecy:

> Tro. What too curious dreg espies my sweet lady in the
> fountain of our love?
> Cres. More dregs than water, if my fears have eyes. *(III.ii.73-75)*

And, in the dazzling manner in which *Troilus and Cressida* works, giving the impression of a blinding flash, a single aesthetic moment, rather than of a discursive composition, Cressida's last note has already had its significant echo in Achilles' pain in the scene that follows it:

> My mind is troubled like a fountain stirr'd,
> And I myself see not the bottom of it. *(III.iii.308-309)*

278

By its last acts the play vibrates at almost every point with this sort of cross-reference. Thus IV.v, a scene crucial to both plots, is larded with motifs and with variants of the theme. Let two excerpts speak for themselves. Agamemnon greets Hector:

> Understand more clear,
> What's past and what's to come is strew'd with husks
> And formless ruin of oblivion;
> But in this extant moment, faith and troth,
> Strain'd purely from all hollow bias-drawing,
> Bids thee with most divine integrity
> From heart of very heart, great Hector, welcome. *(IV.v.166-172)*

And Hector says a few moments later:

> The end crowns all,
> And that old common arbitrator, Time
> Will one day end it.

The last two acts consist primarily in the working out of the ironic prophecies in both plots. In the war plot the decision to keep Helen eventuates not in the glory that Troilus predicted, but in her continuing degradation (recall Diomedes' opinion) and in the utterly ignoble death of Hector himself, presaging the final catastrophe Cassandra has announced. Like a vengeful deity time has decided the debate in the Trojan camp. And in the love plot we have watched Cressida, in a ritualistic prefiguration of her future, passing lightly from the kisses of one Greek to the next. With Troilus we look on at her final act of betrayal; and we watch him arrive at a state, in which reason has become useless, that Ulysses has long since identified as the consequence of the behavior of Troilus' alter ego Achilles:

> O madness of discourse,
> That cause sets up with and against itself!
> Bi-fold authority, where reason can revolt
> Without perdition, and loss assume all reason
> Without revolt. This is, and is not, Cressid. *(V.ii.132-136)*

As "the dragon wing of night o'erspreads the earth" (V.vii.17)—again time is a personal force, the monster of ingratitudes, all too eager to gobble up human achievement—Achilles has ironically regained a reputation which his Myrmidons have stolen for him, and once again, even in the rush of the denouement, we are asked to contemplate the value of reputation. Troilus' last words reveal that he has learned at last the harsh reality that a man is what time proves he is, not what the optimist wishes him to be:

> Hence, broker, lackey; ignomy and shame
> Pursue thy life, and live aye with thy name.

Perhaps it is a signal of the difference between *Troilus and Cressida* and most of Shakespeare's plays that the idealistic hero, with whom for all our awareness of his error we have been led consistently to sympathize, should utter as a last speech words that so clearly reveal the diminution of his stature. Similar reduction affects us in the last appearance of other leading characters whose careers we have followed with concern: Cressida feebly chastizing herself for a disposition to follow Diomedes that she is scarcely capable of recognizing as contemptible, Achilles wretchedly crying the triumph won in fact by his roughneck vassals, Pandarus suddenly aged and bequeathing to the audience his venereal disease. Pandarus, whose coarse and heartless grumbling ends the play, is a paradigm of all the play's characters. In the magical conclusion of III.ii we have virtually seen etymology staged as Pandarus ironically prophesies the way in which he will become his name, and at the end we see the process complete. Regardless of their own intentions and the best potentialities within them, the major characters of the two plots have been transformed by a process over which none of them has control. That process is time, a time presented so consistently in organic terms that one comes finally to understand its inevitability: it grows according to its own will, not according to the desires of any individual.[20] And that process is the play's answer to the question of value: value exists not in the subjective will of the valuer or in the object he sees, but only in that object as time disposes of it. If this is not a satisfactory answer to a legitimate philosophical question, one must admit that very few readers have suspected that it was Shakespeare's intention in *Troilus and Cressida* to satisfy their skepticism or dispel their pessimism. But the play provides another kind of satisfaction which one seeks more legitimately perhaps in the theater, the aesthetic satisfaction of recognizing a structure brilliantly animated and made coherent by its complex relation to a thematic center.

If my account of *Troilus and Cressida* has been inordinately long, it has nevertheless only established the skeletal outline of the play's plan. That plan Shakespeare was shortly to modify in *King Lear,* which similarly but with even more mastery achieves a symphonic network of inner relationships that virtually defies expository analysis. In such plays the double plot has gone as far as it can go; it has become a form which, like all the great forms in the arts, is capable of saying what could not otherwise be said. I have found it almost impossible in discussing *Troilus and Cressida* not to speak at times in the language of the musicologist.[21] Though Pater's dictum that "all art constantly aspires towards the condition of music" has long since received the qualification it needs, it applies with singular aptness to Shakespeare's plays, and particularly to the double plot plays, where he makes the actions play one against the other so swiftly, so subtly, and so interdependently that they form an inseparable whole, a unity created by multiplicity. As the symphonist sets theme against theme, developing now one, now the other, intertwining and then separating them, and finally bringing his movement to a point of stasis at which the formal integrity of the whole releases a sense of completion, so, pre-eminently among the composers of double-plot plays, Shakespeare in such plays as *Troilus and Cressida* sets his plots one against the other, leading us to take pleasure from the insight afforded at each node at which they intersect, and to feel the whole only in the comprehension, conscious or unconscious, of the relation between parts.

Notes:

(1) Jerome H. Buckley, *Tennyson: The Growth of a Poet* (Cambridge, Mass., 1960), p. 257.

(2) S. L. Bethell, *Shakespeare and Dramatic Tradition* (London, 1948), pp. 99-105. Professor Bethell's commitment to Eliot's dramatic practice leads him to regard what sounds like a vice in my paraphrase as a special virtue. The fact that he happens to be attracted to a drama that demands "dual consciousness" on the part of an audience attending to a story and a "philosophy" that work in opposite directions is not the issue with which I am concerned here though it is challenging. The point is rather that Professor Bethell sees a conflict between the play and its theme.

(3) Robert Kimbrough, "The *Troilus* Log," *SQ*, XV (1964), 205-206. Professor Kimbrough elaborates his argument in *Shakespeare's Troilus and Cressida and Its Setting* (Cambridge, Mass., 1964).

(4) Una Ellis-Fermor, " 'Discord in the Spheres': The Universe of *Troilus and Cressida*," *The Frontiers of Drama*, 3rd ed. (London, 1948); L. C. Knights, "The Theme of Appearance and Reality in *Troilus and Cressida*," *Some Shakespearean Themes* (London, 1959). A convenient summary of recent criticism of *Troilus and Cressida* can be found in Mary Ellen Rickey, " 'Twixt the Dangerous Shores: *Troilus and Cressida* Again," *SQ*, XV (1964), 3-13. Professor Rickey's own argument, that the unifying theme of the play is a corruption which consists in mistaking "prideful will and appetite" for honor and glory, will be seen to have its parallels to my own reading, though it stops short of seeing the uses to which this idea is put in the play, and the larger theme which it serves.

(5) I have attempted to formulate a statement about the nature and history of the convention in "The Double Plot: Notes on the History of a Convention," *Renaissance Drama*, I (1964), 55-69.

(6) William Empson's "Double Plots" in *Some Versions of Pastoral*, first published in 1935, has been seminal, particularly with respect to *Troilus and Cressida* and *1 Henry IV*, though his discussions of those plays are more valuable for the avenues they open than for the conclusions they reach. Two recent studies which exemplify the kind of light double-plot analysis can shed on Shakespeare are Cecil C. Seronsy, " 'Supposes' as the Unifying Theme in *The Taming of the Shrew*." *SQ*, XIV (1963), 15-30, and R. W. Dent, "Imagination in *A Midsummer Night's Dream*," *SQ*, XV (1964), 115-130.

(7) Kimbrough, "The *Troilus* Log," p. 205.

(8) Sheldon Sacks, *Fiction and the Shape of Belief* (Berkeley and Los Angeles, 1964), p. 3. Professor Sacks' strictures against the casual use of the concept of "theme" are valuable (e.g., pp. 55-60). Like him, I find myself most concerned not with a writer's beliefs but with the "discernible and vital shape" such beliefs take in his works. Employing Professor Sacks' critical terminology, one might usefully study Shakespeare's plays in terms of their varying uses of the techniques of "represented action" and "apologue"; one of the things one might discover is that *Troilus and Cressida* disturbs its critics and inspires the kind of criticism it does because it is more like an "apologue" than most of Shakespeare's other plays. The debates, followed by episodes which seem to "prove" one or another position taken in them, are unusual in Shakespeare. And so is the fact that most readers, I suspect, though moved by the play's outcome, care less about the

individual fates of the characters than they do about the thesis that has been made so painfully operative in the play's world by the end. Since my study is not taxonomic, however, I am not here concerned with proving that *Troilus and Cressida* is an "apologue."·

(9) My text is George Lyman Kittredge, *The Complete Works of Shakespeare* (Boston, 1936).

(10) The most lucid summary of the arguments over value in *Troilus and Cressida* is Miss Ellis-Fermor's. Her conclusion, that Shakespeare is attacking all value, is not mine.

(11) L. C. Knights, p. 82, calls attention to the importance of time in the world of *Troilus and Cressida.*

(12) *Troilus and Cressida,* ed. Alice Walker, (Cambridge, 1957), p. 169.

(13) O. J. Campbell, *Comicall Satyre and Shakespeare's Troilus and Cressida* (San Marino, 1938).

(14) See Empson (p. 39) on the function in Troilus and Cressida of "the comic character's low jokes" in establishing the play's unity.

(15) *Troilus and Cressida,* ed. H. N. Hillebrand, New Variorum ed. (Philadelphia, 1953), p. 212.

(16) *The Wheel of Fire* (New York, 1957), pp. 65, 68.

(17) The view of A. S. Knowland, in *"Troilus and Cressida,"* SQ, X (1959), that time is identical in the play with mutability is an oversimplification, failing to note the organic metaphors constantly used to describe time's nature and action.

(18) It is significant that Ulysses has already complained that Achilles and Patroclus mock Greek "achievements" (I. iii 81).

(19) Though her interpretation of the phenomenon attempts, as often, to say more about Shakespeare than about what he is doing in a particular play, Miss Spurgeon astutely notices the "extraordinary number of food and cooking images in Troilus," *Shakespeare's Imagery and What It Tells Us* (Cambridge, 1935), Chart VI. Troilus' speech as he awaits Cressida *chez* Pandarus (III ii. 20 ff.) is typical.

(20) For a similar argument about the role of time as a figure for inevitable historical process in a play in which time is not presented organically, see Norman Rabkin, "Structure, Convention, and Meaning in *Julius Caesar," JEGP,* LXIII (1964), 240-254.

(21) For a searching exploration of the appropriateness of such language to the criticism of Shakespeare, see John Palmer, *Political Characters of Shakespeare* (London, 1945), pp. 63-64.

Proteus in Spenser and Shakespeare: the Lover's Identity

by William O. Scott

Whatever we decide about its intrinsic value, *The Two Gentlemen of Verona* at least shows the nascent form and qualities of Shakespeare's comic art. And for either intrinsic or comparative purposes, the character and function of Proteus, and the themes suggested by his role, deserve more scrutiny. His name has a thematic aptness that would scarcely seem to need mentioning—except that the obvious may put us off further questioning and we may conclude that Shakespeare's intent was shallow before we have sounded it.

For the moment we might pass over the notion that Proteus is "significantly named for his fickle nature"[1] and return to it after collecting other suggestions about the name. One of its Renaissance connotations has been used to build a hypothesis of character development. According to Thomas A. Perry, the mythical Proteus, called "god of shapes" by Marlowe, in part suggested to Renaissance authors the changes worked in men by fashion, perhaps through travel.[2] This idea does add to our impression of Proteus' triviality; it seems less valid as an explanation of how he became so. Shakespeare's character is indeed something of a dandy in his wooing of Silvia, but these outward matters are not emphasized, nor is any cause given except Proteus' infatuation. His courtly posturing simply images, without explaining causally, how superficial this infatuation is. Proteus the man of fashion illustrates Proteus the false lover.

But there are other possibilities in the myth. As we might expect, Proteus was a type of lust, or of the variability of passions in the lover. The relevant story is not of Proteus himself, but of another shape-changer sometimes identified with him, Vertumnus,[3] who wooed Pomona by changing his shape (Ovid, *Metamorphoses*, XIV.623f.). Some commentators on Ovid read this as an allegory of trickery or Satanic temptation; and the *Cinque Canti* printed in many editions of *Orlando Furioso* borrowed the name of Vertunno for a deceitful spirit.[4] Or this variable state may figure weakness of soul: in cupidity the human soul changes itself into various forms.[5]

These ideas are implied, along with others, in the remarkable Proteus in Book III of *The Faerie Queene*. After saving Florimell from the lecherous fisherman by carrying her beneath the sea, he in turn forces his intentions on her

> And entertained her the best he might
>
> . . . . .
>
> To winne her liking vnto his delight:
> With flattering words he sweetly wooed her,

And offered faire gifts t'allure her sight,
But she both offers and the offerer
Despysde, and all the fawning of the flatterer.   (viii.38)

This flatterer pushes his temptations further: when she avows that she loves "none, but a Faerie knight," he obligingly changes into that shape, and others (st. 39-40). He tries stronger means: urging "sharpe threates," appearing to her in "dreadfull shapes," and finally casting her in prison.

Several points are important in this passage. The Vertumnus myth is the closest analogue to the tale,[6] which is one of lust and temptation. Proteus appears first as a flatterer; this too is part of the tradition around Vertumnus.[7] Even more significant is the implication, in Proteus' flattery and in his first transformations, that this type of love sacrifices all integrity of the self. Though too late for Spenser or the young Shakespeare to know, an emblem in Otto Veen's *Amorum Emblemata* makes the point well. Cupid is shown holding a chameleon, and one text explains that the lover follows his lady's wishes and aversions, changing faces like Proteus on her account, and imitating the chameleon's changes.[8] Lovers' souls do not stay true to themselves, but are stirred by varied passions.[9] Spenser's Proteus has a compulsion to reshape himself in hopes of becoming what Florimell wants.

A myth of the lover who changes form might end in various ways. Vertumnus threatens to force his lady, but she yields willingly instead (*Met.*, XIV.770). Harington, translating Ariosto, gives a similar outcome in Proteus' affair with the King of Ebuda's daughter: "With her consent he forst the princely wench. . . ."[10] In Spenser rape becomes imprisonment and the lady fails to cooperate, but the source is still the Proteus and Vertumnus myths combined, perhaps through Ariosto. Shakespeare's character would resort to rape, but through a troubling series of events he discovers that he really loves someone else. Both Spenser and Shakespeare vary the outcome of the myth to fit particular ideas.

According to the myth of Proteus, he should be held fast until he resumes his own shape and tells the truth. Thus, says Thomas P. Roche, he was interpreted by mythographers as "a type of nature or the truth of things obscured by material appearance."[11] In Spenser Proteus remains on the level of appearances, as a rival of Florimell's true love, Marinell. In a general sense, as Roche argues, he may represent "the physical attempting to claim beauty for its own" (p.161); a more immediate reading would also take him as the ingratiating lover who has no stability of self. He passes through a variety of moods but can really have no hold on Florimell except force: his phantasms do not interest sensible women.

Though defective as plausible action, the ending of *The Two Gentlemen of Verona* also uses a variant of the Proteus and Vertumnus myths to work out a dialectic of appearance and reality. The mutable Proteus, having perhaps changed somewhat in mood and manner but much more in loyalty, is made to appreciate Valentine's friendship and Julia's love; he returns to his true relations with other people. One might even say that he resumes his true status because Julia has kept him bound fast all the time.

Shakespeare's Proteus shows many of the qualities attributed to the mythic figures. He lies whenever he chooses, and he certainly tries to tempt Silvia, though without success. More important, his change in love is a change of identity, a falling-off from his real self. Just as Valentine defines himself by his love, proclaiming that "Silvia is myself" (III.i.172),[12] so does Proteus. His chop logic satisfies him that pursuit of his new love, regardless of earlier ties to Valentine and Julia, is really self-fulfilment:

> I cannot leave to love, and yet I do;
> But there I leave to love where I should love.
> Julia I lose, and Valentine I lose.
> If I keep them, I needs must lose myself.
>
> . . . . .
>
> I to myself am dearer than a friend,
> For love is still most precious in itself.
>
> . . . . .
>
> I cannot now prove constant to myself,
> Without some treachery us'd to Valentine.   *(II.vi.17f.)*

One overriding interest makes up his whole being, and for it he will cancel all else. But, as he almost seems to recall at first, one cannot discard one's past self that easily; the obligations remain, and he is eventually drawn back to his first state. The transformations of this Proteus are not, as in Spenser and the Vertumnus myth, the stratagems of an insecure lover framing his identity to advance his suit, but an attempt at fundamental changes of loyalty.

Proteus failed to predict a consequence of his altering of identity: Julia changes too. Her new status is shown physically by her disguise, adopted in loneliness before she knew of Proteus' treachery. Her discovery of his behavior prompts the feeling that his choice of a false and shallow self has reduced her to a false existence too. On Proteus' request for Silvia's picture, "to your shadow will I make true love," Julia comments to herself, "If 'twere a substance, you would, sure, deceive it, / And make it but a shadow, as I am" (IV.ii.126f.). Silvia is quite aware that Proteus has departed alike from his better self and from the real world: "your falsehood shall become you well / To worship shadows and adore false shapes."

By taking service as Proteus' page, Julia plunges more actively into the world of illusion. She gains an ironic distance from her plight and contemplates it as an outsider, with dignified pathos. She is not Ariadne but someone who remembers having played the role of Ariadne. The irony of describing herself in the third person leads her to think of her disguise as made up of grief:

> since she did neglect her looking-glass
> And threw her sun-expelling mask away,
> The air hath starv'd the roses in her cheeks
> And pinch'd the lily-tincture of her face,
> That now she is become as black as I.   *(IV.iv.157f.)*

Her appearance itself shows that outside forces divert her from her true identity. Proteus must become himself before she can.

Her disguise has a practical value too; by purporting to be another she can catch Proteus off guard, prove her love by service to him, and eventually appeal to his better self. Meanwhile she uses her supposedly objective viewpoint to give an outsider's pronouncement on his change of love: "It seems you lov'd not her, to leave her token" (l. 79). Earlier (IV.ii.105-106) Proteus had pretended to Silvia that Julia was dead; now Julia tempts him to falsehood again: "She is dead, belike?" He is more honest this time, but he still sends Julia out to woo for him. The tasks she assumes with her disguise contradict her true identity: she cannot be her master's "true servant" unless she is "false traitor" to herself (IV.iv.109-110).[13]

The chameleon, already mentioned as an emblem of the lover's moods along with the Proteus myth, figures in the play. Sir Thurio is one in his anger (II.iv.25-27). In another sense the chameleon resembles lovers since it can live on air, promise-crammed. For Speed this idea is a touchstone of unreality: "though the chameleon Love can feed on the air, I am one that am nourish'd by my victuals and would fain have meat" (II.i.178-180). Lucetta is equally matter-of-fact in her punning complaint against Julia's moodiness in love: "I would it were [near dinner-time], / That you might kill your stomach on your meat, / And not upon your maid" (I.ii.67-69). Here is the self-mockery of Shakespeare's comedies, servants putting us at an ironic distance from the whole action. In Lyly's words, "Loue is a Camelion, which draweth nothing into the mouth but ayre, and nourisheth nothing in the bodie but lunges."[14]

In the final scene of the play Proteus makes his last, most grotesque transformation. It should seem far from his true nature (at least he must admit it is "'gainst the nature of love"), and Valentine promptly recalls him. Two major forces redeem Proteus, both important thematically; he is brought to himself by his friend's generosity and by his lady Julia's steady, though despairing, love. She reveals herself through the ring—that is, through a token of Proteus' former self. Rings are as usual an emblem of remembrance:

> If you turn not, you will return the sooner.[15]
> Keep this remembrance for thy Julia's sake. (II.ii.4-5)
>
> This ring I gave him when he parted from me,
> To bind him to remember my good will. (IV.iv.102-103)

The ring as a sign of Julia's identity is more significant than, say, a strawberry birthmark; it reminds Proteus of his obligations to the past, in contrast to his later intentions toward Silvia (represented by the other ring). But Julia holds both rings, and with them she intercepts Proteus' love. She returns Proteus to his true self by comparing her change of identity with his:

> It is the lesser blot, modesty finds,
> Women to change their shapes than men their minds. (V.iv.108-109)

Once he learns constancy, no more disguises will be needed.

This double return to true identity when lovers are reunited was to appear in later comedies by Shakespeare in which the erring hero really believed the heroine dead and repented his wrong to her. As sign of his reform he might be asked to marry a woman of others' choosing, who turned out to be the heroine after all (*Much Ado, All's Well*). This pattern of returning to old obligations roughly parallels Julia's confusing the rings. *The Winter's Tale* varies the scheme when Leontes is asked to reaffirm his devotion to Hermione and promise not to marry until she breathes again (V.i.76f.). The concepts of true and false identity in all these plays are well expressed by Hero's words of unmasking:

> when I liv'd, I was your other wife;
> And when you lov'd, you were my other husband. *(Much,V.iv.60-61)*

Concern for notions about identity and for the transformations wrought by love had of course been important in *The Comedy of Errors* and *The Taming of the Shrew*.[16] There are hints of these ideas in the well-known sources of *The Two Gentlemen of Verona*; Shakespeare may have started with them, and added the Proteus myth for its suggestions. One hint is Celia's reproach to Don Felix in Montemayor's *Diana*: "Thou saiest I was the cause that made thee forget thy former love. Comfort thy selfe, for there shall not want another to make thee forget thy second. And assure thy selfe of this (Lord *Don Felix*) that there is not any thing more unbeseeming a Gentleman, than to finde an occasion in a Gentlewoman to leese himself [*perderse*] for her love."[17] Though such a reading depends on taking a reflexive verb literally, this strict meaning does describe exactly what Proteus and Don Felix did; they abandoned their true selves, which belonged to Julia and Felismena, for love of another. A later account of the lover's identity comes in the didactic Fourth Book, which borrows from Leone Ebreo's *Dialoghi di Amore*. Felicia discourses on the nature of love, describing the attributes of Cupid: "They paint him with wings, because he simply enters into the lovers soule; and the more perfect he is, with more swiftnes and alienation of himselfe [*enagenamiento de si mismo*] he goeth to seeke the person of the beloved, for which cause *Euripedes* said: That the lover did live in the body of the beloved" (p.249).[18] This is exactly the case with the various lovers—Valentine (III.i.172), Julia (IV.iv.110), and Proteus (II.vi.20). Each of the three, and presumably Silvia too, finds his being or principle of identity in his beloved. Shakespeare uses the idea to present crises of different sorts in the lovers' situations.

Sir Thomas Elyot's *The Boke named The Gouernour* gives much more attention to concepts of identity, applying them to the relations between friends. The story of Titus and Gisippus (II.xii) directly illustrates Elyot's notions of friendship, given in the previous chapter. In the expository chapter xi he uses Cicero's definition, "a parfecte consent of all thinges appertayninge as well to god as to man, with beneuolence and charitie," and he insists that "a frende is proprely named of Philosophers the other I. For that in them is but one mynde and one possession; and that, which more is, a man more reioiseth at his frendes good fortune than at his owne."[19] Elyot is surprisingly thorough in his adaptation of the story of Titus and Gisippus to his sententious aim: he exceeds the other versions of the tale in giving the two friends an exact physical resemblance.[20] Nor is he reticent about explaining how this likeness fits his ideas of friendship: "These two yonge gentil-men, as they semed to be one in fourme and personage, so, shortely after acquaint-aunce, the same nature wrought in their hartes suche a mutuall affection, that their willes and appetites daily more and more so confederated them selfes, that it semed none other, whan their names were declared, but that they hadde onely chaunged their places, issuinge (as I mought saye) out of the one body, and entringe in to the other" (Croft, II,134). Emigration of souls occurs in friends just as Montemayor and Ebreo said it did in lovers. But more wonders result: complete likeness between two persons implies that one will fall in love exactly as the other has, with the same woman. Thus Titus is able to reproach Gisippus for not having foreseen this difficulty;

> Alas, Gysippus, what enuious spirite meued you to bringe me
> with you to her whom ye haue chosen to be your wyfe, where
> I receyued this poison? I saye, Gysippus, where was than your
> wisedom, that ye remembred nat the fragilitie of our commune
> nature? What neded you to call me for a witnesse of your priuate
> delites? Why wolde ye haue me see that, whiche you youre selfe
> coulde nat beholde without rauisshinge of mynde and carnall
> appetite? Alas, why forgate ye that our myndes and appetites
> were euer one? And that also what so ye lyked was euer to me
> in lyke degree pleasaunt? (II,139)

Gisippus has to admit his carelessness.

The rest of the story, though not as emphatic about the matter of identity, de-velops the consequences of the theme. The bed trick works easily because of the friends' likeness; and since the lady is given a perfect facsimile, seemingly she is not expected to have any preferences.[21] The ending carries through the primacy of friendship, without marrying off Gisippus.[22] The theme of identity between friends in fact shapes the major events in the tale and is intended to control the reader's emotional response.

Both Montemayor and Elyot make a point of spiritual likeness or emigration of the soul from the friend or lover to the other person; neither friends nor lovers have distinct, autonomous selves. This is of course a commonplace; but it may well have caught Shakespeare's interest as it is presented in these two books. There is a symmetry in the pairing: one application to friendship and one to love, both important in *The Two Gentlemen*. In both books the theme is prominent: it controls Elyot's whole story, and it is part of the moral instruction in the central book of Montemayor's work.[23]

For Shakespeare the theme of identity is the controlling force in the story— even the concepts of love and friendship are subordinate to it. The basic distinc-tion is between Proteus' true self, defined by his commitment to Julia, and his false one, which arises from his attempt to force his attentions on Silvia. True love corresponds to true self, and false love to false self. Shakespeare plays very heavily on the audience's sense of the happy resolution and their desire for everything to come out well: Julia is around to remind us which love is the true one, and if the ending is to work at all it must rely on the feeling that Proteus has gone momentarily wrong and if something drastic is done in a hurry he may be retrieved. The memory of Proteus' true self is emphasized for the audience through Julia, who loves him.

It is only in Proteus' false self that the conflict of love and friendship arises. The love that puts him in rivalry with his friend is his desire for the wrong woman, Silvia, and for this he betrays his friendship to procure Valentine's banishment and lies about Valentine's death in hopes of winning Silvia. The ending is symmetrical if nothing else, for it unwinds the tangle in reverse order. Valentine reproaches Proteus for his falsehood as a friend, and Proteus is shamed into repentance. When Valentine offers Silvia to Proteus, it would seem that for Valentine friendship has won out over love, just the reverse of Proteus' decision when put in the dilemma. Silvia may have been right when she answered Proteus' question "In love / Who respects friend?" with "All men but Proteus" (V.iv.53-54)—though Valentine's demonstration of sacrifice is extreme. But Julia's response spares us this calamitous generosity, for her love toward Proteus, and the ring she bears which reminds him of his old obligation, convince him that his genuine love is for her and not Silvia. His ungallant question "What is in Silvia's face, but I may spy / More fresh in Julia's with a constant eye?" (ll.114-115) is meant as a recognition of what is best for him, not as a slur on Silvia—though it is best spoken to Julia, out of Silvia's hearing. Thus he is brought to recall his original self (before "Inconstancy" had made him "run through all the sins") and the conflict of love and friendship is dissolved. Proteus has made his last change, from illusion back to his true form, and marriage will fix him there.

Early in the play Proteus states a formula that seems to anticipate Restoration drama when he says of Valentine, "He after honour hunts, I after love" (I.i.63).[24] Matters are soon changed as Valentine falls in love and Proteus abandons his first love for another, but the description is still valid for later events. When his false love for Silvia conflicts with what had been friendship, Proteus chooses love. But when Valentine is forced into a decision between the claims of love and friendship, both of which he feels sincerely, he prefers the honor of yielding to his friend. Though plausibility is sacrificed, the schematization holds.

Luckily Valentine's sacrifice of love for friendship is avoided, and really his friend should not accept it: Proteus must return to Julia. A Titus-and-Gisippus ending will not do here, for in the audience's experience Julia has been made too real to be ignored; her claim to Proteus is valid, and he will not be fully himself again until he acknowledges her. For this reason, even if Valentine's offer of Silvia were credible and were fair to Silvia, it would be no better than a well-intentioned mistake. We expect Proteus to return to both his true friendship and his original love, and Valentine's offer would have left the movement incomplete. But once our expectations have been fulfilled by Proteus' return to Julia, love and honor are seen to be in harmony; Valentine's loyal friendship and Julia's true love both remind Proteus what he has been. The right love and sincere friendship are compatible, and both belong to Proteus' better self.

In this portrayal of a fickle man the myth of Proteus adds meaning by helping to suggest an underlying reality of character which will remain after the fickleness, and its resultant treacheries, have been purged away. The myth does not appear directly in other comedies in which the heroes are changeable, but the contrast between the real self and its illusory variations is implicit in the characters and sometimes in the very structure of the plays. This is true in *A Midsummer Night's Dream,* where all the changes of loyalty (except Titania's) take place in the men, and appear as merely "the fierce vexation of a dream." Events are very lightly treated, with no discredit to the men for their alterations, since we know that superhuman powers are disporting themselves. The joke is against human rationalizations of apparent fickleness—Lysander's excuse that "reason says you are the worthier maid" (II.ii.116), and Demetrius' that "like a sickness did I loathe this food; / But, as in health, come to my natural taste, / Now I do wish it" (IV.i. 177-179). The audience can laugh from a vantage-point that gives them knowledge superior to the deluded lovers; and the changes cancel out to yield a better result that is confirmed as reality by daybreak and Theseus' horns.

In *Twelfth Night* the contrast between false and true self applies to the Duke, who attains his true being (free from melancholy fits of frustrated love) only when he discovers his love for Viola.[25] In some ways he is like the Proteus in Spenser's tale, though he succeeds when he tries the right lady. Like the sea god, he is only too constant to a lady who will have none of him, but he is stable in naught else. Feste makes a wish for the Duke that suits his character:

> Now, the melancholy god protect thee, and the tailor make thy
> doublet of changeable taffeta, for thy mind is a very opal. I
> would have men of such constancy put to sea, that their busi-
> ness might be everything and their intent everywhere; for that's
> it that always makes a good voyage of nothing.   *(II.iv.75-81)*

Orsino himself, describing his character more favorably, compares his love to the sea in its voraciousness; it can devour all values and emotions, can subsume everything into it (I.i.9-14; II.iv.100-104). The Duke glories in his mutability; but it is an unhappy state, and once Viola's love for him is known to us, we trust that when time has untangled the knot Orsino's mutations will cease.

As in both *The Faerie Queene* and *The Two Gentlemen,* events are brought to a crisis by the frustrated lover's threat of force. It is directed first at the obstinate Olivia (ll. 120-122), as in both other stories; then Orsino turns his threat on Viola, though with words implying love.[26] She declares her readiness to sacrifice herself, and all is prepared for their union once her disguise is known. Orsino is taught a new reality in Viola's self-sacrificing devotion, a more convincing lesson than Valentine's unselfishness.

All's Well That Ends Well does not present a strong sense of a real Bertram

290

underlying the proud, fickle, and lustful appearance, and this causes some difficulties; we have to take on faith the love of Helena and his mother for him. But there is the irony that for all his concern with his name and honour, his treatment of Helena makes the Countess disown him and "wash his name out of [her] blood" (III.ii.70). He gives Diana a ring which he describes as symbolic of his honor: "Here, take my ring! / My house, mine honour, yea, my life, be thine, / And I'll be bid by thee" (IV.ii.51-53). In this sense he loses himself, only to be given back both name and honor by Helena's trick. If we are properly hopeful we will expect this honor to be better founded than before, and Bertram to be confirmed in a better self, healed of his sickness.

Just as Julia and Hero had lost identity when spurned by their suitors, so does Helena when Bertram leaves her. On her return she cautiously asserts that she is "but the shadow of a wife, ... The name and not the thing" (V.iii.308-309). This is a hint for Bertram to acknowledge her, as he prudently does: "Both, both. O, pardon!" Only when he recognizes what he should be can she be herself again.

The theme of identity, with its contrast between the real and the false self, gives a meaning and a fittingness to the reform of the erring heroes in some of Shakespeare's comedies. This is the serious subject of *The Two Gentlemen of Verona*, implied in the myth of Proteus. And Shakespeare has added a significant force which continues in later comedies, the redeeming heroine who brings her man to a true concept of himself. If Proteus can be bound firmly, he holds his true shape.

Notes:

(1) Harold Jenkins, "Shakespeare's *Twelfth Night*," *Rice Institute Pamphlet*, XLV (January 1959), 21.

(2) "Proteus, Wry-Transformed Traveller," *SQ*, V (1954), 33-40. For a classical precedent, see Horace, *Epistles*, I.i.90.

(3) DeWitt T. Starnes and Ernest William Talbert, *Classical Myth and Legend in Renaissance Dictionaries* (Chapel Hill, 1955), pp. 72-73—note the cross-reference in Charles Estienne's *Dictionarium*. Cf. Harington's index entry for Proteus: "*Proteus* counted a God of the sea called *Vertumnus*, because he is said to turn himself into all shapes." *Orlando Furioso* (London, 1634), sig. 2O2.

(4) Pierre Bersuire, *Metamorphosis Ouidiana Moraliter explanta* (Paris, 1515), fol. xcviiiᵛ: "Vel dic de diabolo qui scit diuersas formas îduere: & sub diuersis temptationibus & dissimulationibus se mutare: vt homines decipiat" (XIV.xvi); Johan Spreng, *Metamorphoses Ovidii* (Frankfurt, 1563), fol. 170ᵛ: "Hic tibi depingit Sathanam Vertumnus atrocem, / Insidijs animam fallat ut ipse piam. / Mille sibi sumit species, ac mille figuras, / Vertit & in uultus ora subinde nouos" (XIV.viii). *Cinque Conti,* cantos III and V; and in Gower's *Confessio Amantis,* V.6670f., the lover wishes he could use Proteus' arts to convey himself to his lady's chamber.

(5) "... hominem in libidinem habere stultitiam, ferocitatem, dolum: quae dum invicem in uno homine vigent, pars illa quae vicina est divinitati, id est prudentia, non apparet ... " L. G. Giraldi, *Opera Omnia* (Leiden, 1696), col. 168 (Syntagma V). Minoes, commenting on

Alciati's Emblem 182, cites Clement of Alexandria, *Paedagog.*, III.i, in *Emblemata* (Lyons, 1591), p. 643.

(6) Starnes and Talbert, pp. 72-73.

(7) " ... uerbis nimium nobis blanditur amoenis ... " Spreng, 170[v].

(8) (Antwerp, 1608), pp. 64-65: "Quod cupis, id cupio; quod spernis, sperno : tuumque / Velle meum velle est, nolleque nolle meum. / Te propter varios, vt Proteus, induo vultus, / Inque modum chamãe, crede, leontis ago." The emblem seems to combine two ideas in Plutarch's *Life of Alcibiades,* trans. North (London, 1895), II, 106, 117-118: Alcibiades had for his device "the image of Cupide ... holding lightning in his hande," and "he could frame altogether with [men's] manners and facions of life, transforming him selfe more easely to all manner of shapes, then the Camelion."

(9) " ... amantium animi sibi non constant, sed agitantur varijs ac diuersis affectionibus." Georg Sabinus, *Fabularum Ovidii Interpretatio* (Cambridge, 1584),p. 581 (XIV.xvi, on Vertumnus).

(10) VIII.47; her consent is not explicit in Ariosto's corresponding stanza (52).

(11) *The Kindly Flame* (Princeton, 1964), pp. 159-160.

(12) Quotations are from *Complete Plays and Poems,* ed. Neilson and Hill (Cambridge, Mass., 1942).

(13) For this emphasis on conflict with the self, and greater self-sacrifice, cf. Riche's tale "Of Apolonius and Silla": "doe you thinke there could have been a greater torment devised wherewith to afflicte the harte of Silla, then her self to bee made the instrumente to woorke her owne mishapp, and to plaie the atturney in a cause that made so muche againste her self? But Silla, altogether desirous to please her maister, cared nothyng at all to offende herself, followed his businesse with so good a will as if it had been in her owne preferment." Geoffrey Bullough, *Narrative and Dramatic Sources of Shakespeare* (London, 1958), II, 351. Cross-reference to *TGV* is made by Thomas M. Cranfill in his edition of Riche (Austin, 1959), p. 271. Likewise, Montemayor's Felismena is "forced to make warre against [her] owne selfe, and to be the intercessour of a thing so contrarie to [her] owne intent." See T. P. Harrison, Jr., "Shakespeare and Montemayor's *Diana*," *Texas Studies in English,* VI (1926), 88.

(14) *Endimion,* III.iv.129-130, in *Works,* ed. R. W. Bond (Oxford, 1902), III, 50. For the relation between love and food, see *Euphues, Works,* I, 201, 211, 224.

(15) This suggests the usual etymology of Vertumnus' name, as quoted from Harington in n. 3.

(16) Harold Brooks, "Themes and Structure in 'The Comedy of Errors,' " *Stratford-upon-Avon Studies 3* (London, 1961), 55-71.

(17) Trans. Bartholomew Yong (1598), in Bullough, I, 240-241; cf. *Los siete libros de la Diana,* ed. Francisco López Estrada (Madrid, 1946), p. 115.

(18) Cp. López Estrada, p. 196, and, for Ebreo's version, p. 195n.

(19) Ed. H. H. S. Croft (London, 1883), II, 122, 130.

(20) *Early English Versions of Tales from the Decameron,* ed. Herbert G. Wright, EETS O. S. 205, p. xciii.

(21) In *All's Well* and *Measure for Measure* Shakespeare faces more difficult (and realistic) questions about identity, with deceit being used to retrieve the duped person's erring

desires. Though I do not agree with Ralph M. Sargent, in "Sir Thomas Elyot and the Integrity of *The Two Gentlemen of Verona*," *PMLA*, LXV (1950), 1179n., that the bed trick in *Measure* may have come from Elyot (rather it is from *All's Well*, deriving from Boccaccio and Painter), it surely continues and elaborates on problems of identity related to *TGV*.

(22) C. T. Goode, "Sir Thomas Elyot's *Titus and Gysippus*," *MLN*, XXXVII (1922), 7.

(23) For a structural analysis of the *Diana*, see Bruce W. Wardropper, "The *Diana* of Monte-mayor: Revaluation and Interpretation," *SP*, XLVIII (1951), 131-134. Book IV is "pivotal."

(24) In this speech Proteus also claims that he leaves himself for love and that Julia has "metamorphos'd" him and made him neglect his studies. This earlier Proteus who existed before his love has little reality for the audience, who think of him in relation to Julia and define his true self through that love. But this expression of insecurity in his first love may prepare for his change to a second. There is the greatest possible dif-ference from Romeo, whose first love is patently unreal for the audience and whose second is genuine.

(25) Some comparisons between *The Two Gentlemen of Verona* and *Twelfth Night* have been made by Harold Jenkins in the article cited in note 1, and by René Pruvost in "*The Two Gentlemen of Verona, Twelfth Night*, et *Gl'Ingannati*," *Etudes anglaises*, XIII (1960), 1-9.

(26) Porter Williams, Jr., "Mistakes in *Twelfth Night* and their Resolution: A Study in Some Relationships of Plot and Theme," *PMLA*, LXXVI (1961), 198. The first threat, how-ever, does not seem directed at Viola (as Williams thinks) but at Olivia, since "th' Egyptian thief" in Heliodorus (*Aethiopica*, I.xxx) would kill his lady, and since "But hear me this" seems to announce a new thought. Probably Orsino's mind slips over to revenge on another that he loves.

Baroque Passion in Shakespeare and his Contemporaries

by Rolf Soellner

Some of the most interesting discussions of recent years among historians, literary critics, and art critics have arisen on the question of the delimitation of historical periods and period styles. There has been an attempt to push forward the Middle Ages into the Renaissance, and another to draw the Renaissance back into the Middle Ages;[1] the claim of the Renaissance of being an era extending over several centuries, already threatened by the advocates of the Middle Ages on one side, has been attacked by the champions of the Baroque from the other side. The term "Baroque," originally used merely to designate an art style has expanded its field of reference and seems to be in the process of winning out over such competitors as "Late Renaissance" or "Counter-Renaissance" to designate a historical, political, and cultural era thought to have some cohesion.[2] However, the integrity of the Baroque too has been challenged by the identification of one of its earlier phases as "Mannerism," a term which from art history has penetrated into literary terminology.[3]

The literary historian may and should view this discussion with a certain skepticism. The saying, the style is the man, contains an element of truth which no re-classification must obscure. But stylistic classifications have their purpose and use. It may be true that roses smell sweet by any other name; yet biologists have insisted on classifying them by genus and species, and there is no denying that they have advanced our knowledge of roses in this fashion. Literary historians too must aim at precision of nomenclature if they wish to place individual works properly in the stream of the great cultural traditions.

If my parallel to biology be thought irrelevant, the advantages of accurate stylistic analysis are also obvious in art, a field related to literature. The art-historians, whose subject is more demonstrable than that of the literary historian because it is pictorial or plastic, have taken the lead in the analysis of period styles.[4] They have, for instance, taught us that both Rubens and Rembrandt belong to the Baroque. We have become aware that the two painters have a similar mentality of style, that the spirit and temper of the age in which they lived directed and limited the formal possibilities of their work. These resemblances make it possible to set Rubens and Rembrandt apart from Renaissance artists, from, let us say, Dürer and Michaelangelo. Of course, in spite of their common Baroque features, a painting of Rembrandt is also unmistakably different from one of Rubens: the artist's individual sensibility and temperament create the variations of the period style which make the individual style. In addition, there is the accent of quality: few would question that Rembrandt ranks above Rubens; we tend to think of

Rubens as typical of the Baroque and of Rembrandt as transcending it while using its technique.

This seems common sense; yet, fifty years ago, the attribution of Rubens and Rembrandt to the Baroque met with objections almost as great as the horror evinced more recently when it was brought in connection with Shakespeare. The present paper is however not concerned with the "baroqueness" of passionate reactions to the terms "Baroque" or "Mannerism," but it is intended to be a contribution to the discussion on the relative merits of these terms as opposed to "Renaissance" for late Elizabethan and early Jacobean drama. I submit that the treatment of the emotions in this drama gives us one criterion, although only one among several, to decide for "Baroque" in favor of "Renaissance."

The limitations of a short paper require somewhat of a simplification of the situation. I shall be more concerned here with establishing the general trend from the Renaissance to the Baroque, and bypass the question whether there is a need to designate a transitional period, Mannerism. There has been a tendency in art-history and in literary history to apply the term to any production slightly bizarre, neurotic, capricious, or merely unusual. All of Shakespeare's work, together with that of Donne, Montaigne, Machiavelli, Galileo, and many others, has been called "Mannerist."[5] This designation, except for some specified Italian artists, is at present certainly highly problematical. At any rate, before we decide on the need for establishing a transitional period, we must determine whether the change from Elizabethan to Jacobean really does generally correspond to an advance from the Renaissance to or toward the Baroque.

I believe indeed it does. I ascribe the objections of some scholars and critics to the term Baroque for the drama under discussion not only to a common resistance to new terms but also the the specific traditionalism of dramatic analysis. We tend to think of drama, very much like Aristotle, as being composed of plot, characters, diction, thought, spectacle, and rhythm, although we have all experienced the difficulty of establishing such mechanical categories. Even proponents of the Baroque have sometimes weakened their arguments by restricting them to one or two of these categories alone. But if we wish to approximate the precision of the art historians' analysis of period styles, we must consider as many elements as possible: a painting is not Baroque because of organization or coloring alone, but in its totality. The treatment of the emotions in drama includes a sufficient number of traditional categories, in particular, characters, plot, thought, and diction, to be useful in demonstrating the evolution from the Renaissance to the Baroque.

In this idea I have been stimulated by the scholarly criticism which sees in the depiction of passion one of the most significant features of Shakespeare's tragic art, such as Lily Campbell's *Shakespeare's Tragic Heroes: Slaves of Passion* (Cambridge, 1930) although, of course, Miss Campbell does not use the word Baroque and might be surprised to be mentioned in this connection. My immediate stimulation, however, comes from ideas developed by L. L. Schücking in a British Academy lecture on "The Baroque Character of the Elizabethan Hero" (1938) and in a book unfortunately practically unknown in America, *Shakespeare und der Tragödienstil seiner Zeit* (Bern, 1947). Professor Schücking sees tendencies to extreme behavior, such as hyperbolic sensitivity, excessive dynamics of will, grotesque and fantastic actions as characteristic of the Elizabethan tragic hero. Some of these traits might perhaps be identified with the Manneristic style which has come into its own since Professor Schücking wrote. However, the tendency to boundless and ecstatic passion, on which Schücking only touches and which is the criterion applied in this paper, is more clearly associated with the Baroque.

For simplicity's sake, I shall focus on three plays, John Marston's *Antonio and Mellida* (1599), William Shakespeare's *Othello* (1604), and Beaumont and Fletcher's *A King and No King* (1611). At first sight, these three dramas appear utterly different. Marston's *Antonio and Mellida* is a tragedy in two parts; it deals with the suffering of a young prince, Antonio, from the hands of his father's enemy, Duke Piero. This villain not only murders Antonio's father but also becomes guilty of the death of Mellida, his own daughter, with whom Antonio is in love. The second part of the drama is devoted to Antonio's revenge on Piero. The two parts thus present a combination of love and revenge tragedy which bears some resemblance to *Hamlet*. Antonio is a melancholy humor faced with a situation much like Shakespeare's Prince. By contrast, Beaumont and Fletcher's *A King and No King* is a tragicomedy which trifles with the theme of incestuous love. Its hero, King Arbaces, a despot somewhat like Marlowe's Tamburlaine, falls in love with his sister Panthea. He is consumed by desire for her to the point of near insanity but he is saved from destruction by the astonishing discovery that Panthea is not really his sister. Thus the two are allowed to live happily ever after, together.

One may well ask whether these two dramas with such different heroes and plots have any similarity with each other, or, even more, whether they have any kind of resemblance to that relentless tragedy of jealousy, *Othello*. But they do, in so far as they dramatize gigantic passions which break or threaten to break all fetters and to destroy the heroes. Admittedly, all tragedy or tragicomedy intensifies emotions and must do so because our reaction to suffering on the stage is conditioned by the force of its representation; the reasons for suffering sometimes matter less than the energy with which it expresses itself. But in these three dramas, which are three striking links in a chain, passion reached a violence never attained before or after in the history of drama. In them, the emotions are expressed with such dynamic intensity and explosive vehemence that they invite comparison to the contemporaneous painting and sculpture of the continent which abandoned itself to intoxication and ecstasy. "Emotion and movement at all costs," so the Baroque has been characterized.

The impetuous movement of the three plays derives not only, and not even primarily, from the extraordinary events they dramatize, from persecution, violence, disorder, and murder; but most of all, it comes from the turbulence in the heroes' souls. From the beginning, Antonio takes every opportunity to revel in grief. His suffering is emphasized by the parallel suffering of his father, Andrugio, and later, by that of the courtier, Pandulfo, whose son becomes another victim of

Piero. Antonio's quest for grief is almost pathological, as, for instance, when, in disguise, he approaches his beloved Mellida and tearfully reports to her his own death as if it were that of a stranger (*Pt. I*, I.i.187 ff.). His psychic configuration resembles a fever curve, rising from depression to elation and reverting to dejection, from listless inactivity to frantic energy, and back. Thus, when he is forced to flee from the court and believes he has lost Mellida forever, he has a page sing to him and abandons himself to grief, accompanying the melody by beating his chest, wringing his hands, and falling to the ground; but only a moment later, when, unhoped-for, Mellida reappears, he breaks out in ecstatic joy and fervently declaims Italian love-lyrics (*Pt. I*, IV.i.133 ff.).

While Antonio is hysterically aquiver with emotion, Othello is not obviously a passionate nature, at least not in the beginning of the play. He seems all-in-all sufficient, as much in control over himself as over his troops. He is not a youthful sensualist like Antonio, but, as he says, "declined / Into the vale of years" (III.iii.265). Shakespeare has given Iago a formidable task in seducing this mature and moderate man to passion and murder. Iago must convince a man, who has just celebrated his wedding and who deeply loves his wife, that she is deceiving him. To make things even harder, this man is Iago's superior, a famous general, at present as governor of the island of Cyprus supreme over life and death. That Othello is a negro makes the situation more sensational; I doubt that Shakespeare meant it to make the villain's task easier. At any rate, Iago's success in turning the formerly so controlled Othello into a slave of passion is shocking and painful. We wonder with Lodovico whether this later Othello is the noble nature whom passion could not shake.

Paradoxically, Shakespeare has lent verisimilitude to the transformation of Othello into a caricature of himself by motivating it through another polar contrast, that of seducer and seduced. The affectionate and kind Othello, whose martial outside belies his pliable nature, succumbs to the seemingly gruff and honest Iago, endowed with an indomitable will and a coldly calculating brain. The tension and movement of the action derives largely from this contrast. Iago and Othello, as Otto Ludwig said, "go side-by-side through the whole play like theme and counter-theme of a fugue of Bach"[6]—the parallel to Baroque music is felicitous. As Iago drop-by-drop injects the poison of suspicion, Othello becomes perturbed till his fever is past cure. Passion and reason, or, as Shakespeare has it, blood and judgement, struggle with each other in his soul. The prelude to this turbulence is his near-violent reaction to Cassio's drunkenness, stage-managed by Iago. The incident strains Othello's sense of discipline almost to the breaking point. And when Iago has inoculated Othello with his poison, love and hate wrench him apart. In one sentence he pities Desdemona, and in the next, he wants to tear her to pieces; in one scene, he shouts at the perplexed Desdemona in highest passion, and in the next, he enters fatigued and exhausted to a point that an obscene insinuation by Iago brings him to a complete blackout (IV.i.34 ff.).

Othello's psychic polarity between love and hate resembles that of Marston's Antonio between dejection and jubilation. Undoubtedly, ancient theories of the antithesis of the emotions aided Elizabethan dramatists to paint with such contrasting colors; but in the plays under discussion antithesis has become almost schizophrenia. Shakespeare was a master in chiaroscuro paintings of emotions, of portraying hate-in-love, joy-in-grief, hope-in-fear, humor-in-despair, or genius-in-madness. Marston evidently strove at such effect as when, for instance, he had Antonio triumphantly, but tearfully, murder the innocent son of his enemy Piero; but the grotesqueness of this cruelty offends (*Pt. II,* III.ii.192).

The principle and the pitfalls of vehement psychic polarity are even more notable in Beaumont and Fletcher's *A King and No King.* The whole character of Arbaces, for whom, according to Dryden, Alexander the Great provided the model, is built on contrast and antithesis. Even before Arbaces appears for the first time, his loyal general, Mardonius, characterizes him as a bundle of contradictions, "vainglorious and humble, and angry and patient, and merry and dull, and joyful and sorrowful, in extremities, in an hour" (I.i.70). The king exemplifies this characterization when he subsequently enters, intending to console his captive, Tigranes, but unwittingly insulting him by boasting of his own superior strength. Mardonius' reproaches incense him temporarily, but he quickly changes to remorse. Even Leontes in *The Winter's Tale,* who feels himself as a feather for each wind that blows, is a sturdy reed by comparison. Yet Arbaces is no more to be taken as a capricious half-wit than Antonio as a despicable weakling; Mardonius would only like to see his master's valor and passion separated; each of these qualities, he says, might have made an admirable fellow if they had not become mixed (I.i.172).

Surely the taste of the Jacobean public has much to do with the passing-off of such strange mixture of a man for a hero and thus with the trend from the Renaissance to the Baroque. Beaumont and Fletcher's public was more aristocratic than Shakespeare's and Marston's, neither of whom was decidedly bourgeois in his leanings. Middle-class Puritan ideals were represented by dramatists like Thomas Heywood and Thomas Dekker. A total counterpart to Arbaces is, for instance Mr. Frankford in Heywood's *A Woman Killed With Kindness* (1603?), who catches his wife in actual adultery, but does not give way to passion and prays to God for giving him patience; astonishingly, his prayer is granted.

It is true that the Christian virtue of patience, which underlies the puritanical ideal of self-control, is also a significant force in Shakespeare—Desdemona is almost its embodiment; but Shakespeare's tragic heroes reject the counsel of patience. Othello says with grim irony to Iago: "I will be found most cunning in my patience; / But (dost thou hear?) most bloody" (IV.i.91-92). A similar attempt at irony by Beaumont and Fletcher becomes ludicrous when Arbaces in an outbreak of anger boasts of possessing more patience than a God (I.i.234).

Both Arbaces and Othello are symptomatic of the Baroque hero who is lifted above the level of ordinary man and derides patience in agreement with a maxim in *Richard II* (I.ii.33-34): "That which in mean men we entitle patience / Is pale cold cowardice in noble breasts." The taste of the public to which Beaumont and Fletcher and, to some degree, Shakespeare catered demanded a less static hero than Heywood's Mr. Frankford. The irascibility and bad manners of Arbaces, which Beaumont and Fletcher chose to call passion, must have seemed stylish in aristocratic circles. I find Ranke's characterization of King James strangely applicable to Arbaces. James, says Ranke, was even in the trivia of daily life not master over himself; he did often what he later wanted undone. But I realize that it is hazardous to relate art so directly to life, and after all, my subject is the Baroque hero and not Baroque man, if there was such a creature.

Perhaps most clearly, the transition from the Renaissance to the Baroque shows itself in a growing vehemence of stage gestures. From the beginning, Renaissance drama sought the strong mimetic expression of passion by such gestures as wringing of hands or loosening of hair. In dejection, dramatic characters threw themselves to the ground, sometimes announcing this gesture in a sort of spoken stage direction as did the Viceroy in Kyd's *Spanish Tragedy* (ca. 1589): "Here let me lie; now I am at the lowest, *qui jacet in terra non habet unde cadat.*" But subsequent developments of dramatic gestures proved that the ultimate of passionate expression had not yet been reached.[7]

In later drama, passion tended to become ecstasy, madness, or disease, and its accompanying gestures became correspondingly extravagant. In particular, the stage convention of *Hercules Furens*, the model for "fury," that is, temporary, blinding madness of passion, lent itself to be put in the service of violent acting. Antonio's repeated fits, in which he falls to the ground, hammers it with his fists, groans, curses, or howls, are clearly in this tradition. On one such occasion, a bystander suggests, "Belike the falling sickness." This remark, together with references to Hercules, such as Antonio's claim that his is an "Herculean woe" betray the origin of Antonio's seizures. The mythological Hercules' fit of madness, in which he slew his wife and children, was diagnosed by ancient and Renaissance theorists as *Herculanus morbus*, Herculean disease, or epilepsy.[8]

Shakespeare used this dramatic psychology most effectively in *Othello*, when, eaten-up with passion, the Moor breaks down on Iago's insinuation that Cassio has confessed lying with Desdemona (IV.i.34 ff.). The word "lie" hits him like a dagger; his mind disintegrates; he stammers disjointed and incoherent phrases. He trembles and shakes, loses consciousness, and falls to the ground, "in a trance" as the Folio stage direction has it. Iago stands triumphantly over him as Cassio appears on the scene. Iago's explanation for Othello's collapse is that "my lord has fall'n into an epilepsy. / This is his second fit; he had one yesterday." When Cassio suggests rubbing Othello's temples, Iago fends him off: "The lethargy must have his quiet course. / If not he foams at mouth, and by-and-by / Breaks out to savage madness."

The question whether Shakespeare actually thought of Othello's breakdown as an epileptic fit is a matter of dispute. I see little reason why it should not be meant to be one—even modern medicine knows an emotion-induced variant of this disease much like Othello's. But this question is of small importance here; the significance of the terms used in the text, "trance," "epilepsy," "lethargy," and "ecstasy," lies in their emphasis on the titanic or "Herculean" nature of Othello's passion. Othello's as well as Antonio's breakdowns must not be interpreted as merely a tendency to greater realism or naturalism. Realism there is, and in Othello's fit more than in Antonio's—Othello's incoherent phrases could even be called impressionistic in the sensory details which they evoke. Antonio has a similar disarray of grammar in one of his attacks, although he still stutters blank verse and uses mythological images (IV.i.1 ff.). But such realism of Marston's and the greater realism of Shakespeare were in the service of an art form that strove to go beyond nature. The phenomenon is the same as when Rembrandt focused a beam of light in what has been called an impressionistic way on the holy family in order to concentrate the viewer's emotion on his subject. The Baroque used realism not as an end in itself but as a means to create movement and turbulence. It tried, to quote a phrase of the painter in *Timon of Athens,* to be "livelier than life."

This trend is even more striking in *A King and No King.* When Arbaces after long absence sees his sister and falls in love with her, the impression is that of a severe psychic shock. The whole scene (III.i) is a demonstration of the principle of movement and emotion at all costs. Situations change with lightning speed and turn into their opposites. First, the queen-mother, who has plotted against Arbaces, kneels before him and is forgiven by the truly humble king. Then it is Panthea's turn to kneel; but when Arbaces notices her, he is totally ravished, stares at her "like a loathed thing," and begins to stammer. Love seizes him in a kind of visual and sensory hallucination which is anything but pleasant. Although the arrows he complains of are Cupid's, his imagery make them appear to be the claws of a bird of prey he wishes to tear from his flesh. He seems mad to one observer at least. When he comes to and is told that the kneeling lady is his sister, he raves and shouts, vehemently denying any relationship to her. This outbreak is followed by a spell of weakness; he falls on his throne and faints. In his stupor he sees how his prisoner Tigranes in turn is affected by Panthea and confesses his love for her. Arbaces becomes insanely jealous, rises in anger, and orders his rival to be put to prison. In a reversal of the situation, he now kneels down before Panthea, begs her forgiveness, and gives her three "brotherly" kisses. But these stir his passion to the point that he breaks out in a new flare of rage, calls Panthea a temptress and a poisoner, and has her rushed off to jail. He now feels actually as if he were poisoned much like Othello does; he is so weak that he has to support himself on a friend as he exits. With this scene begin his tortures, which, he says, seize his body and mind, but which are most notable in their physical manifestations.

Arbaces' ecstatic states, which appear insufficiently motivated and grossly in excess of the occasion, strike one with amazement. Even Antonio's hysterical fits seem more natural because they are the effect of his suffering through the merciless villainy of Piero. Othello's collapse is much better motivated because it is preceded by a growing infection of his brain and we know the green-eyed monster to be so much more formidable a bird of prey than feathered Cupid.

Yet the comparison of these three scenes shows also a notable similarity and indicates the same mentality of style at work in *Othello* as in *Antonio and Mellida,* and *A King and No King.* The German philosopher Garve said in the eighteenth century that Shakespeare's tragedy was executed in the manner of Buanorotti because it strove toward gigantism and represented passion to a point where it became improbable and incredible[9]—a remark that was not intended to be flattering. The criticism of Garve takes the point of view of classicism; but the observation of gigantic passions in Shakespeare is just. Although these do not become improbable and incredible in Othello, they do become so in *A King and No King*— the Baroque overreaches itself as it does in some of Rubens' larger canvasses. The block, Arbaces, felled by love, reminds me—I hope the comparison will not be thought irreverent—of Bernini's kneeling or recumbent saints, physically massive, but aquiver with ecstasy from the expression of their faces to the folds of their dresses. Emotion and movement at all costs.

The features I have found characteristic of passion in the three dramas occur, with modifications, in a number of other plays of this period. There is surely no better word for these traits than Baroque. They may be summarized as follows:

Passion is in the service of an artistic principle that exploits all opportunities for movement and tension. The particular theme of passion is heavily underlined by parallels and contrasts: Antonio's grief is emphasized by that of his father Andrugio and his friend Pandulfo, Othello's jealousy by that of Iago and Roderigo, Arbaces' desire, by that of Tigranes. Antonio's temperament is set off by the imperturbability of Piero, Othello's warmth, by Iago's coldness, and Arbaces' fire, by Mardonius' logic.

The passion of the Baroque hero becomes overwhelming and immeasurable. His soul is stirred into a whirlpool which threatens to engulf him. The force of passion increases by its collision with an opposing principle: Antonio's grief clashes with his resolution to avenge his father; Othello's jealousy first battles with his reason; after reason is defeated, his jealousy splits into love and hate, which struggle with each other; Arbaces' incestuous love fights with his moral conscience. In these conflicts, the hero is torn from one end of the emotional scale to the other; his abrupt change of mood provides violent contrasts. He mocks himself of the advice of patience, the virtue propagated by dramatists with middle-class leanings. The Baroque hero's sufferings are accompanied by violent gestures and actions. These often climax in pathological states which resemble hallucinations, attacks of hysteria or insanity, or epileptic seizures. Dramatic psychology, generally derived from classical sources, is made subservient to an art which strives to go beyond probability.

In all these features, the later Shakespeare resembles his contemporaries such as Marston and Beaumont and Fletcher. But, I hope to have at least implied that Shakespeare's superiority emerges by comparison. While Othello's passion is even more titanic than that of Arbaces, it strikes us not only with amazement, but also with pity and awe. Shakespeare succeeded in making superhuman passions humanly plausible; he substantiated a titanic outbreak of fury by an equally gigantic motivation. He endowed his heroes with at least a remnant of dignity, even in their greatest fall. Although Shakespeare painted on the canvas of Baroque art, the art of his time, his genius miraculously transcended these limitations to create an art which was for all time.

Notes:

(1) Cf. Douglas Bush, *The Renaissance and English Humanism* (Toronto, 1939).

(2) Cf. Carl J. Friedrich, *The Age of the Baroque 1610-1660* (New York, 1952). For assessments of the validity of the term for literature, see Rene Wellek, "The Concept of Baroque in Literary Scholarship," *Journal of Aesthetics and Art Criticism*, V (1946-47), 77-109, and Helmut Hatzfeld, "The Literary Historian and the Baroque," *Journal of Aesthetics and Art Criticism*, XIV (1955), 156-164.

(3) The terms Baroque and Mannerism are applied to both literature and art by Wylie Sypher, *Five Stages of Renaissance Style* (Garden City, N. Y., 1955) and by Arnold Hauser, *The Social History of Art*, vol. II (New York, 1957). For a diagnosis of Mannerist features in Shakespeare, see Freiherr Kleinschmit von Lengefeld, "Der Manierismus in der Dichtung Shakespeares," *SJ*, XCVII (1961), 62-99.

(4) The epoch-making distinction between Renaissance and Baroque was Heinrich Wölfflin's *Kunstgeschichliche Grundbegriffe* (1915), translated as *Principles of Art History* (New York, 1932). Wölfflin's criteria for the analysis of the Baroque have been most influential also in literary history, and are echoed, sometimes disputed, by Sypher and Hauser, for instance.

(5) E. g. Arnold Hauser, *Mannerism: The Crisis of the Renaissance and the Origin of Modern Art* (London, 1965). For a criticism of the application of the term to such widely different figures and phenomena, see the review of Hauser's book in *TLS* (April 15, 1965), p. 288.

(6) *Shakespeare-Studien* (Halle, 1871), p. 150.

(7) It has been persuasively argued that in the Later Elizabethan period there was change from stylized acting to a more naturalistic, subjective, and passionate fashion, and that this development was due to the shifting cultural climate of the time. See Leonard Goldstein, "On the Transition from Formal to Naturalistic Acting in the Elizabethan and Post-Elizabethan Theater, "*Bull. of the New York Publ. Library*, LXII (1958), 330-349.

(8) Cf. my article on "The Madness of Hercules and the Elizabethans," *CL*, X (1958), 309-324.

(9) Quoted by L. L. Schücking, *Shakespeare und der Tragödienstil seiner Zeit* (Bern, 1947), p. 5.

An Allegory about Allegory. *Review Article*[1]

by Don Cameron Allen

If all metaphysical trappings are torn away and the conceptual process is viewed under purely rhetorical conditions, the articulation of a symbolical nominative by almost any predicate, except, perhaps, a copulative, is likely to result in an allegory. The term itself is a late comer in Greek. "Hyponoia," meaning "an undermeaning," "a hidden significance," is the expression commonly in use until the first century of our era when the word "allegory" begins to appear in the writings of Plutarch, Philo, the pseudo-Heraclitus, and others. Thereafter, thanks to its wide usage by the Fathers, it becomes the proper way to say, "He sets down one thing and means—or, at least, 'I think he means'—something totally different." But when this mode of literary doubletalk began is not so easy to discover.

In the ninth book of the *Iliad* (502-12) old King Phoenix describes the Litai (prayers), halting, wrinkled daughters of God, vainly attempting to follow Ate in her vigorous dance. This is probably a personification, but nothing even similar to it appears elsewhere in the Homeric poems. Sometime between the seventh and sixth centuries, Pherecydes of Syros, eldest of pre-Socratic philosophers, worked out a physical explanation, anticipating the method of the later Stoics, about the myth of the divine marriage of Zas and Chthoniê. Within a generation or two, if Tatian's information is correct, Theagines of Rhegium instituted the custom of searching the Homeric scriptures for deeper and devouter truth. By the fifth century, the practice of looking under the literal for the important is an interpreter's duty. Anaxagoras, Metrodorus of Lampsacus, Stesimbrotus, Glaucon, Democritus, and many others search the poems of Homer and Hesiod, and even the mythology for recollections of ancient wisdom. The pursuit of the second meaning by commentators produced the conscious allegorist. Parmenides expounds his conversion to the contemplative life with an allegory of a journey in the chariot of the senses to the palace of Lady Dike. In the same way, the Sophist, Prodicus of Ceos, increased his fame and fortune by an allegory (still well-known to us) of Hercules' choice between the voluptuous Kakia and the austere Arete.

One hardly needs to comment on the uses made of allegory once the Christian philosophy was in place. It became a handmaiden of mediaeval theology and dominated the thinking of painters, architects, and men of letters in the Renaissance. The regular printing of dictionaries and compendia of symbol and allegory during the sixteenth and seventeenth centuries was not a printer's philanthropy. Most scholars, unfortunately, are inclined to doubt the later importance of allegory; they regard it as a waste-product of an inferior civilization, because they themselves are the naive proponents of a naive theory of undermeaning. Actually, modern man is himself little more than an allegory of chemistry moving rapidly towards a myth of hydrogen.

Although the average American Englishman lives, and always has lived, a life of allegory, there is as yet no history of the mode in the English language, and Fletcher, whose book is before us, attempts nothing of the sort. Departing largely from Honig's excellent *Dark Conceit* (a work he supplements rather than supersedes) and Frye's seminal sections, he attempts to get at the essence of the mode. He has learned from his two predecessors that allegory did not end with the fall of Constantinople. Kafka, Rilke, Stevens, Golding, Updike, and many other modern men of letters have mastered its procedures. In addition the general public battens on T.V. shows, whodunits, westerns, and scientific tales that are peculiarly allegorical. Although, as Berger sagely observed, most allegories contain something in the literal level that is an invitation to second thoughts, there are, Fletcher thinks, no pure allegories, only quasi-allegories. In a sense he is right: all allegories are allegories of allegories.

Allegory is composed of seven chapters held together by the major theme; each chapter, although there are recalled terminologies and allusions backward, is really a discrete essay. The handsomely produced packet of pictures in the appendix is teasing in its manifold symbolisms, but they add, I think, nothing to the general argument and require a richer commentary than Fletcher gives them. Chapter Six on psychoanalytical analogues is a mistake, and a friendly editor should have excised it. Fletcher states that the major agent in an allegory is like an ambivalent compulsive, and, while he insists that it is not so, he leaves us with the impression that the enjoyment of allegory is an obsessive neurosis of a clinical type. This impression is more disturbing, because in the previous chapter, Fletcher objects to J. W. Saunders' use of the word "schizophrenia" in a discussion of literary ambivalence. The remaining six chapters are filled with aperçus that are sometimes nothing short of brilliant. The proper way to review these chapters is to write another book, but since that is impossible, I shall let them pass in review.

In his essay on "The Daemonic Agent," Fletcher distinguishes between the allegorical agent and emblematic personification; in the latter there may be "a remnant of action." The agent stands either for abstract ideas or real people. In "The Phoenix and the Turtle" one sees a pat example of both equivalents. The wide dialectic analysis which provides the structure of such a poem is made broader by the narrowness of irony. In keeping with this hypothesis, Fletcher can say that caricature is "allegorical in essence since it strives for the simplification of character in terms of a single, predominant trait." In the Middle Ages when "depth of significance" implied variability, the singular character was the mode; but as men came to perceive the complexity of their world, they mirrored this perception in more complex allegorical heroes, who reveal, almost as if they were removing garments, one complexity after another.

The central allegorical hero also generated secondary characters like himself that either opposed or aided him. Such a continuous stream of allegorical revelations can be clearly seen in the *Divine Comedy*. The central agent in an allegory is close in nature to what the ancients called a "daemon," by whom one could be possessed. One could listen to its whisperings without ever assuming its shape. Spenser's characters are, for example, fairies; Dante's are all spirits. All of them inhabit a daemonic world "where supernatural energies and consuming appetites are the sole means to existence." But the perfect allegorical agent is not a daemonic man but a bare machine like Spenser's Talus or Frankenstein. The allegorical agent is, however, a division of the "total cosmic organization; he is halfway between god and man," but like the ancient spirits of middle air, he is fixed; he is, in fact, an ideé fixe. Even when it seems to change, the agent is static and bound to necessity without personal control.

In the account of "The Cosmic Image" Fletcher objects to equating allegory with metaphor on the ground of difference in function. A single metaphor is a vehicle of surprise, but surprise becomes, as in the case of Emily Dickinson, anathesia as the metaphor stretches and proliferates. True allegory moves from obscurity to clarity, maintaining until the end a pose of aenigma. Actually, the most striking quality of allegorical images is their separateness. They exist for what they are in perfect isolation. To contain this theory, Fletcher revives Aristotle's term "kosmos," which has been debased, he thinks, by Latin "ornatus" and "decoratio." A part-whole relationship, which includes metonymy, synecdoche, and personification, is implied in the term. It also suggests the daemonic nature of the image, and permits an emphasis on visual modality, especially on visual or symbolic "isolation." Lastly, if it is combined with its similars, large scale double meanings emerge.

"Kosmos" means also a universe and a rank in a hierarchy. As a symbol it can be attached to, associated with, or substituted for "any object the writer wants to place in hierarchical position." Because of its larger Greek meaning, it offers a metonymy-synecdoche relationship between "kosmos" a part and "cosmos" a whole. Besides decorating and specifying, it has the power "to arouse intense emotional response," because like daemons it can lower and elevate. Allegory is, then, a "mode that depends on kosmoi, which in turn depend upon systems of status that are too strict to allow a free play of artistic imagination." As a result of this fact, the allegorist is ethically compelled, and allegory is, consequently, easier in a Christian than in a mechanistic universe. For this reason it seems mediaeval, but it is still a valid literary technique, declining in tone, as in modern sewer fiction, but also expanding as our universe expands.

In the essay on symbolic action, Fletcher observes that all allegories resolve themselves into either progresses or battles. The progress may be a real or fantastic journey or an introspective trip through mental catalogues. It is always a forward journey to a goal, a straight line in keeping with the monomovement of the daemonic agents. The battle may be physical or mental, no more than "an intense rumination." But both processes can blend. Progress supplied by parataxis becomes ritual; battle, depending on juxtaposition or hypotaxis, is symmetry and balance. The paratactic order has that lack of perspective which we associate with the mimetic world and it provides a codelike rythmn that informs us we are in allegory. Like most rituals, progress has no probable limit. Mediaeval allegorists often stopped it by an arbitrary closure. *The Faerie Queene* may have had other than biographical reasons for failing to reach an end.

Now the agents of allegory can help, hurt, change, and affect each other, and the purpose of the essay on "Allegorical Causation" is to spell this out. We can begin by observing that truly allegorical mode of the pastoral, which is ambiguous in its representation of social tensions. The rich persona give power to the poor; the poor give purity to the rich as nobles become shepherds. But magic is required to shift the classes, and it is magic that holds the parts of the ritualized or symmetrical allegorical plot together. To expound this magic, Fletcher goes to the *Golden Bough* for Frazer's theories of imitative and contagious magic. On this great edifice, the whole ritualistic progress of his own speculation flounders and pants as he tries to force his sophisticated perceptions through the doorway of the anthropologist's analysis of primitive superstition. It is simply a nil probatur.

The section on thematic effect, which is one of the best, takes off from Frye's hypothesis that a thematic intensity begets allegory, but Fletcher is not here engaged in separating allegory from mimesis. He is concerned with the dualism that implies the opposition between "two independent, mutually irreducible, mutually antagonistic substances," such as Good versus Evil, Darkness versus Light, etc. But a contention between absolutes is not the foundation of all allegory; in fact, the "polar opposites" are not necessarily more than a half-inch apart. Often they are bound in a philosophical ambivalence similar to a taboo, which is both sacred and profane. This concept can be illustrated by Kafka's four legends of Prometheus, which leaves aside the explanation of the "inexplicable rock," a point made graphically by plates 16-20. The best illustrations are to be found in the eighteenth century's notions on the sublime and picturesque.

Between the telescopically sublime and the microscopically picturesque, Fletcher finds the same ambiguity he found in his earlier statements about allegory. The sublime is an enthusiasm for an ideal in which "the daemonic has been rendered polite." Awe is transferred from religion to aesthetics. One is pushed by a promise of "something more" into the pursuit of a final member of an infinite order until one finds oneself in the limitless plains of the metaphysical. Relying on Uvedal Price for his premises, Fletcher discovers in the picturesque "a more sensuous function" than the veiled language of the Middle Ages. One views a "paysage moralisé" in which effects outweigh organic form. When the picturesque goes morbid, we are in the realm of Gothic excess. The difficult becomes threatening; naturalism stirs in the womb.

The final chapter saddles those weary pegasuses, value and intent. The New Critics objected to allegory because it prescribes how a text must be read and restricts the readers' freedom. The thematic function of allegory immediately suggests its value, and so it is a question, since beauty is not involved, whether an allegory may be aesthetically judged or not. The intent is also under authorial control, but this control may be lessened. One control is to turn an ironical gaze inward, but irony can become sentiment, so other controls must be devised. One must remember that a clinging irony can become a wearisome parody which becomes what it mocks.

In much allegory, however, the abstract is hidden under "difficult ornament" which stirs the curiosity, but there are also texts in which we are not sure of the allegorical intent because the warning signs (daemonism, kosmos, isolation, contagious magic, emotive ambivalence) are never extremely present. Even in the traditional allegories there are degrees. For this reason there have been critics who held that Spenser's tapestries and processions are simply sensuous riches or that Collins and Gray only wrote "highly charged poetry of statement." Sometimes, too, the author—a Dante or William Golding—comments on his symbolism. Dante, in fact, actually allows his commentary to engulph his action, a common enough condition of mediaeval allegory. Swift, on the other hand, prevents this engulphment in the *Tale of a Tub* by satire, whereas Sterne in *Tristram Shandy* allows comment to become burlesque.

If allegory recedes when the literal surface is thick or when commentary takes over the figurative, it also vanishes when, as in Spenser's Garden of Adonis, it becomes mythic. But unlike myth, allegory does not accept doubt (the world of experience). It replaces sensuous testimony with ideas. The reader is left, as a result, the prisoner of his engaged interest as he listens to the commentary he is required to write. After this discourse, Fletcher considers intentional control in political allegory and finds a further intent in the social syncretism that arises from an attack on and defense of the status quo. It is the response to the resulting ambivalence here that alone counts and provides the rationale for allegory. One response is a defensive ritual which carries the ambivalent feeling away and provides a center in a world of flux. But higher than a defensive ritual is a visionary ritual, which allows the agent to move towards an apocalyptic center where the culminating vision is apparent. With this experience, allegory ceases to be allegory "and comes instead to share in the higher order of mysterious language, which we may perhaps call mythical language."

Kosmos, daemonism, and isolation slow the progress and unsettle the balance of *Allegory*. The reader's emotional response is affected by this. Half of the book is given over to footnotes that should be read only after one has finished the main text. To read them with the text is to distract one's attention from a line of argument often difficult to follow. In a generation that avoids footnotes because footnotes indicate that an author has sullied his amateur standing by reading, it is ungracious of this maker of footnotes to complain. Fletcher has read so much that he seems to belong to an earlier generation; his erudition is remarkable and in an age that would rather write than read he deserves the applause of all of us. But the lower half of a page is not the wastepaper basket where one puts all those delightful note slips collected so lovingly and abandoned with such pain. Fletcher's second book in eight point is interesting in the way that Robert Burton's annotations are interesting, but the notes are often unnecessary and are there because they are there.

The text itself is elaborately repetitious. Observations that are excellent when they are first stated are repeated with different phrasing in different places. Repetition is, of course, a sound pedagogical device, but Fletcher's readers probably do not need it to grasp his major ideas. This defect is accompanied by a failure to make easy transitions and by a mandarin mode of expression. Fletcher realized, I think, that each of his chapters is a sequence of insights rather than an organic structure. To smooth out these wrinkles he supplies topics in italics that point out the road for the reader. But only too often he gives us his perceptions the way he got them—the hard way.

The prose style does not reveal the witty man Fletcher is, but rather a garment stiff with technical jargon rented from the rhetorician who seems to costume most literary theoreticians. Honig managed to talk about allegory in prose that is simple but stylish; he was relaxed and puts the reader at ease. Fletcher laments the use of jargon in other disciplines, but slides with excessive ease into the patois of the literary theoreticians. All of the other eccentricities of this school are also visible in *Allegory*. One of these is a kind of prolixity which demands a paragraph of words to make a simple and often obvious statement. Another is the use of an anti-poetic language which requires grammatical decoding. One example of how Fletcher manages this will do. Fletcher quotes Empson—a true master of the boss word— on page 183. "This power of suggestion is the strength of the double plot, once you take the two parts to correspond any character may take on *mana* because he seems to cause what he corresponds to or be the Logos of what he symbolizes." Empson's sentence has to be twice read, but once Fletcher gets his hook into this elephant's ear, the monster he leads out reads: "Here Logos implies a highly charged system of symbolic parallels, presumably imaged in the kosmoi that contain whole universes in small detail of ornament."

Both of the foregoing excerpts contain characteristic symptoms of the unhilarious pose of otherwise humorous men. One must use Greek and Latin words, preferably in italics, or one is not being profound. Fletcher is a victim of the epidemic. On page 41, we learn what *virtus* means in Latin and Italian; on page 92 we are told that banners are *vexilla*; on 118 we have *kosmein* defined; on 172 we read "story (Greek: *mythos*)." This custom of shining a mirror in the eyes of the middle-brows is borrowed from the anthropological theologists whose writings Fletcher obviously respects. With them it is clearly a bulwark against the less literate pious who are thereby revived from spiritual shock by a linguistic display. When they read "And Jesus (*Christos*) sat (*sedi*) at the table (*mensa*)" they think they are listening to the Spiritus Sanctus and ask no questions. If the common reader does not dig this he is, indeed, *infra dig*. For me it is nonsense (*phlyaria*), and I would be delighted if this form of fatty degeneration of the vocabulary were left to the seminary pundits.

These objections do not detract from the grand virtues of this book begotten of hard thinking by a man of undoubted brilliance. It is certainly one of the better works of literary intelligence of the year. My only fear is about what will happen now as the less gifted pick up a detail here and there and use it as a gimmick.

308

History tells us that this will happen, but we need allegory to expound it. When in the past a large and agile fish has swum in pleasing and graceful arabesques through the lush pickerel grass that flourishes on the banks of literary theory, he has usually been followed by a school of small frye incapable of dexterous circling, ignorant of the depths and shallows, of the dark and treacherous holes. These minnows deprived by accident of birth of eyes or gills, of steering tail or finny rudder have only muddied the magic pond of literature until at last they sank into its infinite bottoms where deans lurk and department heads draw red lines through the budget.

Notes:

(1) Angus Fletcher, *Allegory: the Theory of a Symbolic Mode.* Cornell University Press, 1964. Pp. xii + 418. 32 Plates. $6.75

Some Articles and Monographs of Current Interest

July, 1964-65

Charles Barber, "*The Winter's Tale* and Jacobean Society," in *Shakespeare in a Changing World*, ed. Arnold Kettle (London, 1964), pp. 233-252.

This article observes some distinctions initiated by contrasts between court and country in *WT*, the author accounting for a number of elements in the play by reference to his central proposition. Although outside of the scope of his immediate subject, the proneness of non-Shakespearean tragicomedy (i.e. *Philaster*) to court/country antitheses might have been relevant to the author's general discussion.

James T. Bratcher, "The Lorenzo-Jessica Subplot and *Genesis* XXXIV," in *Shakespeare 1964*, ed. Jim W. Corder (Fort Worth, 1965), pp. 33-42.

The story of the marriage between Jacob's daughter, Dinah, and Shechem the gentile in *Genesis* xxxiv is here suggested as a significant parallel to the Lorenzo-Jessica episode. Bringing together the work of Hockey, Nathan, and of several other scholars, Bratcher enlarges on the general relevance of the Jacob story to Shylock's role in the play and observes that the association of Jessica with the monkey she purchased may not only have the usual Renaissance overtones, but may display an unconscious yoking of concepts by the dramatist since the ornamental D of "Dinah," the first word of *Genesis* xxxiv in Bishops' Bible, 1568, itself contains a monkey. The various allusions by Bratcher and others, taken as a whole, raise interesting questions about Shakespeare's early aesthetics, for whether these references were meant to be obtrusive or merely the results of association, they throw light on one or another aspect of artistic intention.

Nicholas Brooke, "The Ending of King Lear," in *Shakespeare 1564-1964*, ed. Edward A. Bloom (Providence, 1964), pp. 71-87.

This is a good companion-piece to the equally well-reasoned article by Myrick (see below). Brooke argues for the tragedy as a negation which does not necessarily illuminate Shakespeare's personal attitudes but does suggest a phase in Shakespeare's theory of tragedy. Calling attention to the phrases "Speak what we feel, not what we ought to say," the author also implies that they might serve as a major ethical motif, for the process of the last two acts continually pits ideas of poetic justice or of avenging gods against the perceptions available from the action of the play.

James L. Calderwood, "*Love's Labour's Lost:* A Wantoning with Words," *SEL*, V (1965), 317-332.

Calderwood suggests some of the ways in which *LLL* would seem to emphasize the role of language not as an instrument of inflating self-expression or of social attack, but of social communion, the activity of the play being shaped towards such a statement.

R. A. Foakes, "Shakespeare's Later Tragedies," in *Shakespeare 1564-1964*, ed. Edward A. Bloom (Providence, 1964), pp. 95-109.

Taking Marston's 1602 revenge plays as parodies for boy-actors, Foakes suggests that such twitting of "heroic tragedy" marked a general turn to new tastes. The greatly good tragic hero of the late 1590's yields to an interest in the deeper complexities of psychological portraiture. Hence Timon, Coriolanus,

310

Antony, and Macbeth, as opposed to Hamlet, Othello, and, in certain respects, Lear. This essay, and the studies of Caputi on this subject, as far as Marston is concerned, might well be supplemented by further research in the matter.

David Frost, "Shakespeare in the Seventeenth Century," *SQ*, XVI (1965), 81-89.

This article is written to correct Bentley's comparison of the reputations of Shakespeare and Jonson in the seventeenth century. — "The evidence of publishing and theatrical performance, which Bentley ignored, indicates an overwhelming preference for Shakespeare among the Jacobeans." Frost is quite right in adducing such evidence, as well as references to the Shakespeare apochrypha, thereby expanding the scope of Shakespeare's reputation among the Jacobeans, but in order to earn the statement quoted above, it would be useful to investigate Jonson's reputation in the same terms; otherwise demonstration is by negatives.

Dean Frye, "The Context of Lear's Unbuttoning," *ELH*, XXXII (1965), 17-31.

The author emphasizes an obverse to the traditional real/artificial dichotomy in Renaissance discussions of existence. In the context of the idea that the "natural" was good in its prelapsarian state, Frye suggests that *Lear* emphasizes the "artificial" (which we may take as civilized custom) as the way of protecting man from the consequences of his postlapsarian (and consequently corrupt) "naturalness." Some additional documentation on the currency of this obverse, as so stated, in Renaissance writings, might have been useful for the author's purpose here.

C. G. Harlow, "The Authorship of *1 Henry VI* (Continued)," *SEL*, V (1965), 269-281.

Harlow demonstrates Shakespeare's personal knowledge of a source drawn upon by Nashe; hence the appearance of certain verbal motifs in *1 Henry VI* would not necessarily point to the hand of Nashe in that play.

Charlton Hinman, "Shakespeare's Text—Then, Now and Tomorrow," *Shakespeare Survey*, 18, for 1965, pp. 23-33.

Originally delivered as a paper at the International Shakespeare Conference in 1964, this article suggests a basis for future study of the quartos, making the following points. 1. The compositor who set the *cancellans* for Sheet E of *2 Henry IV* displays his work-characteristics (*i.e.* at least nine verbal alterations in 165 lines) in his resetting of the previously printed material in E. Effecting approximately 160 *substantive* changes in Q2 of *Richard II* as well, this compositor of *Much Ado*, of most of the bad quarto of *Hamlet*, and of fifty pages of the first good quarto of *Richard II* clearly demands attention. 2. 1597 *Richard II* was set by *formes*, as may have been 1594 *Titus*, 1622 *Othello*, and others, but not 1600 *Much Ado*. 3. Setting by formes will naturally imply casting off, some of the attendant problems of which the author discusses for 1597 *Richard II*. 4. The matter of casting off in quartos most importantly affects concepts of "anticipatory error" which is frequently regarded as characteristic of "reported" texts. Setting by formes would make possible a compositorial sequence of E4^v. E1^v. which would discourage any notion that some errors in the latter can, for instance, be "anticipation" of matter in E4^v. This is Hinman's better line of reasoning on this subject. His other contention, that a compositor will read ahead for inspection and pointing is a "human nature" possibility which implies that the workman will obey Moxon's idealistic desiderata when the very compositor Hinman discusses actually resorts to subterfuge to cover casting-off errors. Nor, in these respects, is it legitimately argued that Shakespeare's copy required careful pre-reading because the poet pointed sparsely, if the contention is based on the *Sir Thomas More* fragment. For such a line of reasoning assumes (a) that no scribe ever copied out Shakespeare's plays (b) that if scribes did copy them out, the printer or Shakespeare preferred setting from authorial manuscript (c) that a presumably busy Shakespeare preferred to copy out his own plays in a fair hand, and, if so, that in his solicitude for his work he still pointed sparsely even though, after all that care, the compositor would re-point (d) that if a scribe were used, he pointed as sparsely as did Shakespeare if the poet himself did so (e) that the *More* fragment is indeed in Shakespeare's hand. General signature-similarities notwithstanding, this document has exhibited no *demonstrably* Shakespearean characteristics. Bibliographical study uses this subjectively-taken fragment at the risk of subverting its own carefully constructed principles of objective verification.

Richard Hosley, "Sources and Analogues of *The Taming of the Shrew,*" *HLQ,* XXVII (1964), 289-308.

This article is grounded on the proposition that *A Shrew* is a bad quarto and hence not a source of *The Shrew.* In terms of this assumption it is then possible for the author to waive the *three* sisters of *A Shrew* when searching for the sources of Shakespeare's play and to present a number of Renaissance stories and motifs in which *two* sisters dominate. "From the present study," the author observes, "there emerges an understanding of Shakespeare's *Taming of The Shrew* as a synthesis of many sources and traditions." This statement is fully supported by the work of the article, but the point of departure, as Hosley himself has suggested, must be based on a postulate, a decision to reject *A Shrew* as written by any one but Shakespeare because in 1593 only he was capable of "devising a three-part structure more impressive than the structure of any extant play by Lyly, Peele, Greene, Marlowe, or Kyd." Considering the percentage of lost plays and, for instance, a Tourneur who only wrote two plays in his life, this line of reasoning is not without its problems.

G. K. Hunter, "Six Notes on *Measure for Measure,*" *SQ,* XV (1964), 167-172.

Notes 2 and 4 are especially informative regarding the tradition of the votarists of St. Clare (2) and the relevance of the Eucharistic controversy to Angelo's lines—"heaven in my mouth, / As if I did but onely chew his name" (4).

Frank L. Huntley, "*Macbeth* and the Background of Jesuitical Equivocation," *PMLA,* LXXIX (1964), 390-400.

This is a balanced investigation of the general context of "equivocation," but the author proceeds to matters not so strongly supported. A 1606 performance of the play is assumed with the consequence that 1611 is taken as the date of a revival. But one of the problems is to demonstrate that the context of equivocation establishes a 1606 date in the first place.

Kenneth Myrick, "Christian Pessimism in King Lear," in *Shakespeare 1564-1964* (Providence, 1964), pp. 56-70.

Myrick's argument is that if *Lear* is pessimistic, it is no more so than was Christianity when it came to evaluating the life of man on earth. But if the play presents no more horror and injustice, stupidity and greed, than were the traditional rationale for a *contemptus mundi,* Myrick observes too that it presents something of the providential assumptions also characteristic of Elizabethan religious writing on the affairs of this world. Consequently, a significant question for the author here concerning the play is "what prompts Cornwall's anonymous servant to make his astonishing attack on his master?"

Douglas L. Peterson, "'Wisdom Consumed in Confidence;' An Examination of Shakespeare's Julius Caesar," *SQ,* XVI (1965), 19-28.

This is an interesting argument to the effect that Caesar's statement, "this ear is deaf," is to be understood proverbially—as a refusal to entertain some one else's suggestion. If accepted, this Renaissance sense of the phrase would resolve the problem of how Shakespeare expected credibly to attribute unhistorical characteristics to perhaps the best known Roman of the poet's day. On the other hand, Peterson does not account for the first interview with the soothsayer, an interview which may operate as the demonstration on stage of a literal deafness.

H. L. Rogers, *"Double Profit" in Macbeth*. Melbourne University Press; New York: Cambridge University Press, 1965. Pp. 65.

This monograph explores with some thoroughness the possible extent to which concepts of "equivocation" inform word and structure in *Macbeth*. The author stresses the relationship between "doubleness" and "equivocation," but he also attends to other matters. He integrates the English-King scene into the play by reference to the association (in *A True and Perfect Relation*) of Edward the Confessor with "those very Walles" within which the Gunpowder Plot was set. From a different viewpoint, the author also argues that Holinshed's pp. 174-175 may be viewed as a center from which many essential features of *Macbeth* radiated (cf. Bratcher, above)—the Hecate scene, for instance, which is therefore defended as authentic. The study is accordingly of great use as further argument to establish the possible topicality of *Macbeth*, and it also furnishes interesting examples of the manner in which Shakespeare related to some of his sources. One aspect of the argument seems, however, dubious. "Equivocation" as a vocabulary-item indeed occurs in the play, and the many allusions to "doubleness" may indeed be complementary, but it is dangerous to point to equivocation "in action," as it were, for Macbeth's various hypocrisies need not warrant the term more than equivalent gestures by Cassius, Brutus, Othello, Iago, Edmund, Goneril, or Regan.

John Hazel Smith, "The Cancel in the Quarto of *2 Henry IV* Revisited," *SQ*, XV (1964), 173-178.

The initial omission of III.i. from the first issue is taken, with Greg, to be a result of accident rather than of deliberate suppression. Smith reconstructs the printing-situation as following this sequence: Qa with III.i. omitted; a setting of the first seven sheets of *Much Ado*; a *cancellans* for E with two extra leaves (E1 and E2 from Qa, E3-E6 newly composed). In this material vv is sometimes substituted for w and S for *S* when a shortage of w and *S* was created by the prior setting of *Much Ado* (cf. Hinman, above). In his conclusion, however, Smith adheres to Greg's assumption that the quartos of *Henry* and *Much Ado* were printed from Shakespeare's foul papers, and hence, that III.i. might have become misplaced. The persistence of this mythology is puzzling, not because the hypothecated situation would have been impossible, but because of the aesthetic naïvete implicit in Greg's decisions as to what constituted "foul papers." Waiving aesthetics, it is nevertheless difficult to demonstrate the nature of Shakespearean foul papers because examples, at this writing, have yet to be found.

Hallett Smith, "Shakespeare's Romances," *HLQ*, XXVII (1964), 279-287.

This article argues that the final comedies may not be so much an accommodation to Blackfriars stage or Fletcherian proclivities as a discovery, through writing *Lear*, of elements suggested by *The Arcadia*, by Holinshed, and by the romance tradition of such popular plays as *Clyomon and Clamydes*, *Mucedorus*, and *King Leir*. The point is well taken, but it explains process, not necessarily causation. The popularity of *Mucedorus* itself implies some stimulus for Shakespeare to meet a demand. Yet Smith's article suggests a wider context for the work of both Fletcher and Shakespeare, each of them, for instance, moving in their own ways to meet tastes which neither of them necessarily initiated.

J. K. Walton, *"Macbeth"* in *Shakespeare in a Changing World* (London, 1964), pp. 102-122.

This is a full discussion of the variations on the concept of "man" throughout *Macbeth*. Taking as a point of departure Lady Macbeth's phrase "the milk of human kindness," Walton places the overly-discussed motif of Macbeth's alienation within the context of traditional distinctions between self-oriented individual and contributing member of human society. A number of sequences are illuminated more strikingly than heretofore as a result.

Robert H. West, "Ariel and the Outer Mystery" in *Shakespeare 1564-1964,*
ed. Edward A. Bloom (Providence, 1964), 115-123.

This article, by the author of *The Invisible World,* suggests some of the ethical ambiguities inherent in the presence of Ariel. There was the possibility, for instance, that a Jacobean audience would understand Prospero's apparently nervous irascibility in the handling of such spirits and sympathize with the amount of labor which must seemingly be expended on the charms throughout the play. In this latter case, there may, however, be a tendency to take "realistic" exit-lines as an indication of the continuousness of Prospero's labors. Since Prospero never has any other activity attributed to him in the play except the practice of magic, these activities would offer a normal excuse for going off stage. However, such arguments can easily become circular.

Robert H. West, "The Christianness of *Othello,*" *SQ,* XV (1964), 333-343.

This is an examination of methodological problems inherent in "Christian" interpretations of *Othello.* West is specifically concerned with those approaches offering quasi-typological analogies as well as predictions as to whether Othello would or would not be damned after his death. Unlike many such articles, West's is concerned with critical and ideological consistencies in one specific play rather than with a blanket condemnation of all suggestions that Tudor and Stuart Christianity might have informed the structure of ideas in given tragedies.

The Editor

Reviews

The Art of Shakespeare by John Arthos. Barnes & Noble. 1964. Pp. ii + 197. $6.00.
Reviewer: Robert Kimbrough.

John Arthos' newest book is misleadingly titled, for instead of an implied discussion of Shakespearean aesthetics *The Art of Shakespeare* offers readings of eight plays in support of a broad, uncritical generalization: "the force of the Shakespearean work, the vast expanse of beauty and strength and life, charms us not by its vitality alone but finally by its containment. The art, like nature itself, holds all in balance, and it arrives at its end in finish and completion" (p.1). Because Professor Arthos' orientation is soundly and safely Elizabethan, he never says anything disturbing, in the negative sense; at the same time, however, his selection of plays is so disparate in kind and his eight essays (four of which have previously appeared in journals) are so loosely held together that he is prevented from saying anything at all disturbing in the positive sense.

The key to the art of Shakespeare, as I deduce it from these essays, lies in appreciating Shakespeare's ability to hold proud and wretched man up to nature, a nature that Arthos repeatedly labels as "reality" and "truth" and seems to believe is ultimately an ideal state: "the idea of truth" governs the tragedies, and the comedies maintain "a fundamental loyalty to the idea of happiness" (p.1). In other words, I suppose, no matter how inadequate man is, individually (tragedy) or collectively (comedy), nature is good, redeeming, beneficent, etc. To illustrate both aspects of his thesis Arthos has taken three tragedies, *Othello*, *Macbeth*, and *Antony and Cleopatra*; three comedies, *The Merchant of Venice*, *All's Well that Ends Well*, and *Troilus and Cressida*; and two of the last plays *Pericles* and *The Winter's Tale*, "which must also be thought of as comedies" (p.1).

The first chapter, on *Othello*, is the longest mainly because one half of it is introductory, establishing the point that in the histories and early tragedies Shakespeare "was learning . . . that the inner life itself was dramatic" (p.16). And the drama of Othello's inner life is tragic because his conception of honor is so willful, so self-contained, that he cannot recognize the truth of the world—the world of love, trust, "order, hierarchy, obedience, faithfulness" (p.26). "The world of the absolute to which Othello is dedicated is both timeless and without grace" (p.31).

Unlike Macbeth, Othello was doomed to lead the totally inner-directed life because he had no imagination, which is the means of apprehending and coming into balance with the truth of the world (to use Arthos' phrase) and "in itself is immaculate" (p.41). But Macbeth has only a touch of the poet, not enough to save him: "his will to live was tremendous, and he meant his imagination to help him live. But his imagination was not under the control of his will" (p.47).

The third chapter among the tragedies does not end the section so much as it provides a way out: because Antony and Cleopatra have an excess of imagination they are able to "deny morality, and although they pay the obvious price in the loss of power and discretion, like the gods they think themselves they escape the tragic judgement" (p.60). In their play, then, "the game has been played out and Shakespeare commences what will provide still other forms for drama in the romances, where instead of men approaching the gods, the gods come to them" (p.67).

Rather than move directly to the last plays, Arthos chose to broaden the base for his eventual study by devoting a section to illustration of what he feels is the essential statement of Shakespearean comedy: no matter how corrupt, confused, and decadent the world may appear, the recurring miracle is that life ends happily. Seemingly lest there be doubt concerning how just this view of his might be, and in order further to tie this section to the previous one, Arthos purposely chose "three of the most serious comedies" (p.1). This section is the most disappointing because it, more than the others, ignores the dramatic logic of each of the three plays chosen. In the chapter on *The Merchant of Venice* we simply must take Arthos' word that "the improbability of the happy ending is its deepest charm, rich with the picture of another existence" (p.91); in the next, we are told that "*All's Well* ends happily, and in doing so it reinforces the central morality of the play, that love is noble and that the ignoble are unworthy of it. We do not yet believe that Bertram is redeemed, but we need to believe he can be. If thus the point the play makes by ending too swiftly by that fact becomes untrue, its very falseness helps relieve our minds, inducing us to renounce the conclusion at the very moment we are needing to accept it" (p.95). And in the third, the major lesson of *Troilus and Cressida* is that "a story that has Troilus survive is the *beginning* for the comment on human aspiration that comedy can provide" (p.119, italics mine). In spite of lingering concern which we might have for what goes on *in* the plays themselves, the way nevertheless has been paved for the third section dealing with the romances, plays which "work upon us in the traditional way of comedy, in submission to the play of thought and fancy, and they avoid involving us in that intimacy of feeling through which in tragedy we identify our own lives with those of the characters" (p.135).

Arthos' point about the last plays (the *TLS* reviewer gave up long before reading the third section) seems to be that the issues raised are more searchingly personal and metaphysical than those of the comedies, even though comic detachment is maintained. But the point is not demonstrated, only asserted through the language of what Alfred Harbage last year called the new idolatry—ritual, romance, revelation, rebirth, redemption, restoration, and the rest. Furthermore, the usual critical objections to the received plots of the two plays which Arthos discusses are transformed into virtues: the fragmented episodes and static activity of *Pericles* are designed to allow the drama to take place "within a man and the resolution of the play is a resolution of a life" (p.137). Thus, at the end, "it is not that we feel sympathy for him [Pericles]—his generalized character gets in the way of that; we feel rather more than sympathy, we are identified with him. That identification without sympathy, that detachment without irony that is possible in our appreciation of character that is generalized, is, I suppose, the very way one looks at oneself, which is to say in a visionary way, neither analytically nor feelingly" (p.156). In *The Winter's Tale,* the divided plot becomes "a pattern of contrast and similarity working in succession, and the various uses of the fantastic, in all their complexity, define the form as well as the burden of the play" (p.173). By the end of *The Winter's Tale* we are "certain that nature is of itself endowed with all manner of excellence, that there are matters in society and in the universe that spoil it, but that all the same life is continually renewed, this is the perennial marvel" (p.187).

Because Arthos here operates on such a level of generality—"characters so limited and extended are marvellous additions to marvellous stories, they progress through fabulous adventures like figures in visions meeting circumstances of an all but inconceivable kind, but they reach a conclusion that is not only conceivable but thought to be realizable—a state of being saved from terror and all loss" (p.157)—it is all but impossible to agree or disagree with him in any logical, specific, critical manner. One simply agrees or disagrees. As a result the last section tends on its own to be an anti-climax, but two other factors reinforce the feeling: the first section is the best of the three, but has less to do with the last than the second, and the book as originally planned was to have ended with a chapter on *The Tempest*. But Arthos leaves it to us to deduce what that chapter would have contained: "I should hope that I have said enough [about *Pericles* and *The Winter's Tale*] to show how what is true of them would apply to *The Tempest* as well." Then he adds paradoxically—and most ironically—"that play, however, is an achievement of such an extraordinary kind that I prefer to put off a study of its form to another time" (p.1).

Although sure that I can tell what he would (or will) say about *The Tempest* in general, I am not at all sure it would apply; at least a demonstration would be interesting in view of the current idea of a cathartic *Tempest*. The absence of *The Tempest* is further felt because Arthos has been operating in obvious triads: Othello, the characters in *The Merchant*, and Pericles are inner-directed; Macbeth, the characters in *All's Well*, and Leontes are suspended between two worlds; and Antony, Cleopatra, Troilus, and, I suppose, Prospero live in the world of the imagination. But the main reason that the section and book are weakened by the absence of *The Tempest* is that that play is Shakespeare's most nearly perfect one which allows any critic free rein to ride his particular hobby horse. On the other hand, good as it is in parts, *Pericles* is far from perfect. As a result, the gap between one's usual experience of the play and Arthos' reading of it as a unified symbolic narrative is very great indeed. With *The Tempest* he will have a worthy objective correlative.

University of Wisconsin

Shakespeare in Germany, 1590-1700 by Ernest Brennecke and Henry Brennecke. The University of Chicago Press, 1964. Pp. viii + 301. $7.50. *Reviewer: R. A. Foakes.*

Anew series under the general editorship of R. C. Bald, and the textual editorship of Fredson Bowers promises well. The first volume in the "Curtain Playwrights" consists of a brief account by Ernest Brennecke of the activities of English actors in Germany from 1590-1700, and translations of five plays based on *Titus Andronicus*, *A Midsummer Night's Dream*, *The Merchant of Venice*, *Twelfth Night* and *Hamlet*. All the German versions are sadly debased and altered from the English originals, but they are all late versions, adapted to the needs of travelling groups, and to tactics that had proved successful for English actors who began by performing in their own language. Evidently clowning and tumbling earned these actors a good deal of their reputation, and the style they developed no doubt persisted strongly after 1600, by when they were able, it seems, to perform their plays in German. One outcome of their stress on the clown was the establishment of Pickelherring as a universal character, given to improvisation and obscenities, and capable of providing comic turns in play after play. Here he appears in the German version of the Pyramus and Thisbe burlesque from *A Midsummer Night's Dream*, in *The Jew of Venice*, a not too close relative of Shylock, and in *The Conflict of Love and Virtue*, a version of the *Twelfth Night* story.

One interesting feature of the repertory of the English players is that it cuts across the divisions between the acting companies in London, which guarded jealously their own plays. So in the German version of *The Merchant of Venice,* some elements are borrowed from another play that had a vogue in Germany, *The Jew of Malta,* and indeed the Jew retains the name Barrabas, while the opening scenes are set in Cyprus. Another is that, through all the perversions of the English plays, some hints may survive of the staging of the original; so Mr. Brennecke points to the *stage-directions* on p.163 of this edition, which instruct the Jew to speak the sum '2000 ducats' slowly, while the emissary of the Prince (Bassanio), here Pickelherring (Gratiano combined with Gobbo), speaks the same words quickly, a shift of emphasis perhaps echoes Shylock's manner in I.iii of *The Merchant of Venice.*

It cannot be said that any of the plays printed here has much merit, but each has its interest, and together they make a useful collection. In his brief introductions to each play, Mr. Brennecke provides a great deal of information very succinctly, and, with its helpful bibliography and index at the end, the volume sets a standard in presentation. Its documentation is not exhaustive, but was not meant to be; the primary aims were to help to throw light on Shakespeare by making available materials relating to some of the plays, and to show how garbled versions of Shakespeare's plays helped to create a new kind of drama on the continent, and became "a part of the foundation of modern theatre" there. Perhaps the most fascinating aspect in all this is that Shakespeare's name remained almost unknown in Germany until well into the eighteenth century, and yet, by 'bypaths and indirect crook'd ways', he was already having a powerful influence on the theatre of a nation which was soon to adopt him as their own.

The University of Kent at Canterbury

The Expulsion of the Triumphant Beast by Giordano Bruno and tr. Arthur D. Imerti. Rutgers University Press, 1964. Pp. ix + 324. $7.50. *Reviewer: Sears Jayne.*

"Shall I apologize translation?" asks Florio. "My olde fellow Nolano told me, and taught publicly, that from translation all Science had its off-spring." Though Bruno probably said nothing of the sort, his own works "apologize" translation sufficiently by their difficulty. One of his most puzzling works, *Spaccio de la bestia trionfante,* has now been translated into English by Professor Arthur D. Imerti, with a 65-page introduction, 35 pages of notes, a bibliography, and an index.

The landscaping around the main edifice requires little attention. The bibliography is only a token, containing little before 1955 and nothing after. The index, also token, does not even include all proper names. The footnotes are all at the back. The introduction merely sketches Bruno's life and comments briefly on the sources and the heresies of the *Spaccio;* the names Aquilecchia, Badaloni, Garin, Sarno, Troilo, and Yates appear nowhere in the book, nor do the names Albright, Hawkins, Levinson, McNulty, or Pellegrini. Everything has gone into the main house, the translation.

And with good reason. Translating a work like the *Spaccio* is an heroic undertaking. Bruno was never one for *sprezzatura,* and in the *Spaccio* he was at the top of his form, laying out vast deserts of rhetoric:

> "Whereas once you formed, while smiling, those two very lovely dimples on your cheeks, two depressions, and two points in the center of those lovable dents, giving you that smile that used to entice the entire world, to add seven times greater grace to its countenance, when, jesting (as he still does from his eyes),

Love was darting his sharp and ardent arrows; now, starting from the corners of your mouth, up to the already commemorated area, from one corner to the other there begins to appear the form of four parentheses, which, geminated, seem to want to prevent your smile, by tightening your mouth, with those circumferential arcs, which appear between your teeth and ears, so as to make you seem like a crocodile. I say that, regardless of whether or not you do smile, the internal geometer within your forehead, who is drying up your vital humor, and making your flesh come closer and closer to the bone, by thinning your skin, deepens the inscription of the parallels, four by four, pointing out to you by those the direct path which leads you, as it were, to the offices of the Dead." (p.101)

rivers of learned allusion:

"Momus", asked Diana, "what action do you think we should take in regard to Boötes, who, so well covered with stars, guides his wagon?" Answered Momus: "Because he is that Arcas, the fruit of that sacrilegious womb, and that noble parturition, which still renders testimony to the horrible thefts of our great father, he must depart from here. Now, make provision for his habitation." (p.123)

mountains of philosophical jargon:

"What you say is true. It must be so, and not otherwise, in the particular, immediate, and natural efficient; because the measure and reason of the particular act, regarding the particular subject, follow according to the reason and measure of the effective particular virtue. However, that is not so in the universal efficient, for it is proportioned, if we can express it thus, to the total infinite effect, which depends on it, according to the reason of all places, times, modes, and subjects, and definitely not to specific places, subjects, times, and modes." (p.135)

and jungles of willful obscurity:

Each one of these natures then, and particularly Jove's, finds itself as such an individual, with such a composition, with such accidents and circumstances, having been placed in number, because of differences which arise from contraries, all of which are reduced to one original and first contrary, which is the first principle of all the others, the proximate efficients of every change and vicissitude. Because of this, just as he, from one who at first was not Jove, afterward was made Jove, so he, from one who at present is Jove, finally will be other than Jove. (p.75)

There, then, where the Bear was, by virtue of the place's being the most eminent part of the heaven, Truth is placed first, who is the highest and most worthy of all things, rather the first, last, and middle; because she fills the area of Entity, Necessity, Goodness, Beginning, Middle, End, and Perfection. She is conceived of in the contemplative, metaphysical, ethical, and logical fields; and with the Bear descend Deformity, Falsity, Defect, Impossibility, Contingency, Hypocrisy, Imposture, and Felony. The seat of the Great Bear, for a reason not to be stated in this place, remains vacant. (p.80)

One can scarcely imagine the patience necessary to translate the whole of such a work, even under ordinary conditions. What must it have been like to fight the battle in braille?

319

Professor Imerti made his translation from a braille transcription of an unidentified text, presumably Gentile's edition. William Morehead's incomplete translation, published in London in 1713, was obviously of little assistance.

Professor Imerti is the Head of the Department of Foreign Languages at The New School for Social Research in Manhattan, and there is no question about the accuracy of his translation. What does deserve some comment is the extraordinary literalness of the translation. The following passages will illustrate:

1. "Maraviglia, che con più del solito frettolose piume mi viene a l'incontro; non lo veggio venir, secondo la sua consuetudine, scherzando col caduceo e battendo si vagamente con l'ali l'aria liquidissimo. Parmi vederlo turbatamente negocioso. Ecco, mi rimira, e talmente ha ver' me converso gli occhi che fa manifesto l'ansioso pensiero non pender da mia causa." (Gentile, p.141)

"It is amazing that he is coming to meet me with wings, speedier than usual. I do not see him coming according to his custom, playing with his caduceus and gently striking the very clear air with his wings. I seem to see him fretfully intent on business. Here he is looking at me, and he has his eyes turned toward me in such a manner that makes it manifest that his disturbed state is not caused by me." (p.195)

2. Dove ancor rimane la fantasia del fiume Eridano, s'ha da trovar qualche cosa nobile, di cui altre volte parlaremo, perche il suo venerando proposito non cape tra questi altri. (Gentile, p.19)

Where there still remains the representation of the river Eridanus, we must find something noble of which we shall speak at other times; because its venerable theme does not fit in among these others. (p.86)

3. Da questa sentenza (da noi, più che par comporte la raggion del presente loco, non senza gran causa distesa) pende l'atto de la penitenza di Giove, il qual s'introduce come volgarmente è discritto: un dio che ebbe de le virtudi e gentilezza, ed ebbe de le dissoluzioni, leggerezze e fragilitadi umane, e talvolta brutali e bestiali; come è figurato, quando è fama, che si cangiasse in que' varii suggetti o forme, per significar la mutazion de gli affetti suoi diversi che incorre il Giove, l'anima, l'uomo, trovandosi in questa fluttuante materia. (Gentile, p.12)

Upon this sentence (elaborated by us more than the plan of the present passage requires, not extended without great reason) depends the act of repentance of Jove, who is introduced, as is vulgarly described, as a god who possessed virtues and kindness, and possessed human and sometimes brutal and bestial dissoluteness, frivolity, and frailty, as it is imagined that he possessed when it is reputed that he changed himself into those various subjects or forms in order to indicate the mutation of the various affects [sic] that Jove, the soul, and man incur, finding themselves in this fluctuating matter. (p.78)

4. "Tutta volta mi pare   piace, per non incusare, ed a fine che non vegna incusata di vituperio la mia figlia Diana, ordino che l'essere carnefice d'uomini sia cosa infame, l'esser beccaio, idest manigoldo d'animali domestici, sia cosa vile, ma l'esser boia di bestie salvatiche sia onore, riputazion buona e gloria." "Ordine," disse Momo, "conveniente non a Giove quando è stazionario o diritto, ma quando è retrogrado." (Gentile, p.214)

320

"Nevertheless, it seems to me and pleases me that in order not to blame my daughter Diana and in order that she be not accused with vituperation, I should ordain that being a slaughterer of men should be deemed an infamous thing, being a butcher, that is, an executioner of domestic animals, should be deemed a contemptible thing, but being an executioner of savage beasts should be deemed worthy of honor, of good reputation, and glory." "A command," said Momus, "fitting to Jove, not when he holds fast to or follows a straight line, but when he retrogresses." (p.261)

Though this literalness complicates the reading and is fatal to grace, the translator's decision to be literal was a wise one in dealing with this work. The contents of the *Spaccio*, according to its title, were "Proposed by Jove, achieved by the council, revealed by Mercury, narrated by Sophia, heard by Saulino, and recorded by the Nolan." It is enough that we have to add to this list, "translated by an American"; any less literal translation would only have obscured even further what Jove "proposed".

Another advantage of Professor Imerti's literalness is that it does not prejudice interpretation of the work. In translating Machiavelli's *Prince* the translator can bias interpretation at once merely by slanting a few critical terms, such as *virtù*, *fortuna*, and *stato*. Similarly in the *Spaccio*, interpretation of the allegory can be biased at once merely by slanting the translation of terms such as *virtù*, *fortuna*, *mutazione*, and *legge*. Such bias as Professor Imerti exhibits in the Introduction is merely that of an admirer of Bruno's personal heroism, but not even this bias colors the translation: he translates *virtù* as virtue, *fortuna* as fortune, *mutazione* as mutation, and *legge* as law, leaving the reader free to interpret the work as a piece of Hermetic magic, an Erasmian satire, a sketch for the *De imaginum*, or what he will.

Among the scholars who will be most grateful to see this translation in print are students of English literature. Professor Kristeller was doubtless right in warning that "the history of philosophy should be primarily the business of students of philosophy," and Bruno himself deplored substituting literary studies for philosophy, but the *Spaccio* is preeminently a work of the imagination, and it not only invites but commands the most vigorous attention from students of Renaissance literature. Thanks to this translation, English-speaking Renaissance specialists are now in a better position than they have ever been before to recognize the force of Miss Yates' arguments for Bruno's Hermetism and for his influence in England. They may also be surprised to notice the many affinities between the *Spaccio* and Rabelais, and between the *Spaccio* and *The Praise of Folly*. Spenser's disputed debt to the *Spaccio* in the Mutability cantos needs to be re-examined now, as does Carew's undisputed debt in *Coelum Britannicum*. These and many other works of the English Renaissance, especially masques and mythological satires and allegories, may well blossom into fresh meaning in the light of Professor Imerti's remarkable achievement.

City University of New York
(Queens)

Shakespeare's Professional Skills by Nevill Coghill. Cambridge University Press, 1964. Pp. xvi + 224. $7.50. *Reviewer: Sylvan Barnet.*

Professor Coghill, who has been directing plays for thirty years, brings to the study of Shakespeare the practical experience that few literary critics have, and the scholarship that few directors have. His book, then, is doubly welcome, the more so because it is gracious, learned, interesting, and humane; and yet it often disappoints. In the following survey of the contents, some specific disappointments will be mentioned.

The Preface reveals Coghill's strength. He keeps the stage in mind, and cautions against the kind of literary reading that moves the play from theater to closet. Because he holds the plays in his mind's eye, not in his mind's ear, he sees the fancifulness of T. S. Eliot's view that Othello's penultimate speech is *Bovarysme,* which Eliot defines as "the human will to see things as they are not." Eliot says Othello is "cheering himself up," but Coghill points out that on the stage the speech simply cannot thus be interpreted. "How is an audience to know," he asks, "whether Othello is cheering himself up for being so gross a fool and failure, or whether he is cheering his audience up by showing once again, and at the last moment, a true flash of that nobility for which they had first honored him?" Othello's speech takes in the spectator as much as it takes in Othello, and if we accept Eliot's view, we must condemn not only Othello but Shakespeare's craftsmanship. On the other hand, had Shakespeare indeed wished to deflate Othello, how easy, Coghill points out, it would have been for Iago, master-deflator, to have said "Thicklips," or "Buzz buzz." Other critics (notably Helen Gardner) have said good things in Othello's defense, but Coghill's arguments ought to put down Eliot's comment once for all. This sort of insight, derived at least in part from visualizing the plays, is the strength of the book, and it pervades the first chapter, "Visual Meaning." A fine discussion of business that may effectively accompany Hamlet's rejection of Ophelia in III.i concludes with a discussion of Hamlet's discovery that Polonius is spying: "There is no need of a crude effect, a fumbling Polonial hand, a protruding foot, a belly-swollen curtain: all that is needed for the audience to have their desire is that Hamlet, facing the arras, should suddenly stop short and stiffen, as might a pointer scenting a brace of partridges, and then turn back and ask the stunningly unexpected question 'Where's your Father?'" There is another good discussion, perhaps even better, of *Lear,* IV.vi, when Gloucester says, "The trick of that voice I do well remember. Is't not the King?" Coghill argues that Gloucester, finding himself in the royal presence, kneels, "but the act of homage that brings Gloucester to his knees, a loyal subject, leaves him there a seeming culprit, for that is how Lear interprets the ambiguity in kneeling." Lear's "I pardon that man's life," and the ensuing lines on copulation, are not a wild soliloquy addressed to the air or to the audience, but to Gloucester.

Much of the second chapter, "Unification," is devoted to the not very remarkable argument that "though *Pericles* lacks pervasive unity, *A Midsummer Night's Dream* is a masterpiece of interweaving." The third chapter, "Juxtaposition of Scenes," calls attention to such contrasts as that between Jessica's disobedience to her father and Portia's submission to her father's will, and Orsino's luxurious melancholy, Viola's starker grief for her lost brother, and Olivia's sham sorrows. But one may doubt that Olivia's sorrows are sham; the word is at least uncharitable. And certainly one may doubt that Olivia's tokens of mourning "are mere tricks for keeping Orsino at arms' length." How, one wonders, does Coghill imagine *this* meaning to be communicated to the audience. Where are the lines in the text that lend it plausibility? Coghill cites Sir Toby's "What a plague means my niece to take the death of her brother thus? I am sure care's an enemy of life"; but Sir Toby doesn't take us very far.

We are a third of the way through the book, and have had ample reason to be grateful to Coghill, but by now we are getting uneasy. The uneasiness is increased by some doubts about the scholarly apparatus. Quotations from Shakespeare are from Elizabethan texts, but as one reads on page 69 a quotation from the Folio version of *1 Henry IV*, to which Coghill adds a note wondering whether "way" (in "Rebellion in this Land shall lose his way") should not be "sway," the reader adds his own wonder: why quote *1 Henry IV* in the Folio text, which was printed from the fifth quarto and has no authority. It is the first quarto that counts, and there indeed we find "sway." In short, the asterisk and square brackets with which Coghill provides his emendation are unnecessary; the text reads "sway" in the first place. A few lines later on the same page we learn that "the rout of the rebels was (in history) achieved by a treacherous betrayal (the blame for which fortunately fell on the cold shoulders of Prince John of Lancaster)," and so gently is the information given in the casual parentheses that we may forget that it is misinformation: Hall, Holinshed, and Daniel all attribute the treachery not to John but to Westmoreland.

The fourth chapter, on *Troilus and Cressida*, evokes similar uneasiness. The gist is that the play was originally performed in the public theater in 1602/3, without the prologue and epilogue; that the play is a tragedy (not a comedy and certainly not a cynical play); and that the prologue and epilogue were added in 1608 to "protect the play . . . from a bad reception by rowdy young cynics" when the play was revived for performance at one of the Inns of Court. All writings on this play make one uneasy, but the next chapter, offering "a structural analysis of *Troilus and Cressida*," does little to mitigate the doubts raised by the fourth chapter. The play is said to be "a straight tragedy, . . . shapely and complete," and we are told that the prologue and especially the epilogue, added to protect the play, ironically have misled critics. But the cynicism is not concentrated in the addition, and to suggest that we do not sufficiently value Troy because we no longer make the Elizabethan identification of Troy with London is odd: Troy has Pandarus and the worthless Helen, and if this is a "straight tragedy" why does it not end, like the other tragedies, with some note of the restoration of order? There are interesting things in these two chapters on *Troilus*, but they do not convince.

The sixth chapter, on the soliloquy, is less daring and more useful; Coghill suggests that seven functions can be distinguished, and he says fresh and good things about the soliloquies. The final chapter, "Revision after Performance," argues that the differences between the 1622 quarto of *Othello* and the Folio text can best be explained by assuming that the Folio text represents Shakespeare's revised version of the play. In the course of this argument, Coghill offers shrewd comments about Emilia's role in the last two acts.

The "Postscript" concluding the book is marred by unpleasant words about Simon Forman and John Manningham. The latter, apparently no brighter than the abused groundlings of the last century's scholarship, was gross enough to write that Olivia was mourning for her husband. "'His Lady Widdoe'!" Coghill repeats, adding an impatient exclamation mark. If Manningham was thus imperceptive, how indeed could he perceive that Olivia's mourning was a mere pretext to keep Orsino at arms' length? I think that Coghill, no less than Forman and Manningham (and everyone else) sometimes fails to see the obvious, and I end with three examples: (1) Coghill says that Iago's improvised versifying in II.i "succeeds completely in taking Desdemona's mind off her worries," but in fact Desdemona has an aside (II.i.120-21) in which she specifically assures the audience that her worries are still in her mind. (2) Coghill says that such terms as "mole," "truepenny," and "Hic and ubique" indicate that Hamlet believes at the outset that the ghost is diabolic. But how explain "It is an honest ghost, that let me tell you"? (3) Coghill says that Horatio's closing lines of I.i ("Let us impart what we have seen tonight / Unto young Hamlet. For upon my life, / This spirit, dumb to us, will speak to him") "create a natural presumption that when at last we are alone with young Hamlet, it will be of his dead father that he will speak. . . . But instead, by a dramatic surprise, he speaks of his mother, as if the soloist in a concerto, at his first entry, were to ignore the first subject just announced by the orchestra and go on to the second." But the subject has not been "just announced"; some 130 lines have intervened to raise other issues, notably the marriage of Gertrude to Claudius. We have no reason to expect Hamlet to speak as Coghill says we expect him to. Nor is it merely of his mother that he does speak. After commenting on the unweeded garden, he says—before he specifically mentions his mother—"But two months dead. . . . So excellent a king. . . . So loving to my mother." The mother enters via thought of the father, rather than unexpectedly. It is hard to see how a critic who so often keeps the play in his mind's eye, and who so often says such good things, could have made these palpable slips—slips worth of Manningham and Forman. But despite their errors we are grateful to Manningham and Forman, and we are no less grateful to Professor Coghill.

Tufts University

Shakespeare and Christian Doctrine by Roland Mushat Frye. Princeton University Press, 1963. Pp. ix + 315. $6.00. *Reviewer: Helen C. White.*

M r. Frye begins his study by excluding any speculation as to Shakespeare's personal religion; he believes that he conformed to the Church of England (p.3). He further believes that in his drama he maintained the secular point of view, being concerned with the temporal order and not with the eternal (p.7).

This was in keeping with the attitude of the most influential theologians of the Reformation in England, Martin Luther, John Calvin, and Richard Hooker (p.14). Mr. Frye reports that, "Luther insisted on the importance of liberal learning, then, as much for the benefit of the state as for the benefit of the church" (p.73). Calvin, too, "was steeped in the Renaissance. . . . Throughout the later editions of the *Institutes,* classical references of all types increase in number, indicating his continued saturation in the Greek and Roman masters" (p.74). Hooker, also, took the same position: "There is in the world no kind of knowledge, whereby any part of truth is seen, but we justly account it precious . . . The bounds of wisdom are large, and within them much is contained. . . . Some things she openeth by the sacred books of Scripture; some things by the glorious works of Nature; with some things she inspireth them from above by spiritual influence; in some things she leadeth and traineth them only by worldly experience and practice" (p.87). On the value of the liberal arts all three leaders were agreed. All three further agreed that there was no "need to 'Christianize' the humane arts and sciences before they may become acceptable for Christians to use and enjoy; on the contrary, they are to be accepted on their own terms, without reinterpretation in terms of Christ-figures and of Christian redemption'" (p.85). Rather, the leaders of the Protestant Reformation tried to preserve the integrity of these arts (pp. 85-86).

Frye believes "that Shakespeare's dramatic interest is almost entirely restricted to what the Reformers called the temporal order" (p.92). Of course, any dramatist must set his action in some context of "ethical evaluation" (p.94). Frye believes "that Shakespeare's appeal to natural law as the norm for evaluating actions in an exclusively temporal setting was again in full accord with the positions of the major theologians of his own age" (p.95). Luther in particular supported the Roman law "for establishing relations between men"

324

(p.96). For civilization Calvin, Luther, and Hooker believed man could achieve that "on the basis of following the guidance of nature, reason, and conscience . . ." (p.107). Shakespeare's own treatment of pagan ethics is in accord with the theologians' teachings on these subjects (p.114).

As for Christ's sacrifice, "Shakespeare makes only quite rare, and even then quite restricted, references" to it (p.122). When it comes to the important subject of Death, "most of the comments on death by Shakespeare's characters could as well be made by Greeks and Romans as by Christians . . ." (p.132). Shakespeare usually "chose to speak in terms of general human wisdom" (p.137). The after-life played little part on Shakespeare's stage (p.139). Mr. Frye distinguishes between two kinds of fear, the godly kind and the natural kind; Macbeth's fear is of the latter kind (pp.150-51).

The author, also, distinguishes between flattery and counsel and in this distinction is in agreement with the theologians' positions (pp.153-56). Shakespeare's characters were also "morally responsible for" their choices of action (p.158). "Christians should act vigorously, making free use of those means which God has provided" (p.164). "Even the general conception of God as merciful in himself and desiring mercy from men is not beyond the reach of non-Christian religion. . . ." (p.169). Furthermore, "There can be little doubt that Shakespeare respects his pagan characters enough to give their paganism its due" (p.170). "A familiar understanding of Christian doctrine in historical perspective thus contributes to a fuller appreciation of Shakespeare's art, but Shakespeare's art is not devoted to theologizing the theater (p.173). . . . Conversely, we may assume that when he did not make theological references clear in his writings, he did not expect us to read them in" (p.184).

As for religious hypocrisy, the fullest portrayal is Richard III (p.185). As for Richmond's prayer before the battle, it is clear that his reliance is on God (p.191). The judgment of God may, also, come in this life (p.193). While "Shakespeare's kings are not, by and large, very pious or even very moral men" (p.195), Shakespeare clearly supported the establishment (p.198).

For Shakespeare, "Man's basic worth and dignity, then, consists in the fact of his humanity, bearing the image of God" (p.200). It is quite clear that for Shakespeare, classical and Christian ethics "interlock and overlap" (p.212). Henry V's prayers of thanksgiving are models (p.223), but it is very doubtful if Claudius could pray (p.224).

Pride held the primacy among sins for sixteenth-century Protestants (p.225); and yet "the fact remains that a kind of secular pride was equally repudiated by non-Christian as by Christian writers" (p.226). It "is Hamlet who seems most aware of the full range of Christian doctrine" (p.234). Shakespeare carefully distinguishes between various types of repentance (p.237). As for self-knowledge, it was universal in both Christian and classical culture (p.247), but Shakespeare's purpose "is still to keep the mirror up to nature and to show the course of human life in this world" (p.255). As for virtue and vice, the main thing is to furnish "a warning against both pride and despair" (p.260).

For the practice of worship, "Shakespeare's knowledge of Roman Catholic practice is what might be expected of a literate Englishman of his time. . . . Even when not precisely correct, Shakespeare's references to worship practices were dramatically appropriate" (p.263). Mr. Frye in his conclusion makes some very important points, and, I think, sound ones: "It has been the general contention of this book that the mirror of Shakespearean drama was held up to nature, and not to saving grace" (p.267). He also insists that "Luther, Calvin, and Hooker, held . . . to an understanding of literature which we also find Shakespeare exemplifying in his dramas. . . . Shakespeare does not speak for himself in the plays, but for the characters he has created. . . . Though the plays do not furnish us evidence of Shakespeare's religious orientation, they do attest to his theological literacy and to his uncanny ability to adapt his impressive religious knowledge to dramatic purposes" (pp. 268-71).

There follows a very interesting appendix on "The Roman Catholic Censorship of Shakespeare: 1641-1651," on which Mr. Frye concludes: "What Sankey's expurgation may do is to put us on our guard, from yet another point of view, against the overly eager identification of Shakespeare's plays with Christian teachings in general and with the Catholic tradition in particular" (p.293). There is also a bibliography and an index of references to the plays, and to the matters taken up in the course of the text. It is a very helpful and interesting book.

University of Wisconsin

The Blazon of Honour: A Study in Renaissance Magnanimity by Margaret Greaves. Methuen, 1964. Pp. 142. $3.75. *Reviewer: Franklin Dickey.*

Miss Greaves writes that her book "makes no claims to originality" but attempts only a useful task—to help us understand the divers metamorphoses of the term "magnanimity" from Aristotle to the Renaissance. This modest book by its careful focus nevertheless accomplishes more than it pretends. An almost old-fashioned study in the history-of-ideas tradition, its clear examination of "magnificence" and "magnanimity" should lend itself to Empsonian analysis if the reader practices this method. The book itself refrains from exploring ambiguities for their own sake and is not concerned with more than historical associations. Instead the author has confined herself to meanings clearly within the ambiance established by the words in their context. Any loss in "richness" is compensated for by gain in precision.

In Aristotle's usage, of course, megalopsychia (translated into Latin as *magnanimitas*) is the sum of the private virtues. Cicero's influence converts the private virtues to public, and medieval authors use the term synonymously with "courage" or *virtus*. The pagan virtues are partially displaced by Christian, and men not only assert but also follow the ideal, the great examples being Alfred and St. Louis among "real," and Hector and Arthur among legendary heroes. Alexander, lost as a historical personage, finds his reincarnation in romance.

A short chapter on Malory points up the heavenly goal of knightly glory seen through the nostalgic eyes of the fifteenth century. A chapter presents Sidney as artist whose own life exemplifies the aim of Joinville's and St. Louis' *prud'homme* but with Renaissance emphasis on delicacy of manners and exquisite balance. The chapter on Spenser suggests that he was not altogether satisfied with magnanimity but looked upon this life as a quest and the sum of virtues as clues to the heavenly magnificence that transcends them. Milton is shown celebrating heavenly magnificence. Marlowe's Tamburlaine appears as archetype of the great and terrible concept of glory. Finally, Chapman and Dryden step forth, as they should, side by side, as masters of the astonishing.

The principal fault of the book—if it can be considered wrong in so slender a book—is that Miss Greaves is forced into only the most rapid survey of her subject so that she is in no position to carry her arguments to their logical conclusions. She is, however, full of suggestions for which both scholarly and general readers will be grateful.

University of New Mexico

Annals of English Drama, 975-1700 by Alfred Harbage as revised by Samuel Schoenbaum. The University of Pennsylvania Press, 1964. Pp. xvii+321. $18.00. *Reviewer: Giles E. Dawson.*

The compiler of a reference book like this one, consisting of a huge number of detailed facts, sticks his neck out a hundred times on every page. Perfection is not to be expected, and today's perfection, if attainable, will be imperfect tomorrow. If it was possible to pick out errors and omissions in Harbage's first edition, the wonder is that there weren't more. Their number has been steadily increased through twenty-five years of accelerating investigation of the early drama. Hence all who work with this drama will raise their voices to bless Sam Schoenbaum for his excellent revision of the *Annals* in the light of that quarter-century of scholarship.

He has retained the whole of Harbage's apparatus and has been at pains to preserve where possible the methods and arrangements, even the words, of the 1940 edition. Schoenbaum's new list of the collections and editions in which plays have most recently appeared adds more to the book's usefulness than would any other practicable innovation I can think of. A list of unprinted dissertations, also new, will be used less often, but when wanted will prove a godsend.

Schoenbaum's biggest job was the reëxamination of every item in every list and index, and he has performed it faithfully. Taking as a random sample the year 1580 in the Chronology, where Harbage has twelve entries, I find that Schoenbaum has added one (moved from an earlier year), queried the authorship of three, improved the titles of four, and narrowed the date-limits of five. Every section of the book has received the same close attention.

A reviewer is expected to point out the more important errors that he finds, and I imagine that I can most usefully perform this function by confining my activity in this sort to the Folger dramatic manuscripts. These are dealt with mainly in the Appendix, "The extant play manuscripts, 975-1700: the location and catalogue numbers".

Macro plays. The shelf number for the three Macro moralities, *The Castle of Perseverance, Mankind,* and *Mind, Will, and Understanding,* omitted in the Appendix, is V.a.354.

Juli and Julian. The date limits ought to be stated as 1560-1570, rather than ca. 1570.

Free-Will. Schoenbaum's curious practice of entering translators' names in the Author column (not mentioned in the introductory explanations) is a source of error in connection with this play. Under 1568 in the Chronology Henry Cheke is named in the Author column for "*Free-Will* (Trans. Bassano's *Tragedia del libero arbitrio.*)". Passing lightly over the playwright's name, which ought to be put down as Francesco Negri (as in the *Enciclopedia Italiana* and elsewhere) or F. Negri de Bassano, I come to column 6, "Earliest Texts", where I find not only the first print, "[1573?]", but also a manuscript. This turns out to be Folger MS. V.b.221—the only manuscript there is. Now things begin to get a little complicated. Under the date 1635 Francis Bristowe is named in the Author column for the same work by Negri, and the same manuscript is again noted in column 6. Finally, in the Appendix list of manuscripts. *Free-Will* is entered under Cheke. All would be well if the manuscript were in all three places entered under Negri instead of under Cheke or Bristowe, for it proves not to be Cheke's translation (though its title-page, quoted on the Folger catalogue card, says it is) and Bristowe's connection with it rests on conflicting and questionable evidence.

Philander, King of Thrace. In the Chronology this anonymous play appears under 1628, represented by a manuscript "author-plot". The title appears also in the Index of English Plays. But it is not to be found in the Appendix devoted to manuscripts. There it ought to be if *Philander, King of Thrace* is its title. In fact it is no more than the first name in the list of *dramatis personae,* and there is no reason for thinking the projected play ever had a title. It ought therefore to be listed among the "Titleless manuscripts and unidentified fragments . . . listed at the end of Supplementary List I". Further, in the Chronology this is called a fragment, and this suggests that part of it has been lost; actually it appears that it was never finished and that all that was written (or copied) is present.

Play without title. Another anonymous Folger item that ought to be listed among the titleless manuscripts is a complete pastoral tragicomedy of about 1630 to 1640, in English, among the leading characters of which are Elaenus, Syringus, Nanthus, Chloris, Charia, and Spiretta. It is in MS.V.b.222, a volume containing three Cambridge plays and part of a fourth, all duly listed in the *Annals.*

Folger Shakespeare Library

A Window to Criticism: Shakespeare's Sonnets and Modern Poetics by Murray Krieger. Princeton University Press, 1964. Pp. ix + 224. $5.00. *Reviewer: Hilton Landry.*

With a few changes and some softening of its asperity, Luther's comment on Erasmus' method of Biblical exegesis might well serve as an appropriate introduction to an estimate of Mr. Krieger's latest work:

> It is the way of all who parry [and present] arguments with figures to hold the text in sovereign contempt, and to concern themselves merely with picking out a word [or theme], torturing it with their figures, and nailing it to the cross of their own chosen meaning, [sometimes] in utter disregard of the surrounding context, of what comes before and after, and of the author's aim and intention. So it is here.

The chief figure of the book, the embodiment of its theoretical principle, is the mirror as window, a reminder that the meaning of a poem is not only locked *in* it but also miraculously comes *through* it. Since the New Criticism, according to Krieger, regarded the poem as a closed system of mirrors (with meaning locked in), to see it as both mirror and window is to move beyond naive limits to the sophisticated and mature position of Contextualism. His aim is to furnish a theoretical justification for this position, and the first and last sections of the book are addressed to this endeavor. But unfortunately his central principle of the mirror as window is never justified or "earned," to use Krieger's term. It is a postulate constantly asserted and claimed as validated, yet there is no reasoned argument supporting it — only superficial surveys of relevant criticism and finally a reference to Krieger's *New Apologists for Poetry* which suffers from the same inability to ground the theoretical claim. The *in* or mirror aspect of a poem's meaning is quite acceptable, partly because it is evident in his discussions of various Sonnets, but the *through* or window aspect is never made clear. In short, despite his repeated serious efforts, Krieger does not fulfill his intention to go beyond the New Criticism and to provide a theoretical basis for doing so.

Scattered throughout the book are transparent signs, not to say confessions, of an inability to validate the principal postulate. The first attempt and failure appear in his summary account of the problem of metaphor as a microcosm of the problem of poetry. In typical language he says,

> The most exciting discussions of metaphor by recent critics, in their desperate attempts finally to explain its mysterious workings and powers, have invariably ended by invoking the miraculous. The form of miracle is one either vaguely or precisely analogous to the Incarnation, the word made body. The reason for this resort to miracle is plain . . . once we see it in light of the implied criteria for metaphor that seem to underlie these discussions. (pp.4-5)

Note well the use of *desperate, mysterious, miraculous,* and *miracle.* It is the essential third criterion of metaphor, a logically discontinuous leap of meaning revealing a new relation of vehicle and tenor, which requires such terms. This relation, "uncovered" in the vehicle,

> enriches the tenor in its reflection, even if we cannot merely re-translate it back. For it is totally *in,* and not merely *through,* the relations within the vehicle that this new relation can now be perceived. *Somehow* [my italics] the vehicle has carried us, step by traceable step, to what startles us in its relevance, its inevitability, and yet its *logical* untraceability. . . . This third criterion requires us to see the vehicle functioning as window for the tenor even as it is its own mirror trapping us within its internalized reflections. (p.6)

Somehow and *miracle* give it all away, for a miracle can only be believed and accepted, never explained or its workings demonstrated. The "reason for this resort to miracle" is indeed plain: it is a disguised pragmatic appeal; and if one must resort to pragmatism, there is clearly no need for contextualism or any other theoretical foundation. The miracle, whether of the "fully incarnating metaphor" or the "fully contextual poem," is invoked from beginning to end; but as Krieger with admirable frankness admits,

> Still the question remains, the old cognitive question which *even our newer formulations cannot evade or quite answer* [my italics]: how, without resorting to a form-content dichotomy, can we depend on the work's context to be an accurate "reflection" of those otherwise unavailable existential forces of the cultural context? (p.208)

"The Mirror as Window in Shakespeare's *Sonnets*" is the title and subject of the book's middle section (pp.73-190). Here Krieger wavers between two different methods of handling the Sonnets and does violence to the collection in both. He claims to be treating it as a metaphorical system, a single body of mythology, as if the Sonnets "were a single entity, written simultaneously," although they obviously are not such a system or body and were not written simultaneously. He also refuses to take a stand on the order of Sonnets found in the quarto of 1609 (Q), for he will not go "beyond assuming that here and there certain sonnets are neighboring to one another" (p.128n.). Yet in the course of his discussion he accepts or ignores the Q order according to his convenience and violates the integrity of the individual Sonnet by taking groups of two and three (15, 16, 17, e.g.) as single poems of 28 or 42 lines. Now the very fact that one may, however improperly, consider as units successive poems such as 5-6, 15-17, 67-68, and 113-114 should suggest that in the Q order Sonnets which fall together belong together and thus its natural groupings may be significant for interpretation. But the groups must be natural, not artifical like Krieger's "curious and unique group of Sonnets 33-39." Although many have rightly found connections among 33, 34, and 35, and a few among 36-39, no one except the too ingenious Dowden ever discovered a direct relationship between 35 and 36. Not only is there no obvious or demonstrable connection between them, but some orthodox editors as well as most rearrangers insist that Sonnet 36 is "out of place."

No one wishes to deny the critic's right to analyze the poems of his choice, yet the capricious treatment of the Q order also implies a manifest arbitrariness in the selection of Sonnets for discussion. Superficial resemblances, especially in the use of certain words and images, often determine what shall be given attention, with the result that important Sonnets which are closely related to those Krieger analyzes are completely ignored. If Sonnet 124 be chosen for discussion (because of "state"), why not 125 which is more closely linked with it than is 64? If 87 be chosen, why not 88 which makes the point of 87 clearer and belongs to a relevant context, whereas 113-114 belong to an unrelated one? If 67-68 be chosen, why not 66 from which they take their departure; if 53, why not 54 since it is crucial to the proper understanding of the former? One begins to wonder what it is that defines a context for the contextualist. Furthermore, one observes that because of the arbitrary principle of selection—it is more or less "thematic"—significant aspects of the collection are glossed over, notably the discrepancy between the physical appearance and the moral reality of the person addressed in a number of poems. One of those poems, although he fails to recognize the fact, is Sonnet 53.

Krieger's reading of 53, the result of stressing a superficial connection with 106 to the exclusion of both the immediate (54) and wider context (43-58), is the most flagrant misinterpretation of the book. A remarkable paragraph, too long to quote in full, indicates the nature of the similarity between the two poems:

> As utter fulfillment of history, the friend is closer to the second coming than to the first coming of Christ—which is why I have spoken of this movement in the Sonnets as eschatological. In Sonnet 106 and in those I turn to next, he is seen to stand at the absolute end of history in that he has fulfilled all the possibilities of the discrete existences that have preceded him. (p.176)

After elaborating on this position he begins his brief discussion of 53 by saying, "The claim that the friend is the one final reality that sustains all the mere images of previous history is made explicitly in Sonnet 53." Despite its Platonic conceit and citation of Helen and Adonis, 53 is concerned with present history (the friend's character) rather than "previous history," and it is not the poem of unqualified praise it is generally understood to be. Like the Sonnets which precede it (43-52) and others using *shadow* and related ideas (27, 37, 43, 61, 98-99, 113-114), Sonnet 53 is written in absence, the fact which governs its thought and feeling. Separation from his friend leads the speaker to find shadows or images of his beauty everywhere and also to have grave doubts about his fidelity (cf.48). After the serious opening question—"What is your substance, whereof are you made, / That millions of strange shaddowes on you tend?"—much of the poem dwells on images of his friend's beauty (l. 12); but the couplet, after stressing his participation in all *external* beauty, ironically questions his internal or moral beauty in the form of constancy: "In all externall grace you have some part, / But you like none, none you for constant heart." Instead of the "common Petrarchan piety" which Krieger finds in the last line (p.178n.) there is a genuine fear that the friend may be all shadow (physical beauty) without substance (fidelity), hence the next Sonnet is a homily on the superiority of beauty which has truth (constancy) as its center: "Oh how much more doth beautie beautious seeme, / By that sweet ornament which truth doth give." In both 53 and 54 the speaker is hoping for the best while fearing the worst and giving precept in the form of praise.

Other Sonnets are distorted or partly misunderstood, among them 5, 6, 12, 23, 24, 64, 87, 106, 113, 116, and 146. Sonnets 5 and 6 do not comprise a unit, however closely the first quatrain of 6 may be linked with the last six lines of 5; each is an independent poem with 5 far superior to its successor. There is nothing distinctively pastoral or Petrarchan about either (pp.112-15), and *refigur'd* in 6 has nothing to do with the *figura* of typology (p.116n.)—neither has *prefiguring* in 106. Above all, *walls of glasse* in 5 (l. 10) does not "most obviously . . . mean the walls of ice that protect the sap even as they 'check' it" (p. 113); lines 9-14, as well as the first quatrain of 6 with its metaphorical *viall*, should make that perfectly clear. In the last quatrain, "Then were not summers distillation left / A liquid prisoner pent in walls of glasse . . .," the speaker has turned from "nature" in order to state how its substance may be preserved, namely, by distilling the fragrant essence of flowers into vials. Why then does Krieger expatiate, for two and a half pages, on *walls of glasse* as an ice metaphor? Because he stresses *sap* in l. 7, regards the conjunction of liquid and "ice" as a "new version of the conventional Petrarchan paradox" (fire-ice), and finds in *glasse* both mirror and window: "Can we see beyond the paradoxical relations between ice and liquid to the one between mirror and window, also two ways with one element? . . . 'glass' . . . may allow us to do it, if we may borrow from the immediate context of the surrounding sonnets . . ." (p.115). Of the first nineteen Sonnets, only one (3) meets his requirements.

A common source of distortion or misreading is the attempt to transfer the meaning of a word or metaphor from one Sonnet to another or from one part of a Sonnet to another. The treatment of *brave* in the second and last lines of 12 (p.100) is a good example of "reassertion" within the Sonnet, the discussion of *state* in 124 and 64 of transference between Sonnets. Now the analysis of 124 in terms of *state* is satisfactory on the whole, although the last line is distorted (pp.143-4), but to connect 64 with it as a similar but more complete "universalizing of the 'accidental' nature of 'state'" is to read the poem too abstractly. There is not only a difference in range of meaning and specific senses for *state* in each poem, there is also a difference in focus. In 124 the range of meaning is in focus while in 64 it is the main senses: estate or condition (l. 9) and stability itself (l. 10). Perhaps another example of misreading because of assimilation or equation, again to 124, occurs in Sonnet 116. The fool of time (l. 9), the link between these Sonnets, is seen to follow and reinforce the aging (l. 3) and destructive action (l. 4) of time and his sickle (p.147). However, the fourth line of 116 refers to inconstancy (*remove*) rather than death, and l. 10 is not its "mirror-image."

One further instance of misinterpretation will enable me to draw attention to another critical defect of the book. The discussion of 87, opening with a characteristically loose application of the term *Petrarchan*, reveals an awareness of what is at stake in the poem— two different views of friendship—but the true disparity between speaker and friend is not elucidated because the couplet and last quatrain are misread. In the language of 116, the friend is a *remover* who never had any "dream of faith and love" (ll. 9-12) and simply made a mistake in his calculations, whereas the speaker has been, and always will be, a true friend under all circumstances (as we learn from Sonnets 88-92). The couplet seems clear in sense and syntax—*I* is the *king*, not *thee* (p.136)—yet it receives more than half the space devoted to the Sonnet. This is a forceful reminder of something one is occasionally aware of—a remarkable lack of proportion in the analysis of individual poems. Some Sonnets, or parts of Sonnets, are handled with comparative brevity and dispatch; others are dealt with at tedious length. Difficulty has almost no bearing on the amount of space expended, for certain difficult Sonnets (53, 113) and parts (l. 8 of 35, l. 14 of 124) are given summary or evasive treatment, while others which are simple and obvious are treated in some detail.

One result of distorting various Sonnets, by whatever means, is distortion of the general character of the collection. This is especially true in those cases where Krieger presses his claim that Shakespeare is "using the body of religious mythology to symbolize the creation of love's faith" (p.190). There is a rather loose and pretentious use of theological language throughout the work, but the alleged instances of the use (even "analogically") of such material as Christ, the Trinity, Biblical typology, and eschatology which appear in the last two chapters are utterly foreign to the Sonnets. That is not to say that the Sonnets are devoid of Biblical or Christian diction and ideas—far from it; it is merely to point out that these "discoveries" are the consequence of reckless and superficial comparisons. It is also a way of saying that however clever and sophisticated the book may seem in its argument, its style is often deplorable. For that style is marked by pretentious and barbaric diction, frequent overstatement, ponderous inflation (often of the obvious), needless repetition, disregard of precision and clarity, and a lamentable self-consciousness. Good horrible examples of these defects may be found on every second or third page.

University of California, Davis

Interpretations in Shakespeare's Sonnets by Hilton Landry. The University of California Press, 1963. Pp. viii + 185. $4.00. *Reviewer: Hallett Smith.*

Mr. Landry's book consists of five chapters of contextual analysis, surveying the interrelations of about twenty-five of Shakespeare's sonnets and providing close readings of some twenty more. The final chapter is called "Some Tentative Conclusions"; the author would perhaps agree that it is more tentative than conclusive.

The order of the 1609 Quarto, we are told, "is generally and essentially right and . . . the burden of proof rests on those who think otherwise," yet Mr. Landry has not addressed himself directly to the whole question of the Quarto order or the merits and shortcomings of such rearrangements as Tucker Brooke's. He bases his belief upon internal thematic and stylistic relationships in the series, and he rigorously eschews any speculation about the identity of Mr. W. H., the fair friend, the dark lady, or the rival poet. He offers no conclusion about the date of composition of the sonnets.

He must, of course, distinguish groups of sonnets, and in this he is like almost everyone else in grouping them by themes: Life through Children, Life through Lines of Verse, Aspects of Absence, Looking toward Death, Rival Poet, Loss of Love Feared, Corruption of Excellence, and The Speaker's Offense against Friendship. Such relationships, he feels, together with the cross-relationships between individual sonnets in different groups, offer the only sure guide to correct interpretation. The plays and the longer poems must not be neglected, and Mr. Landry is always willing to bring in glosses from the Geneva Bible or other sources to define a meaning. His prime focus is on contexts within the series, however, and the reader's agreement or disagreement with his critical findings will usually depend upon whether he selects the same or different contexts.

Sonnet 94, "They that have power to hurt and will do none," first occupies Mr. Landry's attention. His analysis of 94, he says, is "something of an archetypal example" and is the "conceptual matrix . . . from which succeeding chapters arise." This sounds more formidable than the actual treatment turns out to be. The typical interpretation, according to Landry, misunderstands the octave and accordingly distorts the poem. In his view, 94 is a natural bridge between 87-93 and 95-96; the octave looks back to the preceding series and the sestet looks forward. In the octave the offense is potential; in the sestet it is actual. The background of the poem is asserted to be the Parable of the Talents, and Landry provides a Geneva Bible gloss which reads "they that suppress the gifts of God and live in idleness are without all excuse." My own view (as put forth in *Elizabethan Poetry*, pp. 188-191) is quite different, because I include among the contexts the sacred precept "Consider the lilies of the field, how they grow; they toil not, neither do they spin" and a passage in *Lucrece* (ll. 848-875). Mr. Landry declares that there is nothing in recent criticism of the sonnets which would affect his views on sonnet 94, but it is difficult to avoid the suspicion that possibly all of us, in selecting contexts, are somewhat arbitrary.

Shall we read sonnet 69, "Those parts of thee that the world's eye doth view" in the light of sonnet 70, "That thou art blamed shall not be thy defect," or the other way round? And is it legitimate to bring to bear, as Lever does, sonnet 54, "O how much more doth beauty beauteous seem" on a reading of 69? These are matters which Mr. Landry considers in his second chapter, "The Canker in the Rose." He takes 69 more seriously than 70, and minimizes the opposition between them, because to his ear 70 "does have rather uneasy qualifications . . . [and] it does give the impression of being a lame and forced excuse" (p.151, n. 34). One must always interpret poetry as "what it sounds like" to him, of course, but it is the critic's business to give convincing or at least persuasive reasons for hearing the poem as he does. In reading Shakespeare's sonnets, one is likely to force his own sensitivities into the process and then to evade the consequences of this by attributing them to Shakespeare. Mr. Landry is quite severe with L. C. Knights and Miss Mahood for taking the casuistical sonnet 42, "That thou has her, it is not all my grief" as a serio-comic display of wit in which the poet's emotions were not very deeply engaged. "I cannot agree," he says, "that the poet's interests are not very deeply involved. On the contrary, it is because they are involved, because his feelings are running counter to his statements, that what he is saying (perhaps from line 5 on) carries no conviction. I hope it does not classify me as a naïve literalist of the biographical school to say that here the speaker is trying—and clearly without success—to accept disaster with good grace, probably because his attachment to his friend leaves him no alternative" (p. 71). Mr. Landry is here discussing "The Civil War," that ambiguous feeling toward the friend which he finds in the octave of sonnet 94 and in many other sonnets. If this book has a thesis, it must be that the proper (Landry) understanding of the octave of 94 is the key to the literary problem in the sonnets.

In "This Vile World," (a consideration of sonnets 66, "Tired with all these, for restful death I cry," 121, "'Tis better to be vile than vile esteemed," and 129, "The' expense of spirit in a waste of shame,") the author has chosen sonnets to illustrate his conviction "that many of the finer poems of the collection are those which convey negative feelings, whether mixed or relatively pure." When he comes to sonnet 121, he proclaims that "any critic must stand or fall on his interpretation of the details of this difficult sonnet" (p.89). He proceeds to explicate the sonnet, with little that may not be found in the notes in Rollins. His comment on the final line is more novel: "I suggest that Shakespeare's general intention in the last line of sonnet 121 is to present the antithesis of this traditional view of man's nature and his place in the universe. Instead of reigning by virtue of his excellence, whether actual or potential, man rules the world in and by his badness. Since it is unthinkable that the poet's slanderers could actually maintain such a generalization, it serves to destroy the case against him by reducing their position to the absurd." (p.95). In his discussion of sonnet 129, "Th' expense of spirit in a waste of shame," Mr. Landry gives a standard close reading. He quarrels with Riding and Graves but agrees with them in following Q "Made in pursuit" rather than modern editors' "Mad in pursuit."

Sonnets 123, "No, Time, thou shalt not boast that I do change," 124, "If my dear love were but the child of state," and 125, "Were't aught to me I bore the canopy" are discussed under the rubric "Constancy to an Ideal Object," though surely many readers see these poems linked not so much by their professed theme as by their imagery drawn from public affairs (as in the notorious sonnet 107, "Not mine own fears, nor the prophetic soul"). Sonnet 124 Mr. Landry considers "perhaps the most difficult of all the sonnets to interpret in detail" (p.113) and sonnet 125 "one of the finest poems of the entire collection" (p.105). These views are a reflection of his method.

Interpretations in Shakespeare's Sonnets is a useful commentary, not wide in scope but fine in texture. It relates certain sonnets of the series to others in such a way as to illuminate their meaning. It comes at an opportune time, when several new editions of the sonnets are being published.

California Institute of Technology

Orthography in Shakespeare and Elizabethan Drama by A. C. Partridge. The University of Nebraska Press, 1964. Pp. viii + 200. $4.75. *Reviewer: Cyrus Hoy.*

By "Orthography," Professor Partridge means "that part of writing, peculiar to author, scribe, editor or printing-house, which is concerned with accidentals such as spelling, punctuation, elision, syncope and contractions generally." The subject has considerable relevance to the development of the language of Elizabethan drama. The colloquial contractions and weakenings of everyday speech were inevitably transported into dramatic dialogue as more realistic verbal effects were sought. A comedy such as Porter's *Two Angry Women of Abington* demonstrates what, by the 1590's, could be achieved in the way of lively dramatic characterization through an apt mastery of the vigorous patterns of colloquial speech. By the same time, the use of contractions had extended from comedy to the chronicle history play—as Professor Partridge demonstrates with the example of *Thomas of Woodstock*—and thence to Elizabethan tragedy. Professor Partridge rightly points to the debt which *Romeo and Juliet* owes to *The Two Angry Women* in the racy verbal idiom—"marked by a vigorous influx of conventional oaths . . . and colloquial weakenings and contractions (such as *ye* for *you*, *a* for *he*, *a* for the prepositions *of* and *on*; and prepositional or conjunctive combinations with *it* and *the*, the latter being curtailed, e.g. *toote, ont, ast, byth* etc.)."—by means of which Shakespeare characterizes such figures as Capulet, Mercutio, the Nurse, and Peter.

Colloquial contractions, weakenings, and the rest would seem to accommodate themselves naturally enough to dramatic prose. Their effect on dramatic verse is more subtle, and finally more profound, for the elision and slurring of words and combinations of words affect the actual syllabic measure, and hence the whole metrical structure. Professor

Partridge's development of this point is particularly valuable. He says: "Verse dialogue on the stage can only be natural if it cultivates the rhythms of ordinary speech. It needs all the nuances of value-stressing, of slurring and clipping, that accompany intelligent conversation. It is consequently in the drama, and especially the verse drama, that the speech habits of any period are best preserved. . . . Dramatic dialogue aims to conceal the artifices both of education and of metre, and to secure its aesthetic appeal through the subconscious layers of perception. Thus, in the development of Shakespeare's style, colloquial retrenchment of syllables is commoner in the verse than the prose, and as effective in the mouths of the great characters as in those of a grave-digger, an illiterate constable, or a gentle young lady's vulgar nurse."

Professor Partridge's book is essentially a description of the orthography of Elizabethan drama from the 1590's to the publication of the Shakespeare Folio of 1623. In the course of description, he must address himself to a number of other issues: to the varying orthographic practices of different writers (and scribes) of the same period (aptly demonstrated by the sundry authorial hands in the play of *Sir Thomas More*); to the varying orthographic practices of the same writer at different stages of his career (aptly demonstrated by Shakespeare, in whose work "the variety and frequency of colloquial contractions are greater after 1600 than in the plays written before that date"); to the several ways in which an author's orthography could be altered—by scribe or compositor or the editorial practice of a given printing-house—in the process of textual transmission. Partridge's assessment of the extent of editorial intervention in the Folio text of Shakespeare's plays is especially acute. He examines such plays as *Troilus*, *Hamlet*, and *Othello*, preserved both in the Folio and in an earlier quarto edition. Where comparison is possible, the Folio punctuation is regularly found to be far heavier than that of the quarto texts, and of an essentially different kind, being "syntactical" or "logical" rather than "rhythmical" and "elocutionary." Behind the editorial policy of the 1623 Folio, Partridge discerns the influence of Ben Jonson who, if not actively involved in the publication of the volume, had provided an editorial model for it in the elaborate orthography of the folio edition of his own plays seven years earlier.

University of Rochester

Shakespeare's Proverb Lore. His Use of the Sententiae of Leonard Culman and Publius Syrus by Charles G. Smith. The Harvard University Press, 1963. Pp. ix+ 181. $4.00. *Reviewer: Rolf Soellner.*

The subtitle of the book," Professor Smith says rightly, "furnishes a key to its chief concern and limitation." But this subtitle does not only limit the main title, but it also goes far toward contradicting it. Surely it is a simplification to say, as Professor Smith does, that "in the English Renaissance proverbs and *sententiae* were considered to be essentially the same." The most influential of the Renaissance collectors of proverbs, Erasmus, thought differently; as he stated in the Prolegomena to his *Adagia*, *sententiae* are "relatives" of proverbs and can easily be distinguished from them by applying the Erasmian definition of a proverb as a touchstone: "Paroemia est celebre dictum, scita quapiam novitate insigne" ("a proverb is a famous saying marked by a certain clever novelty"). A *sententia*, according to Erasmus, could sometimes "comprehend" a proverb, but only when it corresponded to his definition.

This distinction is admittedly not quite so easy to make for either Renaissance Latin or Elizabethan English as Erasmus thought. There is, as Professor Archer Taylor has remarked, a certain incommunicable quality which tells us this sentence is proverbial and that is not; but we cannot implicitly trust this feeling when it comes to a dead language, and sometimes it fails us altogether. Even so, one wonders whether a majority of the sentences collected by Professor Smith were really thought proverbial by the Elizabethans; many of them do not seem to me to have the certain incommunicable quality. Leaving feelings aside, at least one third clearly do not qualify according to Erasmus' yardstick.

For instance, No. 10 "Do not plunge thyself too far in anger" (*All's Well*, II.iii.222) has no more the distinguishing mark of a proverb than Culman's "Iracundiam tempera" ("moderate your anger") with which Professor Smith parallels it; neither sentence has the "novitas," the unusual turn of phrase or idea, which Erasmus demands of the proverb. To give an example of a related phrase which qualifies, one might quote the Horatian "Ira brevis furor," which was in Shakespeare's grammar and which he knew in Latin and in English. But it is not one of the sentences in Culman and Syrus, and thus it is not in Professor Smith's book.

This is not to deny the significance for Shakespeare study of the two small books, the *Sententiae Pueriles* of Leonard Culman (ca. 1487-1562) and the *Sententiae* of Publilius (or, as usual in the Renaissance, Publius) Syrus (first century A.D.) which Professor Smith has so thoroughly investigated. Malone seems to have been the first to connect them with Shakespeare and Professor T. W. Baldwin has shown that they were likely to have been used in such a grammar-school education as William Shakespeare presumably had. To the previously cited thirteen parallels between Shakespeare and Culman, Professor Smith adds 196 hitherto unnoticed new ones, and to the previously identified 30 parallels from Publilius Syrus he adds 150—104 of these not from the sixteenth century school edition (usually called *Disticha Catonis* for its first component) but from a modern edition.

The difficulty, as Professor Baldwin noted with due scholarly skepticism, is that sentences such as those of Culman and Syrus are so general and were so widely spread throughout the writing of the time that to claim direct influence becomes impossible. Professor Smith seems to argue that his greater number of parallels increases the possibility of direct influence; his parallels give "strong support to the suggestion . . . that Shakespeare memorized Culman's little book." Concerning Syrus he says more modestly that his findings reinforce Baldwin's conclusion that "some of Shakespeare's sentential wisdom thus ultimately derived from Syrus." It is very likely that Baldwin examined and rejected many of the parallels noted by Smith. Smith indeed admits that many of them could be challenged —in my estimate from one third to one half are too general or too vague. The example of No. 10, given above is typical; the Latin sentence has no identifying characteristic such as rhetorical figure or image to mark it as Shakespeare's source; the three supporting analogues (two from Culman and one from Cato) show that the idea as such was common if this requires proof.

Professor Smith has listed such analogues, "striking parallels from Shakespeare's literary environment" as he calls them, to many of the sentences from Cato, Cicero, Horace, Ovid, Seneca, and other classical writers. While these parallels may tend to weaken somewhat the claim for Culman and Syrus, they provide some very useful material for needed studies of the background of Shakespeare's moral thought. One might wish that Professor Smith had gone further in consulting Renaissance Latin sources. Commendably, he used Erasmus' *Adagia;* but Erasmus' *Apothegmata* and *De Parabolis Sive Similitudibus,* or Nannus Mirabellus' *Polyanthea* and similar collections might have rendered other parallels.

It may be objected that collecting such parallels is love's labor lost. There is indeed a tendency among critics to decry moral commonplaces in Shakespeare and the drama of his time as if they were esthetic if not moral lapses. A recent study of the moral vision of Jacobean drama speaks cavalierly of the sententious platitudes which the audiences savored and the dramatists satisfied. This view totally overlooks the obvious moral and literary sensitivity of the authors and their audience. The humanists who were the fathers of Renaissance education impregnated whole generations with the moral and philosophical significances of *sententiae* and proverbs. In *A Treatise of Morall Philosophie* (1547), William Baldwin echoed humanistic pedagogical principles when he distinguished three kinds of teaching moral philosophy, one by counsels, laws, and precepts, the second by proverbs and adages, and the third by parallels and examples. English authors, Shakespeare included, conveyed moral ideas in this fashion. Professor Smith's book shows how vital these were to Shakespeare's thought with its deeply suffused humanism.

This is an unpretentious little book in which the evidence is generally made to speak for itself. In the body of the work, the *sententiae* are listed under general captions with parallels from Shakespeare and analogues from Latin authors. Three indexes, one to Shakespeare, one to Latin, and one to English key words increase the usefulness of the book as a reference work. Even if the evidence does not always support the attribution and even if one finds the focus on Culman and Syrus somewhat limiting, here is a helpful book for tracing Shakespeare's "sentences" and a step in the direction of a much needed index of Shakespeare's moral thought.

Kansas State University

Marlowe: A Critical Study by J. B. Steane. The Cambridge University Press, 1964. Pp. viii + 381. $6.50. Reviewer: Clifford Leech.

This is an informed and most sensitive contribution to Marlowe criticism, and it will be as well to indicate at once the special character of our debt to Mr. Steane. Although he treats the plays as plays and has thought always for the total dramatic effects that performance would or might offer, his writing becomes most vital in his consideration of Marlowe's handling of words, and when he turns to the non-dramatic poems he gives us the best writing yet on *Hero and Leander*, the *Elegies* and the *Lucan*. We may indeed delight to find someone urging us, when we are reading Marlowe's Ovid, to relax and enjoy it. There is strong perceptiveness shown in tracing Marlowe's affinity with Lucan's violence and skepticism, though we may wonder whether it is justifiable to claim that in translating the first book of the *Pharsalia* Marlowe was able to take over a concern with civil disruption and its consequences for "degree" and thus for once to exhibit "no eccentricity of judgment or tone": when one can say that Marlowe found in the original "a certain independence and scepticism" and a "particular brand of sadism", it is strange to think simultaneously in terms of centrality and orthodoxy. On *Hero and Leander*, however, there is a full recognition of the poem's range, of its controlled ambiguities, its alternating rejection of prettiness and use of prettiness for the sake of establishing an ultimate irony which is simultaneously an ultimate affirmation: Mr. Steane speaks of "the sense, always present in the poem, that there is a destructive, painful element strong in the love which is nevertheless the best thing which life offers to man".

337

The high level of Mr. Steane's critical writing is everywhere apparent and can be properly seen only through a close reading of the book, where his demonstration of the special vitality of Marlowe's verbs makes its formidable point. But a reviewer must comment on limitations, in an attempt to encourage the reader to a comprehensive view of the subject, and this may regrettably seem churlish in relation to this book's virtues. Even so, it must be urged that the pattern of Marlowe's career that emerges has an altogether too mechanical appearance. We move up from *Dido* to *Tamburlaine*, from glory to a higher glory; the world shrinks in *Faustus* (for which an early date is here assumed, perhaps rightly), is seen with open mockery (though with eyes still sharp, with a mind still responding to the thrusting individual) in *The Jew*, and goes grey in *Edward II*. A brief note on *The Massacre* recognises the perverted state of the text, but sees in it not much more than horrors often cheaply if energetically presented. It is not a simple journey towards "normalcy" that Mr. Steane finds in Marlowe's career, but a continuing and fluctuating conflict with his own impulse to orthodoxy, a permanent cruel strain, and, it appears, a gradual loss of enthusiasm for the aspiring mind. Now this may have a measure of general validity, but to take the scheme as it stands is likely to predispose one to a fuller recognition of some aspects of the plays than others. *Dido*, for example, coming at the beginning, presents its lovers as "great enough to fill" a universal stage. Mr. Steane is aware of the comedy and the realistic temper of *Dido*, but he strains our belief in taking the love-relationship as one as seriously presented as that between Antony and Cleopatra, to which he compares it, in Shakespeare's play. In *Tamburlaine* he can see that, when Agydas says the hero "Will rattle foorth his facts of war and blood", the effect is deflationary, but he refuses to see the same process working in Marlowe's use of Almeda (or of Wagner in *Faustus*). He is readier to blame on Marlowe the strained effect of Tamburlaine's vaunts and defiance than to see that Marlowe in this play can achieve a distancing through the rhetoric in which he simultaneously glories. He denies the bathos, for Marlowe, in finding "sweet fruition" in "an earthlie crowne", overlooking the successive tarnishings of the crown-symbol that surely begin in quite early scenes of *1 Tamburlaine*. He knows that Zenocrate presents an opposed view to Tamburlaine's but insists that her virtues are womanly, her husband's ideally masculine—missing the contrast between Zenocrate's gradual process of learning, Tamburlaine's refusal to learn even in the face of loss and disappointment and death. For *Faustus* it is rash indeed to take the A-text as the basis for one's analysis of the play, and Mr. Steane seems curiously resistant to the deliberate greyness of *Edward II*'s world, that world where voices are hardly ever raised to eloquence but where the low tones become so shockingly appropriate when the King's shriek rings out through the night. Indeed this book's major limitation seems to be an insufficient recognition of the status of this play. Very much on the credit side, however, is the demonstration of a unity of attitude throughout *The Jew*, its comedy co-existing with its defiant measure of involvement with Barabas.

It should be evident that this book will hold a high place in Marlowe criticism. There is no better (none indeed so good) writing on the poems; the views of the plays put forward are always intelligent, even if the total pattern is sometimes too neat; the complexities of the poet-dramatist under consideration have rarely been so thoroughly and rewardingly recognised. Returning to *Tamburlaine*, however, as Mr. Steane does in his concluding section, we must query the apparent assumption that *Selimus* represents the normal Elizabethan dramatist's attitude to the aspiring mind, in contrast to Marlowe's: before that was written (by Robert Greene himself perhaps) Greene had given the theatre his *Alphonsus King of Aragon*, a play also planned in two parts, though only Part I is extant or perhaps was written, and in that he had quite simply responded to the eloquence and thrust of Marlowe's hero. If we take *Selimus* and *Alphonsus* together, we can see the double effect, the double "intention", of Marlowe himself reflected in the mind of a smaller, though not inconsiderable, contemporary. This may suggest a higher degree of complexity in Marlowe's play than even Mr. Steane's shrewd and subtle interpretation of his writing would suggest.

University of Toronto

Music in Shakespearean Tragedy by F. W. Sternfeld. Routledge and Kegan Paul, 1963. Pp. xxii + 334. Illustrated. $10.00. *Reviewers: Edward Clinkscale, Russell A. Fraser.*

Those who have enjoyed Mr. Sternfeld's articles will be pleased to greet his book. Many of his arguments, and some of his words as well, will already be familiar because of their previous publication in various journals and collections. Musicians should be especially pleased since the individual studies which comprise the book often have a musical accompaniment, appendices containing the relevant tunes. Clearly, Mr. Sternfeld's scholarship involves actual music as well as drama. In these essays he attacks the two elements in reverse order. First, he explores how the music fits the dramatic situation, and then he determines what specific tune might have been used. These tunes are offered in the earliest version known. In some instances, unfortunately, our knowledge is incomplete, and the melodies are not contemporary with the Shakespearian lyrics, but the author is careful to date his material and to inform the reader of the tailoring that he has done to fit the music to the text.

Although Professor Sternfeld does not specifically say so, he has obviously directed his musical discussion more to the literary historian than the musical one. Facts that are considered basic by the working musicologist are carefully explained. Some of the examples have been transposed in order to facilitate comparison—a questionable convenience for the trained musician. The six facsimiles given in the text will gladden the scholar's heart and provide him with a quick means of comparing the original versions with the author's transcriptions, which he has sometimes edited to facilitate modern performance. As Mr. Sternfeld has observed, the notation poses no problems. Many of today's historically oriented lutanists are capable of playing directly from the original sources.

In view of the extensive discussion of the trumpet, one wishes that a few more words had been devoted to the cornett. The brevity seems to assume an expertness on the part of the reader that is probably unwarranted. The cornett was not some different kind of trumpet. In fact, it was not a brass instrument at all, and, although it was capable of a rather large volume of sound—for that time—the characteristic tone quality was similar to that of the human voice. One finds the cornett used to reinforce the voice and to substitute for it.

One also wishes that the book were equipped with a better crafted and more extensive bibliography. There is little excuse for an addendum to the bibliography of a first edition, and one of Mr. Sternfeld's own recent articles, mentioned in his preface, has not found its way even into the addendum.

The reader who is interested in a more convenient collection of this music will want to consult the same author's more recent *Songs from Shakespeare's Tragedies*, published by the Oxford University Press. Though this is designed as a performing edition and though it duplicates many pieces from *Music in Shakespearean Tragedy,* it also contains new matter. Some older versions have been substantially reworked. This new collection must be regarded as Professor Sternfeld's current thinking on this body of material.

The University of California,
Riverside.

The explicit intent of this study of music in Shakespearean tragedy is to yoke together and to exploit a combination of literary, historical, and musical skills. The author's achievement is, however, more notable as a historian and musicologist than as a literary critic. He is capable of observing that "Shakespeare's celebrated blank verse found its glorious expression in the dignified speech of his tragedies," and that "This fact is well known"; or that "There is a common note of pessimism, at times bordering on cynicism, in the plays that appeared in Shakespeare's mature period."

The real value of his work lies in a marshalling of technical information, and in the conclusions, often implicit, which that information engenders. Since the audience envisaged is not exclusively professional, all the songs in the tragedies are transcribed in modern form. (Scholars are promised an edition of the songs alone, for various voices, and in lute tablature.) Appendices record the various extant versions, and Shakespeare's manipulating of them. Sources are given, where ascertainable. When no contemporary melody survives — as for Pandarus's lyric, "Love, love, nothing but love" — a suitable melody is suggested. Though a consideration of music in the comedies is reserved to a subsequent volume, the author attempts a degree of completeness by providing an index of all of Shakespeare's songs, a retrospect of scholarship on Shakespeare and music, and a bibliography on poetry and music in the Renaissance, to 1962. Definitions are given of musical terms for dancing, and of dances specified in the plays. Works relating to Robert Armin, as the chief singer of adult songs, and to the Puritans and music are listed in separate bibliographies. An extensive discussion considers the connection of specific musical instruments to character and social condition, and the tone colors and meanings associated with those instruments. The antagonism of the wind and string families, and the ominous nature of the former are illustrated by the squealing of oboes or the braying of trumpets as Titus Andronicus serves up his gruesome feast, and Claudius and Antony keep wassail, and Duncan enters under the battlements of Macbeth.

Occasionally, Shakespeare's use of song in the plays is seen as affording a clue to chronology. Since Fèste's closing song in *Twelfth Night* is echoed in *King Lear,* the possibility is explored that the two plays are close in date, and that the former is not so early as is commonly supposed, and may even have been revised after the initial performance of *Lear.* Prosodic technique is also illuminated, in its relation to the music. Lyrics sung by boys, as they are magical in tenor, generally maintain the iambic meter of the whole (though employing end-rhyme). Verse is encapsulated in verse: unless the singer, like Ophelia, is mad, in which case the metrical song is surrounded by prose. On the other hand, almost all the adult songs, whose function is to express character and whose tenor is often comic, are enveloped consistently in prose, though their wider context is the blank verse appropriate to tragedy. In this manner, Shakespeare honors his own conception of decorum.

It is not so rigorous a conception as that entertained by his contemporaries, whose general practice is to exclude music from tragedy altogether, or else to admit it, on analogy to the Italian *intermedii,* as a frankly inorganic diversion, "to the intent the people might be refreshed and kept occupied" and to offer "relief . . . if the discourses have been long" (Puttenham). The aversion to mirth in funeral—for example, to the singing of the grave-digger in Hamlet—dictates the conventional Elizabethan hostility to the organic participation in tragic business of the clown, who is also the chief musician of the adult companies. The comic interludes and musical cues in *Doctor Faustus* are admissible in that they are, at least partly, irrelevant. Marlowe mixes Plautus and Seneca, only as he desires to please. Tourneur, in *The Revenger's Tragedy,* and Marston in *Antonio and Mellida,* and Chapman in *The Revenge of Bussy d'Ambois,* enliven their plots but do not enforce them by the interspersing of music and dance. Shakespeare is peculiar in conceiving of music as an integral part of the general artistic design of his tragedies, and not least when the music is comic. The pathos depending on Juliet's supposed death is not relieved but (hopefully) intensified by the incongruous presence of the jesting musicians and Peter the clown. After all it is deeply congruous that Peter in his grief should call for "some merry dump" to ease him: Shakespeare's reading of things is less in debt to the decorous consistency of theory than to the unexpected coupling which is fact. Shakespeare indulges oxymoron, not as Marlowe does, to titillate, but to signallize the paradoxical nature of life itself.

His unwillingness to accept just what theory prescribes is illustrated further in his allotting of song to female protagonists, like Desdemona. In this practice he is aberrant, with respect to his times: excepting Peele's Bethsabe, tragic heroines before Shakespeare are not permitted to sing.

Desdemona's Willow Song is, of course, rendered by a boy. But Shakespeare's use of adult song is also marked by innovation. Although the Elizabethan convention, supposing that "much music marreth men's manners" (Ascham, in *Toxophilus,* 1545), interdicts public singing as improper to aristocratic persons, Shakespeare, very typically, modifies the convention. Pandarus sings in company; so does the gentleman Balthasar, in *Much Ado,* and the noble Amiens, in *As You Like It.* The social prejudice in each case is acknowledged: the singer is made to protest his insufficiency, in accordance with Castiglione's precept that a courtier should "come to show his music as a thing to pass the time withal, and as he were enforced to do it" (Bk. II). His protest is, however, unavailing. Even Hamlet, though he does not sing, delivers snatches from ballads and songs, like Ophelia.

This characteristic refracting of the norm or standard is dramatized most notably in the two songs assigned to Iago. Othello "to hear music . . . does not greatly care": he is known thereby as a man "fit for treasons, strategems, and spoils." Lorenzo, in *The Merchant of Venice,* inveighs against him: "Let no such man be trusted." Iago, conversely, has music in himself: he is known as honest Iago. (Cassius also "hears no music." In this he differs from the gentle Brutus. But Brutus, whom melody pleases, is not less an assassin.) Thus, as the stereotype is distorted, the expectation of the auditor is beguiled. Compelled to repudiate convention and the surface of things, he learns to perceive the visage in the mind.

There is this further yield in the unwonted behavior of the villain. That he should sing lends support to the hypothesis that Robert Armin, as the chief singer of the company, played the part. But Armin is a clown, and Iago a demi-devil, and decorum, in the first decade of the seventeenth century, forbids a mingling of the two. Casting is type-casting, except apparently on Shakespeare's eccentric and more audacious understanding.

The eccentricity which denotes him is vividly manifest in the skepticism he evinces toward the Renaissance view of music as an affective or ethical agent. I should call his

341

skepticism on this head medieval, in the sense that the medieval musician conceives of song, not as expressive but only as imitative. It is no part of his purpose to inspirit the hearer to action. He does not demand an ethical result. The Renaissance, on the other hand, endorses enthusiastically the ancient Pythagorean and Platonic belief in the capacity of music to influence the disposition of men. Antony, as he listens to Dorian music, is impelled to his proper business. This Antony merits our suffrage. But as he indulges soft Lydian airs, he grows slack and effeminate, and so incurs our contempt. That is the customary formulation. I suggest that, in Shakespeare's play, it functions largely as a straw man.

This positing in harmony as in oratory of a power to enthrall and hence to move the soul of man, is glanced at by Shakespeare in a passage from *Measure for Measure*. To Mariana, who confesses that a song had pleased her woe and so assuaged it, the Duke replies,

> 'Tis good; though music oft hath such a charm
> To make bad good, and good provoke to harm.

It is the supposedly kinetic or dynamic property in music to which Orsino adverts, in the opening line of *Twelfth Night*: "If music be the food of love, play on." What may be called the Ethos theory of music descends to the Elizabethans from the *Somnium Scipionis* of Cicero, as interpreted and modified by the commentary of Macrobius and the standard treatments of the art from Boethius and Cassiodorus in the early Middle Ages, to the Renaissance theoreticians, Joannes de Tinctores and Henricus Glareanus. The basic premise is that the music of the planets (*musica mundana*) is mirrored in that of human beings (*musica humana*). If, argues the Platonic proponent of the Ethos theory, appropriate music is performed by men (*musica instrumentalis*), and whether vocal or instrumental or both, virtue and harmony will be engendered in their conduct. The *Republic* (1576) of Jean Bodin cites as illustrative the public banquets (*epulones*) of the Romans, who thought to implant wisdom in their magistrates by a playing of the dulcet music of strings. The music of the spheres is also affective: a psychological or, better, a physiological reality that literally disposes behavior. Pericles, as he hears that "most heavenly music," is nipped "unto listening, and thick slumber hangs upon . . . [his] eyes." But the music must be appropriate: not the pipes of Pan, the wind instruments associated with martial business or with the importunities of the flesh, but the lyre, the strings of Apollo. Gosson, in his famous pamphlet, is alive to this distinction. That is why he describes the *School of Abuse* as containing "a pleasant invective against poets, pipers, players, jesters, and such like caterpillars of a commonwealth."

Shakespeare is not so morose or, depending on one's point of view, so eupeptic. The function of the adult songs, which dominate in the work of his maturity, is not to dispose but mostly to characterize. It is true that Shakespeare resorts often to so-called magic songs, whose office, hypothetically, is to move. Generally, these songs are allotted to boys—for example, to the elves and fairies in *A Midsummer Night's Dream* and *The Merry Wives of Windsor*. But the music, it seems to me, is essentially a blind. Titania and Falstaff are not enchanted; they make love to their employment. Brutus occasions his own demise, and even though the slumbrous song of young Lucius is in prelude to that event. Nor is Ariel's music in *The Tempest* really decisive in allaying the fury and passion of the wicked conspirators. The incantation of the witches in *Macbeth*, ought, as one adheres to the ethical theory, to afford the supreme example of the power of music to conduce to good or ill. But music in *Macbeth*, at least of Shakespeare's contriving, is omitted altogether. It is the protagonist himself who works the fatal imposition. Man at some time is the master of his fate.

Vanderbilt University

342

Elizabethan Drama and Shakespeare's Early Plays by E. W. Talbert. The University of North Carolina Press, 1963. Pp. x +410. $8.00. *Reviewer: G. K. Hunter.*

Professor Talbert is already known as the author of several weighty books, one of which, *The Problem of Order* (1962), is a direct predecessor to this. His aim is one towards which most researchers in the field must feel sympathetic: to describe Shakespeare's dramatic technique "in the light of the probable expectation of contemporary theater-goers and their possible familiarity with current concepts, current representational methods and current features of the Elizabethan scene" (p.323). He takes it for granted that the language of "well-made-play" criticism will not suffice for the Elizabethans; that "multiplicity" is a basic structural principle and that he must begin by describing scenes or even parts of scenes rather than any larger units.

One must, I think, be sympathetic to these aims; but one must report, at the same time, that the critic here has become, to some extent, subdued to the method he is writing about. Mr. Talbert makes a large number of good individual points; but the structure of his book is too close to that of *The Famous Victories* to give any sense of an overall pattern emerging or even beginning to emerge. The author is well aware of the danger: "A study that consists almost entirely of analyses of dramas is not conducive to conclusions" (p.326). Unfortunately, however, the minds of readers tend to require patterns simple and repetitive enough to be lodged in the memory and carried over from one situation to another. It would be a great pity if the reader closed this book convinced that Elizabethan and early Shakespearian drama was a complete muddle, and therefore unworthy of serious consideration. But I would understand the reaction.

The difficulty I have described is one inherent in the subject; but the problem of moving through the book is impeded still further by Mr. Talbert's peculiarly untractable style. He is rather too fond of hard words like "pageantic", "concatenated", "epitatical", and the effect of some sentences is clotted beyond comfort:

> At the same time, in spite of Saturninus' sudden passion for Tamora, the motif of lust is developed explicitly for the first time; and since it is tangential to that of revenge, it seems compatible, on a larger scale, with those rhetorical flowers that are tengential to the main thought of the speeches in which they occur. Even more to the immediate point, perhaps, is the lack of concatenation in Aaron's villainies; for, as a result, they are essentially unexpected and thereby congruent in a structural sense with the imagistic effect noted above. (p.139)

The notes to the book form a solid seventy-page final course, drawing on a vast reading. Bibliographically, however, there are some curiosities. It is strange to hear baldly of "the poet Abercrombie" as if his poetry had obliterated his Christian name. Northrup Frye appears as *Northrup*, Richard David turns into *Richard Davis*, John Munro into *James Munroe*. But the most strange metamorphosis of all is when the Bishop of Carlisle (in *Richard II*) appears as "Carlyle". Inhabitants of Ecclefechan please note!

The University of Warwick
Coventry

A Study of Elizabethan and Jacobean Tragedy by T. B. Tomlinson. The Cambridge University Press, 1964. Pp. viii + 293. $6.00. *Reviewer: Robert Ornstein.*

Mr. Tomlinson's reading of Elizabethan and Jacobean tragedy is interesting, original, and highly argumentative. Skeptical of many earlier assessments of the dramatists, he weighs by his own standards the value and validity of their artistic insights and achievements. Even as F. R. Leavis (whom Tomlinson admires) sought to define the great tradition of the English novel, so also Tomlinson seeks to define the central tradition in Elizabethan and Jacobean tragedy. That central tradition includes only a triumvirate of authors: Shakespeare, of course, and, curiously enough, the Tourneur of *The Revenger's Tragedy,* and Middleton. Kyd and Marlowe are viewed as valuable if minor writers, but most of the Jacobean dramatists receive harsh judgments. Allowing Webster one great scene in *The Duchess of Malfi,* Tomlinson otherwise speaks of the "dangerously uncorrected lyricism" of his plays and of his "hectic search for new sensations of whatever kind" (p. 129). In a similar vein he speaks of Chapman's hollowness, of Ford's irresponsibility, and of Marston's and Beaumont and Fletcher's decadence. Jonson is spared by being ignored as a tragic dramatist.

Unlike earlier critics of the immorality of Jacobean tragedy, Tomlinson is not concerned with the dramatists' treatment of character and plot. These aspects of drama, he feels, have had too much attention, particularly by critics of Shakespeare. Seeking the "true values" of the Elizabethan and Jacobean tragedians in the fabric of their dramatic verse, Tomlinson gives little sense of their plays as actions designed to unfold upon a stage. Like L. C. Knights and G. Wilson Knight, he regards plays as dramatic poems; and like Derek Traversi, he bases interpretation on the intensive study of crucial passages of verse. Tomlinson's key critical terms are familiar enough: tension, texture, paradox, poise, irony, and control. He seems to value complexity as a virtue in itself; and he prizes artistic intelligence and poise, and ironic detachment and control, not only for the poetic effects they achieve, but also as expressions of a socially mature and realistic ability to confront experience. If there is a deeper response to tragedy, however, than sophisticated pleasure in the ironic poise of its verse, this book does not suggest it. Awe and wonder, pity and fear do not concern the author; indeed, implicit in his discussion is the sense that emotion is dangerous unless subjected to the ironic detachment which he sees as the consummate artistic approach to experience. Out of the muddle of Webster's art, he plucks one jewel, the great death scene of the Duchess of Malfi, which he admires not as a supremely haunting portrayal of character and tragic situation but as a superbly fashioned and unified paradoxical image of chaos.

What Tomlinson admires he discusses with engaging enthusiasm and perceptiveness. Especially interesting are the pages on *Dr. Faustus,* the discussion of the "metaphysical wit" of *The Revenger's Tragedy,* and the chapters on Middleton's plays, where dramatic structure, elsewhere ignored, is acutely handled. His main thesis is worth thoughtful consideration: namely, that the great tragedians do not simply offer vibrant characterizations of evil but actually intuit a vital interdependence between good and evil. Unfortunately, however, this hypothesis comes to us in the form of dogma; this intuition of the nature of good and evil is made to be the *sine qua non* of great tragedy, which, according to Tomlinson, necessarily acknowledges the sordidness of experience. And while ascribing profound significance to a minor passage in *Macbeth* which supposedly embodies this intuition, Tomlinson advises readers searching for the true values of Shakespeare not to worry too much about the spiritual destinies of his tragic heroes.

When one considers the narrow range of Tomlinson's critical responses, and the restrictiveness of his critical dogmas, one is awed by his readiness to condemn what he does not admire as decadent if not downright immoral. While the very real flaws or limitations of Tourneur's and Middleton's plays are scarcely noted, the genuine achievements of Chapman, Webster, and Ford are scarcely valued. While Webster's lesser plays are used to indicate "the breakdown of the Elizabethan sensibility," not a word is said of *The Atheist's Tragedy*, which by Tomlinson's standards might convict Tourneur of hollowness or decadence. Of course a scrupulous examination, however unsympathetic, of a writer's failings can be of immense critical value. But Tomlinson's assault on Webster does not come in the form of reasoned and acute analysis; it comes in the form of vaguely defined impressions of the failures of the plays or as pontifical assertions of their triteness and moral confusions. Chapman fares worse in that he is arrogantly patronized: "Perhaps, after all, Chapman is merely a well-intentioned bore and not a writer one would think of as thoroughly hollow and decadent" (p. 265).

This is not a book for the casual reader or the beginning student. Only the chapters on Tourneur and Middleton offer detailed and comprehensive analyses of plays. The other chapters more often than not presume an audience familiar with the plays under discussion and the critical positions which Tomlinson would refute. This is a work intended, I would guess, to influence teachers, critics and scholars — but they will be the readers most aware of the lack of authority in many of the author's pronouncements.

University of Illinois

Hamlet and the Philosophy of Literary Criticism by Morris Weitz. The University of Chicago Press, 1964. Pp. xvi + 335. $6.75. *Reviewer: Joseph Margolis.*

In *Hamlet and the Philosophy of Literary Criticism*, Morris Weitz construes the *Hamlet* literature as "a test case", by which to demonstrate "the logical multiplicity of *Hamlet* criticism, and, consequently, the falsity of the assumption, pervasive in this criticism, that all its discourse is true or false statement" (p.316). Weitz is a philosopher, not a literary critic; he collects and compares in great detail the prominent accounts of the drama, not with an eye to offering an alternative theory of *Hamlet* but rather to exposing the logical properties of the variety of comments critics traditionally offer. His book is usefully divided into two parts: in the first, he summarizes, very carefully indeed, the principal discussions of *Hamlet*, including those of Bradley, Jones, Knight, Eliot, Fergusson, Wilson, Stoll, Schücking, Campbell, Clemen, Spencer as well as selected views from what he calls "the major tradition"; in the second, he brings his philosophical apparatus to bear on these same materials — originally presented with a distinct emphasis on the logical variety of the comments offered and on the problematic aspects of their verification — and isolates, in effect, four distinctive critical procedures (describing, explaining, evaluating, and theorizing) which he takes to be "irreducible" and of which only description may be said to yield "true or false statement" (p.316).

The work may not unfairly be regarded as an expansion, by way of analyzing "the large empirical context of a whole corpus of criticism" (p.xi), of philosophical theories Weitz had proposed in a much-reprinted, independent essay, "The Role of Theory in Aesthetics," *The Journal of Aesthetics and Art Criticism*, XV (1956), 27-35, which is not mentioned in the present text. There, as here, Weitz held that "art" (or "tragedy" and related concepts) cannot, for logically compelling reasons, be defined essentially, defined in terms of necessary and sufficient conditions; that, as he said in the essay, the effort to attempt such a definition, "subtly deceptive as it is, amounts to a transformation of correct criteria for *recognizing* members of certain legitimately closed classes of works of art into recommended criteria for *evaluating* any putative member of the class". The appeal of his effort, apart from an estimate of its success, lies precisely in bringing powerful philosophical distinctions to bear on the sprawling and somewhat philosophically naive critical literature and in informing the somewhat arid and abstract philosophical distinctions with the lively, particular details of criticism addressed to actual cases. I am not myself familiar with any other full-scale study of just this sort.

Having said this much, I must say also that, apart from the enormous value of Weitz's having assembled the *Hamlet* literature in the fresh way in which he has—so that alternative philosophical theories may, quite economically, be brought to bear on the same materials—the philosophical issues are somewhat disappointingly pursued. I should say, in fact, that the *claims* of the *JAAC* article (mentioned above) are simply taken as established and merely applied, however instructively, to the large *Hamlet* literature. On my view, Ch. XVII ("Poetics") is the best and most important portion of the book; and yet it seems to me to offer, from a philosopher's point of view, not the slightest advance beyond the arguments of the *JAAC* article. So, for example, Weitz asserts:

> . . . underlying every theory of tragedy, every purportedly true statement of the essence of tragedy, is the assumption that tragedy has a set of necessary and sufficient properties; this assumption is equivalent to the doctrine that the concept of tragedy or the term, "tragedy", or their adjectival derivatives, have a set of necessary and sufficient conditions for their correct, intelligible use. This doctrine is false. (p.306)

I find no argument to this effect in the text itself; what does appear are reminders of the fuller arguments of the article.

Two things may be said of Weitz's treatment of the problem. For one, the mere collection of the (sometimes stunning) disagreements among the critics about what is or is not tragic about Hamlet (either fixed on the debatable features of Hamlet's conduct and character or on the debatable features of the type of drama called tragedy) cannot in itself possibly secure Weitz's thesis; the simple reason is that his philosophical opponents will *begin* with the same facts Weitz has assembled. And for another, the technical arguments by which Weitz *independently* thought to demonstrate the indefinability of art and tragedy and related concepts are themselves open to serious objection and (at least in the view of this reviewer) definitely inconclusive. This is not to say that these concepts *can* be defined by way of necessary and sufficient conditions but only that the effort is *logically* admissible and that Weitz's reasons for rejecting it rest on a confusion.

He himself correctly observes that Ludwig Wittgenstein, from whom he derives his argument, had held that some of the terms of our language "do not, hence need not, have corresponding essences that guarantee their meanings" (p.308). Weitz exceeds Wittgenstein's argument in holding that the classificatory concepts of our language used in empirically descriptive discourse, *cannot,* for logical reasons, be assigned essences. His case rests on two considerations. The first is that "all the purportedly requisite properties are challengeable, emendable, and corrigible" (p.307). But this is clearly a condition for all genuinely debatable issues and, in itself, is altogether neutral to the question at hand. No one

346

who wished to advance a definition of the requisite sort would deny what Weitz says here; on the contrary, he would insist on it. The second is the more serious and significant: that is that to define tragedy would be to disallow "the ever present possibility of *new* conditions" of tragedy, would be to fail to allow for the *"perennial flexibility"* of the concept of tragedy (pp.307-308). The error here lies with Weitz's failing to observe that *extending* the use of a concept like tragedy to hitherto unclassified items (say, because of the development of the theatre) is logically distinct from, and utterly unrelated to, the *definition* of a concept whose extension is more or less specified. It is not possible even to speak of judging the adequacy of definitions without some commitment on extensional limitation; but to extend the use of a term is, precisely, to disregard *previous* extensional limits. The two notions work at cross-purposes, and it is simply inappropriate to challenge the attempt at one by mentioning the use of the other. This is not to say, of course, that to define a concept like the tragic is at all an important thing to do; nor is it to say that, in fact, for any *given* extension, the required sort of definition can be supplied; nor is it to say that the enterprising critics who have sought to provide definitions of related key concepts were at all aware of the conceptual difficulties involved. It is to say only that Weitz's arguments designed to disqualify the effort are by no means decisive.

I am aware that what I have been saying may be subtly misleading about much of Weitz's book. He himself would probably not be willing to regard the thesis I have isolated as the central one. In fact, he says that his thesis is, rather, that the "assumption—of the *logical univocity* of the language of *Hamlet* criticism—is false; that the realization that it is false is basic to any understanding and solution of the major issues and disagreements of *Hamlet* criticism . . ." (p.213). About this, I should like to say the following. Certainly, critical language is *not* logically univocal, in the sense that all the sentences of criticism have one and only one logical use (as that of stating facts). And certainly, it is important to appreciate this fact in working through critical disputes. But I know of no *philosopher,* that is, of anyone theorizing about the nature of critical discourse, who ever supposed that criticism was logically univocal. And I think it is, frankly, excessive to suppose that *critics,* who enter into their characteristic disputes, hold clearly formulable theories of critical discourse (cf. p.217). Furthermore, even if critics and traditional philosophers did hold to the "particular conception of language" Weitz hopes to expose (p.217), it does not at all follow that exploding this theory serves in itself to describe the *actual functions* of critical discourse. In a word, Weitz's positive views about describing, explaining, and evaluating works of art must be independently assessed. And here, I am bound once again to say that I find his account inconclusive.

He does, as a matter of fact, link himself explicitly to the well-known theories of criticism, regarding description, interpretation, explanation, and evaluation, of C. L. Stevenson, Margaret Macdonald, and Arnold Isenberg (cf. pp. xi, 278). This is not to say that he does not, correctly, insist that "it is simply a false description of the logical behavior of critical evaluations to say that *all* of them recommend, guide our choices, grade, persuade, judge, counsel, or emote" (p.270). He builds a case, for example, designed to show that "critical evaluation is argument" also (pp.270ff.). But his own preferences incline, at the crucial moments, towards those views (mentioned above) that he would be unwilling to accept without qualification. And here, I can only attempt to collect a few clues regarding his convictions.

It is a puzzling fact that Weitz regularly fails to distinguish such functions of language as describing, reporting, and making statements (in Ch. XIV). He freely substitutes locutions

347

referring to one of these uses for any of the others. A difficulty results because he is inclined to speak of descriptions being *true,* when he means to say that certain of the critic's statements are true. For instance, he will say, of Bradley:

> ...as a critic...he also describes: he reports on some of the constituents in
> *Hamlet*...for example, [he] tells us that Hamlet delays....The truth (or falsity)
> of Bradley's claim that Hamlet delays... (p.229; cf. p.244)

The trouble is that though he is primarily concerned with the analysis of the sorts of remarks critics make, Weitz does not actually sort out obvious varieties that will behave in logically distinct ways. This is not a mere quibble, since he nowhere specifies how we are to distinguish between what is description and what merely appears to be description. The distinction between description and interpretation, so obviously important for the present account, is impossible to work out explicitly, in terms of the discussion presented. So, for instance, he asserts (without adequate clarification) that "whether Polonius is (to Hamlet) a male bawd, a panderer, a seller of fish (taken literally), or one who tries to fish out Hamlet's secret is not a descriptive issue, in the way that the problem of extant Elizabethan and Shakespearean usage may be" (p.242). But we are simply not told *how* to decide the issue.

He holds also that interpretation is not "logically distinct from explanation" (p.245), but the thesis is unclear for a number of reasons. For one thing, in speaking of explanation, he evidently has in mind *hypotheses* about *why* things happen as they do (cf. Ch. XV, for instance pp. 252, 256, 259). But Weitz does not seem to be aware that the explanation of human behavior in terms of reasons is itself not infrequently regarded as a *description* or redescription of the data of behavior; consequently, the contrast between description and explanation is altogether unclear in the context of drama. It is, in fact, fundamental to Weitz's argument that "there is no true, best, correct, or right explanation, reading, interpretation, or understanding of *Hamlet,* nor can there be as long as debate and doubt are possible on the categories of explanation and on what is primary in the play" (p.258). But *if* one may speak of true descriptions, it must also be correct to speak of true explanations; and it is certainly curious to hold that the "confirmation" of an explanation depends on ulterior evaluative considerations (cf. pp.254-258). The view, furthermore, that interpretation is explanation, taken in this sense, is simply a flat acceptance of Stevenson's thesis about the inherently evaluative nature of interpretation—which is dubious for the double reason that Stevenson does not consider the implications of the *professional* character of interpreting works of art and that his account is always in the service of his emotive/imperative theory of value judgments. Weitz commits himself to the linkage without discussing these matters. The result is that we cannot clearly distinguish what Weitz means by description, interpretation, and explanation.

The account of evaluation (Ch. XVI) seems especially weak. Weitz says that here he wishes to show that "the central thesis: that critical evaluations are true (or false) descriptive reports on the merits or demerits of works of art or on our responses to them...misrepresents the role of evaluation in criticism" (p.280). For one thing, he should have contrasted evaluative with factual judgments—not with description. For another, if he had, he would have had to face the currently revived theory that factual and evaluative judgments cannot be contrasted in any logically simple and obvious way. Also, he has failed to notice that so-called value judgments are themselves a greatly varied lot and (ironically, against his own master thesis) cannot be characterized as being of a logically uniform kind.

Thus, for instance, it is not entirely appropriate to challenge the view that evaluative judg-ments may be true by drawing attention to such distinctive judgments as "Shakespeare's dramas are great because . . ." (p.277). It might well have proved fair to hold that many (though not all) of the judgments of critics are *not* made in terms of public canons of any reliability but rather in terms of their own varying tastes, that in *some* instances, the value judgments advanced are to be understood in terms of appreciative alternatives. The upshot, I am bound to say, is that, for all its temperate tone and insistence that no general and singleminded theory of critical language could possibly be vindicated, Weitz's account draws us on in the direction of holding that, beyond minimal description, critics work pri-marily by persuasion.

Department of Philosophy
University of Western Ontario

Pericles Prince of Tyre, edited by F. D. Hoeniger. The New Arden Edition. Harvard University Press, 1963. Pp. xci + 188. $3.25 *Reviewer: Charles T. Prouty.*

In his Preface to this edition of *Pericles* Mr. Hoeniger remarks that the play presents "a most uneven and puzzling text" and that "the factual material" poses problems which "are extremely complex." There can be nothing but praise for the thoroughness with which the editor presents the complex problems, but several of these have implications and ramifications which are not indicated by Mr. Hoeniger. Only a variorum edition could cover these in detail, but it seems worthwhile to indicate the direction of some of the major implications.

We can, perhaps, best begin with a factual problem. In 1608 Edward Blount entered *"The booke of Pericles prynce of Tyre"* and *Antony and Cleopatra.* If Blount printed either of these plays no copies survive, and the first extant edition of *Pericles* was printed in 1609 by Henry Gosson, but with no record of a transfer of copyright from Blount to Gosson. In-cidentally this latter fact is not noted by Mr. Hoeniger. Following tradition Mr. Hoeniger regards Blount's entry as "a blocking entry" and quotes Sir Walter Greg on the desire of Shakespeare's company to protect themselves from piracy by "employing a friendly publisher."

This traditional view of "blocking" or "staying entries" constantly reiterated since the days of Alfred Pollard was proved to be erroneous some years ago by Professor C. J. Sisson. In an article "The Laws of Elizabethan Copyright: The Stationers' View", *Library,* 5th Series, XV, No. 1. (March, 1960), pp. 8-20, he drew upon depositions in Chancery arising from a dis-pute about rival claims to copyright in Rider's *Dictionary.*

In the first place the evidence of the Chancery Depositions shows clearly, as stated by Professor Sisson, "that entry in the Register, with the accompanying payment of a fee, was at the will and choice of the Stationer. We must abandon the concept of automatic entry by the clerk in the Stationers' Register of all allowances of copy by the Court or by the Wardens' delegated authority." Thus there is nothing suspicious in Gosson's publication although there is no entry transferring the rights from Blount to him.

Secondly there is no evidence that the entry by Blount was a device to prevent publica-tion. The origin of the theory of blocking or staying entries arises from the famous entry of 4 August 1600 on a spare leaf of Register C where it is noted that *As You Like It, Henry V, Everyman In His Humour,* and *Much Ado About Nothing* are to be "staied." Very simply

Professor Sisson's evidence indicates that mistakes as to the ownership of a given work had been made with some frequency, so that if there were any question, the entry was postponed until the facts were ascertained. Both *Everyman In* and *Much Ado* were regularly registered later in August and duly published. So I think we may safely conclude that Gosson's publication was perfectly legal with no suggestion of piracy or "stolne and surreptitious copies." It is to be hoped that future editors of Elizabethan and Jacobean plays will read and heed Professor Sisson's article.

This question of copyright seems to me to be involved in the problem of the omission of *Pericles* from the First Folio. As far as I can see there is no mystery which would involve us in complicated problems such as once attended discussions of the odd position of *Troilus and Cressida* in the First Folio.

As Sir Walter Greg says (*The Shakespeare First Folio*, pp. 445-47) Walley who with Bonian owned the rights simply refused to allow Jaggard et al to reprint his copy. If we follow the rights of *Pericles* we find that the third quarto of 1611 was printed by S [imon] S [tafford] and the fourth of 1619 was printed for T [homas] P [avier]. In view of the copyright problems which Pavier experienced in his attempted collection of 1619, it seems most reasonable that he would not have looked with favor on the granting of his rights in *Pericles* to Heminge and Condell and/or the syndicate of printers involved in the First Folio. That Pavier had secured the rights to *Pericles* seems quite clear from the fact that his widow transferred her husband's "right in Shakespeares plaies or any of them" to E. Brewster and R. Birde according to an entry in the Stationers' Register for 4 August 1626. The fifth quarto of 1630 was printed by I [ohn] N [orton] for R [obert] B [ird]. From the foregoing I would suggest that we accept the simple explanation that *Pericles* was excluded from the First Folio because of copyright, an explanation which so far as I know has not been hitherto considered. The reader may be interested in comparing the foregoing history of the copyright with Sir Walter Greg's theory (*The Shakespeare First Folio*, p. 98).

> If *Pericles* was indeed wholly Shakespeare's, we should be forced to suppose that its exclusion from the First Folio was due to the editor's inability to replace the 'bad' text by a good one.

The editorial integrity which Sir Walter ascribes to Heminge and Condell demonstrates one of the cardinal fallacies of a great deal of 20th century scholarship and criticism. This is the imposition on the Elizabethan and Jacobean literary and dramatic world of modern standards and ideas. Concern for textual purity such as Sir Walter posits is not to be found in the First Folio, and one need only examine the nature of copy texts used for the printing of this volume as described by both Chambers and Greg to realize the extensive variations with no indication of any standard editorial methodology so dear to the hearts of modern bibliographers. Two sentences from Professor Sisson's article are quite appropriate in this connection: "We are apt, moreover, to fail to allow for the impact of convenience and compromise upon the principles laid down, and upon the machinery devised, by the Stationers' Company for the conduct of their affairs in the common interests of the whole body of their members. The Tudor English were unruly folk, recalcitrant to regulation" (p.9).

Another aspect of the fallacy is illustrated by consideration of the relationship between George Wilkins' novel, *The Painfull Adventures of Pericles Prince of Tyre* (1608). That there is a close relationship between this and the play Mr. Hoeniger makes abundantly clear in a lucid and full comparison. The particular point which interests me is the considerable variation between Wilkins' account of the tournament at Pentapolis and that found in II.ii of the play. As Mr. Hoeniger says "Wilkins' account seems in some respects better than that of the play. Q's stage-directions for this scene are quite inadequate." With this general statement I think that there is general agreement, but the real problem comes in attempting an explanation of why Wilkins gives us details of stage business not found in the play. Here Mr. Hoeniger displays sound judgment and critical sense when he rejects Professor Muir's hypothesis of an "Ur-Pericles" as Wilkins' source and the argument for the rejection seems to me irrefutable. In my view Mr. Hoeniger is a bit too judicious in contenting himself with the statement "that Wilkins based his report, however imperfectly, directly on the play as we know it."

I should like to go a step further and suggest that Wilkins actually did see on the stage all the business which he describes. The rigid modern view that "if it's not in the printed text, it did not exist or was forgotten by the well-known memorial reconstructionists," quite ignores the fact that we are dealing with a play produced by a commercial theatrical company who were playing repertory. Even today a great deal of stage business is developed during rehearsal, so it is not wild imagining to envision what happened during rehearsals of the King's Men where the author was a member of the company. The prompter or book-keeper was not thinking of us and recording every bit of business, or, as far as that goes, new lines or alterations for an anxious posterity. In those plays of the Egerton 1994 MS which show evidence of having been used in the playhouse there is no homogeneity or standardization of stage-directions. As Professors Kirschbaum and Rothwell have pointed out there never was such a thing as a definitive text of an Elizabethan or Jacobean play.

Perhaps the most vexing problem with which Mr. Hoeniger deals is that of "Authorship" where his objectivity and judicious assessment are once again praiseworthy. At first glance there seems to be no question of Shakespeare's authorship, for all six quartos give his name on their respective title pages and the first three also mention "his Maiesties Seruants" and the Globe. All seven of the plays first printed in the second issue of the Third Folio of 1664 are also attributed to Shakespeare either by the use of his name or the initials "W.S." Therefore since George Lillo in 1738 attributed only part of *Pericles* to Shakespeare, and since there is a marked difference between Acts I and II and the remaining three acts both in style and structure, it is natural that scholars have debated the entire question of authorship and/or collaboration. There are a number of references to the play in 17th century literature and perhaps the most curious is Dryden's in the Prologue to Davenant's *Circe* (1667):

> Shakespeare's own Muse her *Pericles* first bore,
> The Prince of *Tyre* was elder than the *Moore*:
> 'Tis miracle to see a first good Play
> All Hawthorns do not bloom on *Christmas-day*, . . .

Among other things this reference has led to the theory of an early play later revised, but there seems to be no general agreement except to excuse Shakespeare of responsibility for Acts I and II. Mr. Hoeniger posits an original play by Day and Wilkins with perhaps a third unknown dramatist which interested Shakespeare to the extent that he revised the final three acts.

It seems to me that the critical problem raised by the variation between Act I and II and the remainder is in an important way connected with the problem of sources. The popularity of the medieval tale of Apollonius of Tyre continued, as Mr. Hoeniger says, "throughout the Renaissance." Just why the tale was popular seems to me the crux of the matter, for if we can understand this appeal in Renaissance terms we may perhaps better understand the form of the play. This approach is a general one which I have discussed on several occasions, and there is no need to labor the point further in this review.

There only remains to compliment Mr. Hoeniger on his excellent handling of a difficult play.

Yale University

Shakespearean Essays, edited by Alwin Thaler and Norman Sanders. The University of Tennessee Press, 1964. Pp. ii + 185. $3.50. Reviewer: Terence Hawkes.

The temptation to deplore the deluge of Shakespeareana produced by the quatercentenary year of 1964 ought to be more strongly resisted than has lately been the case. A mock astringency is easily inculcated thus, and yet the target seems really much too large to afford any satisfaction in the scoring of that sort of bull's eye. A more interesting matter might concern the extent to which the considerable amount of good criticism to which 1964 gave birth no less than any year, may have been submerged by material of a more mediocre sort: the operation, in short, of a literary Gresham's Law. Such an issue is raised in fact by this special number of Tennessee Studies in Literature.

The book's raison d'etre is the quatercentenary, and yet, paradoxically, its all-pervading determination to commemorate remains its least attractive quality. Indeed, a dogged sense of the occasion positively detracts from essays which might, in other surroundings, have proved much more memorable.

Certainly Clifford Leech's contribution, "Shakespeare, Cibber, and the Tudor Myth" deserves to be widely read, for its account of Cibber's version of Richard III sheds interesting light on Shakespeare's own play, especially with regard to the use of conventions in Act V, the scenes before Bosworth. In Cibber's version, of course, the Tudor myth of history is not even hinted at, and there is "no centre of attention beyond Richard himself." By contrast, the essentially tragic structure of Shakespeare's play, its sense of "outraged fate," and its concentration on the hero's theatricality, and consequent neglect of duty in his social, political (and thus, to the Elizabethans, ultimately cosmic) environment is effectively brought out. The vistas forward and backward in the canon afforded by this standpoint are especially rewarding.

The same is true of Paul A. Jorgensen's essay "Hamlet and the Restless Renaissance." In a consideration of the play's intellectual background, Professor Jorgensen notices "an urgency, an impatience in spirit" which characterizes much of the period's writing, and which manifests "an anxiety . . . a time-consciousness that is so general in the Renaissance that it may be loosely called the neurosis of the era." Haunted by a sense of life's shortness, the Elizabethan culture often gave expression to an impatience with its own restrictions clearly discernible in many notable dramatic configurations: Prince Hal, Hotspur, Brutus, Tamburlaine, and, in a sense typically, Hamlet. There can be no doubt that Professor Jorgensen has placed his finger on a hitherto unremarked pulse both in Shakespeare's play and its background. That culture's inherited dichotomy between Action and Contemplation surely has this dimension, and the notion of a Renaissance "restlessness" as an embodiment of the spirit of Action in other playwrights, notably Chapman, suggests the opening of many doors.

George R. Hibbard's essay "The Taming of the Shrew: A Social Comedy" also proves a

352

characteristically valuable contribution. Agreeing with Dr. Johnson that the play has a unity, Mr. Hibbard goes on to argue that it thus comprises ". . . a significant critical comment on the life and society of the England in which it was written." Mr. Hibbard's knowledge of that England is of course extensive, and his contention that the play is "about marriage" and the attitudes of Elizabethan society towards it receives ample support. In pointing out the degree to which Shakespeare was a member, albeit a critical one, of the Elizabethan *bourgeoisie*, sharing many of its social presuppositions, the essay illuminates and informs beyond its nominal scope.

Charles Mitchell's suggestion that *Henry V* puts forward the view that the "social hierarchy should be a reflection of ethical hierarchy" reaches a similar conclusion, whilst running the risk of making the play seem to extol a kind of "moralitocracy", a notion wholly alien, surely, to the callously pragmatic structure of Elizabethan society? However, in so far as the play re-examines the notion of degree, and ends by approving of it on moral grounds whilst disapproving of its merely ceremonial manifestations, Shakespeare may be said to make an ethical virtue of social necessity here with satisfactorily Elizabethan irony.

Other essays exhibit varied interests. Norman Sanders's careful account of the major interpretations of *Hamlet* over the last hundred years constitutes a revealing guide to the changing temper of the times. Kenneth Muir's conclusion that *Venus and Adonis* "cannot easily be categorised" is reached by way of exploring several possible categorizations, each with its own fascination, not least that of the poem as comic. In his consideration of *Measure for Measure*, Alan H. Gilbert seems quite pleased to accept the Johnsonian dictum that Shakespeare ". . . is so much more careful to please than to instruct that he seems to write without any moral purpose." Well and good, perhaps, but dismissive statements such as "Religion does not appear when seemingly required" surely don't work quite so simply for this play. Critics such as Roy Battenhouse have made cases for a Christian interpretation which remain persuasive, and which ought to be met.

The "tail" of the book is a long one, characterized for the most part by articles which, if not undistinguished, would find a more appropriate place in learned journals: their appeal is limited and specialized. Thus, Robert H. West puts a somewhat esoteric interest in magic and pneumatology to sound use in an essay on *The Tempest* which sheds some light on the role of ceremonial magic in the play; John E. Hankins writes briefly but interestingly on the conception of the penalty inflicted on Adam as an element in *As You Like It*; Eric W. Stockton comments, at times coyly, on the sexual experience of Shakespeare's heroines; Clifford P. Lyons demonstrates a similarity in structure between the trysting scenes of *Troilus and Cressida*, and suggests the ironies that a stage-performance, in underlining these, would produce; Thomas P. Harrison sees *Titus Andronicus* as a "prototype" of *King Lear*, convincingly, yet at the same time running the inevitable risk of forcing the lesser play to be a Procrustean bed for the greater; and an "occasional" rôle is unaccountably thrust onto a review article by Mario Praz, first published in *Il Tempo* in 1961, in which some provocative thoughts on "The Ambiguity of Shakespeare" undergo an untypically fugitive expression.

Finally, T. Walter Herbert's essay on *A Midsummer Night's Dream* hints at a number of interesting notions, especially with regard to the complexity of the response demanded in the playing of Pyramus and Thisbe by the "mechanicals". Somehow, however, the book's overall process of diminution crystallizes overpoweringly in the bizarre familiarity here imposed on such luminaries as "twinkling Chaucer" and "wicked old Ovid" and his "raunchy book". Roguishness so ruthlessly pursued may find its own level, but it tends also to determine that of its surroundings.

University College,
Cardiff

Shakespeare's Happy Comedies by J. Dover Wilson. Faber and Faber, 1963. Pp. 224. $4.50. *Reviewer: F. David Hoeniger.*

A hearty welcome to this book however glaring its shortcomings. Weaker than most of Dover Wilson's books, it is yet sufficiently stamped with the mind and personality of this great scholar and teacher to reward the reader richly. The book has style. The lively response is worthy of its great subject. One is constantly made aware of the life-time acquaintance with Shakespeare's plays by this learned yet humble scholar who in his eightieth year responds to the plots, the characters and the poetry with as much enthusiasm and intelligence as he did in his youth. The book is helped, as alas so many on similar subjects are not, by its author's sense of comedy, a perceptive sense of the peculiar comedy which is Shakespeare's.

It seems idle then, if not embarrassing, for a younger and lesser critic to dwell on shortcomings; yet a balanced review demands such comment. The weaknesses are of two basic kinds and in part attributable to the work's long delayed appearance. The analysis of several of the comedies is thinly conventional, especially that of *TGV* (I cannot accept the view of Valentine as "self-effacing" throughout), *Much Ado* (on which much is said that does not need saying after such essays as Rossitter's in *Angel with Horns*), *As You Like It* (though the treatment of Touchstone is enlightening), and *The Merchant* (except for the chapter's brilliant opening, treating the play as the greatest answer to Sidney's condemnation of "mungrel tragi-comedy"). The other shortcoming is simply the lack of reference to, one suspects acquaintance with, much that has been written on Shakespearean comedy since Charlton and Chambers. Dover Wilson announces that he often takes issue with Charlton's book, which he still takes to be "the standard treatment of the subject". But surely this work has by now been adequately rejected or at least superseded in monographs and essays which Wilson fails to mention.

Yet who would wish to accuse such a genial and great senior Shakespearean! Much is anyhow due to the book's long delay. It was first conceived about 1930 as a series of interpretative essays on the plays which Wilson had by then helped Quiller-Couch to edit for the New Cambridge Shakespeare. Many have since wished that Wilson might be granted time to write for these plays his own notes and introductions, but more tactfully Wilson thought instead of writing a book for a different publisher. Most of the work, he tells us, was ready in draft by 1939, based on a series of lectures at Liverpool and Edinburgh. Then came the war, and after it the sense of obligation to complete the New Cambridge Shakespeare. So the work appeared only in 1962. But it is of course a great pity that he then did not revise the draft more thoroughly. For instance, the treatment of *The Merchant* was geared to the age of Hitler in 1937—an age we hope to have passed. Wilson seems to have done little more than add the postscript chapter on *MND*.

But it is more fitting to praise. At a time when younger critics strive for yet further pretentiously involved reinterpretations of the Comedies, the civilized, often subtle but always straightforward approach to the plays in this book is welcome. Sometimes the analysis is thin, sometimes it is anything but: but always it draws attention to the play in question, or to something else in Shakespeare. And even as we learn about one particular play, we move in the context of the whole of Shakespeare's work and art, and of the age he lived in, guided by one who has studied and loved these for a lifetime. And not merely studied and loved. Again and again, Wilson's mind turns to essentials, in the plays as they comment on or imply human experience, or as they are consummate art; and as often we see how Wilson has restlessly tried with all his learning to understand the plays better in detail, down to the meaning of single words, the establishment of the sound text of a line, the interpretation of allusions to contemporary events. Read, for instance, the opening sections of the last chapter.

The best chapter is, I think, that on *Love's Labour's Lost*. Among the twenty odd I have read on this play I know of no better. With typical frankness Wilson admits that the play left him cold until he saw Guthrie's production in 1936. It recalled to him *Cosi fan Tutti* and sent him back to Pater's great essay. His comments on the play's shifting colors, vivacity, sheer gaiety, and on the "smashing hammer-stroke", when "there appears a figure clothed in black from head to foot" would deserve lengthy quotation here if there were space. Instead let me cite from the almost equally impressive chapter on *Twelfth Night*. "The Elizabethans would have called them three melancholics", he says of Orsino, Olivia, and Malvolio. Where do we find such simple telling insights in the longer treatises on Shakespearean comedy? Once more on Malvolio:

> ... in a play by any one but Shakespeare he would appear to a twentieth-century audience a rather stupid butt, upon which an amusing practical joke is played by Maria, and that is all. But in Shakespeare's hands his dream blossoms into a monstrous beauty, expressed in all the magnificent magniloquence of post-Falstaffian prose, a beauty which rivals in its fashion that of Shylock's rhetoric or even Falstaff's itself. As with Shylock, so with Malvolio: Shakespeare let himself go, to the risk of wrenching the drama out of frame. (p.173)

And once more: "For the Malvolio-Sir Toby antithesis stands for a great human issue scarcely less significant than that which concerns Shylock and Antonio" (p.176). And now a comment on Sir Toby: he "knows more about contemporary physiology than most modern editors". Right.

The comedies are treated both individually and as a whole. *Twelfth Night* rounds them off. *Errors* and *TGV* come at the beginning as models of the two main types, merchant comedy and the comedy of romantic love and friendship. Some plays combine elements of both. What Wilson means by "happy" comedies is defined in the second chapter. Omitted are the *Shrew*, the "problem comedies" and the romances. Here and there even in the weaker chapters we encounter statements or single phrases which make us halt, aware that an insight is being expressed in simple concise language, and that so we are indeed helped in understanding an aspect of Shakespeare's art or its context; as when Master Slender's attractiveness for us in *The Merry Wives* is analysed, or when Shakespearean comedy is contrasted with Bergson's famous definition, or when we are reminded how the 'prentice boys among the groundlings took a special interest in such women parts as Rosalind's or Viola's "that their successors in our theatre lack" (pp.145-46). On some of the plays we have probably read more illuminating essays during the last twenty years. But this book will stand on our shelves next to *The Fortunes of Falstaff*.

Victoria College
University of Toronto

Stratford-Upon-Avon Studies 5: Hamlet. Edited by John Russell Brown and Bernard Harris. Edward Arnold, 1963. Pp. 212. $5.75. *Reviewer: Roy W. Battenhouse.*

Most of the essays here assembled are concerned, centrally, with the character of the Prince. Peter Ure discusses the interplay between Hamlet's character and his role. David William, as a theatre director, gives his interpretation of how Hamlet ought to respond to the Ghost in Act I. J. K. Walton, in a long essay on "The Structure of *Hamlet*," attempts to relate the struggle in the hero's soul to the "outer conflict" from scene to scene. G. K. Hunter examines "The Heroism of Hamlet," comparing it with that of Fortinbras, Laertes, and Horatio. Patrick Cruttwell tackles the thorny problem of Hamlet's morality, asking the question: "Sweet Prince" or "Arrant Knave"? He answers that Hamlet is to be admired for bearing himself well in what he believes to be a just war. T. J. B. Spencer, more cautiously, avoids giving any ultimate judgment on Hamlet, simply reviewing samples of criticism in various ages and countries and stressing their relativity to changing fashion. He implies, however, his own skepticism of recent views which have emphasized the "black presence" and "sickly mind" of Hamlet, giving his essay the lugubrious title "The Decline of Hamlet".

On some of the details of argument in these six essays I shall comment in a moment. But first let me review briefly three other contributions to the volume. E. A. J. Honigmann offers a closely reasoned study of Shakespeare's indications of an "elective" monarchy in Denmark. He challenges Dover Wilson's view that we should regard Hamlet as "the rightful heir to the throne" after his father's death, and counter-argues that Claudius has seized the throne "legally, but not perhaps without sharp practice". Claudius has but wrested constitutional law, making it the tool of his sly purpose, thus heightening our impression that in this world, even if not in the world to come, one can "buy out the law". Honigmann's article as a whole is convincing. Equally perceptive is John R. Brown's essay on "The Setting of Hamlet," which focuses on the play's "large and sweeping impression" as theatre. Brown gives us a splendid analysis of the atmosphere created by the play's alternation between "open" and "closed" stage-pictures, and of its rhythm of changing tempos. He shows, further, how the subconscious reaction of characters is conveyed through their movements on stage. The progressive separation of Claudius and Gertrude, for example, is visually presented; and similarly there are stage-signs by which an audience can discriminate between Rosencrantz and Guildenstern as the former takes the lead in guarding Hamlet whereas the latter is more watchful and quick to question. The essay by R. A. Foakes on "Character and Speech in *Hamlet*" I find less illuminating. Most readers, I think, scarcely need to be told, for example, that the orotundity of speech by Claudius suggests a certain hollowness, or that Laertes inherits the assurance of his father's commonplaces, or that Horatio's bare phrases expose by contrast the wordiness of Hamlet, or that the Prince uses quibbles as weapons and, like an actor, escapes into roles to conceal his aims. These observations, while true enough, do little to penetrate the heart of Hamlet's character.

As a further comment I would question the claim made by Foakes that Hamlet "stands apart from (Shakespeare's) other tragic heroes in his relative innocence". Foakes proceeds to quote—as a relevant reaction to Othello or Lear or Macbeth, but *not* to Hamlet—the Prayerbook's cry: "From all blindness of heart; from pride, vainglory, and hypocrisy; from envy, hatred and malice, and all uncharitableness, Good Lord deliver us". But I can not think this litany any less relevant to Hamlet. Blindness of heart and uncharitableness seem to me evident in Hamlet's attitudes. Nor does this fact, for me, cancel out the critical commonplace that almost everyone feels "a smack of Hamlet" in himself. Must we not also, if we are rigorously honest, confess to "smacks" in us sometimes of Othello-like jealousy or Lear-like pride? The litany is our cry for deliverance from all such inclinations—*in us*, not merely outside us. And the literary art of tragedy, on the other hand, seems to me a secular means toward the purging of dangerous "smacks" in ourselves—by giving us an experience vicariously of their disasters. A tragic hero, if we may credit Aristotle, should be like us: not eminently good, hence capable of some great mistake we can pity and fear. By approaching Hamlet as if he were, instead, simply a hero "faced by an impossible dilemma" (a confusing phrase), Foakes evades looking at the initial defect in Hamlet by which Hamlet gets himself into his dilemma.

The moral aspects of Hamlet's character are the ones nowadays most in need of clarification. For this reason I find Cruttwell's essay, mentioned above, an important one even though its answers flounder in ultimate muddle. It succeeds, at least, in posing a crucial question: Are we to take the revenge laid on Hamlet by the ghost as a "true moral duty" or as "a temptation to wrongdoing"? But then Cruttwell's romantic bias betrays him. Seeking to controvert the view of L. C. Knights that part of the corruption in the play is in Hamlet himself, not all in the world around him, Cruttwell argues that Shakespeare "accepted" the ethic of revenge and that Hamlet "cannot be doing wrong". Defensively he thunders against the "quasi-pacifist emotions of many twentieth-century liberals" who, in his view, misunderstand Hamlet's "military virtues". He tries to liken Hamlet to Macduff, who took vengeance on a Macbeth who had killed his wife and children; and to Edgar, who challenged and killed Edmund. But do these two cases present genuine parallels to Hamlet's? On the contrary, I would say, they are instances of an open military challenge on publicly declared charges and under Christian conventions. Surely a forthright political action under the banner of Malcolm's "grace" or Edgar's desire for "charity" is quite distinguishable from the wild justice of Hamlet's "mad" proceedings. Cruttwell believes that both "the play and the character (of Hamlet) are notably Christian". I, too, think the play Christian— but precisely because it shows tragedy arising from variously *un*Christian responses in Hamlet and others. There may be, Cruttwell finally concedes, something of a "moral muddle" in the play, but this could be the result of Shakespeare's "taking over an old story for new times," and we shall never know whether Shakespeare was aware of his play's incongruities. Never? And must Shakespeare be supposed a bungler in order to cover up our own confusions?

Of the other essays on Hamlet's character, those by William and Walton assume, as Cruttwell does, that the ghost's command is valid because he comes from Purgatory. This assumption, however, is highly dubious. It ignores the challenge of certain recent studies which, citing evidence both from the play itself and from traditional theology, see the ghost as a visitor from hell. Since this problem is crucial to interpretation of the play as a whole, all readings which blithely assert, as William does, that the ghost's supernatural soliciting "can not be ill" are proceeding on a very shaky premise.

Walton's essay is disappointing because it relies on a whole series of conventional but unexamined notions: not only that the ghost comes from Purgatory, but that later the mousetrap "succeeds" in plucking out Claudius' mystery, that Hamlet then gives his mother "sound, practical advice" in the closet scene, and that Hamlet is justified in dispatching Rosencrantz and Guildenstern. Further, Walton argues that in the graveyard tussle Shakespeare is emphasizing Hamlet's "restraint"; and he adopts, in preference to the Folio's "solid flesh" Dover Wilson's emendation of "sullied flesh". All of these readings seem to me dubious. Hunter's essay, on the other hand, while sidestepping these pitfalls, comes up with the murky assertion that in *Hamlet*, "for the first time in Shakespeare, and one of the earliest times in European literature," we are shown evil as "not a class of activity but as a description of being". If true, this would indeed be new. It seems to me more likely, however, that Shakespeare understood evil, in this play as elsewhere, in accord with the traditional view that evil is a defect or privation of being, and that Hunter is but voicing a vague impressionism.

Peter Ure's essay carries a thoughtful reply to John Holloway's view that "role predominates over character" in Hamlet and that there is actually no "delay" but rather a phase by phase discharging of the "determinate role" of revenger. Ure sees, instead of a determinate role, a constant "intercourse between character and role, the one modifying the other". He points to Hamlet's own awareness of a gap between undertaking and performance, and emphasizes Hamlet's recurrent attempts to find an adjustment to the role he has formally assumed. Divesting oneself of all "pressures past" proves to be for Hamlet a heavy task; there are times when "it is as though Hamlet had never taken on the role at all, as though all were to be done again". These observations seem to me valid. I can agree also, in part, with Ure's contention that there is a change of character in Hamlet, and that by Act 5 when he submits to providence he is no longer committing himself to the revenger's role in the same way he did earlier when nerving himself by worked-up states of feeling. Yet I am puzzled by Ure's final conclusion: that at the end Hamlet "is able to achieve the act of revenge without ever really becoming a revenger," since now Hamlet's larger perspective of submission to providence "frees his inward self from the role". I would say, rather, that Hamlet's inward self has by now become habituated to abandoning itself to rashness, which he now awaits with a settled "readiness," since rashness in the past has provided him revenges for which he could disclaim responsibility. To say, as Ure does, that Hamlet's role is now "formed by Providence not by character" seems to me a false and unnecessary antithesis. Rather, Hamlet's character has by now become so formed by his recurrent escapes into play-imagined revenges that he can passively await one more such de-naturing of the self into the actor. He can welcome such a destiny as providential—which, by high irony, it in fact is, since Divine Providence does permit this kind of vainglorious transcendence to souls that fixedly long for what amounts to the will's own suicide. But what I am here suggesting needs elaboration beyond the scope of this review.

A seven-page "Reader's Guide to *Hamlet*" by Stanley Wells rounds out the present volume. It is somewhat skimpy on American scholarship, naming only seven works by American critics along with twenty-one by Britishers in the section on twentieth-century criticism. Yet this may be the way the matter looks to an Englishman. The editors in this Stratford series, it may be observed, have not yet ventured to invite American contributors, even though a similar series coming out annually from Stratford, Ontario, regularly does so.

Indiana University

A Knack to Know a Knave, edited by G. R. Proudfoot. Malone Society Reprints, 1964 (for 1963). Pp. xviii+text.

The Miseries of Enforced Marriage by George Wilkins and edited by Glenn H. Blayney. Malone Society Reprints, 1964 (for 1963). Pp. xvi + text. *Reviewer: Robert K. Turner, Jr.*

One of the services rendered by the Malone Society has been the resurrection of obscure plays interesting to the history of the English Renaissance drama but hard for scholars to come by. The two reprints just published are of texts obscure enough and interesting enough in their way, yet neither is unobtainable. *A Knack to Know a Knave*, a latter-day morality in which Kempe's merriments of the madmen of Gotham is embedded, has previously appeared in Collier's *Five Old Plays* (1851), Hazlitt's Dodsley (1874), and a dissertation by P. E. Bennett (1952) which can be had from University Microfilms. *The Miseries of Enforced Marriage*, a domestic drama first-cousin to *The Yorkshire Tragedy,* was included in several editions of Dodsley and in Scott's *Ancient British Drama* (1810). Both plays were published, in addition, in the Tudor Facsimile Texts. While they all are not trustworthy in many particulars, these earlier editions nevertheless furnish versions that are accurate enough for general use, and, if one wants to be sure of a reading, the primitive editions of both plays are at hand in University Microfilms' English Books Before 1640. It might be thought that the Malone Society reprints are still desirable if only because they liberate the scholar from his microfilm reader, but this is not true.

Malone Society reprints are supposed, of course, to do more than furnish reading versions. In the early days of the Society, A. W. Pollard pointed out that "every generation will need to make its own critical editions to suit its own critical taste, but that work of permanent utility can be done by placing in the hands of students at large such reproductions of the original textual authorities as may make constant and continuous reference to these originals themselves unnecessary."[1] The Society's general editors have always subscribed to this policy. Hence, the reprints have as their real reason for being the provision of an authority which, within obvious limitations, can serve as the basis for textual work, and the demanding set of rules for the Society's editors, drawn up by W. W. Greg, the first general editor, were clearly directed toward this end.[2] In 1906 photographic reproductions were both expensive and of uncertain quality; type-facsimiles, then as now, did not exactly reproduce the authority and were subject to the frailties of editors, compositors, and proof-readers. From the outset the Society was faced with Hobson's choice: as Greg later put it, "Photographic reproductions are reliable but illegible, reprints are legible but unreliable."[3] A decision was necessary, however, if the Society's work was to start, and the type-facsimile was chosen; it was cheaper, and it enjoyed the very real advantage of being able to reproduce legibly readings that might be illegible in any one exemplum of the authority.

The choice between photography and type was sometime a paradox, but by the 1920's photography was "so much improved in efficiency and lowered in price" that scholars could question whether the Society should hold to the type-facsimile.[4] Greg himself knew that, when access to the original was barred, the scholar needed both kinds of reproduction.[5] In the subsequent forty years the conflict has been but sharpened, particularly as the microfilm, the photostat, and the xerox print have brought reasonably accurate and reasonably priced reproductions of originals within the means of scholars. Furthermore, scholarly requirements during this period have changed. The type-facsimile was intended for the use of textual critics as distinct from bibliographers, for whose esoteric purposes such a reproduction has always been next to no good at all; today an increasing number of textual critics know and use bibliographical techniques.[6] Ultimately the careful bibliographer has to examine the original authority, but he can do much preliminary work with a good photographic reproduction that cannot be done with a type-facsimile.

One wonders, then, if the Malone reprints are still performing a function important enough to justify the trouble of their preparation and if the Society would not be better advised to put its resources into photographic facsimiles. Professor Arthur Brown, the present general editor, vigorously defends the Society's original choice.[7] Photographs lie, he says; there is the insidious curve of the reproduced surface that distorts spacing, the blind letter that does not appear, the badly inked type that assumes a different appearance when photographed, all dangers because the general likeness of the photograph to the original lulls the textual critic into a false sense of security. Granted. For detailed work the photograph must be checked against the original, but then so must the type-facsimile; and while the photographic reproduction, for all its limitations, has given the bibliographically inclined textual man some help, the type-facsimile has given him very little. If a good scholar has overseen the photographic reproduction, as in the case of the Shakespeare Quarto Facsimiles, and has provided lists of variant and doubtful readings, misprints, and so on, the danger is all the graver, Brown observes, for the textual critic will take on trust what he ought to work out for himself. Perhaps. In crucial matters a scholar should trust no one's judgment but his own, but if such aids are hazards in photographic reproductions, they are equally hazardous in the Malone reprints, which always provide them. The earth has not yet been inherited by the bibliographers, Brown points out. True. But only the most curiously antiquarian general reader is going to prefer a type-facsimile even to Dodsley, and the literary critic, in the final analysis, can rely no more on the reading of a Malone reprint than can the textual critic. On this last point Brown would perhaps demur, for, he remarks, the reader

> can be sure that his Malone Society edition has been prepared by someone carefully chosen for the job, that this editor has had access to the original, that he has spent many hours working on it, that his introduction will contain much, if not all, of the information that a textual critic needs at least to help him on his way to his own examination of the text in question, that all departures from the original have been carried out within carefully defined limits, and that the editor's work has at all stages been checked by another carefully chosen person.[8]

That Malone Society standards are high no one doubts; that they are applied in practice one can doubt, and the two reprints at hand furnish material for a test.

Proudfoot's edition of *A Knack to Know a Knave* was based on photostats of the Bodleian copy. The other extant copies, numbering three, were collated, results being reported in a List of Variant Readings. For the present review, the reprint was collated one time with microfilm of the Huntington copy; the variants noted were confirmed by examination of the Huntington copy itself.[9] Lemmata and line numbers are those of the reprint:

41	Dunston | Dunston.		966 cw	But | Bu
382	teares | teates		1012	them | them
548	And | Aud		1383	what? | what¿
925	Wel | Well			

The Huntington's readings at ll. 925 and 966 cw occur in D(o), uncorrected in that copy but corrected in the Bodleian. They thus probably deserve inclusion in the List of Variant Readings (pp. x and xi of the reprint). The Huntington's turned question mark at l. 1383 occurs in F(o), an invariant forme; it is probably also turned in the Bodleian. Under the provisions of Rule 6(i), the editor seems to have corrected it, but one's doubts could have been put at rest had the matter been mentioned in the general statement on anomalous punctuation (pp. xi and xii), which gives the impression of being exhaustive. The remaining variants do no more than create suspicion, for honest men may disagree as to whether a certain mark is a period or a speck, a u or an n. Yet the Huntington readings seem clear, and one should be cautious in using the readings of the reprint. Minor, but unfortunate, are two misprints in the introduction and apparatus: the inevitable "1954" for "1594" (p. vii) and us? for us? (p. x).

Blayney's reprint of *The Miseries of Enforced Marriage* was based on photostats of the Folger Library copy (the only extant copy with all formes in the corrected state), and variants revealed by a collation with seven other copies, all that are extant, are reported. For the present review, the reprint was compared one time with microfilm of Huntington 79728. The variants noted were checked against Huntington 79728 and against the Folger copy as well.[10] In the following readings both copies agreed but disagreed with the reprint, although in some instances marks of punctuation appear only as specks in the Folger copy. Lemmata and line numbers are again those of the reprint:

18	already that	already, that		2188	Iewels	Iewe ls[12]
569	window an	window, an		2347	cw (Tis)	Tis
697	me duely	me, duely		2495	you your	you, your
1403	himfelcf	himfelfc[11]		2518	him euen	him, euen
1567	chances,	chances		2703	vp but	vp, but
2179	*went*	*went.*				

Here the reprint is clearly wrong, the editor evidently having failed to take seriously enough the injunction of Rule 8 to examine several copies and set right points that are indistinct in the copy-text. The reprint reading at l. 1403 is apparently a misprint. In the following readings the reprint and the Folger copy disagree with Huntington 79728:

227	forbid	forbid		1754	them abfolute	them, abfolute
871	Yet	Yer		2091	you, fay	you fay
1092	afor	afor		2491	*But*	*But.*

The editor, who has seen all extant copies, no doubt ought to be trusted with regard to the readings at ll. 227 and 2091; the first falls in B(o), corrected in Huntington 79728, and the second in H(i), which is invariant. One guesses that the reprint is wrong at ll. 1754 and 2491; the first of these is in G(o) and the second in I(i), both uncorrected in Huntington 79728, but in the first instance the point is desirable and in the second required. It looks as though both were present, but neither printed in the Folger copy. The two remaining variants occur in D(i), uncorrected in Huntington 79728; both are very likely to be genuine uncorrected readings and thus omissions from the List of Variant Readings (pp. x and xi). In addition, the List of Variant Readings, in which lemmata are those of the reprint (the corrected formes) shows

514	percift	pergeft

but the reprint reads "pergeft" as does the List of Irregular and Doubtful Readings (p. xii).

Judged on their own terms, Proudfoot's reprint comes off very well, Blayney's less well, and to impugn their accuracy is somewhat uncharitable, the perfect reproduction of anything in quantity being more luck than cunning. But it would seem clear, if these two can be taken as typical, that the Malone reprints do not entirely satisfy the Society's standards. Greg, as usual, said it: "Reprints are legible but unreliable." If they must be thoroughly checked before use, they are of little more value than photographic prints to the non-bibliographical critic; they are, by their very nature, of no significant help to the bibliographically-minded textual scholar, and his tribe increases. Would it not be better, then, for all scholars to take their chances with photographic reproductions, even ones of modest quality? That is the preference of at least one humble member of the Society.

University of Wisconsin-Milwaukee

Notes:

(1) W. W. Greg, "Type-Facsimiles and Others," *Library,* 4th ser., VI (1925-26), 321.

(2) "Rules for the Guidance of Editors of the Society's Reprints," *Collections Part II* (1908), pp. 113-116, reprinted, with revisions, in *Collections Volume IV* (1956), pp. 66-69.

(3) Greg, p. 322.

(4) "The Discussion," *Library,* 4th ser., VI (1925-26), 327-328.

(5) *Op. cit.,* p. 326.

(6) Cf. John Russell Brown, "The Rationale of Old-Spelling Editions of the Plays of Shakespeare and his Contemporaries," *SB,* XIII (1960), 50-57.

(7) "The Rationale of Old-Spelling Editions of Shakespeare and his Contemporaries: A Rejoinder," *ibid.,* 69-73.

(8) *Ibid.,* 72-73.

(9) I am greatly obliged to Carey S. Bliss, Curator of Rare Books at the Huntington Library, for doing this chore. His readings were agreed in by Dr. Carpenter of the Library staff.

(10) I am again obliged to Mr. Bliss and Dr. Carpenter for examining the Huntington copy as well as to Dr. Giles E. Dawson for examining the Folger copy.

(11) The List of Irregular and Doubtful Readings (p. xiii) reads "himselfc."

(12) According to Rule 3 (see n. 2), spacing in reprints is normalized, but editors sometimes note spacing errors in their Lists of Irregular and Doubtful Readings, as Proudfoot does at, for example, l. 725 (p. xiii) and Blayney regularly does when words are wrongly closed up.

Directory

Gates Kennedy Agnew, *Department of English, Indiana University, Bloomington, Indiana 47405.*

G.P.V. Akrigg, *Department of English, The University of British Columbia, Vancouver 8, B.C., Canada.*

John A. Allen, *Hollins College, Hollins College, Virginia 24020.*

Peter Allen, *431 East 20th Street, New York, N.Y. 10028.*

Ruth L. Anderson, *Department of English, Carthage College, Kenosha, Wisconsin 53140.*

John S. Anson, *2917 Garber Street, Berkeley, California 94705.*

James Applegate, *Wilson College, Chambersburg, Pennsylvania 17201.*

Rosario P. Armato, *Department of English and Comparative Literature, The University of Southern California, Los Angeles, California 90007.*

Professor Aerol Arnold, *The University of Southern California, Los Angeles, California 90007.*

W.E.D. Atkinson, *Department of English, The University of Western Ontario, London, Ontario, Canada.*

Kennith R. Balsley, *The Episcopal Academy, City Line and Berwick Road, Philadelphia, Pennsylvania 19131.*

Professor Betty Bandel, *Department of English, The University of Vermont, Burlington, Vermont 05401.*

Jonas A. Barish, *Department of English, The University of California, Berkeley, California 94720.*

Sylvan Barnet, *51 Trowbridge Street, Cambridge, Massachusetts 02138.*

Mrs. T.C. Barnum, *Hunt Lane, Fayetteville, New York 13066.*

Mary B. Barroll, *416 South Carlisle Street, Philadelphia, Pennsylvania 19146.*

E. Beatrice Batson, *Department of English, Wheaton College, Wheaton, Illinois 60187.*

Bernard Beckerman, *105 Meadowbrook Road, Hempstead, New York.*

John Benedict, *W.W. Norton & Company, 55 Fifth Avenue, New York, N.Y. 10003.*

Josephine Waters Bennett, *200 East 66th Street, New York, N.Y. 10021.*

Ronald Berman, *Department of Literature, The University of California, San Diego, La Jolla, California 92038.*

Rev. Miguel A. Bernad S.J., *Ateneo de Manila, P.O. Box 154, Manila, Philippines.*

Dennis Biggins, *5 Young Street, Cook's Hill, Newcastle, New South Wales, Australia.*

William B. Bjornstad, *Department of English, Drake University, Des Moines, Iowa 50311.*

Ben Black, *Department of English, The University of Kentucky, Lexington, Kentucky 40506.*

Grace T. Blakey, *529 Oak Street, Marquette, Michigan 49855.*

Professor Muriel Bowden, *115 East 82nd Street, New York, N.Y. 10028.*

Professor Hoyt Edwin Bowen, *Box 591, Pfeiffer College, Misenheimer, North Carolina 28109.*

George C. Branam, *Office of Academic Affairs, Louisiana State University, New Orleans, Louisiana 70122.*

Ernest Brennecke, *430 West 116th Street, New York, N.Y. 10027.*

Professor Harriet D. Broeker, *Department of English, Knoxville College, Knoxville, Tennessee 37921.*

Charles B. Brooks, *Department of English, California State College at Long Beach, Long Beach, California 90815.*

Professor Arthur Brown, *Department of English, University College London, Gower Street, London W.C. 1, England.*

William J. Brown, *Department of English, The University of Colorado, Boulder, Colorado 80304.*

Edward S. Brubaker, *114 Race Avenue, Lancaster, Pennsylvania 17603.*

Dr. Albert H. Buford, *The Graduate Office, Villanova University, Villanova, Pennsylvania 19085.*

Dr. Paulina Buhl, *Shorter College, Rome, Georgia 30161.*

C.O. Burgess, *Department of English, Old Dominion College, Norfolk, Virginia 23508.*

Andrew S. Cairncross, *2 New Edinburgh Road, Uddingston, Glasgow, Scotland.*

Mrs. Martin Cannon, *9662 North 29th Street, Omaha, Nebraska.*

Roger W. Calkins, *Box 172, Sackville, New Brunswick, Canada.*

Father Thomas Callan, T.O.R., *Saint Francis College. Loretta, Pennsylvania 15940.*

Louise Callison, *Alderson-Broaddus College, Philippi, West Virginia 26417.*

Otis G. Carnes, *Box 745, Pembroke, North Carolina 28372.*

Professor Félix J. Carrère, *2 Chemin des Fenouillères, Aix-en-Provence, France.*

James E. Carver, *St. Andrews College, Laurinburg, North Carolina 28352.*

Hollis L. Cate, *Box 928, Dahlonega, Georgia 30533.*

Professor Joseph S.M.J. Chang, *Department of English, Tulane University, New Orleans, Louisiana 70118.*

Dr. David R. Cheney, *Department of English, The University of Toledo, Toledo, Ohio 43606.*

H.E. Childs, *1515 Brook Lane, Corvallis, Oregon 97330.*

William S. Clark II, *Department of English, The University of Cincinnati, Cincinnati, Ohio 45221.*

Clarence L. Cline, *Department of English, The University of Texas, Austin, Texas 78712.*

Eileen Z. Cohen, *6445 Greene Street, Philadelphia, Pennsylvania 19119.*

Mr. and Mrs. William Collins, *9 Interwood Place, Cincinnati, Ohio 45220.*

Jackson I. Cope, *Department of English, The Johns Hopkins University, Baltimore, Maryland 21218.*

P.L. Cornett, *Department of English, Wayne State University, Detroit, Michigan 48202.*

Campbell C. Crockett, *Dean of the Graduate School, The University of Cincinnati, Cincinnati, Ohio 45221.*

Miss Elizabeth Cummings, *La Salle-Peru-Oglesby Junior College, La Salle, Illinois 61301.*

L. Cummings, *St. Jerome's College, Waterloo, Ontario, Canada.*

Giles E. Dawson, *The Folger Shakespeare Library, Washington, D.C. 20003.*

Dr. Dayton N. Dennett, *Department of English,*

State College, Fitchburg, Massachusetts 01420.

Robert W. Dent, *Department of English, The University of California, Los Angeles, California 90024.*

Professor Noyes Devor, *Central College, McPherson, Kansas 67460.*

Dr. David O. Dickerson, *Department of English, Greenville College, Greenville, Illinois 62246.*

R.J. Dorius, *1245 California Street, San Francisco, California 94109.*

Alvin W. Druhman, *St. Joseph's College, Rensselaer, Indiana 47979.*

J. Gordon Eaker, *5649 Wickersham Lane, Houston, Texas 77027.*

K.R. Eissler, M.D., *300 Central Park West, New York, N.Y. 10024.*

William A. Elwood, *Department of English, The University of Virginia, Charlottesville, Virginia 22903.*

English Department, *The University of California, Riverside, California 92502.*

English Department, *University of Jyräskylä, Finland.*

English Department, *Miami University, Oxford, Ohio 45056.*

English Department Library, *The Ohio State University, Columbus, Ohio 43210.*

English-Speaking Union, *16 East 69th Street, New York 21, N.Y.*

R.O. Evans, *The University of Kentucky, Lexington, Kentucky 40506.*

S.T. Fisher, *53 Morrison Avenue, Montreal 16, Quebec, Canada.*

Robert E. Fitch, *2223 Marin Avenue, Berkeley, California 94707.*

Professor H. Fluchère, *"Tras-Castel", Sainte-Tulle, France.*

C.L. Ford, *2718 Drake Avenue, Costa Mesa, California 92626.*

Charles R. Forker, *Department of English, Indiana University, Bloomington, Indiana 47405.*

Professor Joseph Barthélémy Fort, *7, Rue Monticelli, Paris 14, France.*

Dr. Levi Fox, O.B.E., *The Shakespeare Birthplace Trust, The Shakespeare Centre, Stratford-upon-Avon, England.*

Russell A. Fraser, *Department of English, Vanderbilt University, Nashville, Tennessee 37205.*

Raymond M. Fredman, *Department of English,*

364

Illinois Wesleyan University, Bloomington, Illinois 61701.

Dean Frye, Department of English, McGill University, Montreal 2, Quebec, Canada.

Roland Mushat Frye, Department of English, The University of Pennsylvania, Philadelphia, Pennsylvania 19104.

Mary N. Gailbreath, 11506 Taber Street, Silver Spring, Maryland 20902.

Professor David Galloway, Department of English, The University of New Brunswick, Fredericton, N.B., Canada.

John W. Gassner, 100 York Street, New Haven, Connecticut 06511.

Lloyd Graham Gibbs, Department of English, The University of South Carolina, Columbia, South Carolina 29208.

John N. Gill, Department of English, Wartburg College, Waverly, Iowa 50677.

Gilbert Godfrey, 43 Fifth Avenue, New York, N.Y. 10003.

Dr. Robert Hillis Goldsmith, Emory and Henry College, Emory, Virginia 24327.

R. Dorset Graves, 501 Shelton Street, Chadron, Nebraska 69337.

Hoke S. Greene, Vice President and Dean of Faculties, The University of Cincinnati, Cincinnati, Ohio 45221.

Thelma Greenfield, Department of English, The University of Oregon, Eugene, Oregon 97403.

Albert J. Guérard, Department of English, Stanford University, Stanford, California 94305.

Miss Annie E. Gunderson, 127 7th Avenue S.W., Valley City, North Dakota 58072.

Dr. Ann Haaker, 1401 Cameo Lane, Fullerton, California.

Margie M. Hankinson, 1824 Ruddell Road, Denton, Texas.

Dean Donald E. Hayden, College of Liberal Arts, The University of Tulsa, Tulsa, Oklahoma 74104.

Ray L. Heffner, Dean of Faculties, Indiana University, Bloomington, Indiana 47405.

Tinsley Helton, Department of English, The University of Wisconsin-Milwaukee, Milwaukee, Wisconsin 53211.

Professor Charles S. Hensley, Department of English, Stanislaus State College, Turlock, California 95380.

George R. Hibbard, Department of English,

The University, Nottingham, England.

Professor Archibald A. Hill, Box 8120 University Station, Austin, Texas 78712.

Dr. Addie Suggs Hilliard, Western Kentucky State College, Bowling Green, Kentucky 42102.

Peter Hilty, 622 Bellevue, Cape Girardeau, Missouri.

Raymond Himelick, Department of English, Purdue University, West Lafayette, Indiana 47906.

Professor Charlton Hinman, Department of English, The University of Kansas, Lawrence, Kansas 66045.

Charles K. Hofling, M.D., 300 Warren Avenue, Cincinnati, Ohio 45220.

Allan Holaday, Department of English, The University of Illinois, Urbana, Illinois 61803.

Irvin B. Horst, Eastern Mennonite College, Harrisonburg, Virginia 22801.

Frank L. Hoskins, Jr., Newberry College, Newberry, South Carolina 29108.

Dr. T.H. Howard-Hill, Brigg's Cottage, Noke, Oxford, England.

Mrs. H.W. Hunsiker, 5622 Northumberland Street, Pittsburgh, Pennsylvania 15217.

Mrs. Donald F. Hyde, 30 Sutton Place, New York, N.Y.

Reginald W. Ingram, Department of English, The University of British Columbia, Vancouver 8, B.C., Canada.

Dr. Maurice Jacobs, 1010 Arch Street, Philadelphia 7, Pennsylvania.

Mrs. Elizabeth T. James, Danbury State College, Danbury, Connecticut.

Hobart Jarrett, Department of English, Brooklyn College, Brooklyn, New York 11210.

James H. Jones, Department of Language and Literature, Northern Michigan University, Marquette, Michigan 49855.

Professor M.T. Jones-Davies, 80 Boulevard de la Duchesse Anne, Rennes, France.

Stanley J. Kahrl, 96 Chadbourne Road, Rochester, New York 14618.

Paul Murray Kendall, Department of English, Ohio University, Athens, Ohio 45701.

William H.J. Kennedy, 3935 Blackstone Avenue, Apt. 6-D, New York, N.Y. 10471.

Arthur F. Kinney, Department of English, Yale University, New Haven, Connecticut.

Joseph P. Klatzkin, 209 Academy Street,

Trenton, New Jersey 08618.

J.W. Knedler, Jr., University College, New York University, Bronx, New York 10453.

James Hisao Kodama, Kyoritsu Women's University, 3-1 Chome Hitotsubashi, Kanda, Chiyoda-Ku, Tokyo, Japan.

Joseph E. Kramer, Department of English, The University of California, Berkeley, California 94720.

Edward A. Langhans, Department of Drama, The University of Hawaii, Honolulu, Hawaii 96822.

President Walter C. Langsam, The University of Cincinnati, Cincinnati, Ohio 45221.

Sr. M. Leandra, O.S.F., Cardinal Stritch College, 6801 North Yates Road, Milwaukee, Wisconsin 53217.

Clifford Leech, Department of English, University College, Toronto 5, Ontario, Canada.

Dr. Maurice Levine, 984 Lenox Place, Cincinnati, Ohio 45229.

John S. Lewis, Department of English, Arlington State College, Arlington, Texas 76010.

Vernon E. Lichtenstein, Department of English, Coe College, Cedar Rapids, Iowa 52402.

J.I. Lindsay, 151 Crescent Road, Burlington, Vermont 05401.

Philip W. London, Department of English, The University of Windsor, Windsor, Ontario, Canada.

W.B. Long, 2773 University Avenue, Bronx, N.Y. 10468.

Clifford P. Lyons, Department of English, The University of North Carolina, Chapel Hill, North Carolina 27515.

Dr. Derick R.C. Marsh, Department of English, The University of Sydney, Sydney, New South Wales, Australia.

Mary H. Marshall, Department of English, Syracuse University, Syracuse, New York 13210.

Mr. and Mrs. Noel Martin, 6226 Robison Road, Cincinnati, Ohio 45213.

Charles D. McCloskey, Department of English, La Salle College, Philadelphia, Pennsylvania 19141.

Robert McDonnell, Department of English, Ohio University, Athens, Ohio 45701.

Dr. George J. Merrill, Lakehead University, Port Arthur, Ontario, Canada.

Sister M. Camillus Mescher, Briar Cliff College, Sioux City, Iowa 51104.

C. William Miller, 119 Gladstone Road, Lansdowne, Pennsylvania 19050.

J.L. Mills, 441 Ridgefield Road, Chapel Hill, North Carolina.

June J. Morgan, Department of English, Kansas State Teachers College, Emporia, Kansas 66802.

Ruth Mortimer, 20 Prescott Street, Cambridge, Massachusetts 02138.

Professor Kenneth Muir, The University of Liverpool, Liverpool 3, England.

Mr. Armour H. Nelson, Division of Humanities, California Lutheran College, Thousand Oaks, California 91360.

Professor Benjamin Nelson, State University, Stony Brook, New York 11790.

Lawrence G. Nelson, Sweet Briar College, Sweet Briar, Virginia 24595.

Nora May Nolan, 3547 St. Charles Place, Cincinnati, Ohio 45208.

Mrs. Robert L. Nutt, Jr., R.F.D. Elliston, Virginia 24087.

Dr. Zelma Odle, 849 E.N. 16th, Abilene, Texas 79601.

Francis R. Olley, 150 Merion Avenue, Narberth, Pennsylvania 19072.

Linwood E. Orange, Box 183, Southern Station, The University of Southern Mississippi, Hattiesburg, Mississippi 39401.

Tucker Orbison, 1402 Jefferson Avenue, Lewisburg, Pennsylvania 17837.

Professor Jiro Ozu, 3-39 Shimouma-cho, Setagaya-ku, Tokyo, Japan.

D.J. Palmer, Department of English, The University, Hull, Yorkshire, England.

Ronald J. Pavone, Department of English, The University of Wisconsin, Madison, Wisconsin 53703.

T.M. Pearce, Department of English, The University of New Mexico, Albuquerque, New Mexico 87106.

Lu Emily Pearson, 4750 Calle Desecada, Route 4, Box 482, Tucson, Arizona 85704.

Margaret I. Pfau, 968 Ottawa Drive, Youngstown, Ohio 44511.

R. Poisson, Department of English, Mount Allison University, Sackville, New Brunswick, Canada.

Professor Lawrence J. Pontrelli, 52 76th Street, Brooklyn 9, New York.

Professor W.W. Powell, Box 2033, Georgia

Southern College, Statesboro, Georgia 30459.

Eleanor Prosser, 657 Los Ninos Way, Los Altos, California 94022.

George Foster Provost, Jr., Department of English, Duquesne University, Pittsburgh, Pennsylvania 15219.

Dr. Edward Quinn, 393 East 7th Street, Brooklyn 18, New York.

Norman Rabkin, Department of English, The University of California, Berkeley, California 94707.

Dr. Donald Radin, 3875 Dakota, Cincinnati, Ohio 45229.

Margaret Loftus Ranald, Department of English, Queens College of the City University of New York, Flushing, New York 11367.

Dr. and Mrs. William Ransohoff, 3536 Biddle Street, Cincinnati, Ohio 45220.

President H.H. Ransom, The University of Texas, Austin, Texas 78712.

Robert R. Reed, Jr., 301 South Garner Street, State College, Pennsylvania 16801.

Victor E. Reichert, 752 Red Bud Avenue, Cincinnati, Ohio 45229.

Ernest L. Rhodes, Old Dominion College, Norfolk, Virginia 23508.

Townsend Rich, Department of English, State University of New York at Albany, Albany, New York 12203.

Mildred Riling, Southeastern State College, Durant, Oklahoma 74701.

Mr. Frederick J. Rogers, 2905 Memory Lane, Kalamazoo, Michigan 49007.

Mr. and Mrs. J.R. Rogers, P.O. Box 7785, Leopoldville, Republic of Congo.

Philip H. Ropp, Hampden-Sydney, Virginia.

Mr. and Mrs. George S. Rosenthal, 3523 Biddle Street, Cincinnati, Ohio 45220.

Sally Ross, 425 Rawson Woods Lane, Cincinnati, Ohio 45220.

James E. Ruoff, Department of English, Wichita State University, Wichita, Kansas 67208.

Professor Andrew J. Sabol, Department of English, Brown University, Providence, Rhode Island 02912.

Alexander Sackton, Department of English, The University of Texas, Austin, Texas 78712.

Norman Sanders, Department of English, The University of Tennessee, Knoxville, Tennessee 37916.

Frank R. Saunders, 65 Westbrooke Avenue, West Hartlepool, Co. Durham, England.

Professor William O. Scott, 1946 Calumet Avenue, Toledo 7, Ohio.

Alice Lyle Scoufos, Department of English, Arizona Western College, Yuma, Arizona 85364.

Professor Daniel Seltzer, Loeb Drama Center, Harvard University, Cambridge, Massachusetts 02138.

Neille Shoemaker, Department of English, Baldwin Wallace College, Berea, Ohio 44017.

Howard Siegel, Ventura College, 4667 Telegraph Road, Ventura, California 93003.

Christopher Spencer, Department of English, Illinois State University, Normal, Illinois 61761.

P.G. Stanwood, Department of English, The University of British Columbia, Vancouver 8, B.C., Canada.

Robert E. Stanton, 4915 Stewart Avenue, Cincinnati, Ohio 45227.

Mr. Jess Stein, Random House, Inc., 501 Madison Avenue, New York, N.Y. 10022.

Richard Stensgaard, 10807 Ramona Avenue, Ontario, California.

David L. Stevenson, Hunter College, The City University of New York, New York, N.Y. 10021.

Frank Sullivan, Loyola University, Los Angeles, California 90045.

G.T. Tanselle, Department of English, The University of Wisconsin, Madison, Wisconsin 53706.

Henry ten Hoor, Hope College, Holland, Michigan 44932.

Bert A. Thompson, Kearney State College Library, Kearney, Nebraska 68847.

Dr. James L. Titchener, 4021 Rose Hill, Cincinnati, Ohio 45229.

B.H. Trask, 21 East 90th Street, New York, N.Y. 10028.

Robert K. Turner, Jr., Department of English, The University of Wisconsin-Milwaukee, Milwaukee, Wisconsin 53211.

Robert Y. Turner, Department of English, The University of Pennsylvania, Philadelphia, Pennsylvania 19104.

Linda van Norden, Department of English, The University of California at Davis, Davis, California 95616.

Professor John W. Velz, *Department of English,
Rice University, Houston, Texas 77005.*

S. Warhaft, *Department of English, The University of Manitoba, Winnipeg, Manitoba,
Canada.*

C.K. Weichert, *Dean of the College of Arts and
Sciences, The University of Cincinnati,
Cincinnati, Ohio 45221.*

Professor John W. Wieler, *19 Park Avenue,
White Plains, New York 10603.*

Marilyn L. Williamson, *315 William Road,
Rochester, Michigan 48063.*

Mrs. Mary M. Wills, *Department of English,*

Central Michigan University, Mount
Pleasant, Michigan 48858.

Graham C. Wilson, *Department of English,
San Jose State College, San Jose,
California 95114.*

James O. Wood, *1056 Carolyn Avenue, San
Jose, California 95125.*

Thomas E. Wright, *Department of English,
San Fernando Valley State College,
Northridge, California 91326.*

R. Zimbardo, *Department of English, City
College of New York, New York, N.Y. 10031.*

II

Agnes Scott College, *Decatur, Georgia 30030.*

Alabama College, *Montevalla, Alabama 35115.*

College of the Albemarle, *Whitehurst Library,
Elizabeth City, North Carolina 27909.*

The University of Alberta, *Edmonton, Alberta,
Canada.*

American International College, *McGown
Memorial Library, Springfield, Massachusetts
01107.*

Anna Maria College, *Paxton, Massachusetts
01612.*

Antioch College, *Olive Kettering Library,
Yellow Springs, Ohio 45387.*

Aquinas College, *Grand Rapids, Michigan 49506.*

The University of Arizona, *Tucson, Arizona
85721.*

Arkansas Polytechnic College, *Russellville,
Arkansas 72801.*

Armstrong State College, *Savannah, Georgia
31401.*

Asheville-Biltmore College, *Asheville, North
Carolina.*

Athens College, *Athens, Alabama 35611.*

Atlantic Christian College, *Wilson, North
Carolina 27893.*

Augsburg College, *Minneapolis, Minnesota
55404.*

Babson Institute, *Babson Park, Massachusetts
02157.*

Barnard College, *New York, New York 10027.*

Bethel College, *St. Paul, Minnesota 55101.*

Bethel College and Seminary, *St. Paul,
Minnesota 55101.*

Black Hawk College, *Moline, Illinois 61265.*

Bob Jones University, *Greenville, South
Carolina 29614.*

Briar Cliff College, *Sioux City, Iowa 51104.*

The University of Bridgeport, *Bridgeport,
Connecticut 06602.*

Brooklyn College, *Brooklyn, New York 11210.*

Bronx Community College, *Bronx, New York
10468.*

Brown University, *Providence, Rhode Island
02912.*

The University of Buffalo, *Buffalo, New York
14214.*

Buffalo and Erie County Public Library, *Buffalo,
New York 14203.*

Butler University, *The Irwin Library,
Indianapolis, Indiana 46207.*

Cabrillo College, *Aptos, California 95003.*

The University of California, *Irvine, California
92650.*

The University of California, *Riverside,
California 92502.*

California Institute of Technology, *Pasadena,
California 91109.*

California Lutheran College, *Mountclef Village,
Thousand Oaks, California 91360.*

California State College at Los Angeles, *Los
Angeles, California 90032.*

Canisius College, *Buffalo, New York 14208.*

Cardinal Cushing College, *Brookline, Massachusetts 02146.*

Cardinal Glennon College, *St. Louis, Missouri
63119.*

Carleton University, *Ottawa 1, Ontario, Canada.*

Carnegie Institute of Technology, *Hunt Library,*

Pittsburgh, Pennsylvania 15213.

Carroll College, Helena, Montana 59601.

Catherine Spalding College, Louisville, Kentucky 40203.

Central College, Pella, Iowa 50219.

The University of Chicago, Chicago, Illinois 60637.

Chicago Teachers College North, Chicago, Illinois 60625.

Chico State College, Chico, California 95927.

Church College of Hawaii, Laie, Oahu, Hawaii.

The University of Cincinnati, Cincinnati, Ohio 45221.

The Cincinnati Bible Seminary Library, Cincinnati, Ohio 45204.

The City College, New York, New York 10031.

Colby College, Waterville, Maine 04901.

The University of Colorado, Boulder, Colorado 80304.

Colorado State College, Greeley, Colorado 80631.

Columbia College, Columbia, South Carolina 29203.

Columbia University, New York, New York 10027.

Concordia Teachers College, Klinck Memorial Library, River Forest, Illinois 60305.

Concordia Teachers College, Link Library, Seward, Nebraska 68435.

Connecticut College, New London, Connecticut 06320.

Cornell University, Ithaca, New York 14850.

Creighton University, Omaha, Nebraska 68131.

C.W. Post College, Greenvale, Long Island, New York 11548.

Daytona Beach Junior College, Daytona Beach, Florida 32015.

The University of Delaware, Newark, Delaware 19711.

De Paul University, Chicago, Illinois 60604.

Dominican College, Racine, Wisconsin 53402.

Drake University, Des Moines, Iowa 50311.

Duke University, Durham, North Carolina 27706.

Earlham College, Lilly Library, Richmond, Indiana 47375.

East Carolina College, Greenville, North Carolina 27834.

Eastern Washington State College, Hargreaves Library, Cheney, Washington 99004.

Elmhurst College, Elmhurst, Illinois 60126.

Elon College, Elon College, North Carolina 27244.

Emory and Henry College, Emory, Virginia 24327.

Erie Public Library, Erie, Pennsylvania 16507.

Erskine College, Due West, South Carolina 29639.

Fairfield University, Fairfield, Connecticut 06433.

The Folger Shakespeare Library, Washington, D.C. 20003.

Fordham University, New York, New York 10458.

Gannon College, Erie, Pennsylvania 16501.

Gardner-Webb College, Boiling Springs, North Carolina 28017.

Gaston-Lincoln Regional Library, Gastonia, North Carolina 28052.

George Mason College of the University of Virginia, Fairfax, Virginia 22030.

Georgetown College, Cooke Memorial Library, Georgetown, Kentucky 40324.

Georgetown University, Washington, D.C. 20007

The University of Georgia, Athens, Georgia 30601.

Gonzago University, Crosby Library, Spokane, Washington 99202.

Goucher College, Julia Rogers Library, Towson, Baltimore, Maryland 21204.

Grinnell College, Grinnell, Iowa 50112.

Guilford College, Guilford College, North Carolina 27410.

Hamline University, St. Paul, Minnesota 55101.

The University of Hartford, Hartford, Connecticut 06117.

Haverford College, Haverford, Pennsylvania 19041.

Church College of Hawaii, Laie, Oahu, Hawaii.

Heidelberg College, Tiffin, Ohio 44883.

The Henry E. Huntington Library and Art Gallery, San Marino 9, California.

Hofstra College, Hempstead, New York 11550.

Hood College, Joseph Henry Apple Library, Frederick, Maryland 21702.

The University of Houston, Houston, Texas 77004.

Huron College, Ella McIntire Library, Huron, South Dakota 57350.

The University of Illinois, Urbana, Illinois 61803.

Illinois State University, Milner Library, Normal, Illinois 61761.

Immaculata College, Immaculata, Pennsylvania 19345.

Incarnate Word College, *San Antonio, Texas 78209.*

Indiana University, *Bloomington, Indiana 47405.*

Iona College, *Ryan Library, New Rochelle, New York 10801.*

State University of Iowa, *Iowa City, Iowa 52240.*

Jersey City Public Library, *Jersey City 2, New Jersey.*

Johns Hopkins University, *Baltimore, Maryland 21218.*

Judson College, *Bowling Library, Marion, Alabama 36756.*

Kansas City Public Library, *Kansas City, Missouri 64106.*

Kansas State University, *Manhattan, Kansas 66504.*

Kent State University, *Kent, Ohio 44240.*

University of Kentucky, *Lexington, Kentucky 40506.*

Knollcrest Campus, *Knollcrest Calvin Library, Grand Rapids, Michigan 49506.*

LaGrange College, *William and Evelyn Banks Library, LaGrange, Georgia 30240.*

Lake-Sumter Junior College, *Leesburg, Florida 32748.*

Lander College, *Greenwood, South Carolina.*

LaSalette Seminary, *Altamont, New York 12009.*

Lehigh University, *Bethlehem, Pennsylvania 18015.*

Le Moyne College, *Syracuse, New York 13214.*

Lewis and Clark College, *Portland, Oregon 97219.*

Lewis College, *Lockport, Illinois 60441.*

Little Rock University, *The John A. Larson Memorial Library, Little Rock, Arkansas 72204.*

Long Island University, *Brooklyn, New York 11201.*

Louisiana State University, *Baton Rouge, Louisiana 70803.*

Loyola College, *Baltimore, Maryland 21210.*

Luther College, *Decorah, Iowa 52101.*

Macalester College, *Weyerhaeuser Library, St. Paul, Minnesota 55101.*

The University of Maine, *Orono, Maine 04473.*

Maria College, *Albany, New York.*

Marshall University, *Huntington, West Virginia 25701.*

Mars Hill College, *Memorial Library, Mars Hill, North Carolina 28754.*

Marycrest College, *Cone Library, Davenport, Iowa 52804.*

Marygrove College, *Detroit, Michigan 48221.*

Mary Holmes Junior College, *West Point, Mississippi 39773.*

Mary Manse College, *Toledo, Ohio 43620.*

McMaster University, *Mills Memorial Library, Hamilton, Ontario, Canada.*

Memphis State University, *John Brister Library, Memphis, Tennessee 38111.*

Miami University, *Oxford, Ohio 45056.*

The University of Michigan, *Ann Arbor, Michigan 48104.*

Millersville State College, *Millersville, Pennsylvania.*

Mills College, *Oakland, California 94613.*

Mississippi State College for Women, *J.C. Fant Memorial Library, Columbus, Mississippi 39701.*

Missouri State Library, *Jefferson City, Missouri 65102.*

Moravian College, *Harvey Memorial Library, Bethlehem, Pennsylvania 18018.*

Mount Holyoke College, *South Hadley, Massachusetts 01075.*

Mount Mary College, *Milwaukee, Wisconsin 53222.*

Mount Mercy College, *Catherine McAuley Library, Cedar Rapids, Iowa 52402.*

Mount Mercy College, *Pittsburgh, Pennsylvania 15213.*

College of Mount St. Joseph-on-the-Ohio, *Mount St. Joseph, Ohio 45051.*

Mount Saint Mary College, *Hooksett, New Hampshire 03106.*

College of Mount Saint Vincent, *Elizabeth Seton Library, Riverdale, New York 10471.*

Mount Union College, *Albiana, Ohio 44601.*

Mount Vernon Seminary, *Washington, D.C. 20007.*

Nazareth College, *Rochester, New York 14610.*

Nebraska Wesleyan University, *Lincoln, Nebraska 68504.*

The Newberry Library, *Chicago 10, Illinois.*

The University of New Hampshire, *Durham, New Hampshire 03824.*

Newton College of the Sacred Heart, *Newton, Massachusetts 02159.*

The City College, *New York, New York* 10031.

Niagara University, *Niagara Falls, New York* 14109.

The University of North Carolina, *Chapel Hill, North Carolina* 27515.

The University of North Carolina at Greensboro, *Greensboro, North Carolina.*

North Carolina Wesleyan College, *Rocky Mount, North Carolina* 27802.

Northeast Louisiana State College, *Monroe, Louisiana.*

North Park College, *Chicago, Illinois* 60625.

Northwest Missouri State College, *Maryville, Missouri* 64468.

Notre Dame College, *St. Louis, Missouri* 63125.

Notre Dame College, *Staten Island, New York* 10301.

Oklahoma City University, *Oklahoma City, Oklahoma* 73106.

The University of Omaha, *Omaha, Nebraska* 68101.

Oregon State University, *Corvallis, Oregon* 97331.

College of Our Lady of Mercy, *Burlingame, California* 94011.

Parsons College, *Fairfield, Iowa* 52556.

The University of Pennsylvania, *Philadelphia, Pennsylvania* 19104.

The Pennsylvania State Library, *Harrisburg, Pennsylvania* 17126.

Pennsylvania State University, *University Park, Pennsylvania* 16802.

Pfeiffer College, Inc., *Misenheimer, North Carolina* 28109.

Philadelphia College of Pharmacy and Science, *Philadelphia, Pennsylvania* 19104.

The University of Pittsburgh, *Pittsburgh, Pennsylvania* 15213.

Point Park Junior College, *Pittsburgh, Pennsylvania* 15222.

C.W. Post College, *Greenvale, Long Island, New York* 11548.

Providence College, *Providence, Rhode Island* 02918.

Providence Public Library, *Providence, Rhode Island* 02903.

The Public Library of Buffalo and Erie County, *Buffalo, New York* 14203.

The Public Library of Erie, *Pennsylvania* 16507.

The Public Library of Jersey City, *New Jersey.*

The Public Library of Kansas City, *Missouri* 64106.

The Public Library of Providence, *Rhode Island* 02903.

The Public Library of Santa Barbara, *California* 93102.

The Public Library of Tampa, *Florida* 33602.

The Public Library of Teaneck, *New Jersey* 07666.

The Public Library of Toledo, *Ohio* 43624.

The Public Library of Worcester, *Massachusetts* 01608.

Purdue University, *Lafayette, Indiana* 47907.

Queen of the Apostles Library, *Harriman, New York* 10926.

The University of Redlands, *Redlands, California* 92373.

Regis College, *Weston, Massachusetts* 02193.

Regis College, *Framingham Campus, Framingham, Massachusetts* 01701.

Rhode Island School of Design, *Providence, Rhode Island* 02903.

Rice University, *Fondren Library, Houston, Texas* 77001.

The University of Rochester, *Rochester, New York* 14627.

Rockhurst College, *Kansas City, Missouri* 64110.

Russell Sage College, *Troy, New York* 12180.

Rutgers University, *New Brunswick, New Jersey* 08901.

St. Ambrose College, *Davenport, Iowa* 52803.

St. Andrews Presbyterian College, *De Tamble Library, Laurinburg, North Carolina* 28352.

College of St. Elizabeth, *Santa Maria Library, Convent Station, New Jersey* 07961.

St. Francis College, *McGarry Library, Brooklyn, New York* 11201.

St. Jerome's College, *Waterloo, Ontario, Canada.*

St. John Fisher College, *Rochester, New York* 14618.

St. John's University, *Jamaica, New York* 11432.

College of St. Joseph, *Albuquerque, New Mexico* 87105.

St. Josephs College, *Calumet Campus, East Chicago, Indiana* 46312.

St. Joseph's College, *North Windham, Maine* 04062.

St. Josephs College, *Rensselaer, Indiana* 47979.

371

St. Joseph Seraphic Seminary,
Callicoon, New York 12723.

St. Louis University, *Pius XII Memorial
Library*, St. Louis, Missouri 63103.

St. Mary's College, *Notre Dame, Indiana 46556.*

St. Mary's Dominican College, *New Orleans,
Louisiana 70118.*

St. Mary's Seminary, *Perryville, Missouri 63775.*

St. Michael's College, *Winooski, Vermont 05404.*

St. Norbert College, *West DePere,
Wisconsin 54178.*

St. Paul's College, *Concordia, Missouri 64020.*

St. Procopius College, *Lisle, Illinois 60532.*

College of St. Rose, *Albany, New York 12203.*

College of Saint Teresa, *Winona,
Minnesota 55987.*

Salem College, *Winston-Salem,
North Carolina 27108.*

Salisbury State College, *Salisbury,
Maryland 21801.*

The University of San Diego, College for Men,
San Diego, California 92110.

Santa Barbara City College, *Santa Barbara,
California.*

The Santa Barbara Public Library, *Santa
Barbara, California 93102.*

The University of Santa Clara, *Orradre Library,
Santa Clara, California 95053.*

Sarah Lawrence College, *Bronxville,
New York 10708.*

Seton Hill College, *Reeves Memorial Library,
Greensburg, Pennsylvania 15601.*

Shippensburg State College, *Ezra Lehman
Memorial Library, Shippensburg,
Pennsylvania 17257.*

Siena College, *Memphis, Tennessee 38117.*

Sir George Williams University, *Montreal 25,
Quebec, Canada.*

Skidmore College, *Saratoga Springs,
New York 12566.*

South East Missouri State College, *Kent
Library, Cape Girardeau, Missouri 67301.*

South Texas Junior College, *Houston,
Texas 77002.*

Southwestern at Memphis, *Burrow Library,
Memphis, Tennessee 38112.*

Southwest Missouri State College, *Springfield,
Missouri 65802.*

Stanislaus State College, *Turlock,
California 95380.*

State University College, *Milne Library,*

Geneseo, *New York 14454.*

State University College, *Benjamin F. Feinberg
Library, Plattsburgh, New York 12901.*

State University of New York at Buffalo,
*Lockwood Memorial Library, Buffalo,
New York 14214.*

Stephen F. Austin State College,
Nacogdoches, Texas 75962.

Stetson University, *DeLand, Florida 32720.*

Stonehill College, *Cushing Martin Library,
North Easton, Massachusetts 02356.*

Suffolk University, *Boston, Massachusetts 02114.*

Swarthmore College, *Swarthmore,
Pennsylvania 19081.*

The University of Tampa, *Tampa, Florida 33606.*

The Tampa Public Library, *Tampa, Florida 33602.*

Taylor University, *Upland, Indiana 46989.*

The Teaneck Public Library, *Teaneck,
New Jersey 07666.*

The University of Tennessee, *Knoxville,
Tennessee 37916.*

Tennessee Polytechnic Institute, *Cookeville,
Tennessee 38500.*

The Toledo Public Library, *Toledo, Ohio 43624.*

Towson State College, *Albert S. Cook Library,
Baltimore, Maryland 21204.*

Trinity College, *Hartford, Connecticut 06106.*

Tufts University, *Medford, Massachusetts 02155.*

Union Junior College, *Cranford,
New Jersey 07016.*

Union University, *Emma Waters Summor
Library, Jackson, Tennessee.*

United States Air Force Academy,
Colorado 80840.

Upsala College, *East Orange, New Jersey 07019.*

The University of Utah, *Salt Lake City,
Utah 84112.*

Utica College of Syracuse University, *Burrstone
Campus, Utica, New York 13502.*

Villa Maria College, *Buffalo, New York 14225.*

The University of Virginia, *The Alderman
Library, Charlottesville, Virginia 22903.*

Weber College, *Ogden, Utah.*

Wellesley College, *Wellesley, Massachusetts
02181.*

Wells College, *Aurora, New York 13026.*

Wesleyan University, *Middletown,
Connecticut 06457.*

West Chester State College, *Francis Harvey
Green Library, West Chester,
Pennsylvania 19380.*

Western Kentucky State College, *Bowling Green, Kentucky.*

Western Reserve University, *Cleveland, Ohio 44106.*

Wheaton College, *Norton, Massachusetts 02766.*

Wichita State University, *Wichita, Kansas 67208.*

College of William and Mary, *Williamsburg, Virginia 23185.*

Wilson College, *Stewart Memorial Library, Chambersburg, Pennsylvania 17201.*

Winthrop College, *The South Carolina College for Women, Rock Hill, South Carolina 29733.*

The University of Wisconsin, *Memorial Library, Madison, Wisconsin 53706.*

Wofford College, *Spartanburg, South Carolina 29301.*

The Worcester Public Library, *Worcester, Massachusetts 01608.*

The University of Wyoming, *Laramie, Wyoming 82071.*

Xavier University, *Cincinnati, Ohio 45207.*

Yale University, *New Haven, Connecticut 06520.*

York University, *Toronto 12, Ontario, Canada.*

III

Auckland, The University of Auckland, *New Zealand.*

Basel, Englisches Seminar der Universität, *Augustinergasse 19, 4000 Basel, Switzerland.*

Besançon, Bibliothèque de l'Université, *Besançon, France.*

Birmingham, City of Birmingham Reference Library, *Ratcliff Place, Birmingham 1, England.*

Birmingham, The Shakespeare Institute, *The University of Birmingham, Birmingham 15, England.*

Birmingham, The University, *Edgbaston, Birmingham 15, England.*

Bordeaux, Faculté des Lettres, *Section d'anglais, 20 Cours Pasteur, Bordeaux, France.*

Campsie, Canterbury Municipal Library, *139 Beamish Street, Campsie, New South Wales, Australia.*

Canterbury, The University of Kent at Canterbury, *4 Station Road West, Canterbury, England.*

Cardiff, The University College of South Wales, *Cathays Park, Cardiff, Great Britain.*

Colchester, The University of Essex, *Wivenhoe Park, Colchester, Essex, England.*

Costa Rica, Universidad de Costa Rica, *Ciudad Universitaria, Costa Rica, A.C.*

Edinburgh, The National Library of Scotland, *Edinburgh 1, Scotland.*

Exeter, Devon County Library, *Barley House, Exeter, Devon, England.*

Freetown, Fourah Bay College, *University College of Sierra Leone, Freetown, West Africa.*

Glasgow, The University, *Glasgow, W.2, Scotland.*

Hull, The University, *Hull, England.*

Kensington, The University of New South Wales, *Kensington, N.S.W., Australia.*

Lausanne, Bibliothèque Cantonale et Universitaire, *6, Place de la Riponne, 1000-Lausanne, Switzerland.*

Lausanne, Bibliotheque Contonale et Universitaire, *6, Place de la Riponne, 1000-Lausanne, Suisse.*

Leopoldville, American School of Leopoldville, *P.O. Box 4702, Leopoldville, Republic of Congo.*

London, Bedford College, *York Gate, Regents Park, London, N.W. 1, England.*

London, Goldsmiths' College, *New Cross, London, S.E. 14, England.*

The London Library, *14, St. James's Square, London, S.W. 1, England.*

London, Orthological Institute, *3, Lincoln's Inn Fields, London, W.C. 2, England.*

London, University College, *Gower Street, London, W.C. 1, England.*

London, The University of London, *Senate House, Malet Street, London, W.C. 1, England.*

The Manchester Public Libraries, *Manchester 2, England.*

Manchester, The University, *Manchester, England.*

Malta, Royal University of Malta, *St. Paul's Street, Valletta, Malta.*

Manila, Ateneo de Manila, *P.O. Box 154, Manila, Philippines.*

Münster, Universitätsbibliothek, *Postfach 1521,*
44 Münster/Westf., Germany.

Newcastle, The University of Newcastle,
Tighes Hill, New South Wales, Australia.

Ottawa, National Library, *Public Archives*
Building, 330 Sussex Drive, Ottawa 2,
Canada.

Oslo, British Institute, *University of Oslo,*
Blindern, Oslo, Norway.

Oxford, Bodleian Library, *Oxford, England.*

St. Andrews, The University, *St. Andrews,*

Scotland.

Sheffield, Central Library, *Surrey Street,*
Sheffield, 1, Yorkshire, England.

Singapore, The University of Singapore,
Bukit Timah Road, Singapore 10.

Southampton, The University, *Highfield,*
Southampton, England.

Tübingen, Die Universitätsbibliothek Tübingen,
Germany.

Wellington, Alexander Turnbull Library,
Box 8016, Wellington, New Zealand.